FORD
ESCORT/TRACER
1991-99 REPAIR MANUAL

Covers all U.S. and Canadian models of Ford Escort, ZX2 and Mercury Tracer

by Thomas A. Mellon, A.S.E., S.A.E.

CHILTON *Automotive Books*

PUBLISHED BY **HAYNES NORTH AMERICA, Inc.**

Haynes

APA
AUTOMOTIVE
PARTS &
ACCESSORIES
ASSOCIATION   MEMBER

Manufactured in USA
© 1998 Haynes North America, Inc.
ISBN 0-8019-9098-X
Library of Congress Catalog Card No. 98-71358
4567890123 9876543210

Haynes Publishing Group
Sparkford Nr Yeovil
Somerset BA22 7JJ England

Haynes North America, Inc
861 Lawrence Drive
Newbury Park
California 91320 USA

ABCDE
FGHI

CHILTON'S

Contents

Contents

SAFETY NOTICE

Proper service and repair procedures are vital to the safe, reliable operation of all motor vehicles, as well as the personal safety of those performing repairs. This manual outlines procedures for servicing and repairing vehicles using safe, effective methods. The procedures contain many NOTES, CAUTIONS and WARNINGS which should be followed, along with standard procedures to eliminate the possibility of personal injury or improper service which could damage the vehicle or compromise its safety.

It is important to note that repair procedures and techniques, tools and parts for servicing motor vehicles, as well as the skill and experience of the individual performing the work vary widely. It is not possible to anticipate all of the conceivable ways or conditions under which vehicles may be serviced, or to provide cautions as to all possible hazards that may result. Standard and accepted safety precautions and equipment should be used when handling toxic or flammable fluids, and safety goggles or other protection should be used during cutting, grinding, chiseling, prying, or any other process that can cause material removal or projectiles.

Some procedures require the use of tools specially designed for a specific purpose. Before substituting another tool or procedure, you must be completely satisfied that neither your personal safety, nor the performance of the vehicle will be endangered.

Although information in this manual is based on industry sources and is complete as possible at the time of publication, the possibility exists that some car manufacturers made later changes which could not be included here. While striving for total accuracy, the authors or publishers cannot assume responsibility for any errors, changes or omissions that may occur in the compilation of this data.

PART NUMBERS

Part numbers listed in this reference are not recommendations by Haynes North America, Inc. for any product brand name. They are references that can be used with interchange manuals and aftermarket supplier catalogs to locate each brand supplier's discrete part number.

SPECIAL TOOLS

Special tools are recommended by the vehicle manufacturer to perform their specific job. Use has been kept to a minimum, but where absolutely necessary, they are referred to in the text by the part number of the tool manufacturer. These tools can be purchased, under the appropriate part number, from your local dealer or regional distributor, or an equivalent tool can be purchased locally from a tool supplier or parts outlet. Before substituting any tool for the one recommended, read the SAFETY NOTICE at the top of this page.

ACKNOWLEDGMENTS

This publication contains material that is reproduced and distributed under a license from Ford Motor Company. No further reproduction or distribution of the Ford Motor Company material is allowed without the express written permission from Ford Motor Company.

1

GENERAL INFORMATION AND MAINTENANCE

HOW TO USE THIS BOOK

Chilton's Total Car Care manual for the 1991–99 Escort/Tracer is intended to help you learn more about the inner workings of your vehicle while saving you money on its upkeep and operation.

The beginning of the book will likely be referred to the most, since that is where you will find information for maintenance and tune-up. The other sections deal with the more complex systems of your vehicle. Operating systems from engine through brakes are covered to the extent that the average do-it-yourselfer becomes mechanically involved. This book will not explain such things as rebuilding a differential for the simple reason that the expertise required and the investment in special tools make this task uneconomical. It will, however, give you detailed instructions to help you change your own brake pads and shoes, replace spark plugs, and perform many more jobs that can save you money, give you personal satisfaction and help you avoid expensive problems.

A secondary purpose of this book is a reference for owners who want to understand their vehicle and/or their mechanics better. In this case, no tools at all are required.

Where to Begin

Before removing any bolts, read through the entire procedure. This will give you the overall view of what tools and supplies will be required. There is nothing more frustrating than having to walk to the bus stop on Monday morning because you were short one bolt on Sunday afternoon. So read ahead and plan ahead. Each operation should be approached logically and all procedures thoroughly understood before attempting any work.

All sections contain adjustments, maintenance, removal and installation procedures, and in some cases, repair or overhaul procedures. When repair is not considered practical, we tell you how to remove the part and then how to install the new or rebuilt replacement. In this way, you at least save the labor costs. Backyard repair of some components is just not practical.

Avoiding Trouble

Many procedures in this book require you to "label and disconnect . . ." a group of lines, hoses or wires. Don't be lulled into thinking you can remember where everything goes—you won't. If you hook up vacuum or fuel lines incorrectly, the vehicle will run poorly, if at all. If you hook up electrical wiring incorrectly, you may instantly learn a very expensive lesson.

You don't need to know the official or engineering name for each hose or line. A piece of masking tape on the hose and a piece on its fitting will allow you to assign your own label such as the letter A or a short name. As long as you remember your own code, the lines can be reconnected by matching similar letters or names. Do remember that tape will dissolve in gasoline or other fluids; if a component is to be washed or cleaned, use another method of identification. A permanent felt-tipped marker can be very handy for marking metal parts. Remove any tape or paper labels after assembly.

Maintenance or Repair?

It's necessary to mention the difference between maintenance and repair. Maintenance includes routine inspections, adjustments, and replacement of parts which show signs of normal wear. Maintenance compensates for wear or deterioration. Repair implies that something has broken or is not working. A need for repair is often caused by lack of maintenance. Example: draining and refilling the automatic transmission fluid is maintenance recommended by the manufacturer at specific mileage intervals. Failure to do this can ruin the transaxle, requiring very expensive repairs. While no maintenance program can prevent items from breaking or wearing out, a general rule can be stated: MAINTENANCE IS CHEAPER THAN REPAIR.

Two basic mechanic's rules should be mentioned here. First, whenever the left side of the vehicle or engine is referred to, it is meant to specify the driver's side. Conversely, the right side of the vehicle means the passenger's side. Second, most screws and bolts are removed by turning counterclockwise, and tightened by turning clockwise.

Safety is always the most important rule. Constantly be aware of the dangers involved in working on an automobile and take the proper precautions. See the information in this section regarding SERVICING YOUR VEHICLE SAFELY and the SAFETY NOTICE on the acknowledgment page.

Avoiding the Most Common Mistakes

Pay attention to the instructions provided. There are 3 common mistakes in mechanical work:

1. Incorrect order of assembly, disassembly or adjustment. When taking something apart or putting it together, performing steps in the wrong order usually just costs you extra time; however, it CAN break something. Read the entire procedure before beginning disassembly. Perform everything in the order in which the instructions say you should, even if you can't immediately see a reason for it. When you're taking apart something that is very intricate, you might want to draw a picture of how it looks when assembled at one point in order to make sure you get everything back in its proper position. We will supply exploded views whenever possible. When making adjustments, perform them in the proper order; often, one adjustment affects another, and you cannot expect even satisfactory results unless each adjustment is made only when it cannot be changed by any other.

2. Overtorquing (or undertorquing). While it is more common for overtorquing to cause damage, undertorquing may allow a fastener to vibrate loose causing serious damage. Especially when dealing with aluminum parts, pay attention to torque specifications and utilize a torque wrench in assembly. If a torque figure is not available, remember that if you are using the right tool to perform the job, you will probably not have to strain yourself to get a fastener tight enough. The pitch of most threads is so slight that the tension you put on the wrench will be multiplied many times in actual force on what you are tightening. A good example of how critical torque is can be seen in the case of spark plug installation, especially where you are putting the plug into an aluminum cylinder head. Too little torque can fail to crush the gasket, causing leakage of combustion gases and consequent overheating of the plug and engine parts. Too much torque can damage the threads or distort the plug, changing the spark gap.

There are many commercial products available for ensuring that fasteners won't come loose, even if they are not torqued just right (a very common brand is Loctite®). If you're worried about getting something together tight enough to hold, but loose enough to avoid mechanical damage during assembly, one of these products might offer substantial insurance. Before choosing a threadlocking compound, read the label on the package and make sure the product is compatible with the materials, fluids, etc. involved.

3. Crossthreading. This occurs when a part such as a bolt is screwed into a nut or casting at the wrong angle and forced. Crossthreading is more likely to occur if access is difficult. It helps to clean and lubricate fasteners, then to start threading with the part to be installed positioned straight in. Then, start the bolt, spark plug, etc. with your fingers. If you encounter resistance, unscrew the part and start over again at a different angle until it can be inserted and turned several times without much effort. Keep in mind that many parts, especially spark plugs, have tapered threads, so that gentle turning will automatically bring the part you're threading to the proper angle, but only if you don't force it or resist a change in angle. Don't put a wrench on the part until it's been tightened a couple of turns by hand. If you suddenly encounter resistance, and the part has not seated fully, don't force it. Pull it back out to make sure it's clean and threading properly.

Always take your time and be patient; once you have some experience, working on your vehicle may well become an enjoyable hobby.

TOOLS AND EQUIPMENT

▶ **See Figures 1 thru 15**

Naturally, without the proper tools and equipment it is impossible to properly service your vehicle. It would also be virtually impossible to catalog every tool that you would need to perform all of the operations in this book. Of course, It would be unwise for the amateur to rush out and buy an expensive set of tools on the theory that he/she may need one or more of them at some time.

The best approach is to proceed slowly, gathering a good quality set of those tools that are used most frequently. Don't be misled by the low cost of bargain tools. It is far better to spend a little more for better quality. Forged wrenches, 6 or 12-point sockets and fine tooth ratchets are by far preferable to their less expensive counterparts. As any good mechanic can tell you, there are few worse experiences than trying to work on a vehicle with bad tools. Your monetary savings will be far outweighed by frustration and mangled knuckles.

Begin accumulating those tools that are used most frequently: those associated with routine maintenance and tune-up. In addition to the normal assortment of screwdrivers and pliers, you should have the following tools:

- Wrenches/sockets and combination open end/box end wrenches in sizes from ⅛–¾ in. or 3mm–19mm (depending on whether your vehicle uses standard or metric fasteners) and a 13⁄16 in. or ⅝ in. spark plug socket (depending on plug type).

➡ **If possible, buy various length socket drive extensions. Universal-joint and wobble extensions can be extremely useful, but be careful when using them, as they can change the amount of torque applied to the socket.**

- Jackstands for support.
- Oil filter wrench.
- Spout or funnel for pouring fluids.
- Grease gun for chassis lubrication (unless your vehicle is not equipped with any grease fittings—for details, please refer to information on Fluids and Lubricants found later in this section).
- Hydrometer for checking the battery (unless equipped with a sealed, maintenance-free battery).
- A container for draining oil and other fluids.
- Rags for wiping up the inevitable mess.

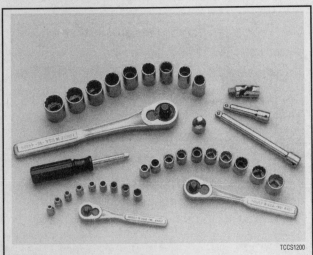

TCCS1200

Fig. 1 All but the most basic procedures will require an assortment of ratchets and sockets

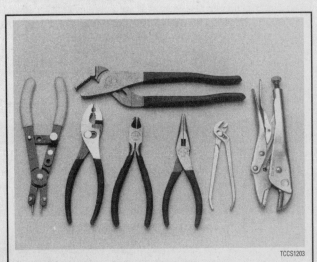

TCCS1202

Fig. 3 A hydraulic floor jack and a set of jackstands are essential for lifting and supporting the vehicle

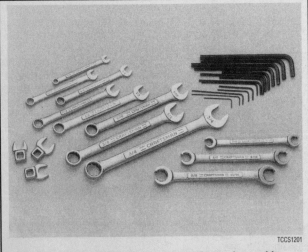

TCCS1201

Fig. 2 In addition to ratchets, a good set of wrenches and hex keys will be necessary

TCCS1203

Fig. 4 An assortment of pliers, grippers and cutters will be handy for old rusted parts and stripped bolt heads

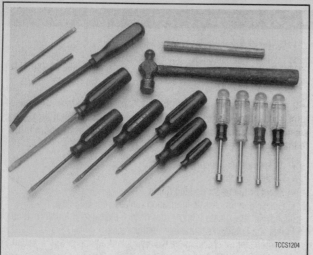

Fig. 5 Various drivers, chisels and prybars are great tools to have in your toolbox

TCCS1204

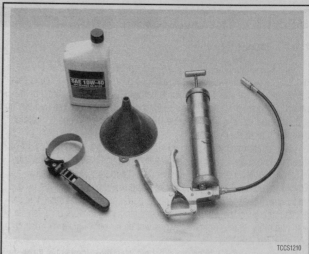

Fig. 8 A few inexpensive lubrication tools will make maintenance easier

TCCS1210

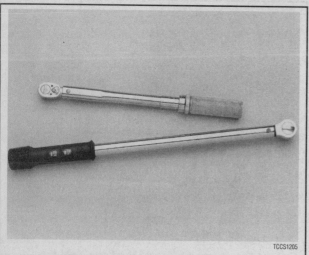

Fig. 6 Many repairs will require the use of a torque wrench to assure the components are properly fastened

TCCS1205

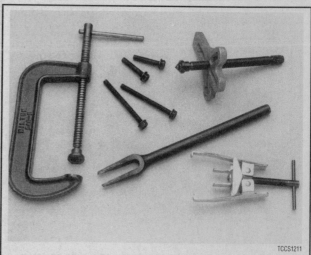

Fig. 9 Various pullers, clamps and separator tools are needed for many larger, more complicated repairs

TCCS1211

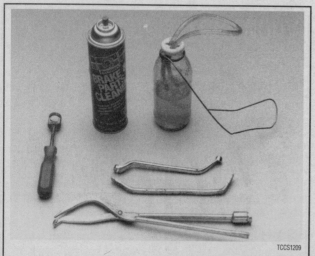

Fig. 7 Although not always necessary, using specialized brake tools will save time

TCCS1209

Fig. 10 A variety of tools and gauges should be used for spark plug gapping and installation

TCCS1212

In addition to the above items there are several others that are not absolutely necessary, but handy to have around. These include Oil Dry® (or an equivalent oil absorbent gravel—such as cat litter) and the usual supply of lubricants, antifreeze and fluids, although these can be purchased as needed. This is a basic list for routine maintenance, but only your personal needs and desire can accurately determine your list of tools.

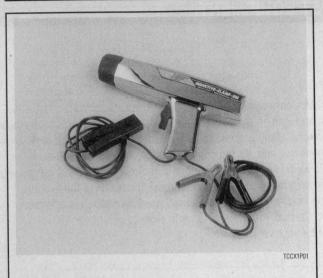

TCCX1P01

Fig. 11 Inductive type timing light

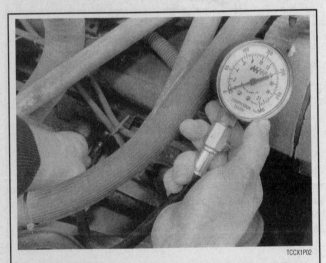

TCCX1P02

Fig. 12 A screw-in type compression gauge is recommended for compression testing

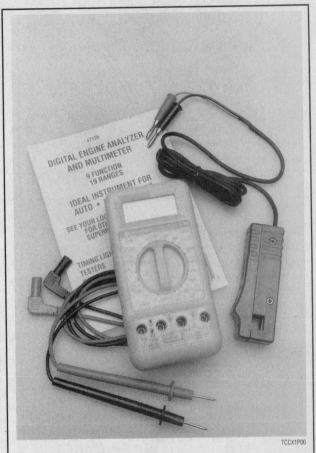

TCCX1P06

Fig. 14 Most modern automotive multimeters incorporate many helpful features

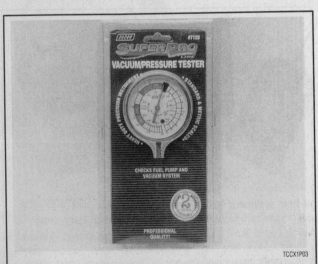

TCCX1P03

Fig. 13 A vacuum/pressure tester is necessary for many testing procedures

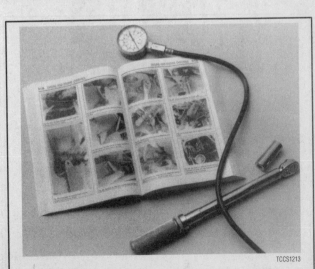

TCCS1213

Fig. 15 Proper information is vital, so always have a Chilton Total Car Care manual handy

DIAGNOSTIC TEST EQUIPMENT

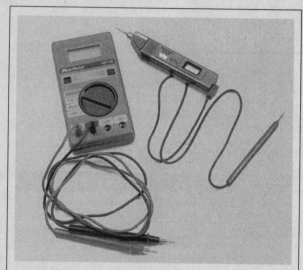

Digital multimeters come in a variety of styles and are a "must-have" for any serious home mechanic. Digital multimeters measure voltage (volts), resistance (ohms) and sometimes current (amperes). These versatile tools are used for checking all types of electrical or electronic components

Modern vehicles equipped with computer-controlled fuel, emission and ignition systems require modern electronic tools to diagnose problems. Many of these tools are designed solely for the professional mechanic and are too costly and difficult to use for the average do-it-yourselfer. However, various automotive aftermarket companies have introduced products that address the needs of the average home mechanic, providing sophisticated information at affordable cost. Consult your local auto parts store to determine what is available for your vehicle.

Trouble code tools allow the home mechanic to extract the "fault' code" number from an on-board computer that has sensed a problem (usually indicated by a Check Engine light). Armed with this code, the home mechanic can focus attention on a suspect system or component

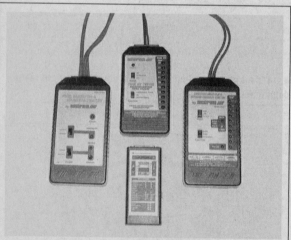

Sensor testers perform specific checks on many of the sensors and actuators used on today's computer-controlled vehicles. These testers can check sensors both on or off the vehicle, as well as test the accompanying electrical circuits

Hand-held scanners represent the most sophisticated of all do-it-yourself diagnostic tools. These tools do more than just access computer codes like the code readers above; they provide the user with an actual interface into the vehicle's computer. Comprehensive data on specific makes and models will come with the tool, either built-in or as a separate cartridge

After performing a few projects on the vehicle, you'll be amazed at the other tools and non-tools on your workbench. Some useful household items are: a large turkey baster or siphon, empty coffee cans and ice trays (to store parts), ball of twine, electrical tape for wiring, small rolls of colored tape for tagging lines or hoses, markers and pens, a note pad, golf tees (for plugging vacuum lines), metal coat hangers or a roll of mechanics's wire (to hold things out of the way), dental pick or similar long, pointed probe, a strong magnet, and a small mirror (to see into recesses and under manifolds).

A more advanced set of tools, suitable for tune-up work, can be drawn up easily. While the tools are slightly more sophisticated, they need not be outrageously expensive. There are several inexpensive tach/dwell meters on the market that are every bit as good for the average mechanic as a professional model. Just be sure that it goes to a least 1200–1500 rpm on the tach scale and that it works on 4, 6 and 8-cylinder engines. (If you have one or more vehicles with a diesel engine, a special tachometer is required since diesels don't use spark plug ignition systems). The key to these purchases is to make them with an eye towards adaptability and wide range. A basic list of tune-up tools could include:

- Tach/dwell meter.
- Spark plug wrench and gapping tool.
- Feeler gauges for valve or point adjustment. (Even if your vehicle does not use points or require valve adjustments, a feeler gauge is helpful for many repair/overhaul procedures).

A tachometer/dwell meter will ensure accurate tune-up work on vehicles without electronic ignition. The choice of a timing light should be made carefully. A light which works on the DC current supplied by the vehicle's battery is the best choice; it should have a xenon tube for brightness. On any vehicle with an electronic ignition system, a timing light with an inductive pickup that clamps around the No. 1 spark plug cable is preferred.

In addition to these basic tools, there are several other tools and gauges you may find useful. These include:

- Compression gauge. The screw-in type is slower to use, but eliminates the possibility of a faulty reading due to escaping pressure.
- Manifold vacuum gauge.
- 12V test light.
- A combination volt/ohmmeter
- Induction Ammeter. This is used for determining whether or not there is current in a wire. These are handy for use if a wire is broken somewhere in a wiring harness.

As a final note, you will probably find a torque wrench necessary for all but the most basic work. The beam type models are perfectly adequate, although the newer click types (breakaway) are easier to use. The click type torque wrenches tend to be more expensive. Also keep in mind that all types of torque wrenches should be periodically checked and/or recalibrated. You will have to decide for yourself which better fits your purpose.

Special Tools

Normally, the use of special factory tools is avoided for repair procedures, since these are not readily available for the do-it-yourself mechanic. When it is possible to perform the job with more commonly available tools, it will be pointed out, but occasionally, a special tool was designed to perform a specific function and should be used. Before substituting another tool, you should be convinced that neither your safety nor the performance of the vehicle will be compromised.

Special tools can usually be purchased from an automotive parts store or from your dealer. In some cases special tools may be available directly from the tool manufacturer.

SERVICING YOUR VEHICLE SAFELY

▶ **See Figures 16, 17, 18 and 19**

It is virtually impossible to anticipate all of the hazards involved with automotive maintenance and service, but care and common sense will prevent most accidents.

The rules of safety for mechanics range from "don't smoke around gasoline," to "use the proper tool(s) for the job." The trick to avoiding injuries is to develop safe work habits and to take every possible precaution.

Do's

- Do keep a fire extinguisher and first aid kit handy.
- Do wear safety glasses or goggles when cutting, drilling, grinding or prying, even if you have 20–20 vision. If you wear glasses for the sake of vision, wear safety goggles over your regular glasses.
- Do shield your eyes whenever you work around the battery. Batteries contain sulfuric acid. In case of contact with the eyes or skin, flush the area with water or a mixture of water and baking soda, then seek immediate medical attention.

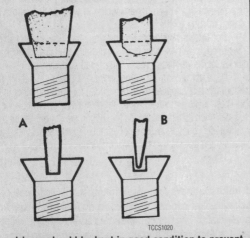

TCCS1020

Fig. 16 Screwdrivers should be kept in good condition to prevent injury or damage which could result if the blade slips from the screw

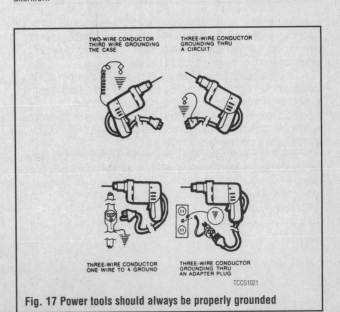

TWO-WIRE CONDUCTOR THIRD WIRE GROUNDING THE CASE

THREE-WIRE CONDUCTOR GROUNDING THRU A CIRCUIT

THREE-WIRE CONDUCTOR ONE WIRE TO A GROUND

THREE-WIRE CONDUCTOR GROUNDING THRU AN ADAPTER PLUG

TCCS1021

Fig. 17 Power tools should always be properly grounded

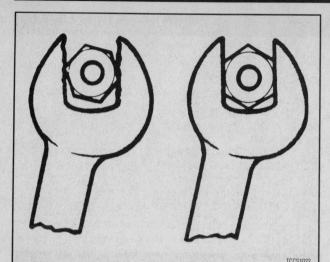

TCCS1022

Fig. 18 Using the correct size wrench will help prevent the possibility of rounding off a nut

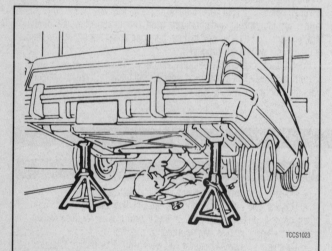

TCCS1023

Fig. 19 NEVER work under a vehicle unless it is supported using safety stands (jackstands)

• Do use safety stands (jackstands) for any undervehicle service. Jacks are for raising vehicles; jackstands are for making sure the vehicle stays raised until you want it to come down. Whenever the vehicle is raised, block the wheels remaining on the ground and set the parking brake.

• Do use adequate ventilation when working with any chemicals or hazardous materials. Like carbon monoxide, the asbestos dust resulting from some brake lining wear can be hazardous in sufficient quantities.

• Do disconnect the negative battery cable when working on the electrical system. The secondary ignition system contains EXTREMELY HIGH VOLTAGE. In some cases it can even exceed 50,000 volts.

• Do follow manufacturer's directions whenever working with potentially hazardous materials. Most chemicals and fluids are poisonous if taken internally.

• Do properly maintain your tools. Loose hammerheads, mushroomed punches and chisels, frayed or poorly grounded electrical cords, excessively worn screwdrivers, spread wrenches (open end), cracked sockets, slipping ratchets, or faulty droplight sockets can cause accidents.

• Likewise, keep your tools clean; a greasy wrench can slip off a bolt head, ruining the bolt and often harming your knuckles in the process.

• Do use the proper size and type of tool for the job at hand. Do select a wrench or socket that fits the nut or bolt. The wrench or socket should sit straight, not cocked.

• Do, when possible, pull on a wrench handle rather than push on it, and adjust your stance to prevent a fall.

• Do be sure that adjustable wrenches are tightly closed on the nut or bolt and pulled so that the force is on the side of the fixed jaw.

• Do strike squarely with a hammer; avoid glancing blows.

• Do set the parking brake and block the drive wheels if the work requires a running engine.

Don'ts

• Don't run the engine in a garage or anywhere else without proper ventilation—EVER! Carbon monoxide is poisonous; it takes a long time to leave the human body and you can build up a deadly supply of it in your system by simply breathing in a little every day. You may not realize you are slowly poisoning yourself. Always use power vents, windows, fans and/or open the garage door.

• Don't work around moving parts while wearing loose clothing. Short sleeves are much safer than long, loose sleeves. Hard-toed shoes with neoprene soles protect your toes and give a better grip on slippery surfaces. Jewelry such as watches, fancy belt buckles, beads or body adornment of any kind is not safe working around a vehicle. Long hair should be tied back under a hat or cap.

• Don't use pockets for toolboxes. A fall or bump can drive a screwdriver deep into your body. Even a rag hanging from your back pocket can wrap around a spinning shaft or fan.

• Don't smoke when working around gasoline, cleaning solvent or other flammable material.

• Don't smoke when working around the battery. When the battery is being charged, it gives off explosive hydrogen gas.

• Don't use gasoline to wash your hands; there are excellent soaps available. Gasoline contains dangerous additives which can enter the body through a cut or through your pores. Gasoline also removes all the natural oils from the skin so that bone dry hands will suck up oil and grease.

• Don't service the air conditioning system unless you are equipped with the necessary tools and training. When liquid or compressed gas refrigerant is released to atmospheric pressure it will absorb heat from whatever it contacts. This will chill or freeze anything it touches. Although refrigerant is normally non-toxic, R-12 becomes a deadly poisonous gas in the presence of an open flame. One good whiff of the vapors from burning refrigerant can be fatal.

• Don't use screwdrivers for anything other than driving screws! A screwdriver used as a prying tool can snap when you least expect it, causing injuries. At the very least, you'll ruin a good screwdriver.

• Don't use a bumper or emergency jack (that little ratchet, scissors, or pantograph jack supplied with the vehicle) for anything other than changing a flat! These jacks are only intended for emergency use out on the road; they are NOT designed as a maintenance tool. If you are serious about maintaining your vehicle yourself, invest in a hydraulic floor jack of at least a 1½ ton capacity, and at least two sturdy jackstands.

FASTENERS, MEASUREMENTS AND CONVERSIONS

Bolts, Nuts and Other Threaded Retainers

▶ See Figures 20, 21, 22 and 23

Although there are a great variety of fasteners found in the modern car or truck, the most commonly used retainer is the threaded fastener (nuts, bolts, screws, studs, etc.). Most threaded retainers may be reused, provided that they are not damaged in use or during the repair. Some retainers (such as stretch bolts or torque prevailing nuts) are designed to deform when tightened or in use and should not be reinstalled.

Whenever possible, we will note any special retainers which should be replaced during a procedure. But you should always inspect the condition of a retainer when it is removed and replace any that show signs of damage. Check all threads for rust or corrosion which can increase the torque necessary to achieve the desired clamp load for which that fastener was originally selected. Additionally, be sure that the driver surface of the fastener has not been compromised by rounding or other damage. In some cases a driver surface may become only partially rounded, allowing the driver to catch in only one direction. In many of these occurrences, a fastener may be installed and tightened, but the driver would not be able to grip and loosen the fastener again. (This could lead to frustration down the line should that component ever need to be disassembled again).

If you must replace a fastener, whether due to design or damage, you must ALWAYS be sure to use the proper replacement. In all cases, a retainer of the same design, material and strength should be used. Markings on the heads of most bolts will help determine the proper strength of the fastener. The same material, thread and pitch must be selected to assure proper installation and safe operation of the vehicle afterwards.

Thread gauges are available to help measure a bolt or stud's thread. Most automotive and hardware stores keep gauges available to help you select the proper size. In a pinch, you can use another nut or bolt for a thread gauge. If the bolt you are replacing is not too badly damaged, you can select a match by finding another bolt which will thread in its place. If you find a nut which threads properly onto the damaged bolt, then use that nut to help select the replacement bolt. If however, the bolt you are replacing is so badly damaged (broken or drilled out) that its threads cannot be used as a gauge, you might start by looking for another bolt (from the same assembly or a similar location on your vehicle) which will thread into the

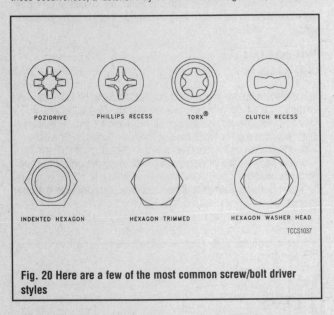

Fig. 20 Here are a few of the most common screw/bolt driver styles

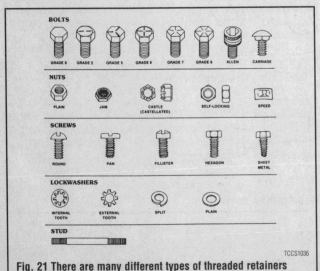

Fig. 21 There are many different types of threaded retainers found on vehicles

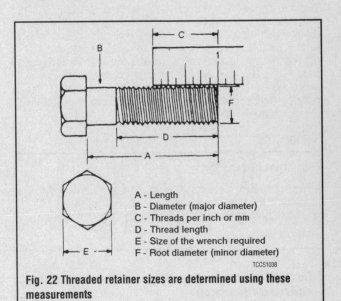

A - Length
B - Diameter (major diameter)
C - Threads per inch or mm
D - Thread length
E - Size of the wrench required
F - Root diameter (minor diameter)

Fig. 22 Threaded retainer sizes are determined using these measurements

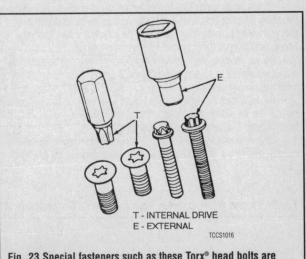

T - INTERNAL DRIVE
E - EXTERNAL

Fig. 23 Special fasteners such as these Torx® head bolts are used by manufacturers to discourage people from working on vehicles without the proper tools

damaged bolt's mounting. If so, the other bolt can be used to select a nut; the nut can then be used to select the replacement bolt.

In all cases, be absolutely sure you have selected the proper replacement. Don't be shy, you can always ask the store clerk for help.

❋❋ WARNING

Be aware that when you find a bolt with damaged threads, you may also find the nut or drilled hole it was threaded into has also been damaged. If this is the case, you may have to drill and tap the hole, replace the nut or otherwise repair the threads. NEVER try to force a replacement bolt to fit into the damaged threads.

Torque

Torque is defined as the measurement of resistance to turning or rotating. It tends to twist a body about an axis of rotation. A common example of this would be tightening a threaded retainer such as a nut, bolt or screw. Measuring torque is one of the most common ways to help assure that a threaded retainer has been properly fastened.

When tightening a threaded fastener, torque is applied in three distinct areas, the head, the bearing surface and the clamp load. About 50 percent of the measured torque is used in overcoming bearing friction. This is the friction between the bearing surface of the bolt head, screw head or nut face and the base material or washer (the surface on which the fastener is rotating). Approximately 40 percent of the applied torque is used in overcoming thread friction. This leaves only about 10 percent of the applied torque to develop a useful clamp load (the force which holds a joint together). This means that friction can account for as much as 90 percent of the applied torque on a fastener.

TORQUE WRENCHES

▶ See Figures 24 and 25

In most applications, a torque wrench can be used to assure proper installation of a fastener. Torque wrenches come in various designs and most automotive supply stores will carry a variety to suit your needs. A torque wrench should be used any time we supply a specific torque value for a fastener. A torque wrench can also be used if you are following the general guidelines in the accompanying charts. Keep in mind that because there is no worldwide standardization of fasteners, the charts are a general guideline and should be used with caution. Again, the general rule of "if you are using the right tool for the job, you should not have to strain to tighten a fastener" applies here.

Beam Type

▶ See Figure 26

The beam type torque wrench is one of the most popular types. It consists of a pointer attached to the head that runs the length of the flexible beam (shaft) to a scale located near the handle. As the wrench is pulled, the beam bends and the pointer indicates the torque using the scale.

Click (Breakaway) Type

▶ See Figure 27

Another popular design of torque wrench is the click type. To use the click type wrench you pre-adjust it to a torque setting. Once the torque is reached, the wrench has a reflex signaling feature that causes a momentary breakaway of the torque wrench body, sending an impulse to the operator's hand.

Pivot Head Type

▶ See Figure 28

Some torque wrenches (usually of the click type) may be equipped with a pivot head which can allow it to be used in areas of limited access. BUT, it must be used properly. To hold a pivot head wrench, grasp the handle lightly, and as you pull on the handle, it should be floated on the pivot point. If the handle comes in contact with the yoke extension during the process of pulling, there is a very good chance the torque readings will be inaccurate because this could alter the wrench loading point. The design of the handle is usually such as to make it inconvenient to deliberately misuse the wrench.

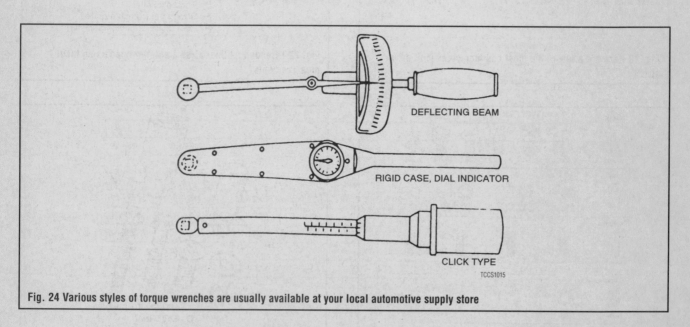

DEFLECTING BEAM

RIGID CASE, DIAL INDICATOR

CLICK TYPE

TCCS1015

Fig. 24 Various styles of torque wrenches are usually available at your local automotive supply store

Standard Torque Specifications and Fastener Markings

In the absence of specific torques, the following chart can be used as a guide to the maximum safe torque of a particular size/grade of fastener.
- There is no torque difference for fine or coarse threads.
- Torque values are based on clean, dry threads. Reduce the value by 10% if threads are oiled prior to assembly.
- The torque required for aluminum components or fasteners is considerably less.

U.S. Bolts

SAE Grade Number	1 or 2			5			6 or 7		
Number of lines always 2 less than the grade number.									
Bolt Size (Inches)—(Thread)	**Maximum Torque**			**Maximum Torque**			**Maximum Torque**		
	Ft./Lbs.	Kgm	Nm	Ft./Lbs.	Kgm	Nm	Ft./Lbs.	Kgm	Nm
¼ — 20	5	0.7	6.8	8	1.1	10.8	10	1.4	13.5
— 28	6	0.8	8.1	10	1.4	13.6			
5/16 — 18	11	1.5	14.9	17	2.3	23.0	19	2.6	25.8
— 24	13	1.8	17.6	19	2.6	25.7			
3/8 — 16	18	2.5	24.4	31	4.3	42.0	34	4.7	46.0
— 24	20	2.75	27.1	35	4.8	47.5			
7/16 — 14	28	3.8	37.0	49	6.8	66.4	55	7.6	74.5
— 20	30	4.2	40.7	55	7.6	74.5			
½ — 13	39	5.4	52.8	75	10.4	101.7	85	11.75	115.2
— 20	41	5.7	55.6	85	11.7	115.2			
9/16 — 12	51	7.0	69.2	110	15.2	149.1	120	16.6	162.7
— 18	55	7.6	74.5	120	16.6	162.7			
5/8 — 11	83	11.5	112.5	150	20.7	203.3	167	23.0	226.5
— 18	95	13.1	128.8	170	23.5	230.5			
¾ — 10	105	14.5	142.3	270	37.3	366.0	280	38.7	379.6
— 16	115	15.9	155.9	295	40.8	400.0			
7/8 — 9	160	22.1	216.9	395	54.6	535.5	440	60.9	596.5
— 14	175	24.2	237.2	435	60.1	589.7			
1 — 8	236	32.5	318.6	590	81.6	799.9	660	91.3	894.8
— 14	250	34.6	338.9	660	91.3	849.8			

Metric Bolts

Relative Strength Marking	4.6, 4.8			8.8		
Bolt Markings						
Bolt Size Thread Size x Pitch (mm)	**Maximum Torque**			**Maximum Torque**		
	Ft./Lbs.	Kgm	Nm	Ft./Lbs.	Kgm	Nm
6 x 1.0	2–3	.2–.4	3–4	3–6	4–.8	5–8
8 x 1.25	6–8	.8–1	8–12	9–14	1.2–1.9	13–19
10 x 1.25	12–17	1.5–2.3	16–23	20–29	2.7–4.0	27–39
12 x 1.25	21–32	2.9–4.4	29–43	35–53	4.8–7.3	47–72
14 x 1.5	35–52	4.8–7.1	48–70	57–85	7.8–11.7	77–110
16 x 1.5	51–77	7.0–10.6	67–100	90–120	12.4–16.5	130–160
18 x 1.5	74–110	10.2–15.1	100–150	130–170	17.9–23.4	180–230
20 x 1.5	110–140	15.1–19.3	150–190	190–240	26.2–46.9	160–320
22 x 1.5	150–190	22.0–26.2	200–260	250–320	34.5–44.1	340–430
24 x 1.5	190–240	26.2–46.9	260–320	310–410	42.7–56.5	420–550

TCCS1098

Fig. 25 Standard and metric bolt torque specifications based on bolt strengths

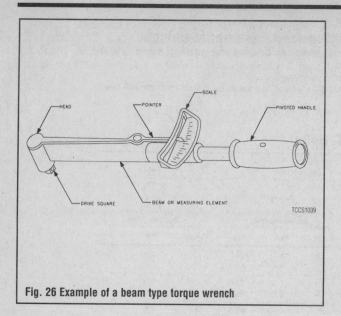

Fig. 26 Example of a beam type torque wrench

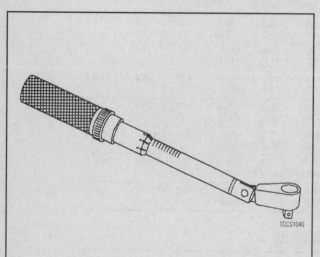

Fig. 27 A click type or breakaway torque wrench—note this one has a pivoting head

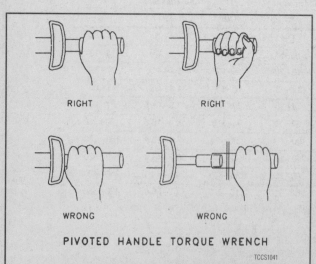

PIVOTED HANDLE TORQUE WRENCH

Fig. 28 Torque wrenches with pivoting heads must be grasped and used properly to prevent an incorrect reading

➡It should be mentioned that the use of any U-joint, wobble or extension will have an effect on the torque readings, no matter what type of wrench you are using. For the most accurate readings, install the socket directly on the wrench driver. If necessary, straight extensions (which hold a socket directly under the wrench driver) will have the least effect on the torque reading. Avoid any extension that alters the length of the wrench from the handle to the head/driving point (such as a crow's foot). U-joint or Wobble extensions can greatly affect the readings; avoid their use at all times.

Rigid Case (Direct Reading)

▶ **See Figure 29**

A rigid case or direct reading torque wrench is equipped with a dial indicator to show torque values. One advantage of these wrenches is that they can be held at any position on the wrench without affecting accuracy. These wrenches are often preferred because they tend to be compact, easy to read and have a great degree of accuracy.

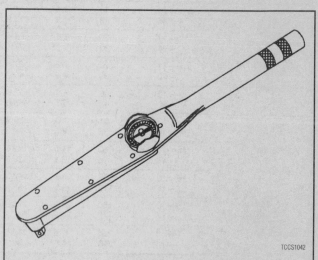

Fig. 29 The rigid case (direct reading) torque wrench uses a dial indicator to show torque

TORQUE ANGLE METERS

▶ **See Figure 30**

Because the frictional characteristics of each fastener or threaded hole will vary, clamp loads which are based strictly on torque will vary as well. In most applications, this variance is not significant enough to cause worry. But, in certain applications, a manufacturer's engineers may determine that more precise clamp loads are necessary (such is the case with many aluminum cylinder heads). In these cases, a torque angle method of installation would be specified. When installing fasteners which are torque angle tightened, a predetermined seating torque and standard torque wrench are usually used first to remove any compliance from the joint. The fastener is then tightened the specified additional portion of a turn measured in degrees. A torque angle gauge (mechanical protractor) is used for these applications.

Standard and Metric Measurements

▶ **See Figure 31**

Throughout this manual, specifications are given to help you determine the condition of various components on your vehicle, or to assist you in their installation. Some of the most common measurements include length (in. or cm/mm), torque (ft. lbs., inch lbs. or Nm) and pressure (psi, in. Hg, kPa or mm Hg). In most cases, we strive to provide the proper measurement as determined by the manufacturer's engineers.

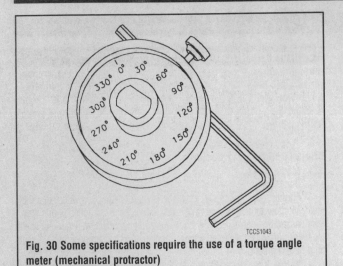

TCCS1043

Fig. 30 Some specifications require the use of a torque angle meter (mechanical protractor)

Though, in some cases, that value may not be conveniently measured with what is available in your toolbox. Luckily, many of the measuring devices which are available today will have two scales so the Standard or Metric measurements may easily be taken. If any of the various measuring tools which are available to you do not contain the same scale as listed in the specifications, use the accompanying conversion factors to determine the proper value.

The conversion factor chart is used by taking the given specification and multiplying it by the necessary conversion factor. For instance, looking at the first line, if you have a measurement in inches such as "free-play should be 2 in." but your ruler reads only in millimeters, multiply 2 in. by the conversion factor of 25.4 to get the metric equivalent of 50.8mm. Likewise, if the specification was given only in a Metric measurement, for example in Newton Meters (Nm), then look at the center column first. If the measurement is 100 Nm, multiply it by the conversion factor of 0.738 to get 73.8 ft. lbs.

CONVERSION FACTORS

LENGTH–DISTANCE

Inches (in.)	x 25.4	= Millimeters (mm)	x .0394	= Inches
Feet (ft.)	x .305	= Meters (m)	x 3.281	= Feet
Miles	x 1.609	= Kilometers (km)	x .0621	= Miles

VOLUME

Cubic Inches (in3)	x 16.387	= Cubic Centimeters	x .061	= in3
IMP Pints (IMP pt.)	x .568	= Liters (L)	x 1.76	= IMP pt.
IMP Quarts (IMP qt.)	x 1.137	= Liters (L)	x .88	= IMP qt.
IMP Gallons (IMP gal.)	x 4.546	= Liters (L)	x .22	= IMP gal.
IMP Quarts (IMP qt.)	x 1.201	= US Quarts (US qt.)	x .833	= IMP qt.
IMP Gallons (IMP gal.)	x 1.201	= US Gallons (US gal.)	x .833	= IMP gal.
Fl. Ounces	x 29.573	= Milliliters	x .034	= Ounces
US Pints (US pt.)	x .473	= Liters (L)	x 2.113	= Pints
US Quarts (US qt.)	x .946	= Liters (L)	x 1.057	= Quarts
US Gallons (US gal.)	x 3.785	= Liters (L)	x .264	= Gallons

MASS–WEIGHT

Ounces (oz.)	x 28.35	= Grams (g)	x .035	= Ounces
Pounds (lb.)	x .454	= Kilograms (kg)	x 2.205	= Pounds

PRESSURE

Pounds Per Sq. In. (psi)	x 6.895	= Kilopascals (kPa)	x .145	= psi
Inches of Mercury (Hg)	x .4912	= psi	x 2.036	= Hg
Inches of Mercury (Hg)	x 3.377	= Kilopascals (kPa)	x .2961	= Hg
Inches of Water (H_2O)	x .07355	= Inches of Mercury	x 13.783	= H_2O
Inches of Water (H_2O)	x .03613	= psi	x 27.684	= H_2O
Inches of Water (H_2O)	x .248	= Kilopascals (kPa)	x 4.026	= H_2O

TORQUE

Pounds–Force Inches (in–lb)	x .113	= Newton Meters (N·m)	x 8.85	= in–lb
Pounds–Force Feet (ft–lb)	x 1.356	= Newton Meters (N·m)	x .738	= ft–lb

VELOCITY

Miles Per Hour (MPH)	x 1.609	= Kilometers Per Hour (KPH)	x .621	= MPH

POWER

Horsepower (Hp)	x .745	= Kilowatts	x 1.34	= Horsepower

FUEL CONSUMPTION*

Miles Per Gallon IMP (MPG)	x .354	= Kilometers Per Liter (Km/L)
Kilometers Per Liter (Km/L)	x 2.352	= IMP MPG
Miles Per Gallon US (MPG)	x .425	= Kilometers Per Liter (Km/L)
Kilometers Per Liter (Km/L)	x 2.352	= US MPG

*It is common to covert from miles per gallon (mpg) to liters/100 kilometers (1/100 km), where mpg (IMP) x 1/100 km = 282 and mpg (US) x 1/100 km = 235.

TEMPERATURE

Degree Fahrenheit (°F)	= (°C x 1.8) + 32
Degree Celsius (°C)	= (°F – 32) x .56

TCCS1044

Fig. 31 Standard and metric conversion factors chart

SERIAL NUMBER IDENTIFICATION

Vehicle Identification Number (VIN)

♦ See Figure 32

The Vehicle Identification Number (VIN) is located on the instrument panel, close to the windshield on the driver's side of the vehicle. It is visible from outside the vehicle.

The 17-character label contains the following information:

- Digits 1, 2 and 3: World manufacturer identifier
- Digit 4: Restraint system type
- Digit 5: 1991–97 models: manufacturer's specification
- Digits 5, 6 and 7: 1998–99 models: line, series and body type
- Digits 6 and 7: 1991–97 models: line, series and body type
- Digit 8: Engine type
- Digit 9: Check digit
- Digit 10: Vehicle model year
- Digit 11: Assembly plant
- Digits 12 through 17: Production sequence number

90981P77

Fig. 32 The Vehicle Identification Number (VIN) is visible from outside the vehicle through the windshield—1991 model shown, others similar

Vehicle Certification Number

A Vehicle Certification Label (VCL) is also affixed on the left front door jamb. The VCL also contains a 17-digit Vehicle Identification Number (VIN). This VIN is used for warranty identification.

This label contains the following information:

- Manufacturer
- Type of restraint system
- Vehicle line
- Model series
- Body type
- Engine
- Model year
- Assembly plant
- Production sequence number
- Exterior color
- Interior trim type and color
- Radio type
- Transaxle ratio
- Transaxle type

Engine

The 8th character of the VIN designates the engine type installed in the vehicle. An engine identification label may also be attached to the engine timing cover.

The codes are as follows on 1991–96 models:

- Code 8: 1.8L DOHC engine
- Code J: 1.9L SOHC engine

The codes are as follows on 1997–99 models:

- Code P: 2.0L SOHC engine
- Code 3: 2.0L DOHC engine

Transaxle

The transaxle code is found on the Vehicle Certification Label (VCL), affixed to the left (driver's) side door lock post. The code is located in the lower right-hand corner of the VCL. This code designates the transaxle type installed in the vehicle. A transaxle identification tag is also affixed to the transaxle assembly.

The codes are as follows:

- Code W: 5-speed manual transaxle
- Code E: 4-speed automatic transaxle

VEHICLE IDENTIFICATION CHART

Engine Series (ID/VIN)	Engine Displacement Liters	Cubic Inches	No. of Cylinders	Fuel System	Eng. Mfg.
8	1.8L DOHC	112	4	MFI	Mazda
J	1.9L SOHC	116	4	SFI	Ford
P	2.0L SOHC	121	4	SFI ①	Ford
3	2.0L DOHC	121	4	SFI	Ford

MFI-Multi-port Fuel Injection

SFI-Sequential Fuel injection

① Also known as Split Port Injection (SPI)

Code	Year
M	1991
N	1992
P	1993
R	1994
S	1995
T	1996
V	1997
W	1998
X	1999

90981C01

GENERAL ENGINE SPECIFICATIONS

Year	Model	Engine ID/VIN	Engine Displacement Liters (cc)	No. of Cyl.	Fuel System Type	Net Horsepower @ rpm	Net Torque @ rpm (ft. lbs.)	Compression Ratio	Oil Pressure (lbs. @ rpm)
1991	Escort/Tracer	8	1.8 (1839)	4	MFI	127@6500	114@4500	9.0:1	28-43@1000
	Escort/Tracer	J	1.9 (1901)	4	SFI	88@4400	108@3800	9.0:1	35-65@2000
1992	Escort/Tracer	8	1.8 (1839)	4	MFI	127@6500	114@4500	9.0:1	28-43@1000
	Escort/Tracer	J	1.9 (1901)	4	SFI	88@4400	108@3800	9.0:1	35-65@2000
1993	Escort/Tracer	8	1.8 (1839)	4	MFI	127@6500	114@4500	9.0:1	28-43@1000
	Escort/Tracer	J	1.9 (1901)	4	SFI	88@4400	108@3800	9.0:1	35-65@2000
1994	Escort/Tracer	8	1.8 (1839)	4	MFI	127@6500	114@4500	9.0:1	28-43@1000
	Escort/Tracer	J	1.9 (1901)	4	SFI	88@4400	108@3800	9.0:1	35-65@2000
1995	Escort/Tracer	8	1.8 (1839)	4	MFI	127@6500	114@4500	9.0:1	28-43@1000
	Escort/Tracer	J	1.9 (1901)	4	SFI	88@4400	108@3800	9.0:1	35-65@2000
1996	Escort/Tracer	8	1.8 (1839)	4	MFI	127@6500	114@4500	9.0:1	28-43@1000
	Escort/Tracer	J	1.9 (1901)	4	SFI	88@4400	108@3800	9.0:1	35-65@2000
1997	Escort/Tracer	P	2.0 (2000)	4	SPI	110@5000	125@3750	9.2:1	35-65@2000
1998	Escort/Tracer	P	2.0 (2000)	4	SPI	110@5000	125@3750	9.2:1	35-65@2000
	Escort/Tracer	3	2.0 (2000)	4	SFI	130@5570	127@4250	9.6:1	54-80@4000
	ZX2	3	2.0 (2000)	4	SFI	130@5570	127@4250	9.6:1	54-80@4000
1999	Escort/Tracer	P	2.0 (2000)	4	SPI	110@5000	125@3750	9.2:1	35-65@2000
	Escort/Tracer	3	2.0 (2000)	4	SFI	130@5570	127@4250	9.6:1	54-80@4000
	ZX2	3	2.0 (2000)	4	SFI	130@5570	127@4250	9.6:1	54-80@4000

MFI-Multi-port Fuel Injection

SFI-Sequential Fuel Injection

SPI-Split Port Injection (SFI system)

90981C2A

ROUTINE MAINTENANCE AND TUNE-UP

Proper maintenance and tune-up is the key to long and trouble-free vehicle life, and the work can yield its own rewards. Studies have shown that a properly tuned and maintained vehicle can achieve better gas mileage than an out-of-tune vehicle. As a conscientious owner and driver, set aside a Saturday morning, say once a month, to check or replace items which could cause major problems later. Keep your own personal log to jot down which services you performed, how much the parts cost you, the date, and the exact odometer reading at the time. Keep all receipts for such items as engine oil and filters, so that they may be referred to in case of related problems or to determine operating expenses. As a do-it-yourselfer, these receipts are the only proof you have that the required maintenance was performed. In the event of a warranty problem, these receipts will be invaluable.

The literature provided with your vehicle when it was originally delivered includes the factory recommended maintenance schedule. If you no longer have this literature, replacement copies are usually available from the dealer. A maintenance schedule is provided later in this section, in case you do not have the factory literature.

Air Cleaner (Element)

REMOVAL & INSTALLATION

1.8L Engines

▶ See Figure 33

1. Loosen the resonance chamber attaching clamp at the Vane Air Flow (VAF) meter and disconnect the chamber from the VAF meter.
2. Disengage the VAF meter electrical connector.
3. Loosen the air cleaner assembly upper cover mounting screws.
4. Remove the VAF meter and the air cleaner assembly upper half.
5. Remove the air cleaner element.

To install:
6. Install the air cleaner element.
7. Install the air cleaner assembly upper half and the VAF meter.
8. Tighten the cover screws to 69–85 inch lbs. (8–11 Nm).

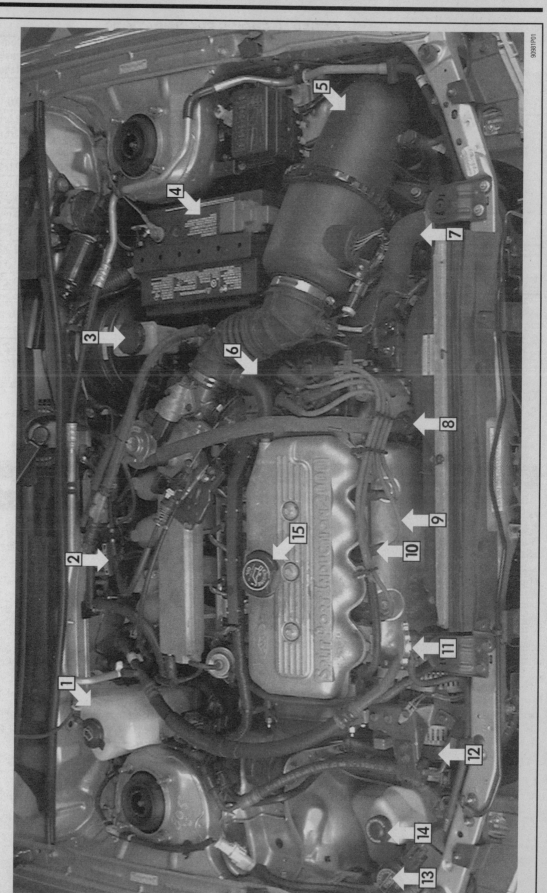

UNDERHOOD MAINTENANCE COMPONENT LOCATIONS—LATE MODELS

1. Windshield washer fluid reservoir
2. Engine oil dipstick
3. Brake master cylinder
4. Battery
5. Air filter element (in housing)
6. Automatic transaxle dipstick
7. Upper radiator hose
8. PCV valve
9. Spark plug wire
10. Spark plug
11. Radiator cap
12. Serpentine belt
13. Coolant reservoir
14. Power steering fluid reservoir
15. Engine oil filler cap

UNDERHOOD MAINTENANCE COMPONENT LOCATIONS—EARLY MODELS

1. Coolant reservoir
2. Power steering fluid reservoir
3. Serpentine belt
4. Radiator cap
5. Spark plug wire
6. Spark plug
7. Upper radiator hose
8. Air filter element (in housing)
9. Exterior fuse panel
10. Engine oil filler cap
11. Engine oil dipstick
12. Automatic transaxle dipstick
13. Battery
14. Brake master cylinder
15. Windshield washer fluid reservoir

90981P21

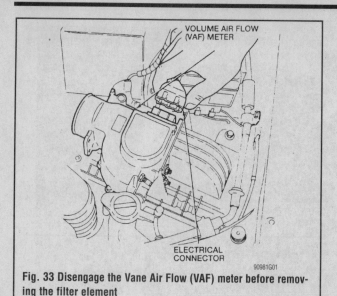

Fig. 33 Disengage the Vane Air Flow (VAF) meter before removing the filter element

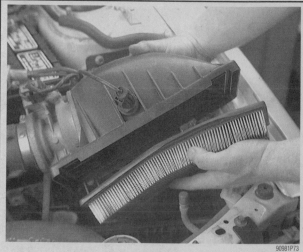

Fig. 35 . . . then lift the housing cover and remove the filter element

9. Engage the VAF meter electrical connector.

10. Engage the resonance chamber to the VAF meter and tighten the attaching clamp.

1.9L Engines

▶ See Figures 34 and 35

1. Release the four air cleaner lid clamps.
2. Lift the lid assembly from the filter housing and remove the filter element.

To install:

3. Hold the air cleaner lid aside and install the filter element in the filter housing.
4. Position the air cleaner lid on the filter housing. Be certain the lid is firmly seated.
5. Engage the air cleaner lid clamps.

2.0L Engines

▶ See Figures 36, 37, 38, 39 and 40

1. Open the air cleaner housing clamp and set the right hand side of the housing aside.

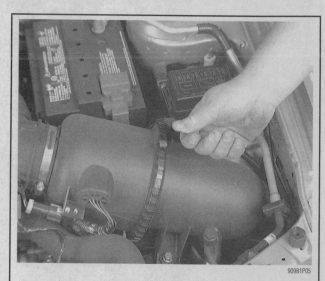

Fig. 36 Open the air cleaner housing clamp . . .

Fig. 34 Release the four air cleaner lid clamps (arrows) . . .

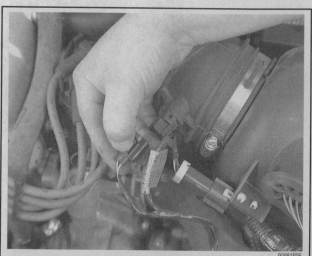

Fig. 37 . . . and, if necessary, unplug the electrical connections from the housing

Fig. 38 In some cases, it may be necessary to loosen the outlet hose-to-housing clamp and separate the hose from the housing

Fig. 39 Separate the housing halves . . .

Fig. 40 . . . then remove the filter element

2. In some cases it may be necessary to unplug the electrical connections from the housing assembly, loosen the outlet hose-to-housing clamp and separate the hose from the housing in order to set the housing aside.

3. Remove the filter element from the left hand side of the housing.

To install:

4. Align the tab on the filter element with the notch in the housing and install the element.

5. Connect the two halves of the housing together and tighten the clamp.

6. If removed, attach the electrical connections and the outlet hose to the housing. Tighten the hose retaining clamp.

Fuel Filter

REMOVAL & INSTALLATION

▶ **See Figures 41 thru 46**

The in-line fuel filter is located in the engine compartment between the fuel tank and the fuel rail.

1. Properly relieve the fuel system pressure.
2. Disconnect the negative battery cable.
3. Position a suitable container below the fuel filter to collect any excess fuel that may leak from the filter and lines.

✷✷ CAUTION

Observe all applicable safety precautions when working around fuel. Whenever servicing the fuel system, always work in a well ventilated area. Do not allow fuel spray or vapors to come in contact with a spark or open flame. Keep a dry chemical fire extinguisher near the work area. Always keep fuel in a container specifically designed for fuel storage; also, always properly seal fuel containers to avoid the possibility of fire or explosion.

4. Remove the retaining clip from the fuel filter upper hose.
5. Disconnect the upper hose from the fuel filter and drain any excess fuel into the container. Plug the hose.
6. Raise and safely support the vehicle.
7. Remove the retaining clip from the fuel filter lower hose.
8. Disconnect the lower hose from the fuel filter and drain any excess fuel into the container. Plug the hose.
9. Lower the vehicle.
10. Unfasten the filter retaining clamp screw and remove the fuel filter.

Fig. 41 The fuel filter is located in the engine compartment, between the fuel tank and fuel rail—1.9L engine's underside shown

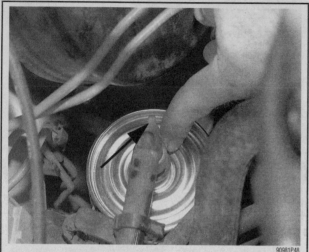

Fig. 42 To remove the fuel filter upper hose clip, grasp the clip (arrow) . . .

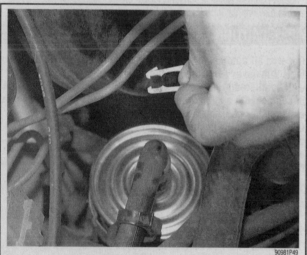

Fig. 43 . . . and gently pull the clip from the hose. (Lower hose clip removal is similar)

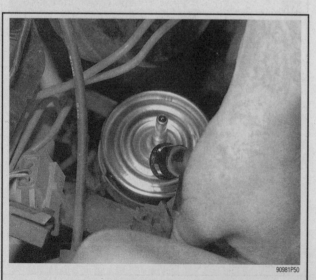

Fig. 44 Grasp the hose and pull it from the fuel filter

Fig. 45 Unfasten the filter retaining clamp screw

Fig. 46 Grasp the filter and remove it from the vehicle

To install:

11. Position the fuel filter and tighten the filter mounting clamp.

12. Remove the plug, then connect the upper hose to the filter and install the hose retaining clip.

13. Raise and safely support the vehicle.

14. Remove the plug, connect the lower hose to the filter and install the hose retaining clip.

15. Lower the vehicle.

16. Connect the negative battery cable.

17. Start the engine and check for leaks.

PCV Valve

REMOVAL & INSTALLATION

1.8L and 1.9L Engines

▶ See Figures 47, 48 and 49

The PCV valve will be located either on the valve cover (1.8L) or on a ventilation tube (1.9L).

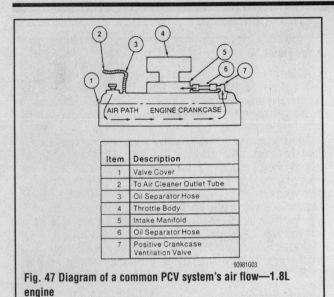

Fig. 47 Diagram of a common PCV system's air flow—1.8L engine

Item	Description
1	Valve Cover
2	To Air Cleaner Outlet Tube
3	Oil Separator Hose
4	Throttle Body
5	Intake Manifold
6	Oil Separator Hose
7	Positive Crankcase Ventilation Valve

90981G03

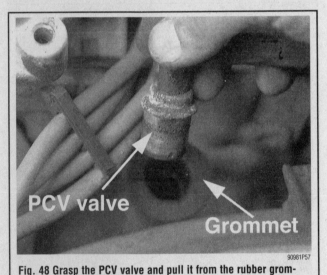

Fig. 48 Grasp the PCV valve and pull it from the rubber grommet—1.9L engine shown; 1.8L engine similar

90981P57

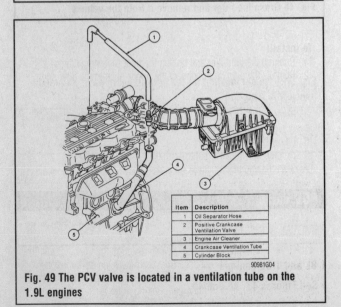

Item	Description
1	Oil Separator Hose
2	Positive Crankcase Ventilation Valve
3	Engine Air Cleaner
4	Crankcase Ventilation Tube
5	Cylinder Block

90981G04

Fig. 49 The PCV valve is located in a ventilation tube on the 1.9L engines

1. Disconnect the hose from the PCV valve.

2. If the hose is secured to the valve by means of a clip, compress the clip with pliers and slide it away from the valve.

3. Grasp the valve and pull it from the rubber grommet in the valve cover or ventilation tube.

To install:

4. Install the new valve into the valve cover or ventilation hose.

5. Connect the hose to the valve.

6. If removed, engage the hose-to-valve retaining clip(s).

2.0L Engines

1997 MODELS

▶ **See Figures 50 and 51**

1. Pull up on the hose to remove the PCV valve from the crankcase vent oil separator.

2. Pull the PCV valve from the crankcase ventilation tube.

3. Installation is the reverse of removal.

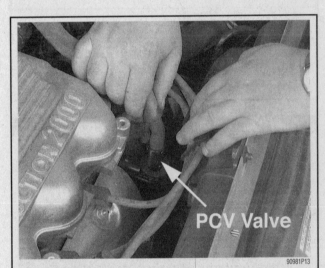

Fig. 50 Pull the PCV hose up to remove the valve from the crankcase vent oil separator . . .

90981P13

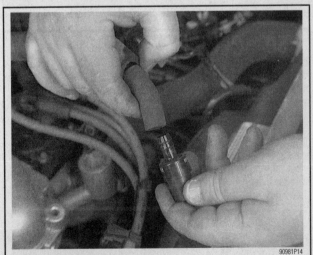

Fig. 51 . . . then pull the PCV valve from the crankcase ventilation tube—1997 2.0L models

90981P14

1998-99 MODELS

▶ See Figure 52

1. Remove the PCV valve from the crankcase ventilation tube.
2. Pull upwards to remove the valve from the grommet.
3. Installation is the reverse of removal.

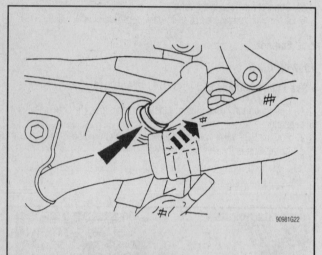

90981G22

Fig. 52 Remove the PCV valve from the grommet by pulling it upward—1998-99 2.0L engines

Evaporative Canister

SERVICING

The evaporative emission canister should be inspected for damage or leaks at the hose fittings. Repair or replace any old or cracked hoses. Replace the canister if it is damaged in any way. The canister is located under the hood, to the right of the engine on 1.8L models, or on a bracket under the air cleaner housing on 1.9L models.

On 1997 models, the canister is located at the front of the engine; on 1998-99 models, the canister is located at the rear of the car.

Battery

PRECAUTIONS

Always use caution when working on or near the battery. Never allow a tool to bridge the gap between the negative and positive battery terminals. Also, be careful not to allow a tool to provide a ground between the positive cable/terminal and any metal component on the vehicle. Either of these conditions will cause a short circuit, leading to sparks and possible personal injury.

Do not smoke, have an open flame or create sparks near a battery; the gases contained in the battery are very explosive and, if ignited, could cause severe injury or death.

All batteries, regardless of type, should be carefully secured by a battery hold-down device. If this is not done, the battery terminals or casing may crack from stress applied to the battery during vehicle operation. A battery which is not secured may allow acid to leak out, making it discharge faster; such leaking corrosive acid can also eat away at components under the hood.

Always visually inspect the battery case for cracks, leakage and corrosion. A white corrosive substance on the battery case or on nearby components would indicate a leaking or cracked battery. If the battery is cracked, it should be replaced immediately.

GENERAL MAINTENANCE

▶ See Figure 53

A battery that is not sealed must be checked periodically for electrolyte level. You cannot add water to a sealed maintenance-free battery (though not all maintenance-free batteries are sealed); however, a sealed battery must also be checked for proper electrolyte level, as indicated by the color of the built-in hydrometer "eye."

Always keep the battery cables and terminals free of corrosion. Check these components about once a year. Refer to the removal, installation and cleaning procedures outlined in this section.

Keep the top of the battery clean, as a film of dirt can help completely discharge a battery that is not used for long periods. A solution of baking soda and water may be used for cleaning, but be careful to flush this off with clear water. DO NOT let any of the solution into the filler holes. Baking soda neutralizes battery acid and will de-activate a battery cell.

Batteries in vehicles which are not operated on a regular basis can fall victim to parasitic loads (small current drains which are constantly drawing current from the battery). Normal parasitic loads may drain a battery on a vehicle that is in storage and not used for 6-8 weeks. Vehicles that have additional accessories such as a cellular phone, an alarm system or other devices that increase parasitic load may discharge a battery sooner. If the vehicle is to be stored for 6-8 weeks in a secure area and the alarm system, if present, is not necessary, the negative battery cable should be disconnected at the onset of storage to protect the battery charge.

Remember that constantly discharging and recharging will shorten battery life. Take care not to allow a battery to be needlessly discharged.

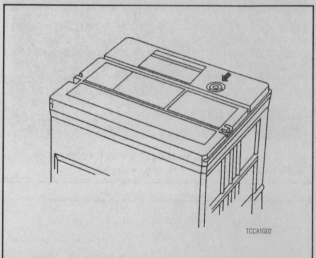

TCCA1G02

Fig. 53 A typical location for the built-in hydrometer on maintenance-free batteries

BATTERY FLUID

Check the battery electrolyte level at least once a month, or more often in hot weather or during periods of extended vehicle operation. On non-sealed batteries, the level can be checked either through the case on translucent batteries or by removing the cell caps on opaque-cased types. The electrolyte level in each cell should be kept filled to the split ring inside each cell, or the line marked on the outside of the case.

If the level is low, add only distilled water through the opening until the level is correct. Each cell is separate from the others, so each must be checked and filled individually. Distilled water should be used, because the chemicals and minerals found in most drinking water are harmful to the battery and could significantly shorten its life.

If water is added in freezing weather, the vehicle should be driven several miles to allow the water to mix with the electrolyte. Otherwise, the battery could freeze.

Although some maintenance-free batteries have removable cell caps for access to the electrolyte, the electrolyte condition and level on all sealed maintenance-free batteries must be checked using the built-in hydrometer "eye." The exact type of eye varies between battery manufacturers, but most apply a sticker to the battery itself explaining the possible readings. When in doubt, refer to the battery manufacturer's instructions to interpret battery condition using the built-in hydrometer.

➡ **Although the readings from built-in hydrometers found in sealed batteries may vary, a green eye usually indicates a properly charged battery with sufficient fluid level. A dark eye is normally an indicator of a battery with sufficient fluid, but one which may be low in charge. And a light or yellow eye is usually an indication that electrolyte supply has dropped below the necessary level for battery (and hydrometer) operation. In this last case, sealed batteries with an insufficient electrolyte level must usually be discarded.**

Checking the Specific Gravity

▶ **See Figures 54, 55 and 56**

A hydrometer is required to check the specific gravity on all batteries that are not maintenance-free. On batteries that are maintenance-free, the specific gravity is checked by observing the built-in hydrometer "eye" on the top of the battery case. Check with your battery's manufacturer for proper interpretation of its built-in hydrometer readings.

✳✳ CAUTION

Battery electrolyte contains sulfuric acid. If you should splash any on your skin or in your eyes, flush the affected area with plenty of clear water. If it lands in your eyes, get medical help immediately.

The fluid (sulfuric acid solution) contained in the battery cells will tell you many things about the condition of the battery. Because the cell plates must be kept submerged below the fluid level in order to operate, maintaining the fluid level is extremely important. And, because the specific gravity of the acid is an indication of electrical charge, testing the fluid can be an

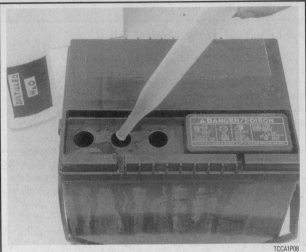

Fig. 55 If the fluid level is low, add only distilled water through the opening until the level is correct

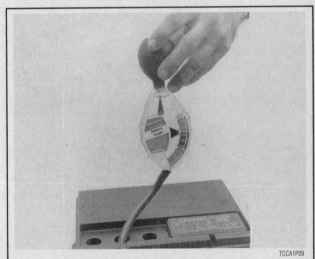

Fig. 56 Check the specific gravity of the battery's electrolyte with a hydrometer

aid in determining if the battery must be replaced. A battery in a vehicle with a properly operating charging system should require little maintenance, but careful, periodic inspection should reveal problems before they leave you stranded.

As stated earlier, the specific gravity of a battery's electrolyte level can be used as an indication of battery charge. At least once a year, check the specific gravity of the battery. It should be between 1.20 and 1.26 on the gravity scale. Most auto supply stores carry a variety of inexpensive battery testing hydrometers. These can be used on any non-sealed battery to test the specific gravity in each cell.

The battery testing hydrometer has a squeeze bulb at one end and a nozzle at the other. Battery electrolyte is sucked into the hydrometer until the float is lifted from its seat. The specific gravity is then read by noting the position of the float. If gravity is low in one or more cells, the battery should be slowly charged and checked again to see if the gravity has come up. Generally, if after charging, the specific gravity between any two cells varies more than 50 points (0.50), the battery should be replaced, as it can no longer produce sufficient voltage to guarantee proper operation.

Fig. 54 On non-maintenance-free batteries, the fluid level can be checked through the case on translucent models; the cell caps must be removed on other models

CABLES

▶ **See Figures 57, 58, 59, 60 and 61**

Once a year (or as necessary), the battery terminals and the cable clamps should be cleaned. Loosen the clamps and remove the cables, negative cable first. On batteries with posts on top, the use of a puller specially made for this purpose is recommended. These are inexpensive and available in most auto parts stores. Side terminal battery cables are secured with a small bolt.

Clean the cable clamps and the battery terminal with a wire brush, until all corrosion, grease, etc., is removed and the metal is shiny. It is especially important to clean the inside of the clamp thoroughly (an old knife is useful here), since a small deposit of foreign material or oxidation there will prevent a sound electrical connection and inhibit either starting or charging. Special tools are available for cleaning these parts, one type for conventional top post batteries and another type for side terminal batteries. It is also a good idea to apply some dielectric grease to the terminal, as this will aid in the prevention of corrosion.

After the clamps and terminals are clean, reinstall the cables, negative cable last; DO NOT hammer the clamps onto battery posts. Tighten the clamps securely, but do not distort them. Give the clamps and termi-

TCCS1208

Fig. 59 Place the tool over the battery posts and twist to clean until the metal is shiny

TCCS1206

Fig. 57 Maintenance is performed with household items and with special tools like this post cleaner

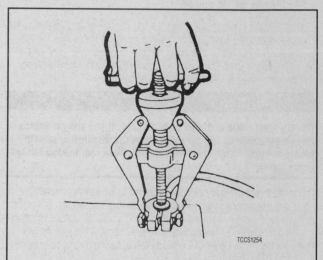

TCCS1254

Fig. 60 A special tool is available to pull the clamp from the post

TCCS1207

Fig. 58 The underside of this special battery tool has a wire brush to clean post terminals

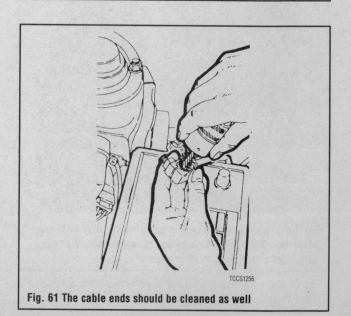

TCCS1256

Fig. 61 The cable ends should be cleaned as well

nals a thin external coating of grease after installation, to retard corrosion.

Check the cables at the same time that the terminals are cleaned. If the cable insulation is cracked or broken, or if the ends are frayed, the cable should be replaced with a new cable of the same length and gauge.

CHARGING

> ※※ **CAUTION**

The chemical reaction which takes place in all batteries generates explosive hydrogen gas. A spark can cause the battery to explode and splash acid. To avoid serious personal injury, be sure there is proper ventilation and take appropriate fire safety precautions when connecting, disconnecting, or charging a battery and when using jumper cables.

A battery should be charged at a slow rate to keep the plates inside from getting too hot. However, if some maintenance-free batteries are allowed to discharge until they are almost "dead," they may have to be charged at a high rate to bring them back to "life." Always follow the charger manufacturer's instructions on charging the battery.

REPLACEMENT

When it becomes necessary to replace the battery, select one with an amperage rating equal to or greater than the battery originally installed. Deterioration and just plain aging of the battery cables, starter motor, and associated wires makes the battery's job harder in successive years. The slow increase in electrical resistance over time makes it prudent to install a new battery with a greater capacity than the old.

Belts

INSPECTION

▶ **See Figures 62, 63, 64, 65 and 66**

Inspect the belts for signs of glazing or cracking. A glazed belt will be perfectly smooth from slippage, while a good belt will have a slight texture of fabric visible. Cracks will usually start at the inner edge of the belt and run outward. All worn or damaged drive belts should be replaced immediately. It is best to replace all drive belts at one time, as a preventive maintenance measure, during this service operation.

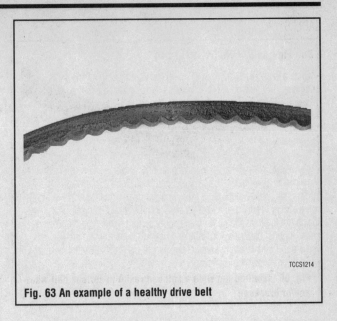

TCCS1214

Fig. 63 An example of a healthy drive belt

TCCS1215

Fig. 64 Deep cracks in this belt will cause flex, building up heat that will eventually lead to belt failure

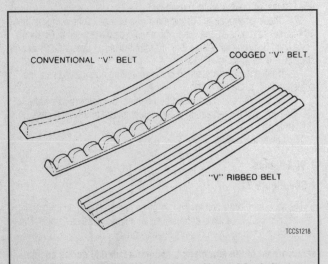

TCCS1218

Fig. 62 There are typically 3 types of accessory drive belts found on vehicles today

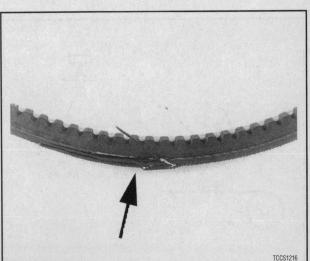

TCCS1216

Fig. 65 The cover of this belt is worn, exposing the critical reinforcing cords to excessive wear

Fig. 66 Installing too wide a belt can result in serious belt wear and/or breakage

ADJUSTMENT

1.8L Engines

ALTERNATOR AND WATER PUMP BELT

▶ **See Figures 67 and 68**

1. Loosen the alternator adjusting bolt.
2. Raise and safely support the vehicle.
3. Loosen the alternator mounting bolt.

➡**Do not pry against the stator frame. Position the prybar against a stronger point, such as the area around a case bolt.**

4. Position a suitable belt tension gauge on the longest accessible span of belt and tighten the belt.
5. Adjust the tension to 86–103 lbs. (383–461 N) for a new belt or 68–86 lbs. (304–383 kg) for a used belt.
6. If a belt tension gauge is not available, adjust the tension to 0.31–0.35 in. (8–9mm) deflection for a new belt or 0.35–0.39 in. (9–10mm) deflection for a used belt.
7. Tighten the alternator adjusting bolt to 14–19 ft. lbs. (19–25 Nm).
8. Tighten the alternator mounting bolt to 27–38 ft. lbs. (37–52 Nm).
9. Lower the vehicle.

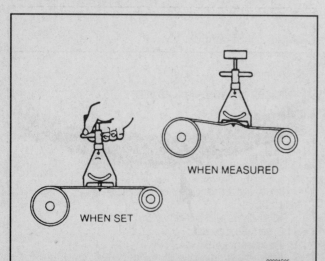

Fig. 67 A belt tension gauge should be placed on the longest span of the belt to check tension—1.8L engine

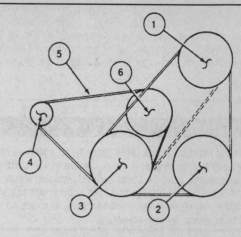

Item	Description
1	Power Steering Pump Pulley
2	A/C Clutch Pulley
3	Crankshaft Pulley
4	Alternator Pulley
5	Tension and Deflection Measuring Point
6	Water Pump Pulley

Fig. 68 Alternator and water pump pulley belt routing—1.8L engine

POWER STEERING PUMP BELT

▶ **See Figures 69 and 70**

1. Raise and safely support the vehicle.
2. Loosen the power steering pump mounting bolt and nuts.
3. Adjust the power steering pump and, if equipped, the air conditioning compressor belt tension by turning the pump adjusting bolt.
4. Tighten the power steering pump mounting nut near the pump adjusting bolt.
5. Position a suitable belt tension gauge on the longest accessible span of belt and tighten the belt.
6. Adjust the tension to 110–132 lbs. (491–589 N) for a new belt or 95–110 lbs. (422–491 N) for a used belt.
7. Check for proper belt deflection. For a new belt (one with less than 10 minutes of run time), the deflection should be 0.31–0.35 in. (8–9mm). For a used belt (one with more than 10 minutes of run time), the deflection should be 0.35–0.39 in. (9–10mm).
8. Tighten the power steering pump mounting nut, located near the adjusting bolt, to 27–38 ft. lbs. (37–52 Nm).
9. Tighten the pump mounting bolt behind the pulley to 27–40 ft. lbs. (36–54 Nm), and the remaining pump mounting nut to 23–34 ft. lbs. (31–46 Nm).
10. Lower the vehicle.

1.9L Engines

▶ **See Figure 71**

The accessory drive belt for 1.9L engines has no provision for manual belt adjustment, since these engines use an automatic belt tensioner. Drive belt slack is taken up by the automatic tensioner.

➡**Movement of the automatic tensioner assembly during engine operation is not a sign of a malfunctioning tensioner. This movement is the tensioner self-adjusting and is required to maintain constant belt tension.**

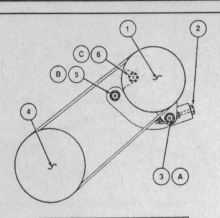

Item	Description
1	Power Steering Pump Pulley
2	Power Steering Pump Adjusting Bolt
3	Power Steering Pump Nut (Near Adjusting Bolt)
4	Crankshaft Pulley
5	Power Steering Pump Nut
6	Power Steering Pump Bolt
A	Tighten to 37-52 N·m (28-38 Lb-Ft)
B	Tighten to 31-46 N·m (23-34 Lb-Ft)
C	Tighten to 36-55 N·m (27-39 Lb-Ft)

90981G07

Fig. 69 Power steering pump belt routing and locations of the mounting bolts, nuts and adjusting nut—models without A/C

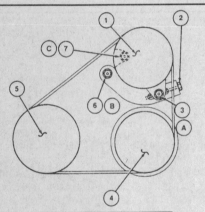

Item	Description
1	Power Steering Pump Pulley
2	Power Steering Pump Adjusting Bolt
3	Power Steering Pump Nut (Near Adjusting Bolt)
4	A/C Clutch Pulley
5	Crankshaft Pulley
6	Power Steering Pump Nut
7	Power Steering Pump Bolt
A	Tighten to 37-52 N·m (28-38 Lb-Ft)
B	Tighten to 31-46 N·m (23-34 Lb-Ft)
C	Tighten to 36-55 N·m (27-39 Lb-Ft)

90981G08

Fig. 70 Power steering pump belt routing and locations of the mounting bolts, nuts and adjusting nut—models with A/C

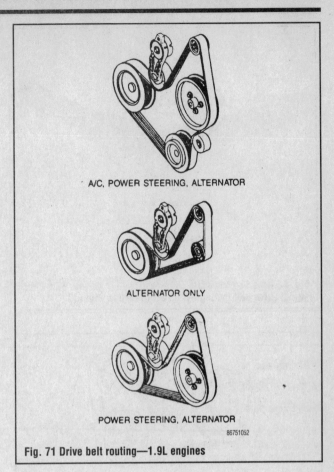

A/C, POWER STEERING, ALTERNATOR

ALTERNATOR ONLY

POWER STEERING, ALTERNATOR

86751052

Fig. 71 Drive belt routing—1.9L engines

2.0L Engines

▶ See Figures 72, 73 and 74

The accessory drive belt for 2.0L engines has no provision for manual belt adjustment, since these engines use an automatic belt tensioner. Drive belt slack is taken up by the automatic tensioner.

➡ **Movement of the automatic tensioner assembly during engine operation is not a sign of a malfunctioning tensioner. This movement is the tensioner self-adjusting and is required to maintain constant belt tension.**

The belt tensioner has a belt length indicator. If the indicator marks are not between the **MIN** and **MAX** marks, the belt must be replaced.

REMOVAL & INSTALLATION

1.8L Engines

ALTERNATOR AND WATER PUMP BELT

▶ See Figure 68

1. Riase the front of the car and support it with safety stands.
2. Loosen the alternator adjusting bolt.
3. If necessary, remove the power steering drive belt .
4. Loosen the alternator mounting bolt.
5. Remove the alternator and water pump drive belt.

To install:

6. Install the alternator and water pump drive belt.
7. Adjust the belt tension.
8. If removed, install the power steering pump belt.
9. Tighten the alternator adjusting bolt to 14–19 ft. lbs. (19–25 Nm).
10. Tighten the alternator mounting bolt to 27–38 ft. lbs. (37–52 Nm).
11. Lower the vehicle.

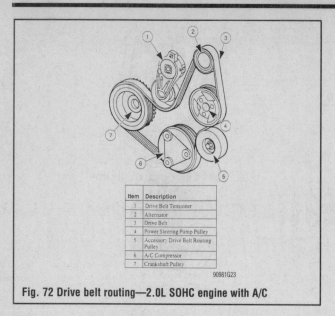

Item	Description
1	Drive Belt Tensioner
2	Alternator
3	Drive Belt
4	Power Steering Pump Pulley
5	Accessory Drive Belt Routing Pulley
6	A/C Compressor
7	Crankshaft Pulley

90981G23

Fig. 72 Drive belt routing—2.0L SOHC engine with A/C

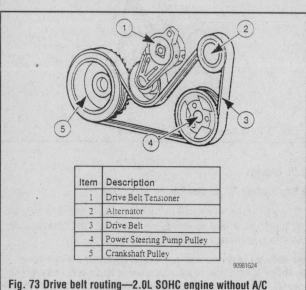

Item	Description
1	Drive Belt Tensioner
2	Alternator
3	Drive Belt
4	Power Steering Pump Pulley
5	Crankshaft Pulley

90981G24

Fig. 73 Drive belt routing—2.0L SOHC engine without A/C

POWER STEERING PUMP BELT

▶ See Figures 69 and 70

1. Raise and safely support the vehicle.
2. Loosen the power steering pump mounting bolt and nuts.
3. Remove the drive belt.

To install:

4. Install the belt and adjust the tension.
5. Tighten the power steering pump mounting nut, located near the adjusting bolt, to 27–38 ft. lbs. (37–52 Nm).
6. Tighten the pump mounting bolt behind the pulley to 27–40 ft. lbs. (36–54 Nm), and the remaining pump mounting nut to 23–34 ft. lbs. (31–46 Nm).
7. Lower the vehicle.

1.9L and 2.0L SOHC Engines

▶ See Figures 75, 76 and 77

1. Insert a ⅜ in. drive ratchet or a breaker bar in the hole on the automatic tensioner, then pull the tool toward the front of the vehicle.
2. While releasing the belt tension, remove the drive belt from the tensioner pulley and slip it off the remaining accessory pulleys.

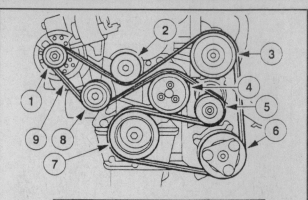

Item	Description
1	Alternator
2	Drive Belt Idler Pulley
3	Power Steering Pump Pulley
4	Water Pump Pulley
5	Drive Belt Tensioner
6	A/C Compressor
7	Crankshaft
8	Drive Belt Idler Pulley
9	Accessory Drive Belt

90981G25

Fig. 74 Drive belt routing—2.0L DOHC engine

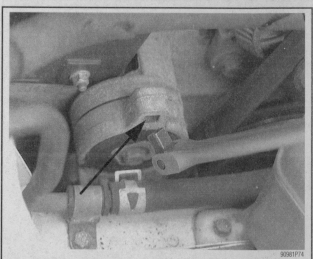

90981P74

Fig. 75 Insert a ⅜ in. drive ratchet or breaker bar into the hole of the automatic tensioner

To install:

3. Position the drive belt over the accessory pulleys.
4. Insert the ⅜ in. drive ratchet or breaker bar into the hole of the automatic tensioner, then pull the tool toward the front of the vehicle.
5. While holding the tool in this position, slip the drive belt behind the tensioner pulley and release the tool.
6. Remove the tool from the automatic tensioner.
7. Check that all V-grooves make proper contact with the pulley.

Fig. 76 Pull the breaker bar or ratchet toward the front of the vehicle to relieve belt tension

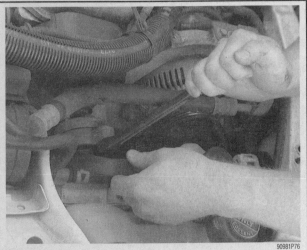

Fig. 77 Once the tension has been released, remove the belt from the pulleys and the vehicle

2.0L DOHC Engines

▶ See Figure 74

1. Raise the car and safely support it with jackstands.
2. Use a 13mm wrench to rotate the tensioner clockwise.
3. Remove the drive belt from the pulleys.

To install:

4. Position the belt on the pulleys.
5. Use a 13mm wrench to rotate the tensioner clockwise.
6. Route the belt as shown in the illustration and release the tensioner.
7. Lower the car.
8. Run the engine for a few minutes to seat the belt in the pulley grooves.

Timing Belts

INSPECTION

▶ See Figures 78 thru 85

The engine in your Escort/Tracer utilizes a timing belt to drive the camshaft from the crankshaft's turning motion, and to maintain proper valve timing. Some manufacturers recommend periodic timing belt replacement to assure optimum engine performance, and to make sure the motorist is never stranded should the belt break (as the engine will stop instantly). On some vehicles (those with "interference" engines), this is especially important to prevent the possibility of severe internal engine damage, should the belt break.

Although the engines covered by this manual are not listed as interference types (engines whose valves might contact the pistons if the camshaft rotates separately from the crankshaft), the first 2 reasons for periodic replacement still apply. Ford specifies that the timing belt on the 1.8L engine should be replaced every 60,000 miles (96,000 km) and inspected every 30,000 miles (48,000 km) after that. Although Ford does not publish a replacement interval for the 1.9L and 2.0L engines, most belt manufacturers recommend intervals anywhere from 45,000 miles (72,500 km) to 90,000 miles (145,000 km). You will have to decide for yourself if the peace of mind offered by a new belt is worth the effort and expense on higher mileage engines.

Whether or not you do decide to replace the timing belt, you would be wise to check it periodically to make sure it has not become damaged or worn. Generally speaking, a severely worn belt may cause engine performance to drop dramatically, but a damaged belt (which could give out suddenly) may not give as much warning. In general, any time the engine

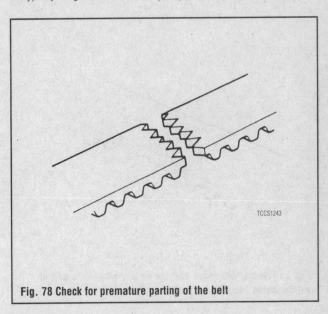

Fig. 78 Check for premature parting of the belt

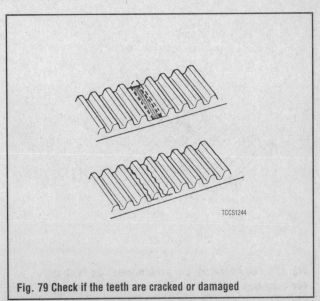

Fig. 79 Check if the teeth are cracked or damaged

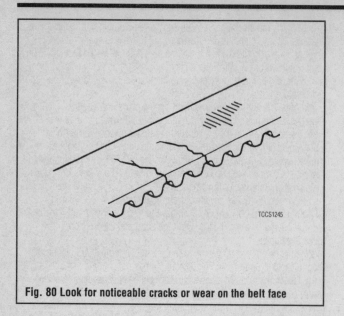

Fig. 80 Look for noticeable cracks or wear on the belt face

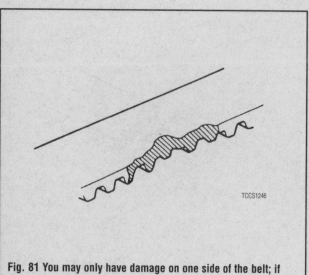

Fig. 81 You may only have damage on one side of the belt; if so, the guide could be the culprit

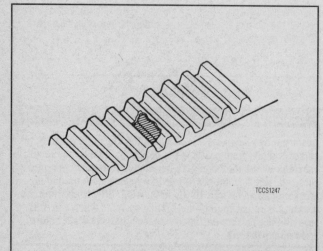

Fig. 82 Foreign materials can get in between the teeth and cause damage

Fig. 83 Inspect the timing belt for cracks, fraying, glazing or damage of any kind

Fig. 84 Damage on only one side of the timing belt may indicate a faulty guide

Fig. 85 ALWAYS replace the timing belt at the interval specified by the manufacturer

timing cover(s) is (are) removed, you should inspect the belt for premature parting, severe cracks or missing teeth. Also, an access plug may be provided in the upper portion of the timing cover, so that camshaft timing can be checked without cover removal. If timing is found to be off, cover removal and further belt inspection or replacement is necessary.

Hoses

INSPECTION

▶ See Figures 86, 87, 88 and 89

Upper and lower radiator hoses along with the heater hoses should be checked for deterioration, leaks and loose hose clamps at least every 15,000 miles (24,000 km). It is also wise to check the hoses periodically in early spring and at the beginning of the fall or winter when you are performing other maintenance. A quick visual inspection could discover a weakened hose which might have left you stranded if it had remained unrepaired.

Whenever you are checking the hoses, make sure the engine and cooling system are cold. Visually inspect for cracking, rotting or collapsed hoses,

Fig. 88 A soft spongy hose (identifiable by the swollen section) will eventually burst and should be replaced

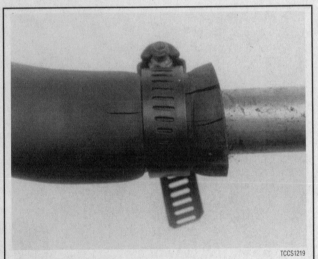

Fig. 86 The cracks developing along this hose are a result of age-related hardening

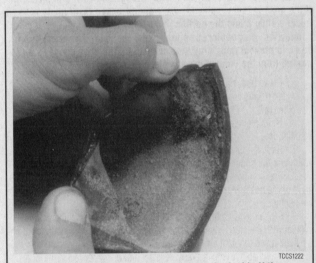

Fig. 89 Hoses are likely to deteriorate from the inside if the cooling system is not periodically flushed

and replace as necessary. Run your hand along the length of the hose. If a weak or swollen spot is noted when squeezing the hose wall, the hose should be replaced.

REMOVAL & INSTALLATION

1. Remove the radiator pressure cap.

❊❊ CAUTION

Never remove the pressure cap while the engine is running, or personal injury from scalding hot coolant or steam may result. If possible, wait until the engine has cooled to remove the pressure cap. If this is not possible, wrap a thick cloth around the pressure cap and turn it slowly to the stop. Step back while the pressure is released from the cooling system. When you are sure all the pressure has been released, use the cloth to turn and remove the cap.

2. Position a clean container under the radiator and/or engine draincock or plug, then open the drain and allow the cooling system to drain to an appropriate level. For some upper hoses, only a little coolant must be

Fig. 87 A hose clamp that is too tight can cause older hoses to separate and tear on either side of the clamp

drained. To remove hoses positioned lower on the engine, such as a lower radiator hose, the entire cooling system must be emptied.

When draining coolant, keep in mind that cats and dogs are attracted by ethylene glycol antifreeze, and are quite likely to drink any that is left in an uncovered container or in puddles on the ground. This will prove fatal in sufficient quantity. Always drain coolant into a sealable container. Coolant may be reused unless it is contaminated or several years old.

3. Loosen the hose clamps at each end of the hose requiring replacement. Clamps are usually either of the spring tension type (which require pliers to squeeze the tabs and loosen) or of the screw tension type (which require screw or hex drivers to loosen). Pull the clamps back on the hose away from the connection.

4. Twist, pull and slide the hose off the fitting, taking care not to damage the neck of the component from which the hose is being removed.

➡If the hose is stuck at the connection, do not try to insert a screwdriver or other sharp tool under the hose end in an effort to free it, as the connection and/or hose may become damaged. Heater connections, especially, may be easily damaged by such a procedure. If the hose is to be replaced, use a single-edged razor blade to make a slice along the portion of the hose which is stuck on the connection, perpendicular to the end of the hose. Do not cut deep, so as to prevent damaging the connection. The hose can then be peeled from the connection and discarded.

5. Clean both hose mounting connections. Inspect the condition of the hose clamps and replace them, if necessary.

To install:

6. Dip the ends of the new hose into clean engine coolant to ease installation.

7. Slide the clamps over the replacement hose, then slide the hose ends over the connections into position.

8. Position and secure the clamps at least ¼ in. (6.35mm) from the ends of the hose. Make sure they are located beyond the raised bead of the connector.

9. Close the radiator or engine drains and properly refill the cooling system with the clean, drained engine coolant or a suitable mixture of fresh ethylene glycol coolant and water.

10. If available, install a pressure tester and check for leaks. If a pressure tester is not available, run the engine until normal operating temperature is reached (allowing the system to naturally pressurize), then check for leaks.

If you are checking for leaks with the system at normal operating temperature, BE EXTREMELY CAREFUL not to touch any moving or hot engine parts. Once temperature has been reached, shut the engine OFF, and check for leaks around the hose fittings and connections which were removed earlier.

CV-Boots

INSPECTION

▶ **See Figures 90 and 91**

The CV (Constant Velocity) boots should be checked for damage each time the oil is changed and any other time the vehicle is raised for service. These boots keep water, grime, dirt and other damaging matter from entering the CV-joints. Any of these could cause early CV-joint failure, which can be expensive to repair. Heavy grease thrown around the inside of the front wheel(s) and on the brake caliper can be an indication of a torn boot. Thor-

TCCS1011

Fig. 90 CV-boots must be inspected periodically for damage

TCCS1010

Fig. 91 A torn boot should be replaced immediately

oughly check the boots for missing clamps and tears. If the boot is damaged, it should be replaced immediately. Please refer to Section 7 for procedures.

Spark Plugs

▶ **See Figure 92**

A typical spark plug consists of a metal shell surrounding a ceramic insulator. A metal electrode extends downward through the center of the insulator and protrudes a small distance. Located at the end of the plug and attached to the side of the outer metal shell is the side electrode. The side electrode bends in at a 90⁻ angle so that its tip is just past and parallel to the tip of the center electrode. The distance between these two electrodes (measured in thousandths of an inch or hundredths of a millimeter) is called the spark plug gap.

The spark plug does not produce a spark but instead provides a gap across which the current can arc. The coil produces anywhere from 20,000 to 50,000 volts (depending on the type and application) which travels through the wires to the spark plugs. The current passes along the center electrode and jumps the gap to the side electrode, and in doing so, ignites the air/fuel mixture in the combustion chamber.

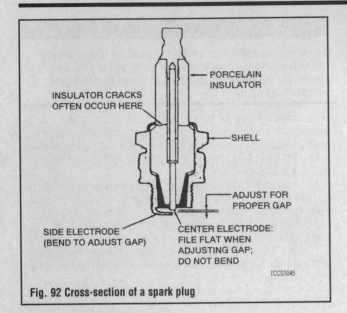

Fig. 92 Cross-section of a spark plug

Labels in figure:
- PORCELAIN INSULATOR
- INSULATOR CRACKS OFTEN OCCUR HERE
- SHELL
- ADJUST FOR PROPER GAP
- SIDE ELECTRODE (BEND TO ADJUST GAP)
- CENTER ELECTRODE: FILE FLAT WHEN ADJUSTING GAP; DO NOT BEND
- TCCS1045

SPARK PLUG HEAT RANGE

▶ **See Figure 93**

Spark plug heat range is the ability of the plug to dissipate heat. The longer the insulator (or the farther it extends into the engine), the hotter the plug will operate; the shorter the insulator (the closer the electrode is to the block's cooling passages) the cooler it will operate. A plug that absorbs little heat and remains too cool will quickly accumulate deposits of oil and carbon since it is not hot enough to burn them off. This leads to plug fouling and consequently to misfiring. A plug that absorbs too much heat will have no deposits but, due to the excessive heat, the electrodes will burn away quickly and might possibly lead to preignition or other ignition problems. Preignition takes place when plug tips get so hot that they glow sufficiently to ignite the air/fuel mixture before the actual spark occurs. This early ignition will usually cause a pinging during low speeds and heavy loads.

The general rule of thumb for choosing the correct heat range when picking a spark plug is: if most of your driving is long distance, high speed travel, use a colder plug; if most of your driving is stop and go, use a hotter plug. Original equipment plugs are generally a good compromise between the 2 styles and most people never have the need to change their plugs from the factory-recommended heat range.

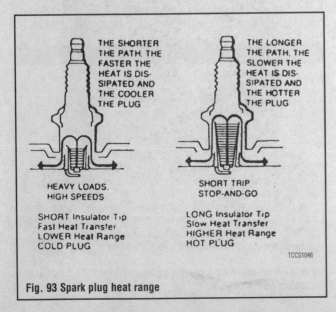

Fig. 93 Spark plug heat range

Labels in figure:
- THE SHORTER THE PATH, THE FASTER THE HEAT IS DISSIPATED AND THE COOLER THE PLUG
- THE LONGER THE PATH, THE SLOWER THE HEAT IS DISSIPATED AND THE HOTTER THE PLUG
- HEAVY LOADS, HIGH SPEEDS
- SHORT Insulator Tip / Fast Heat Transfer / LOWER Heat Range / COLD PLUG
- SHORT TRIP STOP-AND-GO
- LONG Insulator Tip / Slow Heat Transfer / HIGHER Heat Range / HOT PLUG
- TCCS1046

REMOVAL & INSTALLATION

▶ **See Figures 94, 95 and 96**

A set of spark plugs usually requires replacement after about 20,000–30,000 miles (32,000–48,000 km), depending on your style of driving. In normal operation plug gap increases about 0.001 in. (0.025mm) for every 2500 miles (4000 km). As the gap increases, the plug's voltage requirement also increases. It requires a greater voltage to jump the wider gap and about two to three times as much voltage to fire the plug at high speeds than at idle. The improved air/fuel ratio control of modern fuel injection combined with the higher voltage output of modern ignition systems will often allow an engine to run significantly longer on a set of standard spark plugs, but keep in mind that efficiency will drop as the gap widens (along with fuel economy and power).

When you're removing spark plugs, work on one at a time. Don't start by removing the plug wires all at once, because, unless you number them, they may become mixed up. Take a minute before you begin and number the wires with tape.

1. Disconnect the negative battery cable, and if the vehicle has been run recently, allow the engine to thoroughly cool.

2. On all models except the 2.0L DOHC engine, carefully twist the spark plug wire boot to loosen it, then pull upward and remove the boot from the plug. Be sure to pull on the boot and not on the wire, otherwise the connector located inside the boot may become separated.

3. On all 2.0L DOHC engines, remove the appearance cover and disconnect the spark plug wire as follows:

    a. Tag and disconnect all wires, cables and hoses that would interfere with the cover removal.

    b. Unfasten the appearance cover retaining bolts and remove the cover.

    c. Carefully twist the spark plug wire boot to loosen it, then pull upward and remove the boot from the plug. Be sure to pull on the boot and not on the wire, otherwise the connector located inside the boot may become separated.

4. Using compressed air, blow any water or debris from the spark plug well to assure that no harmful contaminants are allowed to enter the combustion chamber when the spark plug is removed. If compressed air is not available, use a rag or a brush to clean the area.

➡**Remove the spark plugs when the engine is cold, if possible, to prevent damage to the threads. If removal of the plugs is difficult, apply a few drops of penetrating oil or silicone spray to the area around the base of the plug, and allow it a few minutes to work.**

5. Using a spark plug socket that is equipped with a rubber insert to properly hold the plug, turn the spark plug counterclockwise to loosen and remove the spark plug from the bore.

❉❉ WARNING

Be sure not to use a flexible extension on the socket. Use of a flexible extension may allow a shear force to be applied to the plug. A shear force could break the plug off in the cylinder head, leading to costly and frustrating repairs.

To install:

6. Inspect the spark plug boot for tears or damage. If a damaged boot is found, the spark plug wire must be replaced.

7. Using a wire feeler gauge, check and adjust the spark plug gap. When using a gauge, the proper size should pass between the electrodes with a slight drag. The next larger size should not be able to pass while the next smaller size should pass freely.

8. Carefully thread the plug into the bore by hand. If resistance is felt before the plug is almost completely threaded, back the plug out and begin threading again. In small, hard to reach areas, an old spark plug wire and boot could be used as a threading tool. The boot will hold the plug while you twist the end of the wire and the wire is supple enough to twist before it would allow the plug to crossthread.

Fig. 94 Grasp the spark plug wire boot and twist to remove it from the spark plug

Fig. 95 Using a spark plug socket, turn the spark plug counter-clockwise to loosen it

Fig. 96 Remove the spark plug from the cylinder head, then check the condition of the spark plug and the plug gap

✳✳ WARNING

Do not use the spark plug socket to thread the plugs. Always carefully thread the plug by hand or using an old plug wire to prevent the possibility of crossthreading and damaging the cylinder head bore.

9. Carefully tighten the spark plug. If the plug you are installing is equipped with a crush washer, seat the plug, then tighten about ¼ turn to crush the washer. If you are installing a tapered seat plug, tighten the plugs to 11–17 ft. lbs. (14–23 Nm) on 1.8L engines and 7–15 ft. lbs. (10–20 Nm) on 1.9L engines.

10. Apply a small amount of silicone dielectric compound to the end of the spark plug lead or inside the spark plug boot to prevent sticking, then install the boot to the spark plug and push until it clicks into place. The click may be felt or heard, then gently pull back on the boot to assure proper contact.

11. On 2.0L DOHC engines, install the appearance cover, tighten the bolts and attach any wires, cables or hoses that were disconnected during the cover removal.

INSPECTION & GAPPING

⬥ **See Figures 97 thru 107**

Check the plugs for deposits and wear. If they are not going to be replaced, clean the plugs thoroughly. Remember that any kind of deposit will decrease the efficiency of the plug. Plugs can be cleaned on a spark plug cleaning machine, which can sometimes be found in service stations, or you can do an acceptable job of cleaning with a stiff brush. If the plugs

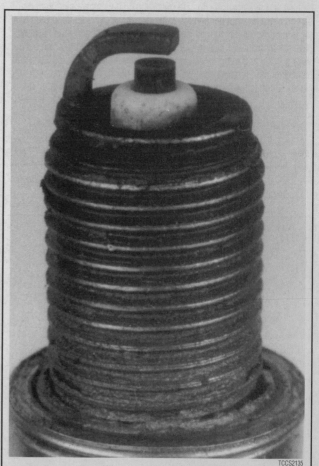

Fig. 97 A normally worn spark plug should have light tan or gray deposits on the firing tip

TCCS2136

Fig. 98 A carbon fouled plug, identified by soft, sooty, black deposits, may indicate an improperly tuned vehicle. Check the air cleaner, ignition components and engine control system

TCCS2137

Fig. 100 A physically damaged spark plug may be evidence of severe detonation in that cylinder. Watch that cylinder carefully between services, as a continued detonation will not only damage the plug, but could also damage the engine

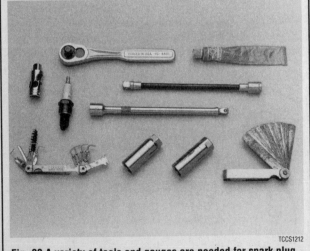

TCCS1212

Fig. 99 A variety of tools and gauges are needed for spark plug service

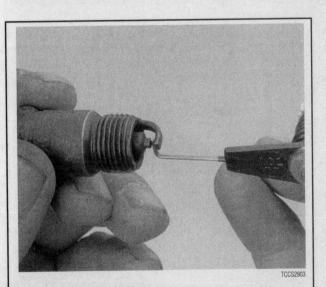

TCCS2903

Fig. 101 Checking the spark plug gap with a feeler gauge

Fig. 102 An oil fouled spark plug indicates an engine with worn piston rings and/or bad valve seals allowing excessive oil to enter the chamber

Fig. 104 This spark plug has been left in the engine too long, as evidenced by the extreme gap—Plugs with such an extreme gap can cause misfiring and stumbling accompanied by a noticeable lack of power

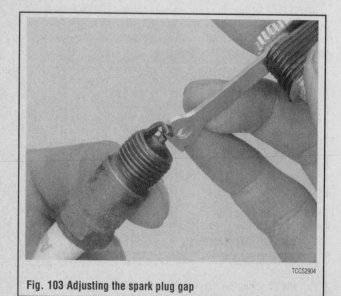

Fig. 103 Adjusting the spark plug gap

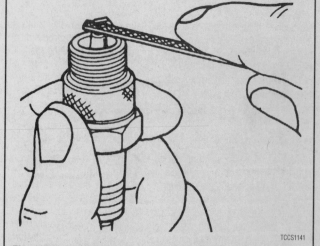

Fig. 105 If the standard plug is in good condition, the electrode may be filed flat—WARNING: do not file platinum plugs

TCCS2140

Fig. 106 A bridged or almost bridged spark plug, identified by a build-up between the electrodes, and caused by excessive carbon or oil build-up on the plug

are cleaned, the electrodes must be filed flat. Use an ignition points file, not an emery board or the like, which will leave deposits. The electrodes must be filed perfectly flat with sharp edges; rounded edges reduce the spark plug voltage by as much as 50%.

Check spark plug gap before installation. The ground electrode (the L-shaped one connected to the body of the plug) must be parallel to the center electrode and the specified size wire gauge (please refer to the Tune-Up Specifications chart for details) must pass between the electrodes with a slight drag.

➡**NEVER adjust the gap on a used platinum type spark plug.**

Always check the gap on new plugs as they are not always set correctly at the factory. Do not use a flat feeler gauge when measuring the gap on a used plug, because the reading may be inaccurate. A round-wire type gapping tool is the best way to check the gap. The correct gauge should pass through the electrode gap with a slight drag. If you're in doubt, try one size smaller and one larger. The smaller gauge should go through easily, while the larger one shouldn't go through at all. Wire gapping tools usually have a bending tool attached. Use that to adjust the side electrode until the

proper distance is obtained. Absolutely never attempt to bend the center electrode. Also, be careful not to bend the side electrode too far or too often as it may weaken and break off within the engine, requiring removal of the cylinder head to retrieve it.

Spark Plug Wires

TESTING

▶ **See Figures 108 and 109**

At every tune-up/inspection, visually check the spark plug cables for burns cuts, or breaks in the insulation. Check the boots and the nipples on the distributor cap and/or coil. Replace any damaged wiring.

Every 50,000 miles (80,000 km) or 60 months, the resistance of the wires should be checked with an ohmmeter. Wires with excessive resistance will cause misfiring, and may make the engine difficult to start in damp weather.

To check resistance, an ohmmeter should be used on each wire to test resistance between the end connectors. Remove and install/replace the wires in order, one-by-one.

Resistance on these wires must not exceed 7,000 ohms per foot. To properly measure this, remove the wires from the plugs, coil, or the distributor cap. Do not pierce any ignition wire for any reason. Measure only from the two ends.

➡**Whenever the high tension wires are removed from the plugs, coil, or distributor, silicone grease must be applied to the boot before reconnection. Coat the entire interior surface with Ford silicone grease D7AZ-19A331-A or its equivalent.**

REMOVAL & INSTALLATION

▶ **See Figures 110 and 111**

When you're removing spark plug wires, work on one at a time. Don't start by removing the plug wires all at once, because, unless you number them, they may become mixed up. Take a minute before you begin and number the wires with tape.

1. Disconnect the negative battery cable, and if the vehicle has been run recently, allow the engine to thoroughly cool.

2. On all models except the 2.0L engines, carefully twist the spark plug wire boot to loosen it, then pull upward and remove the boot from the plug. Be sure to pull on the boot and not on the wire, otherwise the connector located inside the boot may become separated.

3. On all 2.0L DOHC engines, remove the appearance cover and disconnect the spark plug wire as follows:

   a. Tag and disconnect all wires, cables and hoses that would interfere with the cover removal.

   b. Unfasten the appearance cover retaining bolts and remove the cover.

   c. Carefully twist the spark plug wire boot to loosen it, then pull upward and remove the boot from the plug. Be sure to pull on the boot and not on the wire, otherwise the connector located inside the boot may become separated.

4. On all models except the 2.0L engines, carefully twist the spark plug wire boot to loosen it, then pull upward and remove the boot from the distributor towers (1.8L) or coil pack tower (1.9L). Be sure to pull on the boot and not on the wire, otherwise the connector located inside the boot may become separated.

5. On all 2.0L engines, remove the spark plug wire from the coil by squeezing the back tabs and gently pulling the wire from the coil.

To install:

6. Apply a small amount of silicone dielectric compound to the end of the spark plug lead or inside the spark plug boot to prevent sticking, then

Tracking Arc
High voltage arcs between a fouling deposit on the insulator tip and spark plug shell. This ignites the fuel/air mixture at some point along the insulator tip, retarding the ignition timing which causes a power and fuel loss.

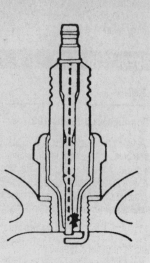

Wide Gap
Spark plug electrodes are worn so that the high voltage charge cannot arc across the electrodes. Improper gapping of electrodes on new or "cleaned" spark plugs could cause a similar condition. Fuel remains unburned and a power loss results.

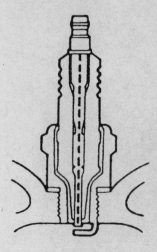

Flashover
A damaged spark plug boot, along with dirt and moisture, could permit the high voltage charge to short over the insulator to the spark plug shell or the engine. A buttress insulator design helps prevent high voltage flashover.

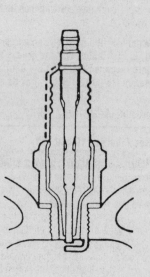

Fouled Spark Plug
Deposits that have formed on the insulator tip may become conductive and provide a "shunt" path to the shell. This prevents the high voltage from arcing between the electrodes. A power and fuel loss is the result.

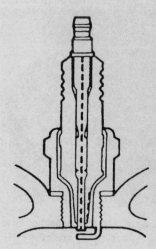

Bridged Electrodes
Fouling deposits between the electrodes "ground out" the high voltage needed to fire the spark plug. The arc between the electrodes does not occur and the fuel air mixture is not ignited. This causes a power loss and exhausting of raw fuel.

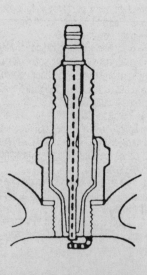

Cracked Insulator
A crack in the spark plug insulator could cause the high voltage charge to "ground out." Here, the spark does not jump the electrode gap and the fuel air mixture is not ignited. This causes a power loss and raw fuel is exhausted.

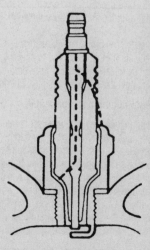

TCCS201A

Fig. 107 Used spark plugs which show damage may indicate engine problems

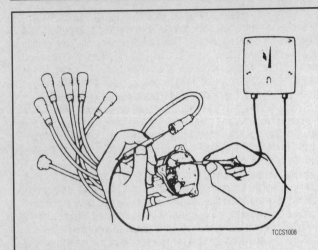

Fig. 108 Checking plug wire resistance through the distributor cap with an ohmmeter

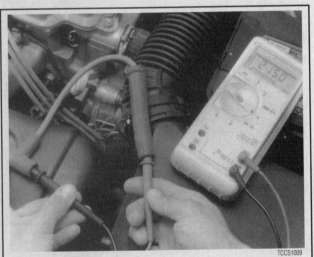

Fig. 109 Checking individual plug wire resistance with a digital ohmmeter

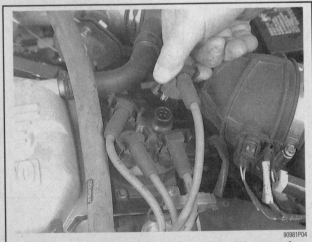

Fig. 110 Remove the spark plug wire from the coil by squeezing the back tabs and gently pulling the wire by the boot—2.0L engines

Fig. 111 The ignition coil towers may be marked with the coil number. Connect the corresponding spark plug lead to the correct tower

install the boot to the spark plug and push until it clicks into place. The click may be felt or heard, then gently pull back on the boot to assure proper contact.

7. On all models except the 2.0L engines, push the boot onto the distributor tower (1.8L) or coil pack tower (1.9L) until it is firmly engaged.

8. On all 2.0L engines, connect the wires to the proper coil pack tower and make sure the back tabs engage.

9. On 2.0L DOHC engines, install the appearance cover, tighten the bolts and attach any wires, cables or hoses that were disconnected during the cover removal.

Distributor Cap and Rotor

REMOVAL & INSTALLATION

1.8L Engine

▶ See Figures 112 and 113

1. Disconnect the negative battery cable.
2. Mark the distributor cap towers with the cylinders numbers to assist during spark plug wire-to-distributor installation.

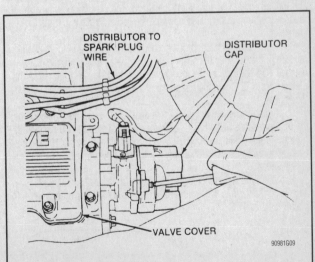

Fig. 112 Loosen the distributor cap retaining screws and remove the cap . . .

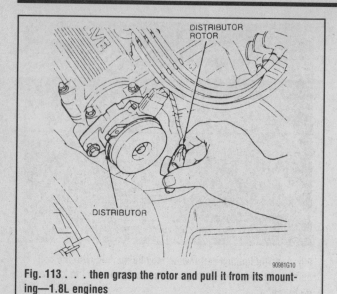

Fig. 113 . . . then grasp the rotor and pull it from its mounting—1.8L engines

3. Disconnect the coil and spark plug wires at the distributor.
4. Loosen the distributor cap retaining screws.
5. Remove the cap and pull the rotor from the distributor.
6. If necessary, remove the distributor boot.

To install:

7. If removed, install the distributor boot.
8. Install the rotor on the distributor.
9. Place the distributor cap into position and install the retaining screws.
10. Connect the coil and the spark plug wires.
11. Connect the negative battery cable.

Ignition Timing

GENERAL INFORMATION

Ignition timing is the measurement, in degrees of crankshaft rotation, of the point at which the spark plugs fire in each of the cylinders. It is measured in degrees before or after Top Dead Center (TDC) of the compression stroke.

Ideally, the air/fuel mixture in the cylinder will be ignited by the spark plug just as the piston passes TDC of the compression stroke. If this happens, the piston will be beginning the power stroke just as the compressed and ignited air/fuel mixture starts to expand. The expansion of the air/fuel mixture then forces the piston down on the power stroke and turns the crankshaft.

Because it takes a fraction of a second for the spark plug to ignite the mixture in the cylinder, the spark plug must fire a little before the piston reaches TDC. Otherwise, the mixture will not be completely ignited as the piston passes TDC and the full power of the explosion will not be used by the engine.

The timing measurement is given in degrees of crankshaft rotation before the piston reaches TDC (BTDC, or Before Top Dead Center). If the setting for the ignition timing is 10°BTDC, each spark plug must fire 10° before each piston reaches TDC. This only holds true, however, when the engine is at idle speed.

As the engine speed increases, the piston go faster. The spark plugs have to ignite the fuel even sooner if it is to be completely ignited when the piston reaches TDC.

If the ignition is set too far advanced (BTDC), the ignition and expansion of the fuel in the cylinder will occur too soon and tend to force the piston down while it is still traveling up. This causes engine ping. If the ignition spark is set too far retarded after TDC (ATDC), the piston will have already passed TDC and started on its way down when the fuel is ignited. This will cause the piston to be forced down for only a portion of its travel. This will result in poor engine performance and lack of power.

Timing marks consist of O marks or scales can be found on the rim of the crankshaft pulley and the timing cover. The mark(s) on the pulley correspond(s) to the position of the piston in the number 1 cylinder. A stroboscopic (dynamic) timing light which is hooked into the circuit of the No. 1 cylinder spark plug.

Every time the spark plug fires, the timing light flashes. By aiming the timing light at the timing marks while the engine is running, the exact position of the piston within the cylinder can be easily read since the stroboscopic flash makes the pulley appear to be standing still. Proper timing is indicated when the mark and scale are in proper alignment.

Because these vehicles utilize high voltage, electronic ignition systems, only a timing light with an inductive pickup should be used. The pickup simply clamps to the No. 1 spark plug wire, eliminating the adapter. It is not susceptible to cross-firing or false triggering, which may occur with a conventional light, due to the greater voltages produced by electronic ignition.

ADJUSTMENT

1.8L Engines

▶ See Figures 114, 115 and 116

1. Clean any dirt from around the timing scale on the timing cover and the yellow timing mark on the crankshaft pulley. This will make it easier to see when you are inspecting the timing.
2. Place the gear selector lever in the **PARK** or **NEUTRAL** position. Apply the parking brake.
3. Turn all accessories and loads **OFF**.
4. Start the engine and allow it to reach operating temperature.
5. Connect an inductive timing light to the engine, following the tool manufacturer's instructions.

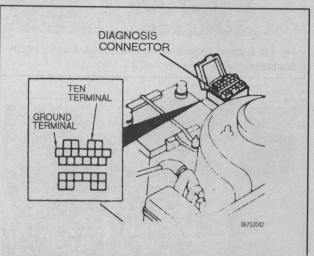

Fig. 114 Connect a jumper wire between the ground and TEN terminals on the DLC—1.8L engine

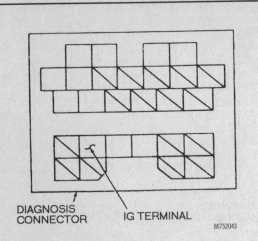

DIAGNOSIS CONNECTOR   IG TERMINAL

86752043

Fig. 115 Connect the tachometer positive lead to the IG terminal on the DLC—1.8L engine

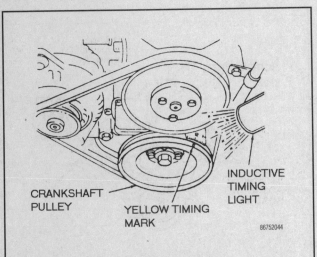

CRANKSHAFT PULLEY   YELLOW TIMING MARK   INDUCTIVE TIMING LIGHT

86752044

Fig. 116 The mark on the pulley should be aligned with the corresponding mark on the timing scale—1.8L engine

6. Using a jumper wire, connect the GROUND terminal to the **TEN** terminal of the Diagnostic Link Connector (DLC).

7. Using Rotunda tachometer 059-00010 or its equivalent, connect the tachometer positive lead to the IG terminal on the DLC and the tachometer negative lead to the battery negative post.

8. Point the timing light at the timing scale.

9. Check the ignition timing. Timing should be 10° BTDC at 700–800 rpm. The mark on the pulley should be aligned with the corresponding mark on the timing scale.

10. If not, loosen the distributor mounting bolt and turn the distributor until the marks are aligned.

11. Tighten the distributor mounting bolt to 14–19 ft. lbs. (19–25 Nm).

12. Check the timing again to make sure it did not change when tightening the distributor mounting bolts.

13. Remove the jumper wire, timing light and tachometer.

1.9L Engine

The 1.9L engine is equipped with an Electronic Distributorless Ignition System (EDIS). Ignition timing adjustment is not possible on the EDIS system.

2.0L Engines

The Powertrain Control Module controls ignition timing on these models. No adjustment is necessary or possible.

Valve Lash

ADJUSTMENT

1.8L, 1.9L and 2.0L SOHC Engines

The 1.8L and 1.9L 2.0L SOHC engines utilize hydraulic lash adjusters. These adjusters eliminate the need for any lash adjustment.

2.0L DOHC Engine

▶ See Figures 117 and 118

1. Remove the valve cover.
2. Remove the timing belt.

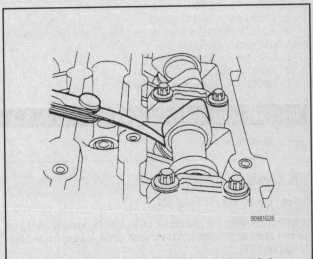

90981G26

Fig. 117 Measure each valve's clearance at the base circle before removing the camshafts—2.0L DOHC engine

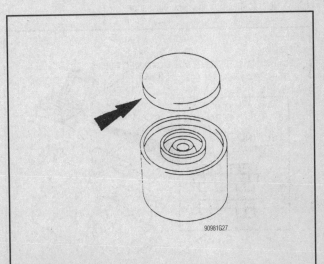

90981G27

Fig. 118 Example of a valve lifter shim (arrow)—2.0L DOHC engine

➡Measure each valve's clearance at the base circle before removing the camshafts. The shims are not serviceable with the camshafts in place. Failure to measure all valve clearances prior to removing the camshafts will result in repeated camshaft removal and installation, and a lot of wasted time.

3. Measure the valve clearances, then remove the camshafts and shims.

➡The shims are marked for thickness. For example: 2.2mm = 222 on shim.

The correct shims allow the following valve clearances:
- Intake valve clearance: 0.0043–0.0071 inch (0.11–0.18mm)
- Exhaust valve clearance: 0.0106–0.0134 inch (0.27–0.34mm)

➡A midrange clearance is the most desirable.

The midrange clearances should be as follows:
- Intake valve clearance: 0.006 inch (0.15mm)
- Exhaust valve clearance: 0.012 inch (0.3mm)

4. Select the shims using the following formula: shim thickness = measured clearance plus the base shim thickness minus the most desirable thickness.

5. Select the correct shims and mark their installation location (where they are going).

6. Replace the shims and install the camshafts.

7. Check the new valve clearances.

8. Adjust the timing of the engine. Refer to the timing belt removal and installation procedure in Section 3.

9. Install the timing belt and covers.

10. Install the valve cover.

11. Start the car and check for proper operation.

Idle Speed and Mixture Adjustments

IDLE SPEED

1.8L Engines

◆ See Figures 119, 120 and 121

➡Before adjusting the idle speed, make sure the ignition timing is correct and that all electrical loads such as the cooling fan and the lamps are OFF.

1. Apply the parking brake and place the transaxle in the **Neutral** (manual) or **PARK** (automatic) position.

2. Use a jumper wire to ground the **TEN** pin at the Data Link Connector (DLC). Refer to the accompanying illustration.

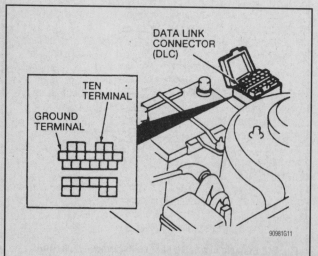

Fig. 119 Use a jumper wire to ground the TEN pin at the Data Link Connector (DLC)

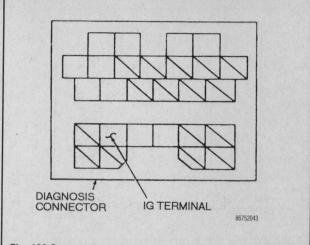

Fig. 120 Connect the tachometer positive lead to the IG terminal on the DLC—1.8L engine

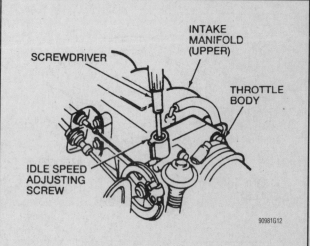

Fig. 121 Use a screwdriver to turn the idle speed adjustment screw, in order to set the idle speed

3. Using Rotunda tachometer 059-00010 or its equivalent, connect the tachometer's positive lead to the IG terminal on the DLC and the tachometer's negative lead to the negative battery post.

4. Start the engine and let it reach normal operating temperature, then note the idle speed.

5. The idle should be 700–800 rpm on an automatic transaxle in **PARK**.

6. If the idle is not as specified, turn the idle speed adjustment screw (refer to the accompanying illustration) until the correct idle speed is reached.

7. Turn the engine **OFF** and let it cool.

8. Remove the jumper wire and the tachometer.

9. After the engine has cooled, start the engine, let it reach normal operating temperature and check the idle speed.

1.9L and 2.0L Engines

The idle adjustment is controlled by the Powertrain Control Module (PCM). No adjustment is necessary or possible.

IDLE MIXTURE

The mixture adjustments are controlled by the Powertrain Control Module (PCM). No adjustment is necessary or possible.

TUNE-UP SPECIFICATIONS

Year	Engine ID/VIN	Engine Displacement Liters (cc)	Spark Plugs Gap (in.)	Ignition Timing (deg.) MT	Ignition Timing (deg.) AT	Fuel Pump (psi)	Idle Speed (rpm) MT	Idle Speed (rpm) AT	Valve Clearance In.	Valve Clearance Ex.
1991	8	1.8 (1839)	0.039-0.043	9-11 B	9-11 B	64-85 ②	700-800	700-800	HYD	HYD
	J	1.9 (1901)	0.052-0.056	8-12 B	8-12 B	30-45 ①	450-750	450-750	HYD	HYD
1992	8	1.8 (1839)	0.039-0.043	9-11 B	9-11 B	64-85 ②	700-800	700-800	HYD	HYD
	J	1.9 (1901)	0.052-0.056	8-12 B	8-12 B	30-45 ①	450-750	450-750	HYD	HYD
1993	8	1.8 (1839)	0.039-0.043	9-11 B	9-11 B	64-85 ②	700-800	700-800	HYD	HYD
	J	1.9 (1901)	0.052-0.056	8-12 B	8-12 B	30-45 ①	450-750	450-750	HYD	HYD
1994	8	1.8 (1839)	0.039-0.043	9-11 B	9-11 B	31-38 ①	700-800	700-800	HYD	HYD
	J	1.9 (1901)	0.052-0.056	8-12 B	8-12 B	30-45 ①	450-750	450-750	HYD	HYD
1995	8	1.8 (1839)	0.039-0.043	9-11 B	9-11 B	31-38 ①	700-800	700-800	HYD	HYD
	J	1.9 (1901)	0.052-0.056	8-12 B	8-12 B	30-45 ①	450-750	450-750	HYD	HYD
1996	8	1.8 (1839)	0.039-0.043	9-11 B	9-11 B	31-38 ①	700-800	700-800	HYD	HYD
	J	1.9 (1901)	0.052-0.056	8-12 B	8-12 B	30-45 ①	450-750	450-750	HYD	HYD
1997	P	2.0 (2000)	0.052-0.056	8-12 B	8-12 B	30-45 ①	③	③	HYD	HYD
1998	P	2.0 (2000)	0.052-0.056	8-12 B	8-12 B	30-45 ①	③	③	HYD	HYD
	3	2.0 (2000)	0.052-0.056	8-12 B	8-12 B	30-45 ①	③	③	MECH ④	MECH ④
1999	P	2.0 (2000)	0.052-0.056	8-12 B	8-12 B	30-45 ①	③	③	HYD	HYD
	3	2.0 (2000)	0.052-0.056	8-12 B	8-12 B	30-45 ①	③	③	MECH ④	MECH ④

NOTE: The Vehicle Emission Control Information label often reflects specification changes made during production.

The label figures must be used if they differ from those in this chart.

BTDC - Before Top Dead Center

HYD - Hydraulic

MECH - Mechanical

① Engine running

② Key on engine off

③ PCM controlled—non-adjustable

④ Intake valve clearance - 0.0043-0.0071 in. (0.11-0.18mm)

Exhaust valve clearance - 0.0106-0.0134 in. (0.27-0.34mm)

90981C3A

Air Conditioning System

SYSTEM SERVICE & REPAIR

➡**It is recommended that the A/C system be serviced by an EPA Section 609 certified automotive technician utilizing a refrigerant recovery/recycling machine.**

The do-it-yourselfer should not service his/her own vehicle's A/C system for many reasons, including legal concerns, personal injury, environmental damage and cost. The following are some of the reasons why you may decide not to service your own vehicle's A/C system.

According to the U.S. Clean Air Act, it is a federal crime to service or repair (involving the refrigerant) a Motor Vehicle Air Conditioning (MVAC) system for money without being EPA certified. It is also illegal to vent R-12 and R-134a refrigerants into the atmosphere. Selling or distributing A/C system refrigerant (in a container which contains less than 20 pounds of refrigerant) to any person who is not EPA 609 certified is also not allowed by law.

State and/or local laws may be more strict than the federal regulations, so be sure to check with your state and/or local authorities for further information. For further federal information on the legality of servicing your A/C system, call the EPA Stratospheric Ozone Hotline.

➡**Federal law dictates that a fine of up to $25,000 may be levied on people convicted of venting refrigerant into the atmosphere. Additionally, the EPA may pay up to $10,000 for information or services leading to a criminal conviction of the violation of these laws.**

When servicing an A/C system you run the risk of handling or coming in contact with refrigerant, which may result in skin or eye irritation or frost-

bite. Although low in toxicity (due to chemical stability), inhalation of concentrated refrigerant fumes is dangerous and can result in death; cases of fatal cardiac arrhythmia have been reported in people accidentally subjected to high levels of refrigerant. Some early symptoms include loss of concentration and drowsiness.

➡**Generally, the limit for exposure is lower for R-134a than it is for R-12. Exceptional care must be practiced when handling R-134a.**

Also, refrigerants can decompose at high temperatures (near gas heaters or open flame), which may result in hydrofluoric acid, hydrochloric acid and phosgene (a fatal nerve gas).

R-12 refrigerant can damage the environment because it is a Chlorofluorocarbon (CFC), which has been proven to add to ozone layer depletion, leading to increasing levels of UV radiation. UV radiation has been linked with an increase in skin cancer, suppression of the human immune system, an increase in cataracts, damage to crops, damage to aquatic organisms, an increase in ground-level ozone, and increased global warming.

R-134a refrigerant is a greenhouse gas which, if allowed to vent into the atmosphere, will contribute to global warming (the Greenhouse Effect).

It is usually more economically feasible to have a certified MVAC automotive technician perform A/C system service on your vehicle. Some possible reasons for this are as follows:

- While it is illegal to service an A/C system without the proper equipment, the home mechanic would have to purchase an expensive refrigerant recovery/recycling machine to service his/her own vehicle.
- Since only a certified person may purchase refrigerant—according to the Clean Air Act, there are specific restrictions on selling or distributing A/C system refrigerant—it is legally impossible (unless certified) for the home mechanic to service his/her own vehicle. Procuring refrigerant in an illegal fashion exposes one to the risk of paying a $25,000 fine to the EPA.

R-12 Refrigerant Conversion

If your vehicle still uses R-12 refrigerant, one way to save A/C system costs down the road is to investigate the possibility of having your system converted to R-134a. The older R-12 systems can be easily converted to R-134a refrigerant by a certified automotive technician by installing a few new components and changing the system oil.

The cost of R-12 is steadily rising and will continue to increase, because it is no longer imported or manufactured in the United States. Therefore, it is often possible to have an R-12 system converted to R-134a and recharged for less than it would cost to just charge the system with R-12.

If you are interested in having your system converted, contact local automotive service stations for more details and information.

PREVENTIVE MAINTENANCE

▶ **See Figures 122 and 123**

Although the A/C system should not be serviced by the do-it-yourselfer, preventive maintenance can be practiced and A/C system inspections can be performed to help maintain the efficiency of the vehicle's A/C system. For preventive maintenance, perform the following:

Fig. 122 A coolant tester can be used to determine the freezing and boiling levels of the coolant in your vehicle

• The easiest and most important preventive maintenance for your A/C system is to be sure that it is used on a regular basis. Running the system for five minutes each month (no matter what the season) will help ensure that the seals and all internal components remain lubricated.

➡**Some newer vehicles automatically operate the A/C system compressor whenever the windshield defroster is activated. When running, the compressor lubricates the A/C system components; therefore, the A/C system would not need to be operated each month.**

• In order to prevent heater core freeze-up during A/C operation, it is necessary to maintain proper antifreeze protection. Use a hand-held coolant tester (hydrometer) to periodically check the condition of the antifreeze in your engine's cooling system.

➡**Antifreeze should not be used longer than the manufacturer specifies.**

• For efficient operation of an air conditioned vehicle's cooling system, the radiator cap should have a holding pressure which meets manufacturer's specifications. A cap which fails to hold these pressures should be replaced.

• Any obstruction of or damage to the condenser configuration will restrict air flow which is essential to its efficient operation. It is, therefore, a good rule to keep this unit clean and in proper physical shape.

➡**Bug screens which are mounted in front of the condenser (unless they are original equipment) are regarded as obstructions.**

• The condensation drain tube expels any water which accumulates on the bottom of the evaporator housing into the engine compartment. If this tube is obstructed, the air conditioning performance can be restricted and condensation buildup can spill over onto the vehicle's floor.

SYSTEM INSPECTION

▶ **See Figure 124**

Although the A/C system should not be serviced by the do-it-yourselfer, preventive maintenance can be practiced and A/C system inspections can be performed to help maintain the efficiency of the vehicle's A/C system. For A/C system inspection, perform the following:

The easiest and often most important check for the air conditioning system consists of a visual inspection of the system components. Visually inspect the air conditioning system for refrigerant leaks, damaged compressor clutch, abnormal compressor drive belt tension and/or condition, plugged evaporator drain tube, blocked condenser fins, disconnected or broken wires, blown fuses, corroded connections and poor insulation.

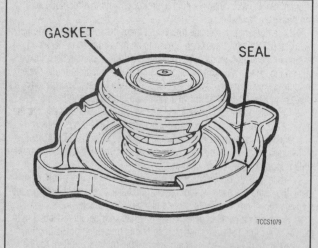

Fig. 123 To ensure efficient cooling system operation, inspect the radiator cap gasket and seal

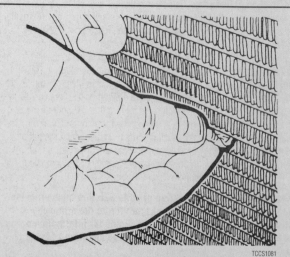

Fig. 124 Periodically remove any debris from the condenser and radiator fins

A refrigerant leak will usually appear as an oily residue at the leakage point in the system. The oily residue soon picks up dust or dirt particles from the surrounding air and appears greasy. Through time, this will build up and appear to be a heavy dirt impregnated grease.

For a thorough visual and operational inspection, check the following:

• Check the surface of the radiator and condenser for dirt, leaves or other material which might block air flow.

• Check for kinks in hoses and lines. Check the system for leaks.

• Make sure the drive belt is properly tensioned. When the air conditioning is operating, make sure the drive belt is free of noise or slippage.

• Make sure the blower motor operates at all appropriate positions, then check for distribution of the air from all outlets with the blower on **HIGH** or **MAX**.

➡**Keep in mind that under conditions of high humidity, air discharged from the A/C vents may not feel as cold as expected, even if the system is working properly. This is because vaporized moisture in humid air retains heat more effectively than dry air, thereby making humid air more difficult to cool.**

• Make sure the air passage selection lever is operating correctly. Start the engine and warm it to normal operating temperature, then make sure the temperature selection lever is operating correctly.

Windshield Wipers

ELEMENT (REFILL) CARE & REPLACEMENT

▶ **See Figures 125 thru 134**

For maximum effectiveness and longest element life, the windshield and wiper blades should be kept clean. Dirt, tree sap, road tar and so on will cause streaking, smearing and blade deterioration if left on the glass. It is advisable to wash the windshield carefully with a commercial glass cleaner at least once a month. Wipe off the rubber blades with the wet rag afterwards. Do not attempt to move wipers across the windshield by hand; damage to the motor and drive mechanism will result.

To inspect and/or replace the wiper blade elements, place the wiper switch in the **LOW** speed position and the ignition switch in the **ACC** position. When the wiper blades are approximately vertical on the windshield, turn the ignition switch to **OFF**.

Examine the wiper blade elements. If they are found to be cracked, broken or torn, they should be replaced immediately. Replacement intervals will vary with usage, although ozone deterioration usually limits element life to about one year. If the wiper pattern is smeared or streaked, or if the blade chatters across the glass, the elements should be replaced. It is easiest and most sensible to replace the elements in pairs.

If your vehicle is equipped with aftermarket blades, there are several different types of refills and your vehicle might have any kind. Aftermarket blades and arms rarely use the exact same type blade or refill as the original equipment. Here are some typical aftermarket blades; not all may be available for your vehicle:

The Anco® type uses a release button that is pushed down to allow the refill to slide out of the yoke jaws. The new refill slides back into the frame and locks in place.

Some Trico® refills are removed by locating where the metal backing strip or the refill is wider. Insert a small screwdriver blade between the frame and metal backing strip. Press down to release the refill from the retaining tab.

Other types of Trico® refills have two metal tabs which are unlocked by squeezing them together. The rubber filler can then be withdrawn from the frame jaws. A new refill is installed by inserting the refill into the front frame jaws and sliding it rearward to engage the remaining frame jaws. There are usually four jaws; be certain when installing that the refill is engaged in all of them. At the end of its travel, the tabs will lock into place on the front jaws of the wiper blade frame.

Another type of refill is made from polycarbonate. The refill has a simple locking device at one end which flexes downward out of the groove into

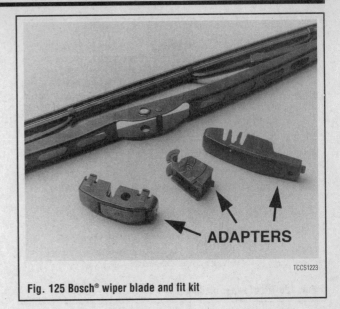

Fig. 125 Bosch® wiper blade and fit kit

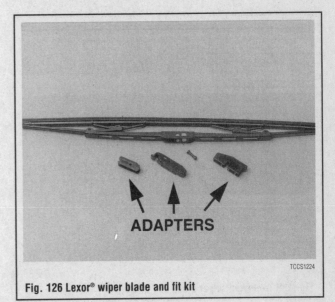

Fig. 126 Lexor® wiper blade and fit kit

Fig. 127 Pylon® wiper blade and adapter

Fig. 128 Trico® wiper blade and fit kit

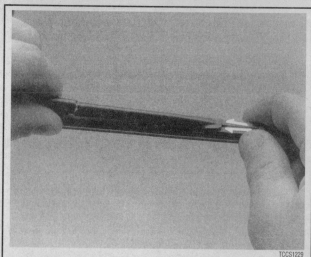

Fig. 131 On Pylon® inserts, the clip at the end has to be removed prior to sliding the insert off

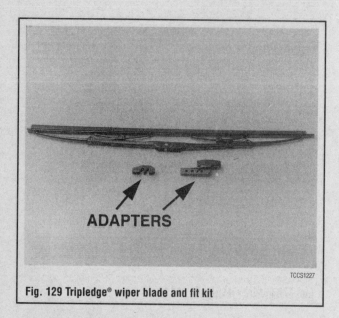

ADAPTERS

Fig. 129 Tripledge® wiper blade and fit kit

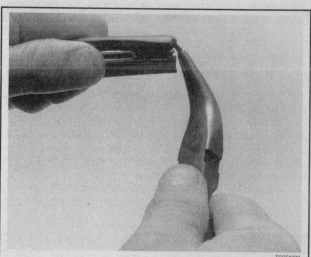

Fig. 132 On Trico® wiper blades, the tab at the end of the blade must be turned up . . .

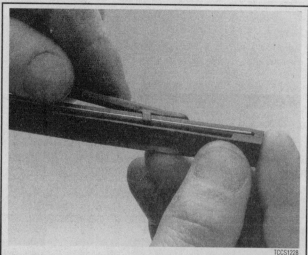

Fig. 130 To remove and install a Lexor® wiper blade refill, slip out the old insert and slide in a new one

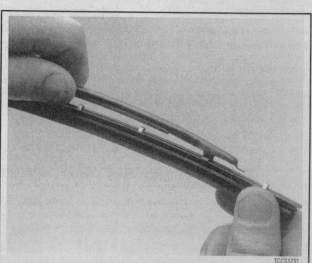

Fig. 133 . . . then the insert can be removed. After installing the replacement insert, bend the tab back

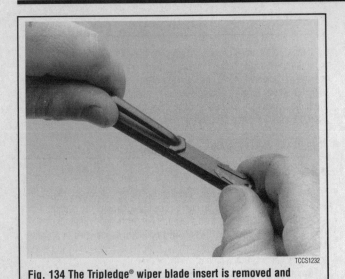

Fig. 134 The Tripledge® wiper blade insert is removed and installed using a securing clip

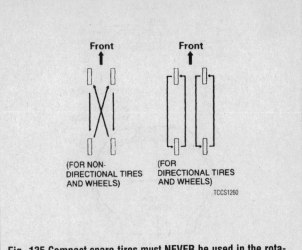

Fig. 135 Compact spare tires must NEVER be used in the rotation pattern

which the jaws of the holder fit, allowing easy release. By sliding the new refill through all the jaws and pushing through the slight resistance when it reaches the end of its travel, the refill will lock into position.

To replace the Tridon® refill, it is necessary to remove the wiper blade. This refill has a plastic backing strip with a notch about 1 in. (25mm) from the end. Hold the blade (frame) on a hard surface so that the frame is tightly bowed. Grip the tip of the backing strip and pull up while twisting counterclockwise. The backing strip will snap out of the retaining tab. Do this for the remaining tabs until the refill is free of the blade. The length of these refills is molded into the end and they should be replaced with identical types.

Regardless of the type of refill used, be sure to follow the part manufacturer's instructions closely. Make sure that all of the frame jaws are engaged as the refill is pushed into place and locked. If the metal blade holder and frame are allowed to touch the glass during wiper operation, the glass will be scratched.

Tires and Wheels

Common sense and good driving habits will afford maximum tire life. Fast starts, sudden stops and hard cornering are hard on tires and will shorten their useful life span. Make sure that you don't overload the vehicle or run with incorrect pressure in the tires. Both of these practices will increase treadwear.

➡For optimum tire life, keep the tires properly inflated, rotate them often and have the wheel alignment checked periodically.

Inspect your tires frequently. Be especially careful to watch for bubbles in the tread or sidewall, deep cuts or underinflation. Replace any tires with bubbles in the sidewall. If cuts are so deep that they penetrate to the cords, discard the tire. Any cut in the sidewall of a radial tire renders it unsafe. Also look for uneven treadwear patterns that may indicate the front end is out of alignment or that the tires are out of balance.

TIRE ROTATION

◆ See Figures 135 and 136

Tires must be rotated periodically to equalize wear patterns that vary with a tire's position on the vehicle. Tires will also wear in an uneven way as the front steering/suspension system wears to the point where the alignment should be reset.

Rotating the tires will ensure maximum life for the tires as a set, so you will not have to discard a tire early due to wear on only part of the tread. Regular rotation is required to equalize wear.

Fig. 136 Unidirectional tires are identifiable by sidewall arrows and/or the word "rotation"

When rotating "unidirectional tires," make sure that they always roll in the same direction. This means that a tire used on the left side of the vehicle must not be switched to the right side and vice-versa. Such tires should only be rotated front-to-rear or rear-to-front, while always remaining on the same side of the vehicle. These tires are marked on the sidewall as to the direction of rotation; observe the marks when reinstalling the tire(s).

Some styled or "mag" wheels may have different offsets front to rear. In these cases, the rear wheels must not be used up front and vice-versa. Furthermore, if these wheels are equipped with unidirectional tires, they cannot be rotated unless the tire is remounted for the proper direction of rotation.

➡The compact or space-saver spare is strictly for emergency use. It must never be included in the tire rotation or placed on the vehicle for everyday use.

TIRE DESIGN

◆ See Figure 137

For maximum satisfaction, tires should be used in sets of four. Mixing of different types (radial, bias-belted, fiberglass belted) must be avoided. In most cases, the vehicle manufacturer has designated a type of tire on which

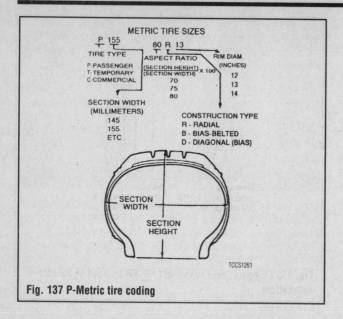

Fig. 137 P-Metric tire coding

the vehicle will perform best. Your first choice when replacing tires should be to use the same type of tire that the manufacturer recommends.

When radial tires are used, tire sizes and wheel diameters should be selected to maintain ground clearance and tire load capacity equivalent to the original specified tire. Radial tires should always be used in sets of four.

✳✳ CAUTION

Radial tires should never be used on only the front axle.

When selecting tires, pay attention to the original size as marked on the tire. Most tires are described using an industry size code sometimes referred to as P-Metric. This allows the exact identification of the tire specifications, regardless of the manufacturer. If selecting a different tire size or brand, remember to check the installed tire for any sign of interference with the body or suspension while the vehicle is stopping, turning sharply or heavily loaded.

Snow Tires

Good radial tires can produce a big advantage in slippery weather, but in snow, a street radial tire does not have sufficient tread to provide traction and control. The small grooves of a street tire quickly pack with snow and the tire behaves like a billiard ball on a marble floor. The more open, chunky tread of a snow tire will self-clean as the tire turns, providing much better grip on snowy surfaces.

To satisfy municipalities requiring snow tires during weather emergencies, most snow tires carry either an M + S designation after the tire size stamped on the sidewall, or the designation "all-season." In general, no change in tire size is necessary when buying snow tires.

Most manufacturers strongly recommend the use of 4 snow tires on their vehicles for reasons of stability. If snow tires are fitted only to the drive wheels, the opposite end of the vehicle may become very unstable when braking or turning on slippery surfaces. This instability can lead to unpleasant endings if the driver can't counteract the slide in time.

Note that snow tires, whether 2 or 4, will affect vehicle handling in all non-snow situations. The stiffer, heavier snow tires will noticeably change the turning and braking characteristics of the vehicle. Once the snow tires are installed, you must re-learn the behavior of the vehicle and drive accordingly.

➡Consider buying extra wheels on which to mount the snow tires. Once done, the "snow wheels" can be installed and removed as needed. This eliminates the potential damage to tires or wheels from seasonal removal and installation. Even if your vehicle has styled wheels, see if inexpensive steel wheels are available. Although the look of the vehicle will change, the expensive wheels will be protected from salt, curb hits and pothole damage.

TIRE STORAGE

If they are mounted on wheels, store the tires at proper inflation pressure. All tires should be kept in a cool, dry place. If they are stored in the garage or basement, do not let them stand on a concrete floor; set them on strips of wood, a mat or a large stack of newspaper. Keeping them away from direct moisture is of paramount importance. Tires should not be stored upright, but in a flat position.

INFLATION & INSPECTION

▶ **See Figures 138 thru 145**

The importance of proper tire inflation cannot be overemphasized. A tire employs air as part of its structure. It is designed around the supporting strength of the air at a specified pressure. For this reason, improper inflation drastically reduces the tire's ability to perform as intended. A tire will lose some air in day-to-day use; having to add a few pounds of air periodically is not necessarily a sign of a leaking tire.

Two items should be a permanent fixture in every glove compartment: an accurate tire pressure gauge and a tread depth gauge. Check the tire pressure (including the spare) regularly with a pocket type gauge. Too often, the

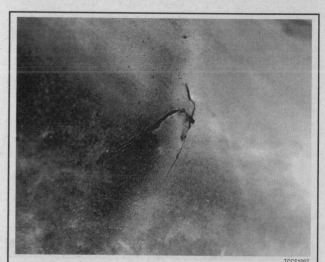

Fig. 138 Tires should be checked frequently for any sign of puncture or damage

Fig. 139 Tires with deep cuts, or cuts which show bulging, should be replaced immediately

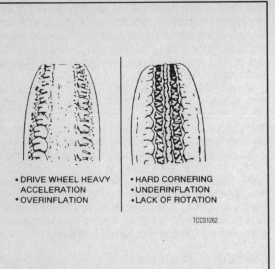

- DRIVE WHEEL HEAVY ACCELERATION
- OVERINFLATION

- HARD CORNERING
- UNDERINFLATION
- LACK OF ROTATION

TCCS1262

Fig. 140 Examples of inflation-related tire wear patterns

gauge on the end of the air hose at your corner garage is not accurate because it suffers too much abuse. Always check tire pressure when the tires are cold, as pressure increases with temperature. If you must move the vehicle to check the tire inflation, do not drive more than a mile before checking. A cold tire is generally one that has not been driven for more than three hours.

A plate or sticker which shows the proper pressure for the tires is normally provided somewhere in the vehicle (door post, hood, tailgate or trunk lid). Never counteract excessive pressure build-up by bleeding off air pressure (letting some air out). This will cause the tire to run hotter and wear quicker.

✳✳ CAUTION

Never exceed the maximum tire pressure embossed on the tire! This is the pressure to be used when the tire is at maximum loading, but it is rarely the correct pressure for everyday driving. Consult the owner's manual or the tire pressure sticker for the correct tire pressure.

Once you've maintained the correct tire pressures for several weeks, you'll be familiar with the vehicle's braking and handling personality. Slight

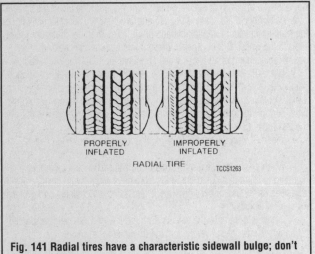

PROPERLY INFLATED

IMPROPERLY INFLATED

RADIAL TIRE

TCCS1263

Fig. 141 Radial tires have a characteristic sidewall bulge; don't try to measure pressure by looking at the tire. Use a quality air pressure gauge

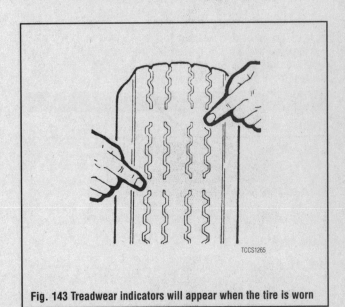

TCCS1265

Fig. 143 Treadwear indicators will appear when the tire is worn

CONDITION	RAPID WEAR AT SHOULDERS	RAPID WEAR AT CENTER	CRACKED TREADS	WEAR ON ONE SIDE	FEATHERED EDGE	BALD SPOTS	SCALLOPED WEAR
EFFECT							
CAUSE	UNDER-INFLATION OR LACK OF ROTATION	OVER-INFLATION OR LACK OF ROTATION	UNDER-INFLATION OR EXCESSIVE SPEED*	EXCESSIVE CAMBER	INCORRECT TOE	UNBALANCED WHEEL — OR TIRE DEFECT *	LACK OF ROTATION OF TIRES OR WORN OR OUT-OF-ALIGNMENT SUSPENSION.
CORRECTION	ADJUST PRESSURE TO SPECIFICATIONS WHEN TIRES ARE COOL ROTATE TIRES			ADJUST CAMBER TO SPECIFICATIONS	ADJUST TOE-IN TO SPECIFICATIONS	DYNAMIC OR STATIC BALANCE WHEELS	ROTATE TIRES AND INSPECT SUSPENSION

*HAVE TIRE INSPECTED FOR FURTHER USE.

TCCS1267

Fig. 142 Common tire wear patterns and causes

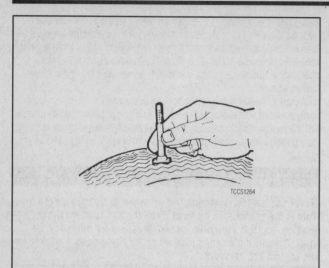

Fig. 144 Accurate tread depth indicators are inexpensive and handy

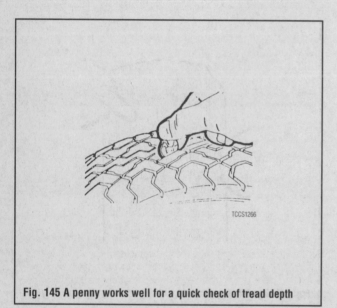

Fig. 145 A penny works well for a quick check of tread depth

adjustments in tire pressures can fine-tune these characteristics, but never change the cold pressure specification by more than 2 psi. A slightly softer tire pressure will give a softer ride, but also yield lower fuel mileage. A slightly harder tire will give crisper dry road handling, but can cause skidding on wet surfaces. Unless you're fully attuned to the vehicle, stick to the recommended inflation pressures.

All tires made since 1968 have built-in treadwear indicator bars that show up as ½ in. (13mm) wide smooth bands across the tire when ⅟₁₆ in. (1.5mm) of tread remains. The appearance of treadwear indicators means that the tires should be replaced. In fact, many states have laws prohibiting the use of tires with less than this amount of tread.

You can check your own tread depth with an inexpensive gauge or by using a Lincoln head penny. Slip the Lincoln penny (with Lincoln's head upside-down) into several tread grooves. If you can see the top of Lincoln's head in 2 adjacent grooves, the tire has less than ⅟₁₆ in. (1.5mm) tread left and should be replaced. You can measure snow tires in the same manner by using the "tails" side of the Lincoln penny. If you can see the top of the Lincoln memorial, it's time to replace the snow tire(s).

CARE OF SPECIAL WHEELS

If you have invested money in magnesium, aluminum alloy or sport wheels, special precautions should be taken to make sure your investment is not wasted and that your special wheels look good for the life of the vehicle.

Special wheels are easily damaged and/or scratched. Occasionally check the rims for cracking, impact damage or air leaks. If any of these are found, replace the wheel. But in order to prevent this type of damage and the costly replacement of a special wheel, observe the following precautions:

• Use extra care not to damage the wheels during removal, installation, balancing, etc. After removal of the wheels from the vehicle, place them on a mat or other protective surface. If they are to be stored for any length of time, support them on strips of wood. Never store tires and wheels upright; the tread may develop flat spots.

• When driving, watch for hazards; it doesn't take much to crack a wheel.

• When washing, use a mild soap or non-abrasive dish detergent (keeping in mind that detergent tends to remove wax). Avoid cleansers with abrasives or the use of hard brushes. There are many cleaners and polishes for special wheels.

• If possible, remove the wheels during the winter. Salt and sand used for snow removal can severely damage the finish of a wheel.

• Make certain the recommended lug nut torque is never exceeded or the wheel may crack. Never use snow chains on special wheels; severe scratching will occur.

FLUIDS AND LUBRICANTS

Fluid Disposal

Used fluids such as engine oil, transmission fluid, antifreeze and brake fluid are hazardous wastes and must be disposed of properly. Before draining any fluids, consult with your local authorities; in many areas, waste oil, antifreeze, etc. are being accepted as a part of recycling programs. A number of service stations and auto parts stores are also accepting waste fluids for recycling.

Be sure of the recycling center's policies before draining any fluids, as many will not accept different fluids that have been mixed together.

Fuel and Engine Oil Recommendations

ENGINE OIL

▶ **See Figures 146 and 147**

➡**Ford recommends that SAE 5W-30 viscosity engine oil should be used for all climate conditions, however, SAE 10W-30 is acceptable for vehicles operated in moderate-to-hot climates.**

When adding oil to the crankcase or changing the oil or filter, it is important that oil of an equal quality to original equipment be used in your car. The use of inferior oils may void the warranty, damage your engine, or both.

The SAE (Society of Automotive Engineers) grade number of oil indicates the viscosity of the oil (its ability to lubricate at a given temperature). The lower the SAE number, the lighter the oil; the lower the viscosity, the easier it is to crank the engine in cold weather but the less the oil will lubricate and protect the engine in high temperatures. This number is marked on every oil container.

Oil viscosity's should be chosen from those oils recommended for the lowest anticipated temperatures during the oil change interval. Due to the need for an oil that embodies both good lubrication at high temperatures and easy cranking in cold weather, multigrade oils have been developed. Basically, a multigrade oil is thinner at low temperatures and thicker at high temperatures. For example, a 10W-40 oil (the W stands for winter) exhibits the characteristics of a 10 weight (SAE 10) oil when the car is first started and the oil is cold. Its lighter weight allows it to travel to the lubricating surfaces quicker and offer less resistance to starter motor cranking than,

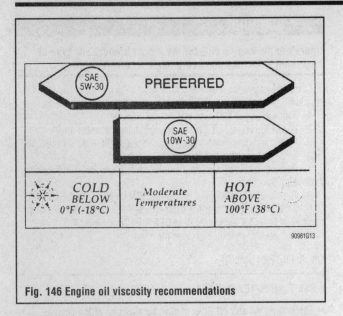

Fig. 146 Engine oil viscosity recommendations

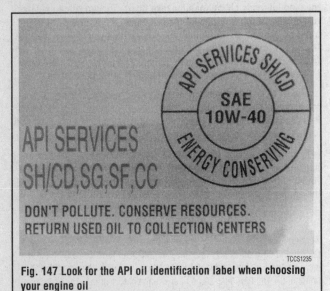

Fig. 147 Look for the API oil identification label when choosing your engine oil

say, a straight 30 weight (SAE 30) oil. But after the engine reaches operating temperature, the 10W-40 oil begins acting like straight 40 weight (SAE 40) oil, its heavier weight providing greater lubrication with less chance of foaming than a straight 30 weight oil.

The API (American Petroleum Institute) designations, also found on the oil container, indicates the classification of engine oil used under certain given operating conditions. Only oils designated for use Service SG heavy duty detergent should be used in your car. Oils of the SG type perform may functions inside the engine besides their basic lubrication. Through a balanced system of metallic detergents and polymeric dispersants, the oil prevents high and low temperature deposits and also keeps sludge and dirt particles in suspension. Acids, particularly sulfuric acid, as well as other by-products of engine combustion are neutralized by the oil. If these acids are allowed to concentrate, they can cause corrosion and rapid wear of the internal engine parts.

✳✳ CAUTION

Non-detergent motor oils or straight mineral oils should not be used in your Ford gasoline engine.

Synthetic Oil

There are many excellent synthetic and fuel-efficient oils currently available that can provide better gas mileage, longer service life and, in some cases, better engine protection. These benefits do not come without a few hitches, however; the main one being the price of synthetic oil, which is significantly more expensive than conventional oil.

Synthetic oil is not for every car and every type of driving, so you should consider your engine's condition and your type of driving. Also, check your car's warranty conditions regarding the use of synthetic oils.

FUEL

Your vehicle is designed to operate using regular unleaded fuel with a minimum of 87 octane. Ford warns that using gasoline with an octane rating lower than 87 can cause persistent and heavy knocking, and may cause internal engine damage.

If your vehicle is having problems with rough idle or hesitation when the engine is cold, it may be caused by low volatility fuel. If this occurs, try a different grade or brand of fuel.

OPERATION IN FOREIGN COUNTRIES

If you plan to drive your car outside the United States or Canada, there is a possibility that fuels will be too low in anti-knock quality and could produce engine damage. It is wise to consult with local authorities upon arrival in a foreign country to determine the best fuels available.

Engine

OIL LEVEL CHECK

▶ **See Figures 148, 149, 150 and 151**

✳✳ CAUTION

The EPA warns that prolonged contact with used engine oil may cause a number of skin disorders, including cancer! You should make every effort to minimize your exposure to used engine oil. Protective gloves should be worn when changing the oil. Wash your hands and any other exposed skin areas as soon as possible after exposure to used engine oil. Soap and water, or waterless hand cleaner should be used.

Fig. 148 On some engines, the type of fluid is clearly marked on the dipstick handle—1997 2.0L engine shown

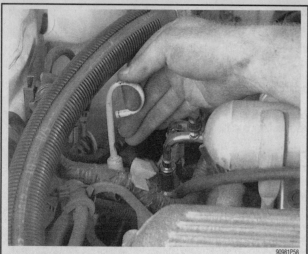

Fig. 149 Grasp the handle and pull the engine oil dipstick from its tube—1.9L engine shown

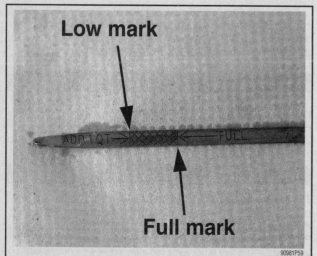

Low mark

Full mark

Fig. 150 The oil level should be at the FULL mark on the engine oil dipstick

Fig. 151 Add oil using a funnel through the opening in the valve cover

✳✳ WARNING

Operating the engine without the proper amount and type of engine oil will result in severe engine damage.

Check the engine oil level every time you fill the fuel tank. The car should be on level ground when checking the oil.
1. Turn the engine **OFF** and wait several minutes.
2. Locate the engine oil dipstick and withdraw it from the tube.
3. Wipe the dipstick with a clean rag and reinsert it in the dipstick tube. Make sure the dipstick is fully seated.
4. Remove the dipstick again, hold the dipstick horizontal and observe the level of the oil.
5. The oil level should be at or near the **FULL** line on the dipstick.
6. If the level is at or near the **ADD** line, replace the dipstick and add fresh oil to bring the level up to the **FULL** line. Do not overfill.
7. Recheck the oil level and close the hood.

OIL & FILTER CHANGE

▶ See Figures 152 thru 161

➡The engine oil and oil filter should be changed at the recommended intervals on the Maintenance Chart. Though some manufacturers have at times recommended changing the filter only at every other oil change, we at Chilton recommend that you always change the filter with the oil. The benefit of fresh oil is quickly lost if the old filter is clogged and unable to do its job. Also, leaving the old filter in place leaves a significant amount of dirty oil in the system.

The oil should be changed more frequently if the vehicle is being operated in a very dusty area. Before draining the oil, make sure that the engine is at operating temperature. Hot oil will hold more impurities in suspension and will flow better, allowing the removal of more oil and dirt.

➡It is usually a good idea to place your ignition key in the box or bag with the bottles of fresh engine oil. In this way, it will be VERY HARD to forget to refill the engine crankcase before you go to start the engine.

1. Raise and support the vehicle safely on jackstands.
2. Before you crawl under the car, take a look at where you will be working and gather all the necessary tools such as: a few wrenches or a ratchet and strip of sockets, a drain pan and clean rags. If the oil filter is more accessible from underneath the vehicle, you will also want to grab a bottle of oil, the new filter and a filter wrench at this time.

✳✳ CAUTION

The EPA warns that prolonged contact with used engine oil may cause a number of skin disorders, including cancer! You should make every effort to minimize your exposure to used engine oil. Protective gloves should be worn when changing the oil. Wash your hands and any other exposed skin areas as soon as possible after exposure to used engine oil. Soap and water, or waterless hand cleaner should be used.

✳✳ WARNING

Operating the engine without the proper amount and type of engine oil will result in severe engine damage.

3. Position the drain pan beneath the oil pan drain plug. Keep in mind that the fast flowing oil, which will spill out as you pull the plug from the pan, will flow with enough force that it could miss the pan. Position the drain pan accordingly and be ready to move the pan more directly beneath the plug as the oil flow lessens to a trickle.
4. Loosen the drain plug with a wrench (or socket and driver), then carefully unscrew the plug with your fingers. Use a rag to shield your fingers from

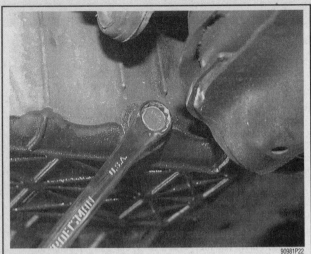

Fig. 152 Loosen the drain plug with a wrench (or socket and driver) . . .

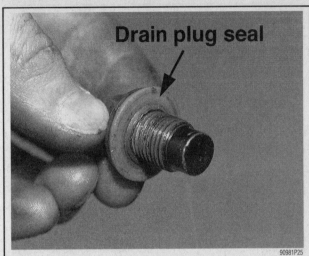

Fig. 155 Check the condition of the drain plug seal and replace it as necessary

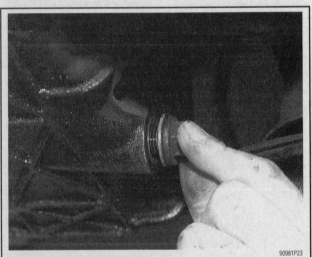

Fig. 153 . . . then carefully unscrew the plug with your fingers . . .

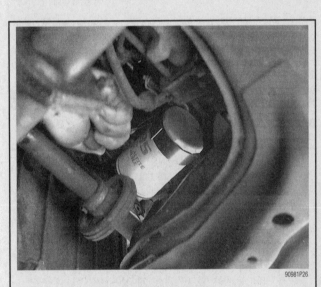

Fig. 156 An oil filter strap type wrench . . .

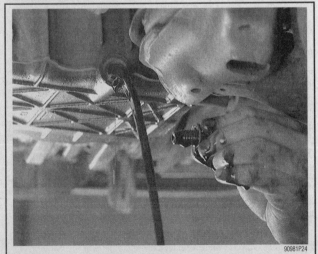

Fig. 154 . . . and remove the plug quickly, to avoid having hot oil run down your arm. Allow the oil to completely drain

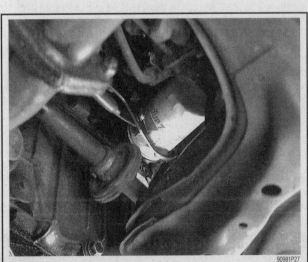

Fig. 157 . . . or oil filter pliers can be used to loosen the engine oil filter

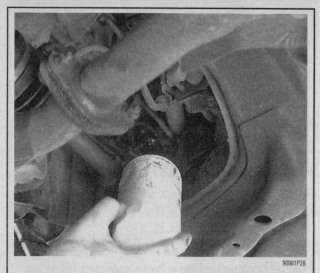

Fig. 158 Unscrew the filter from the boss on the engine

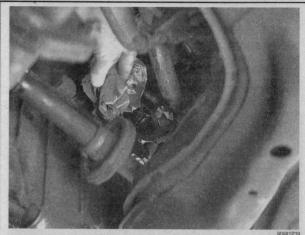

Fig. 159 Before installing a new filter, use a rag to clean the mounting boss and ensure that all the old gasket material is removed

the heat. Push in on the plug as you unscrew it so you can feel when all of the screw threads are out of the hole (and so you will keep the oil from seeping past the threads until you are ready to remove the plug). You can then remove the plug quickly to avoid having hot oil run down your arm. This will also help assure that have the plug in your hand, not in the bottom of a pan of hot oil.

❈❈ CAUTION

Be careful of the oil; when at operating temperature, it is hot enough to cause a severe burn.

5. Allow the oil to drain until nothing but a few drops come out of the drain hole. Check the drain plug to make sure the threads and sealing surface are not damaged. Clean the plug and install a new seal if it is missing or damaged.

6. Carefully thread the plug into position and tighten it with a torque wrench to the correct specification for your vehicle.

7. The drain plug specifications are as follows:
- 1.8L engine: 22–30 ft. lbs. (29–41 Nm)
- 1.9L and 2.0L SOHC engines: 15–22 ft. lbs. (20–30 Nm)
- 2.0L DOHC engines: 22–28 ft. lbs. (29–41 Nm).

8. If a torque wrench is not available, snug the drain plug and give a slight additional turn. You don't want the plug to fall out (as you would quickly become stranded), but the pan threads are EASILY stripped from overtightening (and this can be time consuming and/or costly to fix).

9. Position the drain pan beneath the filter. To remove the filter, you may need an oil filter wrench, since the filter may have been fitted too tightly and/or the heat from the engine may have made it even tighter. A filter wrench can be obtained at any auto parts store and is well-worth the investment. Loosen the filter with the filter wrench. With a rag wrapped around the filter, unscrew the filter from the boss on the engine. Be careful of hot oil that will run down the side of the filter. Make sure that your drain pan is under the filter before you start to remove it from the engine; should some of the hot oil happen to get on you, there will be a place to dump the filter in a hurry and the filter will usually spill a good bit of dirty oil as it is removed.

10. Wipe the base of the mounting boss with a clean, dry cloth. When you install the new filter, smear a small amount of fresh oil on the gasket with your finger, just enough to coat the entire contact surface. When you tighten the filter, rotate it about a half-turn after it contacts the mounting boss (or follow any instructions which are provided on the filter or parts box).

❈❈ WARNING

Never operate the engine without engine oil, otherwise SEVERE engine damage will be the result.

Fig. 160 Before installing a new oil filter, lightly coat the rubber gasket with clean engine oil

11. Remove the jackstands and carefully lower the vehicle, then IMMEDIATELY refill the engine crankcase with the proper amount of oil. DO NOT WAIT TO DO THIS because if you forget and someone tries to start the car severe engine damage will occur.

12. Refill the engine crankcase slowly, checking the level often. You may notice that it usually takes less than the amount of oil listed in the capacity chart to refill the crankcase. But, that is only until the engine is run and the oil filter is filled with oil. To make sure the proper level is obtained, run the engine to normal operating temperature. While the engine is warming, look under the vehicle for any oil leakage; if any leakage is found, shut the engine **OFF** immediately, then fix the leak.

13. Shut the engine **OFF**, allow the oil to drain back into the oil pan, and recheck the level. Top off the oil at this time to the FULL mark.

➡ **If the vehicle is not resting on level ground, the oil level reading on the dipstick may be slightly off. Be sure to check the level only when the car is sitting level.**

14. Drain your used oil in a suitable container for recycling and clean up your tools, as you will be needing them again in a few thousand more miles (kilometers).

Fig. 161 Refill the crankcase with oil through the filler hole in the valve cover

Manual Transaxle

FLUID RECOMMENDATIONS

Ford recommends Mercon Automatic Transmission Fluid (ATF) or its equivalent for use in your manual transaxle.

LEVEL CHECK

▶ **See Figures 162, 163 and 164**

The vehicle speed sensor (speedometer gear), which is located on the transaxle, serves as the manual transaxle's dipstick.

1. Park the car on a level surface, turn the engine **OFF** and apply the parking brake.
2. Locate the speedometer cable assembly where it enters the transaxle.
3. Unplug the electrical connection from the vehicle speed sensor (speedometer gear).
4. Disconnect the speedometer cable from the speed sensor.
5. Wipe the area around the speed sensor with a clean rag, then loosen the speed sensor retaining bolt.

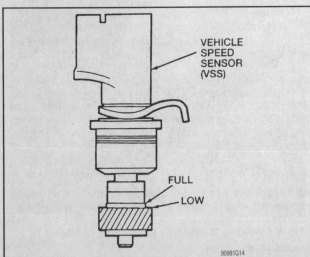

Fig. 162 Location of the manual transaxle's fluid level marks—1.8L engine

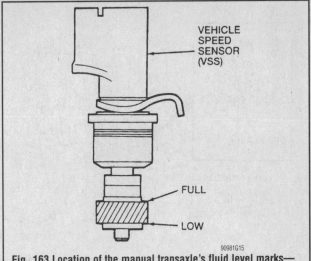

Fig. 163 Location of the manual transaxle's fluid level marks—1.9L and 2.0L engines

Fig. 164 If necessary, add transmission fluid through a funnel into the speed sensor opening

6. Gently pry the speed sensor from the transaxle.
7. Check the condition of the speed sensor O-ring and replace it if it is damaged.
8. Check the fluid level on the speed sensor as illustrated.
9. If the level is low, place a funnel in the speed sensor hole.
10. Add the specified fluid to the transaxle until the FULL level is reached. Do not overfill the transaxle.
11. Install the speed sensor and tighten the retaining bolt to 69–104 inch lbs. (8–12 Nm).
12. Connect the speedometer cable.
13. Engage the speed sensor electrical connection.

DRAIN & REFILL

▶ **See Figures 165 and 166**

1. Locate the speedometer cable assembly where it enters the transaxle.
2. Remove the speed sensor from the transaxle, as outlined in the manual transaxle fluid level check procedure.
3. Raise the vehicle and support it with safety stands.
4. Place a suitable drain pan under the transaxle.

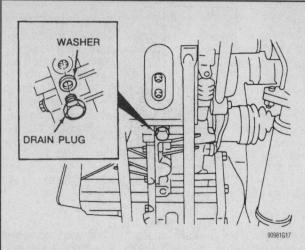

Fig. 165 Location of the manual transaxle drain plug—1.8L and 1.9L engines

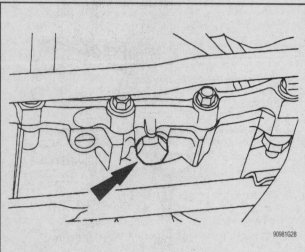

Fig. 166 Location of the manual transaxle drain plug (arrow)—2.0L engines

5. Clean the area around the drain plug with a clean rag.

6. Remove the transaxle drain plug and washer. Allow the fluid to completely drain into the pan.

7. Install the drain plug with a new washer and tighten it to 29–43 ft. lbs. (40–58 Nm) on 1.8L and 1.9L engines. On 2.0L engines, tighten the drain plug to 29–40 ft. lbs. (39–54 Nm).

8. Lower the car.

9. Fill the transaxle as outlined in the manual transaxle fluid level check procedure, earlier in this section.

10. Install the speed sensor in the transaxle.

11. Road test the car and check for proper transaxle operation.

Automatic Transaxle

FLUID RECOMMENDATIONS

Ford recommends that you use Mercon® automatic transmission fluid in your transaxle.

LEVEL CHECK

▶ See Figures 167, 168, 169 and 170

It is very important to maintain the proper fluid level in an automatic transaxle. If the level is either too high or too low, poor shifting operation and internal damage are likely to occur. For this reason, a regular check of the fluid level is essential.

It is best to check fluid at normal operating temperature.

➡There are typically 2 sets of LOW and FULL marks on the dipstick; use the lower set when checking fluid below normal operating temperature, and use the upper set when checking fluid that is at normal operating temperature.

1. Drive the vehicle for 15–20 minutes or idle it at a fast idle speed (about 1200 rpm), allowing the transaxle to reach operating temperature. When the fluid is warm, allow the engine to idle normally.

2. Park the car on a level surface, apply the parking brake and leave the engine idling. Make sure the parking brake is FIRMLY ENGAGED.

Fig. 167 Location of the automatic transaxle dipstick—2.0L engine

Fig. 168 Withdraw the transaxle dipstick from its tube—1.9L engine shown

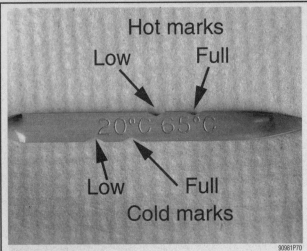

Fig. 169 The transaxle fluid level should be between the FULL and LOW marks

Fig. 170 If the transaxle fluid level is low, use a funnel and add fluid in small quantities through the dipstick filler tube

3. Depress the brake pedal and shift the transaxle engaging each gear, then place the selector in **P** (PARK) position.

4. Keep the engine running and open the hood. Locate the transaxle dipstick. Wipe away any dirt in the area of the dipstick to prevent it from falling into the filler tube. Withdraw the dipstick, wipe it with a clean, lint-free rag and reinsert it until it fully seats.

5. Withdraw the dipstick and hold it horizontally while noting the fluid level. It should be between the upper set of **LOW** and **FULL** marks when the temperature of the fluid is at or above 149°F (65°C).

6. If the level is below the **LOW** mark, use a funnel and add fluid in small quantities through the dipstick filler neck. Keep the engine running while adding fluid and check the level after each small amount. DO NOT overfill, as this could lead to foaming and transaxle damage or seal leaks.

➡Since the transaxle fluid is added through the dipstick tube, if you check the fluid too soon after adding fluid, an incorrect reading may occur. After adding fluid, wait a few minutes to allow it to fully drain into the transaxle.

DRAIN & REFILL

Under normal service (moderate highway driving excluding excessive hot or cold conditions), the manufacturer claims that automatic transaxle fluid should not need periodic changing. However, if a major service is performed to the transaxle, if transaxle fluid becomes burnt or discolored through severe usage, or if the vehicle is subjected to constant stop-and-go driving in hot weather, trailer towing, and/or long periods of highway use at high speeds, the fluid should be changed to prevent transaxle damage. A severe usage preventive maintenance change is, therefore, recommended for most vehicles at least every 30,000 miles (48,000 km) on 1991–94 models and every 42,000 miles (70,000 km) on 1995–96 models. On 1997–99 models, there is no recommended fluid change for severe usage.

1991–96 Models

▶ See Figures 171 thru 184

➡Although not a required service, transaxle fluid changing can help assure a trouble-free transaxle. Likewise, changing the transaxle filter at this time is also added insurance.

1. Raise the car and support it securely on jackstands.
2. Place a large drain pan under the transaxle.
3. Loosen all the pan bolts except the bolts at the four corners.
4. Loosen the front two bolts about three turns and the rear two bolts about six turns.

✳✳ WARNING

DO NOT force the pan while breaking the gasket seal. DO NOT allow the pan flange to become bent or otherwise damaged.

5. Use a prytool to gently separate the pan from the transaxle.
6. As the fluid drains from the pan, keep loosening the bolts in the same two-to-one ratio allowing all the fluid to completely drain.
7. When fluid has drained, remove the pan bolts and the pan, doing your best to drain the rest of the fluid into the drain pan.
8. Loosen the transaxle fluid filter mounting bolts.
9. Remove the filter by pulling it down and off of the valve body. Make sure any gaskets or seals are removed with the old filter.
10. Install the new oil filter screen, making sure all gaskets or seals are in place, then tighten the retaining bolts to 69–95 inch lbs. (8–11 Nm).

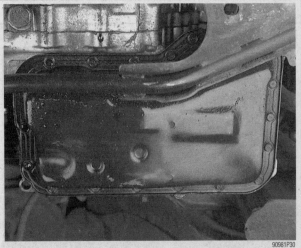

Fig. 171 Raise the front of the car and support it safely with jackstands to gain access to the automatic transaxle fluid pan

Fig. 172 Loosen all the pan bolts except those at the four corners

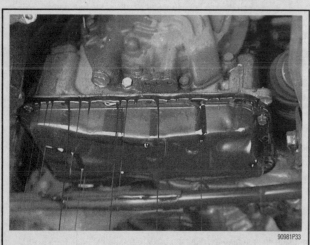

Fig. 173 Loosen the front two bolts three turns and the rear two bolts about six turns. As the fluid drains, keep loosening the bolts in the same two-to-one ratio, allowing all the fluid to drain

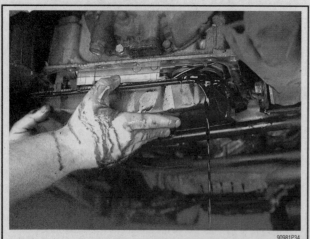

Fig. 174 When the fluid has drained, remove the four pan bolts and the pan, doing your best to drain the remaining fluid into a drain pan

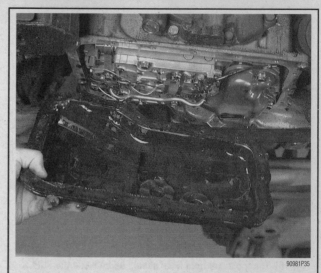

Fig. 175 Remove the pan from the vehicle

Fig. 176 Location of the transaxle filter

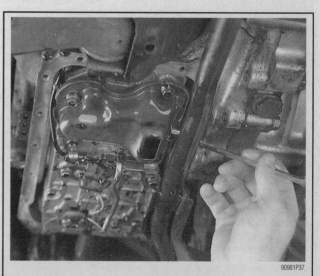

Fig. 177 Unfasten the transaxle filter retaining bolts

Fig. 178 Remove the filter from the transaxle valve body

Fig. 181 Use a scraper to clean the old gasket material from the transaxle pan

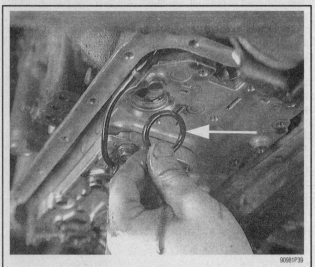

Fig. 179 Remove the transaxle filter O-ring

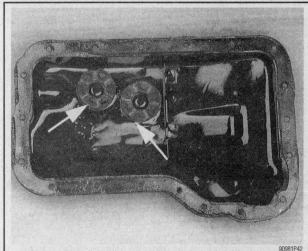

Fig. 182 Inspect the two magnets at the bottom of the pan for large pieces of metal. Small metal shavings, however, are normal

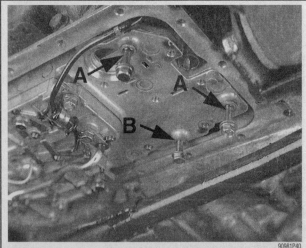

Fig. 180 The filter may use long (A) and short (B) bolts; be careful to thread the correct size bolt into each hole

Fig. 183 Remove the magnets from the pan to thoroughly clean them

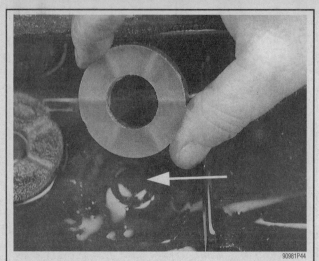

Fig. 184 Once the magnet has been cleaned, position it in its original location on the raised portion of the pan (arrow)

11. Place a new gasket on the fluid pan, then install the pan to the transaxle. Tighten the attaching bolts to 69–95 inch lbs. (8–11 Nm).

12. Remove the jackstands and lower the vehicle.

13. Add 4.1 quarts (3.9L) of fluid through the dipstick tube.

14. The level should always be just below the **F** mark.

15. Start the engine and move the gear selector through all gears in the shift pattern. Allow the engine to reach normal operating temperature.

16. Check the transaxle fluid level. Add fluid, as necessary, to obtain the correct level.

1997–99 Models

➡Although not a required service, transaxle fluid changing can help assure a trouble-free transaxle. Likewise, changing the transaxle filter at this time is also added insurance.

1. Remove the dipstick.

➡Be careful when draining the transaxle fluid, as the oil may be hot and could cause a serious injury.

2. Raise the car and support it securely on jackstands.

3. Place a large drain pan under the transaxle.

4. Loosen the transaxle drain plug and let the fluid drain completely. The plug is accessed through an opening in the support insulator.

5. After the fluid has drained, install the drain plug with a new washer.

6. If you are just changing the fluid, fill the transaxle as outlined in the automatic transaxle fluid level check procedure, earlier in this section. If you also wish to change the transaxle filter, continue with the procedure.

7. Loosen all the pan bolts except the bolts on the four corners.

8. Loosen the front two bolts about three turns and the rear two bolts about six turns.

✳✳ WARNING

DO NOT force the pan while breaking the gasket seal. DO NOT allow the pan flange to become bent or otherwise damaged.

9. Use a prytool to gently separate the pan from the transaxle.

10. As any remaining fluid drains from the pan, keep loosening the bolts in the same two-to-one ratio allowing all the fluid to completely drain.

11. When fluid has drained, remove the remaining pan bolts and the pan, doing your best to drain the rest of the fluid into the drain pan.

12. Loosen the transaxle fluid filter mounting bolts.

13. Remove the filter by pulling it down and off of the valve body. Make sure any gaskets or seals are removed with the old filter.

14. Install the new oil filter screen, making sure all gaskets or seals are in place, then tighten the retaining bolts to 69–95 inch lbs. (8–11 Nm).

15. Place a new gasket on the fluid pan, then install the pan to the transaxle. Tighten the attaching bolts to 70–95 inch lbs. (88–11 Nm).

16. Remove the jackstands and lower the vehicle.

17. Fill the transaxle as outlined in the automatic transaxle fluid level check procedure, earlier in this section.

18. The level should always just be below the **F** mark.

19. Start the engine and move the gear selector through all gears in the shift pattern. Allow the engine to reach normal operating temperature.

20. Check the transaxle fluid level. Add fluid, as necessary, to obtain the correct level.

Cooling System

✳✳ CAUTION

Never remove the radiator cap under any conditions while the engine is running! Failure to follow these instructions could result in damage to the cooling system and/or personal injury. To avoid having scalding hot coolant or steam blow out of the radiator, use extreme care when removing the radiator cap from a hot radiator. Wait until the engine has cooled, then wrap a thick cloth around the radiator cap and turn it slowly to the first stop. Step back while the pressure is released from the cooling system. When you are sure the pressure has been released, press down on the radiator cap (with the cloth still in position), turn and remove the cap.

FLUID RECOMMENDATIONS

▶ See Figures 185, 186 and 187

The recommended coolant for all vehicles covered by this manual is a 50/50 mixture of ethylene glycol and water for year-round use. Choose an aluminum compatible, good quality antifreeze with water pump lubricants, rust inhibitors and other corrosion inhibitors, along with acid neutralizers.

Fig. 185 Remove the recovery tank cap (arrow) to add coolant to the system—2.0L engine shown

Fig. 186 To add fluid to the cooling system, first remove the recovery tank cap . . .

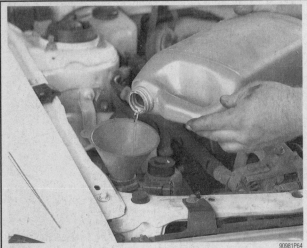

Fig. 187 . . . and add fluid until you reach the FULL mark on the recovery tank, then install the cap on the tank

INSPECTION

▶ See Figure 185

Any time you have the hood open, glance at the coolant recovery tank to make sure it is properly filled. Top off the cooling system using the recovery tank and its markings as a guideline. If you top off the system, make a note of it to check again soon. A coolant level that consistently drops is usually a sign of a small, hard to detect leak, although in the worst case it could be a sign of an internal engine leak (blown head gasket/cracked block? . . . check the engine oil for coolant contamination). In most cases, you will be able to trace the leak to a loose fitting or damaged hose (and you might solve a problem before it leaves you stranded). Evaporating ethylene glycol antifreeze will leave small, white (salt-like) deposits, which can be helpful in tracing a leak.

At least annually or every 15,000 miles (25,000 km), all hoses, fittings and cooling system connections should be inspected for damage, wear or leaks. Hose clamps should be checked for tightness, and soft or cracked hoses should be replaced. Damp spots, or accumulations of rust or dye near hoses or fittings indicate possible leakage. These must be corrected before filling the system with fresh coolant. The pressure cap should be examined for signs of deterioration and aging. The water pump drive belt(s) should be inspected and adjusted to the proper tension. Refer to the information on drive belts found earlier in this section. Finally, if everything looks good, obtain an antifreeze/coolant testing hydrometer in order to check the freeze and boil-over protection capabilities of the coolant currently in your engine. Old or improperly mixed coolant should be replaced.

✳✳ CAUTION

Never open, service or drain the radiator or cooling system when hot; serious burns can occur from the steam and hot coolant. Also, when draining engine coolant, keep in mind that cats and dogs are attracted to ethylene glycol antifreeze and could drink any that is left in an uncovered container or in puddles on the ground. This will prove fatal in sufficient quantities. Always drain coolant into a sealable container. Coolant should be reused unless it is contaminated or is several years old.

At least once every 3 years or 36,000 miles (48,000 km), the engine cooling system should be inspected, flushed and refilled with fresh coolant. If the coolant is left in the system too long, it loses its ability to prevent rust and corrosion. If the coolant has too much water, it won't protect against freezing.

If you experience problems with your cooling system, such as overheating or boiling over, check for a simple cause before expecting the complicated. Make sure the system can fully pressurize (are all the connections tight/is the radiator cap on properly, is the cap seal intact?). Ideally, a pressure tester should be connected to the radiator opening and the system should be pressurized and inspected for leaks. If no obvious problems are found, use a hydrometer antifreeze/coolant tester (available at most automotive supply stores) to check the condition and concentration of the antifreeze in your cooling system. Excessively old coolant or the wrong proportions of water and coolant will adversely affect the coolant's boiling and freezing points.

Check the Radiator Cap

▶ See Figure 188

While you are checking the coolant level, check the radiator cap for a worn or cracked gasket. If the cap doesn't seal properly, fluid will be lost and the engine will overheat. Worn caps should be replaced with new ones.

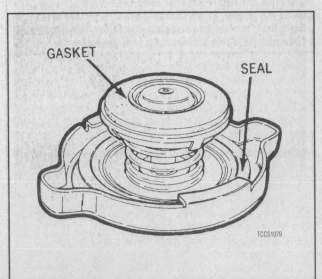

Fig. 188 Check the radiator cap for a worn or cracked gasket

Clean Radiator of Debris

▶ See Figure 189

Periodically, clean any debris—leaves, paper, insects, etc.—from the radiator fins. Pick the large pieces off by hand. The smaller pieces can be washed away with water pressure from a hose.

Carefully straighten any bent radiator fins with a pair of needle-nosed pliers. Be careful; the fins are very soft. Don't wiggle the fins back and forth too much. Straighten them once and try not to move them again.

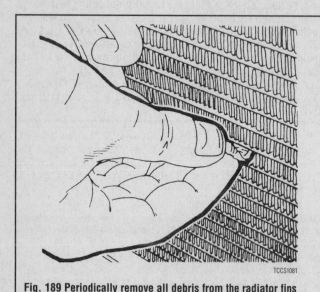

TCCS1081

Fig. 189 Periodically remove all debris from the radiator fins

DRAIN & REFILL

▶ See Figures 190 and 191

✷✷ CAUTION

Never open, service or drain the radiator or cooling system when hot; serious burns can occur from the steam and hot coolant. Also, when draining engine coolant, keep in mind that cats and dogs are attracted to ethylene glycol antifreeze and could drink any that is left in an uncovered container or in puddles on the ground. This will prove fatal in sufficient quantities. Always drain coolant into a sealable container. Coolant should be reused unless it is contaminated or is several years old.

A complete drain and refill of the cooling system at least every 30,000 miles (48,000 km) or 3 years will remove the accumulated rust, scale and other deposits. The recommended coolant is a 50/50 mixture of ethylene glycol and water for year-round use. Choose a good quality antifreeze with water pump lubricants, rust inhibitors and other corrosion inhibitors, along with acid neutralizers.

➡Before opening the radiator petcock, spray it with some penetrating lubricant.

1. Place a suitable container under the petcock.
2. Remove the radiator cap.
3. Attach a length of rubber hose to the draincock. This will help to direct the coolant flow into the drain pan.
4. Drain the existing coolant by opening the radiator petcock.
5. Close the petcock.
6. Determine the capacity of the coolant system, then properly refill the cooling system with a 50/50 mixture of fresh coolant and water, as follows:

90981P45

Fig. 190 Open the radiator petcock by turning the wing nut counterclockwise

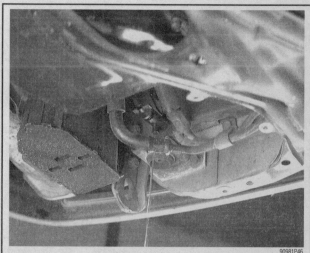

90981P46

Fig. 191 Let the coolant completely drain into a suitable container

a. Fill the radiator with coolant until it reaches the radiator filler neck seat.

b. Start the engine and allow it to idle until the thermostat opens (the upper radiator hose will become hot).

c. Turn the engine **OFF** and refill the radiator until the coolant level is at the filler neck seat.

d. Fill the engine coolant overflow tank with coolant to the FULL HOT mark, then install the radiator cap.

7. If available, install a pressure tester and check for leaks. If a pressure tester is not available, run the engine until normal operating temperature is reached (allowing the system to naturally pressurize), then check for leaks.

✷✷ CAUTION

If you are checking for leaks with the system at normal operating temperature, BE EXTREMELY CAREFUL not to touch any moving or hot engine parts. Once the temperature has been reached, shut the engine OFF, and check for leaks around the hose fittings and connections which were removed earlier.

8. Check the level of protection with an antifreeze/coolant hydrometer.

FLUSHING & CLEANING THE SYSTEM

1991–94 Models

1. Drain the cooling system as outlined in this section.
2. Add water until the radiator is full.
3. Start and idle the engine for three-to-five minutes.
4. Turn the engine **OFF** and drain the cooling system. Be careful of the hot coolant.
5. Repeat Steps 1–4 as many times as necessary until nearly clear water comes out of the radiator. Allow remaining water to drain and then close the petcock.
6. Disconnect the overflow hose from the radiator filler neck nipple.
7. Remove the coolant recovery reservoir from the fender apron and empty the fluid. Flush the reservoir with clean water, drain and install the reservoir and overflow hose and clamp to the radiator filler neck.
8. Refill the cooling system, as outlined earlier in this section.
9. Start the engine and check for leaks.

1995–96 Models

1. Remove the thermostat.
2. Reconnect the water hose connection without the thermostat in place.
3. Close the petcock.

➡ The heater core must be flushed separately from the engine so that deposits from the engine do not plug the core.

4. Tag and disconnect the heater hoses from the heater core at the firewall.

❊❊ CAUTION

the radiator pressure must not exceed 20 psi (138 kPa).

➡ The distributor on the 1.8L engine is located near the heater hose connection. Wrap a clean shop rag around the distributor to protect it from the water.

5. Disconnect the lower radiator hose and attach a high pressure water hose to the radiator hose.
6. Position the lower radiator hose so that the flushed coolant will be emptied into a suitable container.
7. Turn the high pressure hose **ON** and **OFF** several times to break up any sludge or contaminants in the cooling system.
8. Repeat Step 7 until clear water flows from the lower radiator hose.
9. Disconnect the hose and allow the cooling system to completely drain.
10. Install the thermostat and engage the heater hose.
11. Close the petcock and connect the lower radiator hose.
12. Refill the cooling system with the proper mixture and amount of coolant.

1997–99 Models

1. Remove the radiator and turn it upside down.
2. Using a garden hose inserted in the lower hose location, backflush the radiator making sure the radiator internal pressure does not exceed 20 psi (138 kPa).

❊❊ CAUTION

The radiator internal pressure must not exceed 20 psi (138 kPa) or damage may occur.

3. Remove the thermostat, insert the hose into the thermostat opening.

4. Turn the hose on high and let the water backflush the engine block.
5. Tag and disconnect the heater core outlet hose from the water pump fitting and connect a female garden hose-end adapter in the end of the hose and hold it in place with a hose clamp.
6. Connect the garden hose to the hose-end adapter attached to the heater core hose.
7. Tag and disconnect the heater core inlet hose from the block and position it so a container to catch the coolant and water can be placed under it.
8. Place a suitable sized container under the inlet hose.
9. If a check that the valve is open (no vacuum).
10. Turn the water supply on and off several times to loosen sludge and deposits, then turn the full water pressure on and let it run for about five minutes.
11. If a water valve is installed in the heater core inlet hose, apply vacuum to the valve vacuum motor to check for proper operation of the valve with proper closure with no water leakage. If there is water leakage, replace the valve.
12. Remove the garden hose and the adapter from the outlet hose.
13. Connect the heater core inlet and outlet hoses.
14. Install the thermostat and radiator.
15. Properly fill the cooling system.
16. Start the engine and allow it to reach normal operating temperature, then check for leaks.

Brake Master Cylinder

The brake master cylinder reservoir is located under the hood, attached to the firewall on the driver's side of the engine compartment.

FLUID RECOMMENDATIONS

❊❊ WARNING

BRAKE FLUID EATS PAINT. Take great care not to splash or spill brake fluid on painted surfaces. Should you spill a small amount on the car's finish, don't panic, just flush the area with plenty of water.

When adding fluid to the system, ONLY use fresh DOT 3 brake fluid from a sealed container. DOT 3 brake fluid will absorb moisture when it is exposed to the atmosphere, which will lower its boiling point. A container that has been opened once, closed and placed on a shelf will allow enough moisture to enter over time to contaminate the fluid within. If your brake fluid is contaminated with water, you could boil the brake fluid under hard braking conditions and lose all or some braking ability. Don't take the risk, buy fresh brake fluid whenever you must add to the system.

LEVEL CHECK

▶ See Figures 192, 193 and 194

Observe the fluid level indicators on the master cylinder; the fluid level should be between the **MIN** and **MAX** lines.

Before removing the master cylinder reservoir cap, make sure the vehicle is resting on level ground and clean all dirt away from the top of the master cylinder. Unscrew the cap and fill the master cylinder until the level is between the **MIN** and **MAX** lines.

If the level of the brake fluid is less than half the volume of the reservoir, it is advised that you check the brake system for leaks. Leaks in a hydraulic brake system most commonly occur at the wheel cylinder.

Fig. 192 Clean the master cylinder cap and the area around it before removing the cap

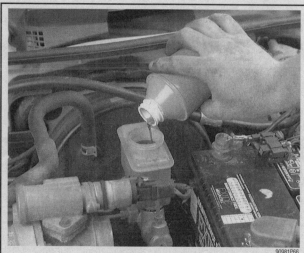

Fig. 193 Add fresh brake fluid to the master cylinder until the fluid level is between the MIN and MAX lines

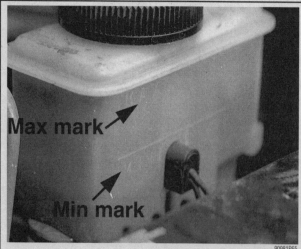

Fig. 194 Location of the brake master cylinder MIN and MAX fluid level marks

Clutch Master Cylinder

▶ See Figure 195

The Escort/Tracer is equipped with a hydraulic clutch control system. The system consists of a fluid reservoir, master cylinder, pressure line and a slave cylinder. The hydraulic clutch control system is tapped into the brake master cylinder reservoir and utilizes brake fluid for its operation.

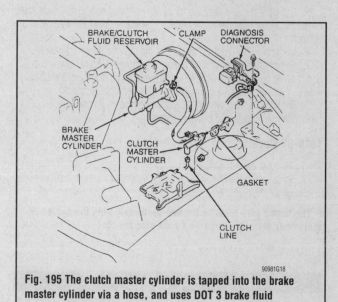

Fig. 195 The clutch master cylinder is tapped into the brake master cylinder via a hose, and uses DOT 3 brake fluid

FLUID RECOMMENDATIONS

Use a DOT 3 brake fluid meeting Ford specifications, such as Ford Heavy Duty Brake Fluid.

FLUID LEVEL CHECK

Inspect the brake master cylinder fluid level through the translucent master cylinder reservoir. It should be between the **MIN** and **MAX** level marks embossed on the side of the reservoir. If the level is found to be low, remove the reservoir cap and fill to the **MAX** level with DOT 3 brake fluid.

➡Never reuse brake fluid that has been drained from the hydraulic system or fluid that has been allowed to stand in an open container for an extended period of time.

Power Steering Pump

FLUID RECOMMENDATIONS

Fill the power steering pump reservoir with a good quality power steering fluid or Automatic Transmission Fluid (ATF) Type **F**.

LEVEL CHECK

▶ See Figures 196 and 197

Position the vehicle on level ground. Run the engine until the fluid is at normal operating temperature. Turn the steering wheel all the way to the left and right several times. Position the wheels in the straight ahead position, then shut off the engine. Check the level in the reservoir; it should be at the **FULL** mark. If fluid is required, remove the cap and add fluid until it reaches the **FULL** mark.

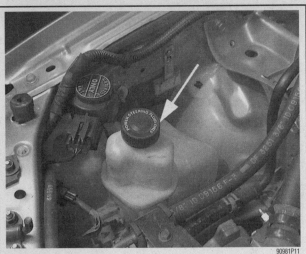

90981P11

Fig. 196 Remove the power steering fluid cap (arrow) to add fluid

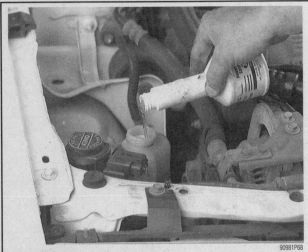

90981P68

Fig. 197 Pour in power steering fluid until it reaches the FULL mark on the reservoir

Steering Gear

The steering gear is factory-filled with steering gear grease. Changing of this lubricant should not be performed and the housing should not be drained; periodic lubrication is not required for the steering gear.

Chassis Lubrication

▶ **See Figure 198**

The chassis lubrication should be performed at least once a year or more, depending on the conditions under which the vehicle is operated.

Refer to the illustration for the lubrication points on the components that require this service.

The components that need lubrication are:

- Rear wheel bearings: Premium long life grease
- Parking brake linkage: Multi-purpose grease
- Clutch linkage: Premium long life grease

Body Lubrication

Whenever you take care of chassis greasing, it is also advised that you walk around the vehicle and give attention to a number of other surfaces which require a variety of lubrication/protection.

Lubricate the door and tailgate hinges, door locks, door latches, and the hood latch when they become noisy or difficult to operate. A high quality multi-purpose grease should be used as a lubricant.

HOOD/DOOR LATCH & HINGES

Wipe clean any exposed surfaces of the door latches and hinges and hood latch, liftgate hinges and latches. Then, treat the surfaces using a multi-purpose grease spray that meets Ford's D7AZ-19584-A specification.

LOCK CYLINDERS

Lock cylinders should be treated with Ford penetrating lubricant, part no. E8AZ-19A501-B or equivalent. Consult your local parts supplier for equivalent lubricants.

DOOR WEATHERSTRIPPING

Spray or wipe the door weatherstripping using a silicone lubricant to help preserve the rubber.

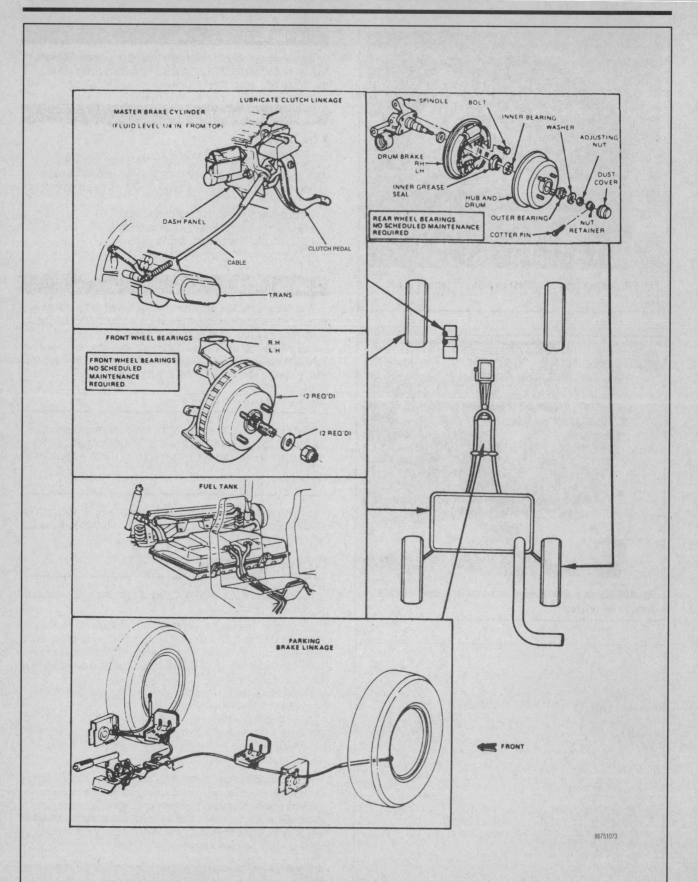

Fig. 198 Common chassis lubrication points

TRAILER TOWING

General Recommendations

Your vehicle was primarily designed to carry passengers and cargo. It is important to remember that towing a trailer will place additional loads on your vehicle's engine, drive train, steering, braking and other systems. However, if you decide to tow a trailer, using the prior equipment is a must.

Local laws may require specific equipment such as trailer brakes or fender mounted mirrors. Check your local laws.

Trailer Weight

The weight of the trailer is the most important factor. A good weight-to-horsepower ratio is about 35:1, 35 lbs. of Gross Combined Weight (GCW) for every horsepower your engine develops. Multiply the engine's rated horsepower by 35 and subtract the weight of the vehicle passengers and luggage. The number remaining is the approximate ideal maximum weight you should tow, although a numerically higher axle ratio can help compensate for heavier weight.

Hitch (Tongue) Weight

▶ See Figure 199

Calculate the hitch weight in order to select a proper hitch. The weight of the hitch is usually 9–11% of the trailer gross weight and should be measured with the trailer loaded. Hitches fall into various categories: those that mount on the frame and rear bumper, the bolt-on type, or the weld-on distribution type used for larger trailers. Axle mounted or clamp-on bumper hitches should never be used.

Check the gross weight rating of your trailer. Tongue weight is usually figured as 10% of gross trailer weight. Therefore, a trailer with a maximum gross weight of 2000 lbs. will have a maximum tongue weight of 200 lbs. Class I trailers fall into this category. Class II trailers are those with a gross weight rating of 2000–3000 lbs., while Class III trailers fall into the 3500–6000 lbs. category. Class IV trailers are those over 6000 lbs. and are for use with fifth wheel trucks, only.

When you've determined the hitch that you'll need, follow the manufacturer's installation instructions, exactly, especially when it comes to fastener torques. The hitch will subjected to a lot of stress and good hitches come with hardened bolts. Never substitute an inferior bolt for a hardened bolt.

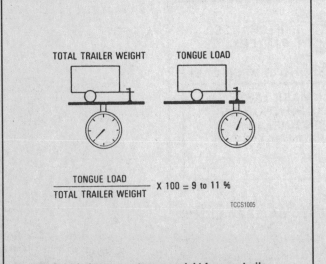

Fig. 199 Calculating proper tongue weight for your trailer

Cooling

ENGINE

Overflow Tank

One of the most common, if not THE most common, problems associated with trailer towing is engine overheating. If you have a cooling system without an expansion tank, you'll definitely need to get an aftermarket expansion tank kit, preferably one with at least a 2 quart capacity. These kits are easily installed on the radiator's overflow hose, and come with a pressure cap designed for expansion tanks.

Flex Fan

Another helpful accessory for vehicles using a belt-driven radiator fan is a flex fan. These fans are large diameter units designed to provide more airflow at low speeds, by using fan blades that have deeply cupped surfaces. The blades then flex, or flatten out, at high speed, when less cooling air is needed. These fans are far lighter in weight than stock fans, requiring less horsepower to drive them. Also, they are far quieter than stock fans. If you do decide to replace your stock fan with a flex fan, note that if your vehicle has a fan clutch, a spacer will be needed between the flex fan and water pump hub.

Oil Cooler

Aftermarket engine oil coolers are helpful for prolonging engine oil life and reducing overall engine temperatures. Both of these factors increase engine life. While not absolutely necessary in towing Class I and some Class II trailers, they are recommended for heavier Class II and all Class III towing. Engine oil cooler systems usually consist of an adapter, screwed on in place of the oil filter, a remote filter mounting and a multi-tube, finned heat exchanger, which is mounted in front of the radiator or air conditioning condenser.

TRANSAXLE

An automatic transaxle is usually recommended for trailer towing. Modern automatics have proven reliable and, of course, easy to operate, in trailer towing. The increased load of a trailer, however, causes an increase in the temperature of the automatic transmission fluid. Heat is the worst enemy of an automatic transaxle. As the temperature of the fluid increases, the life of the fluid decreases.

It is essential, therefore, that you install an automatic transaxle cooler. The cooler, which consists of a multi-tube, finned heat exchanger, is usually installed in front of the radiator or air conditioning compressor, and hooked in-line with the transaxle cooler tank inlet line. Follow the cooler manufacturer's installation instructions.

Select a cooler of at least adequate capacity, based upon the combined gross weights of the vehicle and trailer.

Cooler manufacturers recommend that you use an aftermarket cooler in addition to, and not instead of, the present cooling tank in your radiator. If you do want to use it in place of the radiator cooling tank, get a cooler at least two sizes larger than normally necessary.

→**A transaxle cooler can, sometimes, cause slow or harsh shifting in the transaxle during cold weather, until the fluid has a chance to come up to normal operating temperature. Some coolers can be purchased with or retrofitted with a temperature bypass valve which will allow fluid flow through the cooler only when the fluid has reached above a certain operating temperature.**

Handling a Trailer

Towing a trailer with ease and safety requires a certain amount of experience. It's a good idea to learn the feel of a trailer by practicing turning, stopping and backing in an open area such as an empty parking lot.

TOWING THE VEHICLE

▶ **See Figure 200**

If the vehicle requires towing, it is recommended that a wrecker equipped with a wheel lift be used. The weight of the vehicle should be supported by the lifting device placed under the wheels. Using this technique, the vehicle can be towed from the front or the rear. If the vehicle is to be towed from the rear, the front wheels MUST be placed on a dolly to prevent damage to the transaxle. Make certain the transaxle is in the **Neutral** (manual) or **Park** (automatic) position and that the parking brake is released prior to towing the vehicle.

When towing the vehicle, with driving wheels on the ground, do not exceed 35 mph (56 km/h). Also, do not tow the vehicle for a distance exceeding 50 miles (80 km), or transaxle damage can occur.

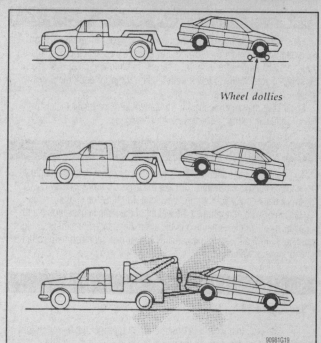

Wheel dollies

90981G19

Fig. 200 When towing the car, the weight of the vehicle should be supported by the lifting device placed under the wheels

JUMP STARTING A DEAD BATTERY

▶ **See Figure 201**

Whenever a vehicle is jump started, precautions must be followed in order to prevent the possibility of personal injury. Remember that batteries contain a small amount of explosive hydrogen gas which is a by-product of battery charging. Sparks should always be avoided when working around batteries, especially when attaching jumper cables. To minimize the possibility of accidental sparks, follow the procedure carefully.

✳✳ WARNING

NEVER hook the batteries up in a series circuit or the entire electrical system will go up in smoke, including the starter!

Vehicles equipped with a diesel engine may utilize two 12 volt batteries. If so, the batteries are connected in a parallel circuit (positive terminal to

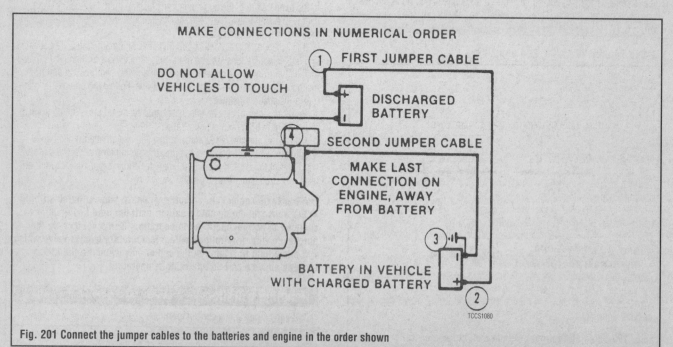

MAKE CONNECTIONS IN NUMERICAL ORDER

DO NOT ALLOW
VEHICLES TO TOUCH

① FIRST JUMPER CABLE

DISCHARGED
BATTERY

SECOND JUMPER CABLE

MAKE LAST
CONNECTION ON
ENGINE, AWAY
FROM BATTERY

③

BATTERY IN VEHICLE
WITH CHARGED BATTERY

②

TCCS1080

Fig. 201 Connect the jumper cables to the batteries and engine in the order shown

positive terminal, negative terminal to negative terminal). Hooking the batteries up in parallel circuit increases battery cranking power without increasing total battery voltage output. Output remains at 12 volts. On the other hand, hooking two 12 volt batteries up in a series circuit (positive terminal to negative terminal, positive terminal to negative terminal) increases total battery output to 24 volts (12 volts plus 12 volts).

Jump Starting Precautions

- Be sure that both batteries are of the same voltage. Vehicles covered by this manual and most vehicles on the road today utilize a 12 volt charging system.
- Be sure that both batteries are of the same polarity (have the same terminal, in most cases NEGATIVE grounded).
- Be sure that the vehicles are not touching or a short could occur.
- On serviceable batteries, be sure the vent cap holes are not obstructed.
- Do not smoke or allow sparks anywhere near the batteries.
- In cold weather, make sure the battery electrolyte is not frozen. This can occur more readily in a battery that has been in a state of discharge.
- Do not allow electrolyte to contact your skin or clothing.

Jump Starting Procedure

1. Make sure that the voltages of the 2 batteries are the same. Most batteries and charging systems are of the 12 volt variety.
2. Pull the jumping vehicle (with the good battery) into a position so the jumper cables can reach the dead battery and that vehicle's engine. Make sure that the vehicles do NOT touch.
3. Place the transaxles of both vehicles in **Neutral** (MT) or **P** (AT), as applicable, then firmly set their parking brakes.

➡**If necessary for safety reasons, the hazard lights on both vehicles may be operated throughout the entire procedure without significantly increasing the difficulty of jumping the dead battery.**

4. Turn all lights and accessories OFF on both vehicles. Make sure the ignition switches on both vehicles are turned to the **OFF** position.
5. Cover the battery cell caps with a rag, but do not cover the terminals.
6. Make sure the terminals on both batteries are clean and free of corrosion or proper electrical connection will be impeded. If necessary, clean the battery terminals before proceeding.

7. Identify the positive (+) and negative (-) terminals on both batteries.
8. Connect the first jumper cable to the positive (+) terminal of the dead battery, then connect the other end of that cable to the positive (+) terminal of the booster (good) battery.
9. Connect one end of the other jumper cable to the negative (-) terminal on the booster battery and the final cable clamp to an engine bolt head, alternator bracket or other solid, metallic point on the engine with the dead battery. Try to pick a ground on the engine that is positioned away from the battery in order to minimize the possibility of the 2 clamps touching should one loosen during the procedure. DO NOT connect this clamp to the negative (-) terminal of the bad battery.

✱✱ CAUTION

Be very careful to keep the jumper cables away from moving parts (cooling fan, belts, etc.) on both engines.

10. Check to make sure that the cables are routed away from any moving parts, then start the donor vehicle's engine. Run the engine at moderate speed for several minutes to allow the dead battery a chance to receive some initial charge.
11. With the donor vehicle's engine still running slightly above idle, try to start the vehicle with the dead battery. Crank the engine for no more than 10 seconds at a time and let the starter cool for at least 20 seconds between tries. If the vehicle does not start in 3 tries, it is likely that something else is also wrong or that the battery needs additional time to charge.
12. Once the vehicle is started, allow it to run at idle for a few seconds to make sure that it is operating properly.
13. Turn ON the headlights, heater blower and, if equipped, the rear defroster of both vehicles in order to reduce the severity of voltage spikes and subsequent risk of damage to the vehicles' electrical systems when the cables are disconnected. This step is especially important to any vehicle equipped with computer control modules.
14. Carefully disconnect the cables in the reverse order of connection. Start with the negative cable that is attached to the engine ground, then the negative cable on the donor battery. Disconnect the positive cable from the donor battery and finally, disconnect the positive cable from the formerly dead battery. Be careful when disconnecting the cables from the positive terminals not to allow the alligator clips to touch any metal on either vehicle or a short and sparks will occur.

JACKING

▶ **See Figures 202, 203, 204 and 205**

Your vehicle was supplied with a jack for emergency road repairs. This jack is fine for changing a flat tire or other short term procedures not requiring you to go beneath the vehicle. If it is used in an emergency situation, carefully follow the instructions provided either with the jack or in your owner's manual. Do not attempt to use the jack on any portions of the vehicle other than specified by the vehicle manufacturer. Always block the diagonally opposite wheel when using a jack.

A more convenient way of jacking is the use of a garage or floor jack. You may use the floor jack to raise the car in the positions indicated in the accompanying photographs.

Never place the jack under the radiator, engine or transaxle components. Severe and expensive damage will result when the jack is raised. Additionally, never jack under the floorpan or bodywork; the metal will deform.

Whenever you plan to work under the vehicle, you must support it on jackstands or ramps. Never use cinder blocks or stacks of wood to support the vehicle, even if you're only going to be under it for a few minutes. Never crawl under the vehicle when it is supported only by the tire-changing jack or other floor jack.

Fig. 202 Raise the front of the vehicle with a hydraulic jack placed beneath the center member

Fig. 203 Place jackstands beneath the frame rails at the front of the vehicle, then lower the jack until the jackstands support the weight of the vehicle

Fig. 205 Place jackstands beneath the frame rails at the rear of the vehicle, then lower the jack until the vehicle rests securely on the jackstands

➡Always position a block of wood or small rubber pad on top of the jack or jackstand to protect the lifting point's finish when lifting or supporting the vehicle.

Small hydraulic, screw, or scissors jacks are satisfactory for raising the vehicle. Drive-on trestles or ramps are also a handy and safe way to both raise and support the vehicle. Be careful though, some ramps may be too steep to drive your vehicle onto without scraping the front bottom panels. Never support the vehicle on any suspension member (unless specifically instructed to do so by a repair manual) or by an underbody panel.

Fig. 204 Raise the rear of the vehicle by placing the hydraulic jack beneath the rear axle

Jacking Precautions

The following safety points cannot be overemphasized:
• Always block the opposite wheel or wheels to keep the vehicle from rolling off the jack.
• When raising the front of the vehicle, firmly apply the parking brake.
• When the drive wheels are to remain on the ground, leave the vehicle in gear to help prevent it from rolling.
• Always use jackstands to support the vehicle when you are working underneath. Place the stands beneath the vehicle's jacking brackets. Before climbing underneath, rock the vehicle a bit to make sure it is firmly supported.

MANUFACTURER RECOMMENDED NORMAL MAINTENANCE INTERVALS
(1991-96 MODELS)

Perform at the Months or Distances Shown, Whichever Occurs First								
Miles x 1000	7.5	15	22.5	30	37.5	45	52.5	60
Kilometers x 1000	12	24	36	48	60	72	84	96
Emission Control Service								
Change engine oil and oil filter — every 6 months OR 7,500 miles, whichever occurs first	x	x	x	x	x	x	x	x
Replace spark plugs				x				x
Replace crankcase ventilation filter (1) (1.9L only)				x(1)				x(1)
Inspect accessory drive belt(s)				x				x
Replace air cleaner filter (1)				x(1)				x(1)
Replace engine coolant (every 36 months) OR				x				x
Check engine coolant protection, hoses and clamps	ANNUALLY							
Replace engine timing belt (1.8L only)	REPLACE EVERY 60,000 MILES (96 000 Km)							x
Replace PCV valve								x

	Miles x 1000	7.5	15	22.5	30	37.5	45	52.5	60
	Kilometers x 1000	12	24	36	48	60	72	84	96
General Maintenance									
Inspect exhaust heat shields					x				x
Inspect disc brake pads and rotors (2)					x(2)				x(2)
Inspect brake linings and drums (2)					x(2)				x(2)
Rotate tires		x		x		x		x	
Inspect halfshaft dust boots									x
Inspect steering operation and linkage					x				x
Inspect front suspension ball joints					x				x
Inspect brake line hoses and connections					x				x
Inspect bolts and nuts on chassis and body					x				x
Inspect clutch pedal operation (if equipped)					x				x

(1) If operating in severe dust, more frequent intervals may be required. Consult your dealer.

(2) If driving includes continuous stop-and-go driving or driving in mountainous areas, more frequent intervals may be required.

Perform maintenance at the same intervals for mileage beyond that on this chart.

90981C04

MANUFACTURER RECOMMENDED SEVERE MAINTENANCE INTERVALS
(1991-96 MODELS)

Perform at the Months or Distances Shown, Whichever Occurs First																				
Miles x 1000 3	6	9	12	15	18	21	24	27	30	33	36	39	42	45	48	51	54	57	60
Kilometers x 1000 4.8	9.6	14.4	19.2	24	28.8	33.6	38.4	43.2	48	52.8	57.6	62.4	67.2	72	76.8	81.6	86.4	91.2	96
Emission Control Service																			
Change engine oil and oil filter (every 3 months) OR 3000 miles whichever occurs first x	x	x	x	x	x	x	x	x	x	x	x	x	x	x	x	x	x	x	x
Replace spark plugs									x										x
Inspect accessory drive belt(s)									x										x
Inspect air cleaner filter (1.8L only)				x(4)									x(4)						
Replace air cleaner filter (all engines) (1)									x(1)										x(1)
Replace crankcase ventilation filter (1) (1.9L only)									x(1)										x(1)
Replace engine coolant EVERY 36 months OR									x										x
Check engine coolant protection, hoses and clamps	ANNUALLY																		
Replace engine timing belt (1.8L only)	REPLACE EVERY 60,000 MILES (96 000 Km)																		x
Replace PCV valve																			x

Miles x 1000 3	6	9	12	15	18	21	24	27	30	33	36	39	42	45	48	51	54	57	60
Kilometers x 1000 4.8	9.6	14.4	19.2	24	28.8	33.6	38.4	43.2	48	52.8	57.6	62.4	67.2	72	76.8	81.6	86.4	91.2	96
General Maintenance																			
Inspect exhaust heat shields									x										x
Change automatic transaxle fluid									x(2)										x(2)
Inspect disc brake pads and rotors (3)									x(3)										x(3)
Inspect brake linings and drums (3)									x(3)										x(3)
Rotate tires	x					x						x				x			
Inspect clutch pedal operation (if equipped)									x										x
Inspect halfshaft dust boots									x										x
Inspect brake line hoses and connections									x										x
Inspect front suspension ball joints									x										x
Inspect bolts and nuts on chassis and body									x										
Inspect steering operation and linkage									x										x

(1) If operating in severe dust, more frequent intervals may be required, consult your dealer.

(2) Change automatic transaxle fluid if your driving habits frequently include one or more of the following conditions:
 • Operation during hot weather (above 90°F, 32°C), carrying heavy loads and in hilly terrain.
 • Towing a trailer or using a car-top carrier.
 • Police, taxi or door-to-door delivery service.

(3) If your driving includes continuous stop-and-go driving or driving in mountainous areas, more frequent intervals may be required.

(4) This item not required to be performed, however, Ford recommends that you also perform maintenance on items designated by a (4) in order to achieve best vehicle operation. Failure to perform this recommended maintenance will not invalidate the vehicle emissions warranty or manufacturer recall liability.

Perform maintenance at the same intervals for mileage beyond that on this chart.

90981C05

MANUFACTURER RECOMMENDED NORMAL MAINTENANCE INTERVALS
(1997-99 MODELS)

Component	Type of Service	Miles (x1000) 5 / km 8	10 / 16	15 / 24	20 / 32	25 / 40	30 / 48	35 / 56	40 / 64	45 / 72	50 / 80	55 / 88	60 / 96	65 / 104	70 / 112	75 / 121	80 / 128
Engine oil and filter	Replace	✓	✓	✓	✓	✓	✓	✓	✓	✓	✓	✓	✓	✓	✓	✓	✓
Tires	Rotate	✓		✓		✓		✓		✓		✓		✓		✓	
Air cleaner	Inspect					✓							✓				
	Replace						✓						✓				
Spark plugs ①	Replace																
Drive belts	Inspect												✓				
Cooling system	Inspect			✓			✓			✓			✓			✓	
Coolant	Replace										✓						✓
PCV valve	Replace												✓				
Exhaust heat shields	Inspect						✓						✓				
Brake linings and drums	Inspect						✓						✓				
Brake pads and rotors	Inspect						✓						✓				
Clutch pedal operation	Inspect												✓				
Halfshaft dust boots	Inspect						✓						✓				
Brake line hoses and connections	Inspect						✓						✓				
Front ball joints	Inspect						✓						✓				
Bolts and nuts on chassis body	Inspect						✓						✓				
Steering linkage operation	Inspect						✓						✓				

Perform maintenace at the same intervals for mileage beyond that on this chart

① Change plugs every 100,000 miles

90981C06

MANUFACTURER RECOMMENDED SEVERE MAINTENANCE INTERVALS
(1997-99 MODELS)

Component	Type of Service	3 / 5	6 / 10	9 / 15	12 / 20	15 / 25	18 / 30	21 / 35	24 / 40	27 / 45	30 / 50	33 / 55	36 / 60	39 / 65	42 / 70	45 / 75	48 / 80
Engine oil and filter	Replace	✓	✓	✓	✓	✓	✓	✓	✓	✓	✓	✓	✓	✓	✓	✓	✓
Tires	Rotate	✓				✓			✓			✓			✓		
Air cleaner	Inspect					✓					✓						
	Replace										✓						
Spark plugs ①	Replace																
Drive belts	Inspect										✓						
Cooling system	Inspect					✓				✓	✓					✓	
Coolant	Replace																✓
PCV valve	Replace										✓						
Exhaust heat shields	Inspect					✓					✓					✓	
Brake linings and drums	Inspect					✓					✓					✓	
Brake pads and rotors	Inspect					✓					✓					✓	
Clutch pedal operation	Inspect										✓						
Halfshaft dust boots	Inspect					✓					✓					✓	
Brake line hoses and connections	Inspect					✓					✓					✓	
Front ball joints	Inspect					✓					✓					✓	
Bolts and nuts on chassis body	Inspect					✓					✓					✓	
Steering linkage operation	Inspect					✓					✓					✓	

Perform maintenace at the same intervals for mileage beyond that on this chart

① Change plugs every 100,000 miles

90981C07

CAPACITIES

Year	Model	Engine ID/VIN	Engine Displacement Liters (cc)	Engine Oil with Filter (qts.)	Transmission (pts.)			Fuel Tank (gals.)	Cooling System (qts.)
					4-Spd	5-Spd	Auto.		
1991	Escort/Tracer	8	1.8 (1839)	4.0	N/A	5.6	12.2	13.2	①
	Escort/Tracer	J	1.9 (1901)	4.0	N/A	7.1	12.2	11.9	①
1992	Escort/Tracer	8	1.8 (1839)	4.0	N/A	5.6	12.2	13.2	①
	Escort/Tracer	J	1.9 (1901)	4.0	N/A	7.1	12.2	11.9	①
1993	Escort/Tracer	8	1.8 (1839)	4.0	N/A	7.1	13.4	13.2	①
	Escort/Tracer	J	1.9 (1901)	4.0	N/A	5.6	13.4	11.9	①
1994	Escort/Tracer	8	1.8 (1839)	4.0	N/A	6.7	8.2	13.2	①
	Escort/Tracer	J	1.9 (1901)	4.0	N/A	5.6	8.2	11.9	①
1995	Escort/Tracer	8	1.8 (1839)	4.0	N/A	6.7	8.2	13.2	①
	Escort/Tracer	J	1.9 (1901)	4.0	N/A	5.6	8.2	11.9	①
1996	Escort/Tracer	8	1.8 (1839)	4.0	N/A	6.7	8.2	13.2	①
	Escort/Tracer	J	1.9 (1901)	4.0	N/A	5.6	8.2	11.9	①
1997	Escort/Tracer	P	2.0 (2000)	4.0	N/A	7.1	8.2	12.7	①
1998	Escort/Tracer	P	2.0 (2000)	4.0	N/A	7.1	8.2	12.7	①
	Escort/Tracer	3	2.0 (2000)	4.0	N/A	7.1	8.2	12.8	①
	ZX2	3	2.0 (2000)	4.25	N/A	7.1	8.2	12.8	①
1999	Escort/Tracer	P	2.0 (2000)	4.0	N/A	7.1	8.2	12.7	①
	Escort/Tracer	3	2.0 (2000)	4.0	N/A	7.1	8.2	12.8	①
	ZX2	3	2.0 (2000)	4.25	N/A	7.1	8.2	12.8	①

① Manual tranaxle: 5.3
Automatic transaxle: 6.3

N/A: Not applicable

90981C8A

ENGLISH TO METRIC CONVERSION: MASS (WEIGHT)

Current mass measurement is expressed in pounds and ounces (lbs. & ozs.). The metric unit of mass (or weight) is the kilogram (kg). Even although this table does not show conversion of masses (weights) larger than 15 lbs, it is easy to calculate larger units by following the data immediately below.

To convert ounces (oz.) to grams (g): multiply th number of ozs. by 28
To convert grams (g) to ounces (oz.): multiply the number of grams by .035

To convert pounds (lbs.) to kilograms (kg): multiply the number of lbs. by .45
To convert kilograms (kg) to pounds (lbs.): multiply the number of kilograms by 2.2

lbs	kg	lbs	kg	oz	kg	oz	kg
0.1	0.04	0.9	0.41	0.1	0.003	0.9	0.024
0.2	0.09	1	0.4	0.2	0.005	1	0.03
0.3	0.14	2	0.9	0.3	0.008	2	0.06
0.4	0.18	3	1.4	0.4	0.011	3	0.08
0.5	0.23	4	1.8	0.5	0.014	4	0.11
0.6	0.27	5	2.3	0.6	0.017	5	0.14
0.7	0.32	10	4.5	0.7	0.020	10	0.28
0.8	0.36	15	6.8	0.8	0.023	15	0.42

ENGLISH TO METRIC CONVERSION: TEMPERATURE

To convert Fahrenheit (°F) to Celsius (°C): take number of °F and subtract 32; multiply result by 5; divide result by 9

To convert Celsius (°C) to Fahrenheit (°F): take number of °C and multiply by 9; divide result by 5; add 32 to total

Fahrenheit (F)	Celsius (C)			Fahrenheit (F)	Celsius (C)			Fahrenheit (F)	Celsius (C)		
°F	°C	°C	°F	°F	°C	°C	°F	°F	°C	°C	°F
−40	−40	−38	−36.4	80	26.7	18	64.4	215	101.7	80	176
−35	−37.2	−36	−32.8	85	29.4	20	68	220	104.4	85	185
−30	−34.4	−34	−29.2	90	32.2	22	71.6	225	107.2	90	194
−25	−31.7	−32	−25.6	95	35.0	24	75.2	230	110.0	95	202
−20	−28.9	−30	−22	100	37.8	26	78.8	235	112.8	100	212
−15	−26.1	−28	−18.4	105	40.6	28	82.4	240	115.6	105	221
−10	−23.3	−26	−14.8	110	43.3	30	86	245	118.3	110	230
−5	−20.6	−24	−11.2	115	46.1	32	89.6	250	121.1	115	239
0	−17.8	−22	−7.6	120	48.9	34	93.2	255	123.9	120	248
1	−17.2	−20	−4	125	51.7	36	96.8	260	126.6	125	257
2	−16.7	−18	−0.4	130	54.4	38	100.4	265	129.4	130	266
3	−16.1	−16	3.2	135	57.2	40	104	270	132.2	135	275
4	−15.6	−14	6.8	140	60.0	42	107.6	275	135.0	140	284
5	−15.0	−12	10.4	145	62.8	44	112.2	280	137.8	145	293
10	−12.2	−10	14	150	65.6	46	114.8	285	140.6	150	302
15	−9.4	−8	17.6	155	68.3	48	118.4	290	143.3	155	311
20	−6.7	−6	21.2	160	71.1	50	122	295	146.1	160	320
25	−3.9	−4	24.8	165	73.9	52	125.6	300	148.9	165	329
30	−1.1	−2	28.4	170	76.7	54	129.2	305	151.7	170	338
35	1.7	0	32	175	79.4	56	132.8	310	154.4	175	347
40	4.4	2	35.6	180	82.2	58	136.4	315	157.2	180	356
45	7.2	4	39.2	185	85.0	60	140	320	160.0	185	365
50	10.0	6	42.8	190	87.8	62	143.6	325	162.8	190	374
55	12.8	8	46.4	195	90.6	64	147.2	330	165.6	195	383
60	15.6	10	50	200	93.3	66	150.8	335	168.3	200	392
65	18.3	12	53.6	205	96.1	68	154.4	340	171.1	205	401
70	21.1	14	57.2	210	98.9	70	158	345	173.9	210	410
75	23.9	16	60.8	212	100.0	75	167	350	176.7	215	414

ENGLISH TO METRIC CONVERSION: LENGTH

To convert inches (ins.) to millimeters (mm): multiply number of inches by 25.4

To convert millimeters (mm) to inches (ins.): multiply number of millimeters by .04

Inches	Decimals	Milli-meters	Inches to millimeters (inches)	mm	Inches	Decimals	Milli-meters	Inches to millimeters (inches)	mm
1/64	0.051625	0.3969	0.0001	0.00254	33/64	0.515625	13.0969	0.6	15.24
1/32	0.03125	0.7937	0.0002	0.00508	17/32	0.53125	13.4937	0.7	17.78
3/64	0.046875	1.1906	0.0003	0.00762	35/64	0.546875	13.8906	0.8	20.32
1/16	0.0625	1.5875	0.0004	0.01016	9/16	0.5625	14.2875	0.9	22.86
5/64	0.078125	1.9844	0.0005	0.01270	37/64	0.578125	14.6844	1	25.4
3/32	0.09375	2.3812	0.0006	0.01524	19/32	0.59375	15.0812	2	50.8
7/64	0.109375	2.7781	0.0007	0.01778	39/64	0.609375	15.4781	3	76.2
1/8	0.125	3.1750	0.0008	0.02032	5/8	0.625	15.8750	4	101.6
9/64	0.140625	3.5719	0.0009	0.02286	41/64	0.640625	16.2719	5	127.0
5/32	0.15625	3.9687	0.001	0.0254	21/32	0.65625	16.6687	6	152.4
11/64	0.171875	4.3656	0.002	0.0508	43/64	0.671875	17.0656	7	177.8
3/16	0.1875	4.7625	0.003	0.0762	11/16	0.6875	17.4625	8	203.2
13/64	0.203125	5.1594	0.004	0.1016	45/64	0.703125	17.8594	9	228.6
7/32	0.21875	5.5562	0.005	0.1270	23/32	0.71875	18.2562	10	254.0
15/64	0.234375	5.9531	0.006	0.1524	47/64	0.734375	18.6531	11	279.4
1/4	0.25	6.3500	0.007	0.1778	3/4	0.75	19.0500	12	304.8
17/64	0.265625	6.7469	0.008	0.2032	49/64	0.765625	19.4469	13	330.2
9/32	0.28125	7.1437	0.009	0.2286	25/32	0.78125	19.8437	14	355.6
19/64	0.296875	7.5406	0.01	0.254	51/64	0.796875	20.2406	15	381.0
5/16	0.3125	7.9375	0.02	0.508	13/16	0.8125	20.6375	16	406.4
21/64	0.328125	8.3344	0.03	0.762	53/64	0.828125	21.0344	17	431.8
11/32	0.34375	8.7312	0.04	1.016	27/32	0.84375	21.4312	18	457.2
23/64	0.359375	9.1281	0.05	1.270	55/64	0.859375	21.8281	19	482.6
3/8	0.375	9.5250	0.06	1.524	7/8	0.875	22.2250	20	508.0
25/64	0.390625	9.9219	0.07	1.778	57/64	0.890625	22.6219	21	533.4
13/32	0.40625	10.3187	0.08	2.032	29/32	0.90625	23.0187	22	558.8
27/64	0.421875	10.7156	0.09	2.286	59/64	0.921875	23.4156	23	584.2
7/16	0.4375	11.1125	0.1	2.54	15/16	0.9375	23.8125	24	609.6
29/64	0.453125	11.5094	0.2	5.08	61/64	0.953125	24.2094	25	635.0
15/32	0.46875	11.9062	0.3	7.62	31/32	0.96875	24.6062	26	660.4
31/64	0.484375	12.3031	0.4	10.16	63/64	0.984375	25.0031	27	690.6
1/2	0.5	12.7000	0.5	12.70					

ENGLISH TO METRIC CONVERSION: TORQUE

To convert foot-pounds (ft. lbs.) to Newton-meters: multiply the number of ft. lbs. by 1.3

To convert inch-pounds (in. lbs.) to Newton-meters: multiply the number of in. lbs. by .11

in lbs	N·m	in lbs	N·m	in lbs	N·m	in lbs	N·m	in lbs	N·m
0.1	0.01	1	0.11	10	1.13	19	2.15	28	3.16
0.2	0.02	2	0.23	11	1.24	20	2.26	29	3.28
0.3	0.03	3	0.34	12	1.36	21	2.37	30	3.39
0.4	0.04	4	0.45	13	1.47	22	2.49	31	3.50
0.5	0.06	5	0.56	14	1.58	23	2.60	32	3.62
0.6	0.07	6	0.68	15	1.70	24	2.71	33	3.73
0.7	0.08	7	0.78	16	1.81	25	2.82	34	3.84
0.8	0.09	8	0.90	17	1.92	26	2.94	35	3.95
0.9	0.10	9	1.02	18	2.03	27	3.05	36	4.0

ENGLISH TO METRIC CONVERSION: TORQUE

Torque is now expressed as either foot-pounds (ft./lbs.) or inch-pounds (in./lbs.). The metric measurement unit for torque is the Newton-meter (Nm). This unit—the Nm—will be used for all SI metric torque references, both the present ft./lbs. and in./lbs.

ft lbs	N-m	ft lbs	N-m	ft lbs	N-m	ft lbs	N-m
0.1	0.1	33	44.7	74	100.3	115	155.9
0.2	0.3	34	46.1	75	101.7	116	157.3
0.3	0.4	35	47.4	76	103.0	117	158.6
0.4	0.5	36	48.8	77	104.4	118	160.0
0.5	0.7	37	50.7	78	105.8	119	161.3
0.6	0.8	38	51.5	79	107.1	120	162.7
0.7	1.0	39	52.9	80	108.5	121	164.0
0.8	1.1	40	54.2	81	109.8	122	165.4
0.9	1.2	41	55.6	82	111.2	123	166.8
1	1.3	42	56.9	83	112.5	124	168.1
2	2.7	43	58.3	84	113.9	125	169.5
3	4.1	44	59.7	85	115.2	126	170.8
4	5.4	45	61.0	86	116.6	127	172.2
5	6.8	46	62.4	87	118.0	128	173.5
6	8.1	47	63.7	88	119.3	129	174.9
7	9.5	48	65.1	89	120.7	130	176.2
8	10.8	49	66.4	90	122.0	131	177.6
9	12.2	50	67.8	91	123.4	132	179.0
10	13.6	51	69.2	92	124.7	133	180.3
11	14.9	52	70.5	93	126.1	134	181.7
12	16.3	53	71.9	94	127.4	135	183.0
13	17.6	54	73.2	95	128.8	136	184.4
14	18.9	55	74.6	96	130.2	137	185.7
15	20.3	56	75.9	97	131.5	138	187.1
16	21.7	57	77.3	98	132.9	139	188.5
17	23.0	58	78.6	99	134.2	140	189.8
18	24.4	59	80.0	100	135.6	141	191.2
19	25.8	60	81.4	101	136.9	142	192.5
20	27.1	61	82.7	102	138.3	143	193.9
21	28.5	62	84.1	103	139.6	144	195.2
22	29.8	63	85.4	104	141.0	145	196.6
23	31.2	64	86.8	105	142.4	146	198.0
24	32.5	65	88.1	106	143.7	147	199.3
25	33.9	66	89.5	107	145.1	148	200.7
26	35.2	67	90.8	108	146.4	149	202.0
27	36.6	68	92.2	109	147.8	150	203.4
28	38.0	69	93.6	110	149.1	151	204.7
29	39.3	70	94.9	111	150.5	152	206.1
30	40.7	71	96.3	112	151.8	153	207.4
31	42.0	72	97.6	113	153.2	154	208.8
32	43.4	73	99.0	114	154.6	155	210.2

TCCS1C03

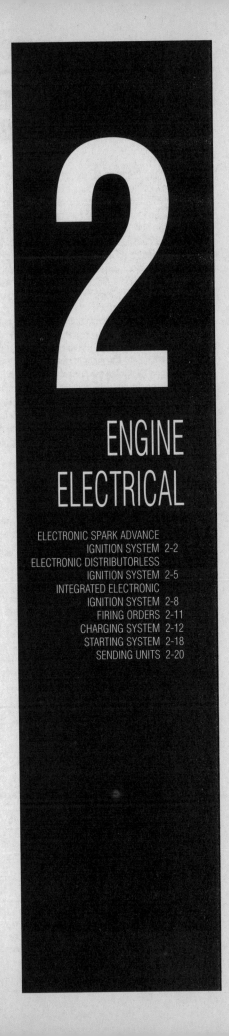

2

ENGINE ELECTRICAL

ELECTRONIC SPARK ADVANCE IGNITION SYSTEM

General Information

♦ See Figure 1

1991–96 Ford Escort and Mercury Tracer models equipped with the 1.8L engine use an ignition system similar to the transistorized systems in other contemporary Ford Motor Company vehicles. The ignition system, known as Electronic Spark Advance (ESA), consists of an ignition coil, ignition module, distributor, spark plugs and spark plug wires. Ignition spark timing correction is accomplished by the Ignition Control Module (ICM), Powertrain Control Module (PCM), Crankshaft Position (CKP) sensor, and a Cylinder Identification (CID) sensor (1991–93 models) or Camshaft Position (CMP) sensor (1994–96 models). This last sensor informs the PCM of camshaft position, and allows the more precise fuel metering provided by Sequential Fuel Injection (SFI).

When the engine is in the starting mode, crankshaft position and engine rpm are sensed by the CKP sensor. Piston travel information is sensed by the CID or CMP sensor. The PCM then signals the ignition module, telling it when to fire the coil. The module controls the current through the ignition primary winding by turning the current **ON** between firing points to build up a magnetic field around the coil windings. It then turns the current **OFF** upon a signal from the pulse generator and the pickup coil. Once the current is turned **OFF**, the field collapses and a high voltage pulse is transmitted to the central terminal in the distributor cap, and through the rotor to the distributor cap terminal for the respective spark plug to fire.

SYSTEM COMPONENTS

Ignition Coil

The ignition coil transforms the primary voltage (battery voltage) into approximately 28,000 volts on its secondary circuit each time it receives an Ignition Diagnostic Monitor (IDM) signal from the ignition module.

Ignition Module

The ignition module receives spark output signal from the PCM and grounds the coil negative side to fire the spark plugs.

Distributor

In addition to a rotor, the distributor houses the Crankshaft Position (CKP) sensor and Cylinder Identification (CID) sensor on 1991–93 models, or the Camshaft Position (CMP) sensor on 1994–96 models. The distributor, with the exception of cap and rotor replacement, is not serviceable. If it is faulty, it must be replaced (along with its built-in sensors) as a unit.

Crankshaft Position (CKP) Sensor

On 1991–93 models, the CKP sensor is located in the distributor assembly. On 1994 and later models, the CKP sensor is located behind the crankshaft pulley. The CKP sensor sends a signal to the PCM to indicate crankshaft speed.

Camshaft Position (CMP) Sensor

The CMP sensor is located in the distributor. This sensor informs the PCM of camshaft position.

➡Instead of a CMP sensor, 1991–93 models contain a Cylinder Identification (CID) sensor, which performs the same function as the CMP sensor.

Diagnosis and Testing

A simple way to check for proper ignition system operation is the secondary spark test. If however, this test fails to show a spark, the individual components of the system must be tested. Refer to the different components in this section for their testing procedures.

SERVICE PRECAUTIONS

Always turn the key **OFF** and isolate both ends of a circuit whenever testing for short or continuity.

Always disconnect solenoids and switches from the harness before measuring for continuity, resistance or energizing by way of a 12 volt source.

✳✳ WARNING

Electronic modules are sensitive to static electrical charges. If the module is exposed to these charges, damage may result.

Before performing any component testing, check for and if necessary repair the following:
- Damaged, corroded, contaminated, carbon tracked or worn distributor cap and rotor
- Damaged, fouled, improperly seated or gapped spark plug
- Damaged or improperly engaged electrically connections, spark plug wires, etc.
- Discharged battery
- Blown fuses

SECONDARY SPARK TEST

♦ See Figure 2

The best way to perform this procedure is to use a spark tester (available at most automotive parts stores). Two types of spark testers are commonly available. The Neon Bulb type is connected to the spark plug wire and flashes with each ignition pulse. The Air Gap type must be adjusted to the individual spark plug gap specified for the engine. This type of tester allows the user to not only detect the presence of spark, but also the intensity (orange/yellow is weak, blue is strong).

1. Disconnect a spark plug wire at the spark plug end.
2. Connect the plug wire to the spark tester and ground the tester to an appropriate location on the engine.
3. Crank the engine and check for spark at the tester.
4. If spark exists at the tester, the ignition system is functioning properly.
5. If spark does not exist at the spark plug wire, remove the distributor cap and ensure the rotor is turning when the engine is cranked.

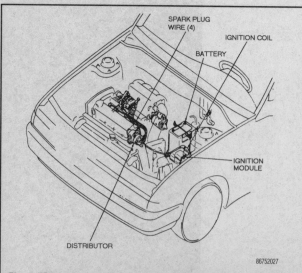

SPARK PLUG
WIRE (4)

IGNITION COIL

BATTERY

IGNITION
MODULE

DISTRIBUTOR

86752027

Fig. 1 ESA ignition system component locations—1.8L engine

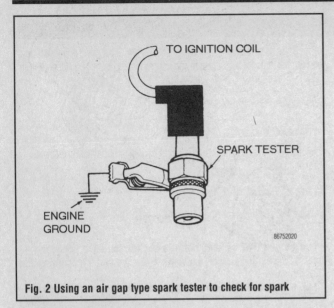

Fig. 2 Using an air gap type spark tester to check for spark

6. If the rotor is turning, perform the spark test again using the ignition coil wire.

7. If spark does not exist at the ignition coil wire, test the ignition coil, and other distributor related components or wiring. Repair or replace components as necessary.

Adjustments

The ignition system functions are controlled by the PCM, so no adjustment is necessary. To check or adjust the ignition timing, refer to Section 1 of this manual.

Ignition Coil

TESTING

▶ See Figure 3

1. Disengage the wire(s) from the coil.
2. Use an ohmmeter, connected as illustrated, to measure the resistance on the primary side of the coil; the resistance should be 0.8–1.6 ohms.

3. Use an ohmmeter, connected as illustrated, to measure the resistance on the secondary side of the coil; as illustrated. the resistance should be 6–30 kilohms.

4. If the resistance readings are not within specifications the coil is defective and must be replaced.

5. If resistance readings are within specifications, there may be a larger problem with the EEC system. It may be necessary to have the system further tested (because of the extensive experience and knowledge necessary, and equipment to perform this testing) by a professional automotive technician.

REMOVAL & INSTALLATION

▶ See Figure 4

1. Disconnect the negative battery cable.
2. Disengage the ignition connector and coil wire from the coil.
3. Loosen the ignition coil mounting nuts and remove the coil and bracket.

To install:
4. If removed, install the bracket to the ignition coil.
5. Place the ignition coil and bracket into its mounting position and tighten the mounting nuts.

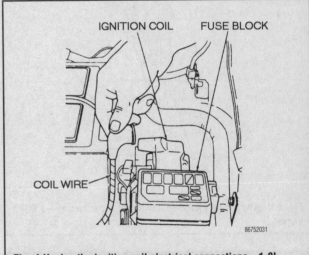

Fig. 4 Unplug the ignition coil electrical connections—1.8L engine

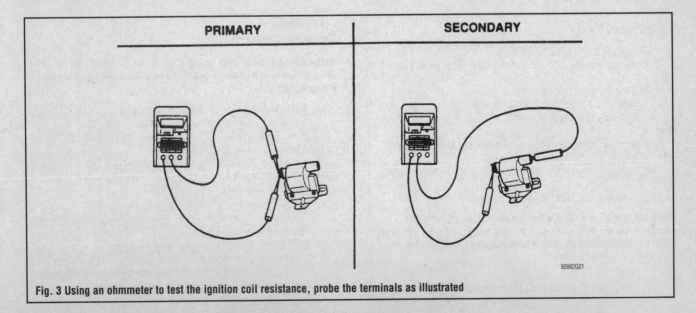

Fig. 3 Using an ohmmeter to test the ignition coil resistance, probe the terminals as illustrated

6. Engage the ignition connector and coil wire to the coil.
7. Connect the negative battery cable.

Ignition Module

REMOVAL & INSTALLATION

▶ **See Figure 5**

1. Disconnect the negative battery cable.
2. Disengage the ignition module electrical connector.
3. Remove the nuts and screws from the ignition module.
4. Remove the ignition module.
   To install:
5. Place the ignition module into its mounting position, then tighten the nuts and screws.
6. Engage the ignition module electrical connector.
7. Connect the negative battery cable.

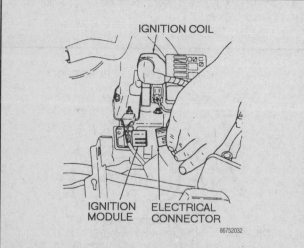

Fig. 5 Unplug the ignition module electrical connection—1.8L engine

Distributor

REMOVAL & INSTALLATION

▶ **See Figures 6 and 7**

1. Disconnect the negative battery cable.
2. Disengage the distributor electrical connector and coil wire at the cap.
3. Remove the distributor cap and rotor.
4. Position it to the side. If the distributor unit is not being replaced, scribe a reference mark across the distributor base flange and the cylinder head.
5. Loosen the distributor mounting bolts and remove the distributor from the engine.
6. If necessary, remove the distributor base gasket from the distributor.
7. If necessary, remove the distributor O-ring.

➡ **Do not rotate the engine while the distributor assembly is removed. Do not attempt to disassemble and service the distributor unit. The distributor unit should be replaced as an assembly.**

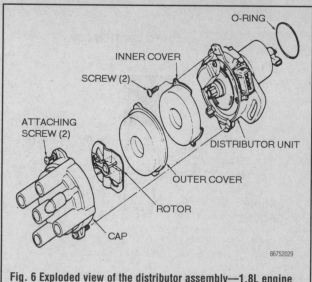

Fig. 6 Exploded view of the distributor assembly—1.8L engine

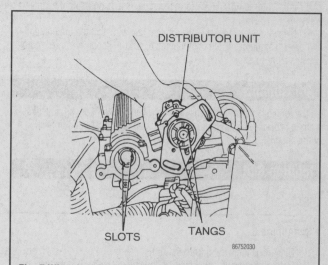

Fig. 7 When installing the distributor, make sure the drive tangs engage the camshaft slots—1.8L engine

To install:
Engine Not Disturbed

➡ **The distributor can only be installed in one direction. Do not force the distributor into position and make sure the drive tangs engage the camshaft slots.**

1. If removed, install a new distributor base gasket.
2. If removed, install a new O-ring on the distributor unit.
3. Install the distributor unit into the engine. Make certain the drive tangs engage with the camshaft slots.
4. If installing the old distributor, make sure the reference marks made during removal are aligned.
5. Tighten the mounting bolts finger-tight.
6. Install the rotor and distributor cap.
7. Engage the distributor electrical connector and coil wire to the cap.
8. Connect the negative battery cable and check ignition timing.
9. If necessary, adjust the ignition timing.
10. Tighten the distributor mounting bolt to 14–19 ft. lbs. (19–25 Nm).

Engine Disturbed

➡When installing the distributor make sure the offset drive tangs engage the camshaft slots.

1. Make sure that the engine is still with the No. 1 piston up on TDC of its compression stroke.

➡If the engine was disturbed while the distributor was removed, it will be necessary to remove the No. 1 spark plug and rotate the engine clockwise until the No. 1 piston is on the compression stroke. Align the timing marks.

2. If installing the old distributor:
   a. Install the distributor and align the marks on the distributor base flange-to-cylinder head and the rotor points toward the mark on the distributor housing made previously. Make certain the rotor is pointing to the No. 1 mark on the distributor base.
3. If installing a new distributor:
   a. Install the rotor and cap (with wires still attached) on the distributor, follow the No. 1 spark plug wire from the plug to the cap, this will be the No.1 tower on the cap. Mark the location of the tower on the distributor housing, then remove the cap.

b. Install the distributor and make sure the rotor aligns with the No.1 tower mark made on the distributor.
4. When all the marks are aligned, install the distributor hold-down bolts and tighten them to 14–19 ft. lbs. (19–25 Nm).
5. Install the cap and tighten the screws.
6. Connect the negative battery cable.
7. Engage the electrical connections.
8. Install the No. 1 spark plug, if removed.
9. Recheck the initial timing and adjust if necessary.

Camshaft Position Sensor

For Camshaft Position (CMP) sensor procedures, please refer to Section 4 in this manual.

Crankshaft Position Sensor

For Crankshaft Position (CKP) sensor procedures, please refer to Section 4 in this manual.

ELECTRONIC DISTRIBUTORLESS IGNITION SYSTEM

Description and Operation

▶ See Figure 8

1991–96 Ford Escort and Mercury Tracer models equipped with the 1.9L engine use a high data rate Electronic Distributorless Ignition System (EDIS). This ignition system is controlled by an EDIS ignition control module and the Powertrain Control Module (PCM) operating in union. The system is designed to deliver a full energy spark at a crank angle selected by the PCM. This system is a modified version of the Distributorless Ignition System (DIS). The EDIS consists of a Crankshaft Position (CKP) sensor, an EDIS ignition control module, PCM and a coil pack.

The CKP sensor is a variable reluctance type sensor triggered by a 36-minus-1 trigger wheel configuration pressed onto the rear of the crankshaft damper. The signal generated by this sensor provides engine position rpm to the ignition control module.

The EDIS ignition control module receives the information on engine position and rpm from the CKP sensor and desired spark advance from the PCM. The module then uses this information to direct which coil to activate, as well as to calculate the **TURN ON** and **TURN OFF** times of the coils required to achieve the correct dwell and spark advance. The module also generates a Profile Ignition Pick-up (PIP) signal and an Ignition Diagnostic Monitor (IDM) signal for use by the PCM. The module signals the PCM of signal failures through the IDM. The PCM then stores this information as trouble codes. A Clean Tach Output (CTO) signal is also provided to drive the tachometer.

The ignition coil pack contains two separate ignition coils which are controlled by the EDIS module through two ignition coil leads. Each coil activates sparks plugs at two cylinders simultaneously. While one plug is active on the compression stroke, the companion plug is active on the exhaust stroke. At the next engine revolution, this process will reverse. The plug that activates on the exhaust stroke uses very little of the coil's stored energy. The majority of the coil's energy is used by the plug active on the compression stroke. Because these two plugs are connected in series, the firing voltage of one plug is negative with respect to ground, and the other plug is positive with respect to ground.

Diagnosis and Testing

PRELIMINARY CHECKS

1. Visually inspect the engine compartment to ensure that all vacuum lines and spark plug wires are properly routed and securely connected.
2. Be certain that the battery is fully charged and that all accessories are **OFF** during the diagnosis.

A simple way to check for proper ignition system operation is the secondary spark test. If however, this test fails to show a spark, the individual components of the system must be tested. Refer to the different components in this section for their testing procedures.

SERVICE PRECAUTIONS

Always turn the key **OFF** and isolate both ends of a circuit whenever testing for short or continuity.

Always disconnect solenoids and switches from the harness before measuring for continuity, resistance or energizing by way of a 12 volt source.

✳✳ WARNING

Electronic modules are sensitive to static electrical charges. If the module is exposed to these charges, damage may result.

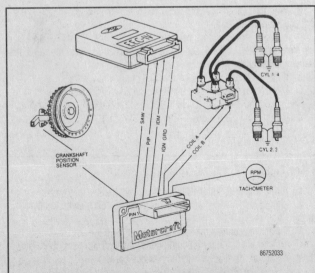

Fig. 8 EDIS system components—1991–96 1.9L engine

Before performing any component testing, check for and if necessary repair the following:
- Damaged, fouled, improperly seated or gapped spark plug
- Damaged or improperly engaged electrically connections, spark plug wires etc.
- Discharged battery
- Blown fuses

SECONDARY SPARK TEST

▶ **See Figure 9**

The best way to perform this procedure is to use a spark tester (available at most automotive parts stores). Two types of spark testers are commonly available. The Neon Bulb type is connected to the spark plug wire and flashes with each ignition pulse. The Air Gap type must be adjusted to the individual spark plug gap specified for the engine. This type of tester allows the user to not only detect the presence of spark, but also the intensity (orange/yellow is weak, blue is strong).

1. Disconnect a spark plug wire at the spark plug end.
2. Connect the plug wire to the spark tester and ground the tester to an appropriate location on the engine.
3. Crank the engine and check for spark at the tester.
4. If spark exists at the tester, the ignition system is functioning properly.
5. If spark does not exist at the wire, test the ignition coil, and other ignition system related components or wiring. Repair or replace components as necessary.

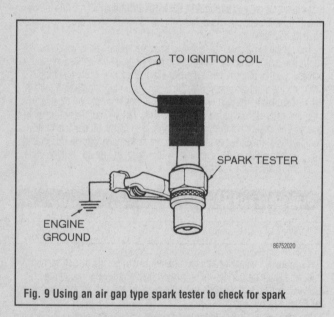

Fig. 9 Using an air gap type spark tester to check for spark

Adjustments

The ignition system functions are controlled by the PCM, so no adjustment is necessary.

Coil Pack

TESTING

▶ **See Figures 10 and 11**

1. Turn the ignition key **OFF**.
2. Unplug the coil pack from the vehicle harness connector.

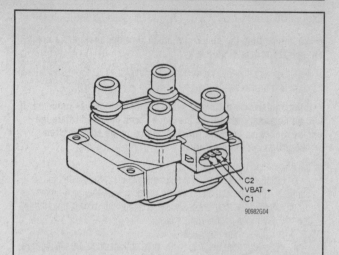

Fig. 10 Probe the terminals of the coil pack with a DVOM to check resistance

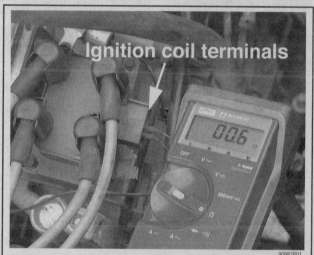

Fig. 11 Measure the resistance between the EDIS coil pack terminals VBAT + and C1 with a DVOM set on the 2 kilohms scale

3. With the EDIS diagnostic cable negative battery lead connected, disengage the positive lead.
4. Measure the resistance between terminals VBAT + and C1 with a Digital Volt Ohmmeter (DVOM) set on the 2 kilohms scale. Refer to the accompanying illustration.
5. If the reading is not greater than 0.4 ohms, replace the coil.
6. Measure the resistance between terminals VBAT + and C2 with a DVOM set on the 2 kilohms scale. Refer to the accompanying illustration.
7. If the reading is not greater than 0.4 ohms, replace the coil.

REMOVAL & INSTALLATION

▶ **See Figures 12, 13, 14, 15 and 16**

1. Turn the ignition key **OFF** and disconnect the negative battery cable.
2. Unplug the harness connectors from the coil pack and capacitor assembly.
3. Tag and disconnect the spark plug wires from the coil.
4. Remove the coil pack retaining bolts and capacitor assembly. Save the capacitor for installation with the new coil pack.

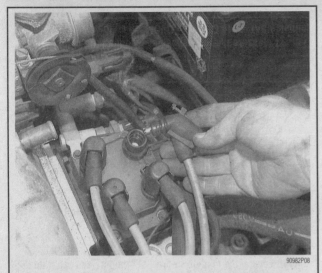

Fig. 12 Disconnect the spark plug wires from the ignition coil

Fig. 13 Unplug the harness connector(s) from the coil

Fig. 14 Remove the coil pack retaining bolts . . .

Fig. 15 . . . along with the capacitor assembly. Save the capacitor for installation with the new coil pack

Fig. 16 After all the bolts have been unfastened and the wires unplugged, remove the coil pack from its bracket

5. Remove the coil pack from the mounting bracket.

To install:

6. Position the coil pack and capacitor assembly on its mounting bracket and install the retaining bolts. Tighten the bolts to 40–61 inch lbs. (5–7 Nm).

7. Connect the spark plug wires to the coil.

8. Engage the coil pack and the capacitor electrical connectors.

9. Connect the negative battery cable.

Ignition Control Module

REMOVAL & INSTALLATION

▶ See Figures 17 and 18

1. Turn the ignition key **OFF** and disconnect the negative battery cable.

2. Remove the Ignition Control Module (ICM) bracket retainers.

3. Carefully pull the bracket and module assembly straight upward and unplug the module electrical connector.

4. Unfasten the module-to-bracket retaining screws and remove the module from the bracket.

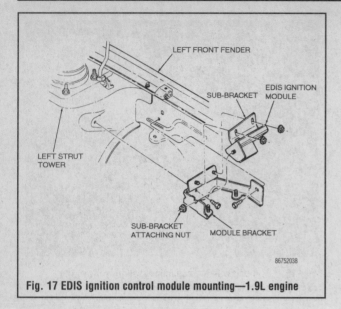

Fig. 17 EDIS ignition control module mounting—1.9L engine

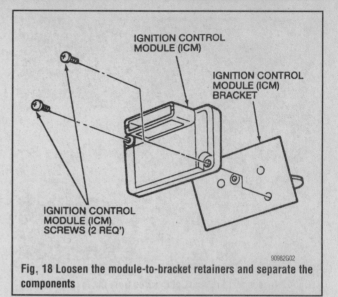

Fig. 18 Loosen the module-to-bracket retainers and separate the components

To install:

5. Position the module on the bracket and install the retaining screws. Tighten the screws to 24–35 inch lbs. (3–4 Nm).

6. Engage the module connector.

7. Place the module and bracket assembly in position and install the retainers. Tighten the retainers to 62–88 inch lbs. (7–10 Nm).

8. Connect the negative battery cable.

INTEGRATED ELECTRONIC IGNITION SYSTEM

Description and Operation

▶ See Figure 19

1997–99 Ford Escort and Mercury Tracers equipped with the 2.0L engine use an integrated electronic ignition system. The ignition system consists of a Crankshaft Position (CKP) sensor, coil pack, wiring and the Powertrain Control Module (PCM). The ignition is controlled by the PCM and is non-adjustable.

The CKP sensor is used to indicate crankshaft position and speed by sensing a missing tooth on a pulse wheel mounted to the crankshaft, and sends this information to the PCM. The PCM then uses this information on when to fire the coil pack.

The coil pack, which contains two separate coils, fires two spark plugs at the same time after it receives the signal from the PCM. The spark plugs are paired so that as one plug fires during the compression stroke, the other plug fires on the exhaust stroke. The next time the coil is fired, the situation is reversed.

The PCM acts like a switch to ground in the coil primary circuit. When the switch is closed, the battery positive voltage applied to the coil primary circuit builds a magnetic field around the primary coil. When the switch opens, the power is interrupted and the primary field collapses, inducing the high voltage in the secondary coil windings, and the spark is fired through the spark plug wire from the coil to the plug. A kickback voltage spike occurs when the primary field collapses. The PCM uses this spike to generate an Ignition Diagnostic Monitor (IDM) signal. The IDM communicates information by pulse width modulation in the PCM.

Camshaft Position Sensor

For Camshaft Position (CMP) sensor procedures, please refer to Section 4 in this manual.

Crankshaft Position Sensor

For Crankshaft Position (CKP) sensor procedures, please refer to Section 4 in this manual.

Diagnosis and Testing

PRELIMINARY CHECKS

1. Visually inspect the engine compartment to ensure that all vacuum lines and spark plug wires are properly routed and securely connected.

2. Be certain that the battery is fully charged and that all accessories are **OFF** during the diagnosis.

3. Measure the spark plug wire resistance. Refer to Section 1 for this procedure.

A simple way to check for proper ignition system operation is the secondary spark test. If however, this test fails to show a spark, the individual components of the system must be tested. Refer to the different components in this section for their testing procedures.

SERVICE PRECAUTIONS

Always turn the key **OFF** and isolate both ends of a circuit whenever testing for short or continuity.

Always disconnect solenoids and switches from the harness before measuring for continuity, resistance or energizing by way of a 12 volt source.

✳ CAUTION

Electronic modules are sensitive to static electrical charges. If the module is exposed to these charges, damage may result.

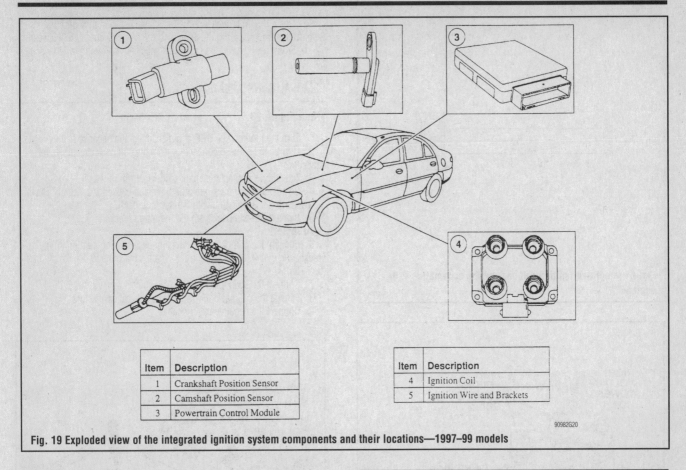

Item	Description
1	Crankshaft Position Sensor
2	Camshaft Position Sensor
3	Powertrain Control Module

Item	Description
4	Ignition Coil
5	Ignition Wire and Brackets

90982G20

Fig. 19 Exploded view of the integrated ignition system components and their locations—1997–99 models

Before performing any component testing, check for and if necessary repair the following:
- Damaged, fouled, improperly seated or gapped spark plug
- Damaged or improperly engaged electrically connections, spark plug wires etc.
- Discharged battery
- Blown fuses

SECONDARY SPARK TEST

▶ See Figure 20

The best way to perform this procedure is to use a spark tester (available at most automotive parts stores). Two types of spark testers are commonly available. The Neon Bulb type is connected to the spark plug wire and flashes with each ignition pulse. The Air Gap type must be adjusted to the individual spark plug gap specified for the engine. This type of tester allows the user to not only detect the presence of spark, but also the intensity (orange/yellow is weak, blue is strong).

1. Disconnect a spark plug wire at the spark plug end.
2. Connect the plug wire to the spark tester and ground the tester to an appropriate location on the engine.
3. Crank the engine and check for spark at the tester.
4. If spark exists at the tester, the ignition system is functioning properly.
5. If spark does not exist at the wire, test the ignition coil, and other ignition system related components or wiring. Repair or replace components as necessary.

Adjustments

The ignition system functions are controlled by the PCM, so no adjustment is necessary.

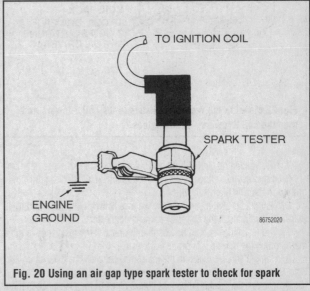

Fig. 20 Using an air gap type spark tester to check for spark

Coil Pack

TESTING

▶ See Figures 21 and 22

1. Turn the ignition key OFF.
2. Unplug the vehicle harness connector from the coil pack.
3. Measure the power supply to the coil by using a high impedance Digital Volt Ohm Meter (DVOM). Measure the voltage between IGN Start/Run terminal at the harness connector and ground.

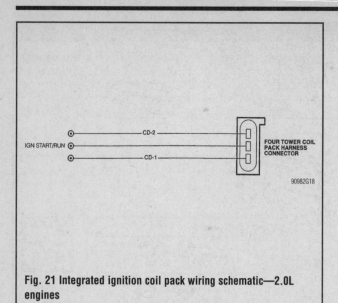

Fig. 21 Integrated ignition coil pack wiring schematic—2.0L engines

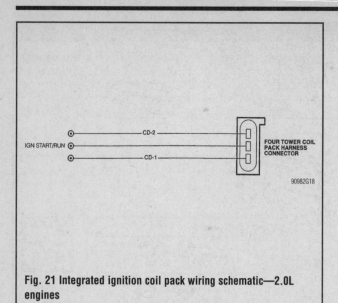

Fig. 22 Measure the resistance between the coil 1 towers and then the coil 2 towers—2.0L engines

4. The voltage reading should be 10 volts.

5. If the reading is incorrect, check for a damaged fuse or a short to ground in the IGN Start/Run wire.

6. Using a DVOM, measure the resistance between the CD-1 and IGN Start/Run terminals at the coil pack harness connector.

7. The resistance should be less than 5 ohms. If the resistance is more than 5 ohms the coil pack is probably defective. *4.8*

8. Using a DVOM, measure the resistance between the CD-2 and IGN Start/Run terminals at the coil pack harness connector.

9. The resistance should be less than 5 ohms. If the resistance is more than 5 ohms, the coil pack is probably defective.

10. Disconnect the spark plug wires from the coil.

11. Use a DVOM to measure the resistance between the coil 1 towers. Refer to the accompanying illustration. The resistance should be between 12–14.5K ohms. If the reading is not as specified, coil 1 is probably defective. *14.59*

12. Use a DVOM to measure the resistance between the coil 2 towers. Refer to the accompanying illustration. The resistance should be between 12–14.5K ohms. If the reading is not as specified, coil 2 is probably defective. *14.8*

REMOVAL & INSTALLATION

▶ See Figure 23

1. Turn the ignition key **OFF** and disconnect the negative battery cable.

2. Unplug the harness connectors from the coil pack assembly and capacitor.

3. Tag and disconnect the spark plug wires from the coil.

4. Remove the coil pack retaining bolts and capacitor assembly. Save the capacitor for installation with the new coil pack.

5. Remove the coil pack from the mounting bracket.

To install:

6. Position the coil pack and capacitor assembly on its mounting bracket and install the retaining bolts. Tighten the bolts to 44–6 inch. lbs. (5–7 Nm).

7. Connect the spark plug wires to the coil.

8. Engage the coil pack and capacitor electrical connectors.

9. Connect the negative battery cable.

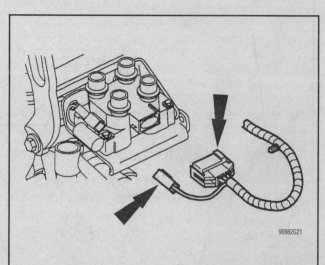

Fig. 23 Unplug the coil pack and radio ignition interference capacitor electrical connections—2.0L engines

Camshaft Position Sensor

For Camshaft Position (CMP) sensor procedures, please refer to Section 4 in this manual.

Crankshaft Position Sensor

For Crankshaft Position (CKP) sensor procedures, please refer to Section 4 in this manual.

FIRING ORDERS

▶ See Figures 24, 25 and 26

➡ **To avoid confusion, remove and tag the spark plug wires one at a time, for replacement.**

If a distributor is not keyed for installation with only one orientation, it could have been removed previously and rewired. The resultant wiring would hold the correct firing order, but could change the relative placement of the plug towers in relation to the engine. For this reason, it is imperative that you label all wires before disconnecting any of them. Also, before removal, compare the current wiring with the accompanying illustrations. If the current wiring does not match, make notes in your book to reflect how your engine is wired.

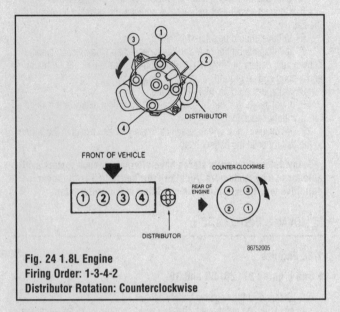

Fig. 24 1.8L Engine
Firing Order: 1-3-4-2
Distributor Rotation: Counterclockwise

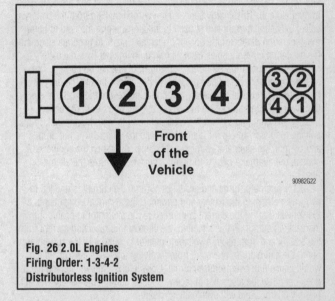

Fig. 26 2.0L Engines
Firing Order: 1-3-4-2
Distributorless Ignition System

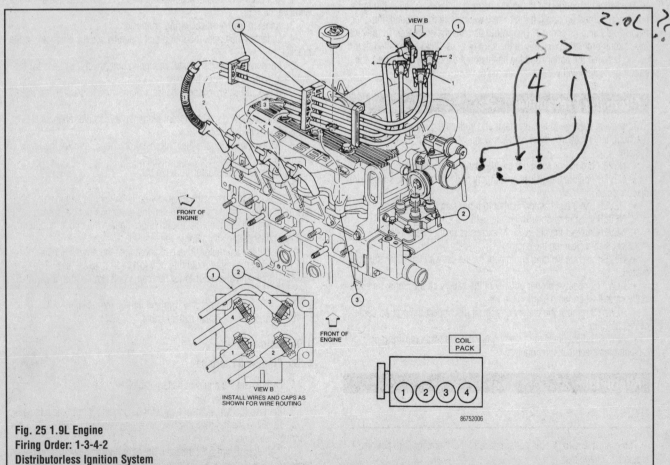

Fig. 25 1.9L Engine
Firing Order: 1-3-4-2
Distributorless Ignition System

CHARGING SYSTEM

General Information

The charging system is a negative (-) ground system which consists of an alternator, a regulator, a charge indicator lamp, a storage battery, circuit protection and wiring connecting the components.

The alternator is belt-driven from the engine. Energy is supplied from the alternator (with integral regulator) to the rotating field through brushes to slip-rings. The slip-rings are mounted on the rotor shaft and are connected to the field coil. This energy supplied to the rotating field from the battery is called excitation current and is used to initially energize the field to begin the generation of electricity. Once the alternator starts to generate electricity, the excitation current comes from its own output rather than the battery.

The alternator produces power in the form of alternating current. The alternating current is rectified by diodes into direct current. The direct current is used to charge the battery and power the rest of the electrical system. When the ignition key is turned on, current flows from the battery, through the charging system indicator light on the instrument panel, to the voltage regulator, and to the alternator. Since the alternator is not producing any current, the alternator warning light comes on. When the engine is started, the alternator begins to produce current and turns the alternator light off.

As the alternator turns and produces current, the current is divided in two ways: charging the battery and powering the electrical components of the vehicle. Part of the current is returned to the alternator to enable it to increase its output. In this situation, the alternator is receiving current from the battery and from itself. A voltage regulator is wired into the current supply to the alternator to prevent it from receiving too much current, which would cause it to overproduce current. Conversely, if the voltage regulator does not allow the alternator to receive enough current, the battery will not be fully charged and will eventually go dead.

The battery is connected to the alternator at all times, whether the ignition key is turned on or off. If the battery were shorted to ground, the alternator would also be shorted. This would damage the alternator. To prevent this, circuit protection (usually in the form of a fuse link) is installed in the wiring between the battery and the alternator. If the battery is shorted, the circuit protection will protect the alternator.

Alternator Precautions

To prevent damage to the alternator and voltage regulator, the following precautionary measures must be taken when working with the electrical system:
- NEVER ground or short out the alternator or regulator terminals.
- NEVER operate the alternator with any of its or the battery's lead wires disconnected.
- NEVER use a fast battery charger to jump start a dead battery.
- NEVER attempt to polarize an alternator.
- NEVER subject the alternator to excessive heat or dampness (for instance, steam cleaning the engine).
- NEVER use arc welding equipment on the car with the alternator connected.
- ALWAYS observe proper polarity of the battery connections; be especially careful when jump starting the car.
- ALWAYS remove the battery or at least disconnect the ground cable while charging.
- ALWAYS disconnect the battery ground cable while repairing or replacing an electrical components.

Alternator

TESTING

The easiest way to test the performance of the alternator is to perform a regulated voltage test.

1. Check the drive belt tension and ensure that it is properly adjusted.
2. Check the battery terminals and make sure they are clean and tight.
3. Check all the charging system wires for insulation damage, corrosion at the connections and make sure they are properly engaged.
4. Start the engine and allow it to reach operating temperature.
5. Connect a voltmeter between the positive and negative terminals of the battery.
6. Voltage should be 14.1–14.7 volts.
7. If voltage is higher or lower than specification, connect a voltmeter between the battery positive (B+) voltage output terminal of the alternator and a good engine ground.
8. Voltage should be 14.1–14.7 volts.
9. If voltage is still out of specification, a problem exists in the alternator or voltage regulator.
10. If voltage is now within specification, a problem exists in the wiring to the battery or in the battery itself.

➡Many automotive parts stores have alternator bench testers available for use by customers. An alternator bench test is the most definitive way to determine the condition of your alternator.

REMOVAL & INSTALLATION

1.8L Engines

▶ **See Figures 27, 28, 29 and 30**

1. Disconnect the negative battery cable.
2. Unfasten the nut that attaches the wiring connector to the alternator. Remove the wire.
3. Remove field terminal wiring connector.
4. Unfasten the upper mounting bolt that attaches the alternator to the bracket.
5. Loosen the lower alternator mounting bolt, pivot the alternator forward and remove the drive belt.
6. Raise and safely support the front of the vehicle securely on jackstands.
7. Unfasten the right-hand front fender splash shield retainers and remove the shield.
8. While supporting the alternator with one hand, remove the lower alternator mounting bolt.
9. Remove the alternator from the car.

To install:
10. Position the alternator assembly onto the vehicle and install the alternator lower mounting bolt. Tighten the lower bolt until it is snug.
11. Lower the car, then install and finger-tighten the upper mounting bolt that attaches the alternator to the bracket.
12. Install the alternator drive belt and adjust the drive belt tension.
13. Tighten the upper mounting bolt to 14–19 ft. lbs. (19–25 Nm).
14. Tighten the alternator lower mounting bolt to 27–38 ft. lbs. (37–52 Nm).
15. Connect the alternator wiring and tighten the retaining nut.
16. Connect the negative battery cable.

1.9L Engines

▶ **See Figures 31 thru 41**

1. Disconnect the negative battery cable.
2. Remove the drive belt.
3. Remove the two snap-in type wiring connectors from the alternator.
4. Unfasten the nut that attaches the wiring connector to the alternator. Remove the connector.
5. If equipped with A/C, unfasten the accumulator tube support clip retainer(s) and remove the clip from the bracket.

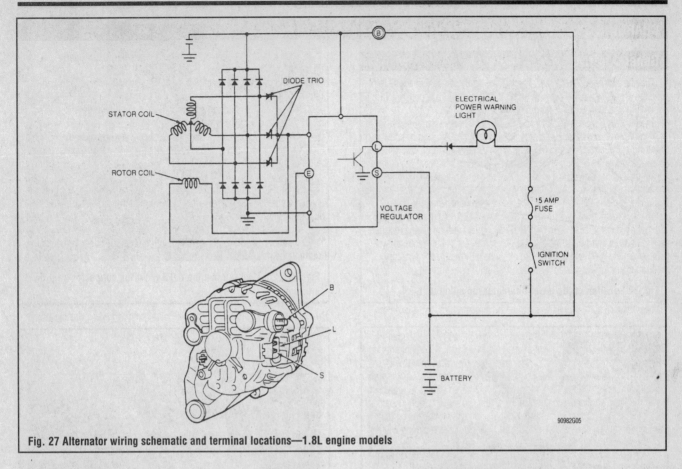

Fig. 27 Alternator wiring schematic and terminal locations—1.8L engine models

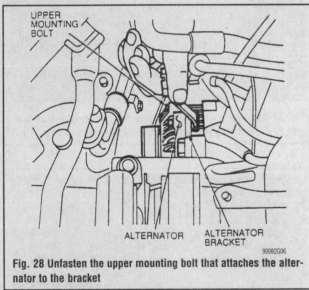

Fig. 28 Unfasten the upper mounting bolt that attaches the alternator to the bracket

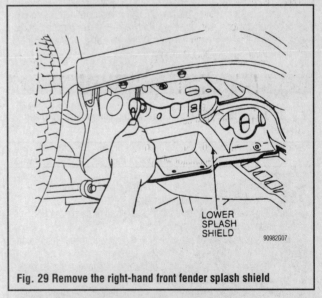

Fig. 29 Remove the right-hand front fender splash shield

6. Remove the upper and lower alternator mounting bolts.

7. Unfasten the power steering pump reservoir bolts and set the reservoir to one side and remove the alternator assembly.

To install:

8. Place the alternator in position and finger-tighten the mounting bolts.

9. Place the power steering pump reservoir in position and tighten the retaining bolts.

10. Tighten the alternator lower bolt to 29–40 ft. lbs. (40–55 Nm) and the upper bolt to 14–22 ft. lbs. (20–30 Nm).

11. If equipped with A/C, install the accumulator tube support clip and tighten the retainer(s).

12. Engage the two snap-in type wiring connectors to the alternator.

13. Engage the wiring connector and tighten the nut.

14. Install the drive belt.

15. Connect the negative battery cable.

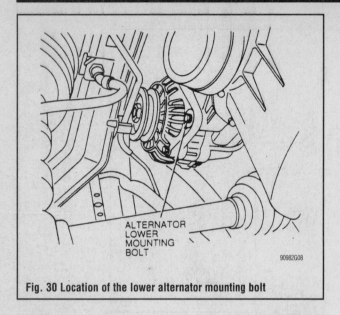

Fig. 30 Location of the lower alternator mounting bolt

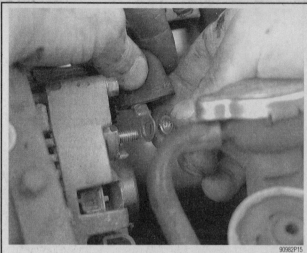

Fig. 33 . . . then remove the nut and wiring connector from the alternator

Fig. 31 Detach the two snap-in type wiring connectors from the alternator

Fig. 34 If equipped with A/C, unfasten the accumulator tube support clip retainer(s) and remove the clip from the bracket

Fig. 32 Loosen the nut that attaches the wiring connector to the alternator . . .

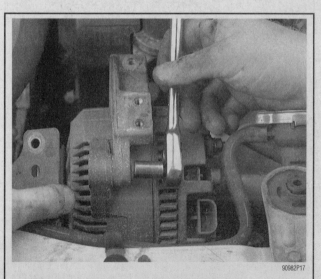

Fig. 35 Remove the upper alternator mounting bolt

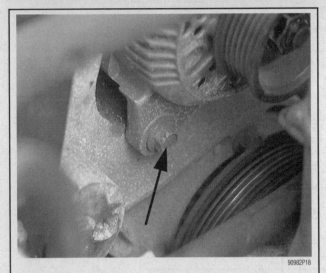

Fig. 36 Location of the lower alternator mounting bolt

Fig. 37 Unfasten the power steering pump reservoir bolts and set the reservoir to one side

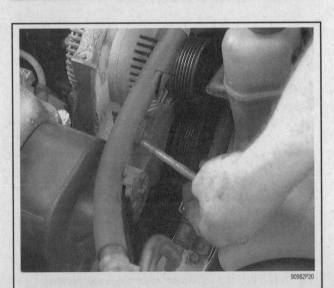

Fig. 38 Unfasten the lower alternator mounting bolt . . .

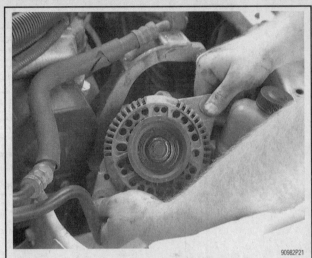

Fig. 39 . . . and remove the alternator from the engine compartment

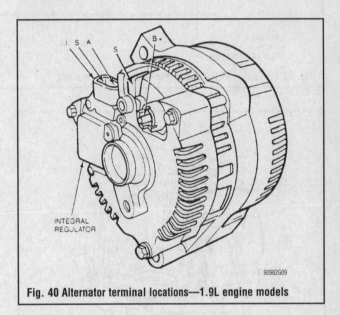

Fig. 40 Alternator terminal locations—1.9L engine models

2.0L Engines

SEDAN AND WAGON

▶ See Figure 42

➡When the battery is disconnected it may cause some abnormal drive symptoms until the Powertrain Control Module (PCM) relearns its adaptive strategy. The vehicle may need to be driven 10 miles (16 km) or more for the PCM to relearn its strategy.

1. Disconnect the negative battery cable.
2. Remove the drive belt.
3. Disconnect the power steering hose bracket from the alternator bracket.
4. Unfasten the alternator mounting bolts and position the assembly so that you can access the electrical connections.
5. Unplug the alternator electrical connectors.
6. Unfasten the battery positive cable retaining nut, then remove the washer and cable.
7. Remove the alternator from the vehicle.

To install:

8. Connect the battery positive cable, then install the nut and the washer. Tighten the nut to 7–9 ft. lbs. (9–12 Nm).

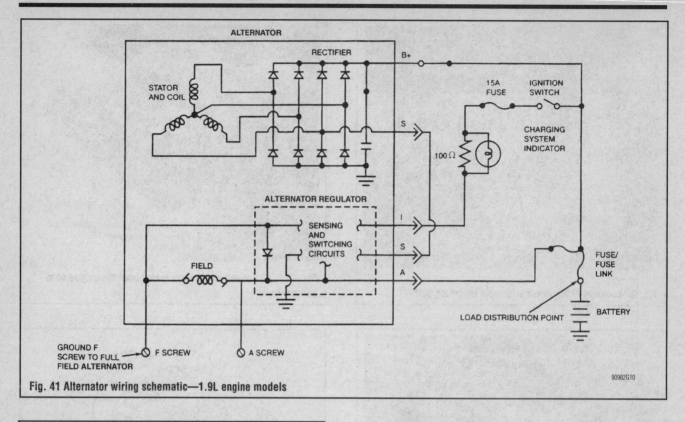

Fig. 41 Alternator wiring schematic—1.9L engine models

Fig. 42 Location of the alternator upper and lower mounting bolts—1997–99 sedan and wagon models

9. Attach the alternator electrical connections.
10. Place the alternator in position and install the mounting bolts. Tighten the upper mounting bolt to 29–40 ft. lbs. (40–55 Nm) and the lower mounting bolt to 15–22 ft. lbs. (20–30 Nm).
11. Connect the power steering hose bracket to the alternator bracket.
12. Install the drive belt.
13. Connect the negative battery cable.

COUPE

▶ See Figure 43

➡When the battery is disconnected it may cause some abnormal drive symptoms until the Powertrain Control Module (PCM) relearns its adaptive strategy. The vehicle may need to be driven 10 miles (16 km) or more for the PCM to relearn its strategy.

1. Disconnect the negative battery cable.
2. Remove the drive belt.
3. Remove the coolant tank reservoir.
4. Unplug the alternator electrical connectors.
5. Unfasten the alternator mounting bolts and position the assembly so that you can access the battery positive cable-to-alternator retaining nut.
6. Unfasten the battery positive cable retaining nut, then remove the washer and cable.
7. Remove the alternator from the vehicle.
To install:
8. Connect the battery positive cable, then install the washer and nut. Tighten the nut to 5–7 ft. lbs. (7–9 Nm).
9. Place the alternator in position and install the mounting bolts. Tighten the mounting bolts to 29–40 ft. lbs. (40–55 Nm).
10. Attach the alternator electrical connections.

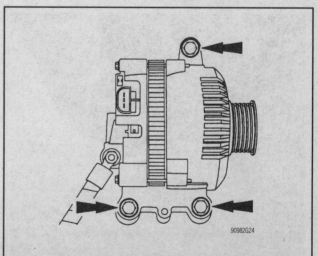

Fig. 43 Location of the alternator upper and lower mounting bolts—1998–99 Escort coupe model

11. Install the coolant tank reservoir.
12. Install the drive belt.
13. Connect the negative battery cable.

Regulator

REMOVAL & INSTALLATION

1.8L Engines

The voltage regulator on models with a 1.8L engine is an internal part of the alternator assembly. If the regulator is found to be defective, replace the alternator, or rebuild it according to the rebuilding kit manufacturer's instructions.

1.9L Engines

▶ **See Figures 44 and 45**

1. Disconnect the negative battery cable.
2. Disconnect the wiring harness from the alternator/regulator assembly.
3. Remove the four screws attaching the regulator to the alternator rear housing.
4. Remove the regulator, with brush holder attached, from the alternator.
5. Pry the cap off the **A** terminal screw with a prytool.
6. Unfasten the brush holder-to-voltage regulator Torx® screws, then separate the regulator from the brush holder.
To install:
7. Engage the voltage regulator to the brush holder and tighten the two screws to 25–35 inch lbs. (3–4 Nm).
8. Install the cap on **A** terminal screw.
9. Depress the brushes into the brush holder and hold the brushes in position by inserting a standard size paper clip or its equivalent through both the location hole in the regulator and the holes in the brushes.
10. Fit the regulator and brush holder assemblies to the alternator rear housing and install the retaining screws. Tighten the screws to 20–30 inch lbs. (2.5–3.5 Nm).
11. Remove the paper clip or equivalent from the alternator.
12. Connect the alternator wiring harness.
13. Connect the negative battery cable.

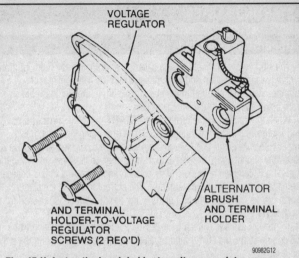

Fig. 45 Unfasten the brush holder-to-voltage regulator screws, and separate the regulator from the brush holder

2.0L Engines

▶ **See Figure 46**

1. Remove the alternator.
2. Remove the four screws attaching the regulator to the alternator rear housing.
3. Remove the regulator, with brush holder attached, from the alternator.
To install:
4. Engage the voltage regulator to the brush holder and tighten the two screws to 25–35 inch lbs. (3–4 Nm).
5. Depress the brushes into the brush holder (A) and hold the brushes in position by inserting a standard size paper clip or its equivalent (B) through both the location hole in the regulator and the holes in the brushes.
6. Fit the regulator and brush holder assemblies to the alternator rear housing and install the retaining screws. Tighten the screws to 20–30 inch lbs. (2.5–3.5 Nm) on 1997 models and 26–41 inch lbs. (3–4.5 Nm) on 1998–99 models.
7. Remove the paper clip or equivalent from the alternator.
8. Install the alternator.

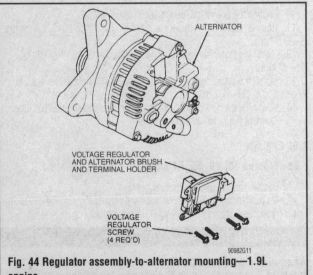

Fig. 44 Regulator assembly-to-alternator mounting—1.9L engine

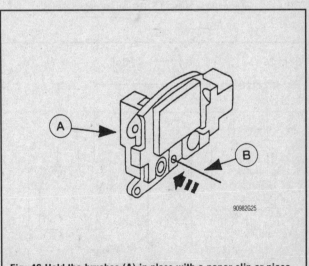

Fig. 46 Hold the brushes (A) in place with a paper clip or piece of wire (B)

STARTING SYSTEM

General Information

The starting system includes the battery, starter motor, solenoid, ignition switch, circuit protection and wiring connecting the components. An inhibitor switch is included in the starting system to prevent the vehicle from being started with the vehicle in gear.

When the ignition key is turned to the **START** position, current flows and energizes the starter's solenoid coil. The iron plunger core is drawn into the solenoid coil. The lever and pin which are connected to the drive assembly engage the starter drive to the ring gear on the flywheel. When the iron core is completely in the coil its contact disc closes the circuit between the battery and starter motor terminals. The current travels to the starter which cranks the engine until it starts or the ignition switch is released from the **START** position.

To prevent damage caused by excessive starter armature rotation when the engine starts, the starter incorporates an over-running clutch in the pinion gear.

Starter

TESTING

Voltage Drop

♦ See Figure 47

➡The battery must be in good condition and fully charged prior to performing these tests.

1. Make sure the battery terminals are clean and tight.
2. Check the starter motor electrical wires for insulation damage, the connections are properly engaged and have no dirt or corrosion.
3. Disengage the electrical connections from the distributor or coil to prevent the engine from starting.
4. Using a Digital Volt Ohmmeter (DVOM) set on the voltage scale, connect the DVOM positive lead to the battery positive terminal and the negative lead engaged to the starter solenoid **M** terminal.
5. Use a remote starter (connected between the battery positive terminal and the starter motor **S** terminal) or with the help an assistant, crank the engine and observe the voltage reading.
6. If the voltage at the **M** Terminal is higher than 0.5 volts, move the DVOM negative lead to the solenoid **B** terminal and repeat the test.

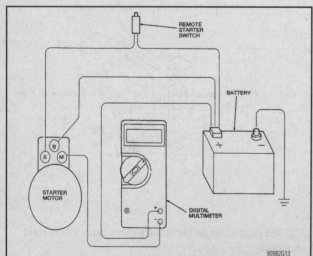

Fig. 47 Wiring schematic of the remote starter and DVOM connections required when performing a voltage drop test

7. If the voltage reading is higher than 0.5 volts there may be a problem with the solenoid or the wires.
8. Disengage, clean and reinstall the **B**, **S** and **M** terminals. Repeat Steps 4–6.
9. If the voltage readings are still the same the solenoid is defective and must be replaced.

REMOVAL & INSTALLATION

1.8L Engines

1. Disconnect the negative battery cable.
2. Remove the air cleaner-to-intake manifold tube.
3. Remove the upper starter motor bolts.
4. Raise and safely support the front of the vehicle securely on jackstands.
5. Unfasten the intake manifold starter support bolts and remove the support.

✱✱ CAUTION

When disengaging the plastic hard shell connector at the solenoid S terminal, grasp the connector and depress the plastic tab, then pull off the lead assembly. Do not pull on the lead.

6. Disengage the **S** terminal connector from the solenoid.
7. Unfasten the solenoid **B** terminal nut and disconnect the cable from the terminal.
8. Unfasten the lower starter motor bolt and remove the starter motor from the car.
   To install:

✱✱ WARNING

Make sure the starter drive housing pilot diameter is fully engaged in the cover plate locating hole and that all mounting surfaces are flush.

➡Install the upper starter motor bolts first to prevent binding or a noisy starter motor.

9. Place the starter motor in position, install the upper mounting bolts and tighten them to 18–20 ft. lbs. (25–27 Nm).
10. Engage the **S** terminal connector to the solenoid.
11. Connect the **B** terminal wire and tighten the nut to 80–120 inch lbs. (9–13.5 Nm).
12. Install the lower starter motor bolt and tighten it to 18–20 ft. lbs. (25–27 Nm).
13. Install the intake manifold starter support and tighten the bolts to 27–38 ft. lbs. (37–52 Nm).
14. Lower the car and connect the air cleaner-to-intake manifold tube.
15. Connect the negative battery cable.

1.9L Engines

♦ See Figures 48, 49, 50, 51 and 52

1. Disconnect the negative battery cable.
2. On models equipped with an automatic transaxle, remove the accelerator (kickdown) cable routing bracket from the block.

✱✱ WARNING

When disengaging the plastic hard shell connector at the solenoid S terminal, grasp the connector and depress the plastic tab, then pull off the lead assembly. Do not pull on the lead.

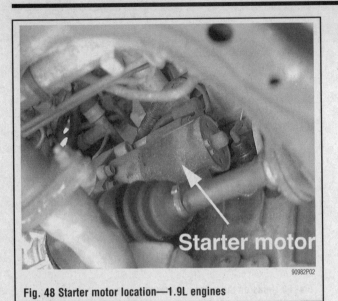

Fig. 48 Starter motor location—1.9L engines

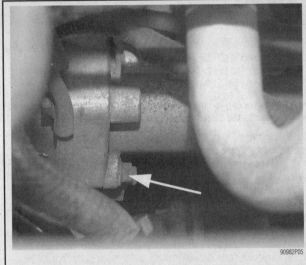

Fig. 51 Location of the lower starter motor mounting bolt (arrow)

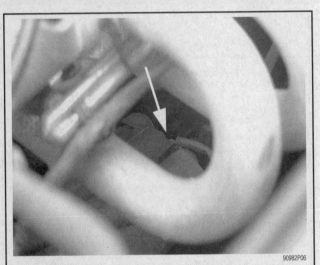

Fig. 49 The arrow indicates the location of the starter motor electrical connections

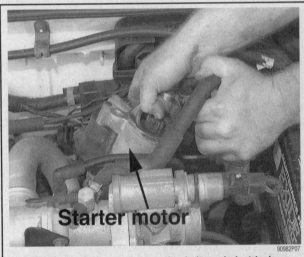

Fig. 52 After unfastening the mounting bolts and electrical connections, remove the starter motor from the vehicle

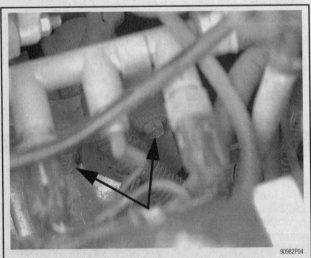

Fig. 50 Location of the upper starter motor mounting bolts (arrows)

3. Disengage the **S** terminal connector from the solenoid.

4. Unfasten the solenoid **B** terminal nut and disconnect the cable from the terminal.

5. Unfasten the starter motor retaining bolts and remove the starter motor from the car.

To install:

➡**Make sure the starter drive housing pilot diameter is fully engaged in the cover plate locating hole and that all mounting surfaces are flush.**

6. Place the starter motor in position, install the retaining bolts and tighten them to 18–20 ft. lbs. (25–27 Nm).

7. Engage the **S** terminal connector to the solenoid.

8. Connect the **B** terminal wire and tighten the nut to 80–120 inch lbs. (9–13.5 Nm).

9. On models equipped with an automatic transaxle, install the accelerator (kickdown) cable routing bracket on the block.

10. Connect the negative battery cable.

2.0L Engines

SOHC ENGINES

1. Disconnect the negative battery cable.
2. Remove the air cleaner outlet tube.
3. Remove the two top starter motor bolts.
4. Raise the car and support it with safety stands.

→**A protective cap is covering the B terminal and must be replaced after servicing the starter motor or solenoid.**

5. Tag and disengage the **S** terminal wire and the **B** terminal nut and cable from the solenoid.
6. Unfasten the lower starter motor bolt and remove the assembly from the car.

To install:

7. Install the starter motor assembly and tighten the lower mounting bolt to 18–20 ft. lbs. (25–27 Nm).
8. Attach the **S** terminal wire, **B** terminal cable and nut. Tighten the nut to 80–120 inch lbs. (9–13.5 Nm).
9. Lower the car and install the top starter motor bolts. Tighten the bolts to 18–20 ft. lbs. (25–27 Nm).
10. Install the air cleaner outlet tube.
11. Connect the negative battery cable.

DOHC ENGINES

1. Disconnect the negative battery cable.
2. Remove the air cleaner outlet tube.
3. Raise the car and support it with safety stands.
4. Unfasten the lower starter motor bolt.
5. Lower the car and unfasten the two starter motor upper bolts.
6. Raise the car and support it with safety stands.
7. Slide the starter motor from its mounting until you can gain access to the wiring.
8. Unfasten the nuts and remove the integral connector.
9. Remove the starter motor from the car.

To install:

10. Install the integral connector and tighten the retaining nuts to 61 inch lbs. (7 Nm).
11. Engage the starter motor to its mounting.
12. Lower the car and install the two starter motor upper bolts. Tighten the bolts to 15–20 ft. lbs. (20–27 Nm).
13. Raise the car and support it with safety stands.
14. Install the lower starter motor bolt. Tighten the bolt to 15–20 ft. lbs. (20–27 Nm).
15. Lower the car and install the air cleaner outlet tube.
16. Connect the negative battery cable.

SOLENOID REPLACEMENT

♦ **See Figures 53 and 54**

1. Remove the starter motor, as described in this section.
2. Remove the positive brush connector from the solenoid motor ``M'' terminal.
3. Unfasten the solenoid retaining screws and remove the solenoid.

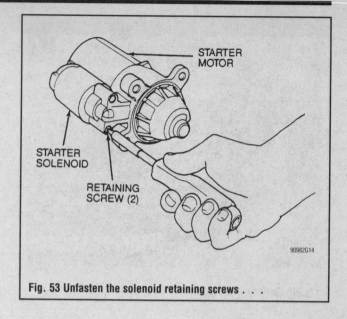

Fig. 53 Unfasten the solenoid retaining screws . . .

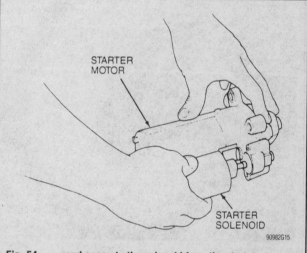

Fig. 54 . . . and separate the solenoid from the starter assembly

To install:

4. Correctly position the solenoid to the drive end housing, making sure the solenoid plunger is attached through the drive lever and pin (the bottom **M** solenoid should have a metal strip attached to it).
5. Install and tighten the solenoid screw(s) to 45–84 inch lbs. (5–9.5 Nm).
6. Attach the positive brush connector nut to the solenoid **M** terminal and tighten the brush connector nut to 80–120 inch lbs. (9–13.5 Nm).
7. Install the starter motor.

SENDING UNITS

→**This section describes the operating principles of sending units, warning lights and gauges. Sensors which provide information to the Powertrain Control Module (PCM) are covered in Section 4 of this manual.**

Instrument panels contain a number of indicating devices (gauges and warning lights). These devices are composed of two separate components. One is the sending unit, mounted on the engine or other remote part of the vehicle, and the other is the actual gauge or light in the instrument panel.

Several types of sending units exist, however most can be characterized as being either a pressure type or a resistance type. Pressure type sending units convert liquid pressure into an electrical signal which is sent to the gauge. Resistance type sending units are most often used to measure temperature and use variable resistance to control the current flow back to the indicating device. Both types of sending units are connected in series by a wire to the battery (through the ignition switch). When the ignition is turned **ON**, current flows from the battery through the indicating device and on to the sending unit.

Coolant Temperature Sender

The coolant temperature sending unit is located either in the cylinder head or on the engine block.

TESTING

▶ See Figure 55

1. Locate and remove the sender.
2. Place the sender in a container of water and heat the water to 176°F (80°C).
3. Using a high impedance Digital Volt Ohmmeter (DVOM), measure the resistance between the wire terminal and the case. The resistance should be between 49 and 58 ohms.
4. Measure the resistance at the same points as the water cools.
5. The resistance should gradually decrease to 24 ohms at 130°F (48°C), and then to 9.7 ohms at 70°F (22°C).
6. If the resistances do not meet specification, replace the sender.
7. If the resistances are as specified, check the circuit wiring for damage or a short to ground.

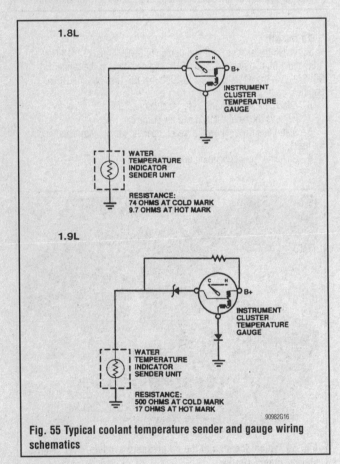

Fig. 55 Typical coolant temperature sender and gauge wiring schematics

REMOVAL & INSTALLATION

1.8L and 1.9L Engines

❋❋ CAUTION

Never open, service or drain the radiator or cooling system when hot; serious burns can occur from the steam and hot coolant. Also, when draining engine coolant, keep in mind that cats and dogs are attracted to ethylene glycol antifreeze and could drink any that is left in an uncovered container or in pud-

dles on the ground. This will prove fatal in sufficient quantities. Always drain coolant into a sealable container. Coolant should be reused unless it is contaminated or is several years old.

1. Locate the coolant temperature sending unit on the engine.
2. Disconnect the sending unit electrical harness.
3. Drain the engine coolant below the level of the switch.
4. Unfasten and remove the sending unit from the engine.
5. If the same sender is to be replaced, remove and discard the O-ring.

To install:

6. If reusing the old sender, install a new O-ring.
7. Coat the new sending unit with Teflon® tape or electrically conductive sealer.
8. Install the sending unit and tighten to 18–22 ft. lbs. (25–29 Nm).
9. Attach the sending unit's electrical connector.
10. Fill the engine with coolant.
11. Start the engine, allow it to reach operating temperature and check for leaks.
12. Check for proper sending unit operation.

2.0L SOHC Engines

▶ See Figure 56

1. Disconnect the negative battery cable.
2. If equipped, raise the car and remove the left-hand splash shield bolts.
3. Loosen the petcock and partially drain the radiator.
4. Lower the car, locate the sender and unplug its electrical connection.
5. Unscrew the sender counterclockwise and remove it from the engine.

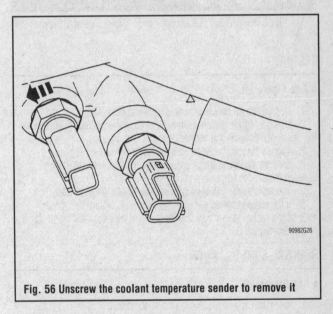

Fig. 56 Unscrew the coolant temperature sender to remove it

To install:

6. Install the sender and tighten it to 13–17 ft. lbs. (17–24 Nm).
7. Attach the sender electrical connection.
8. If equipped, raise the car and install the left-hand splash shield bolts.
9. Lower the car and fill the cooling system.
10. Connect the negative battery cable.

2.0L DOHC Engines

▶ See Figure 57

1. Disconnect the negative battery cable.
2. Loosen the petcock and partially drain the radiator.
3. Locate the sender and unplug its electrical connection.

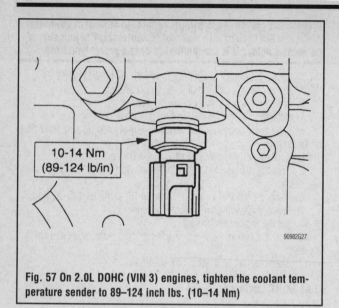

Fig. 57 On 2.0L DOHC (VIN 3) engines, tighten the coolant temperature sender to 89–124 inch lbs. (10–14 Nm)

4. Unscrew the sender counterclockwise and remove it from the engine.
To install:
5. Install the sender and tighten it clockwise to 89–124 inch lbs. (10–14 Nm).
6. Attach the sender electrical connection and fill the cooling system.
7. Connect the negative battery cable.

Oil Pressure Sender

The oil pressure sender is threaded into an oil passage at the rear of the block.

TESTING

▶ See Figure 58

1. Unplug the oil pressure sender electrical connection.
2. Using a high impedance Digital Volt Ohmmeter (DVOM), measure the resistance between the sender terminals and ground.
3. The resistance should be less than approximately 5 ohms.
4. Start the engine and using the DVOM, measure the resistance between the sender terminals and ground.
5. The resistance should be greater than 10.000 ohms at idle.
6. If the resistances do not meet specification, replace the sender.
7. If the resistances are as specified, check the circuit wiring for damage or a short to ground.

REMOVAL & INSTALLATION

▶ See Figure 59

1. Raise the car and support it with safety stands.
2. Locate the oil pressure sending unit on the engine.
3. Disconnect the sending unit electrical harness.
4. Unfasten and remove the sending unit from the engine.

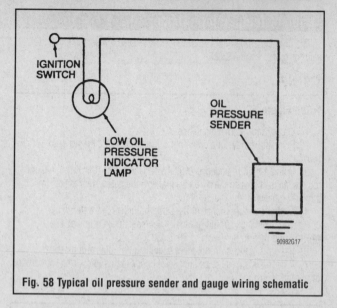

Fig. 58 Typical oil pressure sender and gauge wiring schematic

To install:
5. Install the sending unit and tighten to 9–13 ft. lbs. (12–18 Nm) on 1.8L and 1.9L engines. On 2.0L SOHC engines, tighten the sender to 98–141 inch lbs. (11–16 Nm) and 19 ft. lbs. (27 Nm) on 2.0L DOHC engines.
6. Attach the sending unit's electrical connector.
7. Remove the safety stands and lower the car.
8. Start the engine, allow it to reach operating temperature and check for leaks.
9. Check for proper sending unit operation.

Fig. 59 Typical location of the oil pressure sender—1.9L engine shown, others similar

Troubleshooting Basic Starting System Problems

Problem	Cause	Solution
Starter motor rotates engine slowly	• Battery charge low or battery defective	• Charge or replace battery
	• Defective circuit between battery and starter motor	• Clean and tighten, or replace cables
	• Low load current	• Bench-test starter motor. Inspect for worn brushes and weak brush springs.
	• High load current	• Bench-test starter motor. Check engine for friction, drag or coolant in cylinders. Check ring gear-to-pinion gear clearance.
Starter motor will not rotate engine	• Battery charge low or battery defective	• Charge or replace battery
	• Faulty solenoid	• Check solenoid ground. Repair or replace as necessary.
	• Damaged drive pinion gear or ring gear	• Replace damaged gear(s)
	• Starter motor engagement weak	• Bench-test starter motor
	• Starter motor rotates slowly with high load current	• Inspect drive yoke pull-down and point gap, check for worn end bushings, check ring gear clearance
	• Engine seized	• Repair engine
Starter motor drive will not engage (solenoid known to be good)	• Defective contact point assembly	• Repair or replace contact point assembly
	• Inadequate contact point assembly ground	• Repair connection at ground screw
	• Defective hold-in coil	• Replace field winding assembly
Starter motor drive will not disengage	• Starter motor loose on flywheel housing	• Tighten mounting bolts
	• Worn drive end busing	• Replace bushing
	• Damaged ring gear teeth	• Replace ring gear or driveplate
	• Drive yoke return spring broken or missing	• Replace spring
Starter motor drive disengages prematurely	• Weak drive assembly thrust spring	• Replace drive mechanism
	• Hold-in coil defective	• Replace field winding assembly
Low load current	• Worn brushes	• Replace brushes
	• Weak brush springs	• Replace springs

TCCS2C01

Troubleshooting Basic Charging System Problems

Problem	Cause	Solution
Noisy alternator	• Loose mountings • Loose drive pulley • Worn bearings • Brush noise • Internal circuits shorted (High pitched whine)	• Tighten mounting bolts • Tighten pulley • Replace alternator • Replace alternator • Replace alternator
Squeal when starting engine or accelerating	• Glazed or loose belt	• Replace or adjust belt
Indicator light remains on or ammeter indicates discharge (engine running)	• Broken belt • Broken or disconnected wires • Internal alternator problems • Defective voltage regulator	• Install belt • Repair or connect wiring • Replace alternator • Replace voltage regulator/alternator
Car light bulbs continually burn out—battery needs water continually	• Alternator/regulator overcharging	• Replace voltage regulator/alternator
Car lights flare on acceleration	• Battery low • Internal alternator/regulator problems	• Charge or replace battery • Replace alternator/regulator
Low voltage output (alternator light flickers continually or ammeter needle wanders)	• Loose or worn belt • Dirty or corroded connections • Internal alternator/regulator problems	• Replace or adjust belt • Clean or replace connections • Replace alternator/regulator

TCCS2C02

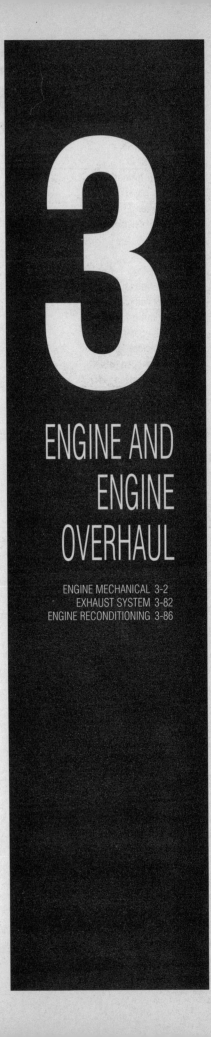

3

ENGINE AND ENGINE OVERHAUL

ENGINE MECHANICAL

1.8L ENGINE MECHANICAL SPECIFICATIONS

Description	English Specifications	Metric Specifications
General Information		
Type	Dual Overhead Cam Engine	
Displacement	112.2 cu. in.	1.8L (1839cc)
Number of cylinders	4	
Bore	3.27 in.	83mm
Stroke	3.35 in.	85mm
Firing order	1-3-4-2	
Compression ratio	9.0:1	
Compression pressure	182 psi @ 300 rpm	1.256 kPa @ 300 rpm
Valve Timing		
Intake-open (BTDC)	5°	
Intake-closed (ABDC)	48°	
Exhaust-open (BBDC)	56°	
Exhaust-closed (ATDC)	14°	
Valve Clearance		
Intake	0 (maintenance-free)	
Exhaust	0 (maintenance-free)	
Idle Speed ① ②		
Manual transaxle	700-800rpm	
Automatic transaxle	700-800rpm	
(Canada)	750-850rpm	
Ignition timing (BTDC) ②		
Timing belt deflection	0.35-0.45 in.	9-11.5mm
Cylinder Head and Valve Train		
Cylinder head distortion	0.004 in. (max.)	0.10mm (max.)
Cylinder head height	5.268-5.276 in.	133.8-134.0mm
Cylinder head grinding surface	0.004 in. (max.)	0.10mm (max.)
Valve head margin thickness		
Intake	0.035-0.0531 in.	0.850-1.350mm
Exhaust	0.0364-0.0581 in.	0.925-1475mm
Valve length		
Standard		
Intake	3.9898 in.	101.34mm
Exhaust	3.9937 in.	101.44mm
Minimum		
Intake	3.9701 in.	100.84mm
Exhaust	3.9740 in.	100.94mm
Valve stem diameter		
Intake	0.2350-0.2356 in.	5.970-5.985mm
Exhaust	0.2348-0.2354 in.	5.965-5.980mm
Valve guide inner diameter		
Intake	0.2366-0.2374 in.	6.01-6.03mm
Exhaust	0.2366-0.2374 in.	6.01-6.03mm
Valve stem-to-valve guide clearance		
Intake	0.0010-0.0024 in.	0.025-0.060mm
Exhaust	0.0012-0.0026 in.	0.030-0.065mm
Valve guide height	0.720-0.744 in.	18.3-18.9mm
Valve seat contact width	0.031-0.055 in.	0.81-1.4mm
Valve stem protruding length (build specification)	1.7539-1.7894 in.	44.55-45.45mm
Maximum valve stem protruding length (wear limit)	1.831 in.	46.5mm

90983C01

1.8L ENGINE MECHANICAL SPECIFICATIONS

Description	English Specifications	Metric Specifications
Cylinder Head and Valve Train (cont.)		
Valve spring		
Standard free length	1.821 in.	46.26mm
Maximum out-of-square	0.064 in.	1.62mm
Camshaft		
Camshaft run-out	0.0012 in.	0.03mm
Camshaft lobe height		
Standard		
Intake	1.736 in.	44.094mm
Exhaust	1.7560 in.	44.600mm
Minimum		
Intake	1.7281 in.	43.894mm
Exhaust	1.7480 in.	44.400mm
Camshaft journal diameter	1.0213-1.022 in.	25.940-25.956mm
Camshaft out-of-round	0.002 in. (max.)	0.005mm (max.)
Camshaft oil clearance	0.0014-0.0032 in.	0.035-0.081mm
Camshaft end-play	0.0028-0.0075 in.	0.07-0.19mm
Camshaft maximum end-play	0.008 in.	0.20mm
Cylinder Block		
Cylinder block distortion	0.006 in.	0.15mm
Cylinder block height	8.720 in.	221.5mm
Cylinder block maximum grinding surface	0.008 in.	0.20mm
Cylinder bore		
Standard	3.2679-3.2682 in.	83.006-83.013mm
0.01 in. (0.25mm) oversize	3.2778-3.2781 in.	83.256-83.263mm
0.020 in. (0.50mm) oversize	3.2876-3.2879 in.	83.506-83.513mm
Cylinder bore taper	0.0007 in. (max.)	0.019mm (max.)
Cylinder out-of-round	0.0007 in.	0.019mm
Crankshaft		
Crankshaft run-out	0.0016 in. (max.)	0.04mm (max.)
Crankshaft end-play	0.012 in. (max.)	0.30mm (max.)
Main journal diameter	1.9661-1.9668 in. (max.)	49.938-49.956mm (max.)
Main journal out-of-round	0.0020 in. (max.)	0.05mm (max.)
Crankpin journal diameter	1.7692-1.7699 in.	44.940-44.956mm
Crankpin journal out-of-round	0.0020 in. (max.)	0.05mm (max.)
Main journal undersize diameter		
0.010 in. (0.25mm) undersize bearing	1.9568-1.9570 in.	49.704-49.708mm
0.020 in. (0.50mm) undersize bearing	1.9470-1.9472 in.	49.454-49.458mm
0.030 in. (0.75mm) undersize bearing	1.9372-1.9373 in.	49.204-49.208mm
Crankpin journal undersize diameter		
0.010 in. (0.25mm) undersize bearing	1.7594-1.7601 in.	44.690-44.706mm
0.020 in. (0.50mm) undersize bearing	1.7496-1.7502 in.	44.440-44.456mm
0.030 in. (0.75mm) undersize bearing	1.7398-1.7404 in.	44.190-44.206mm
Flywheel maximum run-out	0.008 in.	0.2mm
Connecting Rod, Piston and Rings		
Connecting rod bushing inner diameter	0.7875-0.7880 in.	20.003-20.014mm
Connecting rod bushing and piston pin clearance	0.0004-0.0011 in.	0.010-0.027mm
Connecting rod bearing clearance	0.0030 in.	0.075mm
Connecting rod side clearance (assembled to crankshaft)		
Build specifications	0.0045-0.0103 in.	0.110-0.262mm

90983C02

1.8L ENGINE MECHANICAL SPECIFICATIONS

Description	English Specifications	Metric Specifications
Connecting Rod, Piston and Rings (cont.)		
Wear limit	0.012 in. (max.)	0.030mm (max.)
Pistons		
Standard	3.2659-3.2667 in.	82.954-82.974mm
0.010 in. (0.25mm) oversize piston	3.2760-3.2763 in.	83.211-83.217mm
0.020 in. (0.50mm) oversize piston	3.2859-3.286 in.	83.461-83.467mm
Piston-to-cylinder clearance	0.0015-0.0020 in.	0.039-0.052mm
Piston pin hole diameter	0.7869-0.7874 in.	19.988-20.000mm
Piston pin diameter	0.7869-0.7871 in.	19.987-19.993mm
Piston pin-to-piston clearance	-0.0002-0.0005 in.	-0.005-0.013mm
Piston ring-to-ring land clearance		
Top	0.00-12-0.0026 in.	0.030-0.065mm
Second	0.0012-0.0028 in.	0.030-0.070mm
Maximum	0.006 in.	0.15mm
Piston ring end gap		
Top	0.006-0.012 in.	0.15-0.30mm
Second	0.006-0.012 in.	0.15-0.30mm
Oil rail	0.008-0.028 in.	0.20-0.70mm
Maximum	0.039 in.	1.0mm
Lubrication System		
Oil pump type	Gerotor	
Tooth tip clearance	0.0079 in. (max.)	0.20mm (max.)
Outer rotor-to-pump body clearance	0.0087 in. (max.)	0.22mm (max.)
Side clearance	0.0055 in. (max.)	0.14mm (max.)
Oil pressure		
@ 1000 rpm	28-43psi	196-294 kPa
@ 3000 rpm	43-57 psi	294-392 kPa

① With the parking brake applied (Canada)
② STI terminal of Data Link Connector (DLC) grounded
BTDC: Before Top Dead Center
ABDC: After Bottom Dead Center
BBDC: Before Bottom Dead Center
ATDC: After Top Dead Center
Max: Maximum
Min: Minimum
@: At

90983C03

1.9L ENGINE MECHANICAL SPECIFICATIONS

Description	English Specifications	Metric Specifications
General Information		
Type	Single Overhead Cam Engine	
Displacement	116 cu. in.	1.9L (1901 cc)
Number of cylinders	4	
Bore	3.23 in.	82mm
Stroke	3.46 in.	88mm
Firing order	1-3-4-2	
Compression ratio	9.0:1	
Oil pressure (hot @ 2000 rpm)	35-65 psi	240-450 kPa
Cylinder Head and Valve Train		
Combustion chamber volume	39.6cc	2.4156 cu. in.
Valve guide bore diameter		
Intake	0.531-0.5324 in.	13.481-13.519mm
Exhaust	0.531-0.5324 in.	13.481-13.519mm
Valve guide inside diameter		
Intake	0.3174-0.3187 in.	8.063-8.094mm
Exhaust	0.3174-0.3187 in.	8.063-8.094mm
Valve seats		
Width		
Intake	0.069-0.091 in.	1.75-2.32mm
Exhaust	0.069-0.091 in.	1.75-2.32mm
Angle	45°	
Run-out (TIR)	0.0025 in. (max.)	0.064mm (max.)
Bore diameter (insert counterbore diameter)		
Intake	1.572 in. (min.)	39.940mm (min.)
	1.573 in. (max.)	39.965mm (max.)
Exhaust	1.375 in. (min.)	34.940mm (min.)
	1.573 in. (max.)	39.965mm (max.)
Valve stem-to-guide clearance		
Intake	0.0008-0.0027 in.	0.020-0.069mm
Exhaust	0.0018-0.0037 in.	0.046-0.095mm
Valve head diameter		
Intake	1.531-1.539 in.	38.9-39.1mm
Exhaust	1.335-1.343 in.	33.91-34.11mm
Valve face run-out limit		
Intake	0.002 in.	0.05mm
Exhaust	0.002 in.	0.05mm
Valve face angle	45.6°	
Valve stem diameter (standard)		
Intake	0.3159-0.3167 in.	8.025-8.043mm
Exhaust	0.3149-0.3156 in.	7.996-8.017mm
Valve springs		
Compression pressure @ specified length		
Loaded	200 lbs. @ 1.09 in.	892.7 N @ 27.71mm
Unloaded	95 lbs. @ 1.461 in.	422 N+J30 @ 37.1mm
Free length (approximate)	1.86 in.	47.2mm
Assembled height	1.44-1.48 in.	36.9-37.5mm
Service limit	5% pressure loss @ specified height	
Out of square limit	0.060 in.	1.53mm

1.9L ENGINE MECHANICAL SPECIFICATIONS

Description	English Specifications	Metric Specifications
Rocker Arm		
Ratio	1.65	
Valve tappet (hydraulic)		
Diameter (standard)	0.8740-0.8745 in.	22.200-22.212mm
Clearance-to-bore	0.0009-0.0026 in.	0.023-0.065mm
Roundness	0.0005 in.	0.013mm
Run-out	0.00039 in.	0.1mm
Finish	8 micro in.	0.2 micro mm
Service limit	0.127 in.	0.0005 in.
Collapsed tappet gap	0-4.5mm	
Tappet bore diameter	0.8754-0.8766 in.	22.235-22.265mm
Camshaft bore inside diameter		
Nos. 1234 and 5	1.8030-1.8040 in.	45.796-45.821mm
Lobe lift		
Intake	0.245 in.	6.23mm
Exhaust	0.245 in.	6.23mm
Allowable lobe face lift	0.005 in.	0.127mm
Theoretical valve maximum lift		
Intake	0.405 in.	10.28mm
Exhaust	0.405 in.	10.28mm
End-play	0.0018-0.006 in.	0.046-0.152mm
Service limit	0.0078 in.	0.20mm
Journal-to-cylinder head bearing surface clearance	0.0013-0.0033 in.	0.0335-0.0835mm
Journal diameter (standard)	1.8007-1.8017 in.	45.7375-45.7625mm
Run-out limit (run-out of center bearing relative to bearing Nos. 1 and 5)	0.005 in.	0.127mm
Out-of-round limit	0.003 in.	0.08mm
Camshaft drive		
Assembled gear face run-out		
Crankshaft	0.026 in.	0.65mm
Camshaft	0.011 in.	0.275mm
Cylinder Block		
Head gasket surface flatness	0.003 in.	0.076mm
Head gasket surface flatness (CLA)		
Roughness height cutoff	0.031 in.	0.8mm
Dowel height		
Chamfer	0.409 in.	10.40mm
Total	0.462 in.	11.75mm
Cylinder bore		
Diameter	3.23 in.	82mm
Surface finish (RA) each bore	15-38 (min.)	
Average of all bores of a cylinder block (RA)	20-30 (min.)	
Out-of-round limit	0.001 in.	0.025mm
Taper limit (positive)	0.001 in.	0.025mm
Taper limit (negative)	0.0005 in.	0.013mm
Main bearing bore diameter		
@ + or - 30° PF bearing cap P/L	2.4521-2.4533 in.	62.2835-62.3145mm
Other than above	2.4525 in. (+ or - 0.00025 in.)	62.2935mm (+ or - 0.0065mm)
Main bearing journal diameter	2.2827-2.2835 in.	57.98-58.0mm
Out-of-round limit	0.00032 in.	0.008mm

90983C05

1.9L ENGINE MECHANICAL SPECIFICATIONS

Description	English Specifications	Metric Specifications
Cylinder Block (cont.)		
Taper limit (per 1 inch/25.4mm)	0.0003 in.	0.008mm
Journal run-out limit (run-out of bearings 2, 3 and 4)	0.002 in.	0.05mm
Surface finish	12 micro in.	0.3 micro mm
Thrust bearing journal		
Length	1.135-1.136 in.	28.825-28.854mm
Connecting rod journal		
Diameter	1.7279-1.7287 in.	43.89-43.91mm
Out-of-round limit	0.00032 in.	0.008mm
Taper limit (per 1 inch/25.4mm)	0.0003 in.	0.008mm
Surface limit	25 micro in. (rear)	0.6 micro mm (rear)
Main bearing thrust face		
Surface finish	25 micro in.	0.6 micro mm
Rear	35 micro in.	0.9 micro mm
Front run-out limit	0.001 in.	0.025mm
Flywheel clutch face		
Run-out limit (TIR.)	0.007 in.	0.180mm
Flywheel ring gear lateral run-out (TIR.)		
Manual transaxle	0.025 in.	0.64mm
Automatic transaxle	0.06 in.	1.5mm
Crankshaft end-play	0.004-0.008 in.	0.100-0.200mm
Connecting Rod		
Connecting rod bearings		
Clearance-to-crankshaft		
Desired	0.0008-0.0015 in.	0.020-0.038mm
Allowable	0.0008-0.0026 in.	0.020-0.066mm
Bearing wall thickness (standard)	0.0581-0.0586 in.	1.476-1.488mm
Clearance of crankshaft		
Without the cylinder head		
Desired	0.0018-0.0026 in.	0.0457-0.0660mm
Allowable	0.0018-0.0034 in.	0.0461-0.0859mm
With the cylinder head		
Desired	0.0011-0.0019 in.	0.0279-0.0483mm
Allowable	0.0011-0.0027 in.	0.0276-0.0674mm
Bearing wall thickness	0.0833-0.0838 in.	2:117-2.129mm
Connecting rod		
Piston pin bore diameter	0.8106-0.8114 in.	20.589-20.609mm
Crankshaft bearing bore diameter	1.8460-1.8468 in.	46.89-46.91mm
Out-of-round limit<em dash>piston pin bore	0.0003 in.	0.008mm
Taper limit piston pin bore (per i inch/25.4mm)	0.00015 in.	0.0038mm
Length (center-to-center)	5.193-5.196 in.	131.905-131.975mm
Out-of-round limit<em dash>bearing bore	0.0004 in.	0.010mm
Alignment bore-to-bore (max. differential)		
Twist	0.002 in.	0.05mm
Bend	0.0015 in.	0.038mm
Side clearance (assembled to crankshaft)		
Standard	0.004-0.011 in.	0.092-0.268mm
Service limit	0.014 in.	0.356mm

90983C06

1.9L ENGINE MECHANICAL SPECIFICATIONS

Description	English Specifications	Metric Specifications
Pistons		
Piston Diameter		
Coded red	3.224-3.225 in.	81.90-81.92mm
Coded blue	3.225-3.226 in.	81.92-81.94mm
0.004 in. (0.1mm) oversize	3.226-3.227 in.	81.94-81.96mm
Piston-to-bore clearance		
Rebuild	0.0012-0.0020 in.	0.030-0.50mm
Service	0.0012-0.0028 in.	0.030-0.070mm
Piston bore diameter	0.8123-0.8128 in.	20.632-20.644mm
Ring groove width		
Compression (top)	0.0602-0.061 in.	1.53-1.55mm
Compression (bottom)	0.0602-0.061 in.	1.53-1.55mm
Oil	0.1578-0.1587 in.	4.008-4.032mm
Piston pin		
Length	2.606-2.638 in.	66.2-67.0mm
Diameter		
Standard	0.8119-0.8124 in.	20.622-20.634mm
Pin-to-piston clearance	0.0003-0.0005 in.	0.007-0.013mm
Pin-to-rod clearance	Press fit–8 kilonewtons	
Piston rings		
Ring width		
Compression (top)	0.0578-0.0582 in.	1.47-1.49mm
Compression (bottom)	0.0574-0.0586 in.	1.46-1.49mm
Oil ring	Side seal (snug fit)	
Service limit (side clearance)	0.006 in. (max.)	0.15mm (max.)
Ring gap		
Compression (top)	0.010-0.030 in.	0.25-0.28mm
Compression (bottom)	0.010-0.030 in.	0.25-0.28mm
Oil ring (steel ring)	0.016-0.066 in.	0.04-1.68mm
Side clearance		
1st ring	0.0015-0.0032 in.	0.04-0.08mm
2nd ring	0.0015-0.0035 in.	0.04-0.09mm
Lubrication System		
Oil pump		
Relief valve spring tension	9.3-10.3 lbs. @ 1.11 in.	41.4-45.8 N @ 28.1mm
Relief valve-to-bore clearance	0.0008-0.0031 in.	0.02-0.08mm
Oil pump type	Gerotor	
Rotor clearance		
Outer gear-to-housing clearance	0.0029-0.0063 in.	0.0074-0.161mm
Inner and outer gear-to-cover clearance (end-play)	0.0005-0.0035 in.	0.013-0.089mm
Inner-to-outer gear tip clearance	0.002-0.007 in.	0.05-0.18mm

T.I.R: Total Indicated Run-out
Max: Maximum
Min: Minimum
@: At

90983C07

2.0L SOHC ENGINE MECHANICAL SPECIFICATIONS

Description	English Specifications	Metric Specifications
General Information		
Type		Single Overhead Cam Engine
Displacement	121 cu. in.	2.0L (2000cc)
Number of Cylinders		4
Bore	3.34 in.	84.8mm
Stroke	3.46 in.	88.0mm
Firing order		1-3-4-2
Oil pressure (hot @ 2000 rpm)	35-65 psi	240-450 kPa
Drive belt tension	40-70 lbs.	178-311 Nm
Compression ratio		9.2:1
Cylinder Head and Valve Train		
Valve guide inner diameter	0.317-0.319 in.	8.063-8.094mm
Intake and exhaust	0.3174-0.3187 in.	8.03-8.094mm
Valve seats		
Width		
Intake	0.069-0.091 in.	1.75-2.32mm
Exhaust	0.069-0.091 in.	1.75-2.32mm
Angle		45 degrees
Run-out (TIR)	0.0025 in. (max.)	0.064mm (max.)
Bore diameter (ICD)		
Intake	1.572 in. (min.)	39.940mm (min.)
	1.573 in. (max.)	39.965mm (max.)
Exhaust	1.375 in. (min.)	34.940mm (min.)
	1.573 in. (max.)	39.965mm (max.)
Valve stem-to-guide clearance		
Intake	0.0008-0.0027 in.	0.020-0.069mm
Exhaust	0.0018-0.0037 in.	0.046-0.095mm
Valve head diameter		
Intake	1.531-1.539 in.	38.9-39.1mm
Exhaust	1.335-1.343 in.	33.91-34.11mm
Valve face run-out limit		
Intake	0.002 in.	0.005mm
Exhaust	0.002 in.	0.005mm
Valve face angle		45.6 degrees
Valve stem diameter		
Intake	0.3159-0.3167 in.	8.025-8.043mm
Exhaust	0.3149-0.3156 in.	7.996-8.017mm
Valve spring compression		
Loaded	200 lbs. @ 1.09 in.	892.7 N @ 27.71mm
Unloaded	95 lbs. @ 1.461 in.	422 nm @ 37.1mm
Free length	1.701 in.	47.2mm
Installed height	1.86 in.	34.2mm
Valve spring assembled height	1.44-1.48 in.	36.9-37.5mm
Rocker Arm		
Ratio		1.65
Valve tappet (hydraulic)		
Diameter	0.8740-0.8745 in.	22.200-22.212mm
Clearance-to-bore	0.023-0.065 in.	0.0009-0.0026mm
Roundness	0.0005 in.	0.013mm
Service limit	0.0005 in.	0.013mm

2.0L SOHC ENGINE MECHANICAL SPECIFICATIONS

Description	English Specifications	Metric Specifications
Camshaft		
Lobe lift		
Intake	0.245 in.	6.23mm
Exhaust	0.245 in.	6.23mm
Allowable lobe lift loss	0.005 in.	0.127mm
Theoretical valve maximum lift		
Intake	0.405 in.	10.28mm
Exhaust	0.405 in.	10.28mm
End-play	0.0008-0.0078 in.	0.02-0.20mm
Service limit	0.0078 in.	0.20mm
Journal-to-cylinder head bearing surface clearance	0.0013-0.0033 in.	0.03335-0.0835mm
Journal diameter standard	1.8007-1.8017 in.	45.7375-45.7625mm
Run-out limit (run-out of center bearing relative to bearings (Nos. 1 and 5)	0.005 in.	0.127mm
Out-of-round limit	0.003 in.	0.08mm
Cylinder Block		
Head gasket surface overall flatness	0.003 in.	0.076mm
Roughness height	0.15-0.08 in.	3.8-2.0mm
Cylinder bore diameter	3.34 in.	84.8mm
Piston-to-cylinder bore clearance	0.0008-0.0016 in.	0.020-0.040mm
Surface finish (RA) each bore (min.)	15-38 microns	
Average of all bores (RA) of a cylinder block (min.)	20-30 microns	
Out of round limit	0.001 in.	0.025mm
Tappet limit	0.0005 in.	0.013mm
Main bearing bore diameter		
@ + or - 30° PF bearing cap P/L	2.4521-2.4533 in.	62.2835-62.3145mm
Other than above	2.4525 + or - 0.00039 in.	62.2935 + or - 0.0100mm
Crankshaft		
Main bearing journal diameter	2.2827-2.2835 in.	57.980-58.000mm
Out-of-round limit	0.00032 in.	0.008mm
Taper limit	0.0003 in. per 1.0 in.	0.008mm per 25.4mm
Journal run-out limit	0.002 in.	0.05mm
Crankshaft end-play	0.004-0.012 in.	0.100-0.300mm
Clearance-to-crankshaft	0.0008-0.0026 in.	0.020-0.065mm
Thrust bearing journal length]	1.135-1.136 in.	28.825-28.854mm
Connecting rod journal diameter	1.7279-1.7287 in.	43.89-43.91mm
Out-of-round limit	0.00032 in.	0.008mm
Taper limit	0.0003 in. per 1.0 in.	0.008mm per 25.4mm
Flywheel clutch face run-out limit (TIR)	0.007 in.	0.180mm
Flywheel ring gear lateral run-out (TIR)		
Manual transaxle	0.025 in.	0.64mm
Automatic transaxle	0.06 in.	1.5mm
Crankshaft end-play	0.004-0.012 in.	0.100-0.300 mm
Connecting rod		
Connecting rod bearing		
Clearance-to-crankshaft	0.0008-0.0026 in.	0.020-0.065mm
Bearing wall thickness	0.0581-0.0586 in.	1.476-1.488mm
Clearance of crankshaft		
Without the cylinder head		
Desired	0.0018-0.0026 in.	0.0457-0.0660mm
Allowable	0.0018-0.0034 in.	0.0461-0.0859mm

2.0L SOHC ENGINE MECHANICAL SPECIFICATIONS

Description	English Specifications	Metric Specifications
Connecting rod (cont.)		
With the cylinder head		
Desired	0.0011-0.0019 in.	0.0279-0.0483mm
Allowable	0.0833-0.0838 in.	2.117-2.129mm
Bearing wall thickness	0.0833-0.0838 in.	2.117-2.129mm
Connecting rod piston pin bore diameter	0.8098-0.8114 in.	20.570-20.610mm
Crankshaft bearing bore diameter	1.8460-1.8468 in.	46.89-46.91mm
Out-of-round limit		
Piston pin bore	0.0003 in.	0.008mm
Taper limit piston pin bore	0.00015 in./1 in.	0.0038 in./25mm
Length (center-to-center)	5.193-5.196 in.	131.905-131.975mm
Out-of-round limit-bearing bore	0.0004 in.	0.010mm
Taper limit-bearing bore	0.0004 in.	0.010mm
Alignment bore-to-bore (max. differential)		
Twist	0.002 in.	0.05mm
Bend	0.0015 in.	0.038mm
Side clearance (assembled-to-crank)		
Standard	0.004-0.011 in.	0.092-0.268mm
Service limit	0.014 in.	0.356mm
Pistons		
Piston-to-bore clearance		
Rebuild	0.0008-0.0015 in.	0.020-0.040mm
Service	0.0008-0.0027 in.	0.020-0.070mm
Piston diameter	3.3374-3.3386 in.	84.77-84.80mm
Pin bore diameter	0.8123-0.8126 in.	20.632-20.641mm
Ring groove width		
Compression (top)	0.0602-0.061 in.	1.53-1.55mm
Compression (bottom)	0.0602-0.061 in.	1.53-1.55mm
Oil	4.008-4.032 in.	0.1578-0.1587mm
Compression ring-to-ring groove clearance		
Top ring	0.0015-0.0032 in.	0.04-0.08mm
Bottom ring	0.0023-0.0035 in.	0.06-0.09mm
Squish height	0.036-0.073 in.	0.908-1.858mm
Piston pin		
Length	2.606-2.638 in.	66.2-67.0mm
Diameter		
Standard	0.8119-0.8122 in.	20.622-20.631mm
Piston-to-piston clearance	0.0003-0.0005 in.	0.007-0.013mm
Pin-to-rod clearance	Press fit<em dash>8 Kilonewtons	
Ring width		
Upper compression ring	0.0578-0.0582 in.	1.47-1.49mm
Lower compression ring	0.0574-0.0586 in.	1.46-1.49mm
Oil control ring	side seal (snug fit)	
Service limit (side clearance)	0.006 in. (max.)	0.15 (max.)
Ring gap		
Upper compression ring	0.010-0.030 in.	0.25-0.28mm
Lower compression ring	0.010-0.030 in.	0.25-0.28mm
Oil control ring (steel rail)	0.016-0.066 in.	0.04-1.68mm

90983C10

2.0L SOHC ENGINE MECHANICAL SPECIFICATIONS

Description	English Specifications	Metric Specifications
Pistons (cont.)		
Side clearance		
1st ring	0.0015-0.0032 in.	0.04-0.08mm
2nd ring	0.0015-0.0035 in.	0.04-0.09mm
Lubrication system		
Oil pump		
Relief valve spring tension	9.3-10.3 lbs. @ 1.11 in.	41.4-45.8 N @ 28.1mm
Relief valve-to-bore-clearance	0.0008-0.0031 in.	0.02-0.08mm
Oil pump type	Gerotor	
Rotor clearance		
Outer gear-to-housing clearance	0.0029-0.0063 in.	0.074-0.161mm
Inner and outer gear-to-cover clearance (end-play)	0.0005-0.0035 in.	0.013-0.089mm
Inner-to-outer gear tip	0.002-0.007 in.	0.05-0.18mm

SPI: Split Port Injection

TIR: Total Indicated Run-out

ICD: Insert Counterbore Diameter

Max: Maximum

Min: Minimum

90983C11

Troubleshooting the Cooling System

Problem	Cause	Solution
High temperature gauge indication—overheating	• Coolant level low • Improper fan operation • Radiator hose(s) collapsed • Radiator airflow blocked	• Replenish coolant • Repair or replace as necessary • Replace hose(s) • Remove restriction (bug screen, fog lamps, etc.)
	• Faulty pressure cap • Ignition timing incorrect • Air trapped in cooling system • Heavy traffic driving	• Replace pressure cap • Adjust ignition timing • Purge air • Operate at fast idle in neutral intermittently to cool engine • Install proper component(s)
	• Incorrect cooling system component(s) installed • Faulty thermostat • Water pump shaft broken or impeller loose • Radiator tubes clogged • Cooling system clogged • Casting flash in cooling passages	• Replace thermostat • Replace water pump • Flush radiator • Flush system • Repair or replace as necessary. Flash may be visible by removing cooling system components or removing core plugs.
	• Brakes dragging • Excessive engine friction • Antifreeze concentration over 68%	• Repair brakes • Repair engine • Lower antifreeze concentration percentage
	• Missing air seals • Faulty gauge or sending unit	• Replace air seals • Repair or replace faulty component
	• Loss of coolant flow caused by leakage or foaming • Viscous fan drive failed	• Repair or replace leaking component, replace coolant • Replace unit
Low temperature indication—undercooling	• Thermostat stuck open • Faulty gauge or sending unit	• Replace thermostat • Repair or replace faulty component
Coolant loss—boilover	• Overfilled cooling system	• Reduce coolant level to proper specification
	• Quick shutdown after hard (hot) run • Air in system resulting in occasional "burping" of coolant • Insufficient antifreeze allowing coolant boiling point to be too low • Antifreeze deteriorated because of age or contamination • Leaks due to loose hose clamps, loose nuts, bolts, drain plugs, faulty hoses, or defective radiator	• Allow engine to run at fast idle prior to shutdown • Purge system • Add antifreeze to raise boiling point • Replace coolant • Pressure test system to locate source of leak(s) then repair as necessary

TCCS3C11

Troubleshooting the Cooling System

Problem	Cause	Solution
Coolant loss—boilover	• Faulty head gasket • Cracked head, manifold, or block • Faulty radiator cap	• Replace head gasket • Replace as necessary • Replace cap
Coolant entry into crankcase or cylinder(s)	• Faulty head gasket • Crack in head, manifold or block	• Replace head gasket • Replace as necessary
Coolant recovery system inoperative	• Coolant level low • Leak in system • Pressure cap not tight or seal missing, or leaking • Pressure cap defective • Overflow tube clogged or leaking • Recovery bottle vent restricted	• Replenish coolant to FULL mark • Pressure test to isolate leak and repair as necessary • Repair as necessary • Replace cap • Repair as necessary • Remove restriction
Noise	• Fan contacting shroud • Loose water pump impeller • Glazed fan belt • Loose fan belt • Rough surface on drive pulley • Water pump bearing worn • Belt alignment	• Reposition shroud and inspect engine mounts (on electric fans inspect assembly) • Replace pump • Apply silicone or replace belt • Adjust fan belt tension • Replace pulley • Remove belt to isolate. Replace pump. • Check pulley alignment. Repair as necessary.
No coolant flow through heater core	• Restricted return inlet in water pump • Heater hose collapsed or restricted • Restricted heater core • Restricted outlet in thermostat housing • Intake manifold bypass hole in cylinder head restricted • Faulty heater control valve • Intake manifold coolant passage restricted	• Remove restriction • Remove restriction or replace hose • Remove restriction or replace core • Remove flash or restriction • Remove restriction • Replace valve • Remove restriction or replace intake manifold

NOTE: *Immediately after shutdown, the engine enters a condition known as heat soak. This is caused by the cooling system being inoperative while engine temperature is still high. If coolant temperature rises above boiling point, expansion and pressure may push some coolant out of the radiator overflow tube. If this does not occur frequently it is considered normal.*

TCCS3C12

2.0L DOHC ENGINE MECHANICAL SPECIFICATIONS—COUPE MODELS

Description	English Specifications	Metric Specifications
General Information		
Type	Dual Overhead Cam Engine	
Displacement	121 cu. in.	2.0L (2000cc)
Number of cylinders	4	
Bore	3.34 in.	84.8mm
Stroke	3.46 in.	88.0mm
Firing order	1-3-4-2	
Oil Pressure (hot @ 4000 rpm)	54-80 psi	370-550 kPa
Drive belt tension	40-70 lbs.	178-311 Nm
Compression ratio	10.0:1	
Cylinder Head and Valve Train		
Valve-to-valve guide clearance	0.000662-0.0025196 in.	0.017-0.064mm
Valve clearance-intake valve	0.004331-0.007087 in.	0.11-0.18mm
Valve clearance-exhaust valve	0.0106299-0.0133858 in.	0.27-0.34mm
Angle degrees run-out (TIR)	90 degrees	
Valve guide bore diameter (ICD)		
Intake	0.23858 in.	6.06mm
Exhaust	0.23858 in.	6.06mm
Head gasket surface flatness	0.003 in.	0.076mm
Head face surface finish	15 microns (max.)	
Valve head diameter		
Intake	1.2598 in.	32mm
Exhaust	1.10236 in.	28mm
Valve face run-out limit		
Intake	0.0013779 in.	0.035mm
Exhaust	0.0013779 in.	0.035mm
Valve face angle	91 degrees	
Valve stem diameter		
Intake	0.23740 in.	6.03mm
Exhaust	0.23740 in.	6.03mm
Valve spring compression		
Intake	82.1 lbs. @ 0.988 in.	365 Nm @ 25.1mm
Exhaust	94.94 lbs. @ 1.0275 in.	422 nm @ 26.1mm
Free length	1.701 in.	43.2mm
Installed height	1.346 in.	34.2mm
Valve spring assembled	1.346 in.	34.2mm
Height service limit	0.0256 in.	0.65mm
Pressure lost @ specific height		
Intake	32.596 lbs.	145 Nm
Exhaust	40.464 lbs.	180 Nm
Camshaft		
Lobe lift		
Intake	0.3643 in.	9.254mm
Exhaust	0.33858 in.	8.6mm
Theoretical valve maximum lift		
Intake	0.3643 in.	9.254mm
Exhaust	0.33858 in.	8.6mm
End-play service limit	0.00315-0.00866 in.	0.080-0.220mm
Bearing journal diameter	1.0221-1.0227 in.	25.960-25.980mm
Camshaft bearing radial clearance	0.000787-0.002756 in.	0.020-0.070mm

90983C14

2.0L DOHC ENGINE MECHANICAL SPECIFICATIONS—COUPE MODELS

Description	English Specifications	Metric Specifications
Cylinder block		
Cylinder bore diameter		
Class-1	3.338576-3.3389697 in.	84.800-84.810mm
Class-2	3.3389697-3.3393634 in.	84.810-84.820mm
Class-3	3.3393634-3.3397571 in.	84.820-84.830mm
Piston-to-cylinder bore clearance	0.0019685 in.	0.05mm
Surface Finish (RA) each bore (min.)	2-6 microns	
Out-of-round limit	0.0009842 in. (max.)	0.025mm (max.)
Taper limit (max.)	+ 0.0009842-0.0005118 in.	+ 0.025-0.013mm
Main bearing bores inside diameter		
Bearing caps installed	2.28389-2.284956 in.	58.011-58.0380mm
Main bearing bores inside diameter (bearing caps installed)		
Bearing caps graded by size	2.2837749-2.284680 in.	58.008-58.03mm
Main bearing radial clearance	0.000433-0.002833 in.	0.011-0.058mm
Main bearing bores inside diameter (bearing caps graded by size)	0.0007716-0.0017322 in.	0.0196-0.044mm
Crankshaft		
Main bearing journal diameter	2.2826726-2.28346 in.	57.980-58.000mm
Main journal end-play	0.0035433-0.010236 in.	0.09-0.26mm
Connecting rod bearing journal diameter	1.846059-1.850036 in.	46.89-46.91mm
Connecting Rod		
Connecting rod bearing		
Clearance-to-crankshaft	0.0006299-0.0027599 in.	0.016-0.070mm
Connecting rod piston pin bore diameter	0.810589-0.811379 in.	20.589-20.609mm
Crankshaft bearing bore diameter	1.846059-1.846847 in.	46.89-46.91mm
Pistons		
Piston-to-bore clearance	0.0003937-0.0011811 in.	0.010-0.030mm
Piston diameter		
Class-1	3.337828-3.338537 in.	84.781-84.799mm
Class-2	3.357316-3.3358025 in.	85.276-85.294mm
Piston bore diameter	0.7870063-0.7877937 in.	19.99-20.01mm
Ring width		
Upper compression ring	0.011811-0.019685 in.	0.30-0.50mm
Lower compression ring	0.011811-0.019685 in.	0.30-0.50mm
Oil control ring	0.015748-0.055118 in.	0.40-1.40mm
Ring groove width		
Upper compression ring	0.058425 in.	1.484mm
Lower compression ring	0.0682675 in.	1.734mm
Oil control ring	1.1143698 in.	2.905mm
Piston pin length	2.48031-2.51181 in.	63-63.80mm
Piston pin diameter		
White	0.8134629-0.8120062 in.	20.662-20.625mm
Red	0.8120062-0.8121243 in.	20.625-20.628mm
Blue	0.8121243-0.8122424 in.	20.628-20.631mm
Piston-to-piston clearance	0.0003937-0.00005905 in.	0.010-0.015mm
Piston pin clearance in connecting rod bore	0.0006299-0.0019291 in.	0.016-0.049mm
Lubrication System		
Oil pump type	Gerotor	

TIR: Total Indicated Run-out

ICD: Insert Counterbore Diameter

Max: Maximum

Min: Minimum

90983C15

Engine

REMOVAL & INSTALLATION

◆ See Figures 1 thru 11

In the process of removing the engine, you will come across a number of steps which call for the removal of a separate component or system, such as "disconnect the exhaust system" or "remove the radiator." In most instances, a detailed removal procedure can be found elsewhere in this manual.

It is virtually impossible to list each individual wire and hose which must be disconnected, simply because so many different model and engine combinations have been manufactured. Careful observation and common sense are the best possible approaches to any repair procedure.

Removal and installation of the engine can be made easier if you follow these basic points:

- If you have to drain any of the fluids, use a suitable container.
- Always tag any wires or hoses and, if possible, the components they came from before disconnecting them.
- Because there are so many bolts and fasteners involved, store and label the retainers from components separately in muffin pans, jars or coffee cans. This will prevent confusion during installation.
- After unbolting the transmission or transaxle, always make sure it is properly supported.
- If it is necessary to disconnect the air conditioning system, have this service performed by a qualified technician using a recovery/recycling station. If the system does not have to be disconnected, unbolt the compressor and set it aside.
- When unbolting the engine mounts, always make sure the engine is properly supported. When removing the engine, make sure that any lifting devices are properly attached to the engine. It is recommended that if your engine is supplied with lifting hooks, your lifting apparatus be attached to them.
- Lift the engine from its compartment slowly, checking that no hoses, wires or other components are still connected.
- After the engine is clear of the compartment, place it on an engine stand or workbench.
- After the engine has been removed, you can perform a partial or full teardown of the engine using the procedures outlined in this manual.

1. Perform the following basic steps for engine removal.
    a. Remove the hood from the car.
    b. Properly relieve the fuel system pressure.
    c. Disconnect the negative battery cable.

➡ If your vehicle is equipped with air conditioning, refer to Section 1 for information regarding the implications of servicing your A/C system yourself. Only a MVAC-trained, EPA-certified, automotive technician should service the A/C system or its components.

    d. If equipped with A/C, have the system discharged by a qualified technician.
    e. Tag and disconnect all the wires and hoses that would interfere with engine removal.
    f. Tag and disconnect all cables such as the accelerator and kickdown cables (etc.) that would interfere with engine removal.
    g. Remove the drive belt(s).
    h. Drain the cooling system.

✳✳ CAUTION

Never open, service or drain the radiator or cooling system when hot; serious burns can occur from the steam and hot coolant. Also, when draining engine coolant, keep in mind that cats and dogs are attracted to ethylene glycol antifreeze and could drink any that is left in an uncovered container or in puddles on the ground. This will prove fatal in sufficient quantities. Always drain coolant into a sealable container. Coolant should be reused unless it is contaminated or is several years old.

    i. Drain the engine oil.

✳✳ CAUTION

The EPA warns that prolonged contact with used engine oil may cause a number of skin disorders, including cancer! You should make every effort to minimize your exposure to used engine oil. Protective gloves should be worn when changing the oil. Wash your hands and any other exposed skin areas as soon as possible after exposure to used engine oil. Soap and water, or waterless hand cleaner should be used.

2. On 1.8L engines with an automatic transaxle, complete the generic steps for all engines at the start of this procedure, then perform the following steps for removal.
    a. Remove the starter motor.
    b. Remove the splash shields and the starter motor.
    c. Disconnect the transaxle cooling lines from the radiator and plug the lines.
    d. Remove the axle bearing bracket.
    e. Remove flywheel inspection plate from the oil pan.

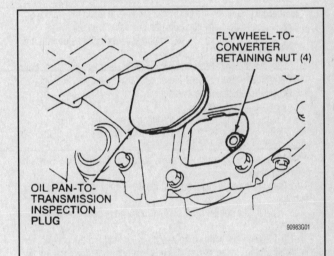

FLYWHEEL-TO-CONVERTER RETAINING NUT (4)

OIL PAN-TO-TRANSMISSION INSPECTION PLUG

90983G01

Fig. 1 Remove the flywheel inspection plate from the oil pan—1.8L engine with an automatic transaxle

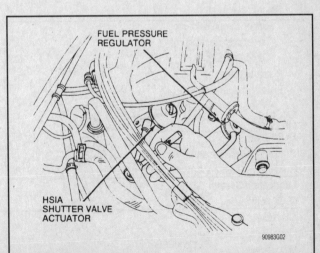

FUEL PRESSURE REGULATOR

HSIA SHUTTER VALVE ACTUATOR

90983G02

Fig. 2 Remove the fuel pressure regulator and High Speed Inlet Air (HSIA) shutter valve actuator—1.8L engine with an automatic transaxle

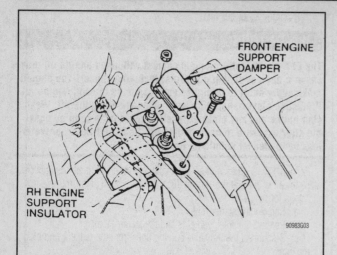

Fig. 3 Remove the right-hand support insulator and the front support damper—1.8L engine with an automatic transaxle

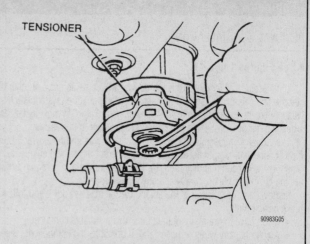

Fig. 5 Loosen the drive belt tensioner mounting bolt and remove the pulley—1.9L engine

f. Place a wrench on the crankshaft pulley and rotate the crankshaft to gain access to the converter nuts, then unfasten the nuts.

g. If equipped, remove the A/C compressor and set it aside with the hoses still attached.

h. Remove the power steering pump, transaxle-to-engine upper bolts, radiator, vacuum reservoir, fuel pressure regulator and the High Speed Inlet Air (HSIA) shutter valve actuator.

i. Remove the alternator.

j. Connect an engine sling to the lifting eyes on the engine.

k. Using an engine hoist, take up the slack on the sling until the engine is supported.

l. Unfasten the oil pan-to-transaxle bolts and the transaxle-to-engine bolts from the block.

m. Remove the right-hand support insulator and the front support damper.

n. Separate the engine from the transaxle and remove the engine from the car.

3. On 1.8L engines with a manual transaxle, complete the generic steps for all engines at the start of this procedure, then perform the following steps for removal.

a. Remove the battery and tray.

b. Remove the radiator upper support brackets.

c. Remove the splash shields.

d. Remove the clutch cylinder hose bracket with the hose still attached and position the assembly aside.

e. Disconnect the transaxle gearshift rod, clevis and lever stabilizer bar from the transaxle.

f. Unbolt the power steering pump and bracket assembly and set it aside with the hoses still connected.

g. Unbolt the A/C compressor and set it aside, if equipped.

h. Remove the A/C accumulator hoses clip from the crossmember and move the hose away from the work area.

i. Remove the A/C hose routing support clips from the radiator and position the hose aside.

j. Disconnect the speedometer cable from the transaxle.

k. Disconnect the exhaust pipe from the manifold.

l. Disconnect the starter motor wiring.

m. Remove the stabilizer bar.

n. Seperate the tie-rod ends from the steering knuckles.

o. Remove the halfshafts.

p. Unbolt the transaxle front and rear mount nuts and remove the mount from the support crossmember.

q. Remove the radiator and fan.

r. Connect an engine sling to the lifting eyes on the engine.

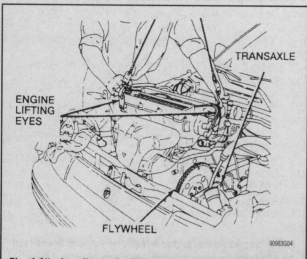

Fig. 4 Attach a sling to the lifting eyes on the engine, and connect the sling to a hoist to remove the engine

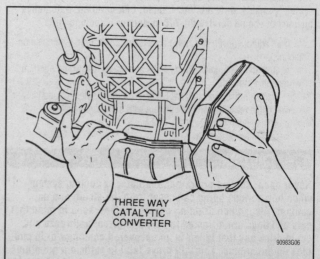

Fig. 6 Remove the catalytic converter—1.9L engine with an automatic transaxle

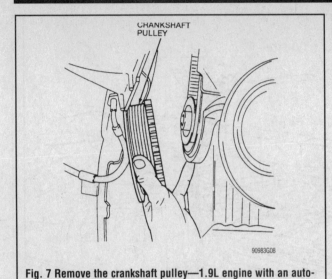

Fig. 7 Remove the crankshaft pulley—1.9L engine with an automatic transaxle

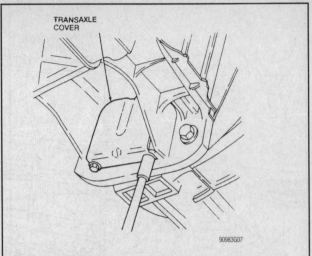

Fig. 8 Remove the transaxle housing cover—1.9L engine with an automatic transaxle

s. Using an engine hoist, take up the slack on the sling until the engine is supported.

t. Remove a crankshaft pulley.

u. Remove the front engine support damper nut and nut.

v. Remove the engine insulator mounting bolt and nut.

w. Remove the right-hand engine support insulator-to-engine nuts.

x. Remove the left-hand transaxle insulator and bracket.

y. Remove the engine and transaxle from the car.

z. Seperate the transaxle from the engine and place the engine on a suitable stand.

4. On 1.9L engines, complete the generic steps for all engines at the start of this procedure, then perform the following steps for removal.

a. Remove the Idle Air Control (IAC) valve.

b. Remove the splash shields.

c. Disconnect the transaxle cooling lines from the radiator and plug the lines.

d. Remove the radiator from the engine compartment.

e. Disconnect the A/C suction manifold and tube from the accumulator/drier.

f. If equipped, disconnect the power steering return hose from the reservoir and the pressure line from the pump.

g. Unbolt the power steering and A/C bracket bolts from the compressor bracket and set the hoses aside.

h. Remove the drive belt tensioner and pulley.

i. Remove the A/C compressor and set it aside with the lines still attached.

j. On models with an automatic transaxle, remove the catalytic converter.

k. On models with an automatic transaxle, remove the transaxle housing cover, four flywheel-to-converter nuts, crankshaft pulley and the starter motor.

l. On models with an automatic transaxle, unbolt the lower transaxle-to-engine mounting bolts.

m. On models with a manual transaxle, disconnect the transaxle gearshift rod, clevis and lever stabilizer bar from the transaxle.

n. On models with an automatic transaxle, unbolt the upper transaxle-to-engine mounting bolts.

o. On models with a manual transaxle, remove the halfshafts. Install transaxle plugs into the differential side gears to prevent them from becoming misaligned.

p. On models with a manual transaxle, remove the halfshafts.

q. On models with a manual transaxle, unbolt the clutch slave cylinder and with the line still attached, set it aside.

r. On models with a manual transaxle, unbolt the transaxle front, rear and left-hand support insulator bolts.

s. On models with a manual transaxle, remove the engine cooling fan motor.

t. Connect an engine sling to the lifting eyes on the engine.

u. Using an engine hoist, take up the slack on the sling until the engine is supported.

v. On models with a manual transaxle, remove the front engine support damper nut and nut.

w. On models with a manual transaxle, remove the engine insulator mounting bolt and nut.

x. On models with a manual transaxle, remove the right-hand engine support bracket and support insulator bolt.

y. On models with a manual transaxle, remove the right-hand insulator.

z. On models with a manual transaxle, remove the engine and transaxle from the car.

a. On models with a manual transaxle, separate the transaxle from the engine and place the engine on a suitable stand.

b. On models with an automatic transaxle, remove the front engine support damper and right-hand engine support insulator, then remove the engine from the car.

5. On 2.0L SOHC engines, complete the generic steps for all engines at the start of this procedure, then perform the following steps for removal.

a. Remove the battery and tray.

b. Remove the air cleaner assembly, then tag and disengage all wiring, hoses, cables and sensors, etc. that would interfere with engine removal.

c. Loosen the power steering pressure hose bracket bolts and set the hose aside.

d. Remove the exhaust manifold heat shield, exhaust manifold-to-catalytic converter nuts and one upper starter motor bolt. Position the starter motor bracket aside.

e. If equipped with an automatic transaxle, disconnect the transaxle cooler lines from the transaxle.

f. Disconnect the A/C manifold tube spring lock coupling at the accumulator/drier and the condenser.

g. Remove the drive belt auto tensioner and if equipped, the accessory drive belt tensioner.

h. Drain the power steering fluid and disconnect the lines from the reservoir.

i. Remove the splash shield, crossmember and the catalytic converter.

j. Remove the drive shafts and the A/C compressor with the lines still attached. Set the compressor aside.

k. Remove the radiator, fan and shroud.

l. Attach a lifting bracket on the left rear side of the cylinder head.

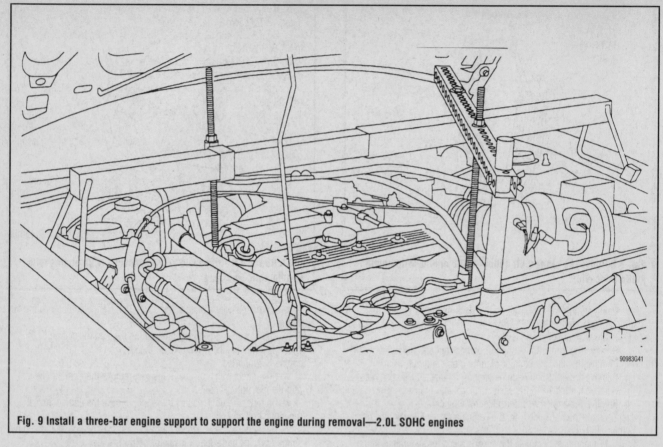

Fig. 9 Install a three-bar engine support to support the engine during removal—2.0L SOHC engines

m. Install a three-bar engine support as illustrated.

n. Remove the transaxle crossmember.

o. Unfasten the transaxle mount nuts and remove the mount.

p. Remove the right-hand engine support insulator through-bolt.

q. Attach a suitable lifting device to the engine.

r. Remove the engine and the transaxle as an assembly.

6. On 2.0L DOHC engines, complete the generic steps for all engines at the start of this procedure, then perform the following steps for removal.

a. Remove the battery and tray.

b. Remove the air cleaner assembly, then tag and disengage all wiring, hoses, cables and sensors, etc. that would interfere with engine removal.

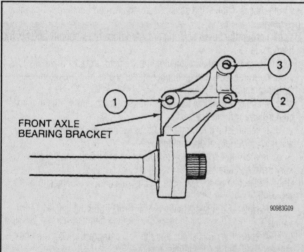

Fig. 10 Tighten the front axle bearing bracket bolts in the sequence illustrated—1.8L engine with an automatic transaxle

c. If equipped with an automatic transaxle, remove the torque converter cover and loosen the converter nuts.

d. Remove the radiator, fan and shroud.

e. Disconnect the power steering return hose and the A/C compressor-to-condenser discharge line.

f. Remove the catalytic converter and the front roll restrictor.

g. Remove the driveshafts and disconnect the hydraulic clutch line.

h. Support the engine with a floor jack.

i. Unfasten all bolts that attach the engine to its compartment.

j. Remove the engine and transaxle as an assembly.

To install:

7. Installation is the reverse of removal, but please note the following important steps.

8. On 1.8L engines with automatic transaxles pay special attention to the following torque specifications:

a. Tighten the transaxle-to-engine upper right-hand bolt to 41–59 ft. lbs. (55–80 Nm).

b. Tighten the right-hand insulator bolt to 49–69 ft. lbs. (67–93 Nm).

c. Tighten the front engine support damper nuts and bolt to 41–59 ft. lbs. (55–80 Nm).

d. Tighten the transaxle-to-engine bolts to 41–59 ft. lbs. (55–80 Nm).

e. Tighten the radiator support upper bracket bolts to 69–95 inch lbs. (7.8–11 Nm).

f. Tighten the oil pan-to-transaxle bolts to 27–38 ft. lbs. (37–52 Nm).

g. Tighten the power steering pump bracket bolts to 27–38 ft. lbs. (37–52 Nm).

h. Tighten the A/C accumulator tube support clip nuts to 56–82 inch lbs. (6–9 Nm).

i. Tighten the flywheel-to-converter nuts to 25–36 ft. lbs. (34–49 Nm).

j. Tighten the front axle bearing bracket bolts in the sequence illustrated to 31–46 ft. lbs. (42–62 Nm).

k. Tighten the exhaust inlet pipe-to-exhaust manifold nuts to 23–34 ft. lbs. (31–46 Nm).

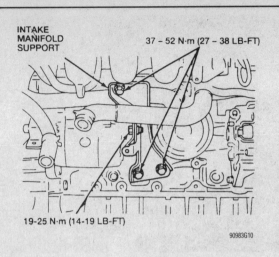

INTAKE
MANIFOLD
SUPPORT

37 – 52 N·m (27 – 38 LB-FT)

19-25 N·m (14-19 LB-FT)

90983G10

Fig. 11 Tighten the intake manifold bolts to the specifications illustrated

l. Tighten the splash shield bolts to 69–95 inch lbs. (7–11Nm).

m. Tighten the throttle cable bracket bolts to 69–95 inch lbs. (7–11Nm).

9. On 1.8L engines with manual transaxles pay special attention to the following torque specifications:

a. Tighten the transaxle-to-engine bolts to 47–66 ft. lbs. (64–89 Nm).

b. Tighten the oil pan-to-transaxle bolts to 27–38 ft. lbs. (37–52 Nm).

c. Tighten the front transaxle support insulator bolts to 27–38 ft. lbs. (37–52 Nm).

d. Tighten the intake manifold bolts to the indicated specifications in the accompanying illustration.

e. Tighten the engine mount through-bolt and nut to 49–69 ft. lbs. (67–93 Nm).

f. Tighten the engine mount-to-engine attaching nuts to 54–76 ft. lbs. (74–103 Nm).

g. Tighten the vibration damper bolt and nut to 41–59 ft. lbs. (55–80 Nm).

h. Tighten the transaxle support bracket bolts to 41–59 ft. lbs. (55–80 Nm).

i. Tighten the transaxle upper mount bolts to 32–45 ft. lbs. (43–61 Nm).

j. Tighten the transaxle upper mount nuts to 49–69 ft. lbs. (67–93 Nm).

k. Tighten the radiator mounting bracket nuts to 69–95 inch lbs. (7.8–11 Nm).

l. Tighten the exhaust mounting flange-to-manifold nuts to 23–34 ft. lbs. (31–46 Nm).

m. Tighten the exhaust pipe support bracket bolts to 27–38 ft. lbs. (37–52 Nm).

n. If equipped, tighten the A/C compressor mounting bolts to 15–22 ft. lbs. (20–30 Nm). And the A/C hose-to-crossmember routing bracket bolt to 56–82 inch lbs. (6.4–9.3 Nm).

o. Tighten the power steering mounting bolts to 27–38 ft. lbs. (37–52 Nm).

p. Tighten the shift control rod attaching nut to 12–17 ft. lbs. (16–23 Nm).

q. Tighten the clutch slave cylinder mounting bolts and the routing bracket bolt to 12–17 ft. lbs. (16–23 Nm).

r. Tighten the splash shield bolts to 69–95 inch lbs. (7.8–11 Nm).

10. On 1.9L engines, pay special attention to the following torque specifications:

a. On models with an automatic transaxle, tighten the crankshaft pulley bolt to 81–96 ft. lbs. (110–130 Nm).

b. If equipped, tighten the A/C compressor-to-bracket bolts to 15–20 ft. lbs. (20–30 Nm).

c. On models with an automatic transaxle, tighten the two upper transaxle-to-engine bolts to 40–59 ft. lbs. (55–80 Nm).

d. On models with an automatic transaxle, tighten the five lower transaxle-to-engine bolts to 27–38 ft. lbs. (37–52 Nm).

e. Tighten the engine insulator mounting bolt to 49–69 ft. lbs. (67–93 Nm).

11. On all models, perform the following steps.

a. Engage all wires and hoses.

b. Have the A/C system evacuated and charged by a qualified technician using approved equipment.

c. Fill the engine with the proper type and quantity of oil.

d. Fill the cooling system with the proper amount and mix of antifreeze.

e. Install the drive belt(s).

f. Fill the transaxle with the proper type and amount of fluid.

12. On 2.0L SOHC engines, pay special attention to the following torque specifications:

a. Tighten the right-hand insulator through-bolt to 50–69 ft. lbs. (67–93 Nm).

b. Tighten the motor mount bolts to 50–69 ft. lbs. (67–93 Nm).

c. Tighten the transaxle support crossmember inner retainers to 28–38 ft. lbs. (38–51 Nm) and the outer retainers to 48–65 ft. lbs. (64–89 Nm).

d. Tighten the A/C compressor mounting bolts to 15–22 ft. lbs. (20–30 Nm).

e. Tighten the muffler-to-catalytic converter to 30–40 ft. lbs. (40–55 Nm).

f. Install the crossmember and tighten the bolts to 69–97 ft. lbs. (94–131 Nm).

g. Tighten the power steering pressure hose connection to 15–18 ft. lbs. (20–25 Nm).

h. Tighten the A/C line bracket bolt to 15–18 ft. lbs. (20–25 Nm).

i. Tighten the exhaust manifold-to-catalytic converter nuts to 26–34 ft. lbs. (34–47 Nm).

13. On 2.0L DOHC engines, pay special attention to the following torque specifications:

a. Tighten the front isolator nuts and bolts to 50–68 ft. lbs. (67–93 Nm).

b. Tighten the front engine support isolator through-bolt to 50–68 ft. lbs. (67–93 Nm).

c. Tighten the front roll restrictor bolts to 48–65 ft. lbs. (64–89 Nm) and the nuts to 50–69 ft. lbs. (67–93 Nm).

d. Tighten the rear roll restrictor nuts to 28–38 ft. lbs. (38–51 Nm).

e. If equipped with an automatic transaxle, tighten the torque converter nuts to 27 ft. lbs. (37 Nm).

Rocker Arm (Valve) Cover

REMOVAL & INSTALLATION

1.8L Engine

▶ See Figure 12

1. Disconnect the negative battery cable.

2. Place fender covers on the aprons.

3. If equipped, unfasten the two uppermost engine front cover bolts from the cover.

4. Remove the air cleaner.

5. Tag and disconnect all vacuum hoses from the rocker arm cover.

6. Disconnect the spark plug wires retainers at the cover and position the wires aside.

7. Loosen the PCV oil separator and allow the hoses to clear the rocker cover.

8. Unfasten the rocker cover retainers.

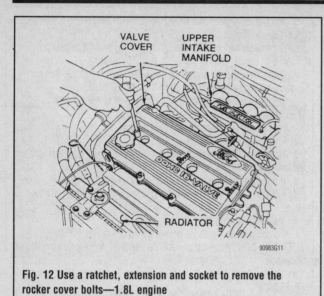

Fig. 12 Use a ratchet, extension and socket to remove the rocker cover bolts—1.8L engine

Fig. 14 Remove the rocker arm cover retaining bolts

9. Remove the rocker arm cover and gasket.

10. Use a gasket scraper to clean the head and rocker arm cover mating surfaces.

To install:

11. Position the gasket and rocker arm cover onto the cylinder head.

12. Install the cover retainers and tighten them to 43–78 inch lbs. (4.9–8.8 Nm).

13. Connect all vacuum hoses and install the air cleaner assembly.

14. Reconnect the spark plug wires retainers.

15. If equipped, install the two uppermost engine front cover bolts and tighten them to 69–95 inch lbs. (8–11 Nm).

16. Connect the negative battery cable, start the engine and check for leaks.

1.9L Engine

▶ See Figures 13, 14, 15 and 16

1. Disconnect the negative battery cable.
2. Place fender covers on the aprons.
3. Disconnect the engine air cleaner-to-valve cover hose.
4. If necessary, disconnect the spark plug wires retainers at the cover and position the wires aside.

Fig. 15 Remove the rocker arm cover from the cylinder head

Fig. 13 Disconnect the engine air cleaner-to-valve cover hose

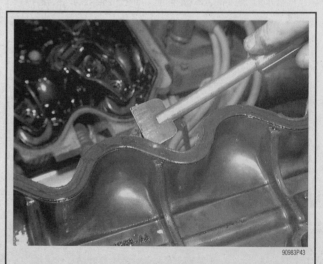

Fig. 16 Use a gasket scraper to clean the cylinder head and rocker arm cover mating surfaces

5. Remove the rocker arm cover retaining bolts.

6. Remove the rocker arm cover and gasket.

7. Use a gasket scraper to clean the head and rocker arm cover mating surfaces.

To install:

➡ **Do not use any sealer with a silicone type gasket.**

8. Position the gasket and rocker arm cover onto the cylinder head.

9. Install the cover retainers and tighten them to 4–9 ft. lbs. (5–12 Nm).

10. If removed, reconnect the spark plug wires retainers.

11. Connect the engine air cleaner-to-valve cover hose.

2.0L Engine

SOHC ENGINE

▶ **See Figures 17, 18, 19 and 20**

1. Disconnect the engine air cleaner-to-valve cover hose from the cover by compressing the hose clamp with pliers and sliding the clamp back, then separate the hose from the cover.

2. Remove the spark plug wire separators from the valve cover and set the wire assemblies aside.

Fig. 19 . . . then disconnect the hose from the valve cover

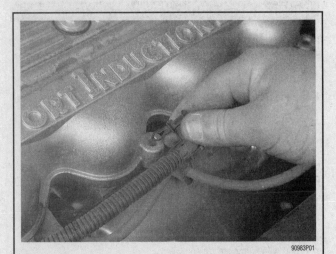

Fig. 17 Remove the spark plug wire separators from the valve cover

Fig. 18 Compress the engine air cleaner-to-valve cover hose clamp with pliers, and slide the clamp back . . .

Fig. 20 Unfasten the valve cover retainers and remove the valve cover—2.0L SOHC engine

3. Unfasten the three valve cover retaining bolts.

4. Remove the valve cover and gasket from the cylinder head.

✳ WARNING

Do not use any abrasive grinding discs to remove gasket material. Use a plastic manual gasket scraper to remove the gasket residue. Be careful not to scratch or gouge the aluminum sealing surfaces when cleaning them.

5. Remove the old gasket material from the cylinder head and valve cover mating surfaces.

To install:

➡ **Do not use any sealer with a silicone type gasket.**

6. Install a new gasket and the valve cover.

7. Install and tighten the valve cover retainers to 71–97 inch lbs. (8–11.5 Nm).

8. Attach the spark plug wire separators to the cylinder head.

9. Connect the engine air cleaner-to-valve cover hose and engage the hose clamp.

DOHC ENGINE

▶ **See Figures 21 and 22**

1. Disconnect the crankcase ventilation hose from the fitting in the valve cover.
2. Unplug the electrical connection from the oil control solenoid.
3. Unfasten the appearance cover bolts and remove the cover.
4. Move the accelerator and speed control cables aside.
5. Remove the spark plug wire and bracket from the spark plug.
6. Unfasten the upper timing cover bolts and remove the cover.
7. Unfasten the valve cover bolts and remove the cover and gasket.
8. Inspect the valve cover for damage and, if necessary, replace the cover.

✳✳ WARNING

Do not use any abrasive grinding discs to remove gasket material. Use a plastic manual gasket scraper to remove the gasket residue. Be careful not to scratch or gouge the aluminum sealing surfaces when cleaning them.

9. Remove the old gasket material from the cylinder head and valve cover mating surfaces. Inspect the mating surfaces to make sure they are clean and flat.

To install:

➡ **The valve cover gasket and valve cover must be installed with the bolts tightened to specification within four minutes of sealer application.**

10. Apply a 0.1 in. (3mm) bead of silicone rubber sealer F4AZ-19562-B, or its equivalent, in two places where the front camshaft bearing cap meets the cylinder head.
11. Place the valve cover gasket and cover in position.
12. Install the cover retainers and tighten them to 53–71 inch lbs. (6–8 Nm).
13. Install the upper timing belt cover and tighten the bolts to 27–44 inch lbs. (3–5 Nm).
14. Install the spark plug wire and bracket.
15. Install the oil control solenoid sensor connector boot in the appearance cover.
16. Attach the oil control solenoid electrical connection.
17. Install the appearance cover, place the accelerator cable bracket on the cover and tighten the cover bolts to 62 inch lbs. (7 Nm).
18. Connect the crankcase ventilation hose to the valve cover.

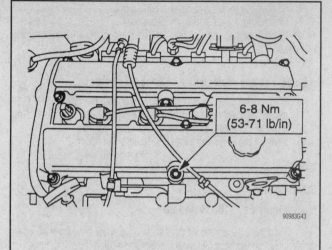

Fig. 22 Tighten the 10 valve cover retaining bolts to the proper specification using a torque wrench—2.0L DOHC engine

Rocker Arms

REMOVAL & INSTALLATION

1.9L Engine

▶ **See Figures 23, 24, 25 and 26**

1. Disconnect the negative battery cable.
2. Place fender covers on the aprons.
3. Remove the rocker arm (valve) cover.

➡ **Keep all parts in order so they can be reinstalled in their original position.**

4. Unfasten and remove the rocker arm bolts.
5. Remove the rocker arms and fulcrums.
To install:
6. Before installation, coat the valve tips, rocker arm and fulcrum contact areas with Lubriplate® or equivalent.
7. Rotate the engine until the lifter is on the base circle of the cam (valve closed).

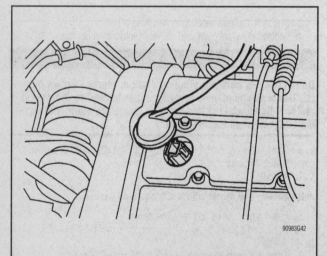

Fig. 21 Unplug the oil control solenoid electrical connection from the appearance cover—2.0L DOHC engine

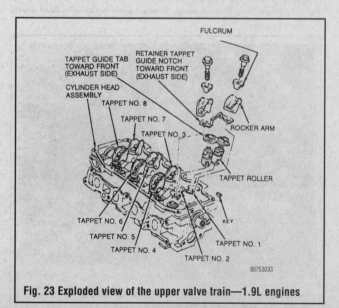

Fig. 23 Exploded view of the upper valve train—1.9L engines

Fig. 24 Unfasten the rocker arm bolts

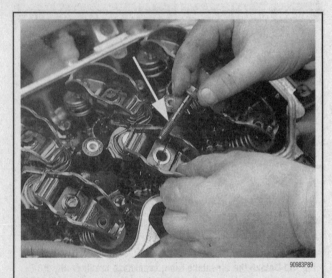

Fig. 25 Remove the rocker arm bolt . . .

Fig. 26 . . . then remove the rocker arm (A) and fulcrum (B)

➡ **Be sure to turn the engine only in the normal direction of rotation. Backward rotation will cause the timing belt to slip or lose teeth, altering the valve timing and causing potentially serious engine damage.**

8. Install the rocker arm and components and tighten the rocker arm bolts to 17–22 ft. lbs. (23–30 Nm). Be sure the lifter is on the base circle of the cam for each rocker arm as it is installed.

9. Install the rocker arm cover.

10. Connect the negative battery cable.

2.0L Engine

SOHC ENGINE

1. Disconnect the negative battery cable.
2. Remove the valve cover.
3. Mark the location of the rocker arms, then unfasten the rocker arm bolts.
4. Remove the rocker arms and seats.

To install:

5. Install the seats and rocker arms in their original positions.
6. Install and tighten the rocker arm bolts to 17–22 ft. lbs. (23–30 Nm).
7. Install the valve cover.
8. Connect the negative battery cable.

Thermostat

REMOVAL & INSTALLATION

1.8L Engine

▶ See Figures 27 and 28

✳✳ CAUTION

Never open, service or drain the radiator or cooling system when hot; serious burns can occur from the steam and hot coolant. Also, when draining engine coolant, keep in mind that cats and dogs are attracted to ethylene glycol antifreeze and could drink any that is left in an uncovered container or in puddles on the ground. This will prove fatal in sufficient quantities. Always drain coolant into a sealable container. Coolant should be reused unless it is contaminated or is several years old.

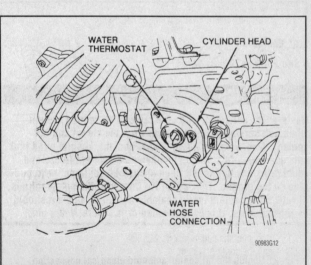

Fig. 27 After unfastening its retainers, separate the thermostat housing from the cylinder head—1.8L engine

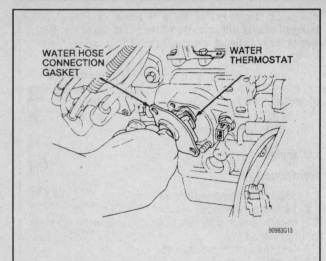

Fig. 28 Remove the thermostat and gasket from the cylinder head—1.8L engine

Fig. 29 Remove the ignition coil pack

1. Disconnect the negative battery cable.
2. Drain the cooling system.
3. Remove the air intake tube.
4. Disengage the water thermoswitch connector.
5. Disconnect the engine wiring harness ground strap from the connector above the housing.
6. Unplug the exhaust gas oxygen sensor electrical connector.
7. Remove the upper radiator hose from the housing.
8. Unfasten the thermostat housing attaching bolt and nut, then remove the housing.
9. Remove the gasket and the thermostat.

To install:

10. Use a scraper to clean the thermostat housing and cylinder head gasket surfaces.
11. Position the thermostat, gasket and housing on the cylinder head.
12. Install the attaching bolt and nut and tighten them to 14–19 ft. lbs. (19–26 Nm).
13. Install the upper radiator hose.
14. Engage the oxygen sensor electrical connector, the engine wiring harness ground strap, and the thermoswitch electrical connector.
15. Install the air intake tube.
16. Connect the negative battery cable.
17. Start the engine and bring to normal operating temperature and check for coolant leaks.
18. Check the coolant level and add as necessary.

1.9L Engine

▶ See Figures 29 thru 42

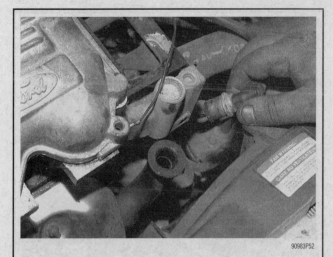

Fig. 30 Detach the air intake tube, crankcase breather and PCV hose

✻✻ CAUTION

Never open, service or drain the radiator or cooling system when hot; serious burns can occur from the steam and hot coolant. Also, when draining engine coolant, keep in mind that cats and dogs are attracted to ethylene glycol antifreeze and could drink any that is left in an uncovered container or in puddles on the ground. This will prove fatal in sufficient quantities. Always drain coolant into a sealable container. Coolant should be reused unless it is contaminated or is several years old.

1. Disconnect the negative battery cable.
2. Drain the cooling system.
3. Remove the air intake tube, crankcase breather and PCV hose.
4. Remove the ignition coil pack and bracket.
5. Remove the upper radiator hose.

Fig. 31 Disconnect the upper radiator hose from the radiator

Fig. 32 Unfasten the ignition coil pack bracket upper bolts . . .

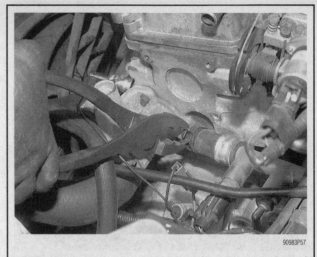

Fig. 35 Unfasten the heater hose inlet tube-to-thermostat housing clamp

Fig. 33 . . . and the lower bracket bolt, then remove the bracket

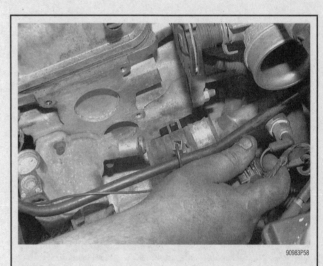

Fig. 36 Disconnect the hose inlet tube from the thermostat housing

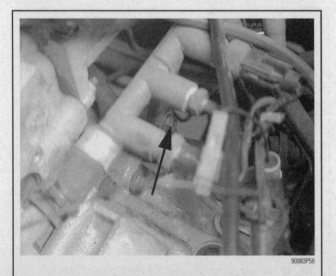

Fig. 34 Unfasten the heater hose inlet tube bracket bolt (arrow)

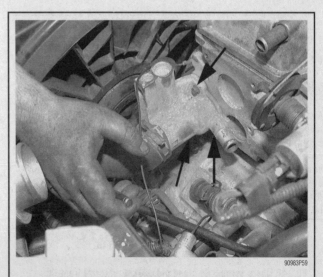

Fig. 37 Unfasten the three thermostat housing bolts

Fig. 38 Separate the thermostat housing from the engine block

Fig. 39 Remove the thermostat from the housing

Fig. 40 Use a scraper to clean old gasket material from the engine block's thermostat housing mating surface . . .

Fig. 41 . . . as well as the thermostat housing

6. Remove the ignition coil pack bracket.

7. Unfasten the heater hose inlet tube bracket bolt and remove the heater hose inlet tube from the thermostat housing.

8. Remove the three thermostat housing attaching bolts, then remove the thermostat housing and gasket.

✳✳ WARNING

Do not pry off the housing.

9. Remove the thermostat and the rubber seal from the housing.

To install:

10. Clean the thermostat housing pocket and cylinder head mating surfaces.

11. Place the thermostat into position. Press it into place to compress the rubber seal inside the housing.

➡**Make sure the thermostat tabs engage properly into the housing slots.**

12. Position the thermostat housing and gasket on the cylinder head.

13. Install the three attaching bolts and tighten them to 71–97 ft. lbs. (8–11 Nm).

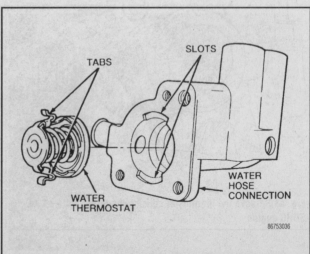

Fig. 42 The thermostat tabs should engage properly into the housing slots—1991–95 1.9L engines

14. Install the heater hose inlet pipe and the heater hose inlet pipe bracket bolt.

15. Install the upper radiator hose.

16. Install the ignition coil and bracket.

17. Install the crankcase breather, PCV hoses and the air intake tube.

18. Connect the negative battery cable.

19. Refill the cooling system.

20. Start the engine and bring to normal operating temperature and check for coolant leaks.

21. Check the coolant level and add as necessary.

2.0L Engine

SOHC ENGINE

▶ See Figure 43

1. Disconnect the negative battery cable.
2. Remove the air cleaner outlet tube.

✸✸ CAUTION

Never open, service or drain the radiator or cooling system when hot; serious burns can occur from the steam and hot coolant. Also, when draining engine coolant, keep in mind that cats and dogs are attracted to ethylene glycol antifreeze and could drink any that is left in an uncovered container or in puddles on the ground. This will prove fatal in sufficient quantities. Always drain coolant into a sealable container. Coolant should be reused unless it is contaminated or is several years old.

3. Drain the cooling system until the level is below the thermostat.

4. Unplug the coolant temperature sender and coolant temperature sensor electrical connections.

5. Disconnect the upper radiator hose and heater coolant hose from the thermostat housing.

6. Unfasten the thermostat housing bolts.

7. Remove the thermostat housing and the thermostat.

8. Clean the gasket surfaces thoroughly until all traces of the old gasket residue are removed.

➡ **Make sure the tabs on the thermostat engage properly into the slots in the housing.**

To install:

9. Install the thermostat in the housing making sure the tabs engage.

10. Install any new gasket required.

11. Install the thermostat, housing and bolts. Tighten the bolts to 8–12 ft. lbs. (10–16 Nm).

12. Connect the upper radiator hose and heater coolant hose to the thermostat housing.

13. Attach the coolant temperature sender and coolant temperature sensor electrical connections.

14. Fill the cooling system.

15. Install the air cleaner outlet tube.

16. Connect the negative battery cable.

17. Start the car and check for leaks.

DOHC ENGINE

▶ See Figures 44 and 45

1. Disconnect the negative battery cable.

✸✸ CAUTION

Never open, service or drain the radiator or cooling system when hot; serious burns can occur from the steam and hot coolant. Also, when draining engine coolant, keep in mind that cats and dogs are attracted to ethylene glycol antifreeze and could drink any that is left in an uncovered container or in puddles on the ground. This will prove fatal in sufficient quantities. Always drain coolant into a sealable container. Coolant should be reused unless it is contaminated or is several years old.

2. Drain the cooling system until the level is below the thermostat.

3. Unplug the Camshaft Position (CMP) sensor electrical connection.

4. Unfasten the water hose connection retaining bolts and move the connection aside.

5. Remove the thermostat and seal from the housing.

To install:

6. Inspect the seal and replace it if damaged.

7. Install the thermostat and seal in the housing.

8. Install the water hose connection and bolts. Tighten the bolts to 71–97 inch lbs. (8–11 Nm).

9. Attach the Camshaft Position (CMP) sensor electrical connection.

Fig. 43 Remove the thermostat housing mounting bolts—2.0L SOHC engine

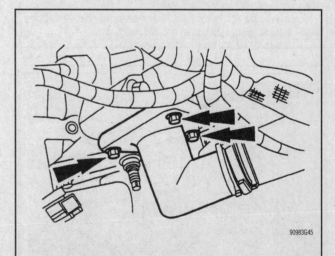

Fig. 44 Location of the water hose connection mounting bolts—2.0L DOHC engine

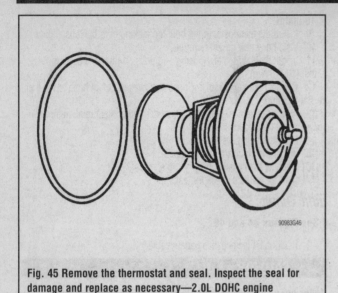

Fig. 45 Remove the thermostat and seal. Inspect the seal for damage and replace as necessary—2.0L DOHC engine

10. Fill the cooling system.
11. Start the car and check for leaks.

Intake Manifold

REMOVAL & INSTALLATION

1.8L Engine

UPPER MANIFOLD

▶ See Figures 46 and 47

1. Properly relieve the fuel system pressure.
2. Disconnect the negative battery cable.
3. Partially drain the cooling system.
4. Remove the air cleaner outlet tube from the throttle body and intake air resonator.
5. Disconnect the throttle cable and throttle valve control actuating cable from the throttle body control lever.
6. Unfasten the accelerator cable throttle valve control actuating cable bracket bolt and remove the bracket from the manifold.
7. Unplug the throttle body electrical connections.

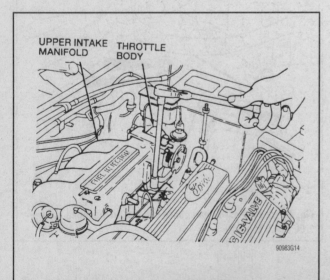

Fig. 46 Loosen the upper intake manifold bolts . . .

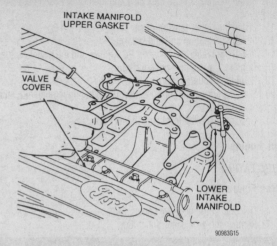

Fig. 47 . . . then remove the upper intake manifold and gasket—1.8L engine

8. Tag and disconnect all necessary vacuum hoses from the upper manifold.
9. Disconnect the air bypass and idle air control hoses from the manifold.
10. Remove the idle air control hose.
11. Unfasten the upper intake manifold upper bolts.
12. Raise the car and support it with safety stands.
13. Unfasten the upper intake lower bolts and lower the car.
14. Remove the manifold with the throttle body attached.
15. Remove the upper intake manifold gasket.

To install:

16. Use a gasket scraper to clean the upper intake mounting surfaces.
17. Install a new upper intake manifold gasket.
18. Place the upper intake manifold in position.
19. Install the manifold upper bolts and nuts, then tighten them to 14–19 ft. lbs. (19–25 Nm).
20. Raise the car and support it with safety stands.
21. Install the manifold lower bolts and nuts, then tighten them to 14–19 ft. lbs. (19–25 Nm) and lower the car.
22. Install the idle air control hose.
23. Connect the air bypass and idle air control hoses to the manifold.
24. Connect all the vacuum hoses to the upper manifold.
25. Engage the throttle body electrical connections.
26. Install the accelerator cable throttle valve control actuating cable bracket and tighten the bolt to 69–95 inch lbs. (8–11 Nm).
27. Connect the throttle cable and throttle valve control actuating cable to the throttle body control lever.
28. Install the air cleaner outlet tube.
29. Make sure all wires and hoses are connected.
30. Fill the cooling system
31. Connect the negative battery cable.
32. Start the car and check for proper operation.

LOWER MANIFOLD

▶ See Figures 48, 49, 50 and 51

❈❈ CAUTION

Never open, service or drain the radiator or cooling system when hot; serious burns can occur from the steam and hot coolant. Also, when draining engine coolant, keep in mind that cats and dogs are attracted to ethylene glycol antifreeze and could drink any that is left in an uncovered container or in puddles on the ground. This will prove fatal in sufficient quantities. Always drain coolant into a sealable container. Coolant should be reused unless it is contaminated or is several years old.

1. Properly relieve the fuel system pressure.
2. Disconnect the negative battery cable.
3. Partially drain the cooling system.
4. Tag and disconnect all necessary vacuum hoses from the upper manifold and throttle body.
5. Remove the vacuum reservoir from the upper intake manifold.
6. Tag and disconnect the coolant hoses from the valves.
7. Disconnect the throttle cable and throttle valve control actuating cable from the throttle body control lever.
8. Unfasten the accelerator cable throttle valve control actuating cable bracket bolt and remove the bracket from the manifold.
9. Unplug the throttle body electrical connections.
10. Disconnect the fuel and vapor line spring lock couplings.
11. Disconnect the PCV hose from the upper intake manifold and valve cover.
12. Disconnect the vacuum hose from the fuel pressure regulator.
13. Unplug the fuel charging harness electrical connectors.
14. Unfasten the fuel rail retaining bolts and remove the fuel rail and injectors.
15. Unfasten the transaxle breather tube and separate the tube from the manifold.
16. Unfasten the five uppermost intake manifold-to-cylinder head nuts.

17. Raise the car and support it with safety stands.
18. Unfasten the bolts attaching the intake manifold support and remove the support.
19. Unfasten the four lowermost intake manifold-to-cylinder block nuts.
20. Lower the car.
21. Remove the lower intake manifold, upper intake manifold and throttle body from the engine compartment as an assembly.
22. Remove the intake manifold gasket.
23. If necessary, separate the upper manifold from the lower manifold.
To install:
24. Use a scraper to clean the manifold mating surfaces.
25. Install a new intake manifold gasket.
26. Install the lower intake manifold, upper intake manifold and throttle body onto the studs.
27. Install the intake manifold-to-cylinder head nuts and tighten them in the sequence illustrated to 14–19 ft. lbs. (19–25 Nm).
28. Raise the car and support it with safety stands.
29. Install the intake manifold support and tighten the bolts to the specifications illustrated. Refer to the accompanying illustration.
30. Lower the car.
31. Install the fuel rail and the transaxle breather tube.

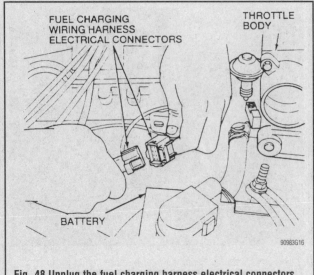

Fig. 48 Unplug the fuel charging harness electrical connectors

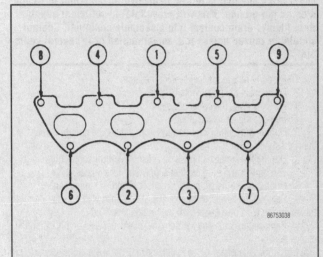

Fig. 50 Tighten the intake manifold-to-cylinder head nuts in the indicated sequence—1.8L engine

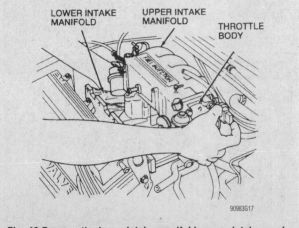

Fig. 49 Remove the lower intake manifold, upper intake manifold and throttle body from the engine compartment as an assembly

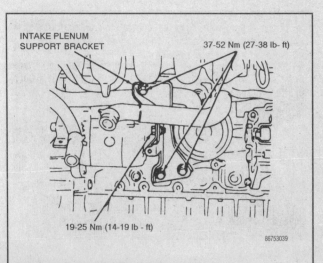

Fig. 51 Tighten the intake manifold support bolts to the indicated specifications—1.8L engine

32. Install the vacuum reservoir and engage the throttle body electrical connections.

33. Connect all vacuum, coolant and valve hoses

34. Install the accelerator cable throttle valve control actuating cable bracket and tighten the bolt to 69–95 inch lbs. (8–11 Nm).

35. Connect the throttle cable and throttle valve control actuating cable to the throttle body control lever.

36. Install the air cleaner outlet tube.

37. Make sure all wires and hoses are connected.

38. Fill the cooling system.

39. Connect the negative battery cable.

40. Start the car and check for proper operation.

1.9L Engine

▶ See Figures 52 thru 69

✳✳ CAUTION

Never open, service or drain the radiator or cooling system when hot; serious burns can occur from the steam and hot coolant. Also, when draining engine coolant, keep in mind that cats and dogs are attracted to ethylene glycol antifreeze and could drink any that is left in an uncovered container or in puddles on the ground. This will prove fatal in sufficient quantities. Always drain coolant into a sealable container. Coolant should be reused unless it is contaminated or is several years old.

---

1. Properly relieve the fuel system pressure.
2. Disconnect the negative battery cable.
3. Partially drain the cooling system.
4. Remove the air intake tube.
5. Unplug the fuel injector harness from the engine control harness at the right shock tower.
6. Unplug the crankshaft position sensor electrical connection.
7. Disconnect and plug the fuel supply and return lines.
8. Unplug the camshaft position sensor electrical connection.
9. Remove the accelerator cable and, if equipped with an automatic transaxle, the kickdown cable from the throttle lever.
10. Remove the cable bracket from the intake manifold and position the cables aside.
11. Remove the power brake supply hose, PCV line and the vacuum line from the bottom of the throttle body.
12. Remove the seven attaching nuts from the intake manifold studs.

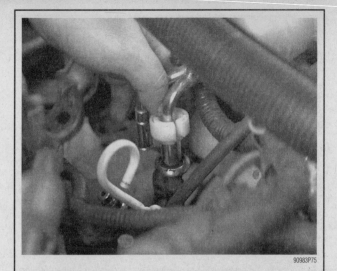

Fig. 53 Install the fuel line disconnect tool on the fuel line

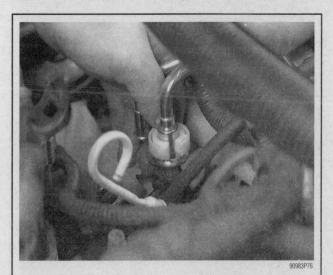

Fig. 54 Press the tool into the spring lock coupling . . .

Fig. 52 Unplug the fuel injector harness from the engine control harness at the right shock tower

Fig. 55 . . . and separate the fuel line fitting from the hose

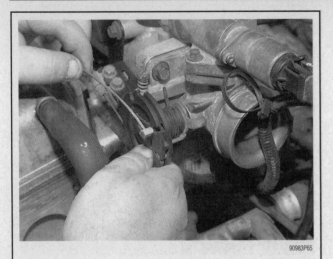

Fig. 56 If equipped with an automatic transaxle, disconnect the kickdown cable from the throttle lever

Fig. 59 . . . then set the bracket and cable(s) aside

Fig. 57 Disconnect the accelerator cable from the throttle lever

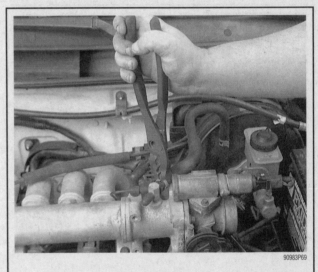

Fig. 60 Unfasten the power brake supply hose clamp with pliers

Fig. 58 Unfasten the two throttle lever bracket bolts . . .

Fig. 61 Disconnect the brake supply hose from the intake manifold

Fig. 62 Disconnect the PCV hose . . .

Fig. 65 Unfasten the intake manifold mounting bolts

Fig. 63 . . . and the vacuum hose from the intake manifold

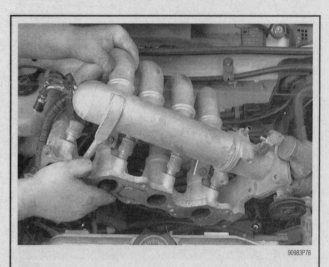

Fig. 66 Remove the intake manifold from the engine compartment

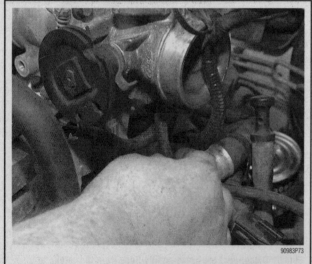

Fig. 64 Unplug the vacuum hose from the throttle body

Fig. 67 Use a scraper to remove the old gasket from the intake manifold-to-cylinder head mating surface

Fig. 68 Clean the gasket material from the intake manifold mating surface

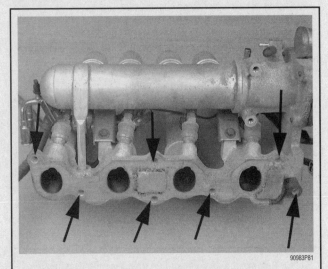

Fig. 69 Location of the intake manifold mounting bolts

13. Slide the manifold assembly off of the studs and remove it from the cylinder head.

14. Remove and discard the intake manifold gasket.

To install:

15. Use a scraper to clean and inspect the mounting faces of the intake manifold and cylinder head. Both surfaces must be clean and flat.

16. Clean and oil the manifold studs and position a new gasket over them.

17. Install the intake manifold and the attaching nuts. Tighten the nuts to 12–15 ft. lbs. (16–20 Nm).

18. Install the vacuum line on the bottom of the throttle body, the power brake supply hose and the PCV line.

19. Install the accelerator cable bracket and connect the accelerator cable and, if equipped, kickdown cable on the throttle lever.

20. Connect the fuel supply and return lines. Install the fuel line retaining clips.

21. Attach the two fuel injector harness connectors to the engine control harness at the right shock tower.

22. Attach the crankshaft position sensor and camshaft position sensor electrical connections.

23. Install the air intake tube.

24. Refill the cooling system.

25. Connect the negative battery cable.

26. Start the engine and bring to normal operating temperature, then check for fuel and coolant leaks.

27. Stop the engine and check the coolant level.

2.0L Engine

SOHC ENGINE

▶ See Figures 70 and 71

1. Disconnect the negative battery cable.

> **✷✷ CAUTION**
>
> Never open, service or drain the radiator or cooling system when hot; serious burns can occur from the steam and hot coolant. Also, when draining engine coolant, keep in mind that cats and dogs are attracted to ethylene glycol antifreeze and could drink any that is left in an uncovered container or in puddles on the ground. This will prove fatal in sufficient quantities. Always drain coolant into a sealable container. Coolant should be reused unless it is contaminated or is several years old.

2. Partially drain the cooling system.
3. Remove the air cleaner outlet tube.
4. Tag and disconnect the vacuum hoses from the following components:
- EGR valve
- PCV valve
- Throttle body
- Fuel pressure regulator.
- Intake manifold
5. Disconnect the accelerator cable, throttle control lever and if equipped, the speed control cable.
6. If equipped, remove the speed control cable bracket bolt.
7. Unplug the Idle Air Control (IAC) valve and Throttle Position (TP) sensor electrical connections.
8. Unfasten the engine oil dipstick tube bracket bolt that attaches the tube to the intake manifold.
9. Disconnect the EGR manifold tube located below the EGR valve.
10. Raise the car and support it with safety stands.
11. Remove the engine oil dipstick tube from the block.
12. Unfasten the intake manifold lower nuts, then lower the car.
13. Unfasten the intake manifold upper nuts and remove the manifold. Discard the manifold gasket.

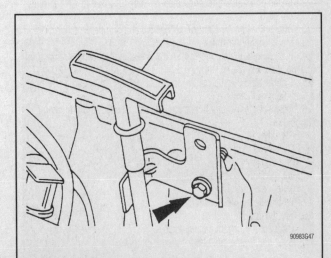

Fig. 70 Remove the engine oil dipstick tube bracket bolt that attaches the tube to the intake manifold

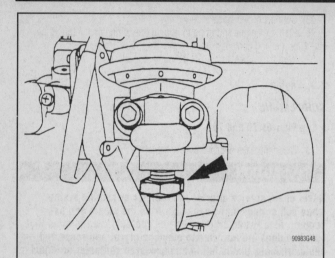

Fig. 71 Disconnect the EGR manifold tube located below the EGR valve

To install:

14. Clean the gasket surfaces thoroughly until all traces of the old gasket residue are removed. Inspect the gasket mating surfaces, both must be clean and flat.

15. Clean and oil the intake manifold mounting studs.

16. Install the intake manifold and hand-tighten the upper nuts.

17. Raise the car and support it with safety stands.

18. Install the lower manifold nuts and tighten them to 15–22 ft. lbs. (20–30 Nm).

19. Connect the engine oil dipstick tube to the block.

20. Lower the car and tighten the manifold upper nuts to 15–22 ft. lbs. (20–30 Nm).

21. Connect the EGR manifold tube and tighten it to 15–20 ft. lbs. (20–28 Nm).

22. Install and tighten the engine oil dipstick tube bolt to 71–97 inch lbs. (8–11 Nm).

23. Attach the Idle Air Control (IAC) valve and Throttle Position (TP) sensor electrical connections.

24. If equipped, install and tighten the speed control cable bracket bolt to 71–88 inch lbs. (8–10 Nm).

25. Connect the throttle control lever, accelerator cable and if equipped, the speed control cable.

26. Connect the vacuum hoses tagged and removed to the following components:
- EGR valve
- PCV valve
- Throttle body
- Fuel pressure regulator
- Intake manifold

27. Install the air cleaner outlet tube.

28. Fill the cooling system.

29. Connect the negative battery cable.

30. Start the engine and check for coolant leaks.

DOHC ENGINE

▶ **See Figures 72, 73 and 74**

1. Properly relieve the fuel system pressure.
2. Disconnect the negative battery cable.
3. Remove the air cleaner outlet tube.
4. Unplug the Throttle Position (TP) sensor electrical connection.
5. Raise the car and support it with safety stands.

6. Drain the cooling system into a suitable container.

7. Remove the bolt that secures the pipe located by the crankshaft pulley, then lower the car.

8. Disconnect the heater hoses from the core.

9. Unplug the main engine control sensor wiring.

10. Remove the connectors from the mounting bracket.

11. Tag and disconnect the vacuum hoses from the intake manifold by squeezing the tabs, twisting the hoses and pulling them away from the manifold.

12. Disconnect the crankcase ventilation hose from the valve cover.

13. Remove the drive belt.

14. Unfasten the alternator mounting bolts and move the alternator aside.

15. Disconnect the fuel lines.

16. Unfasten the intake manifold nuts and bolts in the sequence illustrated.

17. Remove the intake manifold and gasket.

To install:

18. Clean all dirt and gasket residue from the intake manifold mating surfaces.

19. Install a new gasket and place the manifold in position.

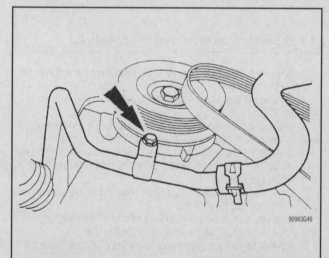

Fig. 72 Unfasten the bolt that secures the pipe near the crankshaft pulley

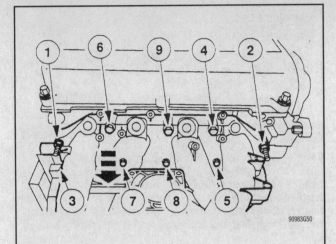

Fig. 73 Remove the intake manifold bolts and nuts in this sequence—2.0L DOHC engine

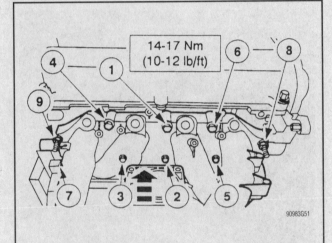

Fig. 74 Tighten the manifold bolts and nuts to 10–12 ft. lbs. (14–17 Nm) in this sequence—2.0L DOHC engine

20. Install and tighten the manifold bolts and nuts in the sequence illustrated to 10–12 ft. lbs. (14–17 Nm).

21. Connect the fuel lines and install the alternator.

22. Install the drive belt and connect the crankcase ventilation hose to the valve cover.

23. Connect the vacuum hoses to the manifold making sure the tabs are firmly engaged.

24. Install the connectors in the mounting bracket and attach the main engine control sensor wiring.

25. Connect the heater hoses to the heater core.

26. Install the bolt that secures the pipe located by the crankshaft pulley. Tighten the bolt to 71–97 inch lbs. (8–11 Nm).

27. Attach the Throttle Position (TP) sensor electrical connection.

28. Install the air cleaner outlet tube.

29. Fill the cooling system.

30. Connect the negative battery cable.

Exhaust Manifold

REMOVAL & INSTALLATION

1.8L Engine

▶ See Figure 75

1. Disconnect the negative battery cable.

2. Partially drain the cooling system and disconnect the upper radiator hose.

3. Remove the engine intake air resonator (duct).

4. Disconnect the upper radiator hose.

5. Remove the cooling fan motor.

6. Raise and safely support the vehicle.

7. If equipped, remove the engine and transaxle splash shield.

8. Remove the exhaust inlet pipe from the exhaust manifold and remove the gasket.

9. Remove the two bolts from the exhaust pipe support bracket.

10. Unfasten the cooling fan lower mounting bolts

11. Lower the vehicle.

12. Unplug the oxygen sensor electrical connector.

13. Unfasten the exhaust manifold heat shield mounting bolts and remove the shield.

14. Unfasten the exhaust manifold mounting nuts and remove the assembly.

15. Using a scraper, remove all gasket material from the cylinder head and exhaust manifold.

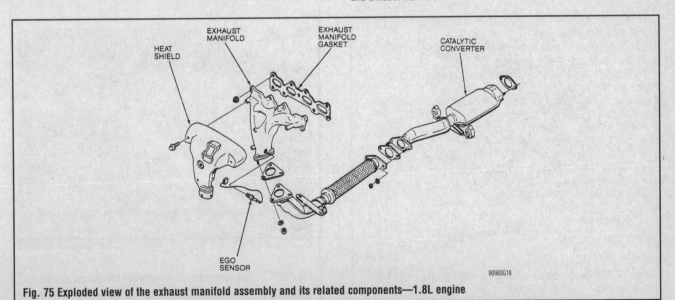

Fig. 75 Exploded view of the exhaust manifold assembly and its related components—1.8L engine

To install:

16. Install a new gasket onto the exhaust manifold mounting studs.

17. Place the exhaust manifold onto the mounting studs and install the manifold mounting nuts. Tighten the nuts to 28–34 ft. lbs. (38–46 Nm).

18. Place the heat shield into its mounting position and install the shield mounting bolts. Tighten the bolts to 69–95 inch lbs. (8–11 Nm).

19. Attach the oxygen sensor electrical connector.

20. Install the cooling fan.

21. Connect the upper radiator hose.

22. Install the intake air duct.

23. Raise and safely support the vehicle.

24. Install the exhaust pipe support bracket.

25. Install a new gasket and attach the exhaust pipe to the exhaust manifold. Tighten the attaching nuts to 23–34 ft. lbs. (31–46 Nm).

26. Install the splash shields and tighten the bolts to 69–95 inch lbs. (7.8–11.0 Nm).

27. Lower the vehicle.

28. Refill the cooling system.

29. Connect the negative battery cable.

1.9L Engine

▶ **See Figures 76 thru 86**

1. Disconnect the negative battery cable.

2. Remove the accessory drive belt.

3. Remove the alternator.

4. Remove the radiator cooling fan motor and the shroud assembly.

5. On 1991–93 models, remove the exhaust manifold heat shield.

6. On 1994–96 models, perform the following steps to remove the EGR valve-to-exhaust manifold tube:

    a. Hold the EGR valve tube-to-manifold connector with a wrench and loosen the valve-to-exhaust manifold tube nut.

    b. Unfasten the two EGR valve-to-exhaust manifold tube bolts from the ignition coil bracket.

    c. Remove the EGR valve tube.

7. On 1994–96 models, remove the exhaust manifold heat shield.

8. Raise and safely support the vehicle.

9. Remove the two catalytic converter inlet pipe-to-exhaust manifold attaching nuts.

10. Lower the vehicle.

11. Unfasten the eight exhaust manifold attaching nuts and remove the exhaust manifold and gasket.

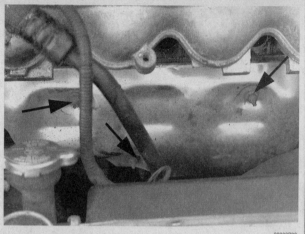

Fig. 77 Location of the exhaust manifold heat shield retaining nuts

Fig. 78 Unfasten the heat shield nuts . . .

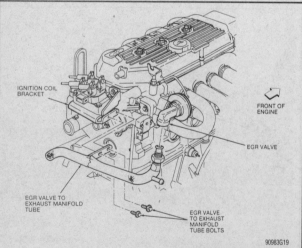

Fig. 76 EGR valve tube-to-exhaust manifold routing—1994–96 1.9L engine

IGNITION COIL BRACKET

FRONT OF ENGINE

EGR VALVE

EGR VALVE TO EXHAUST MANIFOLD TUBE

EGR VALVE TO EXHAUST MANIFOLD TUBE BOLTS

Fig. 79 . . . and remove the heat shield from the engine compartment

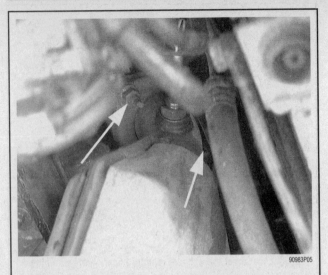

Fig. 80 Location of the exhaust pipe-to-manifold nuts

Fig. 83 . . . then remove the exhaust manifold from the engine compartment

Fig. 81 Unfasten the exhaust pipe-to-manifold nuts and separate the pipe from the manifold

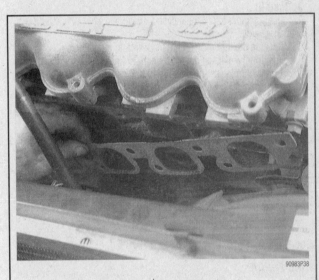

Fig. 84 Remove the exhaust manifold gasket

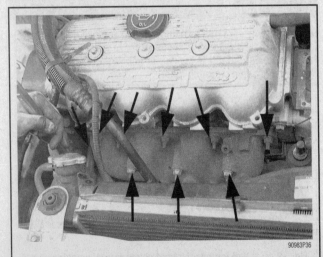

Fig. 82 Unfasten the eight exhaust manifold attaching nuts (arrows) . . .

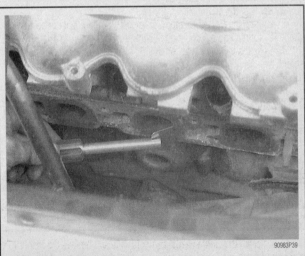

Fig. 85 Use a scraper to clean the gasket residue from the manifold mating surfaces

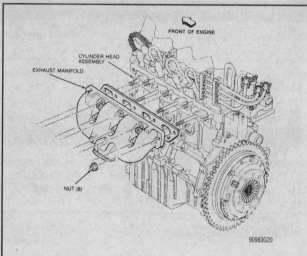

NUT (8)

90983G20

Fig. 86 Exploded view of the exhaust manifold mounting—1.9L engine

To install:

12. Use a scraper to clean the cylinder head and exhaust manifold gasket surfaces.

13. Position the new gasket onto the manifold mounting studs.

14. Position the exhaust manifold on the cylinder head and install the attaching nuts. Tighten the nuts to 16–19 ft. lbs. (21–26 Nm).

15. Raise and safely support the vehicle.

16. Install the catalytic converter inlet pipe-to-exhaust manifold attaching nuts. Tighten the nuts to 25–33 ft. lbs. (34–47 Nm).

17. Lower the vehicle.

18. Install the exhaust manifold heat shield. Tighten the nuts to 3–5 ft. lbs. (5–7 Nm).

19. Install the EGR valve-to-exhaust manifold tube and tighten the nuts to 18–25 ft. lbs. (25–35 Nm).

20. Install the radiator cooling fan and shroud assembly.

21. Install the alternator and the accessory drive belt.

22. Connect the negative battery cable.

2.0L Engine

SOHC ENGINE

▶ **See Figures 87 and 88**

1. Disconnect the negative battery cable.
2. Remove the drive belt.
3. Unplug the Heated Oxygen Sensor (HO2S) electrical connection which is mounted on the cooling fan shroud.
4. Unfasten the five exhaust manifold heat shield nuts and remove the shield.
5. Unfasten the two EGR tube-to-exhaust manifold stud nuts.
6. Unfasten the power steering pressure hose bracket bolts, then position the bracket and hose aside.
7. Loosen the alternator lower bolt, unfasten the alternator upper bolt and pivot the alternator forward.
8. Unfasten the four exhaust manifold-to-catalytic converter nuts.

✳✳ WARNING

Do not work on aluminum engine components until the engine is cold.

9. Unfasten the eight exhaust manifold nuts and remove the manifold and gasket.

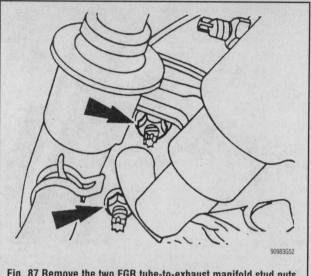

90983G52

Fig. 87 Remove the two EGR tube-to-exhaust manifold stud nuts

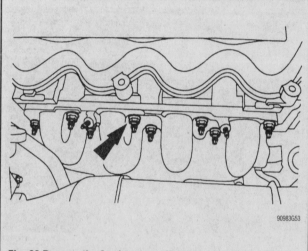

90983G53

Fig. 88 Remove the 8 exhaust manifold retaining nuts—2.0L SOHC engine

✳✳ WARNING

Do not use any abrasive grinding discs to remove gasket material. Use a plastic manual gasket scraper to remove the gasket residue. Be careful not to scratch or gouge the aluminum sealing surfaces when cleaning them.

10. Clean the gasket surfaces thoroughly until all traces of the old gasket residue are removed. Inspect the gasket mating surfaces; both must be clean and flat.

To install:

11. Install a new gasket and the exhaust manifold.

12. Install and tighten the manifold retaining nuts to 15–18 ft. lbs.(20–24 Nm).

13. Install and tighten the exhaust manifold-to-catalytic converter nuts to 26–34 ft. lbs. (34–47 Nm).

14. Place the alternator in position and tighten the upper and lower mounting bolts.

15. Place the power steering pressure hose and bracket in position, then tighten the retaining bolts.

16. Tighten the two EGR tube-to-exhaust manifold nuts studs to 45–62 inch lbs. (5–7 Nm).

17. Install the exhaust manifold heat shield and tighten the nuts to 45–61 inch lbs. (5–7 Nm).

18. Attach the Heated Oxygen Sensor (HO2S) electrical connection.

19. Install the drive belt.

20. Connect the negative battery cable.

DOHC ENGINE

▶ **See Figures 89 and 90**

1. Disconnect the negative battery cable.
2. Unplug the fan motor electrical connection.
3. Remove the fan shroud.
4. Raise the vehicle and support it with safety stands..
5. Unplug the Heated Oxygen Sensor (HO2S) electrical connection.
6. Unfasten the catalytic converter-to-exhaust manifold bolt and nut, the disconnect the converter from the manifold.
7. Lower the vehicle.

❊❊ WARNING

Do not break the threadlock seal on the engine oil dipstick tube. If the seal is broken, relock it to prevent any oil leaks from the block.

8. Unfasten the engine oil dipstick tube bracket bolt.
9. Unfasten the exhaust manifold heat shield bolts and nuts, then remove the shield.

❊❊ WARNING

Do not work on aluminum engine components until the engine is cold.

10. On Escort coupe models, unfasten the seven exhaust manifold bolts and two studs, then remove the manifold and gasket.

11. On Escort/Tracer (non-coupe) models, unfasten the exhaust manifold nuts and bolts in the sequence illustrated.

❊❊ WARNING

Do not use any abrasive grinding discs to remove gasket material. Use a plastic manual gasket scraper to remove the gasket residue. Be careful not to scratch or gouge the aluminum sealing surfaces when cleaning them.

12. Clean the gasket surfaces thoroughly until all traces of the old gasket residue are removed. Inspect the gasket mating surfaces, both must be clean and flat.
To install:
13. Install a new gasket and the exhaust manifold.
14. On Escort coupe models, install and tighten the manifold retaining bolts and nuts to 13–16 ft. lbs. (14–17 Nm).
15. On Escort/Tracer (non-coupe) models, install and tighten the exhaust manifold nuts and bolts in the sequence illustrated to 10–12 ft. lbs. (14–17 Nm).
16. Install the exhaust manifold heat shield retainers and tighten them to 71–101 inch lbs. (8–11 Nm).

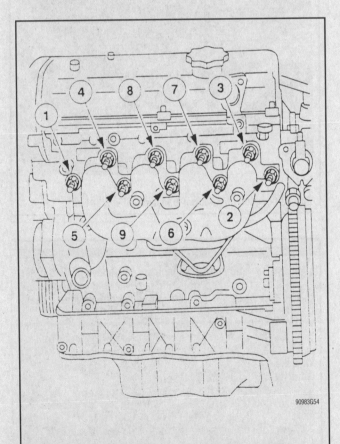

Fig. 89 Remove the exhaust manifold nuts and bolts in the sequence illustrated—ZX2 models

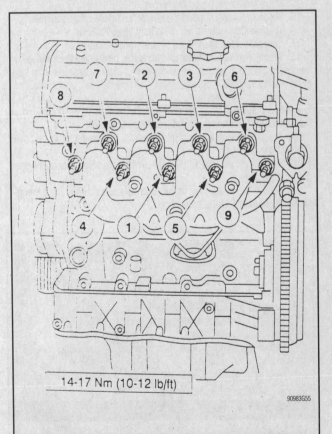

14-17 Nm (10-12 lb/ft)

Fig. 90 Tighten the exhaust manifold nuts and bolts in the sequence illustrated to the proper specification—ZX2 models

17. Tighten the engine oil dipstick tube bracket bolt to 71–101 inch lbs. (8–11 Nm).

18. Install and tighten the exhaust manifold-to-catalytic converter bolt and nut.

19. Attach the Heated Oxygen Sensor (HO2S) electrical connection.

20. Install the fan shroud and attach the fan motor wiring.

21. Connect the negative battery cable.

Radiator

REMOVAL & INSTALLATION

1.8L and 1.9L Engines

▶ See Figures 91 thru 99

✳✳ CAUTION

Never open, service or drain the radiator or cooling system when hot; serious burns can occur from the steam and hot coolant. Also, when draining engine coolant, keep in mind that cats and dogs are attracted to ethylene glycol antifreeze and could drink any that is left in an uncovered container or in puddles on the ground. This will prove fatal in sufficient quantities. Always drain coolant into a sealable container. Coolant should be reused unless it is contaminated or is several years old.

1. Disconnect the negative battery cable.

2. Place fender covers on the aprons.

3. Raise and safely support the vehicle. Drain the cooling system.

4. Remove the right and left-hand front splash shields.

5. Disconnect the lower radiator hose from the radiator.

6. If equipped with an automatic transaxle, disconnect the lower oil cooler line from the radiator. Remove the oil cooler line brackets from the bottom of the radiator.

7. Lower the vehicle.

8. If equipped with an automatic transaxle and air conditioning, remove the seal located between the radiator and the fan shroud.

9. If equipped with an automatic transaxle, remove the upper oil cooler line from the radiator.

10. If equipped with the 1.8L engine, remove the resonance duct from the radiator mounts.

11. Unplug the cooling fan motor electrical connector and the cooling fan thermoswitch electrical connector.

Fig. 92 . . . then disconnect the lower hose from the radiator

Fig. 93 Location of the lower transaxle oil cooler line

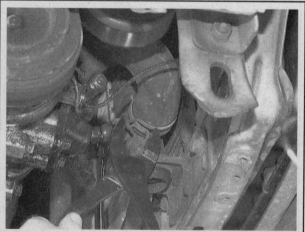

Fig. 91 Use pliers to compress the lower radiator hose clamp and move the clamp out of the way . . .

Fig. 94 Use an appropriate size wrench to loosen the lower transaxle oil cooler line fitting

Fig. 95 Disconnect the cooler line from the radiator; make sure to remove and not lose any washers (arrow)

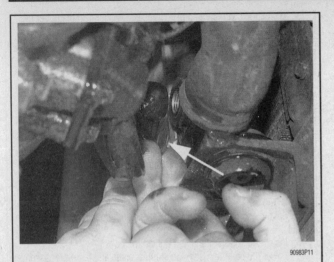

Fig. 98 . . . and remove the brackets

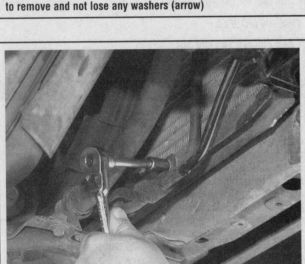

Fig. 96 If equipped, unfasten any cooler line-to-bracket bolts

Fig. 99 Remove the radiator from the engine compartment

12. If necessary, remove the cooling fan thermoswitch for clearance.

13. Remove the three fan shroud attaching bolts and remove the shroud assembly by pulling it straight up.

14. On some 1.9L engines equipped with A/C, remove the upper radiator air deflector from the radiator and set it aside.

15. Remove the upper radiator hose and the two upper radiator mounts.

16. If equipped, remove the fluid cooler tube bracket bolts and coolant overflow hose from the radiator.

17. Remove the radiator from the engine compartment by lifting it straight up.

To install:

18. Make sure the radiator lower mounting insulators are installed over the bolts on the radiator support.

19. Position the radiator to the support, making sure the lower brackets are positioned properly on the lower mounts.

20. Install the radiator upper brackets, making sure the locating pegs are positioned correctly.

21. Install the fluid cooler tube bracket bolts which secure the fluid cooler tube and the upper radiator hose.

22. On some 1.9L engines equipped with A/C, install the upper radiator air deflector on the radiator.

Fig. 97 Unfasten the radiator upper bracket retaining bolts . . .

23. Lower the cooling fan shroud assembly into place and install the three shroud attaching bolts.

24. Attach the cooling fan motor and thermoswitch electrical connections.

25. If removed, install the cooling fan thermoswitch.

26. If equipped with the 1.8L engine, install the resonance duct on the radiator mounts.

27. If equipped with an automatic transaxle, install the upper oil cooler line on the radiator.

28. If equipped with an automatic transaxle and air conditioning, install the seal between the radiator and fan shroud.

29. Raise and safely support the vehicle.

30. If equipped with an automatic transaxle, install the lower oil cooler line on the radiator.

31. Install the lower radiator hose and install the right and left-hand front splash shields.

32. Lower the vehicle and fill the cooling system.

33. Connect the negative battery cable, start the engine and check for coolant leaks.

2.0L Engine

1997 MODELS

1. Remove the fan motor, blade and shroud assembly.
2. Raise the car and support it with safety stands.
3. Unfasten the left-hand splash shield bolts and remove the shield.

✳✳ CAUTION

Never open, service or drain the radiator or cooling system when hot; serious burns can occur from the steam and hot coolant. Also, when draining engine coolant, keep in mind that cats and dogs are attracted to ethylene glycol antifreeze and could drink any that is left in an uncovered container or in puddles on the ground. This will prove fatal in sufficient quantities. Always drain coolant into a sealable container. Coolant should be reused unless it is contaminated or is several years old.

4. Drain the cooling system into a suitable container.

5. Disconnect the lower radiator hose and if equipped with an automatic transaxle, the lower oil cooler outlet tube.

6. If equipped with an automatic transaxle, Unfasten the oil cooler tube bracket bolts.

7. Lower the car and disconnect the upper radiator hose.

8. Remove the radiator cap and disconnect the radiator overflow hose.

9. If equipped with an automatic transaxle, disconnect the upper oil cooler outlet tube.

10. Unfasten the four radiator bracket bolts and remove the radiator from the engine compartment.

To install:

11. Install the radiator and tighten the bracket bolts.

12. If equipped with an automatic transaxle, connect the upper oil cooler outlet tube.

13. Install the radiator cap and connect the radiator overflow hose.

14. Connect the upper radiator hose, then raise the car and support it with safety stands.

15. If equipped with an automatic transaxle, tighten the oil cooler tube bracket bolts.

16. Connect the lower radiator hose and if equipped with an automatic transaxle, the lower oil cooler outlet tube.

17. Fill the cooling system with the specified amount and mixture of coolant.

18. Install the splash shield and tighten the bolts.

19. Lower the car and install the shroud, blade and fan motor assembly.

20. Start the car and check for coolant leaks.

1998–99 MODELS

▶ **See Figures 100 and 101**

1. Raise the car and support it with safety stands.

✳✳ CAUTION

Never open, service or drain the radiator or cooling system when hot; serious burns can occur from the steam and hot coolant. Also, when draining engine coolant, keep in mind that cats and dogs are attracted to ethylene glycol antifreeze and could drink any that is left in an uncovered container or in puddles on the ground. This will prove fatal in sufficient quantities. Always drain coolant into a sealable container. Coolant should be reused unless it is contaminated or is several years old.

2. Drain the cooling system into a suitable container.

3. Unfasten the right-hand splash shield bolts and remove the shield.

4. Disconnect the lower radiator hose and if equipped with an automatic transaxle, the lower oil cooler outlet tube.

5. Lower the car, disconnect the upper radiator hose and if equipped with an automatic transaxle, disconnect the upper oil cooler outlet tube.

6. Unplug the fan motor electrical connection.

7. Remove the radiator cap and disconnect the radiator overflow hose.

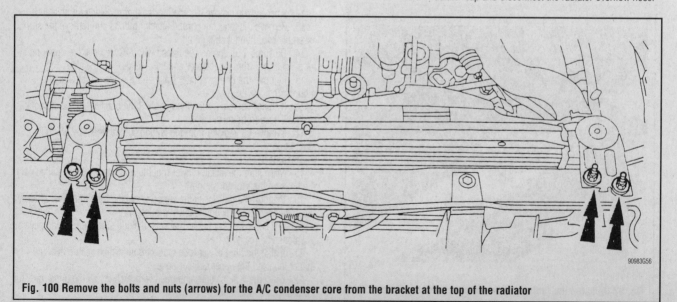

Fig. 100 Remove the bolts and nuts (arrows) for the A/C condenser core from the bracket at the top of the radiator

90983G56

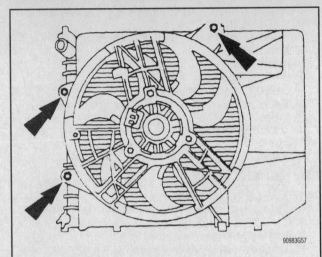

Fig. 101 Unfasten the retainers and separate the fan shroud from the radiator

8. Unfasten the bolts and nuts for the A/C condenser core from the bracket at the top of the radiator.

9. Remove the radiator and fan shroud assembly from the engine compartment.

10. Unfasten the retainers and separate the fan shroud from the radiator.

To install:

11. Engage the fan shroud to the radiator and tighten the retaining bolts to 24–48 inch lbs. (3–5.5 Nm).

12. Install the radiator and shroud assembly in the engine compartment.

13. Tighten the bolts and nuts for the A/C condenser core bracket at the top of the radiator.

14. Attach the radiator cap and connect the radiator overflow hose.

15. Connect the upper radiator hose and if equipped with an automatic transaxle, the upper oil cooler outlet tube.

16. Raise the car and support it with safety stands.

17. Connect the lower radiator hose and if equipped with an automatic transaxle, the lower oil cooler outlet tube.

18. Install the splash shield and tighten the bolts.

19. Lower the car and fill the cooling system with the proper amount and mixture of coolant.

20. Start the car and check for coolant leaks.

Electric Cooling Fan

REMOVAL & INSTALLATION

1.8L and 1.9L Engines

1. Disconnect the negative battery cable.

2. Place fender covers on the aprons.

3. On 1.8L engine equipped vehicles, remove the resonance duct from the radiator mounts.

4. Unplug the cooling fan motor electrical connector.

5. Unfasten the three shroud attaching bolts and remove the cooling fan shroud assembly by pulling it straight up.

6. Place the assembly on a bench, remove the cooling fan retainer clip.

7. Remove the cooling fan from the motor shaft.

8. Unclip the cooling fan motor electrical harness retainers and remove the harness from the retainers.

9. Unfasten the cooling fan motor attaching screws and remove the cooling fan motor from the shroud assembly.

To install:

10. Place the cooling fan motor in the shroud assembly and install the attaching screws.

11. Position the cooling fan motor electrical harness in the harness retainers and clip the retainers shut.

12. Install the cooling fan on the cooling motor shaft and engage the retainer clip.

13. Carefully lower the cooling fan shroud assembly into place and install the attaching bolts.

14. Attach the cooling fan motor electrical connector.

15. If equipped with 1.8L engine, install the resonance duct on the radiator mounts.

16. Connect the negative battery cable.

17. Check the fan for proper operation.

2.0L Engine

1997 MODELS

➡The fan motor, blade and shroud assembly are not serviced separately.

1. Disconnect the negative battery cable.

2. Remove the air cleaner outlet tube.

3. Unplug the fan and the upstream Heated oxygen Sensor (HO2S) electrical connections.

4. Unfasten the three fan shroud bolts and remove the assembly from the engine compartment.

To install:

5. Position the fan assembly in the engine compartment and tighten the retaining bolts.

6. Attach the fan and the upstream Heated oxygen Sensor (HO2S) electrical connections

7. Install the air cleaner outlet tube.

8. Connect the negative battery cable.

1998–99 MODELS

➡The fan motor, blade and shroud assembly are not serviced separately.

1. Disconnect the negative battery cable.

2. Remove the two push pins and the main wiring harness from the fan shroud.

3. Unplug the main wiring harness connector and move the harness to one side.

4. Unfasten the shroud bolts and remove the assembly from the engine compartment.

To install:

5. Place the fan assembly in the engine compartment and tighten the retaining bolts to 24–48 inch lbs. (3–5.5 Nm).

6. Attach the main wiring harness connector. Attach the main wiring harness and the two push pins to the fan shroud.

7. Connect the negative battery cable.

TESTING

1.8L and 1.9L Engines

1. Make sure the ignition key is **OFF**.

2. Apply 12 volts to the yellow wire at the cooling fan motor on all except 1.8L vehicles equipped with a 4EAT automatic transaxle and 1.9L vehicles equipped with air conditioning. Replace the motor if it does not run.

3. On 1.8L vehicles equipped with 4EAT automatic transaxle or 1.9L vehicles equipped with air conditioning, apply 12 volts to the blue wire on the 1.8L engine or the light green/yellow wire on the 1.9L engine at the cooling fan motor. Replace the motor if it does not run.

2.0L Engines

1. Make sure the ignition key is **OFF**.

2. Apply 12 volts to the yellow wire at the cooling fan motor and the fan should operate normally, then apply 12 volts to the green wire with the yel-

low stripe and the fan should again operate properly. If the fan does not run it may be defective.

Water Pump

REMOVAL & INSTALLATION

☀ CAUTION

Never open, service or drain the radiator or cooling system when hot; serious burns can occur from the steam and hot coolant. Also, when draining engine coolant, keep in mind that cats and dogs are attracted to ethylene glycol antifreeze and could drink any that is left in an uncovered container or in puddles on the ground. This will prove fatal in sufficient quantities. Always drain coolant into a sealable container. Coolant should be reused unless it is contaminated or is several years old.

1.8L Engine

▶ See Figure 102

1. Disconnect the negative battery cable.
2. Drain the cooling system.
3. Remove the timing belt.
4. Raise and safely support the vehicle.
5. Remove the engine oil dipstick tube bracket bolt(s) from the w water pump.
6. Remove the two bolts and the gasket from the water inlet pipe.
7. Remove all but the uppermost water pump mounting bolt.
8. Lower the vehicle.
9. Remove the remaining bolts and the water pump assembly.
10. If the water pump is being reused, remove all gasket material from the water pump.
11. Remove all gasket material from the engine block.

To install:
12. Install a new gasket onto the water pump.
13. Place the water pump into its mounting position, then install the uppermost bolt.
14. Raise and safely support the vehicle.
15. Install the remaining water pump mounting bolts and tighten all bolts to 14–19 ft. lbs. (19–25 Nm).
16. Install a new gasket onto the water inlet pipe.

17. Install the two bolts from the water inlet pipe to the water pump and tighten to 14–19 ft. lbs. (19–25 Nm).
18. Install the bolt to the engine oil dipstick tube bracket.
19. Lower the vehicle.
20. Install the timing belt.
21. Fill the cooling system.
22. Connect the negative battery cable.
23. Start the engine and allow it to reach operating temperature. Check for coolant leaks.
24. Check the coolant level and add coolant, as necessary.

1.9L Engine

▶ See Figures 103 thru 108

1. Disconnect the negative battery cable.
2. Drain the cooling system.
3. Remove the timing belt cover and the timing belt.
4. Raise and safely support the vehicle.
5. Remove the lower radiator hose from the water pump.
6. Remove the heater hose from the water pump.
7. Lower the vehicle.
8. Support the engine with a suitable hydraulic floor jack.
9. Remove the right engine mount attaching bolts and roll the engine mount aside.
10. Remove the water pump attaching bolts.
11. Using the floor jack, raise the engine enough to provide clearance for removing the water pump.
12. Remove the water pump and gasket from the engine through the top of the engine compartment.

To install:
13. Make sure the mating surfaces of the cylinder block and water pump are clean and free of gasket material.
14. If the water pump is to be replaced, transfer the timing belt tensioner components to the new water pump.
15. With the engine supported and raised with a suitable floor jack, place the water pump and the gasket on the cylinder block and install the four attaching bolts. Tighten the bolts to 15–22 ft. lbs. (20–30 Nm).
16. Install the timing belt and cover.
17. Roll the engine mount into position and install the mount bolts. Remove the floor jack.
18. Raise and safely support the vehicle.
19. Connect the heater hose to the pump.
20. Lower the vehicle.
21. Connect the negative battery cable.
22. Refill the cooling system.

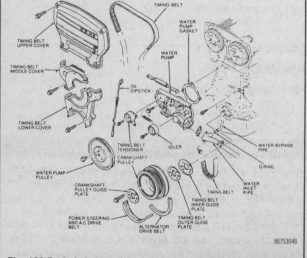

Fig. 102 Exploded view of a water pump mounting—1.8L engine

Fig. 103 Disconnect the lower radiator hose (A) from the water pump (B)

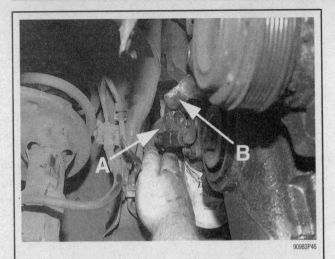

Fig. 104 Disconnect the heater hose (A) from the water pump (B)

Fig. 105 Remove the water pump's lower mounting bolts (arrows) . . .

Fig. 106 . . . and the upper mounting bolts

Fig. 107 After raising the engine enough to provide clearance, remove the pump from the engine compartment

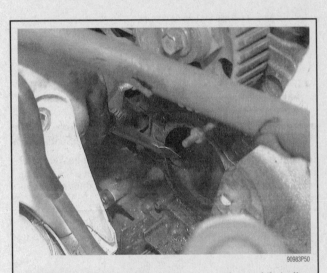

Fig. 108 Use a scraper to clean the mating surfaces of the cylinder block and water pump

23. Start the engine, allow it to reach normal operating temperature and check for coolant leaks.
24. Check the coolant level and add as necessary.

2.0L Engine

SOHC ENGINE

♦ See Figure 109

1. Disconnect the negative battery cable.
2. Raise the car and support it with safety stands.

✳✳ CAUTION

Never open, service or drain the radiator or cooling system when hot; serious burns can occur from the steam and hot coolant. Also, when draining engine coolant, keep in mind that cats and dogs are attracted to ethylene glycol antifreeze and could drink any that is left in an uncovered container or in puddles on the ground. This will prove fatal in sufficient quantities. Always drain coolant into a sealable container. Coolant should be reused unless it is contaminated or is several years old.

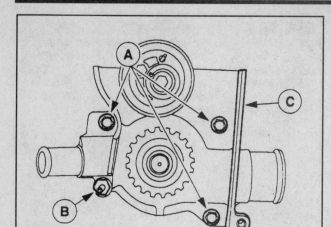

Fig. 109 Location of the water pump mounting bolts (A) and stud (B)—2.0L SOHC engine

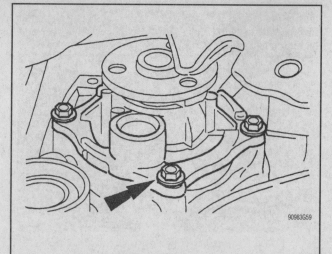

Fig. 110 Remove the water pump mounting retainers—2.0L DOHC engine

3. Drain and recycle the engine coolant.
4. Remove the timing belt.
5. Unfasten the timing belt tensioner bolt and remove the tensioner.
6. Disconnect the lower radiator hose from the water pump.
7. Lower the car and disconnect the heater hose from the water pump.
8. Unfasten the three bolts and one stud from the water pump.
9. Remove the water pump.
To install:

✳✳ WARNING

Do not use any abrasive grinding discs to remove gasket material. Use a plastic manual gasket scraper to remove the gasket residue. Be careful not to scratch or gouge the aluminum sealing surfaces when cleaning them.

10. Clean the gasket surfaces thoroughly until all traces of the old gasket residue are removed. Inspect the gasket mating surfaces, both must be clean and flat.
11. Install a new gasket and the water pump.
12. Install the water pump bolts and stud to 15–22 ft. lbs. (20–30 Nm).
13. Connect the heater hose to the pump.
14. Raise the car and support it with safety stands.
15. Connect the lower radiator hose to the pump.
16. Install the timing belt tensioner and tighten the bolt to 15–22 ft. lbs. (20–30 Nm).
17. Install the timing belt and lower the car.
18. Fill the cooling system with the proper amount and mixture of coolant.
19. Start the engine and check for leaks.

DOHC ENGINE

▶ See Figure 110

1. Disconnect the negative battery cable.

✳✳ CAUTION

Never open, service or drain the radiator or cooling system when hot; serious burns can occur from the steam and hot coolant. Also, when draining engine coolant, keep in mind that cats and dogs are attracted to ethylene glycol antifreeze and could drink any that is left in an uncovered container or in puddles on the ground. This will prove fatal in sufficient quantities. Always drain coolant into a sealable container. Coolant should be reused unless it is contaminated or is several years old.

2. Drain and recycle the engine coolant.
3. Raise the car and support it with safety stands.
4. Unfasten the splash shield bolts and remove the shield.
5. Loosen the water pump pulley retaining bolts, then remove the drive belt.
6. Remove the A/C compressor bolts and move the compressor aside.
7. Unfasten the water pump retainers and remove the pump from the middle timing belt cover.
To install:
8. Install the water pump and tighten the retainers to 17 ft. lbs. (24 Nm).
9. Place the A/C compressor in position and tighten the mounting bolts.
10. Install the drive belt and tighten the water pump pulley bolts.
11. Install the splash shield and tighten the bolts.
12. Fill the cooling system with the proper amount and mixture of coolant.
13. Connect the negative battery cable.
14. Start the engine and check for leaks.

Cylinder Head

REMOVAL & INSTALLATION

✳✳ WARNING

To reduce the possibility of cylinder head warpage and/or distortion, do not remove the cylinder head while the engine is warm. Always allow the engine to cool entirely before disassembly.

1.8L Engine

▶ See Figures 111, 112, 113, 114 and 115

1. Properly relieve the fuel system pressure.
2. Disconnect the negative battery cable.
3. Drain the cooling system.

✳✳ CAUTION

Never open, service or drain the radiator or cooling system when hot; serious burns can occur from the steam and hot coolant. Also, when draining engine coolant, keep in mind that cats and dogs are attracted to ethylene glycol antifreeze and

11. Loosen the air cleaner outlet tube clamps and disconnect it from the resonance chamber and throttle body.

12. Disconnect the accelerator cable and, if equipped with automatic transaxle, the kickdown cable from the throttle cam. Remove the cable bracket from the intake manifold.

13. Tag and remove all vacuum lines from the intake manifold.

14. Tag and unplug all necessary electrical connectors from the cylinder head, exhaust manifold, intake manifold, and throttle body.

15. Disconnect the ground straps.

16. Loosen the upper radiator hose clamps and remove the hose.

17. Unfasten the transaxle-to-engine block upper-right bolt.

18. If equipped, remove the safety clips from the fuel rail.

19. Disconnect the fuel pressure and return lines, then plug the lines.

20. Disconnect the ignition coil high-tension lead from the distributor.

21. Tag and disengage the necessary hoses connected to the cylinder head and intake manifold.

22. Remove the two bolts from the transaxle vent tube routing brackets.

23. Raise and safely support the vehicle.

24. Remove the bolt from the water pump-to-cylinder head hose bracket.

25. Remove the front exhaust mounting flange and exhaust pipe support bracket from the exhaust manifold.

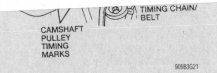

CAMSHAFT PULLEY TIMING MARKS

TIMING CHAIN/ BELT

90983G21

Fig. 111 Make sure the timing marks on the camshaft pulleys and seal plate are aligned—1.8L engine

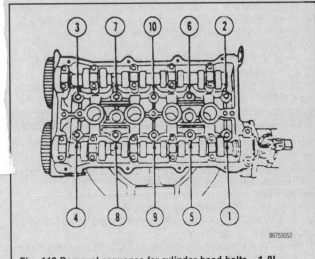

86753052

Fig. 113 Removal sequence for cylinder head bolts—1.8L engine

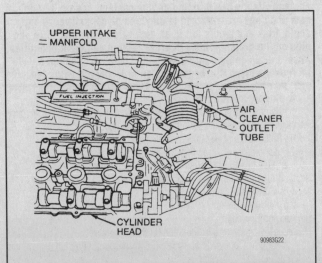

UPPER INTAKE MANIFOLD

FUEL INJECTION

AIR CLEANER OUTLET TUBE

CYLINDER HEAD

90983G22

Fig. 112 Disconnect the air cleaner outlet tube from the resonance chamber and throttle body

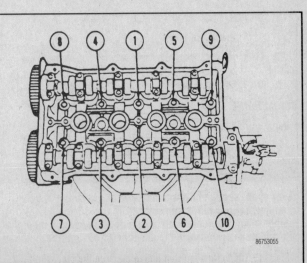

86753055

Fig. 114 Tighten the cylinder head bolts in this sequence to the proper specification—1.8L engine

26. Remove the intake manifold support bracket.
27. Lower the vehicle.
28. Remove the cylinder head bolts in the sequence illustrated.
29. Remove the cylinder head assembly, with the intake manifold, exhaust manifold and distributor still attached, from the vehicle.
30. Remove the intake manifold and exhaust manifold.

To install:

31. Remove all dirt, oil and old gasket material from all gasket contact surfaces.
32. Install the intake manifold and exhaust manifold.
33. Install a new head gasket onto the top of the engine block, using the dowel pins for reference.
34. Place the cylinder head into its mounting position on top of the engine block.
35. Lubricate the cylinder head bolts with engine oil and install them finger-tight. Tighten the bolts in the proper sequence (refer to the accompanying illustration) in two or three steps to 56–60 ft. lbs. (76–81 Nm).
36. Install the two bolts to the transaxle vent tube routing brackets.
37. Connect the heater hoses to the cylinder head and tighten the clamps.
38. Connect the ignition coil high-tension lead to the distributor.
39. Connect the fuel pressure and return lines to the fuel supply manifold and install the safety clips.
40. Install the transaxle-to-engine block upper-right bolt. If equipped with a manual transaxle, tighten the bolt to 47–66 ft. lbs. (64–89 Nm). If equipped with an automatic transaxle, tighten the bolt to 41–59 ft. lbs. (55–80 Nm).
41. Install the upper radiator hose and tighten the clamps.
42. Connect the ground straps.
43. Attach the electrical connectors that were unplugged at the cylinder head, exhaust manifold, intake manifold, and throttle body.
44. Connect the vacuum lines to the intake manifold.
45. Install the accelerator and kickdown cable bracket onto the intake manifold and tighten the bolts to 69–95 inch lbs. (8–11 Nm). Connect the cable(s) to the throttle cam.
46. Install the valve cover and gasket, then connect the hose running from the manifold to the valve cover. Tighten the cover bolts to 43–78 inch lbs. (5–9 Nm).
47. Install and connect the spark plug wires.
48. Connect the air cleaner outlet tube to the resonator and throttle body and tighten the clamps.
49. Connect the hose going from the air duct to the cylinder head cover.
50. Raise and safely support the vehicle.
51. Install the intake manifold support bracket. Tighten the bolts to 27–38 ft. lbs. (37–52 Nm) and the nut to 14–19 ft. lbs. (19–25 Nm).

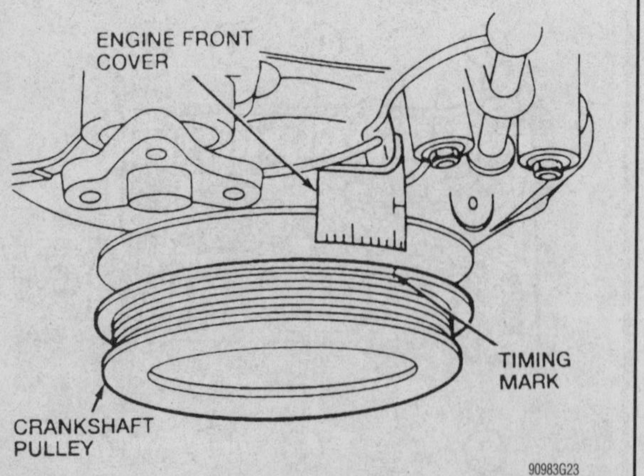

Fig. 115 The yellow ignition timing mark on the crankshaft pulley should be aligned with the TDC mark on the timing belt cover

52. Install the bolt to the water pump-to-cylinder head hose bracket.
53. Install the exhaust front mounting flange with a new gasket to the exhaust manifold. Tighten the flange-to-manifold attaching nuts to 23–34 ft. lbs. (31–46 Nm).
54. Install the exhaust pipe support bracket. Tighten the bracket attaching bolts to 27–38 ft. lbs. (37–52 Nm).
55. Make sure the yellow ignition timing mark on the crankshaft pulley is aligned with the TDC mark on the timing belt cover.
56. Lower the vehicle.
57. Make sure the timing marks on the camshaft pulleys and seal plate are aligned. Install the timing belt so there is no looseness at the idler pulley side or between the two camshaft pulleys.

➡Do not turn the crankshaft counterclockwise.

58. Turn the crankshaft two turns clockwise by hand and verify that the yellow ignition timing mark on the crankshaft pulley is aligned with the timing mark on the timing belt cover. Verify that the timing marks on the camshaft pulley and seal plate are aligned.

➡If the timing marks are not aligned, remove the timing belt and repeat the procedure.

59. Turn the crankshaft 1⅚ turns clockwise by hand and align the 4th tooth to the right of the **I** and **E** timing marks on the camshaft pulleys with the seal plate alignment marks.
60. Loosen the timing belt tensioner lockbolt and apply tension to the timing belt. Tighten the tensioner lockbolt to 27–38 ft. lbs. (37–52 Nm).
61. Turn the crankshaft 2⅙ (780 degrees) turns clockwise and verify that the timing marks on the camshaft pulleys and the seal plate are aligned.
62. Install new gaskets onto the timing belt upper and middle covers and install the covers. Tighten the mounting bolts to 69–95 inch lbs. (8–11 Nm).
63. Fill the cooling system.
64. Connect the negative battery cable.
65. Start the engine and check for leaks.

1.9L Engine

➧ See Figures 116 thru 131

1. Properly relieve the fuel system pressure.
2. Disconnect the negative battery cable.
3. Drain the cooling system.

✲✲ CAUTION

Never open, service or drain the radiator or cooling system when hot; serious burns can occur from the steam and hot coolant. Also, when draining engine coolant, keep in mind that cats and dogs are attracted to ethylene glycol antifreeze and could drink any that is left in an uncovered container or in puddles on the ground. This will prove fatal in sufficient quantities. Always drain coolant into a sealable container. Coolant should be reused unless it is contaminated or is several years old.

4. Remove the air intake duct.
5. Remove the crankcase breather hose from the rocker arm cover and the vacuum hose from the bottom of the throttle body.
6. Remove the power brake supply hose.
7. Tag and unplug the following the electrical connectors:
   a. Fuel charging harness (right-hand strut tower).
   b. Alternator harness (back of the alternator).
   c. Crank angle sensor.
   d. Oxygen sensor.
   e. Ignition coil.
   f. Radio suppresser (mounted on the coil bracket).
   g. Engine Coolant Temperature (ECT) sensor, cooling fan sensor and temperature sending unit.
8. Remove the ground strap from the stud on the left side of the cylinder head.

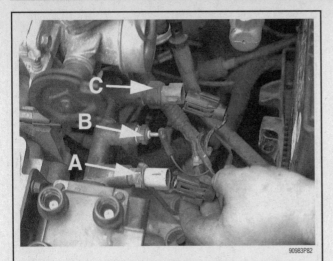

Fig. 116 Disconnect the Engine Coolant Temperature (ECT) sensor (A), cooling fan sensor (C) and temperature sending unit (B)

Fig. 117 Remove the ground strap from the stud on the left side of the cylinder head

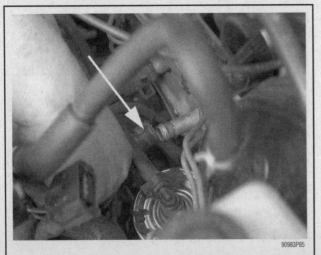

Fig. 118 Disconnect the heater hose containing the coolant temperature switches at the firewall

Fig. 119 Remove the oil level indicator tube mounting nut from the cylinder head stud

Fig. 120 Remove the alternator bracket-to-cylinder head mounting bolt

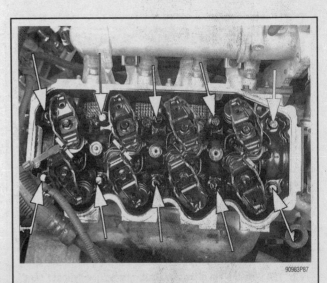

Fig. 121 Location of the cylinder head mounting bolts

Fig. 122 Use a breaker bar and socket to loosen the cylinder head bolts

Fig. 123 Remove all of the cylinder head bolts

Fig. 124 With the aid of an assistant, remove the cylinder head, intake manifold and exhaust manifold as an assembly

Fig. 125 If the cylinder head gasket is stuck, insert a scraper under the gasket to loosen it . . .

Fig. 126 . . . and remove the cylinder head gasket

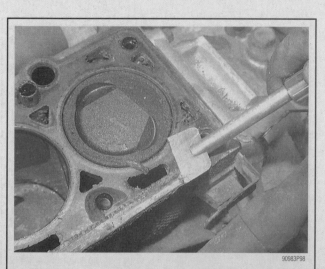

Fig. 127 Use a scraper to clean old gasket material from the engine block's cylinder head mounting surface . . .

Fig. 128 . . . and from the cylinder head's mating surface

Fig. 129 Use a torque wrench to tighten the cylinder head bolts to the correct specification in the proper sequence

9. Disconnect the accelerator and the transaxle kickdown cables from the throttle lever and remove the cable bracket from the intake manifold.

10. Disconnect the heater hose containing the coolant temperature switches at the firewall.

11. Remove the upper radiator hose.

12. Disconnect and plug the fuel supply and return lines.

13. Remove the oil level indicator tube mounting nut from the cylinder head stud.

14. Remove the power steering hose and the air conditioner line retainer bracket bolts from the alternator bracket.

15. Remove the accessory drive belt, alternator, and the drive belt automatic tensioner.

16. Raise and safely support the vehicle.

17. Remove the catalytic converter inlet pipe.

18. Remove the starter wiring harness from the retaining clip below the intake manifold.

19. Set the engine No. 1 cylinder on TDC.

20. On 1991 models, perform the following steps:

    a. Place a block of wood on a hydraulic jack and support the weight of the engine with the jack.

    b. Remove the passenger side engine mount. Unfasten the right-hand engine mount bolt and roll the mount out of the way

21. Lower the vehicle.

22. Remove the timing belt.

23. Remove the heater hose support bracket retaining bolt and the alternator bracket-to-cylinder head mounting bolt.

24. Remove the rocker arm cover.

25. Remove the cylinder head bolts. The old bolts can be used to check the piston squish height before discarding them.

26. Remove the cylinder head with the exhaust and intake manifolds attached.

27. Remove the cylinder head gasket. Keep the gasket to check the piston squish height, then after checking the squish height, discard the gasket

➡ Do not lay the cylinder head flat. Damage to the spark plugs, valves or gasket surfaces may result.

To install:

28. Clean all gasket material from the mating surfaces on the cylinder head and block and clean out the head bolt holes in the block.

29. Check the piston squish height. Refer to the procedure in this section.

➡ No cylinder block deck machining, or use of replacement crankshaft, piston or connecting rod causing the assembled squish height to be over or under tolerance specification, is permitted. If no parts other than the head gasket are replaced, the squish height should

be within specification. If parts other than the head gasket are replaced, check the squish height. If the squish height is out of specification, replace the parts again and recheck the squish height.

30. Install the dowels in the cylinder block, if removed. Check the dowel height, it should be 0.407–0.40 inch (10.40–11.75mm) above the surface of the block. A dowel that is too long will not allow the cylinder head to sit properly.

31. Position the cylinder head gasket on the cylinder block.

➡ The cylinder head attaching bolts cannot be tightened to the specified torque more than once and must, therefore, be replaced when installing a cylinder head.

32. Install the cylinder head and install new bolts and washers in the following order:

    a. Apply a light coat of engine oil to the threads of the new cylinder head bolts and install the new bolts into the head.

    b. Tighten the cylinder head bolts in sequence (refer to the illustration) to 44 ft. lbs. (60 Nm).

    c. Loosen the cylinder head bolts approximately two turns and then tighten them again in the same sequence to 44 ft. lbs. (60 Nm).

    d. After bolts have all been tightened, turn the head bolts 90° in

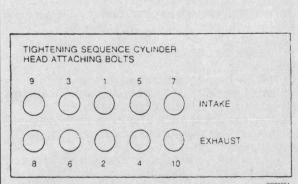

Fig. 130 Cylinder head bolt tightening sequence—1.9L engine

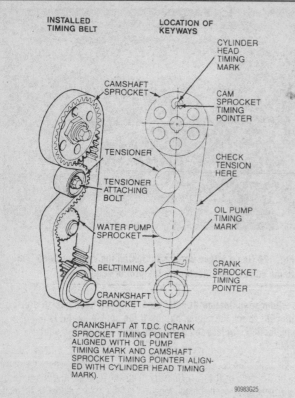

INSTALLED
TIMING BELT

LOCATION OF
KEYWAYS

CYLINDER
HEAD
TIMING
MARK

CAMSHAFT
SPROCKET

CAM
SPROCKET
TIMING
POINTER

TENSIONER

CHECK
TENSION
HERE

TENSIONER
ATTACHING
BOLT

OIL PUMP
TIMING
MARK

WATER PUMP
SPROCKET

BELT-TIMING

CRANK
SPROCKET
TIMING
POINTER

CRANKSHAFT
SPROCKET

CRANKSHAFT AT T.D.C. (CRANK
SPROCKET TIMING POINTER
ALIGNED WITH OIL PUMP
TIMING MARK AND CAMSHAFT
SPROCKET TIMING POINTER ALIGN-
ED WITH CYLINDER HEAD TIMING
MARK).

90983G25

Fig. 131 Make sure the timing marks are aligned so that the engine is at Top Dead Center (TDC) before installing the timing belt—1.9L engine

sequence and to complete the head bolt installation, turn the head bolts an additional 90° in the same torque sequence.

33. Install the rocker arm cover and the alternator bracket-to-cylinder head bolt.

34. With the timing marks aligned so that the engine is at Top Dead Center (TDC), install the timing belt and timing belt cover.

35. Raise and safely support the vehicle.

36. On 1991 models, install the lower right-hand mount.

37. Install the starter wiring harness on the retaining clip below the intake manifold.

38. Install the catalytic converter inlet pipe.

39. Lower the vehicle.

40. Install the alternator and the accessory drive belt automatic tensioner. Install the accessory drive belt.

41. Install both the power steering hose and air conditioner line retainer bracket bolts. Install the oil level indicator tube retainer bolt.

42. Connect the fuel supply and return lines.

43. Install the upper radiator hose and connect the heater hose at the firewall.

44. Install the heater hose support bracket retaining bolt.

45. Install the accelerator cable bracket on the intake manifold and connect the accelerator and kickdown cables to the throttle lever.

46. Install the ground strap at the left side of the cylinder head.

47. Attach all the remaining electrical connectors according to their positions marked during the removal procedure.

48. Connect the power brake supply hose, crankcase breather hose and the vacuum line at the bottom of the throttle body.

49. Install the air intake duct.

50. Connect the negative battery cable.

51. Fill and bleed the cooling system.

52. Start the engine and check for leaks. Stop the engine and check the coolant level. Add fluid as necessary.

2.0L Engine

SOHC ENGINE

▶ See Figure 132

➡ Never work on aluminum engine parts when the engine is warm.

1. Disconnect the negative battery cable.

2. Properly relieve the fuel system pressure.

3. Remove the timing belt and engine air cleaner intake tube.

4. Tag and disconnect the vacuum hoses from the following components:
- EGR valve
- PCV valve
- Throttle body
- Fuel pressure regulator
- Intake manifold

5. Disconnect the accelerator cable, throttle control lever and if equipped, the speed control cable.

6. If equipped, remove the speed control cable bracket bolt.

7. Unplug the two fuel charging wiring electrical connections.

8. Unplug the Crankshaft Position (CKP) sensor and Heated Oxygen sensor (HO2S) electrical connections.

9. Using tool D87L-9280-A or its equivalent, disconnect the fuel supply line from the fuel rail.

10. Unfasten the power steering pressure hose bracket bolts, then position the bracket and hose aside.

11. Loosen the alternator lower bolt, unfasten the alternator upper bolt and pivot the alternator forward.

12. Unfasten the engine oil dipstick tube bracket bolt that attaches the tube to the intake manifold.

13. Disconnect the EGR manifold tube located below the EGR valve.

14. Unfasten the exhaust manifold heat shield nuts and remove the heat shield.

15. Unfasten the catalytic converter-to-exhaust manifold nuts and separate the components.

16. Raise the car and support it with safety stands.

✳✳ CAUTION

Never open, service or drain the radiator or cooling system when hot; serious burns can occur from the steam and hot coolant. Also, when draining engine coolant, keep in mind that cats and dogs are attracted to ethylene glycol antifreeze and could drink any that is left in an uncovered container or in puddles on the ground. This will prove fatal in sufficient quantities. Always drain coolant into a sealable container. Coolant should be reused unless it is contaminated or is several years old.

17. Drain the cooling system into a suitable container.

18. Unfasten the right-hand splash shield bolts and remove the shield.

19. Remove the engine oil dipstick tube from the cylinder block.

20. Unplug the A/C compressor electrical connection.

21. Unbolt the A/C compressor retainers and set the compressor aside with the lines still attached.

22. Loosen but do not remove, the four bolts and nut that attach the front engine accessory drive bracket about four turns.

23. Lower the car and unfasten the uppermost front engine accessory drive bracket-to-cylinder head bolt.

24. Unfasten the A/C line bracket-to-front engine accessory drive bracket bolt.

25. Remove the valve cover, then disconnect the upper radiator hose from the thermostat housing water hose connection.

26. Disconnect the heater hose from the thermostat housing.

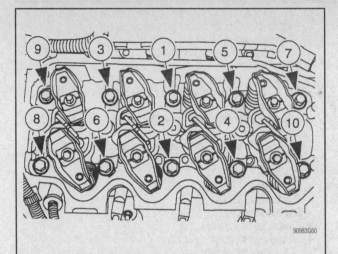

Fig. 132 Tighten the cylinder head bolts in the specified sequence—2.0L SOHC engines

※ CAUTION

The removal of the cylinder head requires two people; please do not remove the head without the aid of a helper.

➡**Maintain a balanced pressure when removing the cylinder head bolts.**

27. Unfasten the cylinder head bolts, remove the head and gasket.
28. Discard the old bolts and the gasket.
To install:

※ WARNING

Do not use any abrasive grinding discs to remove gasket material. Use a plastic manual gasket scraper to remove the gasket residue. Be careful not to scratch or gouge the aluminum sealing surfaces when cleaning them.

29. Clean the gasket surfaces thoroughly until all traces of the old gasket residue are removed. Inspect the gasket mating surfaces, both must be clean and flat.
30. Install a new head gasket on the cylinder block.

※ CAUTION

Do not attempt to install the cylinder head without the aid of an assistant; it takes two people.

➡**Always use new bolts when installing the cylinder head.**

31. Lubricate the new cylinder bolts when engine oil.
32. Install the cylinder head and tighten the bolts in the illustrated sequence, using the following steps:
   a. Tighten all the bolts in sequence to 30–44 ft. lbs. (40–60 Nm).
   b. Back all the bolts off ½ turn.
   c. Retighten all the bolts to 30–44 ft. lbs. (40–60 Nm).
33. Rotate all the bolts in sequence an additional 180°, in two steps of 90°.
34. Install and tighten the uppermost accessory drive bracket bolt to 30–40 ft. lbs. (40–55 Nm).
35. Install the A/C line bracket and tighten the bolt to 15–18 ft. lbs. (20–25 Nm).
36. Install the valve cover, then raise and support the car on safety stands.
37. Install and tighten the four front engine accessory drive bracket bolts and the nut to 30–40 ft. lbs. (40–55 Nm).

38. Install the A/C compressor and tighten the retaining bolts.
39. Install the right-hand splash shield and tighten its retainers.
40. Install the engine oil dipstick tube and lower the car.
41. Connect the heater and upper radiator hoses.
42. Install the timing belt and alternator.
43. Install the power steering pressure hose.
44. Attach the CKP sensor and two main fuel charging electrical connections
45. Install and tighten the engine oil dipstick tube bolt.
46. Install and tighten the EGR valve manifold tube connection.
47. Connect the EGR valve manifold tube to the exhaust manifold.
48. Connect the fuel supply line to the fuel rail.
49. Connect the catalytic converter to the exhaust manifold using a new gasket and tighten the nuts.
50. Install the heat shield and tighten the nuts.
51. If equipped, install the speed control cable bracket.
52. Connect the throttle control lever, accelerator cable and if equipped, the speed control cable.
53. Connect the vacuum hoses tagged and removed to the following components:
   - EGR valve
   - PCV valve
   - Throttle body
   - Fuel pressure regulator
   - Intake manifold
54. Install the air cleaner outlet tube.
55. Fill the cooling system.
56. Connect the negative battery cable.
57. Start the engine and check for leaks.

DOHC ENGINE

◆ See Figure 133

1. Disconnect the negative battery cable.
2. Properly relieve the fuel system pressure.
3. Remove the air cleaner assembly outlet tube.
4. Remove the timing belt.
5. Tag and disconnect the vacuum hoses from the following components:
   - PCV valve
   - Throttle body
   - Fuel pressure sensor
   - Intake manifold
6. Disconnect the speed control and accelerator cables from the control lever.

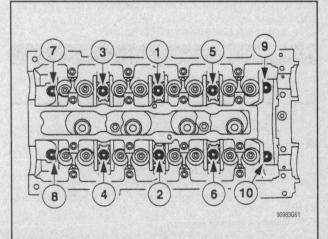

Fig. 133 Tighten the cylinder head bolts in the following sequence in the order specified—2.0L DOHC engines

7. Unplug the fuel charging electrical connectors at the main engine connector.

8. Unplug the Crankshaft Position (CKP) sensor and Heated Oxygen sensor (HO2S) electrical connections.

9. Disconnect the fuel line.

10. Unbolt the power steering pump and bracket, then set them aside with the lines still attached.

11. Remove the alternator and engine oil dipstick tube.

12. Raise the car and support it with safety stands.

✳✳ CAUTION

Never open, service or drain the radiator or cooling system when hot; serious burns can occur from the steam and hot coolant. Also, when draining engine coolant, keep in mind that cats and dogs are attracted to ethylene glycol antifreeze and could drink any that is left in an uncovered container or in puddles on the ground. This will prove fatal in sufficient quantities. Always drain coolant into a sealable container. Coolant should be reused unless it is contaminated or is several years old.

13. Drain the cooling system into a suitable container.

14. Unfasten the splash shield bolts and remove the shield.

15. Unplug the A/C compressor electrical connection.

16. Unbolt the A/C compressor retainers and set the compressor aside with the lines still attached.

17. Lower the car, tag and disconnect the spark plug wires and remove the plugs.

18. Remove the valve cover, then disconnect the upper radiator hose from the thermostat housing water hose connection.

19. Disconnect the heater hose from the thermostat housing.

20. Remove the camshafts and the ignition coil.

21. Remove the thermostat housing.

22. Unfasten the cylinder head bolts, then remove the head and the gasket.

To install:

➡️Always use new bolts when installing the cylinder head.

✳✳ WARNING

Do not use any abrasive grinding discs to remove gasket material. Use a plastic manual gasket scraper to remove the gasket residue. Be careful not to scratch or gouge the aluminum sealing surfaces when cleaning them.

23. Clean the gasket surfaces thoroughly until all traces of the old gasket residue are removed. Inspect the gasket mating surfaces, both must be clean and flat.

24. Install a new head gasket on the cylinder block.

✳✳ CAUTION

Do not attempt to install the cylinder head without the aid of an assistant; it takes two people.

25. Lubricate the new cylinder head bolts with clean engine oil.

26. Install the cylinder head and tighten the bolts in the illustrated sequence, using the following steps:

   a. Tighten all the bolts in sequence to 12–18 ft. lbs. (15–25 Nm).

   b. Tighten all the bolts to 26–33 ft. lbs. (35–45 Nm).

   c. On Escort/Tracer (non-coupe) models, tighten all the bolts an additional 105°. On Escort coupe models, tighten the bolts an additional 90°.

27. Install the thermostat housing.

28. Install the ignition coil and the camshafts.

29. Connect the heater and upper radiator hoses.

30. Install the valve cover, spark plugs and connect the spark plug wires.

31. Install the A/C compressor and tighten the retaining bolts.

32. Attach the A/C compressor electrical connection.

33. Install the splash shield and tighten its retainers.

34. Install the engine oil dipstick tube.

35. Install the alternator and the power steering reservoir and bracket.

36. Connect the fuel line.

37. Attach the CKP sensor, HO2S sensor, and two main fuel charging electrical connections

38. Connect accelerator cable and if equipped, the speed control cable to the control lever.

39. Connect the vacuum hoses tagged and removed to the following components:

- PCV valve
- Throttle body
- Fuel pressure sensor
- Intake manifold

40. Install the timing belt.

41. Install the air cleaner outlet tube.

42. Fill the cooling system.

43. Connect the negative battery cable.

44. Start the engine and check for leaks.

PISTON SQUISH HEIGHT

1.9L Engines

▶ **See Figures 134 and 135**

Before final installation of the cylinder head to the engine, piston "squish height" must be checked. Squish height is the clearance of the piston dome to the cylinder head dome at piston TDC. No rework of the head gasket surfaces (slabbing) or use of replacement parts (crankshaft, piston and connecting rod) that causes the assembled squish height to be over or under the tolerance specification is permitted.

➡️**If no parts other than the head gasket are replaced, the piston squish height should be within specification. If parts other than the head gasket are replaced, check the squish height. If out of specification, replace the parts again and recheck the squish height.**

1. Clean all gasket material from the mating surfaces on the cylinder head and engine block.

2. Place a small amount of soft lead solder or lead shot of an appropriate thickness on the piston spherical areas.

3. Rotate the crankshaft to lower the piston in the bore and install the head gasket and cylinder head.

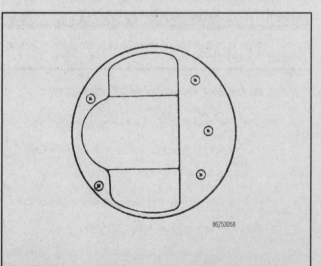

86753058

Fig. 134 Place the lead shot or solder on the positions illustrated to measure the piston squish height

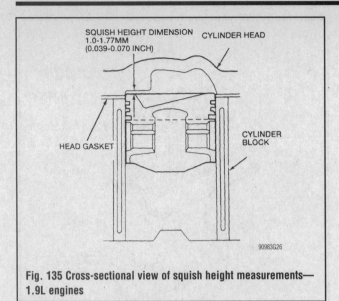

Fig. 135 Cross-sectional view of squish height measurements—1.9L engines

➡A compressed (used) head gasket is preferred for checking squish height.

4. Install used head bolts and tighten them to 30–44 ft. lbs. (40–60 Nm) following the proper sequence.
5. Rotate the crankshaft to move the piston through its TDC position.
6. Remove the cylinder head and measure the thickness of the compressed solder to determine squish height at TDC. The compressed lead piece should be 0.039–0.070 inch (1.0–1.77mm).

Oil Pan

REMOVAL & INSTALLATION

✳✳ CAUTION

The EPA warns that prolonged contact with used engine oil may cause a number of skin disorders, including cancer! You should make every effort to minimize your exposure to used engine oil. Protective gloves should be worn when changing the oil. Wash your hands and any other exposed skin areas as soon as possible after exposure to used engine oil. Soap and water, or waterless hand cleaner should be used.

1.8L Engine

▶ See Figures 136, 137 and 138

1. Disconnect the negative battery cable. Remove the oil filler cap.
2. Raise and safely support the vehicle.
3. Remove the drain plug and drain the engine oil into a suitable container.
4. Remove the upper right and lower right and left splash shields.
5. Remove the exhaust pipe front mounting flange and exhaust pipe support bracket from the exhaust manifold. Discard the pipe bracket.
6. Unfasten the oil pan-to-transaxle attaching bolts.
7. Place a block of wood on a suitable jackstand and support the oil pan with jackstand.
8. Unfasten oil pan-to-engine block attaching bolts.
9. Only at the points of the oil pan illustrated, use a suitable tool to carefully pry the oil pan away from the engine block and remove the oil pan.

➡Do not force a prying tool between the engine block and the oil pan contact surface when trying to remove the oil pan. This may damage the oil pan contact surface and cause oil leakage.

10. Use a prytool to remove the oil pan reinforcements away from the block.
11. Remove the front and rear oil pan seals. Remove all sealant material from the engine block and oil pan.

➡When removing the oil pan flange reinforcements and sealant material from the oil pan and engine block, be careful not to damage the oil pan and engine block contact surfaces.

To install:
12. Apply a bead of silicone sealant to the oil pan flange reinforcements along the inside of the bolt holes.
13. Install the oil pan flange reinforcements.

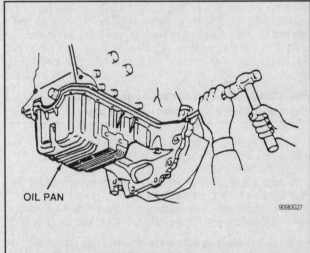

Fig. 136 Use a suitable tool to carefully pry the oil pan away from the engine block

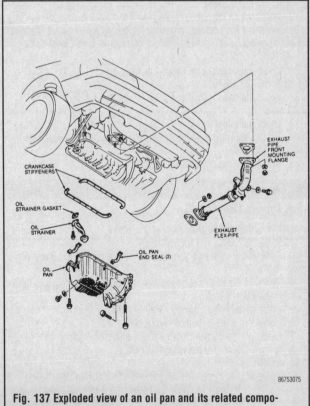

Fig. 137 Exploded view of an oil pan and its related components—1.8L engines

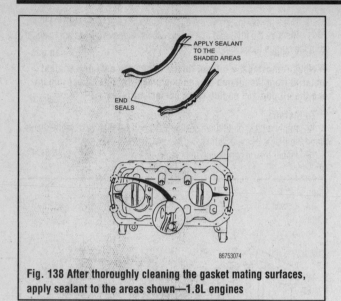

Fig. 138 After thoroughly cleaning the gasket mating surfaces, apply sealant to the areas shown—1.8L engines

14. Apply sealant to the areas of the end seals as illustrated. Be sure to install the end seals with the projections in the notches.

15. Install the front and rear end seals onto the oil pan.

16. Apply a continuous bead of silicone sealant to the oil pan along the inside of the bolt holes. Overlap the sealant ends.

17. Place the oil pan into its mounting position and install the oil pan-to-engine block attaching bolts. Tighten the bolts to 69–95 inch lbs. (8–11 Nm).

➡If the oil pan attaching bolts are to be reused, the old sealant must be removed from the bolt threads. Tightening the old attaching bolts with old sealant still on them may cause cracking inside the bolt holes.

18. Install the oil pan-to-transaxle attaching bolts and tighten them to 27–38 ft. lbs. (37–52 Nm).

19. Install the oil drain plug and tighten it to 22–30 ft. lbs. (29–41 Nm).

20. Install the front exhaust mounting flange and a new gasket. Tighten the mounting flange-to-exhaust manifold attaching nuts to 23–34 ft. lbs. (31–46 Nm).

21. Install the exhaust pipe support bracket, then tighten the bolts to 27–38 ft. lbs. (37–52 Nm).

22. Install the splash shields. Tighten the bolts to 69–95 inch lbs. (8–11 Nm).

23. Lower the vehicle.

24. Fill the crankcase with the proper type and quantity of engine oil. Install the filler cap.

25. Connect the negative battery cable.

1.9L Engines

▶ See Figures 139 and 140

1. Disconnect the negative cable at the battery.

2. Raise the vehicle and support safely.

3. Remove the drain plug and drain the engine oil into a suitable container.

4. Remove the catalytic converter from the exhaust manifold and from the inlet pipe and resonator.

5. Unfasten the two oil pan-to-transaxle bolts.

6. Unfasten the ten oil pan-to-engine bolts.

7. Gently pry the oil pan from the block and remove the oil pan

8. Remove the oil pan gasket and discard.

To install:

9. Use a scraper to clean the oil pan gasket surface and the mating surface on the cylinder block. Wipe the oil pan rail with a solvent-soaked, lint-free cloth to remove all traces of oil.

10. Remove the two oil pump screen cover screws to clean the oil pump

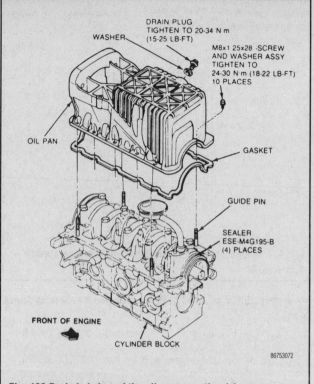

Fig. 139 Exploded view of the oil pan mounting (shown inverted)—1.9L engine

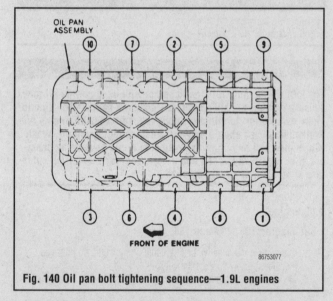

Fig. 140 Oil pan bolt tightening sequence—1.9L engines

pick up tube and screen assembly. Install tube and screen assembly using a new tube gasket. Tighten the screen screws and tube bolts to 7–9 ft. lbs. (10–13 Nm).

➡Install the pan within 10 minutes of applying the sealant.

11. Apply a bead of suitable silicone rubber sealer approximately 0.125 inch (3.0mm) wide at the corners of the block and at the oil pump-to-block and the crankshaft rear oil seal retainer-to-block joints.

12. Install the oil pan gasket in the pan ensuring the press fit tabs are fully engaged in the gasket channel.

13. Install the oil pan and attaching bolts. Tighten the bolts lightly until the two oil pan-to-transaxle bolts can be installed.

➡️**If the oil pan is installed on the engine outside of the vehicle, a transaxle case or equivalent, fixture must be bolted to the block to line-up the oil pan flush with the rear face of the block.**

14. Tighten the two pan-to-transaxle bolts to 30–40 ft. lbs. (40–54 Nm), then loosen them one half turn.

15. Tighten the oil pan flange-to-cylinder block bolts to 15–22 ft. lbs. (20–30 Nm) in the sequence illustrated.

16. Retighten the two pan-to-transaxle bolts to 30–40 ft. lbs. (40–54 Nm).

17. Install the catalytic converter.

18. Install the oil pan drain plug and tighten it to 15–22 ft. lbs. (20–30 Nm).

19. Lower the vehicle and fill the crankcase.

20. Connect negative battery cable.

21. Start the engine and check for oil leaks.

2.0L Engine

SOHC ENGINE

▶ **See Figure 141**

1. Raise the car and support it with safety stands.
2. Remove the catalytic converter.
3. Drain the engine oil.
4. Unfasten the oil pan-to-catalytic converter bracket bolts and remove the bracket.
5. Unfasten the ten oil pan bolts evenly, then remove the oil pan and gasket.
6. Discard the old gasket.

❊❊ CAUTION

Do not use any abrasive grinding discs to remove gasket material. Use a plastic manual gasket scraper to remove the gasket residue. Be careful not to scratch or gouge the aluminum sealing surfaces when cleaning them.

7. Clean the gasket surfaces thoroughly until all traces of the old gasket residue are removed. Inspect the gasket mating surfaces, both must be clean, flat and dry.

To install:

➡️**Install the oil pan within ten minutes of applying the silicone sealer.**

8. Apply a 0.125 in. (3mm) wide bead of silicone sealant F6AZ-19562-

AA or its equivalent at the oil pump-to-cylinder block joints and the crankshaft rear oil seal retainer-to-cylinder block joints.

➡️**Make sure the press fit tabs are fully engaged in the oil pan gasket channel when installing the pan and gasket.**

9. Install the gasket.

10. When installing the oil pan, make sure the rear of the pan is aligned with the cylinder block by using a straight edge as a guide.

11. Install and tighten the oil pan bolts in the sequence illustrated to 15–22 ft. lbs. (20–30 Nm).

12. Install the oil pan-to-catalytic converter bracket and tighten the bolts to 30–40 ft. lbs. (40–55 Nm).

13. Install the catalytic converter and oil pan drain plug. Tighten the drain plug to 15–22 ft. lbs. (20–30 Nm).

14. Lower the car and fill the engine with the proper type and quantity of engine oil.

15. Start the car and check for oil leaks.

DOHC ENGINE

▶ **See Figure 142**

1. Raise the car and support it with safety stands.
2. Drain the engine oil.
3. Remove the catalytic converter.
4. Unfasten the 17 oil pan bolts evenly, then remove the oil pan.

❊❊ CAUTION

Do not use any abrasive grinding discs to remove gasket material. Use a plastic manual gasket scraper to remove the gasket residue. Be careful not to scratch or gouge the aluminum sealing surfaces when cleaning them.

5. Clean the gasket surfaces thoroughly until all traces of the old gasket residue are removed. Inspect the gasket mating surfaces, both must be clean, flat and dry.

To install:

➡️**Install the oil pan within four minutes of applying the silicone sealer.**

6. Apply a 0.1in. (3.0mm) wide bead of silicone sealant F6AZ-19562-AA or its equivalent to the oil pan.

7. Install the oil pan and the bolts. Tighten the oil pan bolts in the sequence illustrated to 15–22 ft. lbs. (20–30 Nm).

8. Install the oil pan drain plug.

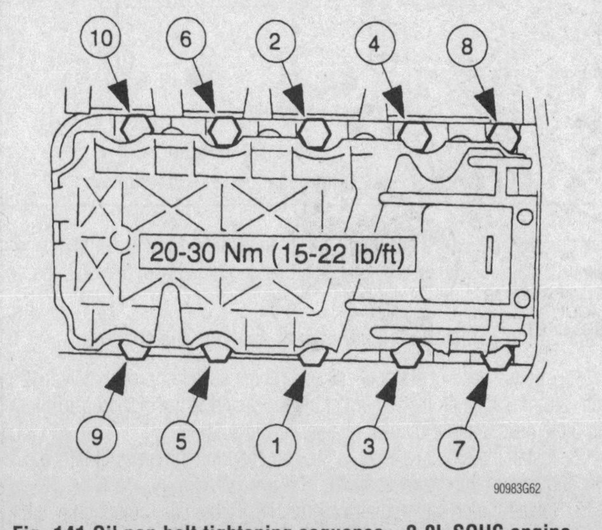

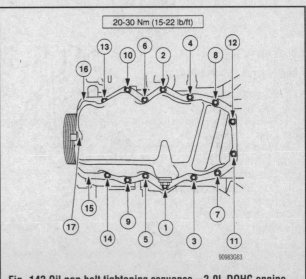

Fig. 141 Oil pan bolt tightening sequence—2.0L SOHC engine

Fig. 142 Oil pan bolt tightening sequence—2.0L DOHC engine

9. Lower the car and fill the engine with the proper type and quantity of engine oil.

10. Start the car and check for oil leaks.

Oil Pump

REMOVAL & INSTALLATION

✳✳ CAUTION

The EPA warns that prolonged contact with used engine oil may cause a number of skin disorders, including cancer! You should make every effort to minimize your exposure to used engine oil. Protective gloves should be worn when changing the oil. Wash your hands and any other exposed skin areas as soon as possible after exposure to used engine oil. Soap and water, or waterless hand cleaner should be used.

1.8L Engine

▶ See Figure 143

1. Disconnect the negative battery cable.
2. Remove the timing belt and timing belt pulley.
3. Remove the oil pan.
4. Remove the oil pump screen cover and tube.
5. If equipped, remove the A/C compressor mounting bolts and position the compressor so it is free from the work area.
6. Remove the A/C compressor mounting bracket.
7. Unbolt the mounting bolt from the engine oil dipstick tube bracket and the alternator lower mounting bolt.
8. Unfasten all oil pump mounting bolts and remove the oil pump.
9. Use a scraper to remove all gasket material from the oil pump mounting surfaces.

To install:

10. Install a new gasket onto the oil pump.
11. Place the oil pump into its mounting position and install the pump mounting bolts. Tighten the bolts to 14–19 ft. lbs. (19–25 Nm).
12. Place the dipstick tube bracket bolt into its mounting position and install the mounting bolt. Tighten the bolt to 68–95 inch lbs. (8–11 Nm).
13. Install the alternator lower mounting bolt and tighten it to 27–38 ft. lbs. (37–52 Nm).
14. Install a new gasket onto the oil strainer, place the strainer into its mounting position and install the mounting bolts. Tighten the bolts to 69–95 inch lbs. (8–11 Nm).
15. Install the oil pan.
16. If equipped, place the A/C compressor bracket into its mounting position and install the mounting bolts. Tighten the bolts to 30–40 ft. lbs. (40–55 Nm).
17. If equipped, install A/C compressor side bolt. Tighten the bolts to 14–19 ft. lbs. (19–25 Nm).
18. Install the timing belt pulley and timing belt.
19. Connect the negative battery cable.
20. Start the engine and check for oil leaks. Make sure the oil pressure indicator lamp has gone out after a second or two. If the lamp remains on after several seconds, immediately shut off the engine. Determine the cause and correct the condition.

1.9L Engine

▶ See Figure 144

1. Make sure the No. 1 cylinder is at TDC.
2. Disconnect the negative battery cable.
3. Remove the accessory drive belt and the automatic tensioner.
4. Support the engine with a suitable floor jack.
5. Remove the right engine mount dampener and remove the right engine mount bolts from the mount bracket.
6. Loosen the mount through-bolt and roll the mount aside.

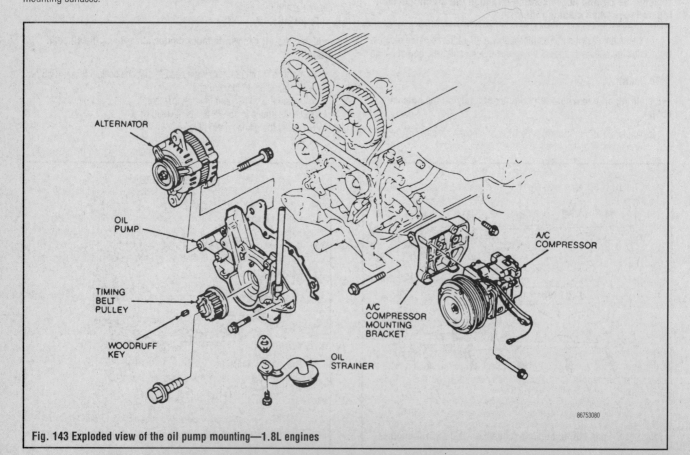

Fig. 143 Exploded view of the oil pump mounting—1.8L engines

86753080

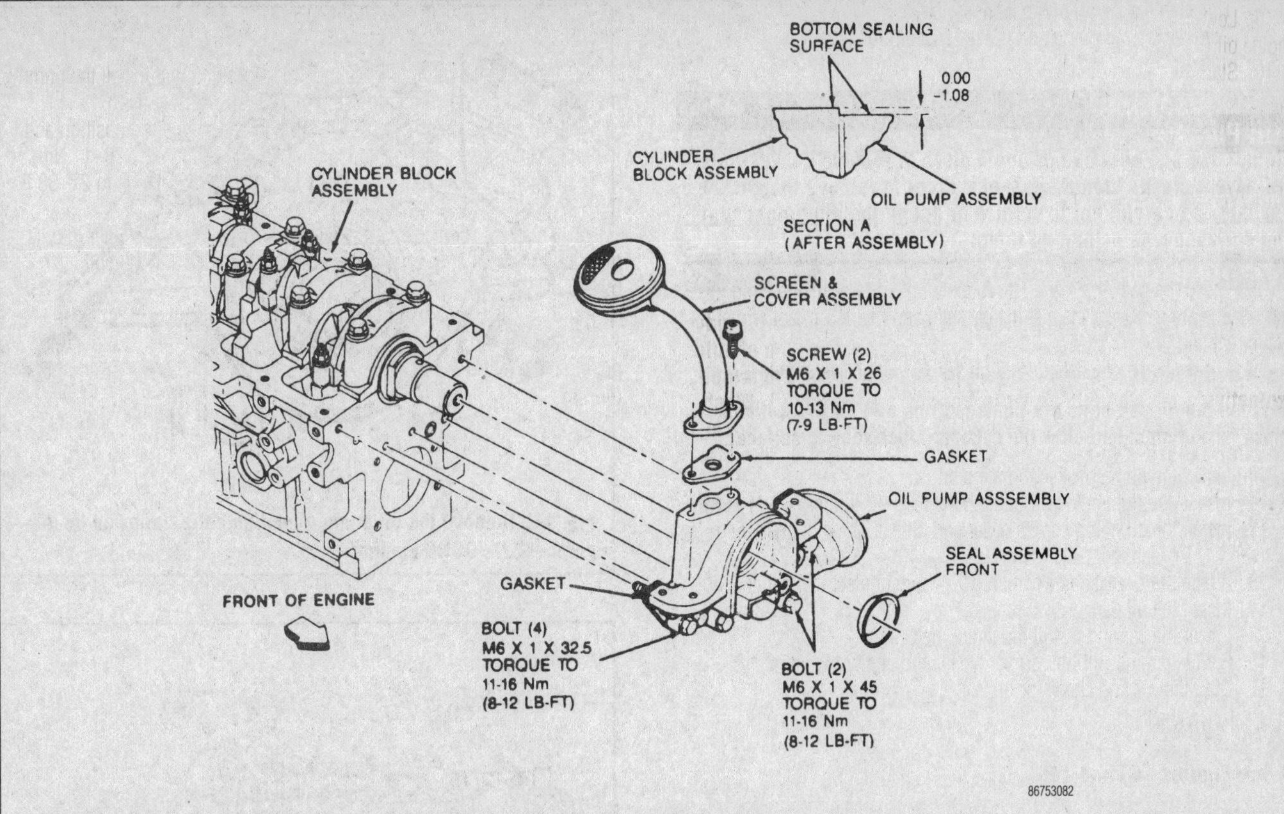

Fig. 144 Exploded view of the oil pump mounting (shown inverted)—1.9L engines

7. Remove the timing belt cover.

8. Roll the engine mount back into place and install the two mount bolts. Remove the floor jack.

9. Loosen the belt tensioner attaching bolt and pry the tensioner to the rear of the engine. Tighten the attaching bolt.

10. Raise and safely support the vehicle.

11. Remove the right side splash shield.

12. Remove the catalytic converter inlet pipe.

13. Drain and remove the oil pan. Remove the oil filter.

14. Remove the crankshaft dampener and the timing belt.

15. Remove the crankshaft sprocket and the timing belt guide from the crankshaft.

16. Disconnect the crankshaft position sensor.

17. Unfasten the 6 oil pump-to-engine bolts and remove the oil pump assembly from the engine. Remove and discard the gasket.

18. Remove the crankshaft seal from the pump and discard.

To install:

19. Make sure the pump mating surfaces on the cylinder block and oil pump are clean and free of gasket material.

20. Remove the oil pickup tube and screen assembly from the pump for cleaning.

21. Lubricate the outside diameter of the crankshaft seal with engine oil and install the seal with a suitable installation tool. Lubricate the seal lip with clean engine oil.

22. Position the oil pump gasket on the cylinder block.

23. Using a suitable tool, position the pump drive gear to allow the pump to pilot over the crankshaft and seat firmly on the cylinder block.

➡**The pump drive gear can be accessed through the oil pickup hole in the body of the pump. Do not install the oil pump pickup tube and screen until the pump has been correctly installed on the cylinder block.**

24. Install the six oil pump bolts and tighten to 8–12 ft. lbs. (11–16 Nm).

➡**When the oil pump bolts are tightened, the gasket must not be below the cylinder block sealing surface.**

25. Install the pickup tube and screen assembly on the oil pump using a new gasket. Tighten the attaching screws to 7–9 ft. lbs. (10–13 Nm).

26. Install the timing belt guide over the end of the crankshaft and install the crankshaft sprocket.

27. Make sure the No. 1 cylinder is at TDC.

28. Position the timing belt over the sprockets.

29. Connect the crank angle sensor.

30. Install the oil pan and the crankshaft dampener.

31. Install the catalytic converter inlet pipe.

32. Install the splash shield and lower the vehicle.

33. Install the timing belt. Tighten the tensioner attaching bolt to 17–22 ft. lbs. (23–30 Nm).

34. Support the engine with a suitable floor jack.

35. Remove the right engine mount bolts and roll the mount back.

36. Install the timing belt cover.

37. Roll the engine mount back into place and install the attaching bolts. Tighten the mount through-bolt and install the mount dampener.

38. Remove the floor jack.

39. Install the accessory drive belt automatic tensioner and the accessory drive belt.

40. Fill the crankcase with the proper type and amount of engine oil.

41. Connect the negative battery cable, start the engine and check for leaks.

2.0L Engine

SOHC ENGINE

1. Remove the timing belt.

2. Raise the car and support it with safety stands.

3. Remove the oil pan.

4. Unplug the Crankshaft Position (CKP) sensor electrical connection.

5. Unfasten the oil pump screen cover and tube bolts and remove the cover and tube.

6. Unfasten the six oil pump retaining bolts.
7. Remove the old pump and gasket. Discard the gasket.

To install:

✳✳ WARNING

Do not use any abrasive grinding discs to remove gasket material. Use a plastic manual gasket scraper to remove the gasket residue. Be careful not to scratch or gouge the aluminum sealing surfaces when cleaning them.

8. Clean the gasket surfaces thoroughly until all traces of the old gasket residue are removed. Inspect the gasket mating surfaces, both must be clean, flat and dry.
9. Lubricate the crankshaft front oil seal lip with clean engine oil.

➡ **When the oil pan bolts are tightened, the oil pump-to-cylinder block gasket must be below the cylinder block sealing surface.**

10. Install the pump gasket and the pump.
11. Install and tighten the oil pump bolts to 8–12 ft. lbs. (11–16 Nm).
12. Install the oil pump screen cover and tube. Tighten the retaining bolts to 71–97 inch lbs. (8–11 Nm).
13. Attach the Crankshaft Position (CKP) sensor electrical connection.
14. Install the oil pan.
15. Lower the car and install the timing belt.
16. Fill the engine with the proper type and quantity of engine oil.
17. Start the car and check for oil leaks.

DOHC ENGINE

▶ **See Figures 145 and 146**

1. Remove the timing covers and belt.
2. Raise the car and support it with safety stands.
3. Remove the crankshaft pulley, sprocket and the timing chain guide.
4. Remove the oil pan.
5. Unfasten the oil pump cover and screen bolts and remove the cover and screen.
6. If necessary, remove the lower cylinder block shims.
7. If necessary, remove the lower cylinder block, the gasket and the crankshaft front oil seal.
8. Unfasten the oil pump retaining bolts, then remove the pump and gasket.

To install:

✳✳ WARNING

Do not use any abrasive grinding discs to remove gasket material. Use a plastic manual gasket scraper to remove the gasket residue. Be careful not to scratch or gouge the aluminum sealing surfaces when cleaning them.

9. Clean the gasket surfaces thoroughly until all traces of the old gasket residue are removed. Inspect the gasket mating surfaces, both must be clean, flat and dry.

➡ **The clearance between the lower cylinder block sealing surfaces on the oil pump and the cylinder block cannot exceed 0.012–0.031 inch (0.3–0.8mm).**

10. Install a new oil pump gasket and the pump.
11. Install and tighten the oil pump bolts to 88–97 inch. lbs. (10–11 Nm).
12. If removed, install the crankshaft front oil seal.
13. If removed, install the lower cylinder block and gasket. Tighten the lower cylinder block bolts to 15–17 ft. lbs. (20–24 Nm) in the sequence illustrated.
14. Install the oil pump screen cover and tube. Tighten the retaining bolts to 71–97 inch lbs. (8–11 Nm).

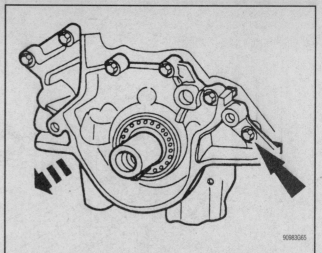

Fig. 145 Remove the oil pump mounting bolts, followed by the pump—2.0L DOHC engine

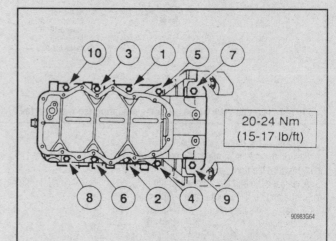

Fig. 146 Tighten the lower cylinder block bolts in the sequence illustrated—2.0L DOHC engine

15. Install the oil pan, timing chain guide, crankshaft sprocket and the pulley.
16. Lower the car, then install the timing belt and covers.
17. Fill the engine with the proper type and quantity of engine oil.
18. Start the car and check for oil leaks.

Crankshaft Damper

REMOVAL & INSTALLATION

1.8L Engine

▶ **See Figure 147**

The 1.8L engine does not use a crankshaft damper, but it does employ a conventional pulley.

1. Remove the drive belts.
2. Raise and support the front of the car with jackstands.
3. Remove the right-hand wheel.
4. Remove the right-hand front fender, engine and transaxle splash shields.

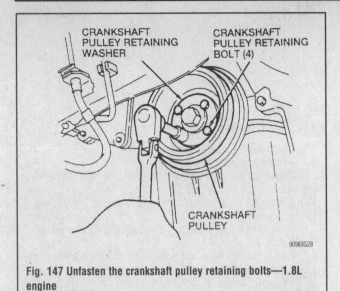

Fig. 147 Unfasten the crankshaft pulley retaining bolts—1.8L engine

Fig. 149 . . . and remove the crankshaft damper (pulley) bolt . . .

5. Remove the four crankshaft pulley retaining bolts and the retaining washer.

6. Remove the crankshaft pulley.

To install:

7. Place the crankshaft pulley and the retaining washer on the crankshaft.

8. Install the pulley retaining bolts and tighten them to 109–152 inch lbs. (12–17 Nm).

9. Install the splash shields and tighten the bolts to 69–95 inch lbs. (8–11 Nm).

10. Install the right-hand wheel.

11. Lower the car and install the drive belts.

1.9L Engine

▶ See Figures 148, 149 and 150

1. Disconnect the negative battery cable.
2. Remove the accessory drive belt.
3. Raise and safely support the vehicle.
4. Remove the right side front fender splash shield.
5. Remove the transmission cover.
6. Using a suitable tool to hold the flywheel, unfasten the crankshaft damper (pulley) bolt and washer.

Fig. 148 After immobilizing the flywheel, use a wrench to loosen . . .

Fig. 150 . . . then remove the crankshaft pulley from the engine

7. Remove the crankshaft pulley.

To install:

8. Position the damper on the crankshaft and install the retaining bolt and washer. Tighten to 81–96 ft. lbs. (110–130 Nm).

9. Install the splash shield and transmission cover.

10. Lower the vehicle.

11. Install the accessory drive belt.

12. Connect the negative battery cable.

2.0L Engine

1. Disconnect the negative battery cable.
2. Remove the accessory drive belt.
3. Raise and safely support the vehicle.
4. If equipped, remove the splash shield(s).
5. Unfasten the crankshaft pulley bolt and remove the pulley.

To install:

6. Install the pulley and the bolt. Tighten the bolt to 81–98 ft. lbs. (110–120 Nm).

7. If removed, install the splash shield(s).

8. Lower the car and install the drive belt.

9. Connect the negative battery cable.

Timing Belt Cover

REMOVAL & INSTALLATION

1.8L Engine

▶ **See Figure 151**

1. Disconnect the negative battery cable.
2. Unfasten the timing belt upper cover retaining bolts, then remove the timing belt upper cover and gasket.
3. Loosen the water pump pulley bolts.
4. Remove water pump/alternator drive belt.
5. Remove the water pump pulley bolts and the pulley.
6. Raise and safely support the vehicle.
7. Remove the right wheel and tire assembly.
8. Remove the right side front fender, engine and transaxle splash shields.
9. Remove the power steering and A/C (if equipped) drive belt.
10. If necessary, remove the crankshaft pulley, crankshaft pulley guide plate and timing belt outer and inner guide plates.
11. Unfasten the timing belt middle and lower covers, then remove the covers and the gaskets.

To install:

12. Install the timing belt middle and lower covers, along with the gaskets.
13. If removed, install the timing belt inner and outer guide plates, the crankshaft pulley and the crankshaft pulley guide plate. Tighten the bolts to 109–152 inch lbs. (12–17 Nm).
14. Install the air conditioning belt, if equipped, and power steering accessory drive belt.
15. Install the splash shields and tighten the bolts to 69–95 inch lbs. (8–11 Nm).
16. Install the water pump pulley and tighten the bolts to 69–95 inch lbs. (8–11 Nm).
17. Install the alternator and water pump accessory drive belt.
18. Install the right wheel and tire assembly and lower the vehicle.
19. Install the timing belt upper cover and gasket. Tighten the bolts to 69–95 inch lbs. (8–11 Nm).
20. Connect the negative battery cable.

1.9L Engine

▶ **See Figures 152 thru 162**

1. Disconnect the negative battery cable.
2. Remove the accessory drive belt(s).
3. Remove the drive belt automatic tensioner by unfastening the tensioner bolt.
4. To remove the tensioner, you may have to unfasten the A/C hose bracket and move the hose aside.
5. Using a block of wood, support the weight of the engine with a hydraulic jack.
6. Remove the right-hand front engine dynamic damper and support insulator and bracket retainers.
7. Remove the damper and the support insulator.
8. Unfasten the two timing belt cover attaching nuts and remove the timing belt cover from the mounting studs.

To install:

9. Position the timing belt cover on the mounting studs.
10. Install the attaching nuts and tighten to 3–5 ft. lbs. (5–7 Nm).
11. Install the support insulator bracket in position and tighten the bolt to 49–69 ft. lbs. (67–93 Nm).
12. Install the damper and tighten its retainers.
13. Install the drive belt automatic tensioner as follows:
    a. Make sure the locating pin on the tensioner is inserted in the hole on the alternator bracket as you install the tensioner.
    b. Install the tensioner bolt and tighten it to 30–41 ft. lbs. (40–55 Nm).

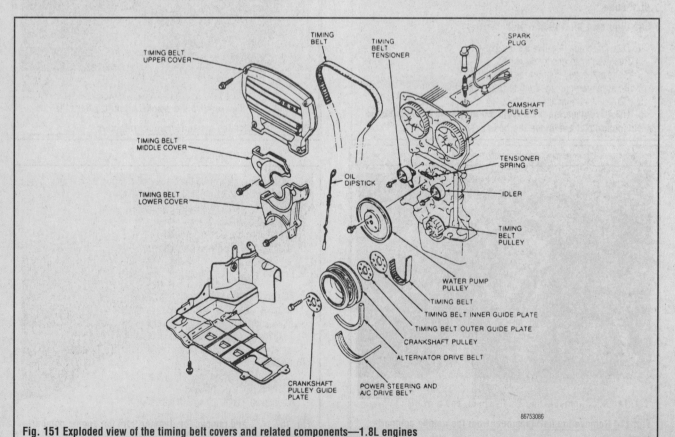

Fig. 151 Exploded view of the timing belt covers and related components—1.8L engines

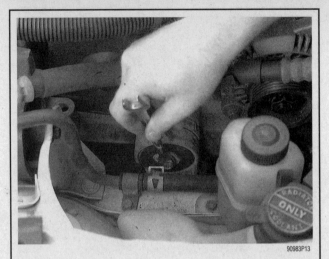

Fig. 152 Unfasten the drive belt automatic tensioner retaining bolt

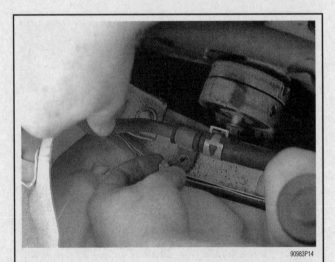

Fig. 153 To remove the tensioner, you may have to unfasten the A/C hose bracket and move the hose aside

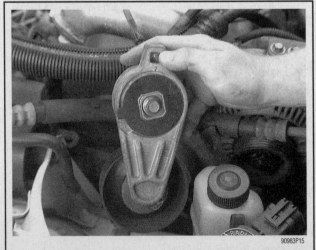

Fig. 154 Remove the belt tensioner from the engine compartment

Fig. 155 Using a block of wood, support the weight of the engine with a hydraulic jack

Fig. 156 Unfasten the dynamic damper retainers . . .

Fig. 157 . . . and remove the damper from the engine compartment

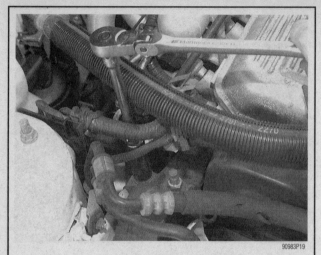

Fig. 158 Unfasten the right-hand support insulator-to-engine retainers

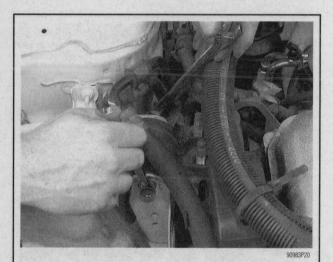

Fig. 159 Using two wrenches, unfasten the right-hand support insulator nut and bolt . . .

Fig. 160 . . . then remove the support insulator from the vehicle

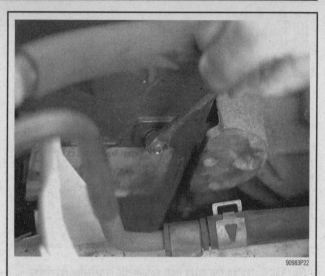

Fig. 161 Unfasten the timing cover retaining nuts

Fig. 162 Lift the timing cover up and off the engine block

14. If removed, place the A/C hose into position and fasten the bracket attaching bolt.
15. Install the drive belt.
16. Connect the negative battery cable.

2.0L Engine

SOHC ENGINE

1. Unfasten the three nuts and three bolts from the timing belt cover.
2. Remove the cover.
3. Installation is the reverse of removal.
4. Tighten the nuts and bolts to 71–97 inch lbs. (8–11 Nm).

DOHC ENGINE

1. Disconnect the negative battery cable.
2. Unfasten the upper timing belt cover bolts and remove the cover.
3. Loosen but do not remove the water pump pulley bolts and remove the drive belt.
4. Remove the idler pulley.
5. Remove the water pump pulley bolts and the pulley.
6. Raise the car and support it with safety stands.

7. Unfasten the middle timing cover bolts and remove the cover.

8. Remove the crankshaft pulley.

9. Unfasten the lower timing cover bolts and remove the cover.

To install:

10. Install the lower cover and bolts. Tighten the bolts to 62 inch lbs. (7 Nm).

11. Install the crankshaft pulley.

12. Install the middle timing cover and tighten the bolts to 9.5 ft. lbs. (13 Nm).

13. Lower the car and install the water pump pulley and finger-tighten the bolts.

14. Install the idler pulley and tighten the bolt to 35 ft. lbs. (48 Nm).

15. Install the drive belt and tighten the water pump pulley bolts to 17 ft. lbs. (23.5 Nm).

16. Install the upper timing cover and tighten the bolts to 27–44 inch lbs. (3–5 Nm).

17. Connect the negative battery cable.

Timing Belt

REMOVAL & INSTALLATION

1.8L Engine

▶ **See Figures 163, 164, 165 and 166**

1. Disconnect the negative battery cable.

2. Remove the timing belt covers.

3. Rotate the crankshaft and align the timing marks located on the camshaft pulleys and the seal plate.

4. Remove the crankshaft pulley and hub.

5. If the timing belt is to be reused, mark an arrow on the belt to indicate its rotational direction to enable correct re-installation.

6. Loosen the timing belt tensioner lockbolt and remove the timing belt.

To install:

7. Temporarily secure the timing belt tensioner in the far left position with the spring fully extended, then tighten the lockbolt.

8. Make sure the timing marks on the timing belt pulley (crankshaft sprocket) and the engine block (oil pump housing) are aligned.

9. Make sure the timing marks on the camshaft pulleys and the seal plate are aligned.

10. Install the timing belt.

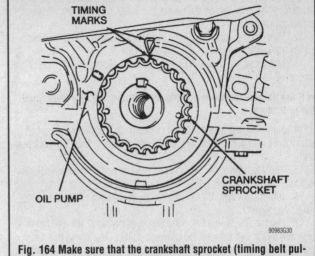

Fig. 164 Make sure that the crankshaft sprocket (timing belt pulley) and oil pump timing marks are aligned—1.8L engines

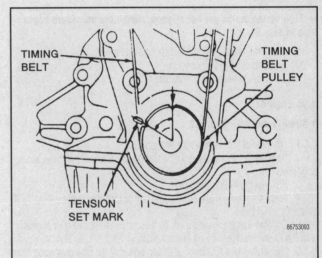

Fig. 165 Align the timing belt pulley mark with the tension set mark, at approximately the 10 o'clock position—1.8L engines

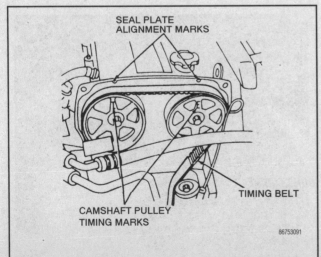

Fig. 163 Timing marks are located on the camshaft pulleys as shown—1.8L engines

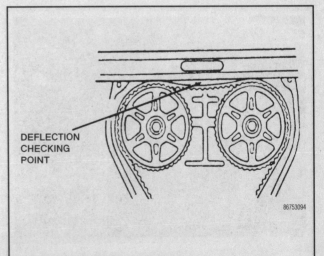

Fig. 166 Check the timing belt deflection at the location shown—1.8L engines

11. Loosen the tensioner lockbolt. Using a suitable prying tool, position the timing belt tensioner so the timing belt is taut, then tighten the tensioner lockbolt.

12. Turn the crankshaft two turns clockwise and align the timing belt pulley mark with the mark on the engine block.

13. Make sure the camshaft pulley marks are aligned with the seal plate marks.

➡ If the timing marks are not aligned, remove the belt and repeat the procedure.

14. Turn the crankshaft 1⅚ turns clockwise and align the timing belt pulley mark with the tension set mark, at approximately the 10 o'clock position.

15. Apply tension to the timing belt tensioner and install the tensioner lockbolt. Tighten the bolt to 27–38 ft. lbs. (37–52 Nm).

16. Turn the crankshaft 2⅙ turns clockwise and make sure the timing marks are aligned.

17. Measure the timing belt deflection by applying 22 lbs. (10 kg) of pressure on the belt between the camshaft pulleys. The timing belt deflection should be 0.35–0.45 in. (9.0–11.5mm). If necessary, adjust the timing belt deflection.

18. Turn the crankshaft two turns clockwise and make sure the timing marks are aligned.

➡ If the timing marks are not aligned, repeat the procedure beginning at Step 9.

19. Install the crankshaft pulley hub, bolt and pulley.

20. Install the timing belt covers.

21. Connect the negative battery cable.

1.9L Engine

▶ See Figures 167 thru 172

1. Disconnect the negative battery cable.

2. Remove the accessory drive belt automatic tensioner and the accessory drive belt.

3. Remove the timing belt cover.

4. Align the timing mark on the camshaft sprocket with the timing mark on the cylinder head.

5. Confirm that the timing mark on the crankshaft sprocket is aligned with the timing mark on the oil pump housing.

6. Loosen the belt tensioner attaching bolt, pry the tensioner away from the timing belt and retighten the bolt.

7. Remove the spark plugs.

Fig. 168 Confirm that the timing mark on the crankshaft sprocket is aligned with the timing mark on the oil pump housing

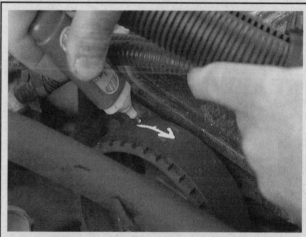

Fig. 169 If reinstalling the old timing belt, mark the direction of belt rotation; this will aid during installation

Fig. 167 Align the timing mark on the camshaft sprocket (arrow) with the timing mark on the cylinder head

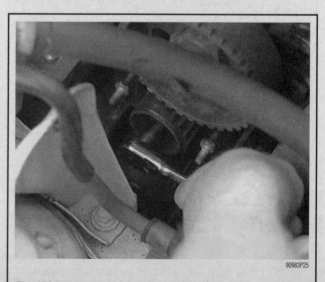

Fig. 170 Loosen the belt tensioner attaching bolt

Fig. 171 Pry the tensioner away from the timing belt and retighten the bolt, then slide the belt off the pulleys

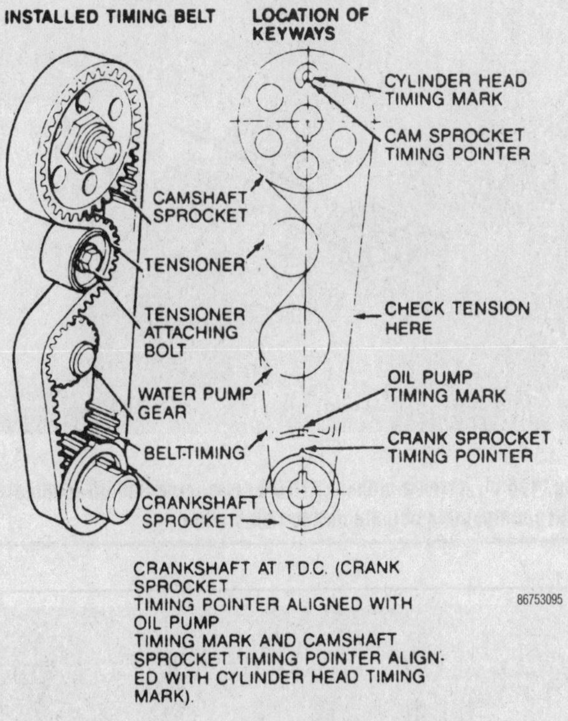

INSTALLED TIMING BELT

LOCATION OF KEYWAYS

CYLINDER HEAD TIMING MARK

CAM SPROCKET TIMING POINTER

CAMSHAFT SPROCKET

TENSIONER

CHECK TENSION HERE

TENSIONER ATTACHING BOLT

WATER PUMP GEAR

OIL PUMP TIMING MARK

BELT-TIMING

CRANK SPROCKET TIMING POINTER

CRANKSHAFT SPROCKET

CRANKSHAFT AT T.D.C. (CRANK SPROCKET TIMING POINTER ALIGNED WITH OIL PUMP TIMING MARK AND CAMSHAFT SPROCKET TIMING POINTER ALIGNED WITH CYLINDER HEAD TIMING MARK).

86753095

Fig. 172 Timing belt installation guide and alignment marks—1.9L engines

8. Remove the right-hand engine mount.
9. Raise and safely support the vehicle.
10. Remove the right side splash shield.
11. Remove the crankshaft pulley.
12. Remove the timing belt.

➡With the timing belt removed and the No. 1 piston at TDC, do not rotate the camshaft.

To install:

➡Do not mix ½ round and trapezoidal belt tooth profiles, this would cause premature belt wear. Also no belt dressing or oil should be used on the belt.

13. Install the timing belt over the sprockets in a counterclockwise direction starting at the crankshaft. Keep the belt span from the crankshaft to the camshaft tight while positioning the belt over the remaining sprockets.
14. Loosen the belt tensioner attaching bolt, then allow the tensioner to snap against the belt.
15. Rotate the crankshaft clockwise two complete revolutions (720 degrees) stopping at TDC. This will allow the tensioner spring to properly load the timing belt.

➡Do not turn the engine counterclockwise to align the timing marks.

16. Tighten the tensioner attaching bolt to 17–22 ft. lbs. (23–30 Nm).
17. Install the crankshaft dampener and the bolt and washer. Tighten the bolt to 81–96 ft. lbs. (110–130 Nm).
18. Install the right-hand engine mount.
19. Install the splash shield and lower the vehicle.
20. Install the spark plugs.
21. Install the timing belt cover.
22. Install the accessory drive belt automatic tensioner and the accessory drive belt.
23. Connect the negative battery cable.

2.0L Engine

SOHC ENGINE

▶ See Figures 173 and 174

1. Remove the drive belt and timing cover.
2. Raise the car and support it with safety stands.
3. Remove the right-hand splash shield and the crankshaft pulley.
4. Align the timing marks as illustrated in the accompanying illustration.
5. Refer to the accompanying illustration and remove the timing belt as follows:
  a. Loosen the timing belt tensioner bolt (1).
  b. Use an 8mm Allen wrench, and turn the tensioner (2) counterclockwise ¼ turn.
  c. Insert a ⅛ inch drill bit in the hole (3) to lock the belt tensioner in place.
  d. Remove the timing belt (4).
  e. Inspect the belt for damage and signs of oil leakage.

To install:

➡Install the timing belt over the sprocket in a counterclockwise direction starting at the crankshaft. Keep the belt span between the crankshaft and camshaft tight when installing the belt over the camshaft.

6. Install the timing belt and remove the drill bit.
7. Tighten the tensioner bolt to 15–22 ft. lbs. (20–30 Nm).
8. Rotate the engine two complete revolutions and make sure the timing marks are aligned.
9. Install the timing belt cover and crankshaft pulley.
10. Install the right-hand splash shield and the drive belt.
11. Start the car and check for proper operation.

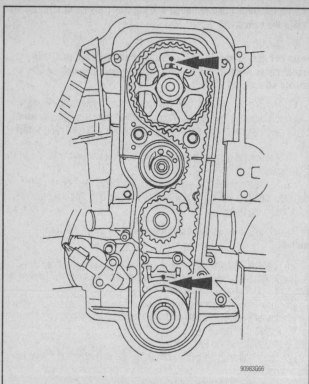

Fig. 173 The timing marks on both the camshaft and crankshaft pulleys must be aligned like this before removing or installing the timing belt—2.0L SOHC engines

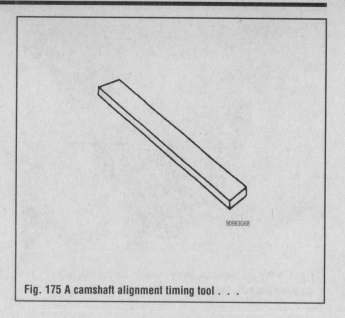

Fig. 175 A camshaft alignment timing tool . . .

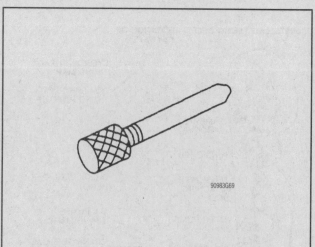

Fig. 176 . . . and a crankshaft TDC timing peg tool are required when removing and installing the timing belt

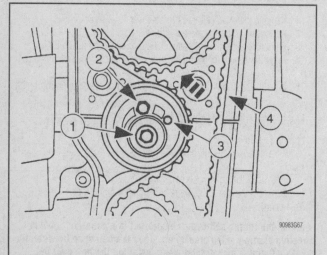

Fig. 174 Remove the timing belt by following these 4 numbered steps (refer to the text for an explanation)—2.0L SOHC engine

DOHC ENGINE

▶ See Figures 175 thru 183

➡A camshaft alignment timing tool (No. T94P-6256-CH or equivalent) and a crankshaft Top Dead Center (TDC) timing peg tool (No. T97P-6000-A or equivalent) are required for this procedure.

➡Make sure the correct notch in the pulley is indexed to the lower cylinder block. Refer to the accompanying illustration.

1. Remove the spark plugs.
2. Rotate the crankshaft to TDC.

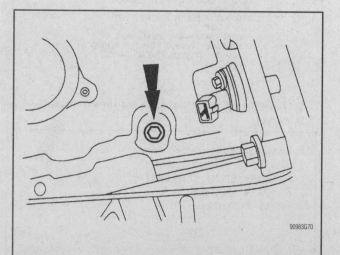

Fig. 177 Remove the plug bolt by the Crankshaft Position (CKP) sensor and install the TDC timing peg

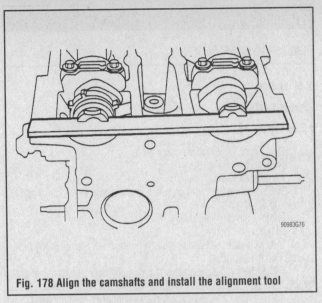

Fig. 178 Align the camshafts and install the alignment tool

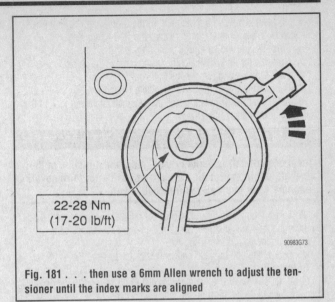

Fig. 181 . . . then use a 6mm Allen wrench to adjust the tensioner until the index marks are aligned

22-28 Nm
(17-20 lb/ft)

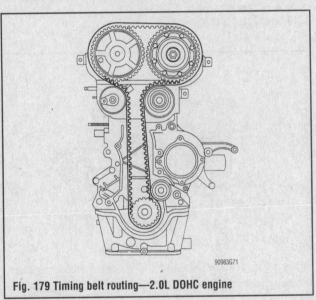

Fig. 179 Timing belt routing—2.0L DOHC engine

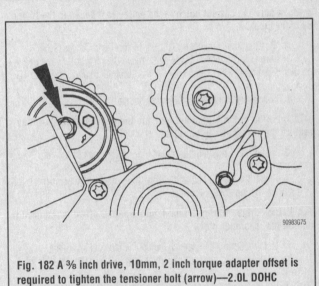

Fig. 182 A ⅜ inch drive, 10mm, 2 inch torque adapter offset is required to tighten the tensioner bolt (arrow)—2.0L DOHC engine

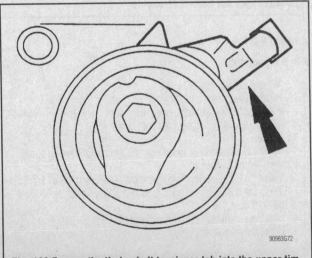

Fig. 180 Engage the timing belt tensioner tab into the upper timing cover backplate . . .

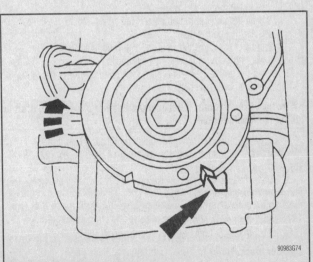

Fig. 183 Rotate the crankshaft clockwise against the TDC alignment peg

3. Locate and remove the plug bolt by the Crankshaft Position (CKP) sensor (refer to the illustration) and install the TDC timing peg.

4. Raise the car and support it with safety stands.

5. Unfasten the splash shields bolts and remove the shield.

6. Lower the car and remove the water pump pulley.

7. Remove the valve cover and the timing belt covers.

8. Align the camshafts and install the camshaft alignment tool on the back of the camshafts as illustrated.

✳✳ WARNING

If the camshaft belt is being reused, mark the direction of the camshaft belt to the rotation of the camshaft prior to removal, or premature wear and belt failure could occur.

9. Loosen the tensioner pulley bolt and relieve the tension on the belt by disconnecting the tensioner tab from the timing cover back plate.

10. Slide the belt off the sprockets.

11. Inspect the belt for wear and replace as necessary.

To install:

12. If, for any reason, the engine was disturbed, the camshafts moved or the sprockets replaced, perform the following procedure:

➡**Make sure the correct notch in the pulley is indexed to the lower cylinder block.**

a. Position the crankshaft just prior to Top Dead Center (TDC).

b. If not already done, locate and remove the plug bolt by the Crankshaft Position (CKP) sensor (refer to the illustration) and install the TDC timing peg.

c. Rotate the crankshaft clockwise against the TDC peg.

➡**Installation of the alignment tool into the exhaust camshaft may require the camshafts to be rotated clockwise.**

d. Install the camshaft alignment tool on the back of the camshafts.

e. Install the timing belt and engage the timing belt tensioner tab into the upper timing cover backplate.

➡**A ⅜ inch drive, 10mm, 2 inch torque adapter offset is required to tighten the tensioner bolt.**

f. Using a 6mm Allen wrench, adjust the tensioner until the index marks are aligned and tighten the bolt to 17–20 ft. lbs. (22–28 Nm).

g. Rotate the crankshaft clockwise against the TDC alignment peg, then remove the camshaft alignment tool.

h. Remove the TDC peg tool and install the plug bolt.

i. Install the timing and valve covers.

j. Install the water pump pulley and the splash shield.

k. Install the spark plugs.

If the engine or the camshaft were not disturbed in any way, or the sprockets were not removed, perform the following procedure:

13. Install the timing belt and engage the timing belt tensioner tab into the upper timing cover backplate.

➡**A ⅜ inch drive, 10mm, 2 inch torque adapter offset is required to tighten the tensioner bolt.**

14. Using a 6mm Allen wrench, adjust the tensioner until the index marks are aligned and tighten the bolt to 17–20 ft. lbs. (22–28 Nm).

15. Rotate the crankshaft clockwise against the TDC alignment peg, then remove the camshaft alignment tool.

16. Remove the TDC peg tool and install the plug bolt.

17. Install the timing and valve covers.

18. Install the water pump pulley and the splash shield.

19. Install the spark plugs.

Timing Sprockets

REMOVAL & INSTALLATION

1.8L Engine

CAMSHAFT(S)

◆ **See Figure 184**

1. Disconnect the negative battery cable.

2. Remove the timing belt.

3. Remove the valve cover.

4. While holding the camshaft with a wrench, remove the camshaft sprocket lockbolt.

5. Remove the camshaft pulley.

To install:

6. Install the camshaft pulley with the timing mark aligned to the timing mark on the seal plate.

7. While holding the camshaft with a wrench, install the camshaft pulley lockbolt. Tighten the bolt to 36–45 ft. lbs. (49–61 Nm).

8. Install a new cylinder head cover gasket onto the cylinder head.

9. Install the valve cover.

10. Install the timing belt.

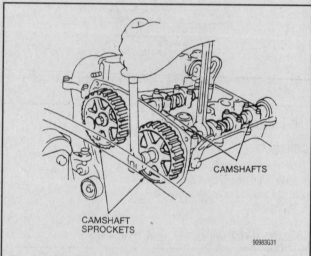

Fig. 184 While holding the camshaft with a wrench, remove the camshaft sprocket bolt—1.8L engine

CRANKSHAFT

◆ **See Figure 185**

1. Remove the crankshaft pulley.

2. Remove the crankshaft pulley bolt and hub.

3. If necessary, use a suitable puller to remove crankshaft sprocket.

4. Remove the Woodruff key from the crankshaft.

To install:

5. Install the crankshaft sprocket onto the shaft while making sure to match the alignment grooves.

6. Install the Woodruff key with the tapered end facing the oil pump.

7. Install the crankshaft sprocket locking bolt and tighten to 80–87 ft. lbs. (108–118 Nm).

8. Install the crankshaft pulley hub and bolt.

9. Install the crankshaft pulley.

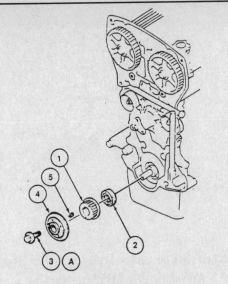

Item	Description
1	Crankshaft Sprocket
2	Crankshaft Front Seal
3	Crankshaft Pulley Bolt
4	Crankshaft Pulley Hub
5	Crankshaft Key
A	Tighten to 108-118 N·m (80-87 Lb-Ft)

90983G32

Fig. 185 Exploded view of the crankshaft sprocket assembly—1.8L engine

1.9L Engine

CAMSHAFT

1. Remove the timing belt.
2. Remove the camshaft sprocket lockbolt.
3. Remove the camshaft sprocket.
To install:
4. Install the camshaft sprocket and tighten the retaining bolt to 70–85 ft. lbs. (95–115 Nm).
5. Install the timing belt.

CRANKSHAFT

▶ See Figure 186

1. Remove the timing belt.
2. Remove the crankshaft damper.
3. Remove the crankshaft sprocket.
4. Installation is the reverse of removal.

2.0L SOHC Engine

CAMSHAFT

Perform the timing drive components' timing alignment procedure (as described elsewhere in this section) after removing the sprockets.
1. Align the timing marks and remove the timing belt.
2. Using a camshaft sprocket holding/removing tool, unfasten the camshaft sprocket bolt.
3. Remove the sprocket bolt, washer and sprocket.
To install:
4. Install the camshaft sprocket, washer and bolt. Tighten the bolt to 70–80 ft. lbs. (95–115 Nm).
5. Install the timing belt.

CRANKSHAFT

Perform the timing drive components timing alignment adjustment procedure in this section after removing the sprockets.
1. Remove the timing belt.
2. Remove the crankshaft pulley.
3. Remove the crankshaft sprocket.
4. Installation is the reverse of removal.

Fig. 186 Removing the crankshaft sprocket

2.0L DOHC Engine

CAMSHAFT(S)

1. Remove the timing belt.

✳✳ WARNING

Do not use the camshaft alignment tool to hold the camshafts in position while loosening the camshaft sprocket bolts.

2. Using an open wrench to keep the intake camshaft from turning, loosen the intake camshaft sprocket bolt and remove the sprocket.
3. Using an open wrench to keep the exhaust camshaft from turning, remove the Variable Camshaft Timing (VCT) oil plug, unfasten the sprocket bolt and remove the sprocket.
To install:
4. Using an open wrench to keep the intake camshaft from turning, install intake camshaft sprocket. Finger tighten the bolt.
5. Rotate the oil control bushing one full turn and inspect it for binding. Position the bushing with the single hole at the 12 o'clock position.
6. Install a new O-ring into the exhaust sprocket.

✳✳ WARNING

The VCT sprocket has a rectangular tab on the backside of the sprocket which has to align with the hole on the front face of the thrust bushing. Failure to align the tab will result in poor engine performance.

7. Using an open wrench to keep the exhaust camshaft from turning, install the sprocket, (VCT) oil plug and bolt. Finger tighten the bolt.
8. Install the timing belt.
9. Tighten the intake camshaft sprocket bolt to 48–53 ft. lbs. (64–72 Nm).
10. Tighten the exhaust camshaft sprocket bolt to 88 ft. lbs. (120 Nm) and the oil plug to 26–30 ft. lbs. (35–40 Nm).

CRANKSHAFT

1. Remove the timing belt.
2. Remove the crankshaft pulley.
3. Remove the crankshaft sprocket.
4. Installation is the reverse of removal.

Crankshaft Front Oil Seal

REMOVAL & INSTALLATION

1.8L Engine

▶ **See Figure 187**

1. Disconnect the negative battery cable.
2. Remove the crankshaft sprocket.
3. If necessary, cut the lip of the front oil seal with a razor to ease removal.
4. Use seal removal tool T92C-6700-CH or its equivalent to remove the seal.

To install:

5. Lubricate the lip of the new oil seal with clean engine oil.
6. Using crankshaft front seal replacer T88C-6701-AH or equivalent tool, install the seal evenly until it is flush with the edge of the oil pump body.
7. Install the crankshaft sprocket.
8. Connect the negative battery cable.

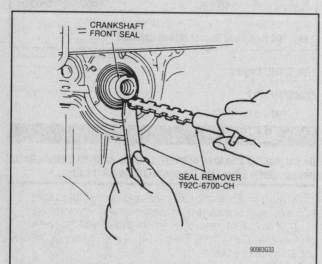

Fig. 187 Use an appropriate seal removal tool to remove the crankshaft front oil seal—1.8L engine

1.9L Engine

▶ **See Figure 188**

1. Disconnect the negative battery cable.
2. Remove the accessory drive belt.
3. Raise and safely support the vehicle.
4. Remove the right side splash shield.
5. Remove the transmission housing cover.
6. Use a suitable tool to hold the flywheel in place.
7. Remove the crankshaft dampener.
8. Remove the timing belt.
9. Remove the crankshaft sprocket and belt guide.
10. Using a seal removal tool T92C-6700-CH or equivalent, remove the crankshaft seal from the oil pump body.

To install:

11. Install the new seal using seal installation tool T81P-6700-A or equivalent.

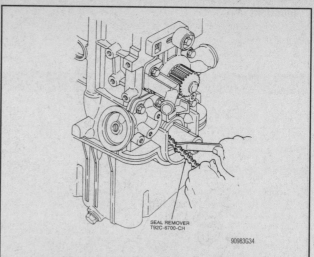

Fig. 188 Removing the front crankshaft oil seal using tool T92C-6700-CH or equivalent—1.9L engine

12. Install the belt guide and crankshaft sprocket.
13. Install the timing belt.
14. Install the crankshaft dampener.
15. Remove the flywheel holding tool and install the transmission housing cover.
16. Install the right splash shield and lower the vehicle.
17. Install the accessory drive belt.
18. Connect the negative battery cable.
19. Start the engine and check for leaks.

2.0L Engines

▶ **See Figure 189**

1. Remove the timing belt and crankshaft sprocket.

✳✳ CAUTION

Be careful not to damage the crankshaft surface when removing the seal.

2. Using seal remover tool T92C-6700-CH or its equivalent, remove the crankshaft front oil seal.

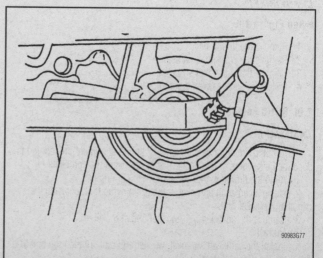

Fig. 189 Use an appropriate tool to remove the crankshaft front oil seal—2.0L engines

To install:

3. Using seal replacer tool T81P-6700-A or its equivalent, install the new seal.

4. Install the crankshaft sprocket and the timing belt.

Camshaft(s)

REMOVAL & INSTALLATION

1.8L Engine

♦ See Figures 190, 191, 192 and 193

1. Disconnect the negative battery cable.
2. Remove the distributor assembly.
3. Remove the camshaft sprockets.
4. Unbolt the seal plate mounting bolts and remove the seal plate.
5. Loosen the camshaft cap bolts in the correct sequence (see accompanying illustration).
6. Remove the camshaft caps and note their mounting locations for installation reference.

➡ The camshaft caps are numbered and have arrow marks for installation and direction reference.

7. Remove the camshaft and camshaft oil seal.

To install:

8. Apply clean engine oil to the camshaft journals and bearings.
9. Place the camshaft into its mounting position.

➡ The exhaust camshaft has a groove which must be aligned with the distributor drive gear.

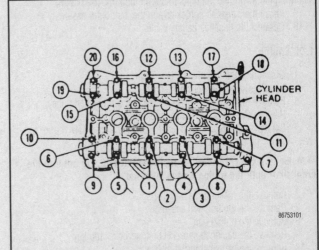

Fig. 192 Tighten the cap bolts in the sequence shown—1.8L engines

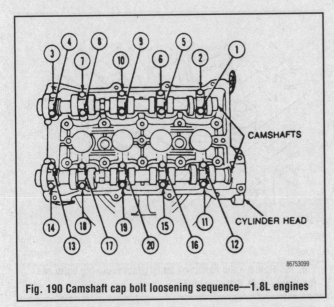

Fig. 190 Camshaft cap bolt loosening sequence—1.8L engines

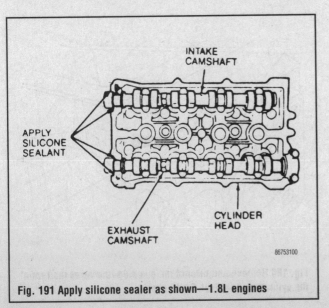

Fig. 191 Apply silicone sealer as shown—1.8L engines

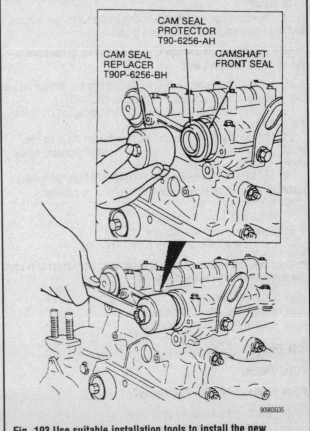

Fig. 193 Use suitable installation tools to install the new camshaft seal

10. Apply silicone sealant to the required areas (see accompanying illustration).

11. Install the camshaft caps according to the cap numbers and arrow marks.

12. Install the camshaft cap bolts and tighten them in the proper sequence to 100–126 inch lbs. (11–14 Nm).

13. Apply a small amount of clean engine oil to the lip of a new camshaft oil seal. Using a suitable installation tool, install the new seal. Refer to the accompanying illustration.

14. Place the seal plate into its mounting position and install the mounting bolts. Tighten the bolts to 69–95 inch lbs. (8–11 Nm).

15. Install the camshaft sprockets and the distributor assembly.

16. Connect the negative battery cable.

1.9L Engine

1. Disconnect the negative battery cable.
2. Remove the air cleaner intake duct.
3. Remove the accessory drive belts and the crankshaft pulley.
4. Remove the timing belt cover and the rocker arm cover.
5. Set the engine No. 1 cylinder at Top Dead Center (TDC) prior to removing the timing belt.

➡ **Make sure the crankshaft is positioned at TDC. Do not turn the crankshaft until the timing belt is installed.**

6. Remove the rocker arms and lifters.
7. Remove the ignition coil assembly.
8. Remove the timing belt.
9. Remove the camshaft sprocket bolt, sprocket and key.
10. Remove the camshaft thrust plate.
11. Remove the cup plug from the back of the cylinder head.
12. Remove the camshaft through the back of the head toward the transaxle.
13. Remove and discard the camshaft seal.

To install:

14. Thoroughly coat the camshaft bearing journals, cam lobe surfaces and thrust plate groove with a suitable lubricant.

➡ **Before installing the camshaft, apply a thin film of lubricant to the lip of the camshaft seal.**

15. Install a new camshaft seal and install the camshaft through the rear of the cylinder head. Rotate the camshaft during installation.

16. Install the camshaft thrust plate. Tighten attaching bolts to 6–9 ft. lbs. (8–13 Nm).

17. Align and install the cam sprocket over the cam key. Install the attaching washer and bolt. While holding the camshaft stationary, tighten the bolt to 70–85 ft. lbs. (95–115 Nm).

18. Install the cup plug using a sealer EOAZ-19554-BA. Use the sealer sparingly, as excess sealer may clog the oil holes in the camshaft.

19. Install the timing belt.
20. Install the timing belt cover.
21. Install the ignition coil assembly.
22. Install a new rocker arm cover gasket, if required.

➡ **Make sure the surfaces on the cylinder head and rocker arm cover are clean and free of sealant material.**

23. Install the valve cover.
24. Install the air cleaner intake tube.
25. Connect the negative battery cable.

2.0L Engine

SOHC ENGINE

▸ **See Figures 194, 195, 196 and 197**

1. Disconnect the negative battery cable.
2. Remove the air cleaner and valve cover.
3. Remove the camshaft front seal as follows:

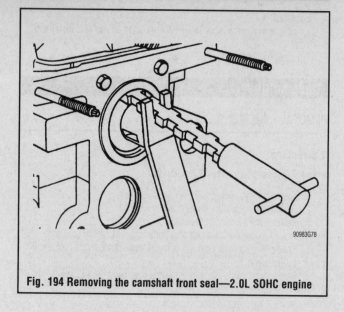

Fig. 194 Removing the camshaft front seal—2.0L SOHC engine

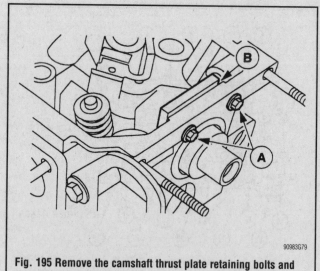

Fig. 195 Remove the camshaft thrust plate retaining bolts and the plate—2.0L SOHC engine

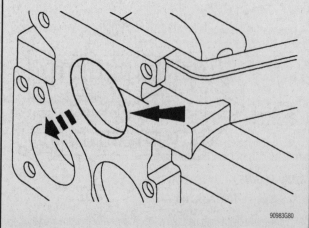

Fig. 196 Remove and discard the cup plug located at the rear of the cylinder head—2.0L SOHC engine

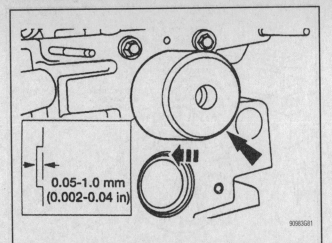

Fig. 197 Using an appropriate seal replacement tool, install the camshaft front seal 0.002–0.04 inch (0.05–1.0mm) below the cylinder head's front face—2.0L SOHC engine

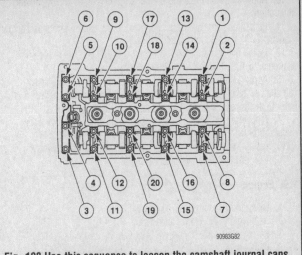

Fig. 198 Use this sequence to loosen the camshaft journal caps in several two-turn passes—2.0L DOHC engine

a. Align the timing marks and remove the timing belt.

b. Use cam sprocket holding/removing tool T74P-6256-B or its equivalent, and remove the camshaft sprocket.

c. Unfasten the timing belt tensioner bolt and remove the tensioner.

d. Remove the inner engine front cover.

e. Use seal removal tool T92C-6700-CH or its equivalent to remove the camshaft front seal.

4. Remove the ignition coil and bracket.

5. Remove the rocker arms and valve tappets.

6. Unfasten the camshaft thrust plate bolts and remove the plate.

7. Remove and discard the cup plug from the rear of the cylinder head.

8. Carefully remove the camshaft from the rear of the cylinder head.

To install:

➡Liberally coat the cam bore in the cylinder with clean 5W-30 motor oil.

9. Install the camshaft through the rear of the cylinder head.

10. Install the camshaft thrust plate and the bolts. Tighten the bolts to 71–115 inch lbs. (8–13 Nm).

11. Install a new cup plug and the tappets.

12. Install the rocker arms.

13. Install the ignition coil bracket and coil.

14. Install the camshaft front seal as follows:

a. Apply a thin film of 5W-30 motor oil to the lip of the seal.

➡The seal depth should be 0.002–0.04 inch (0.05–1.0mm) below flush with the cylinder head front face.

b. Use seal replacer T81P-6292-A or equivalent to install the camshaft front seal.

c. Install the inner engine front cover.

d. Install the timing belt tensioner. Tighten the tensioner bolt to 15–22 ft. lbs. (20–30 Nm).

e. Install the camshaft sprocket and the timing belt

15. Install the valve cover and the air cleaner assembly.

16. Connect the negative battery cable.

DOHC ENGINE

◢ **See Figures 198, 199 and 200**

1. Remove the timing belt, valve cover and camshaft sprockets.

➡It may be necessary to rotate the oil control solenoid flange 90° prior to removal.

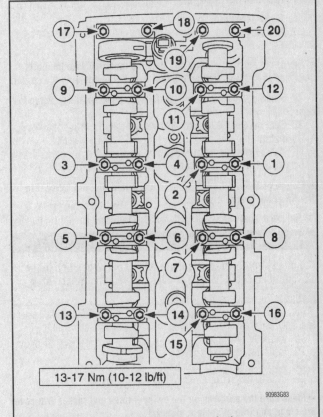

13-17 Nm (10-12 lb/ft)

Fig. 199 Tighten the camshaft journal caps in the sequence illustrated to the proper specification—2.0L DOHC engine

2. Unfasten the oil control solenoid flange bolts and remove the flange.

➡Mark the camshaft journal caps with a number to identify their location as they must be replaced in their original position.

3. Loosen the camshaft journal caps in several two turn passes in the sequence illustrated, then remove the bolts and caps.

4. Remove the camshafts from the cylinder head.

5. Remove the oil control sensor and bushing.

6. Inspect the camshafts for damage and wear.

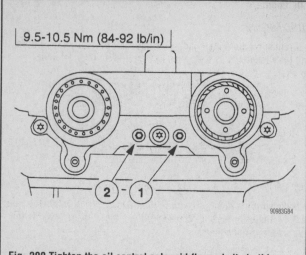

Fig. 200 Tighten the oil control solenoid flange bolts in this sequence—2.0L DOHC engine

9.5-10.5 Nm (84-92 lb/in)

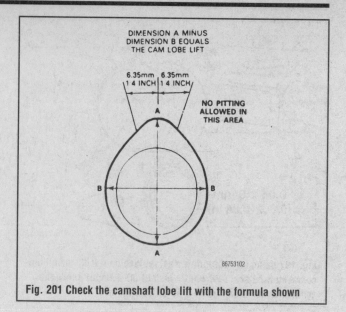

DIMENSION A MINUS DIMENSION B EQUALS THE CAM LOBE LIFT

6.35mm 1 4 INCH   6.35mm 1 4 INCH

NO PITTING ALLOWED IN THIS AREA

Fig. 201 Check the camshaft lobe lift with the formula shown

To install:

7. Make sure the valve clearance is correct. Refer to Section 1 of this manual for the procedure.

8. Install the oil control solenoid bushing and flange on the exhaust camshaft.

➡ The front camshaft journal cap must be installed with the bolts tightened to specification within four minutes of applying the sealer.

9. Coat the surface of the front camshaft journal cap with gasket maker E2AZ-19562-B or its equivalent.

10. Place the camshafts in position and lubricate the bearing surfaces with engine assembly lubricant D9AZ-19579-D or its equivalent.

11. Install new camshaft front oil seals.

12. Apply a thin coat of silicone gasket and sealant F6AZ-19562-AA or its equivalent to the sealing surface of the of the front camshaft journal bearing cap.

13. Install the caps and tighten the bolts in several two turn passes in the sequence illustrated to 10–12 ft. lbs. (13–17 Nm).

✳✳ WARNING

The oil control O-ring seals must not fall out of position in the oil control solenoid flange, or poor engine performance may occur.

14. Inspect the oil control solenoid flange O-rings for damage or wear and replace as necessary.

15. Install the oil control solenoid flange and tighten the bolts to 84–92 inch lbs. (9.5–10.5 Nm) in the sequence illustrated.

16. Rotate the camshafts a full turn and check for binding.

17. Install the camshaft sprockets and timing belt.

18. Install the valve cover.

INSPECTION

▶ See Figures 201, 202 and 203

Degrease the camshaft using safe solvent, clean all oil grooves. Visually inspect the cam lobes and bearing journals for excessive wear. If a lobe is questionable, check all lobes and journals with a micrometer.

Measure the lobes from nose to base and again at 90°. The lift is determined by subtracting the second measurement from the first. If all exhaust lobes and all intake lobes are not identical, the camshaft must be reground or replaced. Measure the bearing journals and compare to the specifications. If a journal is worn there is a good chance that the cam bearings are worn too, requiring replacement.

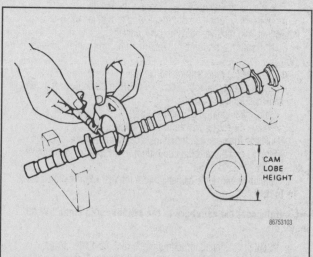

CAM LOBE HEIGHT

Fig. 202 Measure the camshaft lobe height using a precision micrometer

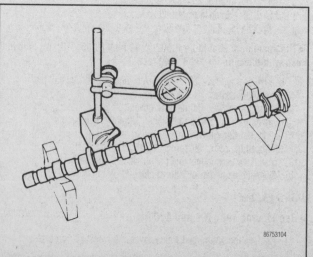

Fig. 203 To measure camshaft run-out, revolve the shaft and measure with a dial indicator

If the lobes and journals appear intact, place the front and rear camshaft journals in V-blocks and rest a dial indicator on the center journal. Rotate the camshaft to check for straightness, if deviation exceeds 0.001 in. (0.025mm), replace the camshaft.

Valve Lifters

All engines covered in this manual, except the 2.0L DOHC engine, employ hydraulic (oil pressurized) valve lifters. These lifters operate more quietly and do not require periodic adjustments.

For the 2.0L DOHC engine's valve clearance adjustment, refer to Section 1 of this manual.

REMOVAL & INSTALLATION

1.8L Engine

1. Disconnect the negative battery cable.
2. Remove the camshafts.
3. Mark the hydraulic lash adjusters and the cylinder head with alignment marks so the hydraulic lash adjusters can be installed in their original positions.
4. Remove the hydraulic lash adjusters from the cylinder head.

To install:

5. Apply clean engine oil to the hydraulic lash adjuster friction surfaces.
6. If the hydraulic lash adjusters are being reused, install them in the positions from which they were removed.
7. Make sure the hydraulic lash adjusters move smoothly in their bores.
8. Install the camshafts.
9. Connect the negative battery cable.

1.9L Engines

1. Disconnect the negative battery cable.
2. Remove rocker arm cover and gasket.
3. Remove the rocker arms.
4. Remove the lifer valve guides plates, retainers and the eight lifters.

➡ **Always return the lifters to their original bores unless they are being replaced.**

5. Lubricate each lifter bore with clean engine oil.
6. If equipped with flat bottom lifters, install with the oil hole in the plunger upward. If equipped with roller lifters, install with the plunger upward and position the guide flats of lifters to be parallel with the centerline of the camshaft. The color orientation dots on the lifters should be opposite the oil feed holes in the cylinder head.
7. For roller lifters only, install the lifter guide plates over the tappet guide flats with the notch toward the exhaust side. For flat lifters, no guide plate is required.
8. Lubricate the lifter plunger cap and valve tip with engine oil.
9. Install the lifter guide plate retainers into rocker arm fulcrum slots, in both the intake and exhaust side. Align the notch to be with the exhaust valve lifter.
10. Install four rocker arms in lifter position Nos. 3, 6, 7 and 8.
11. Lubricate the rocker arm surface that will contact the fulcrum surface with engine oil.
12. Install four fulcrums. The fulcrums must be fully seated in the slots of cylinder head.
13. Install four bolts. Tighten to 17–22 ft. lbs. (23–30 Nm).
14. Rotate the engine until the camshaft sprocket keyway is in the 6 o'clock position.
15. Repeat steps 9–12 in lifter position Nos. 1, 2, 4 and 5.
16. Install the rocker arm cover and gasket. Install the air cleaner assembly.
17. Connect the negative battery cable.

2.0L Engine

SOHC ENGINE

➡ **If removing more than one valve lifter (tappet), mark the lifters and their locations as they must be installed in their original bores.**

1. Remove the valve cover and the rocker arm(s).
2. Unfasten the lifter guide plate retainer.
3. Remove the guide plate and the lifter.

To install:

4. The oil feed hole in the lifter must face away from the oil feed hole in the cylinder head.
5. Lubricate the lifter(s) with clean 5W-30 engine oil and install them in their original bores.

➡ **Make sure the lifter guide plate retainer tabs are towards the rear of the cylinder head, and the lifter guide plate tabs are towards the front of the cylinder head.**

6. Install the lifter guide plate and tighten the retainer.
7. Install the rocker arm and the valve cover.

DOHC ENGINE

➡ **If the camshafts and lifters are to be reused, mark the lifters and their locations as they must be installed in their original bores.**

1. Remove the camshafts.
2. Remove the lifters from the cylinder head.

To install:

3. Lubricate the lifter(s) with clean 5W-30 engine oil and install them in their original bores.
4. Install the camshafts.

INSPECTION

1. Throughly clean the lifter and its bore, then check for pitting, scoring or excessive wear.
2. On flat lifters, the bottom should be flat and not concave.
3. If equipped with a roller, the roller should rotate freely without excessive play.

Rear Main Seal

REMOVAL & INSTALLATION

1.8L engines

▶ **See Figures 204, 205 and 206**

1. Remove the flywheel (MT) or flex plate (AT).
2. If necessary, unfasten the rear cover attaching bolts and remove the cover.
3. Using a prytool with a rag over the end (refer to the accompanying illustration) or seal removal tool such T92C-6700-CH or its equivalent, pry out the rear oil seal.

To install:

4. If removed install the rear cover and tighten its retaining bolts to 69–95 inch lbs. (8–11 Nm).
5. Coat the lip of the new seal wit clean engine oil.
6. Use seal replacer T87C-6701-A or its equivalent, and tighten the bolts to install the seal. Keep tightening the bolts until the seal is flush with the rear cover.
7. Install the flywheel or flexplate.

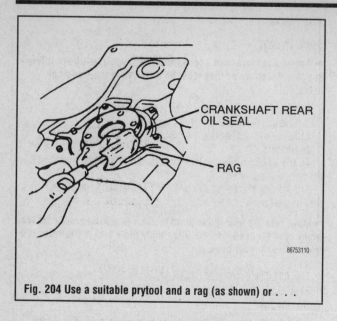

Fig. 204 Use a suitable prytool and a rag (as shown) or . . .

1.9L Engines

▶ See Figures 207 and 208

1. Remove the flywheel.
2. Remove the engine or transmission housing cover..

➡️Use care to avoid damaging the crankshaft surface.

3. Using a seal removal tool such T92C-6700-CH or its equivalent, pry out the rear oil seal.
   To install:
4. Inspect the oil seal area for damage. If damage is found, service or replace the crankshaft
5. Coat the lip of the new seal wit clean engine oil.

➡️Make sure the rear oil seal is properly aligned and that the edges are not rolled up.

6. Place crankshaft rear seal pilot T88P-6701-B2 (or equivalent) into the crankshaft rear seal replacer T88P-6701-B1 (or equivalent) and lubricate the pilot replacer with clean engine oil.
7. Slide the rear oil seal over the pilot onto the replacer.
8. Remove the rear seal pilot T88P-6701-B2 (or equivalent) from seal replacer T88P-6701-B1 (or equivalent).

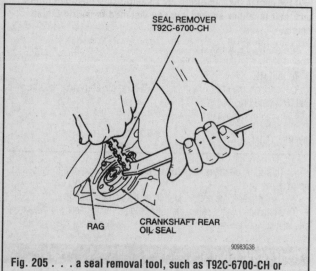

Fig. 205 . . . a seal removal tool, such as T92C-6700-CH or equivalent, to remove the rear crankshaft oil seal—1.8L

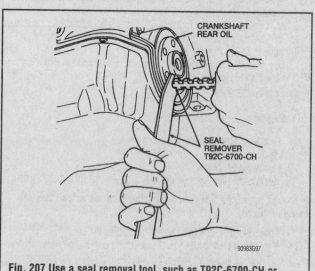

Fig. 207 Use a seal removal tool, such as T92C-6700-CH or equivalent, to pry out the rear oil seal—1.9L engines

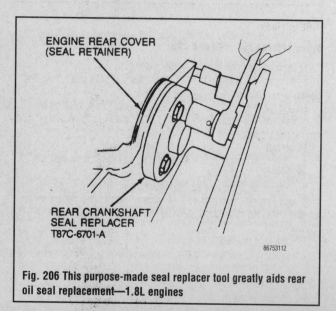

Fig. 206 This purpose-made seal replacer tool greatly aids rear oil seal replacement—1.8L engines

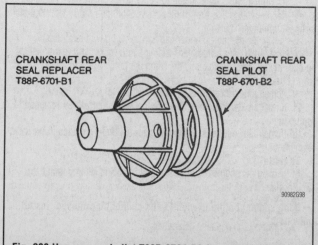

Fig. 208 Use rear seal pilot T88P-6701-B2 (or equivalent) and crankshaft rear seal replacer T88P-6701-B1 (or equivalent) when installing the seal—1.9L engines

9. Place the rear oil seal and replacer over the crankshaft and install the seal.

10. Remove the seal installer tool and install the flywheel.

2.0L Engines

1. Remove the transaxle and flywheel.

➡**Be careful not to damage the crankshaft surface when removing the seal.**

2. Use seal replacer tool T92C-6700-CH or its equivalent to remove the old seal.

To install:

3. Coat the lip of the new seal with clean 5W-30 engine oil.

➡**Make sure the crankshaft rear oil seal is on correctly and that the edges are not rolled over.**

4. Install the new seal using crankshaft rear seal pilot tool T88P-6701-B2 and rear seal replacer tool T88P-6701-B1, or their equivalents.

5. Install the flywheel and the transaxle.

Flywheel/Flexplate

REMOVAL & INSTALLATION

1.8L Engine

WITH MANUAL TRANSAXLE

▶ See Figure 209

1. Remove the transaxle assembly.
2. Remove the clutch assembly.
3. Install a suitable holding tool and unfasten the flywheel retaining bolts.
4. Remove the flywheel.

To install:

5. Inspect the flywheel for cracks, heat checks or other damage that would make it unfit for further service. Replace with a new one, if required.

➡**If the sealant on the flywheel bolts cannot be removed, install new bolt.**

6. Install the flywheel. Use a suitable holding tool, tighten the retaining bolts to 71–76 ft. lbs. (96–103 Nm) using the tightening sequence as illustrated.

7. Install the clutch assembly, if equipped.
8. Install the transaxle assembly.
9. Reconnect the negative battery cable. Start the engine and check for proper starter gear meshing.

WITH AUTOMATIC TRANSAXLE

▶ See Figure 209

1. Remove the transaxle assembly.
2. Install a suitable holding tool and unfasten the flywheel retaining bolts.
3. Remove the flywheel reinforcing plate, flywheel and crankshaft converter adapter.

To install:

4. Inspect the flywheel for cracks, heat checks or other damage that would make it unfit for further service. Replace with a new one, if required.

➡**If the sealant on the flywheel bolts cannot be removed, install new bolt.**

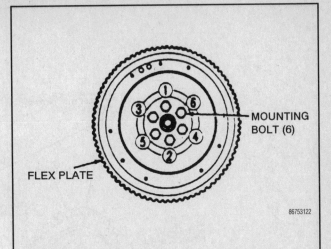

Fig. 209 The flywheel/flexplate bolts should be correctly tightened using the illustrated sequence—1.8L engines

5. Install the crankshaft converter adapter.
6. Install the flywheel and the reinforcing plate.
7. Using a suitable holding tool, tighten the retaining bolts to 71–76 ft. lbs. (96–103 Nm) using the tightening sequence illustrated.
8. Install the transaxle assembly.

1.9L Engine

WITH MANUAL TRANSAXLE

▶ See Figure 210

1. Remove the transaxle assembly.
2. Remove the clutch assembly.
3. Install a suitable holding tool and unfasten the flywheel retaining bolts.
4. Remove the flywheel.

To install:

5. Inspect the flywheel for cracks, heat checks or other damage that would make it unfit for further service. Replace with a new one, if required.

➡**Line up the mark on the flywheel with the untapped hole in the crankshaft flange.**

6. Place the flywheel in position.
7. Apply pipe sealant with Teflon® to the flywheel attaching bolt threads.
8. Install the flywheel retaining bolts and using a suitable holding tool, tighten the retaining bolts to 54–67 ft. lbs. (73–91 Nm).
9. Install the clutch assembly, if equipped.
10. Install the transaxle assembly.

WITH AUTOMATIC TRANSAXLE

1. Remove the transaxle assembly.
2. Install a suitable holding tool and unfasten the flywheel retaining bolts.
3. Remove the flywheel reinforcing plate and flywheel.

To install:

4. Inspect the flywheel for cracks, heat checks or other damage that would make it unfit for further service. Replace with a new one, if required.
5. Install the flywheel and the reinforcing plate.
6. Apply pipe sealant with Teflon® to the flywheel attaching bolt threads.

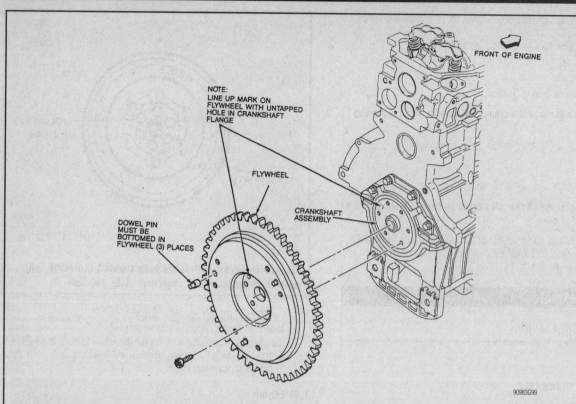

FRONT OF ENGINE

NOTE:
LINE UP MARK ON
FLYWHEEL WITH UNTAPPED
HOLE IN CRANKSHAFT
FLANGE

FLYWHEEL

CRANKSHAFT
ASSEMBLY

DOWEL PIN
MUST BE
BOTTOMED IN
FLYWHEEL (3) PLACES

90983G99

Fig. 210 Make sure you line up the mark on the flywheel with the untapped hole in the crankshaft flange—1.9L engines with a manual transaxle

7. Using a suitable holding tool, align the bolt holes and tighten the retaining bolts to 54–67 ft. lbs. (73–91 Nm).

8. Install the transaxle assembly.

2.0L Engines

♦ See Figure 211

1. Remove the transaxle assembly.
2. If equipped, remove the clutch assembly.
3. Install a suitable holding tool and unfasten the flywheel retaining bolts.
4. On models with an automatic transaxle, remove the flywheel reinforcing plate and flywheel.

To install:

5. Inspect the flywheel for cracks, heat checks or other damage that would make it unfit for further service. Replace with a new one, if required.
6. Install the flywheel and if equipped, the reinforcing plate.
7. Apply threadlock and sealer E0AZ-19554-AA or its equivalent to the flywheel retaining bolts.
8. Using a suitable holding tool, align the bolt holes and tighten the retaining bolts to 54–67 ft. lbs. (73–91 Nm) in the sequence illustrated.
9. If equipped, install the clutch assembly.
10. Install the transaxle assembly.

73-91 Nm (54-67 lb/ft)

90983G85

Fig. 211 Tighten the flywheel bolts in the sequence illustrated—2.0L engines

EXHAUST SYSTEM

Inspection

♦ See Figures 212 thru 221

➡ Safety glasses should be worn at all times when working on or near the exhaust system. Older exhaust systems will almost always be covered with loose rust particles which will shower you when disturbed. These particles are more than a nuisance and could injure your eye.

✳✳ CAUTION

DO NOT perform exhaust repairs or inspection with the engine or exhaust hot. Allow the system to cool completely before attempting any work. Exhaust systems are noted for sharp edges, flaking metal and rusted bolts. Gloves and eye protection are required. A healthy supply of penetrating oil and rags is highly recommended.

Your vehicle must be raised and supported safely to inspect the exhaust system properly. By placing 4 safety stands under the vehicle for support should provide enough room for you to slide under the vehicle and inspect the system completely. Start the inspection at the exhaust manifold or turbocharger pipe where the header pipe is attached and work your way to the back of the vehicle. On dual exhaust systems, remember to inspect both

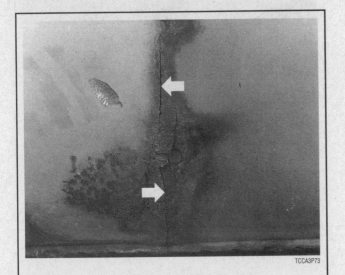

Fig. 212 Cracks in the muffler are a guaranteed leak

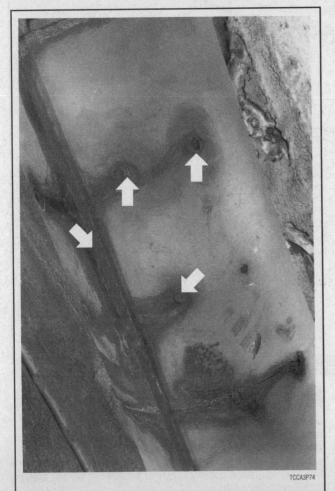

Fig. 213 Check the muffler for rotted spot welds and seams

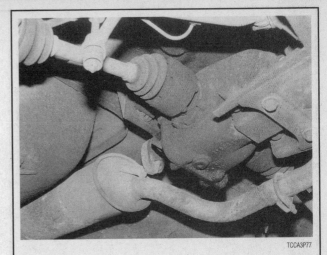

Fig. 214 Make sure the exhaust components are not contacting the body or suspension

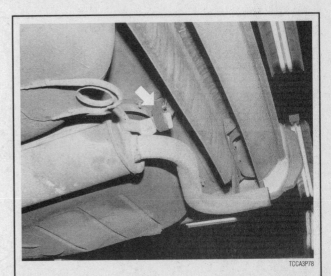

Fig. 215 Check for overstretched or torn exhaust hangers

Fig. 216 Example of a badly deteriorated exhaust pipe

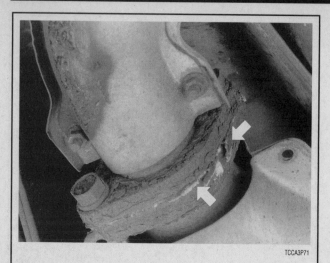

Fig. 217 Inspect flanges for gaskets that have deteriorated and need replacement

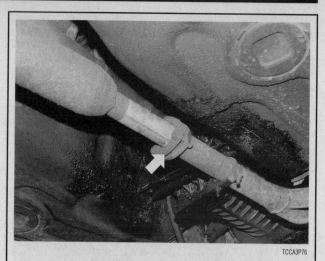

Fig. 218 Some systems, like this one, use large O-rings (donuts) in between the flanges

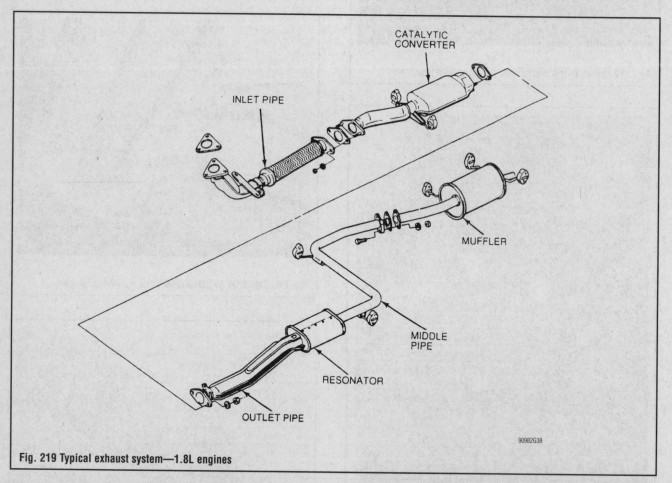

Fig. 219 Typical exhaust system—1.8L engines

sides of the vehicle. Check the complete exhaust system for open seams, holes loose connections, or other deterioration which could permit exhaust fumes to seep into the passenger compartment. Inspect all mounting brackets and hangers for deterioration, some models may have rubber O-rings that can be overstretched and non-supportive. These components will need to be replaced if found. It has always been a practice to use a pointed tool to poke up into the exhaust system where the deterioration spots are to see whether or not they crumble. Some models may have heat shield covering certain parts of the exhaust system , it will be necessary to remove these shields to have the exhaust visible for inspection also.

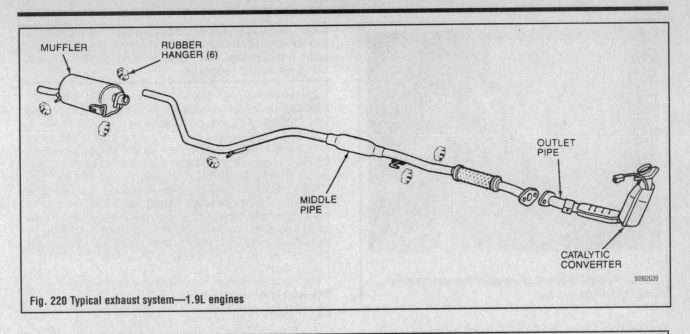

Fig. 220 Typical exhaust system—1.9L engines

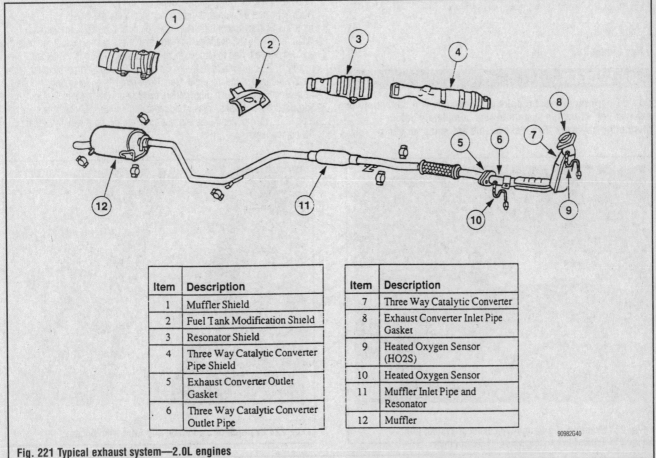

Item	Description
1	Muffler Shield
2	Fuel Tank Modification Shield
3	Resonator Shield
4	Three Way Catalytic Converter Pipe Shield
5	Exhaust Converter Outlet Gasket
6	Three Way Catalytic Converter Outlet Pipe

Item	Description
7	Three Way Catalytic Converter
8	Exhaust Converter Inlet Pipe Gasket
9	Heated Oxygen Sensor (HO2S)
10	Heated Oxygen Sensor
11	Muffler Inlet Pipe and Resonator
12	Muffler

Fig. 221 Typical exhaust system—2.0L engines

REPLACEMENT

▶ See Figure 222

There are basically two types of exhaust systems. One is the flange type where the component ends are attached with bolts and a gasket in-between. The other exhaust system is the slip joint type. These components slip into one another using clamps to retain them together.

✳✳ CAUTION

Allow the exhaust system to cool sufficiently before spraying a solvent exhaust fasteners. Some solvents are highly flammable and could ignite when sprayed on hot exhaust components.

Before removing any component of the exhaust system, ALWAYS squirt a liquid rust dissolving agent onto the fasteners for ease of removal. A lot of

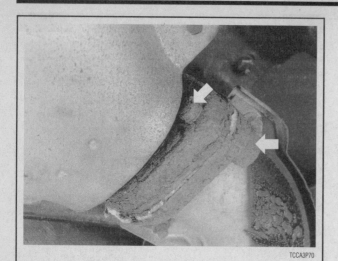

TCCA3P70

Fig. 222 Nuts and bolts will be extremely difficult to remove when deteriorated with rust

knuckle skin will be saved by following this rule. It may even be wise to spray the fasteners and allow them to sit overnight.

Flange Type

▶ See Figure 223

> ❊❊ **CAUTION**
>
> Do NOT perform exhaust repairs or inspection with the engine or exhaust hot. Allow the system to cool completely before attempting any work. Exhaust systems are noted for sharp

edges, flaking metal and rusted bolts. Gloves and eye protection are required. A healthy supply of penetrating oil and rags is highly recommended. Never spray liquid rust dissolving agent onto a hot exhaust component.

Before removing any component on a flange type system, ALWAYS squirt a liquid rust dissolving agent onto the fasteners for ease of removal. Start by unbolting the exhaust piece at both ends (if required). When unbolting the headpipe from the manifold, make sure that the bolts are free before trying to remove them. if you snap a stud in the exhaust manifold, the stud will have to be removed with a bolt extractor, which often means removal of the manifold itself. Next, disconnect the component from the mounting; slight twisting and turning may be required to remove the component completely from the vehicle. You may need to tap on the component with a rubber mallet to loosen the component. If all else fails, use a hacksaw to separate the parts. An oxy-acetylene cutting torch may be faster but the sparks are DANGEROUS near the fuel tank, and at the very least, accidents could happen, resulting in damage to the under-car parts, not to mention yourself.

Slip Joint Type

▶ See Figure 224

Before removing any component on the slip joint type exhaust system, ALWAYS squirt a liquid rust dissolving agent onto the fasteners for ease of removal. Start by unbolting the exhaust piece at both ends (if required). When unbolting the headpipe from the manifold, make sure that the bolts are free before trying to remove them. if you snap a stud in the exhaust manifold, the stud will have to be removed with a bolt extractor, which often means removal of the manifold itself. Next, remove the mounting U-bolts from around the exhaust pipe you are extracting from the vehicle. Don't be surprised if the U-bolts break while removing the nuts. Loosen the exhaust pipe from any mounting brackets retaining it to the floor pan and separate the components.

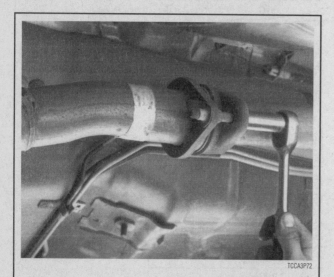

TCCA3P72

Fig. 223 Example of a flange type exhaust system joint

TCCA3P79

Fig. 224 Example of a common slip joint type system

ENGINE RECONDITIONING

Determining Engine Condition

Anything that generates heat and/or friction will eventually burn or wear out (for example, a light bulb generates heat, therefore its life span is limited). With this in mind, a running engine generates tremendous amounts of both; friction is encountered by the moving and rotating parts inside the engine and heat is created by friction and combustion of the fuel. However,

the engine has systems designed to help reduce the effects of heat and friction and provide added longevity. The oiling system reduces the amount of friction encountered by the moving parts inside the engine, while the cooling system reduces heat created by friction and combustion. If either system is not maintained, a break-down will be inevitable. Therefore, you can see how regular maintenance can affect the service life of your vehicle. If you do not drain, flush and refill your cooling system at the proper intervals, deposits will begin to accumulate in the radiator, thereby reducing the amount of heat it can extract from the coolant. The same applies to your oil and filter; if it is not changed often enough it becomes laden with contaminates and is unable to properly lubricate the engine. This increases friction and wear.

There are a number of methods for evaluating the condition of your engine. A compression test can reveal the condition of your pistons, piston rings, cylinder bores, head gasket(s), valves and valve seats. An oil pressure test can warn you of possible engine bearing, or oil pump failures. Excessive oil consumption, evidence of oil in the engine air intake area and/or bluish smoke from the tail pipe may indicate worn piston rings, worn valve guides and/or valve seals. As a general rule, an engine that uses no more than one quart of oil every 1000 miles is in good condition. Engines that use one quart of oil or more in less than 1000 miles should first be checked for oil leaks. If any oil leaks are present, have them fixed before determining how much oil is consumed by the engine, especially if blue smoke is not visible at the tail pipe.

COMPRESSION TEST

▶ **See Figure 225**

A noticeable lack of engine power, excessive oil consumption and/or poor fuel mileage measured over an extended period are all indicators of internal engine wear. Worn piston rings, scored or worn cylinder bores, blown head gaskets, sticking or burnt valves, and worn valve seats are all possible culprits. A check of each cylinder's compression will help locate the problem.

➡**A screw-in type compression gauge is more accurate than the type you simply hold against the spark plug hole. Although it takes slightly longer to use, it's worth the effort to obtain a more accurate reading.**

1. Make sure that the proper amount and viscosity of engine oil is in the crankcase, then ensure the battery is fully charged.
2. Warm-up the engine to normal operating temperature, then shut the engine **OFF**.
3. Disable the ignition system.
4. Label and disconnect all of the spark plug wires from the plugs.
5. Thoroughly clean the cylinder head area around the spark plug ports, then remove the spark plugs.
6. Set the throttle plate to the fully open (wide-open throttle) position. You can block the accelerator linkage open for this, or you can have an assistant fully depress the accelerator pedal.
7. Install a screw-in type compression gauge into the No. 1 spark plug hole until the fitting is snug.

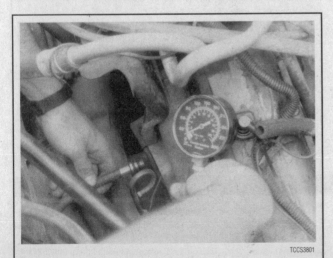

TCCS3801

Fig. 225 A screw-in type compression gauge is more accurate and easier to use without an assistant

Be careful not to crossthread the spark plug hole.

8. According to the tool manufacturer's instructions, connect a remote starting switch to the starting circuit.
9. With the ignition switch in the **OFF** position, use the remote starting switch to crank the engine through at least five compression strokes (approximately 5 seconds of cranking) and record the highest reading on the gauge.
10. Repeat the test on each cylinder, cranking the engine approximately the same number of compression strokes and/or time as the first.
11. Compare the highest readings from each cylinder to that of the others. The indicated compression pressures are considered within specifications if the lowest reading cylinder is within 75 percent of the pressure recorded for the highest reading cylinder. For example, if your highest reading cylinder pressure was 150 psi (1034 kPa), then 75 percent of that would be 113 psi (779 kPa). So the lowest reading cylinder should be no less than 113 psi (779 kPa).
12. If a cylinder exhibits an unusually low compression reading, pour a tablespoon of clean engine oil into the cylinder through the spark plug hole and repeat the compression test. If the compression rises after adding oil, it means that the cylinder's piston rings and/or cylinder bore are damaged or worn. If the pressure remains low, the valves may not be seating properly (a valve job is needed), or the head gasket may be blown near that cylinder. If compression in any two adjacent cylinders is low, and if the addition of oil doesn't help raise compression, there is leakage past the head gasket. Oil and coolant in the combustion chamber, combined with blue or constant white smoke from the tail pipe, are symptoms of this problem. However, don't be alarmed by the normal white smoke emitted from the tail pipe during engine warm-up or from cold weather driving. There may be evidence of water droplets on the engine dipstick and/or oil droplets in the cooling system if a head gasket is blown.

OIL PRESSURE TEST

Check for proper oil pressure at the sending unit passage with an externally mounted mechanical oil pressure gauge (as opposed to relying on a factory installed dash-mounted gauge). A tachometer may also be needed, as some specifications may require running the engine at a specific rpm.

1. With the engine cold, locate and remove the oil pressure sending unit.
2. Following the manufacturer's instructions, connect a mechanical oil pressure gauge and, if necessary, a tachometer to the engine.
3. Start the engine and allow it to idle.
4. Check the oil pressure reading when cold and record the number. You may need to run the engine at a specified rpm, so check the specifications chart located earlier in this section.
5. Run the engine until normal operating temperature is reached (upper radiator hose will feel warm).
6. Check the oil pressure reading again with the engine hot and record the number. Turn the engine **OFF**.
7. Compare your hot oil pressure reading to that given in the chart. If the reading is low, check the cold pressure reading against the chart. If the cold pressure is well above the specification, and the hot reading was lower than the specification, you may have the wrong viscosity oil in the engine. Change the oil, making sure to use the proper grade and quantity, then repeat the test.

Low oil pressure readings could be attributed to internal component wear, pump related problems, a low oil level, or oil viscosity that is too low. High oil pressure readings could be caused by an overfilled crankcase, too high of an oil viscosity or a faulty pressure relief valve.

Buy or Rebuild?

Now that you have determined that your engine is worn out, you must make some decisions. The question of whether or not an engine is worth rebuilding is largely a subjective matter and one of personal worth. Is the engine a popular one, or is it an obsolete model? Are parts available? Will it get acceptable gas mileage once it is rebuilt? Is the car it's being put into worth keeping? Would it be less expensive to buy a new engine, have your engine rebuilt by a pro, rebuild it yourself or buy a used engine from a salvage yard? Or would it be simpler and less expensive to buy another car? If you have considered all these matters and more, and have still decided to rebuild the engine, then it is time to decide how you will rebuild it.

➡**The editors at Chilton feel that most engine machining should be performed by a professional machine shop. Don't think of it as wasting money, rather, as an assurance that the job has been done right the first time. There are many expensive and specialized tools required to perform such tasks as boring and honing an engine block or having a valve job done on a cylinder head. Even inspecting the parts requires expensive micrometers and gauges to properly measure wear and clearances. Also, a machine shop can deliver to you clean, and ready to assemble parts, saving you time and aggravation. Your maximum savings will come from performing the removal, disassembly, assembly and installation of the engine and purchasing or renting only the tools required to perform the above tasks. Depending on the particular circumstances, you may save 40 to 60 percent of the cost doing these yourself.**

A complete rebuild or overhaul of an engine involves replacing all of the moving parts (pistons, rods, crankshaft, camshaft, etc.) with new ones and machining the non-moving wearing surfaces of the block and heads. Unfortunately, this may not be cost effective. For instance, your crankshaft may have been damaged or worn, but it can be machined undersize for a minimal fee.

So, as you can see, you can replace everything inside the engine, but, it is wiser to replace only those parts which are really needed, and, if possible, repair the more expensive ones. Later in this section, we will break the engine down into its two main components: the cylinder head and the engine block. We will discuss each component, and the recommended parts to replace during a rebuild on each.

Engine Overhaul Tips

Most engine overhaul procedures are fairly standard. In addition to specific parts replacement procedures and specifications for your individual engine, this section is also a guide to acceptable rebuilding procedures. Examples of standard rebuilding practice are given and should be used along with specific details concerning your particular engine.

Competent and accurate machine shop services will ensure maximum performance, reliability and engine life. In most instances it is more profitable for the do-it-yourself mechanic to remove, clean and inspect the component, buy the necessary parts and deliver these to a shop for actual machine work.

Much of the assembly work (crankshaft, bearings, piston rods, and other components) is well within the scope of the do-it-yourself mechanic's tools and abilities. You will have to decide for yourself the depth of involvement you desire in an engine repair or rebuild.

TOOLS

The tools required for an engine overhaul or parts replacement will depend on the depth of your involvement. With a few exceptions, they will be the tools found in a mechanic's tool kit (see Section 1 of this manual). More in-depth work will require some or all of the following:
- A dial indicator (reading in thousandths) mounted on a universal base
- Micrometers and telescope gauges
- Jaw and screw-type pullers
- Scraper
- Valve spring compressor
- Ring groove cleaner
- Piston ring expander and compressor
- Ridge reamer
- Cylinder hone or glaze breaker
- Plastigage®
- Engine stand

The use of most of these tools is illustrated in this section. Many can be rented for a one-time use from a local parts jobber or tool supply house specializing in automotive work.

Occasionally, the use of special tools is called for. See the information on Special Tools and the Safety Notice in the front of this book before substituting another tool.

OVERHAUL TIPS

Aluminum has become extremely popular for use in engines, due to its low weight. Observe the following precautions when handling aluminum parts:
- Never hot tank aluminum parts (the caustic hot tank solution will eat the aluminum.
- Remove all aluminum parts (identification tag, etc.) from engine parts prior to the tanking.
- Always coat threads lightly with engine oil or anti-seize compounds before installation, to prevent seizure.
- Never overtighten bolts or spark plugs especially in aluminum threads.

When assembling the engine, any parts that will be exposed to frictional contact must be prelubed to provide lubrication at initial start-up. Any product specifically formulated for this purpose can be used, but engine oil is not recommended as a prelube in most cases.

When semi-permanent (locked, but removable) installation of bolts or nuts is desired, threads should be cleaned and coated with Loctite® or another similar, commercial non-hardening sealant.

CLEANING

▶ **See Figures 226, 227, 228 and 229**

Before the engine and its components are inspected, they must be thoroughly cleaned. You will need to remove any engine varnish, oil sludge and/or carbon deposits from all of the components to insure an accurate inspection. A crack in the engine block or cylinder head can easily become overlooked if hidden by a layer of sludge or carbon.

Most of the cleaning process can be carried out with common hand tools and readily available solvents or solutions. Carbon deposits can be chipped away using a hammer and a hard wooden chisel. Old gasket material and varnish or sludge can usually be removed using a scraper and/or cleaning solvent. Extremely stubborn deposits may require the use of a power drill with a wire brush. If using a wire brush, use extreme care around any critical machined surfaces (such as the gasket surfaces, bearing saddles, cylinder bores, etc.). USE OF A WIRE BRUSH IS NOT RECOMMENDED ON ANY ALUMINUM COMPONENTS. Always follow any safety recommendations given by the manufacturer of the tool and/or solvent. You should always wear eye protection during any cleaning process involving scraping, chipping or spraying of solvents.

An alternative to the mess and hassle of cleaning the parts yourself is to drop them off at a local garage or machine shop. They will, more than

TCCS3132

Fig. 226 Use a gasket scraper to remove the old gasket material from the mating surfaces

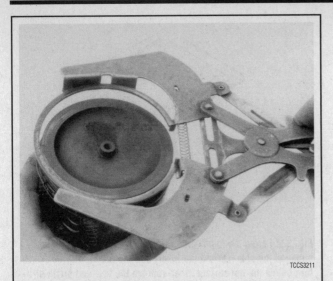

Fig. 227 Use a ring expander tool to remove the piston rings

Fig. 228 Clean the piston ring grooves using a ring groove cleaner tool, or . . .

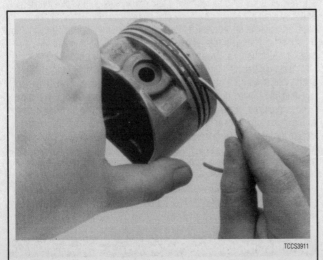

Fig. 229 . . . use a piece of an old ring to clean the grooves. Be careful, the ring can be quite sharp

likely, have the necessary equipment to properly clean all of the parts for a nominal fee.

Remove any oil galley plugs, freeze plugs and/or pressed-in bearings and carefully wash and degrease all of the engine components including the fasteners and bolts. Small parts such as the valves, springs, etc., should be placed in a metal basket and allowed to soak. Use pipe cleaner type brushes, and clean all passageways in the components. Use a ring expander and remove the rings from the pistons. Clean the piston ring grooves with a special tool or a piece of broken ring. Scrape the carbon off of the top of the piston. You should never use a wire brush on the pistons. After preparing all of the piston assemblies in this manner, wash and degrease them again.

When cleaning the cylinder head, remove carbon from the combustion chamber with the valves installed. This will avoid damaging the valve seats.

REPAIRING DAMAGED THREADS

▶ See Figures 230, 231, 232, 233 and 234

Several methods of repairing damaged threads are available. Heli-Coil® (shown here), Keenserts® and Microdot® are among the most widely used. All involve basically the same principle—drilling out stripped threads, tapping the hole and installing a prewound insert—making welding, plugging and oversize fasteners unnecessary.

Two types of thread repair inserts are usually supplied: a standard type for most inch coarse, inch fine, metric course and metric fine thread sizes and a spark lug type to fit most spark plug port sizes. Consult the individual tool manufacturer's catalog to determine exact applications. Typical thread repair kits will contain a selection of prewound threaded inserts, a tap (corresponding to the outside diameter threads of the insert) and an installation tool. Spark plug inserts usually differ because they require a tap equipped with pilot threads and a combined reamer/tap section. Most manufacturers also supply blister-packed thread repair inserts separately in addition to a master kit containing a variety of taps and inserts plus installation tools.

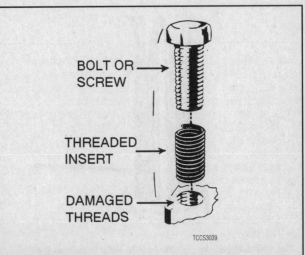

Fig. 230 Damaged bolt hole threads can be replaced with thread repair inserts

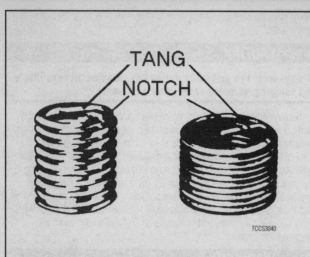

Fig. 231 Standard thread repair insert (left), and spark plug thread insert

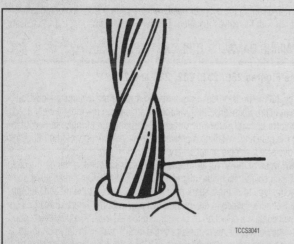

Fig. 232 Drill out the damaged threads with the specified size bit. Be sure to drill completely through the hole or to the bottom of a blind hole

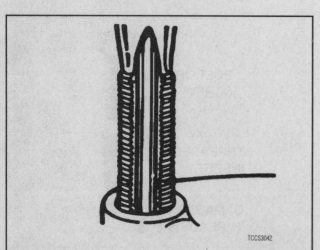

Fig. 233 Using the kit, tap the hole in order to receive the thread insert. Keep the tap well oiled and back it out frequently to avoid clogging the threads

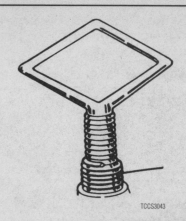

Fig. 234 Screw the insert onto the installer tool until the tang engages the slot. Thread the insert into the hole until it is ¼–½ turn below the top surface, then remove the tool and break off the tang using a punch

Before attempting to repair a threaded hole, remove any snapped, broken or damaged bolts or studs. Penetrating oil can be used to free frozen threads. The offending item can usually be removed with locking pliers or using a screw/stud extractor. After the hole is clear, the thread can be repaired, as shown in the series of accompanying illustrations and in the kit manufacturer's instructions.

Engine Preparation

To properly rebuild an engine, you must first remove it from the vehicle, then disassemble and diagnose it. Ideally you should place your engine on an engine stand. This affords you the best access to the engine components. Follow the manufacturer's directions for using the stand with your particular engine. Remove the flywheel or flexplate before installing the engine to the stand.

Now that you have the engine on a stand, and assuming that you have drained the oil and coolant from the engine, it's time to strip it of all but the necessary components. Before you start disassembling the engine, you may want to take a moment to draw some pictures, or fabricate some labels or containers to mark the locations of various components and the bolts and/or studs which fasten them. Modern day engines use a lot of little brackets and clips which hold wiring harnesses and such, and these holders are often mounted on studs and/or bolts that can be easily mixed up. The manufacturer spent a lot of time and money designing your vehicle, and they wouldn't have wasted any of it by haphazardly placing brackets, clips or fasteners on the vehicle. If it's present when you disassemble it, put it back when you assemble, you will regret not remembering that little bracket which holds a wire harness out of the path of a rotating part.

You should begin by unbolting any accessories still attached to the engine, such as the water pump, power steering pump, alternator, etc. Then, unfasten any manifolds (intake or exhaust) which were not removed during the engine removal procedure. Finally, remove any covers remaining on the engine such as the rocker arm, front or timing cover and oil pan. Some front covers may require the vibration damper and/or crank pulley to be removed beforehand. The idea is to reduce the engine to the bare necessities (cylinder head(s), valve train, engine block, crankshaft, pistons and connecting rods), plus any other `in block' components such as oil pumps, balance shafts and auxiliary shafts.

Finally, remove the cylinder head(s) from the engine block and carefully place on a bench. Disassembly instructions for each component follow later in this section.

Cylinder Head

There are two basic types of cylinder heads used on today's automobiles: the Overhead Valve (OHV) and the Overhead Camshaft (OHC). The latter can also be broken down into two subgroups: the Single Overhead Camshaft (SOHC) and the Dual Overhead Camshaft (DOHC). Generally, if there is only a single camshaft on a head, it is just referred to as an OHC head. Also, an engine with an OHV cylinder head is also known as a pushrod engine.

Most cylinder heads these days are made of an aluminum alloy due to its light weight, durability and heat transfer qualities. However, cast iron was the material of choice in the past, and is still used on many vehicles today. Whether made from aluminum or iron, all cylinder heads have valves and seats. Some use two valves per cylinder, while the more hi-tech engines will utilize a multi-valve configuration using 3, 4 and even 5 valves per cylinder. When the valve contacts the seat, it does so on precision machined surfaces, which seals the combustion chamber. All cylinder heads have a valve guide for each valve. The guide centers the valve to the seat and allows it to move up and down within it. The clearance between the valve and guide can be critical. Too much clearance and the engine may consume oil, lose vacuum and/or damage the seat. Too little, and the valve can stick in the guide causing the engine to run poorly if at all, and possibly causing severe damage. The last component all cylinder heads have are valve springs. The spring holds the valve against its seat. It also returns the valve to this position when the valve has been opened by the valve train or camshaft. The spring is fastened to the valve by a retainer and valve locks (sometimes called keepers). Aluminum heads will also have a valve spring shim to keep the spring from wearing away the aluminum.

An ideal method of rebuilding the cylinder head would involve replacing all of the valves, guides, seats, springs, etc. with new ones. However, depending on how the engine was maintained, often this is not necessary. A major cause of valve, guide and seat wear is an improperly tuned engine. An engine that is running too rich, will often wash the lubricating oil out of the guide with gasoline, causing it to wear rapidly. Conversely, an engine which is running too lean will place higher combustion temperatures on the valves and seats allowing them to wear or even burn. Springs fall victim to the driving habits of the individual. A driver who often runs the engine rpm to the redline will wear out or break the springs faster then one that stays well below it. Unfortunately, mileage takes it toll on all of the parts. Generally, the valves, guides, springs and seats in a cylinder head can be machined and re-used, saving you money. However, if a valve is burnt, it may be wise to replace all of the valves, since they were all operating in the same environment. The same goes for any other component on the cylinder head. Think of it as an insurance policy against future problems related to that component.

Unfortunately, the only way to find out which components need replacing, is to disassemble and carefully check each piece. After the cylinder head(s) are disassembled, thoroughly clean all of the components.

DISASSEMBLY

▶ **See Figures 235 and 236**

Whether it is a single or dual overhead camshaft cylinder head, the disassembly procedure is relatively unchanged. One aspect to pay attention to is careful labeling of the parts on the dual camshaft cylinder head. There will be an intake camshaft and followers as well as an exhaust camshaft and followers and they must be labeled as such. In some cases, the components are identical and could easily be installed incorrectly. DO NOT MIX THEM UP! Determining which is which is very simple; the intake camshaft and components are on the same side of the head as was the intake manifold. Conversely, the exhaust camshaft and components are on the same side of the head as was the exhaust manifold.

CUP TYPE CAMSHAFT FOLLOWERS

▶ **See Figures 237, 238 and 239**

Most cylinder heads with cup type camshaft followers will have the valve spring, retainer and locks recessed within the follower's bore. You will need a C-clamp style valve spring compressor tool, an OHC spring removal tool (or equivalent) and a small magnet to disassemble the head.

1. If not already removed, remove the camshaft(s) and/or followers. Mark their positions for assembly.

TCCA3P54

Fig. 235 Exploded view of a valve, seal, spring, retainer and locks from an OHC cylinder head

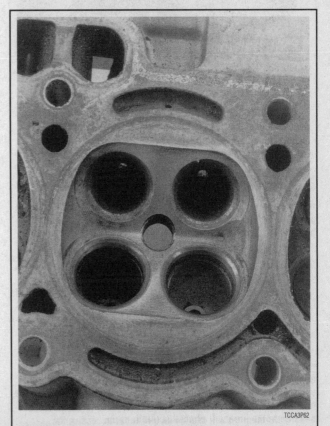

TCCA3P62

Fig. 236 Example of a multi-valve cylinder head. Note how it has 2 intake and 2 exhaust valve ports

Fig. 237 C-clamp type spring compressor and an OHC spring removal tool (center) for cup type followers

Fig. 239 Position the OHC spring tool in the follower bore, then compress the spring with a C-clamp type tool

Fig. 238 Most cup type follower cylinder heads retain the camshaft using bolt-on bearing caps

2. Position the cylinder head to allow use of a C-clamp style valve spring compressor tool.

➡It is preferred to position the cylinder head gasket surface facing you with the valve springs facing the opposite direction and the head laying horizontal.

3. With the OHC spring removal adapter tool positioned inside of the follower bore, compress the valve spring using the C-clamp style valve spring compressor.

4. Remove the valve locks. A small magnetic tool or screwdriver will aid in removal.

5. Release the compressor tool and remove the spring assembly.

6. Withdraw the valve from the cylinder head.

7. If equipped, remove the valve seal.

➡Special valve seal removal tools are available. Regular or needlenose type pliers, if used with care, will work just as well. If using ordinary pliers, be sure not to damage the follower bore. The follower and its bore are machined to close tolerances and any damage to the bore will effect this relationship.

8. If equipped, remove the valve spring shim. A small magnetic tool or screwdriver will aid in removal.

9. Repeat Steps 3 through 8 until all of the valves have been removed.

ROCKER ARM TYPE CAMSHAFT FOLLOWERS

▶ **See Figures 240 thru 248**

Most cylinder heads with rocker arm-type camshaft followers are easily disassembled using a standard valve spring compressor. However, certain models may not have enough open space around the spring for the standard tool and may require you to use a C-clamp style compressor tool instead.

1. If not already removed, remove the rocker arms and/or shafts and the camshaft. If applicable, also remove the hydraulic lash adjusters. Mark their positions for assembly.

2. Position the cylinder head to allow access to the valve spring.

3. Use a valve spring compressor tool to relieve the spring tension from the retainer.

➡Due to engine varnish, the retainer may stick to the valve locks. A gentle tap with a hammer may help to break it loose.

4. Remove the valve locks from the valve tip and/or retainer. A small magnet may help in removing the small locks.

5. Lift the valve spring, tool and all, off of the valve stem.

6. If equipped, remove the valve seal. If the seal is difficult to remove with the valve in place, try removing the valve first, then the seal. Follow the steps below for valve removal.

7. Position the head to allow access for withdrawing the valve.

Fig. 240 Example of the shaft mounted rocker arms on some OHC heads

Fig. 241 Another example of the rocker arm type OHC head. This model uses a follower under the camshaft

Fig. 242 Before the camshaft can be removed, all of the followers must first be removed . . .

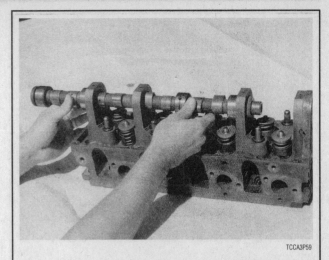

Fig. 243 . . . then the camshaft can be removed by sliding it out (shown), or unbolting a bearing cap (not shown)

Fig. 244 Compress the valve spring . . .

Fig. 245 . . . then remove the valve locks from the valve stem and spring retainer

Fig. 246 Remove the valve spring and retainer from the cylinder head

Fig. 247 Remove the valve seal from the guide. Some gentle prying or pliers may help to remove stubborn ones

Fig. 248 All aluminum and some cast iron heads will have these valve spring shims. Remove all of them as well

➥Cylinder heads that have seen a lot of miles and/or abuse may have mushroomed the valve lock grove and/or tip, causing difficulty in removal of the valve. If this has happened, use a metal file to carefully remove the high spots around the lock grooves and/or tip. Only file it enough to allow removal.

8. Remove the valve from the cylinder head.

9. If equipped, remove the valve spring shim. A small magnetic tool or screwdriver will aid in removal.

10. Repeat Steps 3 though 9 until all of the valves have been removed.

INSPECTION

Now that all of the cylinder head components are clean, it's time to inspect them for wear and/or damage. To accurately inspect them, you will need some specialized tools:

- A 0–1 in. micrometer for the valves
- A dial indicator or inside diameter gauge for the valve guides
- A spring pressure test gauge

If you do not have access to the proper tools, you may want to bring the components to a shop that does.

Valves

▶ See Figures 249 and 250

The first thing to inspect are the valve heads. Look closely at the head, margin and face for any cracks, excessive wear or burning. The margin is the best place to look for burning. It should have a squared edge with an even width all around the diameter. When a valve burns, the margin will look melted and the edges rounded. Also inspect the valve head for any signs of tulipping. This will show as a lifting of the edges or dishing in the center of the head and will usually not occur to all of the valves. All of the heads should look the same, any that seem dished more than others are probably bad. Next, inspect the valve lock grooves and valve tips. Check for any burrs around the lock grooves, especially if you had to file them to remove the valve. Valve tips should appear flat, although slight rounding with high mileage engines is normal. Slightly worn valve tips will need to be machined flat. Last, measure the valve stem diameter with the micrometer. Measure the area that rides within the guide, especially towards the tip where most of the wear occurs. Take several measurements along its length and compare them to each other. Wear should be even along the length with little to no taper. If no minimum diameter is given in the specifications, then the stem should not read more than 0.001 in. (0.025mm) below the specification. Any valves that fail these inspections should be replaced.

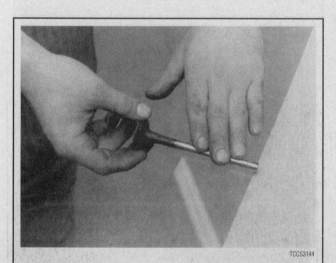

Fig. 249 Valve stems may be rolled on a flat surface to check for bends

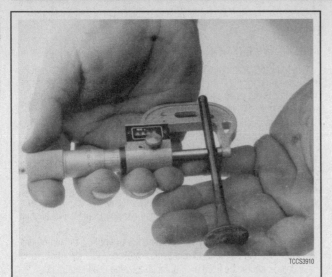

Fig. 250 Use a micrometer to check the valve stem diameter

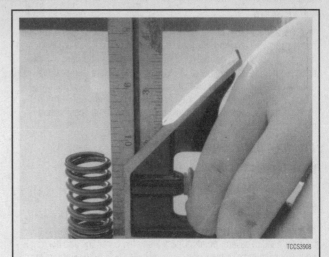

Fig. 252 Check the valve spring for squareness on a flat surface; a carpenter's square can be used

Springs, Retainers and Valve Locks

▶ See Figures 251 and 252

The first thing to check is the most obvious, broken springs. Next check the free length and squareness of each spring. If applicable, insure to distinguish between intake and exhaust springs. Use a ruler and/or carpenters square to measure the length. A carpenters square should be used to check the springs for squareness. If a spring pressure test gauge is available, check each springs rating and compare to the specifications chart. Check the readings against the specifications given. Any springs that fail these inspections should be replaced.

The spring retainers rarely need replacing, however they should still be checked as a precaution. Inspect the spring mating surface and the valve lock retention area for any signs of excessive wear. Also check for any signs of cracking. Replace any retainers that are questionable.

Valve locks should be inspected for excessive wear on the outside contact area as well as on the inner notched surface. Any locks which appear worn or broken and its respective valve should be replaced.

Cylinder Head

There are several things to check on the cylinder head: valve guides, seats, cylinder head surface flatness, cracks and physical damage.

VALVE GUIDES

▶ See Figure 253

Now that you know the valves are good, you can use them to check the guides, although a new valve, if available, is preferred. Before you measure anything, look at the guides carefully and inspect them for any cracks, chips or breakage. Also if the guide is a removable style (as in most aluminum heads), check them for any looseness or evidence of movement. All of the guides should appear to be at the same height from the spring seat. If any seem lower (or higher) from another, the guide has moved. Mount a dial indicator onto the spring side of the cylinder head. Lightly oil the valve stem and insert it into the cylinder head. Position the dial indicator against the valve stem near the tip and zero the gauge. Grasp the valve stem and wiggle towards and away from the dial indicator and observe the readings. Mount the dial indicator 90 degrees from the initial point and zero the gauge and again take a reading. Compare the two readings for a out of round condition. Check the readings against the specifications given. An Inside Diameter (I.D.) gauge designed for valve guides will give you an accurate valve guide bore measurement. If the I.D. gauge is used, compare the readings with the specifications given. Any guides that fail these inspections should be replaced or machined.

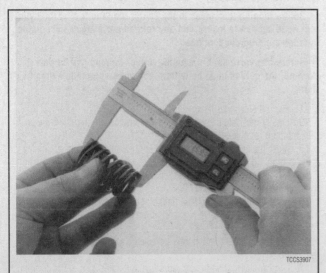

Fig. 251 Use a caliper to check the valve spring free-length

Fig. 253 A dial gauge may be used to check valve stem-to-guide clearance; read the gauge while moving the valve stem

VALVE SEATS

A visual inspection of the valve seats should show a slightly worn and pitted surface where the valve face contacts the seat. Inspect the seat carefully for severe pitting or cracks. Also, a seat that is badly worn will be recessed into the cylinder head. A severely worn or recessed seat may need to be replaced. All cracked seats must be replaced. A seat concentricity gauge, if available, should be used to check the seat run-out. If run-out exceeds specifications the seat must be machined (if no specification is given use 0.002 in. or 0.051mm).

CYLINDER HEAD SURFACE FLATNESS

▶ See Figures 254 and 255

After you have cleaned the gasket surface of the cylinder head of any old gasket material, check the head for flatness.

Place a straightedge across the gasket surface. Using feeler gauges, determine the clearance at the center of the straightedge and across the cylinder head at several points. Check along the centerline and diagonally on the head surface. If the warpage exceeds 0.003 in. (0.076mm) within a 6.0 in. (15.2cm) span, or 0.006 in. (0.152mm) over the total length of the head, the cylinder head must be resurfaced. After resurfacing the heads of a V-type engine, the intake manifold flange surface should be checked, and if

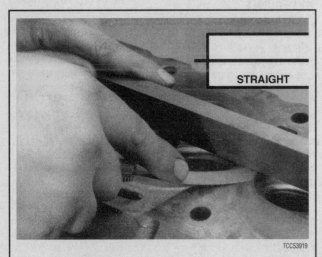

TCCS3919

Fig. 254 Check the head for flatness across the center of the head surface using a straightedge and feeler gauge

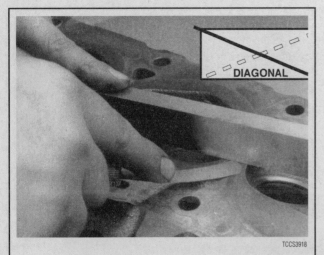

TCCS3918

Fig. 255 Checks should also be made along both diagonals of the head surface

necessary, milled proportionally to allow for the change in its mounting position.

CRACKS AND PHYSICAL DAMAGE

Generally, cracks are limited to the combustion chamber, however, it is not uncommon for the head to crack in a spark plug hole, port, outside of the head or in the valve spring/rocker arm area. The first area to inspect is always the hottest: the exhaust seat/port area.

A visual inspection should be performed, but just because you don't see a crack does not mean it is not there. Some more reliable methods for inspecting for cracks include Magnaflux®, a magnetic process or Zyglo®, a dye penetrant. Magnaflux® is used only on ferrous metal (cast iron) heads. Zyglo® uses a spray on fluorescent mixture along with a black light to reveal the cracks. It is strongly recommended to have your cylinder head checked professionally for cracks, especially if the engine was known to have overheated and/or leaked or consumed coolant. Contact a local shop for availability and pricing of these services.

Physical damage is usually very evident. For example, a broken mounting ear from dropping the head or a bent or broken stud and/or bolt. All of these defects should be fixed or, if unrepairable, the head should be replaced.

Camshaft and Followers

Inspect the camshaft(s) and followers as described earlier in this section.

REFINISHING & REPAIRING

Many of the procedures given for refinishing and repairing the cylinder head components must be performed by a machine shop. Certain steps, if the inspected part is not worn, can be performed yourself inexpensively. However, you spent a lot of time and effort so far, why risk trying to save a couple bucks if you might have to do it all over again?

Valves

Any valves that were not replaced should be refaced and the tips ground flat. Unless you have access to a valve grinding machine, this should be done by a machine shop. If the valves are in extremely good condition, as well as the valve seats and guides, they may be lapped in without performing machine work.

It is a recommended practice to lap the valves even after machine work has been performed and/or new valves have been purchased. This insures a positive seal between the valve and seat.

LAPPING THE VALVES

➡ Before lapping the valves to the seats, read the rest of the cylinder head section to insure that any related parts are in acceptable enough condition to continue.

➡ Before any valve seat machining and/or lapping can be performed, the guides must be within factory recommended specifications.

1. Invert the cylinder head.
2. Lightly lubricate the valve stems and insert them into the cylinder head in their numbered order.
3. Raise the valve from the seat and apply a small amount of fine lapping compound to the seat.
4. Moisten the suction head of a hand-lapping tool and attach it to the head of the valve.
5. Rotate the tool between the palms of both hands, changing the position of the valve on the valve seat and lifting the tool often to prevent grooving.
6. Lap the valve until a smooth, polished circle is evident on the valve and seat.
7. Remove the tool and the valve. Wipe away all traces of the grinding compound and store the valve to maintain its lapped location.

Do not get the valves out of order after they have been lapped. They must be put back with the same valve seat with which they were lapped.

Springs, Retainers and Valve Locks

There is no repair or refinishing possible with the springs, retainers and valve locks. If they are found to be worn or defective, they must be replaced with new (or known good) parts.

Cylinder Head

Most refinishing procedures dealing with the cylinder head must be performed by a machine shop. Read the sections below and review your inspection data to determine whether or not machining is necessary.

VALVE GUIDES

➡ **If any machining or replacements are made to the valve guides, the seats must be machined.**

Unless the valve guides need machining or replacing, the only service to perform is to thoroughly clean them of any dirt or oil residue.

There are only two types of valve guides used on automobile engines: the replaceable-type (all aluminum heads) and the cast-in integral-type (most cast iron heads). There are four recommended methods for repairing worn guides.
- Knurling
- Inserts
- Reaming oversize
- Replacing

Knurling is a process in which metal is displaced and raised, thereby reducing clearance, giving a true center, and providing oil control. It is the least expensive way of repairing the valve guides. However, it is not necessarily the best, and in some cases, a knurled valve guide will not stand up for more than a short time. It requires a special knurlizer and precision reaming tools to obtain proper clearances. It would not be cost effective to purchase these tools, unless you plan on rebuilding several of the same cylinder head.

Installing a guide insert involves machining the guide to accept a bronze insert. One style is the coil-type which is installed into a threaded guide. Another is the thin-walled insert where the guide is reamed oversize to accept a split-sleeve insert. After the insert is installed, a special tool is then run through the guide to expand the insert, locking it to the guide. The insert is then reamed to the standard size for proper valve clearance.

Reaming for oversize valves restores normal clearances and provides a true valve seat. Most cast-in type guides can be reamed to accept an valve with an oversize stem. The cost factor for this can become quite high as you will need to purchase the reamer and new, oversize stem valves for all guides which were reamed. Oversizes are generally 0.003 to 0.030 in. (0.076 to 0.762mm), with 0.015 in. (0.381mm) being the most common.

To replace cast-in type valve guides, they must be drilled out, then reamed to accept replacement guides. This must be done on a fixture which will allow centering and leveling off of the original valve seat or guide, otherwise a serious guide-to-seat misalignment may occur making it impossible to properly machine the seat.

Replaceable-type guides are pressed into the cylinder head. A hammer and a stepped drift or punch may be used to install and remove the guides. Before removing the guides, measure the protrusion on the spring side of the head and record it for installation. Use the stepped drift to hammer out the old guide from the combustion chamber side of the head. When installing, determine whether or not the guide also seals a water jacket in the head, and if it does, use the recommended sealing agent. If there is no water jacket, grease the valve guide and its bore. Use the stepped drift, and hammer the new guide into the cylinder head from the spring side of the cylinder head. A stack of washers the same thickness as the measured protrusion may help the installation process.

VALVE SEATS

➡ **Before any valve seat machining can be performed, the guides must be within factory recommended specifications.**

➡ **If any machining or replacements were made to the valve guides, the seats must be machined.**

If the seats are in good condition, the valves can be lapped to the seats, and the cylinder head assembled. See the valves section for instructions on lapping.

If the valve seats are worn, cracked or damaged, they must be serviced by a machine shop. The valve seat must be perfectly centered to the valve guide, which requires very accurate machining.

CYLINDER HEAD SURFACE

If the cylinder head is warped, it must be machined flat. If the warpage is extremely severe, the head may need to be replaced. In some instances, it may be possible to straighten a warped head enough to allow machining. In either case, contact a professional machine shop for service.

➡ **Any OHC cylinder head that shows excessive warpage should have the camshaft bearing journals align bored after the cylinder head has been resurfaced.**

Failure to align bore the camshaft bearing journals could result in severe engine damage including but not limited to: valve and piston damage, connecting rod damage, camshaft and/or crankshaft breakage.

CRACKS AND PHYSICAL DAMAGE

Certain cracks can be repaired in both cast iron and aluminum heads. For cast iron, a tapered threaded insert is installed along the length of the crack. Aluminum can also use the tapered inserts, however welding is the preferred method. Some physical damage can be repaired through brazing or welding. Contact a machine shop to get expert advice for your particular dilemma.

ASSEMBLY

The first step for any assembly job is to have a clean area in which to work. Next, thoroughly clean all of the parts and components that are to be assembled. Finally, place all of the components onto a suitable work space and, if necessary, arrange the parts to their respective positions.

OHC Engines

▶ **See Figure 256**

CUP TYPE CAMSHAFT FOLLOWERS

To install the springs, retainers and valve locks on heads which have these components recessed into the camshaft follower's bore, you will need a small screwdriver-type tool, some clean white grease and a lot of patience. You will also need the C-clamp style spring compressor and the OHC tool used to disassemble the head.

1. Lightly lubricate the valve stems and insert all of the valves into the cylinder head. If possible, maintain their original locations.
2. If equipped, install any valve spring shims which were removed.
3. If equipped, install the new valve seals, keeping the following in mind:
- If the valve seal presses over the guide, lightly lubricate the outer guide surfaces.
- If the seal is an O-ring type, it is installed just after compressing the spring but before the valve locks.
4. Place the valve spring and retainer over the stem.
5. Position the spring compressor and the OHC tool, then compress the spring.

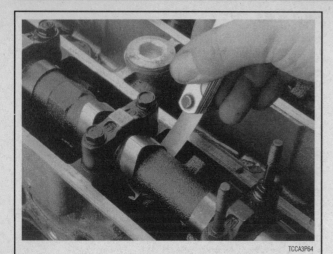

Fig. 256 Once assembled, check the valve clearance and correct as needed

6. Using a small screwdriver as a spatula, fill the valve stem side of the lock with white grease. Use the excess grease on the screwdriver to fasten the lock to the driver.

7. Carefully install the valve lock, which is stuck to the end of the screwdriver, to the valve stem then press on it with the screwdriver until the grease squeezes out. The valve lock should now be stuck to the stem.

8. Repeat Steps 6 and 7 for the remaining valve lock.

9. Relieve the spring pressure slowly and insure that neither valve lock becomes dislodged by the retainer.

10. Remove the spring compressor tool.

11. Repeat Steps 2 through 10 until all of the springs have been installed.

12. Install the followers, camshaft(s) and any other components that were removed for disassembly.

ROCKER ARM TYPE CAMSHAFT FOLLOWERS

1. Lightly lubricate the valve stems and insert all of the valves into the cylinder head. If possible, maintain their original locations.

2. If equipped, install any valve spring shims which were removed.

3. If equipped, install the new valve seals, keeping the following in mind:
• If the valve seal presses over the guide, lightly lubricate the outer guide surfaces.
• If the seal is an O-ring type, it is installed just after compressing the spring but before the valve locks.

4. Place the valve spring and retainer over the stem.

5. Position the spring compressor tool and compress the spring.

6. Assemble the valve locks to the stem.

7. Relieve the spring pressure slowly and insure that neither valve lock becomes dislodged by the retainer.

8. Remove the spring compressor tool.

9. Repeat Steps 2 through 8 until all of the springs have been installed.

10. Install the camshaft(s), rockers, shafts and any other components that were removed for disassembly.

Engine Block

GENERAL INFORMATION

A thorough overhaul or rebuild of an engine block would include replacing the pistons, rings, bearings, timing belt/chain assembly and oil pump. For OHV engines also include a new camshaft and lifters. The block would then have the cylinders bored and honed oversize (or if using removable cylinder sleeves, new sleeves installed) and the crankshaft would be cut undersize to provide new wearing surfaces and perfect clearances. However,

your particular engine may not have everything worn out. What if only the piston rings have worn out and the clearances on everything else are still within factory specifications? Well, you could just replace the rings and put it back together, but this would be a very rare example. Chances are, if one component in your engine is worn, other components are sure to follow, and soon. At the very least, you should always replace the rings, bearings and oil pump. This is what is commonly called a "freshen up".

Cylinder Ridge Removal

Because the top piston ring does not travel to the very top of the cylinder, a ridge is built up between the end of the travel and the top of the cylinder bore.

Pushing the piston and connecting rod assembly past the ridge can be difficult, and damage to the piston ring lands could occur. If the ridge is not removed before installing a new piston or not removed at all, piston ring breakage and piston damage may occur.

→It is always recommended that you remove any cylinder ridges before removing the piston and connecting rod assemblies. If you know that new pistons are going to be installed and the engine block will be bored oversize, you may be able to forego this step. However, some ridges may actually prevent the assemblies from being removed, necessitating its removal.

There are several different types of ridge reamers on the market, none of which are inexpensive. Unless a great deal of engine rebuilding is anticipated, borrow or rent a reamer.

1. Turn the crankshaft until the piston is at the bottom of its travel.

2. Cover the head of the piston with a rag.

3. Follow the tool manufacturers instructions and cut away the ridge, exercising extreme care to avoid cutting too deeply.

4. Remove the ridge reamer, the rag and as many of the cuttings as possible. Continue until all of the cylinder ridges have been removed.

DISASSEMBLY

▶ **See Figures 257 and 258**

The engine disassembly instructions following assume that you have the engine mounted on an engine stand. If not, it is easiest to disassemble the engine on a bench or the floor with it resting on the bell housing or transmission mounting surface. You must be able to access the connecting rod fasteners and turn the crankshaft during disassembly. Also, all engine covers (timing, front, side, oil pan, whatever) should have already been removed. Engines which are seized or locked up may not be able to be completely disassembled, and a core (salvage yard) engine should be purchased.

Fig. 257 Place rubber hose over the connecting rod studs to protect the crankshaft and cylinder bores from damage

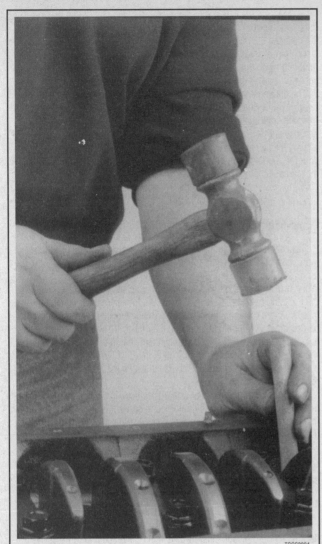

Fig. 258 Carefully tap the piston out of the bore using a wooden dowel

OHC Engines

If not done during the cylinder head removal, remove the timing chain/belt and/or gear/sprocket assembly. Remove the oil pick-up and pump assembly and, if necessary, the pump drive. If equipped, remove any balance or auxiliary shafts. If necessary, remove the cylinder ridge from the top of the bore. See the cylinder ridge removal procedure earlier in this section.

Rotate the engine over so that the crankshaft is exposed. Use a number punch or scribe and mark each connecting rod with its respective cylinder number. The cylinder closest to the front of the engine is always number 1. However, depending on the engine placement, the front of the engine could either be the flywheel or damper/pulley end. Generally the front of the engine faces the front of the vehicle. Use a number punch or scribe and also mark the main bearing caps from front to rear with the front most cap being number 1 (if there are five caps, mark them 1 through 5, front to rear).

✴✴ WARNING

Take special care when pushing the connecting rod up from the crankshaft because the sharp threads of the rod bolts/studs will score the crankshaft journal. Insure that special plastic caps are installed over them, or cut two pieces of rubber hose to do the same.

Again, rotate the engine, this time to position the number one cylinder bore (head surface) up. Turn the crankshaft until the number one piston is at the bottom of its travel, this should allow the maximum access to its connecting rod. Remove the number one connecting rods fasteners and cap and place two lengths of rubber hose over the rod bolts/studs to protect the crankshaft from damage. Using a sturdy wooden dowel and a hammer, push the connecting rod up about 1 in. (25mm) from the crankshaft and remove the upper bearing insert. Continue pushing or tapping the connecting rod up until the piston rings are out of the cylinder bore. Remove the piston and rod by hand, put the upper half of the bearing insert back into the rod, install the cap with its bearing insert installed, and hand-tighten the cap fasteners. If the parts are kept in order in this manner, they will not get lost and you will be able to tell which bearings came form what cylinder if any problems are discovered and diagnosis is necessary. Remove all the other piston assemblies in the same manner. On V-style engines, remove all of the pistons from one bank, then reposition the engine with the other cylinder bank head surface up, and remove that banks piston assemblies.

The only remaining component in the engine block should now be the crankshaft. Loosen the main bearing caps evenly until the fasteners can be turned by hand, then remove them and the caps. Remove the crankshaft from the engine block. Thoroughly clean all of the components.

INSPECTION

Now that the engine block and all of its components are clean, it's time to inspect them for wear and/or damage. To accurately inspect them, you will need some specialized tools:

• Two or three separate micrometers to measure the pistons and crank-shaft journals
• A dial indicator
• Telescoping gauges for the cylinder bores
• A rod alignment fixture to check for bent connecting rods

If you do not have access to the proper tools, you may want to bring the components to a shop that does.

Generally, you shouldn't expect cracks in the engine block or its components unless it was known to leak, consume or mix engine fluids, it was severely overheated, or there was evidence of bad bearings and/or crankshaft damage. A visual inspection should be performed on all of the components, but just because you don't see a crack does not mean it is not there. Some more reliable methods for inspecting for cracks include Magnaflux®, a magnetic process or Zyglo®, a dye penetrant. Magnaflux® is used only on ferrous metal (cast iron). Zyglo® uses a spray on fluorescent mixture along with a black light to reveal the cracks. It is strongly recommended to have your engine block checked professionally for cracks, especially if the engine was known to have overheated and/or leaked or consumed coolant. Contact a local shop for availability and pricing of these services.

Engine Block

ENGINE BLOCK BEARING ALIGNMENT

Remove the main bearing caps and, if still installed, the main bearing inserts. Inspect all of the main bearing saddles and caps for damage, burrs or high spots. If damage is found, and it is caused from a spun main bearing, the block will need to be align-bored or, if severe enough, replacement. Any burrs or high spots should be carefully removed with a metal file.

Place a straightedge on the bearing saddles, in the engine block, along the centerline of the crankshaft. If any clearance exists between the straightedge and the saddles, the block must be align-bored.

Align-boring consists of machining the main bearing saddles and caps by means of a flycutter that runs through the bearing saddles.

DECK FLATNESS

The top of the engine block where the cylinder head mounts is called the deck. Insure that the deck surface is clean of dirt, carbon deposits and old gasket material. Place a straightedge across the surface of the deck along its centerline and, using feeler gauges, check the clearance along several points. Repeat the checking procedure with the straightedge placed along both diagonals of the deck surface. If the reading exceeds 0.003 in. (0.076mm) within a 6.0 in. (15.2cm) span, or 0.006 in. (0.152mm) over the total length of the deck, it must be machined.

CYLINDER BORES

▶ See Figure 259

The cylinder bores house the pistons and are slightly larger than the pistons themselves. A common piston-to-bore clearance is 0.0015–0.0025 in. (0.0381mm–0.0635mm). Inspect and measure the cylinder bores. The bore should be checked for out-of-roundness, taper and size. The results of this inspection will determine whether the cylinder can be used in its existing size and condition, or a rebore to the next oversize is required (or in the case of removable sleeves, have replacements installed).

The amount of cylinder wall wear is always greater at the top of the cylinder than at the bottom. This wear is known as taper. Any cylinder that has a taper of 0.0012 in. (0.305mm) or more, must be rebored. Measurements are taken at a number of positions in each cylinder: at the top, middle and bottom and at two points at each position; that is, at a point 90 degrees from the crankshaft centerline, as well as a point parallel to the crankshaft centerline. The measurements are made with either a special dial indicator or a telescopic gauge and micrometer. If the necessary precision tools to check the bore are not available, take the block to a machine shop and have them mike it. Also if you don't have the tools to check the cylinder bores, chances are you will not have the necessary devices to check the pistons, connecting rods and crankshaft. Take these components with you and save yourself an extra trip.

For our procedures, we will use a telescopic gauge and a micrometer. You will need one of each, with a measuring range which covers your cylinder bore size.

1. Position the telescopic gauge in the cylinder bore, loosen the gauges lock and allow it to expand.

➡ **Your first two readings will be at the top of the cylinder bore, then proceed to the middle and finally the bottom, making a total of six measurements.**

2. Hold the gauge square in the bore, 90 degrees from the crankshaft centerline, and gently tighten the lock. Tilt the gauge back to remove it from the bore.

3. Measure the gauge with the micrometer and record the reading.

4. Again, hold the gauge square in the bore, this time parallel to the crankshaft centerline, and gently tighten the lock. Again, you will tilt the gauge back to remove it from the bore.

5. Measure the gauge with the micrometer and record this reading. The difference between these two readings is the out-of-round measurement of the cylinder.

6. Repeat steps 1 through 5, each time going to the next lower position, until you reach the bottom of the cylinder. Then go to the next cylinder, and continue until all of the cylinders have been measured.

The difference between these measurements will tell you all about the wear in your cylinders. The measurements which were taken 90 degrees from the crankshaft centerline will always reflect the most wear. That is because at this position is where the engine power presses the piston against the cylinder bore the hardest. This is known as thrust wear. Take your top, 90 degree measurement and compare it to your bottom, 90 degree measurement. The difference between them is the taper. When you measure your pistons, you will compare these readings to your piston sizes and determine piston-to-wall clearance.

Crankshaft

Inspect the crankshaft for visible signs of wear or damage. All of the journals should be perfectly round and smooth. Slight scores are normal for a used crankshaft, but you should hardly feel them with your fingernail. When measuring the crankshaft with a micrometer, you will take readings at the front and rear of each journal, then turn the micrometer 90 degrees and take two more readings, front and rear. The difference between the front-to-rear readings is the journal taper and the first-to-90 degree reading is the out-of-round measurement. Generally, there should be no taper or out-of-roundness found, however, up to 0.0005 in. (0.0127mm) for either can be overlooked. Also, the readings should fall within the factory specifications for journal diameters.

If the crankshaft journals fall within specifications, it is recommended that it be polished before being returned to service. Polishing the crankshaft insures that any minor burrs or high spots are smoothed, thereby reducing the chance of scoring the new bearings.

Pistons and Connecting Rods

PISTONS

▶ See Figure 260

The piston should be visually inspected for any signs of cracking or burning (caused by hot spots or detonation), and scuffing or excessive wear on the skirts. The wrist pin attaches the piston to the connecting rod. The piston should move freely on the wrist pin, both sliding and pivoting. Grasp the connecting rod securely, or mount it in a vise, and try to rock the piston back and forth along the centerline of the wrist pin. There should not be any excessive play evident between the piston and the pin. If there are

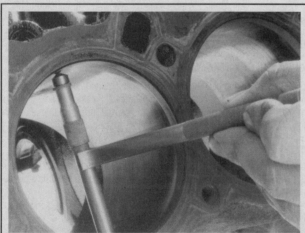

TCCS3209

Fig. 259 Use a telescoping gauge to measure the cylinder bore diameter—take several readings within the same bore

TCCS3210

Fig. 260 Measure the piston's outer diameter, perpendicular to the wrist pin, with a micrometer

C-clips retaining the pin in the piston then you have wrist pin bushings in the rods. There should not be any excessive play between the wrist pin and the rod bushing. Normal clearance for the wrist pin is approx. 0.001–0.002 in. (0.025mm–0.051mm).

Use a micrometer and measure the diameter of the piston, perpendicular to the wrist pin, on the skirt. Compare the reading to its original cylinder measurement obtained earlier. The difference between the two readings is the piston-to-wall clearance. If the clearance is within specifications, the piston may be used as is. If the piston is out of specification, but the bore is not, you will need a new piston. If both are out of specification, you will need the cylinder rebored and oversize pistons installed. Generally if two or more pistons/bores are out of specification, it is best to rebore the entire block and purchase a complete set of oversize pistons.

CONNECTING RODS

You should have the connecting rods checked for straightness at a machine shop. If a connecting rod is bent, it will unevenly wear the bearing and piston, as well as place greater stress on these components. Any bent or twisted connecting rods must be replaced. If the rods are straight and the wrist pin clearance is within specifications, then only the bearing end of the rod need be checked. Place the connecting rod into a vice, with the bearing inserts in place, install the cap to the rod and torque the fasteners to specifications. Use a telescoping gauge and carefully measure the inside diameter of the bearings. Compare this reading to the rods original crankshaft journal diameter measurement. The difference is the oil clearance. If the oil clearance is not within specifications, install new bearings in the rod and take another measurement. If the clearance is still out of specifications, and the crankshaft is not, the rod will need to be reconditioned by a machine shop.

➡You can also use Plastigage® to check the bearing clearances. The assembling section has complete instructions on its use.

Camshaft

Inspect the camshaft and lifters/followers as described earlier in this section.

Bearings

All of the engine bearings should be visually inspected for wear and/or damage. The bearing should look evenly worn all around with no deep scores or pits. If the bearing is severely worn, scored, pitted or heat blued, then the bearing, and the components that use it, should be brought to a machine shop for inspection. Full-circle bearings (used on most camshafts, auxiliary shafts, balance shafts, etc.) require specialized tools for removal and installation, and should be brought to a machine shop for service.

Oil Pump

➡The oil pump is responsible for providing constant lubrication to the whole engine and so it is recommended that a new oil pump be installed when rebuilding the engine.

Completely disassemble the oil pump and thoroughly clean all of the components. Inspect the oil pump gears and housing for wear and/or damage. Insure that the pressure relief valve operates properly and there is no binding or sticking due to varnish or debris. If all of the parts are in proper working condition, lubricate the gears and relief valve, and assemble the pump.

REFINISHING

▶ See Figure 261

Almost all engine block refinishing must be performed by a machine shop. If the cylinders are not to be rebored, then the cylinder glaze can be removed with a ball hone. When removing cylinder glaze with a ball hone, use a light or penetrating type oil to lubricate the hone. Do not allow the hone to run dry as this may cause excessive scoring of the cylinder bores and wear on the hone. If new pistons are required, they will need to be installed to the connecting rods. This should be performed by a machine

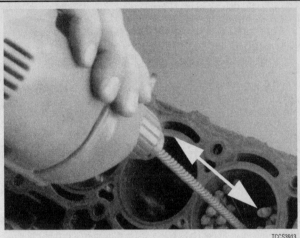

Fig. 261 Use a ball type cylinder hone to remove any glaze and provide a new surface for seating the piston rings

shop as the pistons must be installed in the correct relationship to the rod or engine damage can occur.

Pistons and Connecting Rods

▶ See Figure 262

Only pistons with the wrist pin retained by C-clips are serviceable by the home-mechanic. Press fit pistons require special presses and/or heaters to remove/install the connecting rod and should only be performed by a machine shop.

All pistons will have a mark indicating the direction to the front of the engine and the must be installed into the engine in that manner. Usually it is a notch or arrow on the top of the piston, or it may be the letter F cast or stamped into the piston.

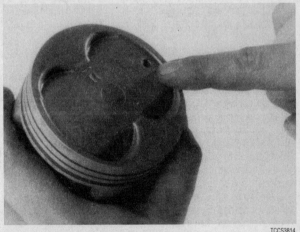

Fig. 262 Most pistons are marked to indicate positioning in the engine (usually a mark means the side facing the front)

C-CLIP TYPE PISTONS

1. Note the location of the forward mark on the piston and mark the connecting rod in relation.
2. Remove the C-clips from the piston and withdraw the wrist pin.

➡Varnish build-up or C-clip groove burrs may increase the difficulty of removing the wrist pin. If necessary, use a punch or drift to carefully tap the wrist pin out.

3. Insure that the wrist pin bushing in the connecting rod is usable, and lubricate it with assembly lube.

4. Remove the wrist pin from the new piston and lubricate the pin bores on the piston.

5. Align the forward marks on the piston and the connecting rod and install the wrist pin.

6. The new C-clips will have a flat and a rounded side to them. Install both C-clips with the flat side facing out.

7. Repeat all of the steps for each piston being replaced.

ASSEMBLY

Before you begin assembling the engine, first give yourself a clean, dirt free work area. Next, clean every engine component again. The key to a good assembly is cleanliness.

Mount the engine block into the engine stand and wash it one last time using water and detergent (dishwashing detergent works well). While washing it, scrub the cylinder bores with a soft bristle brush and thoroughly clean all of the oil passages. Completely dry the engine and spray the entire assembly down with an anti-rust solution such as WD-40® or similar product. Take a clean lint-free rag and wipe up any excess anti-rust solution from the bores, bearing saddles, etc. Repeat the final cleaning process on the crankshaft. Replace any freeze or oil galley plugs which were removed during disassembly.

Crankshaft

▶ **See Figures 263, 264, 265 and 266**

1. Remove the main bearing inserts from the block and bearing caps.

2. If the crankshaft main bearing journals have been refinished to a definite undersize, install the correct undersize bearing. Be sure that the bearing inserts and bearing bores are clean. Foreign material under inserts will distort bearing and cause failure.

3. Place the upper main bearing inserts in bores with tang in slot.

➡ **The oil holes in the bearing inserts must be aligned with the oil holes in the cylinder block.**

4. Install the lower main bearing inserts in bearing caps.

5. Clean the mating surfaces of block and rear main bearing cap.

6. Carefully lower the crankshaft into place. Be careful not to damage bearing surfaces.

7. Check the clearance of each main bearing by using the following procedure:

  a. Place a piece of Plastigage® or its equivalent, on bearing surface across full width of bearing cap and about ¼ in. off center.

  b. Install cap and tighten bolts to specifications. Do not turn crankshaft while Plastigage® is in place.

  c. Remove the cap. Using the supplied Plastigage® scale, check width of Plastigage® at widest point to get maximum clearance. Difference between readings is taper of journal.

  d. If clearance exceeds specified limits, try a 0.001 in. or 0.002 in. undersize bearing in combination with the standard bearing. Bearing clearance must be within specified limits. If standard and 0.002 in. undersize bearing does not bring clearance within desired limits, refinish crankshaft journal, then install undersize bearings.

8. Install the rear main seal.

9. After the bearings have been fitted, apply a light coat of engine oil to the journals and bearings. Install the rear main bearing cap. Install all bearing caps except the thrust bearing cap. Be sure that main bearing caps are installed in original locations. Tighten the bearing cap bolts to specifications.

10. Install the thrust bearing cap with bolts finger-tight.

11. Pry the crankshaft forward against the thrust surface of upper half of bearing.

12. Hold the crankshaft forward and pry the thrust bearing cap to the rear. This aligns the thrust surfaces of both halves of the bearing.

13. Retain the forward pressure on the crankshaft. Tighten the cap bolts to specifications.

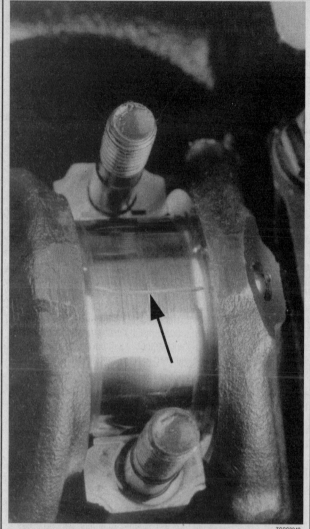

TCCS3243

Fig. 263 Apply a strip of gauging material to the bearing journal, then install and torque the cap

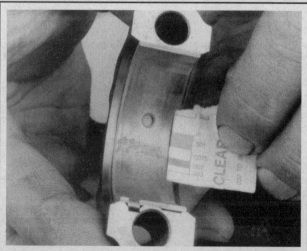

TCCS3912

Fig. 264 After the cap is removed again, use the scale supplied with the gauging material to check the clearance

Fig. 265 A dial gauge may be used to check crankshaft end-play

Fig. 266 Carefully pry the crankshaft back and forth while reading the dial gauge for end-play

b. Position the ring in the bore in which it is going to be used.

c. Push the ring down into the bore area where normal ring wear is not encountered.

d. Use the head of the piston to position the ring in the bore so that the ring is square with the cylinder wall. Use caution to avoid damage to the ring or cylinder bore.

e. Measure the gap between the ends of the ring with a feeler gauge. Ring gap in a worn cylinder is normally greater than specification. If the ring gap is greater than the specified limits, try an oversize ring set.

f. Check the ring side clearance of the compression rings with a feeler gauge inserted between the ring and its lower land according to specification. The gauge should slide freely around the entire ring circumference without binding. Any wear that occurs will form a step at the inner portion of the lower land. If the lower lands have high steps, the piston should be replaced.

2. Unless new pistons are installed, be sure to install the pistons in the cylinders from which they were removed. The numbers on the connecting rod and bearing cap must be on the same side when installed in the cylinder bore. If a connecting rod is ever transposed from one engine or cylinder to another, new bearings should be fitted and the connecting rod should be numbered to correspond with the new cylinder number. The notch on the piston head goes toward the front of the engine.

Fig. 267 Checking the piston ring-to-ring groove side clearance using the ring and a feeler gauge

14. Measure the crankshaft end-play as follows:

a. Mount a dial gauge to the engine block and position the tip of the gauge to read from the crankshaft end.

b. Carefully pry the crankshaft toward the rear of the engine and hold it there while you zero the gauge.

c. Carefully pry the crankshaft toward the front of the engine and read the gauge.

d. Confirm that the reading is within specifications. If not, install a new thrust bearing and repeat the procedure. If the reading is still out of specifications with a new bearing, have a machine shop inspect the thrust surfaces of the crankshaft, and if possible, repair it.

15. Rotate the crankshaft so as to position the first rod journal to the bottom of its stroke.

Pistons and Connecting Rods

♦ See Figures 267, 268, 269 and 270

1. Before installing the piston/connecting rod assembly, oil the pistons, piston rings and the cylinder walls with light engine oil. Install connecting rod bolt protectors or rubber hose onto the connecting rod bolts/studs. Also perform the following:

a. Select the proper ring set for the size cylinder bore.

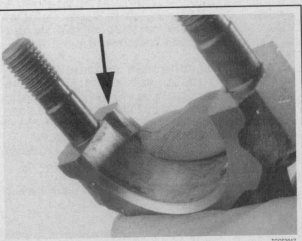

Fig. 268 The notch on the side of the bearing cap matches the tang on the bearing insert

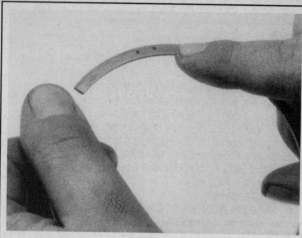

Fig. 269 Most rings are marked to show which side of the ring should face up when installed to the piston

Fig. 270 Install the piston and rod assembly into the block using a ring compressor and the handle of a hammer

3. Install all of the rod bearing inserts into the rods and caps.

4. Install the rings to the pistons. Install the oil control ring first, then the second compression ring and finally the top compression ring. Use a piston ring expander tool to aid in installation and to help reduce the chance of breakage.

5. Make sure the ring gaps are properly spaced around the circumference of the piston. Fit a piston ring compressor around the piston and slide the piston and connecting rod assembly down into the cylinder bore, pushing it in with the wooden hammer handle. Push the piston down until it is only slightly below the top of the cylinder bore. Guide the connecting rod onto the crankshaft bearing journal carefully, to avoid damaging the crankshaft.

6. Check the bearing clearance of all the rod bearings, fitting them to the crankshaft bearing journals. Follow the procedure in the crankshaft installation above.

7. After the bearings have been fitted, apply a light coating of assembly oil to the journals and bearings.

8. Turn the crankshaft until the appropriate bearing journal is at the bottom of its stroke, then push the piston assembly all the way down until the connecting rod bearing seats on the crankshaft journal. Be careful not to allow the bearing cap screws to strike the crankshaft bearing journals and damage them.

9. After the piston and connecting rod assemblies have been installed, check the connecting rod side clearance on each crankshaft journal.

10. Prime and install the oil pump and the oil pump intake tube.

11. Install the cylinder head(s) using new gaskets.

12. Install the timing sprockets/gears and the belt/chain assemblies. Install the timing cover(s) and oil pan. Refer to your notes and drawings made prior to disassembly and install all of the components that were removed. Install the engine into the vehicle.

Engine Start-up and Break-in

STARTING THE ENGINE

Now that the engine is installed and every wire and hose is properly connected, go back and double check that all coolant and vacuum hoses are connected. Check that you oil drain plug is installed and properly tightened. If not already done, install a new oil filter onto the engine. Fill the crankcase with the proper amount and grade of engine oil. Fill the cooling system with a 50/50 mixture of coolant/water.

1. Connect the vehicle battery.

2. Start the engine. Keep your eye on your oil pressure indicator; if it does not indicate oil pressure within 10 seconds of starting, turn the vehicle off.

✷✷ WARNING

Damage to the engine can result if it is allowed to run with no oil pressure. Check the engine oil level to make sure that it is full. Check for any leaks and if found, repair the leaks before continuing. If there is still no indication of oil pressure, you may need to prime the system.

3. Confirm that there are no fluid leaks (oil or other).

4. Allow the engine to reach normal operating temperature (the upper radiator hose will be hot to the touch).

5. If necessary, set the ignition timing.

6. Install any remaining components such as the air cleaner (if removed for ignition timing) or body panels which were removed.

BREAKING IT IN

Make the first miles on the new engine, easy ones. Vary the speed but do not accelerate hard. Most importantly, do not lug the engine, and avoid sustained high speeds until at least 100 miles. Check the engine oil and coolant levels frequently. Expect the engine to use a little oil until the rings seat. Change the oil and filter at 500 miles, 1500 miles, then every 3000 miles past that.

KEEP IT MAINTAINED

Now that you have just gone through all of that hard work, keep yourself from doing it all over again by thoroughly maintaining it. Not that you may not have maintained it before, heck you could have had one to two hundred thousand miles on it before doing this. However, you may have bought the vehicle used, and the previous owner did not keep up on maintenance. Which is why you just went through all of that hard work. See?

1.8L ENGINE TORQUE SPECIFICATIONS

Components	Ft. Lbs.	Nm
A/C compressor mounting bolts	15-22	20-30
A/C compressor mounting bracket side bolt	14-19	19-25
A/C hose routing bracket nuts	56-82 inch lbs.	6.4-93
Accelerator and kickdown cable bracket bolts	69-95 inch lbs.	8-11
Alternator lower mounting bolt	27-38	37-52
Battery duct bolts	69-95 inch lbs.	8-11
Camshaft cap bolts	100-126 inch lbs.	11-14
Camshaft pulley lockbolt	36-45	49-61
Clutch release cylinder bolts	12-17	16-23
Clutch slave cylinder pipe routing bracket bolt	12-17	16-23
Connecting rod cap nuts	35-37	47-50
Crankshaft pulley bolts	109-152 inch lbs.	12-17
Crankshaft rear cover bolts	69-95 inch lbs.	8-11
Crankshaft rear cover plate bolts	69-95 inch lbs.	8-11
Cylinder head ②	56-60	76-81
Distributor mounting bolts	14-19	19-25
Engine lifting bracket bolts	27-38	37-52
Engine mount bolt and nuts	49-69	67-93
Engine mount through-bolt and nut	49-69	67-93
Engine mount-to-engine nuts	54-76	74-103
Engine oil dipstick tube bolts	69-95 inch lbs.	8-11
Engine support bracket bolts	69-86	93-117
Engine vibration damper bolt and nuts	41-59	55-80
Exhaust flange-to-manifold nuts	23-34	31-46
Exhaust flange-to-manifold nuts	30-40	41-55
Exhaust flex pipe-to-converter nuts	23-34	31-46
Exhaust manifold heat shield bolts	69-95 inch lbs.	8-11
Exhaust manifold mounting nuts	28-34	38-46
Exhaust mounting flange-to-exhaust manifold nuts	23-34	31-46
Exhaust pipe support bracket bolts	27-38	37-52
Extension bar-to-transaxle nut	23-34	31-46
Flywheel/flexplate bolts ①	71-76	96-103
Fuel rail mounting bolts	14-19	19-25
Halfshaft bearing support bolts	31-46	45-62
Idler mounting bolt	27-38	37-52
Intake plenum and manifold assembly-to-cylinder head nuts	14-19	19-25
Main bearing cap bolts	40-43	54-59
Oil cooler mounting nut	22-29	29-39
Oil jet bolt	104-156 inch lbs.	12-18
Oil pan drain plug	22-30	29-41
Oil pan-to-engine block bolts	69-95 inch lbs.	8-11
Oil pan-to-transaxle bolts	27-38	37-52
Oil pressure switch	9-13	12-18
Oil pump cover screws	52-78 inch lbs.	6-9
Oil pump mounting bolts	14-19	19-25
Oil pump mounting bolts	14-19	19-25
Oil strainer bolts	69-95 inch lbs.	8-11
Power steering pump bracket bolts	27-38	37-52
Radiator mounting bracket bolts	69-95 inch lbs.	8-11
Seal plate mounting bolts	69-95 inch lbs.	8-11
Shift control rod-to-transaxle nut	12-17	16-23
Spark plugs	11-17	15-23
Splash shield bolts	69-95 inch lbs.	8-11
Starter motor bolts	27-38	37-52
Thermostat housing bolt and nut	14-19	19-25

90983C16

1.8L ENGINE TORQUE SPECIFICATIONS

Components	Ft. Lbs.	Nm
Timing belt lower cover bolts	69-95 inch lbs.	8-11
Timing belt middle cover bolts	69-95 inch lbs.	8-11
Timing belt pulley locking bolt	80-87	108-118
Timing belt tensioner lockbolt	37-52	27-38
Timing belt upper cover bolts	69-95 inch lbs.	8-11
Torque converter nuts	25-36	34-49
Transaxle front mount nuts	27-38	37-52
Transaxle support bracket bolts	41-59	55-80
Transaxle upper mount bolts	32-45	43-61
Transaxle upper mount nuts	49-69	67-93
Transaxle-to-engine bolts (automatic transaxle)	41-59	55-80
Transaxle-to-engine bolts (manual transaxle)	47-66	64-89
Valve cover bolts	43-78 inch lbs.	5-9
Water pump bolts	14-19	19-25
Water pump inlet fitting-to-water pump bolts	14-19	19-25
Water pump pulley bolts	69-95 inch lbs.	8-11

① Refer to the text for the tightening sequence

② Use new bolts; refer to the text for the tightening sequence

90983C17

1.9L ENGINE TORQUE SPECIFICATIONS

Components	Ft. Lbs.	Nm
A/C compressor mounting bolts	15-22	20-30
Camshaft sprocket retaining bolt	70-85	95-115
Camshaft thrust plate bolts	72-108 inch lbs.	8-13
Catalytic converter-to-exhaust manifold nuts	25-33	34-47
Clutch pressure plate bolt	13-20	18-26
Connecting rod nuts	26-30	35-41
Crankcase vent oil separator bracket bolt	72-108 inch lbs.	8-11
Crankshaft position sensor bolts	48-60 inch lbs.	5-7
Crankshaft pulley bolt	81-96	110-130
Crankshaft rear oil seal retainer bolt	15-22	20-30
Cylinder head stud ①	30-44	40-60
EGR valve bolt	13-19	18-26
EGR valve-to-exhaust manifold tube nut	18-25	25-35
Engine front cover nuts	36-60 inch lbs.	5-7
Engine front cover studs	84-108 inch lbs.	9-11
Engine insulator mounting bolt	49-69	67-93
Engine insulator mounting bolt	49-69	67-93
Engine lifting eye bolt	30-41	40-55
Engine oil dipstick tube bracket bolt	72-96 inch lbs.	8-10
Engine-to-transaxle bolts	27-38	37-52
Exhaust manifold nuts	16-19	21-26
Exhaust manifold shield-to-exhaust manifold nut	35-60 inch lbs.	5-7
Exhaust manifold stud	18-84 inch lbs.	2-10
Flywheel-to-converter nuts	25-36	34-49
Flywheel-to-crankshaft bolts	54-67	73-91
Front engine support mounting bracket bolt	69-86	93-117
Fuel rail bolt	15-22	20-30
Idle air control valve bolt	72-108 inch lbs.	8-11
Ignition coil mounting bolt	36-60 inch lbs.	4.5-7
Ignition coil mounting bracket bolt	15-30	20-40
Ignition coil screws	72-96 inch lbs.	8-11
Intake manifold nuts	12-15	16-20
Intake manifold stud	18-84 inch lbs.	2-10
Main bearing cap bolts	67-80	90-108
Oil pan drain plug	15-22	20-30
Oil pan-to-cylinder block bolts ①	15-22	20-30
Oil pan-to-transaxle bolts	30-40	40-55
Oil pressure sender	9-13	12-18
Oil pump bolts	8-12	11-16
Oil pump screen cover and tube bolts	84-108 inch lbs.	10-13
Rocker arm bolts	17-22	23-30
Spark plugs	8-15	10-20
Starter motor support bolts	15-20	20-27
Throttle body bolt	15-22	20-30
Timing belt tensioner bolt	17-22	23-30
Transaxle-to-engine bolts	40-59	55-80
Valve cover bolts	48-108 inch lbs.	5-12
Water hose connection bolts	72-108 inch lbs.	8-11
Water pump bolts	15-22	20-30

① Refer to the text for the tightening sequence

90983C18

2.0L SOHC ENGINE TORQUE SPECIFICATIONS

Components	Ft. Lbs.	Nm
A/C compressor bolts	15-22	20-30
A/C line bracket bolt	15-18	20-25
Alternator ground strap bolt	64-87 inch lbs.	8-11
Camshaft sprocket bolt	70-85	95-115
Camshaft thrust plate bolts	71-115 inch lbs.	8-13
Catalytic converter bracket bolts	15-20	20-28
Catalytic converter-to-muffler inlet pipe and resonator bolts	30-40	40-55
Catalytic converter-to-oil pan bracket bolts	30-40	40-55
Connecting rod cap nuts	26-30	35-41
Constant control relay bolts	70-101 inch lbs.	8-11.5
Crankshaft main bearing cap bolts	66-79	90-108
Crankshaft pulley bolt	81-96	110-130
Cylinder head bolts ①		
Step 1	30-44	40-60
Step 2	Back off bolts one-half turn	
Step 3	30-44	40-60
Step 4	Tighten all bolts an additional 180° in two steps of 90°	
EGR manifold tube-to-EGR valve	15-20	20-28
EGR manifold tube-to-exhaust manifold	45-62 inch lbs.	5-7
Engine front cover bolts and nuts	71-101 inch lbs.	8-11.5
Engine lifting eye bolts	29-40	40-55
Engine mounting bracket bolts	31-42	41-57
Engine oil dipstick tube bolt	71-101 inch lbs.	8-11.5
Exhaust manifold heat shield nuts	45-61 inch lbs.	5-7
Exhaust manifold nuts	15-18	20-24
Exhaust manifold-to-catalytic converter nuts	26-34	34-47
Flywheel bolts	54-67	73-91
Front engine accessory drive bracket bolts	30-40	40-55
Front engine accessory drive bracket nuts	30-40	40-55
Ignition coil bolts	40-61 inch lbs.	4.5-7
Ignition coil bracket bolts	71-101 inch lbs.	8-11.5
Intake manifold nuts	15-22	20-30
Intake manifold runner control actuator bolts	71-101 inch lbs.	8-11.5
Left-hand splash shield bolts	69-98 inch lbs.	8-11
Lower alternator bolt	15-22	20-30
Motor mount nuts	50-69	67-93
Oil pan baffle bolts	15-22	20-30
Oil pan bolts	15-22	20-30
Oil pan drain plug	15-22	20-30
Oil pressure sender	8-12	10-16.5
Oil pump bolts	8-12	11-16
Oil pump screen cover and tube bolts	71-102 inch lbs.	8-11.5
Power steering pressure hose bracket bolts	64-87 inch lbs.	8-11
Power steering pressure line fitting	15-18	20-25
Power steering pump bolts	30-41	40-55
Power steering pump pulley bolt	15-22	20-30
Right-hand engine support insulator through-bolt	50-69	67-93
Right-hand splash shield assembly	69-98 inch lbs.	8-11
Rocker arm bolts	17-22	23-30
Speed control cable bracket bolts	64-87 inch lbs.	8-11
Starter motor bolt	18-20	25-27
Timing belt tensioner bolt	15-22	20-30
Upper alternator bolt	30-40	40-55
Vacuum tree bolts	70-101 inch lbs.	8-11.5
Valve cover bolts	71-101 inch lbs.	8-11.5
Water outlet connection bolts	8-11	10-16
Water pump bolts	15-22	20-30

① Refer to the text for the tightening sequence

90983C19

2.0L DOHC ENGINE TORQUE SPECIFICATIONS

Components	Ft. Lbs.	Nm
A/C compressor bolts	15-22	20-30
Alternator bolts	34	47
Appearance cover bolts	62 inch lbs.	7
Camshaft journal cap bolts	10-12	13-17
Crankshaft main bearing cap bolts	59-66	80-90
Crankshaft pulley bolt	81-89	110-120
Crankshaft rear seal retainer bolt	14-16	18-22
Cylinder head bolts ①		
First pass	12-18	15-25
Second pass	26-33	35-45
Final pass	Tighten the bolts an additional 105°	
Engine lifting eye bolts	29-40	39-55
Engine oil dipstick tube bolt	71-97 inch lbs.	8-11
Engine-to-automatic transaxle bolts	28-38	38-51
Engine-to-manual transaxle bolt	41-59	55-80
Exhaust camshaft (VCT) sprocket bolt	88	120
Exhaust camshaft (VCT) sprocket plug	27	37
Exhaust manifold heat shield bolts	71-97 inch lbs.	8-11
Exhaust manifold nuts	10-12	14-17
Flywheel bolts	75-85	102-115
Front engine support isolator nuts and bolt	50-68	67-93
Front roll restrictor bolts	50-69	67-93
Front roll restrictor nuts	48-65	64-89
Fuel charging wiring bolt	71-97 inch lbs.	8-11
Heater tube bolts	79 inch lbs.	9
Intake camshaft sprocket bolt	50	68
Intake manifold nuts	12-15	16-20
Lower cylinder block bolts	15-17	20-24
Lower timing belt cover switch	61 inch lbs.	7
Middle timing belt cover bolts	10	13
Oil control solenoid flange bolts	88 inch lbs.	10
Oil pan bolts	15-22	20-30
Oil pan drain plug	22-28	29-41
Oil pressure sender	19	27
Oil pump bolts	88-97 inch lbs.	10-11
Oil pump screen cover and tube bolts	71-97 inch lbs.	8-11
Oil separator bolt	71-97 inch lbs.	8-11
Power steering pump bolts	15	20
Rear roll restrictor nuts	28-38	38-51
Splash shield assembly	62-97 inch lbs.	7-11
Throttle body bolts	71-106 inch lbs.	8-12
Timing belt backplate bolts	80-97 inch lbs.	9-11
Timing belt idler pulley bolt	35	48
Timing belt tensioner bolt	17-20	22-28
Torque converter inspection cover bolt	28-38	38-51
Transaxle oil cooler line bolts	71-106 inch lbs.	8-12
Upper timing cover bolts	27-44 inch lbs.	3-5
Valve cover bolts	54-70 inch lbs.	6-8
Water pump bolts	17	24

VCT: Variable Cam Timing

① Refer to the text for the tightening sequence

90983C21

USING A VACUUM GAUGE

White needle = steady needle   *Dark needle = drifting needle*

The vacuum gauge is one of the most useful and easy-to-use diagnostic tools. It is inexpensive, easy to hook up, and provides valuable information about the condition of your engine.

Indication: Normal engine in good condition

Gauge reading: Steady, from 17–22 in./Hg.

Indication: Sticking valve or ignition miss

Gauge reading: Needle fluctuates from 15–20 in./Hg. at idle

Indication: Late ignition or valve timing, low compression, stuck throttle valve, leaking carburetor or manifold gasket.

Gauge reading: Low (15–20 in./Hg.) but steady

Indication: Improper carburetor adjustment, or minor intake leak at carburetor or manifold

NOTE: Bad fuel injector O-rings may also cause this reading.

Gauge reading: Drifting needle

Indication: Weak valve springs, worn valve stem guides, or leaky cylinder head gasket (vibrating excessively at all speeds).

NOTE: A plugged catalytic converter may also cause this reading.

Gauge reading: Needle fluctuates as engine speed increases

Indication: Burnt valve or improper valve clearance. The needle will drop when the defective valve operates.

Gauge reading: Steady needle, but drops regularly

Indication: Choked muffler or obstruction in system. Speed up the engine. Choked muffler will exhibit a slow drop of vacuum to zero.

Gauge reading: Gradual drop in reading at idle

Indication: Worn valve guides

Gauge reading: Needle vibrates excessively at idle, but steadies as engine speed increases

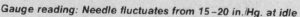

TCCS3C01

Troubleshooting Engine Mechanical Problems

Problem	Cause	Solution
External oil leaks	• Cylinder head cover RTV sealant broken or improperly seated	• Replace sealant; inspect cylinder head cover sealant flange and cylinder head sealant surface for distortion and cracks
	• Oil filler cap leaking or missing	• Replace cap
	• Oil filter gasket broken or improperly seated	• Replace oil filter
	• Oil pan side gasket broken, improperly seated or opening in RTV sealant	• Replace gasket or repair opening in sealant; inspect oil pan gasket flange for distortion
	• Oil pan front oil seal broken or improperly seated	• Replace seal; inspect timing case cover and oil pan seal flange for distortion
	• Oil pan rear oil seal broken or improperly seated	• Replace seal; inspect oil pan rear oil seal flange; inspect rear main bearing cap for cracks, plugged oil return channels, or distortion in seal groove
	• Timing case cover oil seal broken or improperly seated	• Replace seal
	• Excess oil pressure because of restricted PCV valve	• Replace PCV valve
	• Oil pan drain plug loose or has stripped threads	• Repair as necessary and tighten
	• Rear oil gallery plug loose	• Use appropriate sealant on gallery plug and tighten
	• Rear camshaft plug loose or improperly seated	• Seat camshaft plug or replace and seal, as necessary
Excessive oil consumption	• Oil level too high	• Drain oil to specified level
	• Oil with wrong viscosity being used	• Replace with specified oil
	• PCV valve stuck closed	• Replace PCV valve
	• Valve stem oil deflectors (or seals) are damaged, missing, or incorrect type	• Replace valve stem oil deflectors
	• Valve stems or valve guides worn	• Measure stem-to-guide clearance and repair as necessary
	• Poorly fitted or missing valve cover baffles	• Replace valve cover
	• Piston rings broken or missing	• Replace broken or missing rings
	• Scuffed piston	• Replace piston
	• Incorrect piston ring gap	• Measure ring gap, repair as necessary
	• Piston rings sticking or excessively loose in grooves	• Measure ring side clearance, repair as necessary
	• Compression rings installed upside down	• Repair as necessary
	• Cylinder walls worn, scored, or glazed	• Repair as necessary

TCCS3C02

Troubleshooting Engine Mechanical Problems

Problem	Cause	Solution
Excessive oil consumption (cont.)	• Piston ring gaps not properly staggered	• Repair as necessary
	• Excessive main or connecting rod bearing clearance	• Measure bearing clearance, repair as necessary
No oil pressure	• Low oil level	• Add oil to correct level
	• Oil pressure gauge, warning lamp or sending unit inaccurate	• Replace oil pressure gauge or warning lamp
	• Oil pump malfunction	• Replace oil pump
	• Oil pressure relief valve sticking	• Remove and inspect oil pressure relief valve assembly
	• Oil passages on pressure side of pump obstructed	• Inspect oil passages for obstruction
	• Oil pickup screen or tube obstructed	• Inspect oil pickup for obstruction
	• Loose oil inlet tube	• Tighten or seal inlet tube
Low oil pressure	• Low oil level	• Add oil to correct level
	• Inaccurate gauge, warning lamp or sending unit	• Replace oil pressure gauge or warning lamp
	• Oil excessively thin because of dilution, poor quality, or improper grade	• Drain and refill crankcase with recommended oil
	• Excessive oil temperature	• Correct cause of overheating engine
	• Oil pressure relief spring weak or sticking	• Remove and inspect oil pressure relief valve assembly
	• Oil inlet tube and screen assembly has restriction or air leak	• Remove and inspect oil inlet tube and screen assembly. (Fill inlet tube with lacquer thinner to locate leaks.)
	• Excessive oil pump clearance	• Measure clearances
	• Excessive main, rod, or camshaft bearing clearance	• Measure bearing clearances, repair as necessary
High oil pressure	• Improper oil viscosity	• Drain and refill crankcase with correct viscosity oil
	• Oil pressure gauge or sending unit inaccurate	• Replace oil pressure gauge
	• Oil pressure relief valve sticking closed	• Remove and inspect oil pressure relief valve assembly
Main bearing noise	• Insufficient oil supply	• Inspect for low oil level and low oil pressure
	• Main bearing clearance excessive	• Measure main bearing clearance, repair as necessary
	• Bearing insert missing	• Replace missing insert
	• Crankshaft end-play excessive	• Measure end-play, repair as necessary
	• Improperly tightened main bearing cap bolts	• Tighten bolts with specified torque
	• Loose flywheel or drive plate	• Tighten flywheel or drive plate attaching bolts
	• Loose or damaged vibration damper	• Repair as necessary

TCCS3C03

Troubleshooting Engine Mechanical Problems

Problem	Cause	Solution
Connecting rod bearing noise	• Insufficient oil supply	• Inspect for low oil level and low oil pressure
	• Carbon build-up on piston	• Remove carbon from piston crown
	• Bearing clearance excessive or bearing missing	• Measure clearance, repair as necessary
	• Crankshaft connecting rod journal out-of-round	• Measure journal dimensions, repair or replace as necessary
	• Misaligned connecting rod or cap	• Repair as necessary
	• Connecting rod bolts tightened improperly	• Tighten bolts with specified torque
Piston noise	• Piston-to-cylinder wall clearance excessive (scuffed piston)	• Measure clearance and examine piston
	• Cylinder walls excessively tapered or out-of-round	• Measure cylinder wall dimensions, rebore cylinder
	• Piston ring broken	• Replace all rings on piston
	• Loose or seized piston pin	• Measure piston-to-pin clearance, repair as necessary
	• Connecting rods misaligned	• Measure rod alignment, straighten or replace
	• Piston ring side clearance excessively loose or tight	• Measure ring side clearance, repair as necessary
	• Carbon build-up on piston is excessive	• Remove carbon from piston
Valve actuating component noise	• Insufficient oil supply	• Check for: (a) Low oil level (b) Low oil pressure (c) Wrong hydraulic tappets (d) Restricted oil gallery (e) Excessive tappet to bore clearance
	• Rocker arms or pivots worn	• Replace worn rocker arms or pivots
	• Foreign objects or chips in hydraulic tappets	• Clean tappets
	• Excessive tappet leak-down	• Replace valve tappet
	• Tappet face worn	• Replace tappet; inspect corresponding cam lobe for wear
	• Broken or cocked valve springs	• Properly seat cocked springs; replace broken springs
	• Stem-to-guide clearance excessive	• Measure stem-to-guide clearance, repair as required
	• Valve bent	• Replace valve
	• Loose rocker arms	• Check and repair as necessary
	• Valve seat runout excessive	• Regrind valve seat/valves
	• Missing valve lock	• Install valve lock
	• Excessive engine oil	• Correct oil level

TCCS3C04

Troubleshooting Engine Performance

Problem	Cause	Solution
Hard starting (engine cranks normally)	• Faulty engine control system component • Faulty fuel pump • Faulty fuel system component • Faulty ignition coil • Improper spark plug gap • Incorrect ignition timing • Incorrect valve timing	• Repair or replace as necessary • Replace fuel pump • Repair or replace as necessary • Test and replace as necessary • Adjust gap • Adjust timing • Check valve timing; repair as necessary
Rough idle or stalling	• Incorrect curb or fast idle speed • Incorrect ignition timing • Improper feedback system operation • Faulty EGR valve operation • Faulty PCV valve air flow • Faulty TAC vacuum motor or valve • Air leak into manifold vacuum • Faulty distributor rotor or cap • Improperly seated valves • Incorrect ignition wiring • Faulty ignition coil • Restricted air vent or idle passages • Restricted air cleaner	• Adjust curb or fast idle speed (If possible) • Adjust timing to specification • Refer to Chapter 4 • Test EGR system and replace as necessary • Test PCV valve and replace as necessary • Repair as necessary • Inspect manifold vacuum connections and repair as necessary • Replace rotor or cap (Distributor systems only) • Test cylinder compression, repair as necessary • Inspect wiring and correct as necessary • Test coil and replace as necessary • Clean passages • Clean or replace air cleaner filter element
Faulty low-speed operation	• Restricted idle air vents and passages • Restricted air cleaner • Faulty spark plugs • Dirty, corroded, or loose ignition secondary circuit wire connections • Improper feedback system operation • Faulty ignition coil high voltage wire • Faulty distributor cap	• Clean air vents and passages • Clean or replace air cleaner filter element • Clean or replace spark plugs • Clean or tighten secondary circuit wire connections • Refer to Chapter 4 • Replace ignition coil high voltage wire (Distributor systems only) • Replace cap (Distributor systems only)
Faulty acceleration	• Incorrect ignition timing • Faulty fuel system component • Faulty spark plug(s) • Improperly seated valves • Faulty ignition coil	• Adjust timing • Repair or replace as necessary • Clean or replace spark plug(s) • Test cylinder compression, repair as necessary • Test coil and replace as necessary

Troubleshooting Engine Performance

Problem	Cause	Solution
Faulty acceleration (cont.)	• Improper feedback system operation	• Refer to Chapter 4
Faulty high speed operation	• Incorrect ignition timing • Faulty advance mechanism	• Adjust timing (if possible) • Check advance mechanism and repair as necessary (Distributor systems only)
	• Low fuel pump volume • Wrong spark plug air gap or wrong plug • Partially restricted exhaust manifold, exhaust pipe, catalytic converter, muffler, or tailpipe • Restricted vacuum passages • Restricted air cleaner	• Replace fuel pump • Adjust air gap or install correct plug • Eliminate restriction • Clean passages • Cleaner or replace filter element as necessary
	• Faulty distributor rotor or cap	• Replace rotor or cap (Distributor systems only)
	• Faulty ignition coil • Improperly seated valve(s)	• Test coil and replace as necessary • Test cylinder compression, repair as necessary
	• Faulty valve spring(s)	• Inspect and test valve spring tension, replace as necessary
	• Incorrect valve timing	• Check valve timing and repair as necessary
	• Intake manifold restricted	• Remove restriction or replace manifold
	• Worn distributor shaft	• Replace shaft (Distributor systems only)
	• Improper feedback system operation	• Refer to Chapter 4
Misfire at all speeds	• Faulty spark plug(s) • Faulty spark plug wire(s) • Faulty distributor cap or rotor	• Clean or relace spark plug(s) • Replace as necessary • Replace cap or rotor (Distributor systems only)
	• Faulty ignition coil • Primary ignition circuit shorted or open intermittently • Improperly seated valve(s)	• Test coil and replace as necessary • Troubleshoot primary circuit and repair as necessary • Test cylinder compression, repair as necessary
	• Faulty hydraulic tappet(s) • Improper feedback system operation • Faulty valve spring(s)	• Clean or replace tappet(s) • Refer to Chapter 4 • Inspect and test valve spring tension, repair as necessary
	• Worn camshaft lobes • Air leak into manifold	• Replace camshaft • Check manifold vacuum and repair as necessary
	• Fuel pump volume or pressure low • Blown cylinder head gasket • Intake or exhaust manifold passage(s) restricted	• Replace fuel pump • Replace gasket • Pass chain through passage(s) and repair as necessary
Power not up to normal	• Incorrect ignition timing • Faulty distributor rotor	• Adjust timing • Replace rotor (Distributor systems only)

Troubleshooting Engine Performance

Problem	Cause	Solution
Power not up to normal (cont.)	• Incorrect spark plug gap	• Adjust gap
	• Faulty fuel pump	• Replace fuel pump
	• Faulty fuel pump	• Replace fuel pump
	• Incorrect valve timing	• Check valve timing and repair as necessary
	• Faulty ignition coil	• Test coil and replace as necessary
	• Faulty ignition wires	• Test wires and replace as necessary
	• Improperly seated valves	• Test cylinder compression and repair as necessary
	• Blown cylinder head gasket	• Replace gasket
	• Leaking piston rings	• Test compression and repair as necessary
	• Improper feedback system operation	• Refer to Chapter 4
Intake backfire	• Improper ignition timing	• Adjust timing
	• Defective EGR component	• Repair as necessary
	• Defective TAC vacuum motor or valve	• Repair as necessary
Exhaust backfire	• Air leak into manifold vacuum	• Check manifold vacuum and repair as necessary
	• Faulty air injection diverter valve	• Test diverter valve and replace as necessary
	• Exhaust leak	• Locate and eliminate leak
Ping or spark knock	• Incorrect ignition timing	• Adjust timing
	• Distributor advance malfunction	• Inspect advance mechanism and repair as necessary (Distributor systems only)
	• Excessive combustion chamber deposits	• Remove with combustion chamber cleaner
	• Air leak into manifold vacuum	• Check manifold vacuum and repair as necessary
	• Excessively high compression	• Test compression and repair as necessary
	• Fuel octane rating excessively low	• Try alternate fuel source
	• Sharp edges in combustion chamber	• Grind smooth
	• EGR valve not functioning properly	• Test EGR system and replace as necessary
Surging (at cruising to top speeds)	• Low fuel pump pressure or volume	• Replace fuel pump
	• Improper PCV valve air flow	• Test PCV valve and replace as necessary
	• Air leak into manifold vacuum	• Check manifold vacuum and repair as necessary
	• Incorrect spark advance	• Test and replace as necessary
	• Restricted fuel filter	• Replace fuel filter
	• Restricted air cleaner	• Clean or replace air cleaner filter element
	• EGR valve not functioning properly	• Test EGR system and replace as necessary
	• Improper feedback system operation	• Refer to Chapter 4

TCCS3C07

Troubleshooting the Serpentine Drive Belt

Problem	Cause	Solution
Tension sheeting fabric failure (woven fabric on outside circumference of belt has cracked or separated from body of belt)	• Grooved or backside idler pulley diameters are less than minimum recommended • Tension sheeting contacting (rubbing) stationary object • Excessive heat causing woven fabric to age • Tension sheeting splice has fractured	• Replace pulley(s) not conforming to specification • Correct rubbing condition • Replace belt • Replace belt
Noise (objectional squeal, squeak, or rumble is heard or felt while drive belt is in operation)	• Belt slippage • Bearing noise • Belt misalignment • Belt-to-pulley mismatch • Driven component inducing vibration • System resonant frequency inducing vibration	• Adjust belt • Locate and repair • Align belt/pulley(s) • Install correct belt • Locate defective driven component and repair • Vary belt tension within specifications. Replace belt.
Rib chunking (one or more ribs has separated from belt body)	• Foreign objects imbedded in pulley grooves • Installation damage • Drive loads in excess of design specifications • Insufficient internal belt adhesion	• Remove foreign objects from pulley grooves • Replace belt • Adjust belt tension • Replace belt
Rib or belt wear (belt ribs contact bottom of pulley grooves)	• Pulley(s) misaligned • Mismatch of belt and pulley groove widths • Abrasive environment • Rusted pulley(s) • Sharp or jagged pulley groove tips • Rubber deteriorated	• Align pulley(s) • Replace belt • Replace belt • Clean rust from pulley(s) • Replace pulley • Replace belt
Longitudinal belt cracking (cracks between two ribs)	• Belt has mistracked from pulley groove • Pulley groove tip has worn away rubber-to-tensile member	• Replace belt • Replace belt
Belt slips	• Belt slipping because of insufficient tension • Belt or pulley subjected to substance (belt dressing, oil, ethylene glycol) that has reduced friction • Driven component bearing failure • Belt glazed and hardened from heat and excessive slippage	• Adjust tension • Replace belt and clean pulleys • Replace faulty component bearing • Replace belt
"Groove jumping" (belt does not maintain correct position on pulley, or turns over and/or runs off pulleys)	• Insufficient belt tension • Pulley(s) not within design tolerance • Foreign object(s) in grooves	• Adjust belt tension • Replace pulley(s) • Remove foreign objects from grooves

Troubleshooting the Serpentine Drive Belt

Problem	Cause	Solution
"Groove jumping" (belt does not maintain correct position on pulley, or turns over and/or runs off pulleys)	• Excessive belt speed • Pulley misalignment • Belt-to-pulley profile mismatched • Belt cordline is distorted	• Avoid excessive engine acceleration • Align pulley(s) • Install correct belt • Replace belt
Belt broken (Note: identify and correct problem before replacement belt is installed)	• Excessive tension • Tensile members damaged during belt installation • Belt turnover • Severe pulley misalignment • Bracket, pulley, or bearing failure	• Replace belt and adjust tension to specification • Replace belt • Replace belt • Align pulley(s) • Replace defective component and belt
Cord edge failure (tensile member exposed at edges of belt or separated from belt body)	• Excessive tension • Drive pulley misalignment • Belt contacting stationary object • Pulley irregularities • Improper pulley construction • Insufficient adhesion between tensile member and rubber matrix	• Adjust belt tension • Align pulley • Correct as necessary • Replace pulley • Replace pulley • Replace belt and adjust tension to specifications
Sporadic rib cracking (multiple cracks in belt ribs at random intervals)	• Ribbed pulley(s) diameter less than minimum specification • Backside bend flat pulley(s) diameter less than minimum • Excessive heat condition causing rubber to harden • Excessive belt thickness • Belt overcured • Excessive tension	• Replace pulley(s) • Replace pulley(s) • Correct heat condition as necessary • Replace belt • Replace belt • Adjust belt tension

TCCS3C10

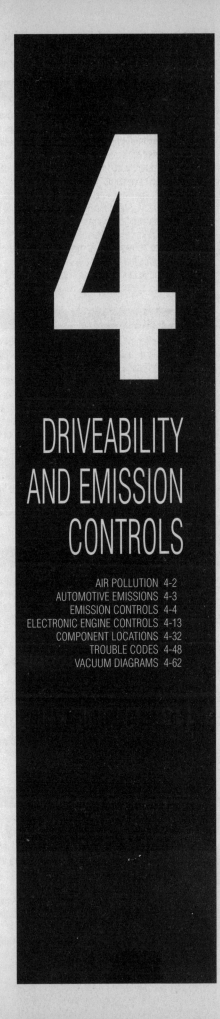

4

DRIVEABILITY AND EMISSION CONTROLS

AIR POLLUTION

The earth's atmosphere, at or near sea level, consists approximately of 78 percent nitrogen, 21 percent oxygen and 1 percent other gases. If it were possible to remain in this state, 100 percent clean air would result. However, many varied sources allow other gases and particulates to mix with the clean air, causing our atmosphere to become unclean or polluted.

Some of these pollutants are visible while others are invisible, with each having the capability of causing distress to the eyes, ears, throat, skin and respiratory system. Should these pollutants become concentrated in a specific area and under certain conditions, death could result due to the displacement or chemical change of the oxygen content in the air. These pollutants can also cause great damage to the environment and to the many man made objects that are exposed to the elements.

To better understand the causes of air pollution, the pollutants can be categorized into 3 separate types, natural, industrial and automotive.

Natural Pollutants

Natural pollution has been present on earth since before man appeared and continues to be a factor when discussing air pollution, although it causes only a small percentage of the overall pollution problem. It is the direct result of decaying organic matter, wind born smoke and particulates from such natural events as plain and forest fires (ignited by heat or lightning), volcanic ash, sand and dust which can spread over a large area of the countryside.

Such a phenomenon of natural pollution has been seen in the form of volcanic eruptions, with the resulting plume of smoke, steam and volcanic ash blotting out the sun's rays as it spreads and rises higher into the atmosphere. As it travels into the atmosphere the upper air currents catch and carry the smoke and ash, while condensing the steam back into water vapor. As the water vapor, smoke and ash travel on their journey, the smoke dissipates into the atmosphere while the ash and moisture settle back to earth in a trail hundreds of miles long. In some cases, lives are lost and millions of dollars of property damage result.

Industrial Pollutants

Industrial pollution is caused primarily by industrial processes, the burning of coal, oil and natural gas, which in turn produce smoke and fumes. Because the burning fuels contain large amounts of sulfur, the principal ingredients of smoke and fumes are sulfur dioxide and particulate matter. This type of pollutant occurs most severely during still, damp and cool weather, such as at night. Even in its less severe form, this pollutant is not confined to just cities. Because of air movements, the pollutants move for miles over the surrounding countryside, leaving in its path a barren and unhealthy environment for all living things.

Working with Federal, State and Local mandated regulations and by carefully monitoring emissions, big business has greatly reduced the amount of pollutant introduced from its industrial sources, striving to obtain an acceptable level. Because of the mandated industrial emission clean up, many land areas and streams in and around the cities that were formerly barren of vegetation and life, have now begun to move back in the direction of nature's intended balance.

Automotive Pollutants

The third major source of air pollution is automotive emissions. The emissions from the internal combustion engines were not an appreciable problem years ago because of the small number of registered vehicles and the nation's small highway system. However, during the early 1950's, the trend of the American people was to move from the cities to the surrounding suburbs. This caused an immediate problem in transportation because the majority of suburbs were not afforded mass transit conveniences. This lack of transportation created an attractive market for the automobile manufacturers, which resulted in a dramatic increase in the number of vehicles produced and sold, along with a marked increase in highway construction between cities and the suburbs. Multi-vehicle families emerged with a growing emphasis placed on an individual vehicle per family member. As the increase in vehicle ownership and usage occurred, so did pollutant levels in and around the cities, as suburbanites drove daily to their businesses and employment, returning at the end of the day to their homes in the suburbs.

It was noted that a smoke and fog type haze was being formed and at times, remained in suspension over the cities, taking time to dissipate. At first this "smog," derived from the words "smoke" and "fog," was thought to result from industrial pollution but it was determined that automobile emissions shared the blame. It was discovered that when normal automobile emissions were exposed to sunlight for a period of time, complex chemical reactions would take place.

It is now known that smog is a photo chemical layer which develops when certain oxides of nitrogen (NOx) and unburned hydrocarbons (HC) from automobile emissions are exposed to sunlight. Pollution was more severe when smog would become stagnant over an area in which a warm layer of air settled over the top of the cooler air mass, trapping and holding the cooler mass at ground level. The trapped cooler air would keep the emissions from being dispersed and diluted through normal air flows. This type of air stagnation was given the name "Temperature Inversion."

TEMPERATURE INVERSION

In normal weather situations, surface air is warmed by heat radiating from the earth's surface and the sun's rays. This causes it to rise upward, into the atmosphere. Upon rising it will cool through a convection type heat exchange with the cooler upper air. As warm air rises, the surface pollutants are carried upward and dissipated into the atmosphere.

When a temperature inversion occurs, we find the higher air is no longer cooler, but is warmer than the surface air, causing the cooler surface air to become trapped. This warm air blanket can extend from above ground level to a few hundred or even a few thousand feet into the air. As the surface air is trapped, so are the pollutants, causing a severe smog condition. Should this stagnant air mass extend to a few thousand feet high, enough air movement with the inversion takes place to allow the smog layer to rise above ground level but the pollutants still cannot dissipate. This inversion can remain for days over an area, with the smog level only rising or lowering from ground level to a few hundred feet high. Meanwhile, the pollutant levels increase, causing eye irritation, respiratory problems, reduced visibility, plant damage and in some cases, even disease.

This inversion phenomenon was first noted in the Los Angeles, California area. The city lies in terrain resembling a basin and with certain weather conditions, a cold air mass is held in the basin while a warmer air mass covers it like a lid.

Because this type of condition was first documented as prevalent in the Los Angeles area, this type of trapped pollution was named Los Angeles Smog, although it occurs in other areas where a large concentration of automobiles are used and the air remains stagnant for any length of time.

HEAT TRANSFER

Consider the internal combustion engine as a machine in which raw materials must be placed so a finished product comes out. As in any machine operation, a certain amount of wasted material is formed. When we relate this to the internal combustion engine, we find that through the input of air and fuel, we obtain power during the combustion process to drive the vehicle. The by-product or waste of this power is, in part, heat and exhaust gases with which we must dispose.

The heat from the combustion process can rise to over 4000°F (2204°C). The dissipation of this heat is controlled by a ram air effect, the use of cooling fans to cause air flow and a liquid coolant solution surrounding the combustion area to transfer the heat of combustion through the cylinder walls and into the coolant. The coolant is then directed to a thin-finned, multi-tubed radiator, from which the excess heat is transferred to the atmosphere by 1 of the 3 heat transfer methods, conduction, convection or radiation.

The cooling of the combustion area is an important part in the control of exhaust emissions. To understand the behavior of the combustion and transfer of its heat, consider the air/fuel charge. It is ignited and the flame front burns progressively across the combustion chamber until the burning charge reaches the cylinder walls. Some of the fuel in contact with the walls is not hot enough to burn, thereby snuffing out or quenching the combustion process. This leaves unburned fuel in the combustion chamber. This unburned fuel is then forced out of the cylinder and into the exhaust system, along with the exhaust gases.

Many attempts have been made to minimize the amount of unburned fuel in the combustion chambers due to quenching, by increasing the coolant temperature and lessening the contact area of the coolant around the combustion area. However, design limitations within the combustion chambers prevent the complete burning of the air/fuel charge, so a certain amount of the unburned fuel is still expelled into the exhaust system, regardless of modifications to the engine.

AUTOMOTIVE EMISSIONS

Before emission controls were mandated on internal combustion engines, other sources of engine pollutants were discovered along with the exhaust emissions. It was determined that engine combustion exhaust produced approximately 60 percent of the total emission pollutants, fuel evaporation from the fuel tank and carburetor vents produced 20 percent, with the final 20 percent being produced through the crankcase as a by-product of the combustion process.

Exhaust Gases

The exhaust gases emitted into the atmosphere are a combination of burned and unburned fuel. To understand the exhaust emission and its composition, we must review some basic chemistry.

When the air/fuel mixture is introduced into the engine, we are mixing air, composed of nitrogen (78 percent), oxygen (21 percent) and other gases (1 percent) with the fuel, which is 100 percent hydrocarbons (HC), in a semi-controlled ratio. As the combustion process is accomplished, power is produced to move the vehicle while the heat of combustion is transferred to the cooling system. The exhaust gases are then composed of nitrogen, a diatomic gas (N_2), the same as was introduced in the engine, carbon dioxide (CO_2), the same gas that is used in beverage carbonation, and water vapor (H_2O). The nitrogen (N_2), for the most part, passes through the engine unchanged, while the oxygen (O_2) reacts (burns) with the hydrocarbons (HC) and produces the carbon dioxide (CO_2) and the water vapors (H_2O). If this chemical process would be the only process to take place, the exhaust emissions would be harmless. However, during the combustion process, other compounds are formed which are considered dangerous. These pollutants are hydrocarbons (HC), carbon monoxide (CO), oxides of nitrogen (NOx) oxides of sulfur (SOx) and engine particulates.

HYDROCARBONS

Hydrocarbons (HC) are essentially fuel which was not burned during the combustion process or which has escaped into the atmosphere through fuel evaporation. The main sources of incomplete combustion are rich air/fuel mixtures, low engine temperatures and improper spark timing. The main sources of hydrocarbon emission through fuel evaporation on most vehicles used to be the vehicle's fuel tank and carburetor float bowl.

To reduce combustion hydrocarbon emission, engine modifications were made to minimize dead space and surface area in the combustion chamber. In addition, the air/fuel mixture was made more lean through the improved control which feedback carburetion and fuel injection offers and by the addition of external controls to aid in further combustion of the hydrocarbons outside the engine. Two such methods were the addition of air injection systems, to inject fresh air into the exhaust manifolds and the installation of catalytic converters, units that are able to burn traces of hydrocarbons without affecting the internal combustion process or fuel economy.

To control hydrocarbon emissions through fuel evaporation, modifications were made to the fuel tank to allow storage of the fuel vapors during periods of engine shut-down. Modifications were also made to the air intake system so that at specific times during engine operation, these vapors may be purged and burned by blending them with the air/fuel mixture.

CARBON MONOXIDE

Carbon monoxide is formed when not enough oxygen is present during the combustion process to convert carbon (C) to carbon dioxide (CO_2). An increase in the carbon monoxide (CO) emission is normally accompanied by an increase in the hydrocarbon (HC) emission because of the lack of oxygen to completely burn all of the fuel mixture.

Carbon monoxide (CO) also increases the rate at which the photo chemical smog is formed by speeding up the conversion of nitric oxide (NO) to nitrogen dioxide (NO_2). To accomplish this, carbon monoxide (CO) combines with oxygen (O_2) and nitric oxide (NO) to produce carbon dioxide (CO_2) and nitrogen dioxide (NO_2). ($CO + O_2 + NO = CO_2 + NO_2$).

The dangers of carbon monoxide, which is an odorless and colorless toxic gas are many. When carbon monoxide is inhaled into the lungs and passed into the blood stream, oxygen is replaced by the carbon monoxide in the red blood cells, causing a reduction in the amount of oxygen supplied to the many parts of the body. This lack of oxygen causes headaches, lack of coordination, reduced mental alertness and, should the carbon monoxide concentration be high enough, death could result.

NITROGEN

Normally, nitrogen is an inert gas. When heated to approximately 2500°F (1371°C) through the combustion process, this gas becomes active and causes an increase in the nitric oxide (NO) emission.

Oxides of nitrogen (NOx) are composed of approximately 97–98 percent nitric oxide (NO). Nitric oxide is a colorless gas but when it is passed into the atmosphere, it combines with oxygen and forms nitrogen dioxide (NO_2). The nitrogen dioxide then combines with chemically active hydrocarbons (HC) and when in the presence of sunlight, causes the formation of photochemical smog.

Ozone

To further complicate matters, some of the nitrogen dioxide (NO_2) is broken apart by the sunlight to form nitric oxide and oxygen. (NO_2 + sunlight = NO + O). This single atom of oxygen then combines with diatomic (meaning 2 atoms) oxygen (O_2) to form ozone (O_3). Ozone is one of the smells associated with smog. It has a pungent and offensive odor, irritates the eyes and lung tissues, affects the growth of plant life and causes rapid deterioration of rubber products. Ozone can be formed by sunlight as well as electrical discharge into the air.

The most common discharge area on the automobile engine is the secondary ignition electrical system, especially when inferior quality spark plug cables are used. As the surge of high voltage is routed through the secondary cable, the circuit builds up an electrical field around the wire, which acts upon the oxygen in the surrounding air to form the ozone. The faint glow along the cable with the engine running that may be visible on a dark night, is called the "corona discharge." It is the result of the electrical field passing from a high along the cable, to a low in the surrounding air, which forms the ozone gas. The combination of corona and ozone has been a major cause of cable deterioration. Recently, different and better quality insulating materials have lengthened the life of the electrical cables.

Although ozone at ground level can be harmful, ozone is beneficial to the earth's inhabitants. By having a concentrated ozone layer called the "ozonosphere," between 10 and 20 miles (16–32 km) up in the atmosphere, much of the ultra violet radiation from the sun's rays are absorbed and screened. If this ozone layer were not present, much of the earth's surface would be burned, dried and unfit for human life.

OXIDES OF SULFUR

Oxides of sulfur (SOx) were initially ignored in the exhaust system emissions, since the sulfur content of gasoline as a fuel is less than $\frac{1}{10}$ of 1 percent. Because of this small amount, it was felt that it contributed very little to the overall pollution problem. However, because of the difficulty in solving the sulfur emissions in industrial pollutions and the introduction of catalytic converter to the automobile exhaust systems, a change was mandated. The automobile exhaust system, when equipped with a catalytic converter, changes the sulfur dioxide (SO_2) into sulfur trioxide (SO_3).

When this combines with water vapors (H_2O), a sulfuric acid mist (H_2SO_4) is formed and is a very difficult pollutant to handle since it is extremely corrosive. This sulfuric acid mist that is formed, is the same mist that rises from the vents of an automobile battery when an active chemical reaction takes place within the battery cells.

When a large concentration of vehicles equipped with catalytic converters are operating in an area, this acid mist may rise and be distributed over a large ground area causing land, plant, crop, paint and building damage.

PARTICULATE MATTER

A certain amount of particulate matter is present in the burning of any fuel, with carbon constituting the largest percentage of the particulates. In gasoline, the remaining particulates are the burned remains of the various other compounds used in its manufacture. When a gasoline engine is in good internal condition, the particulate emissions are low but as the engine wears internally, the particulate emissions increase. By visually inspecting the tail pipe emissions, a determination can be made as to where an engine defect may exist. An engine with light gray or blue smoke emitting from the tail pipe normally indicates an increase in the oil consumption through burning due to internal engine wear. Black smoke would indicate a defective fuel delivery system, causing the engine to operate in a rich mode. Regardless of the color of the smoke, the internal part of the engine or the fuel delivery system should be repaired to prevent excess particulate emissions.

Diesel and turbine engines emit a darkened plume of smoke from the exhaust system because of the type of fuel used. Emission control regulations are mandated for this type of emission and more stringent measures are being used to prevent excess emission of the particulate matter. Electronic components are being introduced to control the injection of the fuel at precisely the proper time of piston travel, to achieve the optimum in fuel ignition and fuel usage. Other particulate after-burning components are being tested to achieve a cleaner emission.

Good grades of engine lubricating oils should be used, which meet the manufacturers specification. Cut-rate oils can contribute to the particulate emission problem because of their low flash or ignition temperature point. Such oils burn prematurely during the combustion process causing emission of particulate matter.

The cooling system is an important factor in the reduction of particulate matter. The optimum combustion will occur, with the cooling system operating at a temperature specified by the manufacturer. The cooling system must be maintained in the same manner as the engine oiling system, as each system is required to perform properly in order for the engine to operate efficiently for a long time.

Crankcase Emissions

Crankcase emissions are made up of water, acids, unburned fuel, oil fumes and particulates. These emissions are classified as hydrocarbons (HC) and are formed by the small amount of unburned, compressed air/fuel mixture entering the crankcase from the combustion area (between the cylinder walls and piston rings) during the compression and power strokes. The head of the compression and combustion help to form the remaining crankcase emissions.

EMISSION CONTROLS

Crankcase Ventilation System

OPERATION

▶ See Figure 1

The Positive Crankcase Ventilation (PCV) system vents blow-by gases from the crankcase back into the intake manifold where they are burned.

Since the first engines, crankcase emissions were allowed into the atmosphere through a road draft tube, mounted on the lower side of the engine block. Fresh air came in through an open oil filler cap or breather. The air passed through the crankcase mixing with blow-by gases. The motion of the vehicle and the air blowing past the open end of the road draft tube caused a low pressure area (vacuum) at the end of the tube. Crankcase emissions were simply drawn out of the road draft tube into the air.

To control the crankcase emission, the road draft tube was deleted. A hose and/or tubing was routed from the crankcase to the intake manifold so the blow-by emission could be burned with the air/fuel mixture. However, it was found that intake manifold vacuum, used to draw the crankcase emissions into the manifold, would vary in strength at the wrong time and not allow the proper emission flow. A regulating valve was needed to control the flow of air through the crankcase.

Testing, showed the removal of the blow-by gases from the crankcase as quickly as possible, was most important to the longevity of the engine. Should large accumulations of blow-by gases remain and condense, dilution of the engine oil would occur to form water, soots, resins, acids and lead salts, resulting in the formation of sludge and varnishes. This condensation of the blow-by gases occurs more frequently on vehicles used in numerous starting and stopping conditions, excessive idling and when the engine is not allowed to attain normal operating temperature through short runs.

Evaporative Emissions

Gasoline fuel is a major source of pollution, before and after it is burned in the automobile engine. From the time the fuel is refined, stored, pumped and transported, again stored until it is pumped into the fuel tank of the vehicle, the gasoline gives off unburned hydrocarbons (HC) into the atmosphere. Through the redesign of storage areas and venting systems, the pollution factor was diminished, but not eliminated, from the refinery standpoint. However, the automobile still remained the primary source of vaporized, unburned hydrocarbon (HC) emissions.

Fuel pumped from an underground storage tank is cool but when exposed to a warmer ambient temperature, will expand. Before controls were mandated, an owner might fill the fuel tank with fuel from an underground storage tank and park the vehicle for some time in warm area, such as a parking lot. As the fuel would warm, it would expand and should no provisions or area be provided for the expansion, the fuel would spill out of the filler neck and onto the ground, causing hydrocarbon (HC) pollution and creating a severe fire hazard. To correct this condition, the vehicle manufacturers added overflow plumbing and/or gasoline tanks with built in expansion areas or domes.

However, this did not control the fuel vapor emission from the fuel tank. It was determined that most of the fuel evaporation occurred when the vehicle was stationary and the engine not operating. Most vehicles carry 5–25 gallons (19–95 liters) of gasoline. Should a large concentration of vehicles be parked in one area, such as a large parking lot, excessive fuel vapor emissions would take place, increasing as the temperature increases.

To prevent the vapor emission from escaping into the atmosphere, the fuel systems were designed to trap the vapors while the vehicle is stationary, by sealing the system from the atmosphere. A storage system is used to collect and hold the fuel vapors from the carburetor (if equipped) and the fuel tank when the engine is not operating. When the engine is started, the storage system is then purged of the fuel vapors, which are drawn into the engine and burned with the air/fuel mixture.

The PCV valve varies the amount of blow-by gas fed to the intake manifold in relation to engine demand and also prevents combustion backfiring from traveling into the crankcase.

The amount of blow-by gas allowed into the intake manifold from the crankcase is controlled by the PCV valve. The PCV valve acts like a one-way check valve and does not allow anything from the intake manifold to pass into the crankcase.

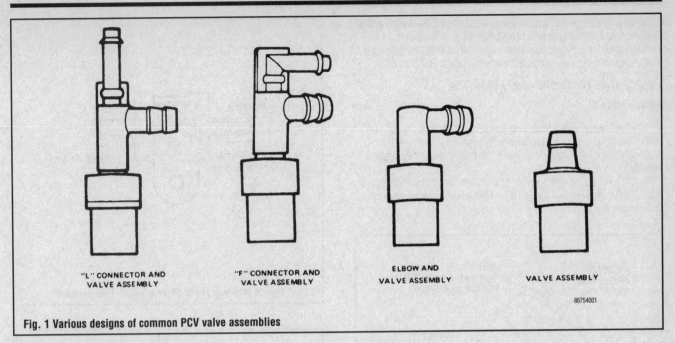

"L" CONNECTOR AND VALVE ASSEMBLY

"F" CONNECTOR AND VALVE ASSEMBLY

ELBOW AND VALVE ASSEMBLY

VALVE ASSEMBLY

86754001

Fig. 1 Various designs of common PCV valve assemblies

COMPONENT TESTING

1. With the engine **OFF**, remove the PCV valve.
2. Shake the PCV valve.
3. If the valve rattles when shaken, re-connect it.
4. If it does not rattle, replace it.
5. Start the engine and allow it to idle. Disconnect the hose from the air cleaner or air outlet tube (the tube which connects the Mass Air Flow sensor and the throttle body).
6. Place a piece of paper over the end of the hose. The vacuum should hold the paper in place.
7. If vacuum does not exist, the system is plugged or the evaporative valve is leaking.
8. Disconnect the evaporative hose, cap the tee and recheck the system. If vacuum exists, the PCV system is functioning. Check the evaporative emission system.
9. If vacuum still does not exist at the PCV, check for vacuum back through the system (filler cap, PCV valve, hoses and the rocker cover bolt torque). Service the defective components as required.

REMOVAL & INSTALLATION

➡️**For details on PCV valve removal and installation, refer to Section 1.**

Remove the PCV hoses by pulling and twisting them from their ports. Always check the hoses for clogging, breaks and deterioration.

Evaporative Emission Controls

OPERATION

The evaporative emission system prevents the escape of fuel vapors into the atmosphere when the engine is off. When the vehicle is not in operation the fuel vapors are stored in the Evaporative emission canister (EVAP).

The fuel vapors trapped in the tank are vented through hoses located on top of the tank to the EVAP canister. When the vehicle is operated the stored fuel vapors are purged from the EVAP canister to the intake manifold assembly and the vapors are burned as part of the normal combustion process.

TESTING

System Inspection

1. Check the electrical connections of the Canister Purge (CANP) solenoid.
2. Check the Powertrain Control Module (PCM), throttle body and the air flow meter for looseness or corrosion.
3. Check the fuel tank, fuel vapor lines, vacuum lines and the connections for leakage, looseness, pinching, damage or other any other obvious signs that would cause a malfunction.
4. If all these components are in good working order, procedure with the component testing.

1.8L Engines

CANISTER PURGE (CANP) SOLENOID

◆ **See Figure 2**

1. Unplug the solenoid electrical connection.
2. Tag and disconnect the vacuum hoses from the solenoid.

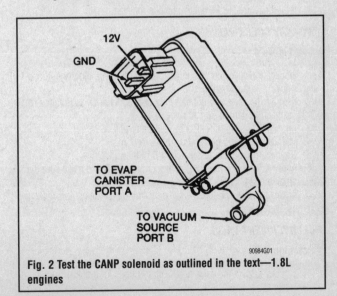

12V
GND
TO EVAP CANISTER PORT A
TO VACUUM SOURCE PORT B

90984G01

Fig. 2 Test the CANP solenoid as outlined in the text—1.8L engines

3. Blow air through port **A** and make sure that no air exits through port **B**.
4. Apply 12 volts and ground to the solenoid as illustrated.
5. Blow air through port **A** and make sure that air exits through port **B**.
6. If the solenoid does not pass these tests, it must be replaced.

EVAPORATIVE EMISSIONS (EVAP) CANISTER

▶ See Figure 3

1. Start the engine and let it reach operating temperature.
2. Turn the engine off and remove the canister.
3. Check the EVAP canister for liquid fuel (strong odor or excessive weight).
4. Blow into the air vent port **C** and make sure that air flows from port **B**.
5. If the canister contains liquid fuel or the air does not flow as specified, replace the canister.

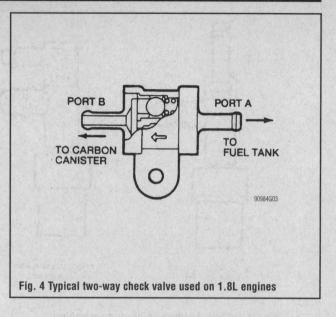

Fig. 4 Typical two-way check valve used on 1.8L engines

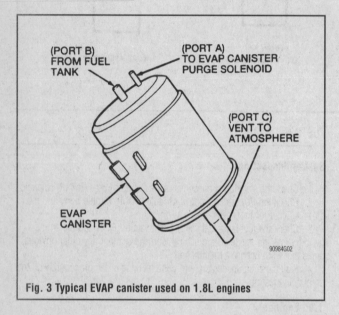

Fig. 3 Typical EVAP canister used on 1.8L engines

PURGE LINES

1. Tag and disconnect the purge lines from the EVAP canister to the engine air intake.
2. Blow through the lines to make sure that air flows freely through them.
3. If the lines are blocked, they must be replaced.

TWO-WAY CHECK VALVE

▶ See Figure 4

1. Inspect the valve and its connections for pinching, blockage, looseness or any other damage/looseness.
2. Remove the valve and connect a vacuum tester such as Rotunda 021-00037 or its equivalent to port **A** of the valve.
3. Apply 1.46 in. Hg (4.9 kPa) of vacuum to port **A**.
4. The valve should open and not hold vacuum.
5. Connect the vacuum tester to port **B** of the valve.
6. Apply 1.73 in. Hg (5.8 kPa) of vacuum to port **B** and make sure the valve remains open.
7. If the valve does not open when performing these tests, it is defective and must be replaced.

ROLLOVER/VENT VALVE

▶ See Figure 5

1. Visually inspect the valve and its connections for blockage, pinching or damage.
2. Remove the valve.

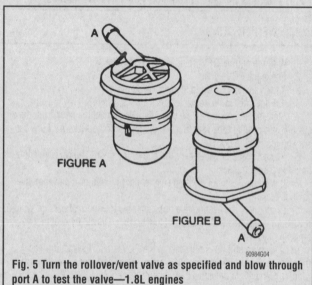

Fig. 5 Turn the rollover/vent valve as specified and blow through port A to test the valve—1.8L engines

3. Hold the valve as shown in Figure A.
4. Blow into port **A** and make sure that air flows through the valve.
5. Turn the valve as shown in Figure B.
6. Blow into port **A** and make sure that air does not flow through the valve.

EVAPORATIVE EMISSION SEPARATOR

1. Visually inspect the separator, hoses and connections for damage, blockage, looseness or pinching.
2. Replace and/or repair any damaged component of the separator assembly.

1.9L Engines

EVAPORATIVE EMISSIONS (EVAP) CANISTER

▶ See Figure 6

1. Start the engine and let it reach operating temperature.
2. Turn the engine off and remove the canister.
3. Check the EVAP canister for liquid fuel (strong odor or excessive weight).
4. Connect a hand pump to port **C** of the canister and block port **A**.

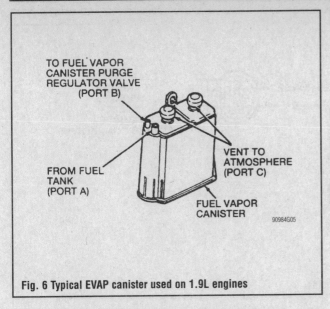

Fig. 6 Typical EVAP canister used on 1.9L engines

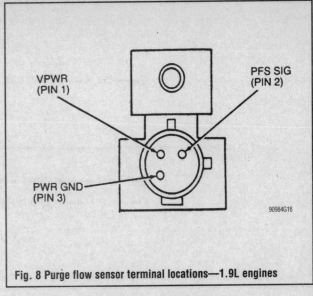

Fig. 8 Purge flow sensor terminal locations—1.9L engines

5. Blow into the air vent port **C** and make sure that air flows from port **B**.
6. If the canister contains liquid fuel or the air does not flow as specified, replace the canister.

CANISTER PURGE (CANP) SOLENOID

▶ See Figure 7

1. Unplug the solenoid electrical connection.
2. Tag and disconnect the vacuum hoses from the solenoid.
3. Apply 9–14 volts DC to the solenoid.
4. Using a vacuum pump attached to the vacuum side of the valve, apply 16 in. Hg (53 kPa) of vacuum to the valve.
5. The solenoid should open and air should pass freely.
6. If the solenoid does not pass this test, it may be defective.

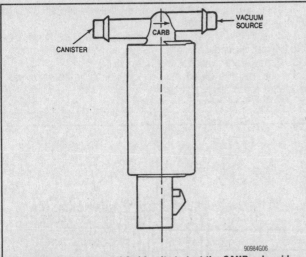

Fig. 7 Apply vacuum and 9–14 volts to test the CANP solenoid—1.9L engines

PURGE FLOW SENSOR

▶ See Figure 8

1. Turn the ignition key **OFF**.
2. Plug the open end of the intake manifold vacuum hose to the purge flow sensor vacuum port to EVAP canister purge solenoid.
3. Disconnect the vacuum hose at the intake manifold at the intake manifold port on the purge flow sensor.

4. Install a vacuum pump to the intake manifold port on the purge flow sensor.
5. Apply 4.1 in. Hg (13.6 kPa) of vacuum to the sensor.
6. The sensor should not bleed off all the vacuum in less than 20 seconds.
7. With the car and sensor at a room temperature of 50°–80°F (10°–17°C), unplug the sensor electrical connection.
8. Using a Digital Volt Ohmmeter (DVOM) set on the resistance scale, measure the resistance between the PFS SIG and VPWR terminals on the sensor.
9. The resistance should be between 40 and 230 ohms.
10. Using a DVOM set on the resistance scale, measure the resistance between the PFS SIG and PWR GND terminals on the sensor.
11. The resistance should not be less than 25.5 ohms.
12. If the sensor does not pass these tests, it may be defective.

2.0L Engines

EVAPORATIVE EMISSIONS (EVAP) CANISTER

1. Visually inspect the canister and hoses for damage.
2. Start the engine and let it reach operating temperature.
3. Turn the engine off and remove the canister.
4. Check the EVAP canister for liquid fuel (strong odor or excessive weight).
5. If the canister is damaged or contains liquid fuel, it may be defective and should be replaced.

EVAPORATIVE EMISSION CANISTER PURGE VALVE— 1997 MODELS

▶ See Figure 9

1. Turn the ignition key **OFF**.
2. Unplug the valve electrical connection.
3. Turn the ignition key **ON**.
4. Using a high impedance Digital Volt Ohmmeter (DVOM) set to read voltage, probe the VPWR terminal at the valve harness connection with the positive lead of the DVOM and touch the negative lead of the DVOM to battery ground.
5. The voltage reading should be greater than 10.5 volts.
6. If a low or no voltage is present, check the VPWR wire for a short to ground and repair as necessary.
7. Turn the ignition key **OFF**.
8. Unplug the valve electrical connection.
9. Using a high impedance Digital Volt Ohmmeter (DVOM) set to read resistance, probe the EVAP Canister purge and VPWR terminal on the valve.
10. The resistance should be between 30 and 90 ohms.

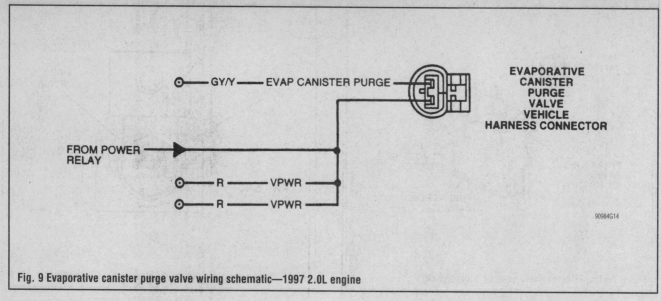

Fig. 9 Evaporative canister purge valve wiring schematic—1997 2.0L engine

11. Measure the resistance between the EVAP Canister purge terminal and the valve casing. The resistance reading should be greater than 90 ohms.

12. Measure the resistance between the VPWR terminal and the valve casing. The resistance reading should be greater than 90 ohms.

13. If the resistance readings are not within specifications, the sensor may be defective and should be replaced.

EVAPORATIVE EMISSION CANISTER PURGE VALVE— 1998–99 MODELS

▶ See Figure 10

1. Turn the ignition key **OFF**.
2. Unplug the valve electrical connection.
3. Turn the ignition key **ON**.
4. Using a high impedance Digital Volt Ohmmeter (DVOM) set to read voltage, probe the VPWR terminal at the valve harness connection with the positive lead of the DVOM and touch the negative lead of the DVOM to battery ground.
5. The voltage reading should be greater than 10.5 volts.
6. If a low or no voltage is present, check the VPWR wire for a short to ground and repair as necessary.
7. Turn the ignition key **OFF**.

8. Using a high impedance Digital Volt Ohmmeter (DVOM) set to read resistance, probe the two terminals on the valve.

9. The resistance should be between 30 and 38 ohms.

10. If the resistance reading is not within specifications, the sensor may be defective and should be replaced.

PURGE FLOW SENSOR—1997 MODELS

▶ See Figure 11

1. Turn the ignition key **OFF**.
2. Unplug the valve electrical connection.
3. The engine temperature should be 55°–80°F (13°–27°C).
4. Using a high impedance Digital Volt Ohmmeter (DVOM) set to read resistance, probe the PF and VPWR terminals on the sensor.
5. The resistance should not be greater than 160 ohms.
6. Using the DVOM, measure the resistance between the PWR GND and VPWR terminals on the sensor.
7. Using the DVOM, measure the resistance between the PF and PWR GND terminals on the sensor.
8. The resistance should not be less than 25.5 ohms.
9. If the resistance reading is not within specifications, the sensor may be defective and should be replaced.

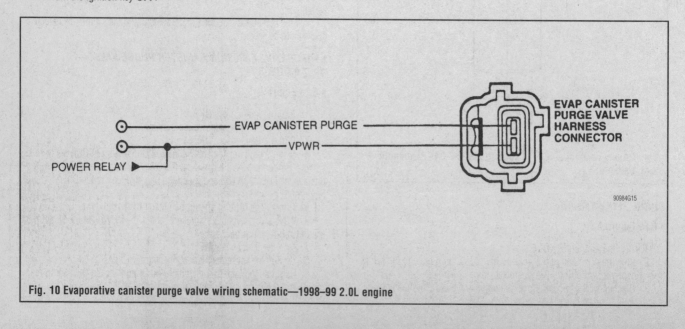

Fig. 10 Evaporative canister purge valve wiring schematic—1998–99 2.0L engine

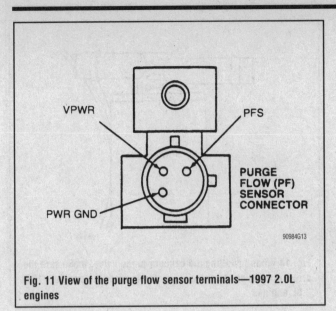

Fig. 11 View of the purge flow sensor terminals—1997 2.0L engines

REMOVAL & INSTALLATION

1.8L Engines

EVAPORATIVE EMISSIONS CANISTER

1. Open the hood.
2. Tag and disconnect the hoses from the canister.
3. Lift the canister from the bracket.
4. Installation is the reverse of removal.

FUEL VAPOR FRONT HOSE

1. Tag and disconnect the hose from the EVAP canister and the purge regulator valve.
2. Remove the hose from the dash panel clips and remove it from the car.
3. Installation is the reverse of removal.

CANISTER PURGE (CANP) SOLENOID

1. Disconnect the negative battery cable.
2. Unplug the electrical connection at the CANP solenoid.
3. Tag and disconnect the vacuum lines from the valve.
4. Unfasten the bolt and remove the valve.
To install:
5. Install the valve and tighten the bolt until it is snug.
6. Attach the vacuum lines and the electrical connection to the valve.
7. Connect the negative battery cable.

FUEL VAPOR VALVES

The fuel vapor valves are the two-way check valve and the rollover/vent valve.
1. Remove the fuel tank.
2. Remove the valves from the tank.
3. Installation is the reverse of removal.

1.9L Engines

EVAPORATIVE EMISSIONS CANISTER

1. Open the hood.
2. Tag and disconnect the hoses from the canister.
3. Unfasten the bolt at the top of the canister.

4. Lift the canister from the bracket.
5. Installation is the reverse of removal.

PURGE FLOW SENSOR

1. Tag and disconnect the vacuum hose.
2. Tag and disconnect the vacuum hose from the intake manifold.
3. Remove the sensor from the car.
4. Installation is the reverse of the removal.

EVAPORATIVE EMISSION (EVAP) CANISTER PURGE VALVE

1. Disconnect the negative battery cable.
2. Unplug the canister purge valve electrical connection.
3. Tag and disconnect the vacuum lines from the valve.
4. Remove the valve from the car.
To install:
5. Install the valve and connect the vacuum hose.
6. Attach the valve electrical connection.
7. Connect the negative battery cable.

FUEL VAPOR VALVES

1. Remove the fuel tank.
2. Tag and disconnect the valve-to-EVAP canister hose.
3. Remove the fuel tank vent tube from the vapor valve.
4. Remove the valve from the tank.
To install:
5. Install the valve and connect the vent tube.
6. Connect the valve-to-EVAP canister hose.
7. Install the fuel tank.

2.0L Engines

EVAPORATIVE EMISSIONS (EVAP) CANISTER—1997 MODELS

▶ See Figure 12

1. Raise the front of the car and support it with safety stands.
2. Tag and disconnect the fuel vapor lines from the canister.
3. Unfasten the canister retaining bolt, then remove the canister.
To install:
4. Install the canister and tighten the retaining bolt.
5. Connect the fuel vapor hoses and lower the car.

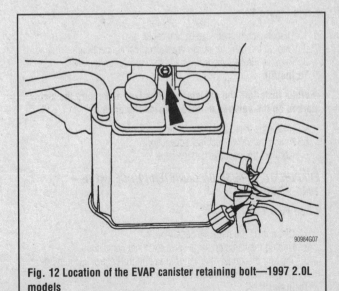

Fig. 12 Location of the EVAP canister retaining bolt—1997 2.0L models

EVAPORATIVE EMISSIONS (EVAP) CANISTER—
1998–99 MODELS

▶ See Figure 13

1. Raise the rear of the car and support it with safety stands.
2. Tag and disconnect the fuel vapor lines from the canister.
3. If necessary on coupe models, remove the vapor hose from the tube.
4. Unfasten the canister bracket retaining bolts, then remove the canister and bracket.
5. Separate the canister from the bracket.

To install:

6. Attach the canister to the bracket.
7. Install the canister assembly and tighten the bolts to 43–63 inch lbs. (5–7 Nm).
8. If removed, install the fuel vapor hose in the tube.
9. Connect the fuel vapor hoses and lower the car.

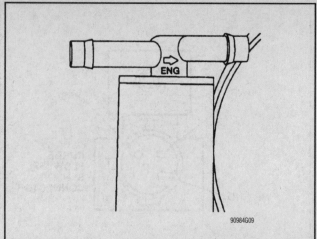

Fig. 14 When installing the canister purge valve, make sure the arrow marked on the valve is pointed towards the engine—1997 2.0L engines

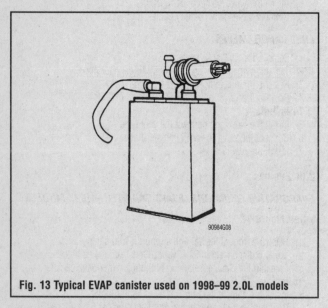

Fig. 13 Typical EVAP canister used on 1998–99 2.0L models

EVAPORATIVE EMISSION CANISTER PURGE VALVE—
1997 MODELS

▶ See Figure 14

1. Disconnect the negative battery cable.
2. Unplug the canister purge valve electrical connection.
3. Remove the two vapor lines and the canister purge valve.

To install:

➡ When installing the canister purge valve, make sure the arrow marked on the valve is pointed towards the engine.

4. Install the valve and connect the vapor lines.
5. Attach the valve electrical connection.
6. Connect the negative battery cable.

EVAPORATIVE EMISSION CANISTER PURGE VALVE—
1998–99 MODELS

▶ See Figure 15

1. Disconnect the negative battery cable.
2. Unplug the canister purge valve electrical connection.
3. Tag and disconnect the vapor lines and the control vacuum line.
4. Unfasten the valve retaining nuts and remove the valve.

To install:

5. Install the valve and tighten the nuts to 43–63 inch lbs. (5–7 Nm).
6. Connect the vapor lines and the control vacuum line.
7. Attach the valve electrical connection.
8. Connect the negative battery cable.

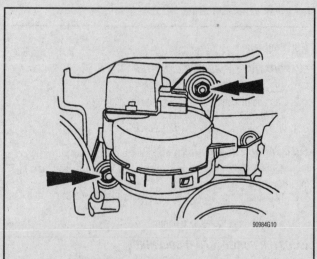

Fig. 15 Location of the canister purge valve retainers—1998–99 2.0L models

PURGE FLOW SENSOR—1997 MODELS

1. Disconnect the negative battery cable.
2. Unplug the purge flow sensor electrical connections.
3. Remove the vapor lines and the sensor.

To install:

4. Install the sensor and the vapor lines.
5. Attach the sensor electrical connection.
6. Connect the negative battery cable.

FUEL VAPOR VENT VALVE—1998–99 MODELS

▶ See Figure 16

1. Disconnect the negative battery cable.
2. Remove the fuel tank.
3. Grasp the valve assembly and remove it from the tank.

To install:

4. Install the valve assembly grommets in the tank.
5. Install the valve assembly.
6. Install the fuel tank.
7. Disconnect the negative battery cable.

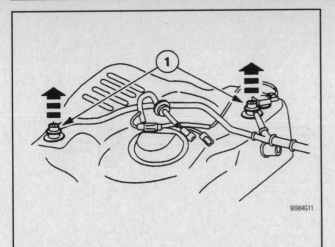

Fig. 16 Pull the fuel vapor vent valve assembly (1) from the fuel tank—1998–99 Escort/Tracer models

CANISTER VENT SOLENOID VALVE—1998–99 MODELS

▶ See Figure 17

1. Disconnect the negative battery cable.
2. Remove the EVAP canister.
3. Unplug the vent solenoid valve electrical connection.
4. Remove the valve by pulling it from its mounting.

To install:

5. If necessary, lubricate the valve O-ring with Merpol O-ring seal lubricant seal or its equivalent.

➡ **If the valve is marked with a direction arrow, make sure it is pointed towards the engine.**

6. Install the valve and attach its electrical connection.
7. Install the EVAP canister.
8. Connect the negative battery cable.

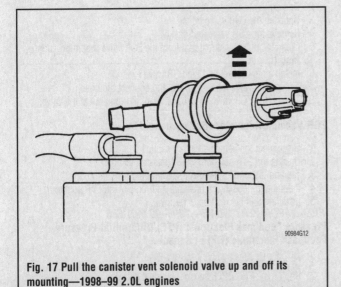

Fig. 17 Pull the canister vent solenoid valve up and off its mounting—1998–99 2.0L engines

Exhaust Gas Recirculation System

OPERATION

The Exhaust Gas Recirculation (EGR) system is designed to reintroduce small amounts of exhaust gas into the combustion cycle, thus reducing the generation of Nitrous Oxides (NOx). The amount of exhaust gas reintroduced and the timing of the cycle varies by calibration and is controlled by various factors such as engine speed, altitude, engine vacuum, exhaust system backpressure, coolant temperature and throttle angle.

➡ **1.8L engine equipped models, as well as the 1998–99 Escort coupe are not equipped with an EGR valve.**

A malfunctioning EGR valve can cause one or more of the following:
- Detonation
- Rough idle or stalling on deceleration
- Hesitation or surge
- Abnormally low power at wide-open throttle

COMPONENT TESTING

Before performing any test on the EGR system components, make sure the hoses are not kinked or damaged, any electrical connection are loose, corroded or damaged.

Exhaust Gas Recirculation (EGR) Valve

▶ See Figure 18

1. Start the car and let the engine reach normal operating temperature.
2. Turn the engine **OFF** and connect a vacuum tester (pump) to the EGR valve vacuum source port.
3. Turn the engine **ON** and idle the engine.
4. Slowly apply 5–10 in. Hg (16–33 kPa) of vacuum; if the engine idles roughly or stalls, the EGR valve is functioning properly.
5. If the engine does not idle rough replace the EGR valve.

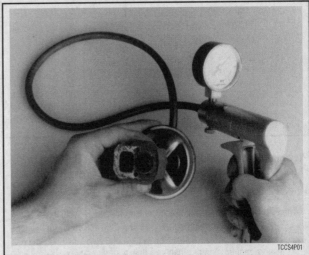

Fig. 18 Some EGR valves may be tested using a vacuum pump by watching for diaphragm movement

EGR Vacuum Regulator (EVR) Solenoid

▶ **See Figure 19**

1. Unplug the EVR solenoid electrical connection.
2. Using a high impedance Digital Volt Ohmmeter (DVOM), probe the terminals of the solenoid.
3. The resistance should be 20–70 ohms on 1991–96 models, or 26–40 ohms on 1997–99 models.

➥ **There are two types of EVR solenoids used. One is a normally open solenoid and the other is a normally closed solenoid. Follow both testing procedures to determine which type of solenoid you are testing.**

4. For a normally open solenoid, test it as follows:
    a. Trace the hose that runs from the solenoid to the EGR valve and unplug the hose from the solenoid.
    b. Using a hand pump, apply 10–15 in. Hg (33–50 kPa) of vacuum to the solenoid. The vacuum should hold.
    c. Apply 12 volts to the solenoid and the vacuum should be released.
5. For a normally closed solenoid, test it as follows:
    a. Trace the hose that runs from the solenoid to the EGR valve and unplug the hose from the solenoid.
    b. Using a hand pump, apply 10–15 in. Hg (33–50 kPa) of vacuum to the solenoid. The vacuum should not hold.
    c. Apply 12 volts to the solenoid, then re-apply 10–15 in. Hg (33–50 kPa) of vacuum and it should hold.
6. If the solenoid does not meet the specifications outlined in the tests, it may be defective and must be replaced.

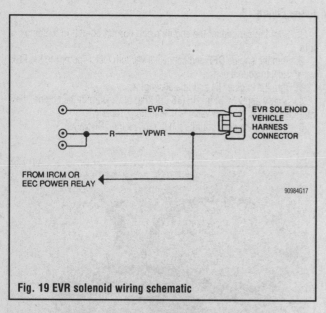

Fig. 19 EVR solenoid wiring schematic

Pressure Feedback Electronic (PFE)/Differential Pressure Feedback Electronic (DPFE) EGR System

▶ **See Figure 20**

The PFE type system is a subsonic, closed loop EGR system that controls EGR flow rate by monitoring the pressure drop across a remotely located sharp-edge orifice. With a PFE system, the EGR valve only serves as a pressure regulator, rather than as a flow metering device. The Differential Pressure Feedback EGR (DPFE) system operates in the same manner, except that it also monitors the pressure drop across the metering orifice. This allows for a more accurate assessment of EGR flow requirements.

1. Unplug the PFE/DPFE sensor electrical connection.

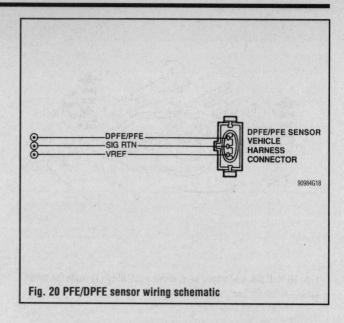

Fig. 20 PFE/DPFE sensor wiring schematic

2. Turn the ignition key to the **ON** position, but do not start the engine.
3. Using a high impedance Digital Volt Ohmmeter (DVOM) set to read voltage, probe the DPFE/PFE terminal of the sensor. The voltage should be approximately 0.45 volts.
4. Using a hand held vacuum pump, apply 8–9 in. Hg (27–30 kPa).
5. The voltage should be above 4 volts.
6. Quickly release the vacuum from the sensor and the voltage should drop to less than one volt in three seconds.
7. If the readings are not as specified, the sensor may be defective and should be replaced.

REMOVAL & INSTALLATION

EGR Valve

1. Loosen the Exhaust Gas Recirculation (EGR) valve-to-exhaust manifold tube nut at the valve.
2. Unplug the EGR valve hose.
3. Unfasten the EGR valve bolts.
4. Remove the EGR valve and gasket.
5. Clean the old gasket material from the EGR valve mounting surface.
To install:
6. Install a new gasket and the EGR valve.
7. Tighten the valve retaining bolts and connect the hose.
8. Tighten the EGR valve-to-exhaust manifold tube nut at the valve.

EGR Vacuum Regulator (EVR) Solenoid

1. Disconnect the negative battery cable.
2. Unplug the EVR solenoid's electrical connection.
3. Tag and disconnect the hose(s) from the EVR solenoid.
4. If equipped, loosen the retainers and remove the EVR solenoid.
5. Installation is the reverse of removal.

Pressure Feedback Electronic (PFE)/Differential Pressure Feedback Electronic (DPFE) Sensor

1. Disconnect the negative battery cable.
2. Unplug the PFE/DPFE sensor electrical connection.
3. Tag and disengage the hose(s) from the sensor.
4. Unfasten the retainers and remove the sensor.
5. Installation is the reverse of removal.

ELECTRONIC ENGINE CONTROLS

✳✳ WARNING

Electronic modules are very sensitive to Electrostatic Static Discharge (ESD). If the modules are exposed to these charges, they may be damaged. While most vehicles display a label informing you that their electronic components may be damaged by ESD, some do not have labels, but they may be damaged also. To avoid possible damage to any of these components, follow the steps outlined below in Handling Electrostatic Discharge (ESD) Sensitive Parts.

Handling Electrostatic Discharge (ESD) Sensitive Parts

1. Body movement produces an electrostatic charge. To discharge personal static electricity, touch a ground point (metal) on the vehicle. This should be performed any time you:
- Slide across the vehicle seat
- Sit down or get up
- Do any walking

2. Do not touch any exposed terminals on components or connectors with your fingers or any tools.

3. Never use jumper wires, ground a terminal on a component, use test equipment on any component or terminal unless instructed to in a diagnostic or testing procedure. When using test equipment, always connect the ground lead first.

Powertrain Control Module

OPERATION

➡ **Models covered by this manual employ the fourth and fifth generation Electronic Engine Control systems, commonly designated EEC-IV or EEC-V, to manage fuel, ignition and emissions on vehicle engines.**

Typically the EEC-IV system was used on 1991–95 models and the EEC-V system was used on 1996–99 models.

The Powertrain Control Module (PCM) detects the engine operating and driving conditions, along with the exhaust gas oxygen content. Various switches, sensors and components provide the PCM with information which allows it to control the air/fuel ratio (mixture), emissions and driveability.

REMOVAL & INSTALLATION

1.8L Engine

The PCM is located behind the center of the instrument panel.
1. Disconnect the negative battery cable.
2. Remove the control box side covers.
3. Remove the air duct located in front of the PCM.
4. Unfasten the PCM retainers and unplug the PCM electrical connections.
5. Unfasten the nut from the relay mounting bracket and separate the relay from the PCM.
6. Remove the PCM.
To install:
7. Install the PCM, then connect the relay to the PCM and tighten the nut.
8. Attach the PCM electrical connectors and tighten the PCM retainers.
9. Install the air duct and the control box side covers.
10. Connect the negative battery cable.

1.9L Engine

The PCM is located on the floor tunnel, ahead of the shift console in the PCM bracket. The PCM and fuel pump relays are mounted on the PCM bracket.
1. Disconnect the negative battery cable.
2. Remove the shift console and control box side covers.
3. Unplug the electrical connector from the PCM.
4. Remove the relays from the PCM bracket.
5. Remove the plastic duct and pad from the top of the PCM bracket.
6. Unfasten the PCM retainers.
7. Remove the PCM and the bracket from the floor tunnel.
8. Remove the plastic clip from the bracket.
9. Slide the PCM straight out from the bracket to remove it.
To install:
10. Slide the PCM onto the bracket and engage the plastic clip.
11. Install the PCM and bracket. Tighten the retainers to 6 ft. lbs. (8 Nm).
12. Install the plastic duct and pad to the top of the PCM bracket.
13. Install the relays on the PCM bracket.
14. Attach the electrical connector to the PCM.
15. Install the control box side covers and shift console.
16. Connect the negative battery cable.

2.0L Engines

EXCEPT ESCORT COUPE MODELS

1. Disconnect the negative battery cable.
2. Remove the parking brake and shift consoles.
3. Place the gearshift lever in the **LOW** position and unfasten the 4 transaxle control selector dial bezel screws.
4. Turn the transaxle control selector dial bezel ¼ turn counterclockwise.
5. Unfasten the PCM electrical connector retaining bolt, then unplug the connector.
6. Slide the PCM straight out from its mounting.
To install:
7. Install the PCM, attach the electrical connector and tighten the connector bolt to 55 inch lbs. (6 Nm).
8. Turn the transaxle control selector dial bezel ¼ turn clockwise.
9. Tighten the 4 transaxle control selector dial bezel screws.
10. Place the gearshift lever in the **PARK** position.
11. Install the shift consoles and the parking brake.
12. Connect the negative battery cable.

ESCORT COUPE MODELS

1. Disconnect the negative battery cable.
2. Remove the parking brake and shift consoles
3. Remove the gearshift knob and boot.
4. Unfasten the PCM electrical connector retaining bolt, then unplug the connector.
5. Slide the PCM straight out from its mounting.
To install:
6. Install the PCM, attach the electrical connector and tighten the connector bolt to 55 inch lbs. (6 Nm).
7. Install the gearshift knob and boot.
8. Install the shift consoles and the parking brake.
9. Connect the negative battery cable.

Oxygen Sensor

OPERATION

An Oxygen Sensor (O2S) is used on 1991–94 1.8L engines. The sensor is mounted in the exhaust manifold. The sensor protrudes into the exhaust stream and monitors the oxygen content of the exhaust gases. The difference between the oxygen content of the exhaust gases and that of the outside air generates a voltage signal to the PCM. The PCM monitors this voltage and, depending upon the value of the signal received, issues a command to adjust for a rich or a lean condition.

TESTING

1. Perform a visual inspection on the sensor as follows:
   a. Remove the sensor from the exhaust.
   b. If the sensor tip has a black/sooty deposit, this may indicate a rich fuel mixture.
   c. If the sensor tip has a white gritty deposit, this may indicate an internal anti-freeze leak.
   d. If the sensor tip has a brown deposit, this could indicate oil consumption.

➡**All these contaminants can destroy the sensor; if the problem is not repaired, the new sensor will also be damaged.**

2. Reinstall the sensor and disengage its electrical connection.
3. Connect jumper wires from the sensor connector to the wiring harness. This permits the engine to operate normally while you check the engine.

❊❊ WARNING

Never disengage any sensor while the ignition is ON.

4. Start the engine and allow it to reach normal operating temperature. This will take around ten minutes.
5. Engage the positive lead of a high impedance Digital Volt Ohmmeter (DVOM) to the sensor signal wire and the negative lead to a good known engine ground, such as the negative battery terminal.
6. The voltage reading should fluctuate as the sensor detects varying levels of oxygen in the exhaust stream.
7. If the sensor voltage does not fluctuate, the sensor may be defective or the fuel mixture could be extremely out of range.
8. If the sensor reads above 550 millivolts constantly, the fuel mixture may be too lean or you could have an exhaust leak near the sensor.
9. Under normal conditions, the sensor should fluctuate high and low. Prior to condemning the sensor, try forcing the system to have a rich fuel mixture by restricting the air intake, or a lean mixture by removing a vacuum line. If this causes the sensor to respond, look for problems in other areas of the system.

REMOVAL & INSTALLATION

▶ **See Figure 21**

1. Disconnect the negative battery cable.
2. Unplug the oxygen sensor electrical connection.
3. Remove the exhaust manifold heat shield.
4. Raise the front of the car and support it with safety stands.
5. Using the appropriate size wrench, remove the oxygen sensor.
To install:
6. Install the new sensor and tighten it to 22–36 ft. lbs. (29–49 Nm).
7. Lower the car and install the heat shield.
8. Attach the oxygen sensor electrical connection.
9. Connect the negative battery cable.

Heated Oxygen Sensor

OPERATION

A Heated Oxygen Sensor (HO2S) monitors the oxygen content in the three-way catalytic converter and transmits this information to the Powertrain Control Module (PCM). The PCM then adjusts the air/fuel ratio to provide a rich (more fuel) or lean (less fuel) condition.

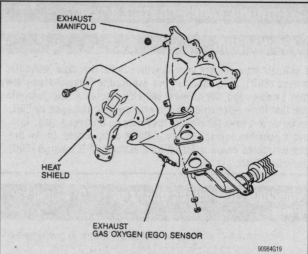

Fig. 21 The Oxygen Sensor (O2S) is located in the exhaust manifold on 1991–94 1.8L engines

TESTING

▶ **See Figures 22 and 23**

1. Perform a visual inspection on the sensor as follows:
   a. Remove the sensor from the exhaust.
   b. If the sensor tip has a black/sooty deposit, this may indicate a rich fuel mixture.
   c. If the sensor tip has a white gritty deposit, this may indicate an internal anti-freeze leak.
   d. If the sensor tip has a brown deposit, this could indicate oil consumption.

➡**All these contaminates can destroy the sensor, if the problem is not repaired the new sensor will also be damaged.**

2. Reinstall the sensor.
3. Disconnect the Heated Oxygen Sensor (HO2S). Measure resistance between PWR and GND (heater) terminals of the sensor.
4. With the engine hot-to-warm, the resistance should be 5–30 ohms.
5. At room temperature, the resistance should be 2–5 ohms. If the readings are within specification, the sensor's heater element is okay.

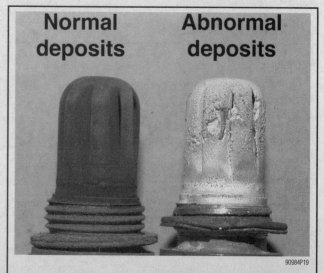

Fig. 22 Inspect the oxygen sensor tip for abnormal deposits

Fig. 23 Probe the terminals of the Heated Oxygen Sensor (HO2S) harness to test the heating element resistance

Fig. 24 Unplug the Heated Oxygen Sensor (HO2S) electrical connection

6. With the O₂S connected and engine running, measure voltage with a DVOM by backprobing the **SIG RTN** wire of the oxygen sensor connector. The voltage readings at idle should stay below 1 volt. When the speed is increased or decreased, the voltage should fluctuate between 0 and 1 volt; if so, the sensor is okay.

REMOVAL & INSTALLATION

1995–96 1.8L Engines

1. Disconnect the negative battery cable.
2. Raise the car and support it with safety stands.
3. Unplug the Heated Oxygen Sensor (HO2S) electrical connection.
4. Using the appropriate size wrench, remove the oxygen sensor.

To install:

5. Install the new sensor and tighten it to 22–36 ft. lbs. (29–49 Nm).
6. Lower the car and install the heat shield.
7. Attach the oxygen sensor electrical connection.
8. Connect the negative battery cable.

1.9L and 2.0L Engines

▶ See Figures 24, 25 and 26

➡On models equipped with an upstream HO2S, it can be accessed without raising the car. On models with a downstream HO2S, the car must be raised and supported with safety stands to facilitate removal.

1. Open and support the hood with the prop rod.
2. Disconnect the negative battery cable.
3. If equipped, remove the exhaust manifold heat shield.
4. If equipped and replacing a downstream oxygen sensor, raise the car and support it with safety stands.
5. Unplug the Heated Oxygen Sensor (HO2S) electrical connection.
6. Using the appropriate size wrench or socket, remove the oxygen sensor.

To install:

7. Install and tighten the new sensor.
8. If raised, lower the car.
9. If removed, install the heat shield.
10. Attach the oxygen sensor electrical connection.
11. Connect the negative battery cable.

Fig. 25 Using the appropriate size wrench or socket, loosen the oxygen sensor . . .

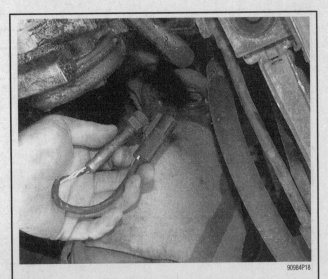

Fig. 26 . . . and remove the oxygen sensor from the vehicle

Coolant Temperature Sensor

OPERATION

The Engine Coolant Temperature (ECT) sensor is a thermistor (a device which changes resistance or voltage as temperature changes). The sensor detects the temperature of engine coolant and provides a corresponding signal to the PCM.

The ECT sensor is mounted in the following locations:
- 1.8L engines: in the cylinder head
- 1.9L engines: threaded into the heater hose inlet pipe
- 2.0L engines: at the left rear of the engine

TESTING

▶ **See Figures 27, 28 and 29**

1. Disengage the temperature sensor electrical connection.
2. Connect jumper wires from the sensor connector to the wiring harness. This permits the engine to operate normally while you check the sensor.

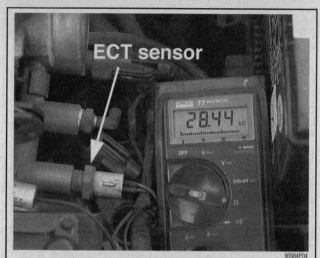

Fig. 29 Connect a Digital Volt Ohmmeter (DVOM) between the sensor terminals and measure the resistance or voltage

Coolant Temperature °C (°F)	ECT Sensor Resistance (kohms)
-20 (-4)	14.6 - 17.8
20 (68)	2.2 - 2.7
80 (176)	0.25 - 0.35

Fig. 27 ECT sensor temperature versus resistance chart—1.8L engines

Temperature		Engine Coolant/Intake Air Temperature Sensor Values	
°C	°F	Voltage (volts)	Resistance (K ohms)
120	248	0.27	1.18
110	230	0.35	1.55
100	212	0.46	2.07
90	194	0.60	2.80
80	176	0.78	3.84
70	158	1.02	5.37
60	140	1.33	7.70
50	122	1.70	10.97
40	104	2.13	16.15
30	86	2.60	24.27
20	68	3.07	37.30
10	50	3.51	58.75

Fig. 28 ECT/IAT sensor temperature versus resistance/voltage chart—1.9L and 2.0L engines

3. Connect a Digital Volt Ohmmeter (DVOM) between the sensor terminals.

4. Measure the voltage or resistance with the engine off and cool and with the engine running and warmed up. Compare the temperature versus voltage or resistance values obtained with the chart(s).

5. Replace the sensor if the readings are incorrect.

REMOVAL & INSTALLATION

1.8L Engines

▶ See Figure 30

> **⁂ CAUTION**
>
> **Never open, service or drain the radiator or cooling system when hot; serious burns can occur from the steam and hot coolant. Also, when draining engine coolant, keep in mind that cats and dogs are attracted to ethylene glycol antifreeze and could drink any that is left in an uncovered container or in puddles on the ground. This will prove fatal in sufficient quantities. Always drain coolant into a sealable container. Coolant should be reused unless it is contaminated or is several years old.**

1. Disconnect the negative battery cable.
2. Partially drain the cooling system until the level is below the ECT sensor.
3. Locate the ECT sensor and unplug its electrical connection.
4. Using a suitable size wrench, remove the ECT sensor.

To install:

5. Install the new sensor and tighten it to 18–22 ft. lbs. (25–29 Nm).
6. Attach the sensor electrical connection.
7. Fill the cooling system.
8. Connect the negative battery cable.

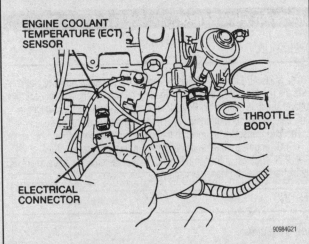

Fig. 30 Unplug the electrical connector from the ECT sensor—1.8L engines

1.9L and 2.0L Engines

▶ See Figure 31

> **⁂ CAUTION**
>
> **Never open, service or drain the radiator or cooling system when hot; serious burns can occur from the steam and hot coolant. Also, when draining engine coolant, keep in mind that cats and dogs are attracted to ethylene glycol antifreeze and could drink any that is left in an uncovered container or in pud-**

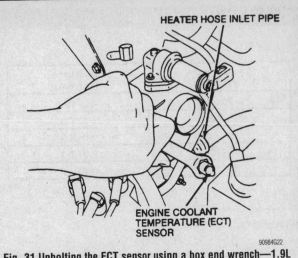

Fig. 31 Unbolting the ECT sensor using a box end wrench—1.9L engines

dles on the ground. This will prove fatal in sufficient quantities. Always drain coolant into a sealable container. Coolant should be reused unless it is contaminated or is several years old.

1. Disconnect the negative battery cable.
2. Partially drain the cooling system until the level is below the ECT sensor.
3. On 1.9L engines, remove the engine air intake duct.
4. Locate the ECT sensor and unplug its electrical connection.
5. Using a suitable size wrench, remove the ECT sensor.

➡ **It may be necessary to brace the heater hose inlet pipe with your free hand while removing or installing the ECT sensor.**

To install:

6. Coat the threads of the new sensor with pipe sealant that contains Teflon®.
7. Install the new sensor and tighten it to 18–22 ft. lbs. (25–29 Nm) on 1.9L engines, or to 89–123 inch lbs. (10–14 Nm) on 2.0L engines.
8. Attach the sensor electrical connection.
9. On 1.9L engines, install the air intake duct.
10. Fill the cooling system.
11. Connect the negative battery cable.

Intake Air Temperature Sensor

OPERATION

The Intake Air Temperature (IAT) sensor is a thermistor that changes the resistance in response to the intake air temperature. The IAT senses the intake air temperature and sends that information to the Powertrain Control Module (PCM). The PCM uses this information to calculate the correct amount of fuel injection.

The IAT sensor is mounted in the following locations:

- 1.8L engines: integrated with the Vane Air Flow (VAF) meter
- 1.9L engines: threaded into the air cleaner lid
- 2.0L engines: at the top left front of the engine compartment, on the front of the air cleaner

TESTING

▶ See Figures 28, 32 and 33

1. Disengage the Intake Air Temperature (IAT) sensor electrical connection.

Temperature °C (°F)	Resistance (kohms)
-20 (-4)	10.0 - 20.0
0 (32)	4.0 - 7.0
20 (68)	2.0 - 3.0
40 (104)	0.9 - 1.3
60 (140)	0.4 - 0.7

90984G43

Fig. 32 IAT sensor temperature versus resistance chart—1.8L engines

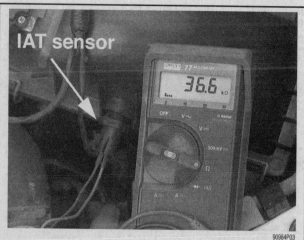

90984P03

Fig. 33 Probe the terminals of the IAT sensor and measure the voltage or resistance, then compare the readings to the appropriate chart

2. Connect jumper wires from the sensor connector to the wiring harness. This permits the engine to operate normally while you check the sensor.

3. Connect a Digital Volt Ohmmeter (DVOM) between the sensor terminals.

4. Measure the voltage or ohms with the engine off and cool, as well as with the engine running and warmed up. Compare the temperature versus voltage or resistance values obtained with those in the chart.

5. Replace the sensor if the readings are incorrect.

6. If the reading for a given temperature is about that shown in the table, the IAT sensor is okay.

REMOVAL & INSTALLATION

1.8L Engines

The Intake Air Temperature (IAT) sensor used on 1.8L engines is an integral part of the Vane Air Flow (VAF) meter, and is not serviced separately.

1.9L and 2.0L Engines

▶ See Figure 34

1. Disconnect the negative battery cable.

2. If necessary for access on some 2.0L engines, remove the air cleaner outlet tube.

3. Unplug the sensor electrical connection.

4. Using a suitable tool, remove the sensor.

To install:

5. Install the sensor and attach its electrical connection.

6. If removed, install the air cleaner outlet tube.

7. Connect the negative battery cable.

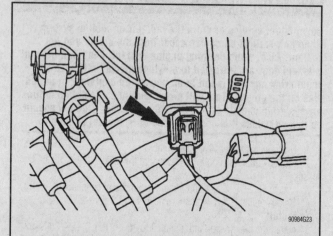

90984G23

Fig. 34 The IAT sensor is located at the top left front side of the engine compartment, on front of the air cleaner assembly—2.0L engines

Mass Air Flow Sensor

OPERATION

The Mass Air Flow (MAF) sensor detects the intake air quantity and converts the measurement to a voltage reading by way of a heated resistor. The voltage signal is sent to the Powertrain Control Module (PCM) which, in turn, determines such things as injection quantities and engine speed.

The MAF sensor is mounted in the following locations:

• 1.9L engines: on the outside of the air cleaner assembly lid

• 2.0L engines: at the top left-hand front of the engine compartment, on the inside of the air cleaner assembly

TESTING

OBD-I Systems

▶ See Figures 35, 36 and 37

1. Make sure the ignition key is **OFF**.

2. Connect jumper wires from the sensor connector to the wiring harness. This permits the engine to operate normally while you check the sensor.

3. Turn the ignition key **ON**, but do not start the engine.

4. Connect a Digital Volt Ohmmeter (DVOM), set to read voltage, between harness terminal VPWR and the negative battery terminal.

5. The voltage reading should be more than 10.5 volts.

6. If the reading is incorrect, check for an open in the VPWR circuit.

7. Connect the DVOM between harness terminals VPWR and PWR GND.

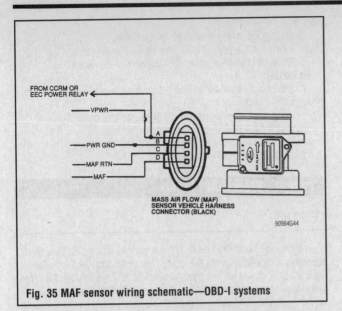

Fig. 35 MAF sensor wiring schematic—OBD-I systems

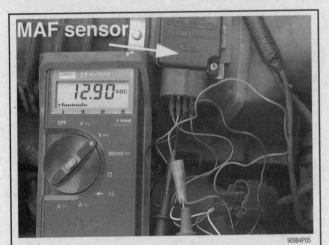

Fig. 36 Connect a DVOM between MAF sensor harness terminal VPWR and the negative battery terminal; the voltage should exceed 10.5 volts

Fig. 37 With the DVOM connected between the MAF terminal and negative battery terminal, the voltage reading should be 0.36–1.50 volts

8. The voltage reading should be more than 10.5 volts.

9. If the reading is incorrect, check for an open in the PWR GND circuit.

10. Start the engine.

11. Connect the DVOM between the MAF terminal and the negative battery terminal.

12. The voltage reading should be between 0.36 and 1.50 volts.

13. Connect the DVOM between the MAF and MAF RTN terminals.

14. The voltage reading should be between 0.36 and 1.50 volts.

15. If the voltage readings are not within specifications, replace the sensor.

OBD-II Systems

▶ See Figure 38

1. Make sure the ignition key is **OFF**.

2. Connect jumper wires from the sensor connector to the wiring harness. This permits the engine to operate normally while you check the sensor.

3. Connect a Digital Volt Ohmmeter (DVOM), set to read voltage, between harness terminal VPWR and the negative battery terminal.

4. The voltage reading should be approximately 10.5 volts.

5. If the reading is incorrect, check for an open in the VPWR circuit.

6. Connect the DVOM between harness terminals VPWR and PWR GND.

7. The voltage reading should be 10.5 volts.

8. If the reading is incorrect, check for an open in the PWR GND circuit.

9. Start the engine.

10. Connect the DVOM between the MAF terminal and the negative battery terminal.

11. The voltage reading should be between 0.34 and 1.96 volts.

12. Connect the DVOM between the MAF and MAF RTN terminals.

13. The voltage reading should be between 0.34 and 1.96 volts.

14. If the voltage readings are not within specifications, replace the sensor.

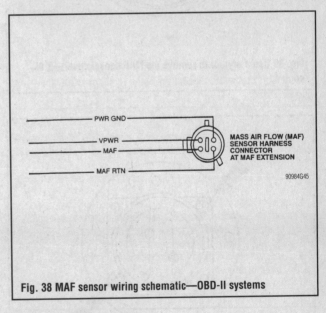

Fig. 38 MAF sensor wiring schematic—OBD-II systems

REMOVAL & INSTALLATION

1.9L Engines

1. Disconnect the negative battery cable.

2. Remove the air cleaner-to-intake manifold tube.

3. Unplug the MAF sensor electrical connector.

4. Unfasten the four sensor retaining screws.

5. Remove the MAF sensor and gasket.

To install:

6. Inspect the sensor mounting surfaces for damage and replace them as necessary.

7. Clean the old gasket material with from the mounting surfaces being very careful not to damage them.

8. Install a new gasket and the MAF sensor.

9. Install and tighten the sensor retaining screws to 72–108 inch lbs. (8–12 Nm).

10. Attach the sensor electrical connection.

11. Install the air cleaner-to-intake manifold tube.

12. Connect the negative battery cable.

2.0L Engines

▶ **See Figures 39 and 40**

1. Disconnect the negative battery cable.

2. Remove the air cleaner outlet tube and air cleaner.

3. Slide the MAF sensor electrical connector grommet out of the air

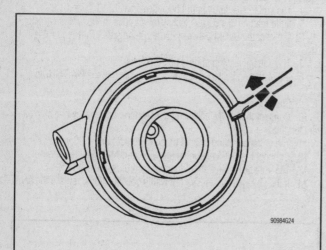

Fig. 39 Use a prytool to remove the MAF sensor cover—2.0L engines

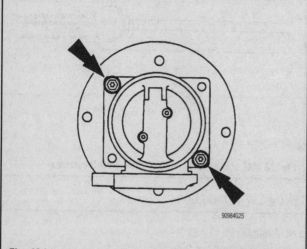

Fig. 40 Location of the MAF sensor retaining nuts—2.0L engines

cleaner.

4. Unplug the MAF sensor electrical connection.

5. Use a suitable prytool to remove the MAF sensor cover.

6. Unfasten the two retaining nuts and remove the sensor.

To install:

7. Position the MAF sensor and tighten the retaining nuts to 71–106 inch lbs. (8–12 Nm).

8. Install the sensor cover and attach its electrical connection.

9. Install the sensor electrical connector grommet.

10. Install the air cleaner and air cleaner outlet tube.

11. Connect the negative battery cable.

Vane Air Flow (VAF) Meter

OPERATION

The Vane Air Flow (VAF) meter, also known as a Volume Air Flow Meter, measures the air flowing into the engine. The meter contains a movable vane which is connected to a potentiometer. As air flows through the meter, the movable vane and potentiometer change position and provide an input to the PCM. The PCM can then translate the vane position into the volume of air flowing into the engine.

The VAF meter is mounted in the following locations:

• 1.8L engines: between the air cleaner and throttle body

TESTING

▶ **See Figure 41**

1. Make sure the ignition key is **OFF**.

2. Connect jumper wires from the sensor connector to the wiring harness. This permits the engine to operate normally while you check the sensor.

3. Connect a Digital Volt Ohmmeter (DVOM), set to read voltage, between sensor terminals VAF and SIG RTN.

4. Turn the key **ON** and access the VAF meter measuring vane.

5. With the vane fully closed, the voltage reading should be 4.5–5 volts.

6. Slowly move the vane to the fully open position. As the vane moves through its travel, the voltage should drop slowly and smoothly. When the vane reaches the end of its travel, the voltage reading should be 0.5–1.5 volts.

7. If the voltage readings are not within specifications, replace the VAF meter.

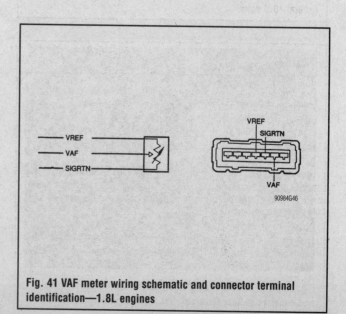

Fig. 41 VAF meter wiring schematic and connector terminal identification—1.8L engines

REMOVAL & INSTALLATION

▶ **See Figure 42**

1. Disconnect the negative battery cable.
2. Disconnect the engine intake air resonator from the VAF meter and position the resonator and air duct away from the work area.
3. Unplug the VAF meter electrical connection.
4. Unfasten the ignition coil wire routing bracket nut and remove the bracket.
5. Unfasten the VAF meter nuts, then remove the VAF meter and gasket.

To install:

6. Install the VAF mater gasket and meter.
7. Install and tighten the meter retainers.
8. Install the ignition coil wire routing bracket and tighten the retaining nut.
9. Attach the VAF meter electrical connection.
10. Connect the air duct and engine intake air resonator to the VAF meter.
11. Connect the negative battery cable.

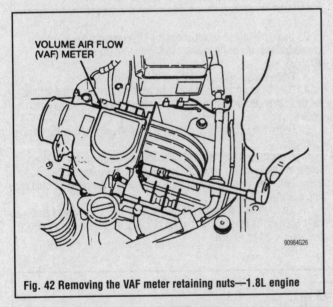

VOLUME AIR FLOW (VAF) METER

90984G26

Fig. 42 Removing the VAF meter retaining nuts—1.8L engine

Throttle Position Sensor

OPERATION

The Throttle Position (TP) sensor detects the throttle plate opening angle and supplies the PCM with an input signal indicating throttle position.

On 1991–95 1.8L engines with a manual transaxle, the TP sensor consists of a two-position switch sensing only closed or open throttle positions. These two positions are monitored by the Idle (IDL) switch and the Wide Open Throttle (WOT) switch.

On 1991–95 1.8L engines with automatic transaxles, the TP sensor consists of a combination switch and idle switch. The TP sensor sends a range of signals to the PCM indicating throttle plate position. This range of signals could range from idle to off idle.

On 1996 1.8L engines, the TP sensor consists of a combination switch and idle switch. The TP sensor sends a range of signals to the PCM indicating throttle plate position. This range of signals could range from idle to off idle.

On 1.9L and 2.0L engines, the TP sensor is a rotary potentiometer which consists of either a rigid or flexible thick film resistive substrate, and a moving wiper that is mounted on a rotor. As the TP sensor is rotated by the throttle shaft blade, the PCM receives information on the throttle plate position.

TESTING

1.8L Engines

1991–95 MODELS

▶ **See Figure 43**

1. Connect jumper wires from the sensor connector to the wiring harness. This permits the engine to operate normally while you check the sensor.
2. Using the jumper wires, probe the TP terminal at the TP sensor connector, with the positive lead of a Digital Volt Ohmmeter (DVOM).
3. Using the jumper wire, probe the SIG RTN terminal with the negative lead.
4. Have an assistant turn the ignition key **ON** and depress the accelerator pedal in ⅛ increments to the wide open position.
5. Observe the voltmeter at each of these positions and note the voltage displayed. Compare your readings with the accompanying charts.
6. If the TP sensor readings match the values in the chart, the sensor is working properly. If, however, the TP sensor readings are not as specified, continue with the test procedure.
7. Turn the ignition key **OFF**.
8. Unplug the TP sensor electrical connector, then attach the positive lead of the DVOM to the VREF terminal of the wiring harness connector.
9. Turn the ignition key **ON** and observe the voltage reading on the DVOM; it should be between 4.5 and 5.5 volts.
10. If the VREF voltage is within specifications and the TP voltage readings do not agree with the values displayed in the chart, replace the TP sensor.

THROTTLE POSITION	VOLTS
1/8	.998
2/8	1.60
3/8	2.37
4/8	2.74
5/8	3.15
6/8	3.43
7/8	3.60
8/8	4.02

NOTE: Voltage and Resistance values may vary ± 15%.

90984G47

Fig. 43 Throttle position sensor voltage chart—1991–95 1.8L engines

1996 MODELS

▶ **See Figure 44**

1. Connect jumper wires from the sensor connector to the wiring harness. This permits the engine to operate normally while you check the sensor.
2. Using the jumper wires, probe the TP terminal at the TP sensor connector, with the positive lead of a Digital Volt Ohmmeter (DVOM).
3. Probe the SIG RTN terminal with the negative lead.
4. Have an assistant turn the ignition key **ON** and depress the accelerator pedal to the ¼ open, ½ open, ¾ open and wide open positions.
5. Observe the voltmeter at each of these positions and note the voltage displayed. Compare your readings with the accompanying charts.

Throttle Position	Volts
1/4	0.5
HALF	2.75
3/4	3.88
FULL	5.0

NOTE: Voltage and Resistance values may vary ± 15%.

90984G48

Fig. 44 Throttle position sensor voltage chart—1996 1.8L engines

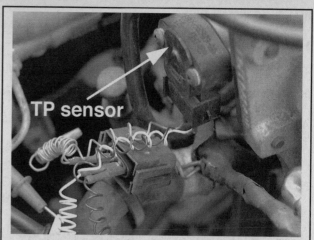

90984P07

Fig. 46 Attach jumper wires from the TP sensor connector to the wiring harness. This permits the engine to operate normally while you check the sensor

6. If the TP sensor readings match the values in the chart, the sensor is working properly. If, however, the TP sensor readings are not as specified, continue with the test procedure.

7. Turn the ignition key **OFF**.

8. Unplug the TP sensor electrical connector, then attach the positive lead of the DVOM to the VREF terminal of the wiring harness connector.

9. Turn the ignition key **ON** and observe the voltage reading on the DVOM; it should be between 4.5 and 5.5 volts.

10. If the VREF voltage is within specifications and the TP voltage readings do not agree with the values displayed in the chart, replace the TP sensor.

1.9L and 2.0L Engines

♦ See Figures 45 and 46

1. Connect jumper wires from the sensor connector to the wiring harness. This permits the engine to operate normally while you check the sensor.

2. Using the jumper wires, probe the TP terminal at the TP sensor connector, with the positive lead of a Digital Volt Ohmmeter (DVOM).

3. Probe the SIG RTN terminal with the negative lead.

4. Have an assistant turn the ignition key **ON** and depress the accelerator pedal in small, smooth increments from the fully closed to the wide open position.

5. Observe the voltmeter at each of these positions and note the voltage displayed.

6. The voltage at the closed position should be approximately 0 volts. As the throttle is moved slowly through its travel, the voltage should rise evenly until you reach the fully open position, where the voltage should be approximately 4.5 volts.

7. If the voltage does not meet specifications, or jumps around erratically when moving the throttle through its travel, the sensor may be defective and should be replaced.

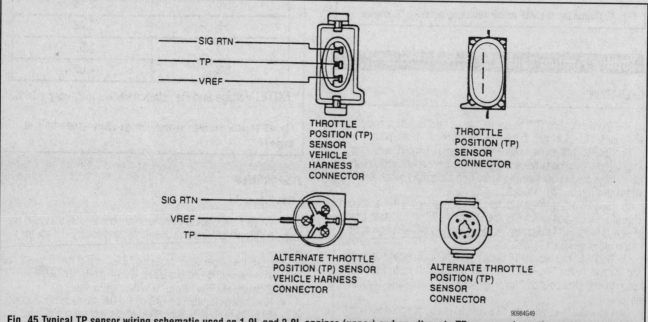

Fig. 45 Typical TP sensor wiring schematic used on 1.9L and 2.0L engines (upper) and an alternate TP sensor schematic used on some 1.9L models (lower)

REMOVAL & INSTALLATION

1.8L Engines

▶ **See Figure 47**

1. Disconnect the negative battery cable.
2. Unplug the TP sensor electrical connection.
3. Unfasten the sensor retaining screws and remove the sensor.

To install:

4. Install the sensor and tighten the retaining screws.
5. Attach the TP sensor electrical connection.
6. Connect the negative battery cable.
7. Adjust the TP sensor, as outlined later in this section.

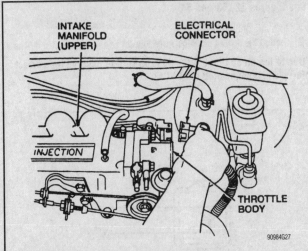

Fig. 47 Unplug the TP sensor electrical connection—1.8L engines

1.9L and 2.0L Engines

▶ **See Figures 48 and 49**

1. Disconnect the negative battery cable.
2. Remove the air cleaner-to-intake manifold tube.

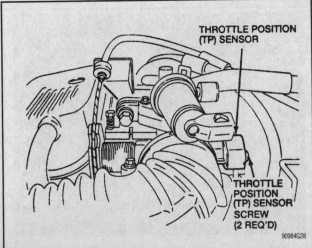

Fig. 48 Location of the TP sensor and its retaining screws—1.9L engines

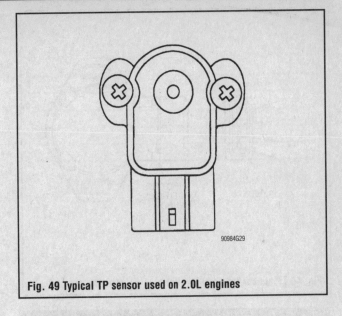

Fig. 49 Typical TP sensor used on 2.0L engines

3. Unplug the TP sensor electrical connection.
4. Unfasten the sensor retaining screws and remove the sensor.

To install:

5. Place the sensor on the throttle body. Make sure the tangs on the sensor are properly aligned and the wires are pointing down. Slide the rotary tangs of the TP sensor, rotated 90 degrees clockwise away from their final installed position, into place over the throttle shaft blade, then rotate the sensor counterclockwise to the installed position.

❋❋ WARNING

Failure to install the sensor in this way could result in high idle speeds.

6. Install and tighten the sensor retainers to 25–30 inch lbs. (3–3.5 Nm) on 1.9L engines and 26 inch lbs. (3 Nm) on 2.0L engines.

➡ **The TP sensor on 1.9L and 2.0L engines is not adjustable.**

7. Attach the TP sensor electrical connection.
8. Install the air cleaner-to-intake manifold tube.
9. Connect the negative battery cable.

ADJUSTMENT

1.8L Engines

▶ **See Figure 50**

1. Unplug the TP sensor electrical connection.
2. Connect the leads of a high impedance Digital Volt Ohmmeter (DVOM) to terminals to the IDL and E terminals of the sensor. Refer to the accompanying illustration for terminal locations.
3. Loosen the sensor screws and insert a 0.01 inch (0.25mm) feeler gauge between the throttle stop screw and stop lever.
4. Rotate the sensor clockwise about 30 degrees, then rotate it counterclockwise until a continuity reading is showing on the DVOM.
5. Replace the 0.01 inch (0.25mm) feeler gauge and replace it with a 0.016 inch (0.4mm) feeler gauge and insert it between the throttle stop screw and stop lever.
6. Verify that continuity no longer is present. If continuity still exists, repeat steps 3 through 6.
7. Tighten the sensor retaining screws.
8. Open the throttle plate to its wide open position several times and verify that the resistance between the E and VT terminals on the sensor is approximately 5 kilohms.

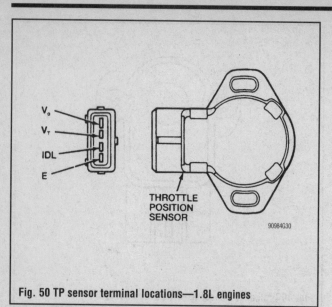

Fig. 50 TP sensor terminal locations—1.8L engines

Idle Air Control Valve

OPERATION

The Idle Air Control (IAC) valve is used to control idle speed. The amount of air allowed to bypass the throttle plate is determined by the PCM.

When the engine is cold, air flows through the valve during all modes of engine operation to maintain the factory set idle speed.

TESTING

1.8L Engines

▶ See Figure 51

1. Turn the ignition key **OFF**.
2. Connect jumper wires from the sensor connector to the wiring harness. This permits the engine to operate normally while you check the sensor.
3. Connect a Digital Volt Ohmmeter (DVOM), set to read resistance, between sensor terminal SIG and the negative battery cable.

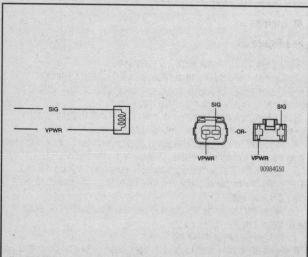

Fig. 51 Typical IAC valve wiring schematic and connector terminal identification—1.8L engines

4. The resistance should not be greater than 10,000 ohms.
5. Connect the DVOM, set to read resistance, between sensor terminal VPWR and the negative battery cable.
6. The resistance should not be greater than 10,000 ohms.
7. Turn the ignition key **ON**.
8. Connect the DVOM, set to read voltage, between sensor terminal VPWR and the negative battery cable.
9. The voltage should be more than 1 volt.
10. Connect the DVOM, set to read voltage, between sensor terminal SIG and the negative battery cable.
11. The voltage should be more than 1 volt.
12. If the readings are not within specifications, replace the IAC valve.

1.9L and 2.0L Engines

▶ See Figures 52, 53 and 54

1. Turn the ignition key **OFF**.
2. Unplug the sensor electrical connection.

➡Due to the diode in the IAC valve, be sure to observe the correct polarity when connecting the DVOM.

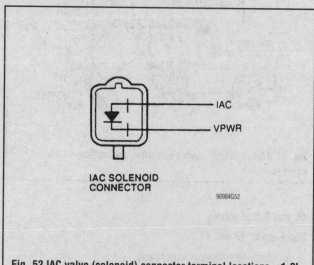

Fig. 52 IAC valve (solenoid) connector terminal locations—1.9L and 2.0L engines

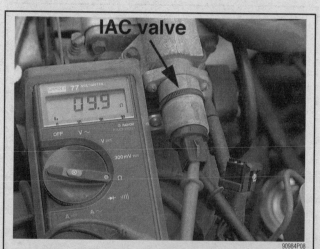

Fig. 53 Connect the DVOM positive lead to the VPWR terminal and the negative lead to the IAC terminal. The resistance should be between 6 and 13 ohms

Fig. 54 Measure resistance between either of the valve terminals and the valve body. The resistance should be greater than 10,000 ohms

3. Connect a Digital Volt Ohmmeter (DVOM), set to read resistance, between the sensor terminals as follows. Connect the positive lead to the VPWR terminal and the negative lead to the IAC terminal.

4. The resistance should be between 6 and 13 ohms.

5. Measure the resistance between either of the valve terminals and the valve body. The resistance should be greater than 10,000 ohms.

6. If the resistances are not within specification, replace the sensor.

REMOVAL & INSTALLATION

1.8L Engines

▶ See Figure 55

1. Disconnect the negative battery cable.
2. Remove the throttle body.
3. Unfasten the IAC valve retaining screws and remove the valve.
4. Remove and discard the valve gasket.

To install:

5. Install a new valve gasket.
6. Install the valve and tighten its retaining screws to 25–36 inch lbs. (3–4 Nm).

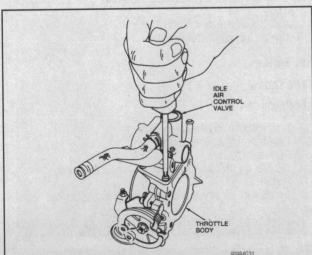

Fig. 55 Unfasten the IAC valve retaining screws and remove the valve—1.8L engines

7. Install the throttle body.
8. Connect the negative battery cable.

1.9L and 2.0L Engines

▶ See Figure 56

1. Disconnect the negative battery cable.
2. If necessary on 2.0L engines, remove the air cleaner outlet tube for easier access.
3. Unplug the IAC valve electrical connection.
4. Unfasten the valve retainers, then remove the valve and gasket.

To install:

5. Use a scraper to CAREFULLY clean the IAC valve mating surfaces.
6. Install a new IAC valve gasket and valve.
7. Install and tighten the valve retainers to 71–97 inch lbs. (8–11 Nm).
8. Attach the IAC valve electrical connection.
9. If removed, install the air cleaner outlet tube.
10. Connect the negative battery cable.

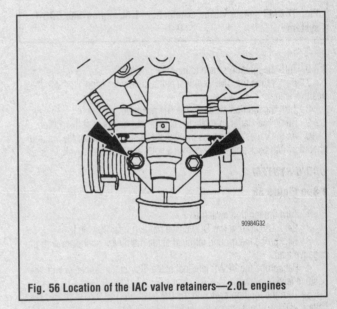

Fig. 56 Location of the IAC valve retainers—2.0L engines

Camshaft Position Sensor

OPERATION

➡ **The Camshaft Position (CMP) sensor provides camshaft position and rpm information to the PCM when the No. 1 piston is on the compression stroke.**

TESTING

1.8L Engines

OBD-I SYSTEM

▶ See Figure 57

1. Turn the ignition switch **OFF**.
2. Set a DVOM to a low DC voltage range (under 20 volts).
3. Backprobe the ground terminal of the distributor connector with the negative lead.
4. Backprobe the VPWR terminal of the distributor connector with the positive lead.
5. Turn the ignition switch to the **ON** position. The DVOM should read battery voltage. If not, check the wiring to the PCM.

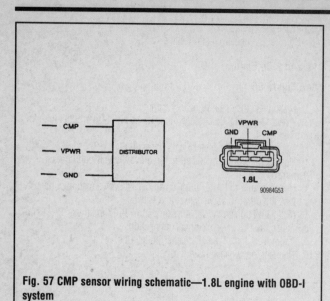

Fig. 57 CMP sensor wiring schematic—1.8L engine with OBD-I system

6. Turn the ignition switch to the **OFF** position.
7. Back probe the CMP terminal of the distributor connector with the positive lead.
8. Turn the ignition switch to the **ON** position.
9. Bump the starter to rotate the engine, but do not start the engine.
10. As the vanes of the pass through the Hall effect sensor the voltage should switch back and forth between 5 volts and less than 1 volt.

OBD-II SYSTEM

▶ See Figure 58

1. Turn the ignition switch **OFF**.
2. Set a DVOM to a low DC voltage range (under 20 volts).
3. Backprobe the ground terminal of the distributor connector with the negative lead.
4. Backprobe the VPWR terminal of the distributor connector with the positive lead.
5. Turn the ignition switch to the **ON** position. The DVOM should read battery voltage. If not, check the wiring to the PCM.
6. Turn the ignition switch to the **OFF** position.

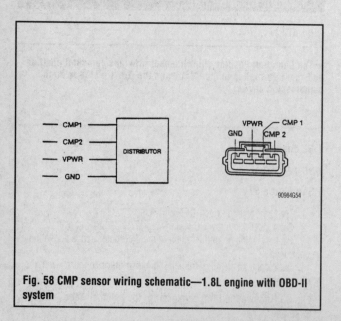

Fig. 58 CMP sensor wiring schematic—1.8L engine with OBD-II system

7. Back probe the CMP1 terminal of the distributor connector with the positive lead.
8. Turn the ignition switch to the **ON** position.
9. Bump the starter to rotate the engine, but do not start the engine.
10. As the vanes in the distributor pass through the Hall effect sensor the voltage should switch back and forth between 5 volts and less than 1 volt.
11. Perform the same test on the CMP 2 terminal.
12. If the voltage doesn't vary, check that the distributor is rotating. If the distributor is rotating, the CMP sensor may be defective.

1.9L and 2.0L Engines

▶ See Figures 59, 60, 61 and 62

1. Turn the ignition switch **OFF**.
2. Set a DVOM on the AC scale to read less than 5 volts.
3. Connect jumper wires from the CMP sensor connector to the wiring harness. This permits the engine to operate normally while you check the sensor.
4. Backprobe the CID (–) or CMP (–) terminal of the sensor with the negative lead.
5. Backprobe the CID (+) or CMP (+) terminal of the sensor with the positive lead.
6. Vary the engine rpm by turning the throttle assembly.
7. The voltage reading should vary by more than 0.1 volt AC.
8. If the voltage is not as specified, replace the CMP sensor.

REMOVAL & INSTALLATION

1.8L Engines

The CMP sensor is an integral part of the distributor assembly. If the CMP sensor is defective, the distributor assembly must be replaced.

1.9L engines

▶ See Figure 63

1. Disconnect the negative battery cable.
2. Remove the intake manifold assembly.
3. Unfasten the CMP sensor retaining screws and remove the sensor from the cylinder head.

To install:
4. Inspect the O-rings for damage and replace them if necessary.
5. Lubricate the O-rings with light engine oil and install the CMP sensor in the cylinder head.
6. Install and tighten the sensor retaining screws to 15–22 ft. lbs. (20–30 Nm).
7. Install the intake manifold.
8. Connect the negative battery cable.

2.0L Engines

SOHC ENGINE

▶ See Figure 64

1. Disconnect the negative battery cable.
2. Relieve the fuel system pressure.
3. Remove the fuel rail.
4. Unfasten the CMP sensor retainer and remove the sensor.

To install:
5. Inspect the CMP sensor O-ring for damage and replace it as necessary.
6. Lubricate the O-ring with light engine oil and install the CMP sensor.
7. Install and tighten the sensor retaining bolt to 54–79 inch lbs. (6–9 Nm).
8. Install the fuel rail.
9. Connect the negative battery cable.

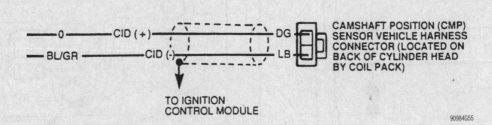

O —— CID (+) —— DG

BL/GR —— CID (-) —— LB

TO IGNITION
CONTROL MODULE

CAMSHAFT POSITION (CMP)
SENSOR VEHICLE HARNESS
CONNECTOR (LOCATED ON
BACK OF CYLINDER HEAD
BY COIL PACK)

90984G55

Fig. 59 Common CMP sensor wiring schematic—1.9L and 2.0L engines

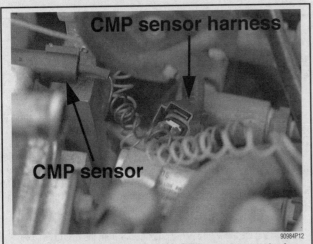

Fig. 60 Attach jumper wires from the CMP sensor connector to
the wiring harness. This permits the engine to operate normally
while you check the sensor

Fig. 62 . . . then move the throttle assembly to vary the engine
rpm and observe the CMP sensor voltage reading

Fig. 61 Measure the CMP sensor voltage with the throttle
assembly closed . . .

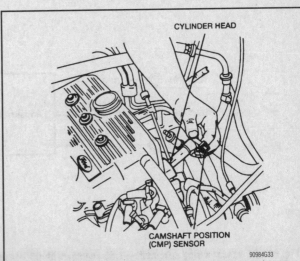

Fig. 63 Remove the CMP sensor from the cylinder head—1.9L
engines

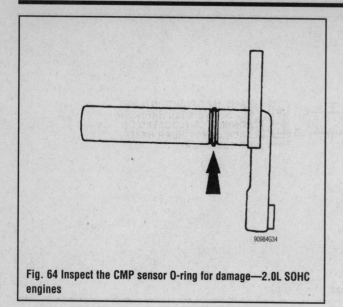

Fig. 64 Inspect the CMP sensor O-ring for damage—2.0L SOHC engines

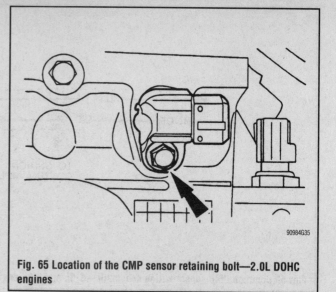

Fig. 65 Location of the CMP sensor retaining bolt—2.0L DOHC engines

DOHC ENGINES

▶ See Figure 65

1. Disconnect the negative battery cable.
2. Unplug the CMP sensor electrical connection.
3. Unfasten the CMP sensor retainer and remove the sensor.

To install:
4. Inspect the CMP sensor O-ring for damage and replace it as necessary.
5. Lubricate the O-ring with light engine oil and install the CMP sensor.
6. Install and tighten the sensor retaining bolt to 62–70 inch lbs. (7–8 Nm).
7. Connect the negative battery cable.

Crankshaft Position Sensor

The Crankshaft Position (CKP) sensor relays engine speed and crankshaft position to the Powertrain Control Module (PCM).

TESTING

1.8L Engines

OBD-I SYSTEM

▶ See Figure 66

1. Turn the ignition key **OFF**.
2. Using a Digital Volt Ohmmeter (DVOM), backprobe the CKP terminal of the CKP sensor connector with the DVOM's positive lead. Attach the DVOM's negative lead to a good engine ground.
3. While an assistant cranks the engine with the starter motor (using the ignition switch), observe the voltage displayed on the DVOM.
4. The CKP sensor voltage should fluctuate between approximately 0 and 5 volts. If the CKP sensor performs as specified, it is functioning properly. If, however, the voltage is not as specified, continue with the test procedure.
5. Turn the ignition key **OFF**.
6. Disengage the wiring harness connector from the distributor, then attach the positive lead of the DVOM to the VPWR terminal on the wiring harness connector. Attach the negative lead to a good ground.

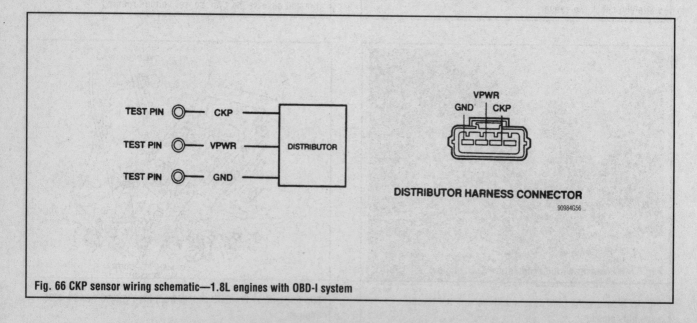

Fig. 66 CKP sensor wiring schematic—1.8L engines with OBD-I system

7. Turn the ignition key **ON** and observe the voltage displayed on the DVOM. The voltage should be greater than 10 volts. If not, the CKP sensor is not receiving the proper voltage from the PCM; the problem lies elsewhere in the electrical system.

8. If the VPWR voltage is satisfactory and the CKP output is not as specified, replace the CKP sensor.

OBD-II SYSTEM

▶ See Figure 67

1. Turn the ignition key **OFF**.
2. Using a Digital Volt Ohmmeter (DVOM), backprobe the CKP (-) terminal of the harness and ground.
3. The resistance should be less than 5 volts. If not check for a short in the GND circuit.
4. Measure the resistance between CKP (+) and the negative battery terminal.
5. The resistance should be approximately 10, 000 ohms. If the resistance is greater than specified resistance, replace the sensor. If the resistance is less than 10,000 ohms, check for a wiring harness for short circuits.
6. Measure the resistance between CKP (-) and the negative battery terminal.
7. The resistance should be approximately 10, 000 ohms. If the resistance is greater than specified resistance, replace the sensor. If the resistance is less than 10,000 ohms, check for a wiring harness for short circuits.

➡ **To perform this test accurately, the ambient air temperature should be 68°F (20°C).**

8. Turn the ignition key **OFF**.
9. Unplug the CKP electrical connection.
10. Using a Digital Volt Ohmmeter (DVOM), set to read resistance, probe the CKP (+) terminal of the CKP sensor connector with the DVOM's positive lead. Attach the DVOM's negative lead to a good engine ground. Note the reading.
11. Backprobe the CKP (+) terminal of the CKP sensor connector with the DVOM's positive lead in the same manner and note the resistance reading.
12. The resistance should be 520–580 ohms at 68°F (20°C). If readings are not as specified, replace the CKP sensor.

1.9L and 2.0L Engines

▶ See Figures 68 and 69

1. Visually inspect the CKP sensor and the trigger wheel for damage.
2. Unplug the CKP harness.
3. Probe the CKP (-) wire on the wiring harness connector and turn the ignition key **ON**. The voltage should be greater than 0.8 volts and less than 2.2 volts DC.
4. If no voltage is present, check the continuity of the CKP (-) wire between the wiring connector and the EDIS module. If the wire has continuity, check the EDIS module is getting power, If power is present, replace the EDIS module and retest the system.
5. Attach jumper wires from the CKP sensor connector to the wiring harness. This permits the engine to operate normally while you check the sensor.
6. Set a Digital Volt Ohmmeter (DVOM) on the AC voltage scale.
7. Start the engine and observe the voltage reading while varying the rpm, the voltage should also vary.

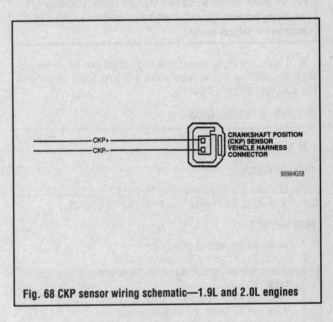

Fig. 68 CKP sensor wiring schematic—1.9L and 2.0L engines

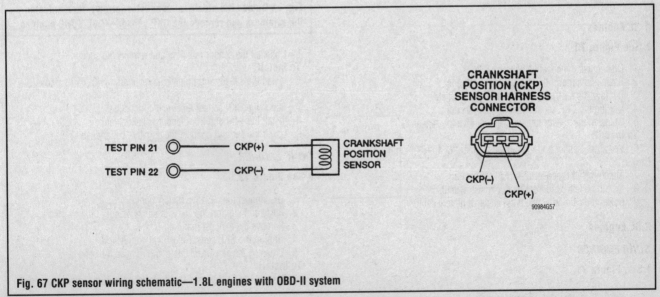

Fig. 67 CKP sensor wiring schematic—1.8L engines with OBD-II system

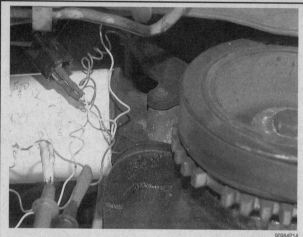

Fig. 69 Attach jumper wires from the CKP sensor connector to the wiring harness, connect a voltmeter, start the engine and observe the voltage reading

Fig. 70 Location of the CKP sensor—1.9L engines

8. If there is no signal, unplug the wiring harness from the sensor and check the harness for continuity and shorts to ground. Repair as necessary and attach the harness to the sensor.

REMOVAL & INSTALLATION

1.8L Engines

1991–95 MODELS

The CKP sensor is an integral part of the distributor assembly. If the CKP sensor is defective, the distributor assembly must be replaced.

1996 MODELS

1. Disconnect the negative battery cable.
2. Unplug the CKP sensor electrical connection.
3. Unfasten the sensor bolt and remove the sensor.
To install:
4. Install the sensor and tighten the bolt to 70–95 inch lbs. (8–10 Nm).
5. Attach the CKP sensor electrical connection.
6. Connect the negative battery cable.

1.9L Engines

▶ See Figure 70

1. Disconnect the negative battery cable.
2. Raise and support the car with safety stands.
3. Remove the left-hand front fender splash shield.
4. Unplug the CKP sensor electrical connection.
5. Unfasten the sensor retainers and remove the sensor.
To install:
6. Install the sensor and tighten the retainers to 40–61 inch lbs. (5–7 Nm).
7. Attach the CKP sensor electrical connection.
8. Install the left-hand front fender splash shield.
9. Lower the car and connect the negative battery cable.

2.0L Engines

SOHC ENGINES

▶ See Figure 71

1. Disconnect the negative battery cable.
2. Raise and support the car with safety stands.
3. Remove the left-hand front fender splash shield.
4. Unplug the CKP sensor electrical connection.

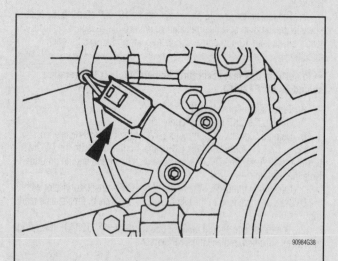

Fig. 71 Detach the electrical connector (arrow), then unfasten the retainers and remove the CKP sensor—2.0L SOHC engines

5. Unfasten the sensor retainers and remove the sensor.
To install:
6. Install the sensor and tighten the retainers to 40–61 inch lbs. (5–7 Nm).
7. Attach the CKP sensor electrical connection.
8. Install the left-hand front fender splash shield.
9. Lower the car and connect the negative battery cable.

DOHC ENGINES

▶ See Figure 72

1. Disconnect the negative battery cable.
2. Raise and support the car with safety stands.
3. Remove the exhaust manifold.
4. Unplug the CKP sensor electrical connection.
5. Unfasten the sensor retainers and remove the sensor.
To install:
6. Inspect the CKP sensor O-ring for damage and replace it as necessary.
7. Lubricate the O-ring with light engine oil and install the CKP sensor.
8. Install the sensor and tighten the retainers to 53–80 inch lbs. (6–9 Nm).

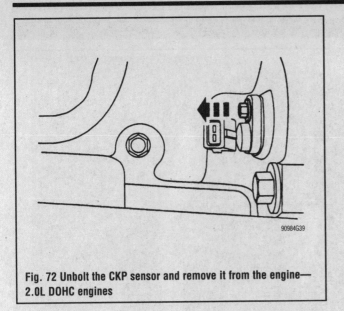

Fig. 72 Unbolt the CKP sensor and remove it from the engine— 2.0L DOHC engines

9. Attach the CKP sensor electrical connection.
10. Install the exhaust manifold.
11. Lower the car and connect the negative battery cable.

Variable Camshaft Timing Oil Control Solenoid

OPERATION

➡The oil control solenoid is part of the Variable Camshaft Timing (VCT) unit.

The VCT unit used on the 2.0L DOHC engine is connected to the exhaust camshaft, and the rotation of the exhaust camshaft takes place in the VCT unit. The unit is oil filled to move the pistons inside the unit. Oil and piston movement inside the unit can retard the exhaust camshaft without affecting the intake camshaft.

Adjustment of the VCT unit permits every piston position between maximum advance and maximum retardation.

TESTING

▶ See Figure 73

1. Turn the ignition switch **OFF**.
2. Unplug the wiring harness from the sensor and check the harness for continuity and shorts to ground. Repair as necessary and attach the harness to the sensor.
3. Using a Digital Volt Ohmmeter (DVOM), set to read resistance, probe the terminals of the solenoid.
4. The resistance should be between 3.0 and 6.0 volts.
5. If the resistance is not within specification, replace the sensor.

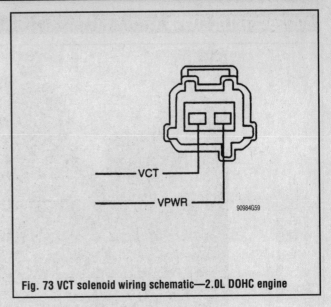

Fig. 73 VCT solenoid wiring schematic—2.0L DOHC engine

REMOVAL & INSTALLATION

▶ See Figure 74

1. Remove the camshafts.
2. Slide the oil control solenoid from the camshaft.
3. Installation is the reverse of removal.

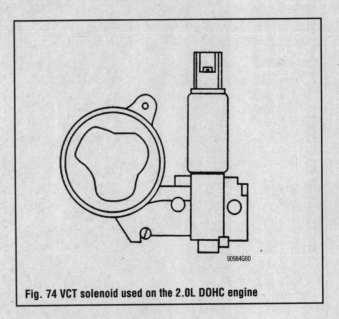

Fig. 74 VCT solenoid used on the 2.0L DOHC engine

COMPONENT LOCATIONS

TYPICAL ENGINE ELECTRONIC COMPONENT LOCATIONS — 1.9L ENGINE SHOWN

1. Engine Coolant Temperature (ECT) sensor (under hose)
2. Intake Air Temperature (IAT) sensor
3. Throttle Position (TP) sensor
4. Idle Air Control (IAC) solenoid
5. Camshaft Position (CMP) sensor
6. Mass Air Flow (MAF) sensor
7. Diagnostic Link Connector (DLC)
8. Fuel rail and pressure regulator
9. Fuel injector

90984P15

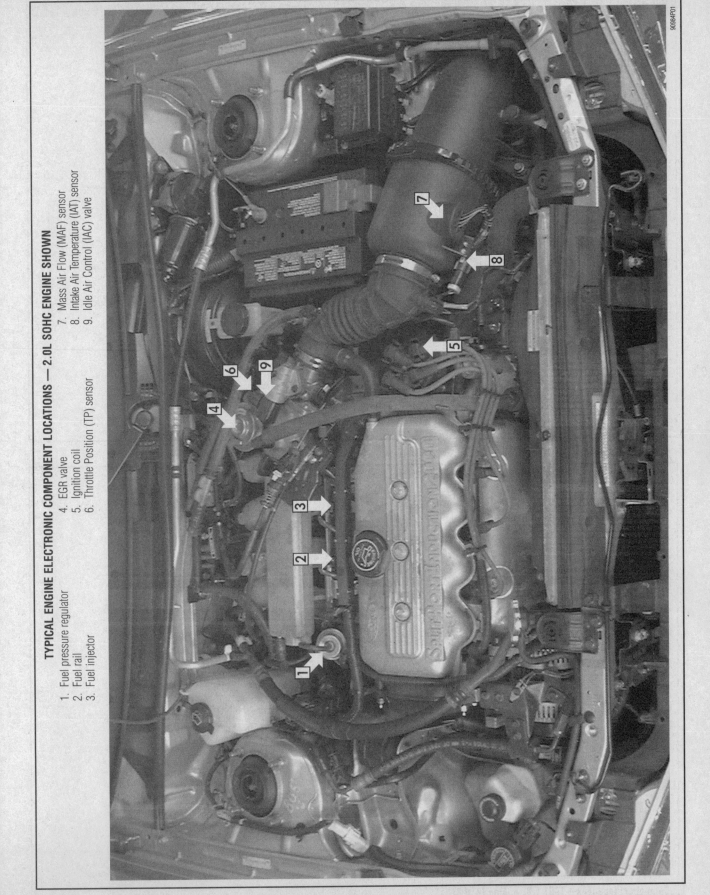

TYPICAL ENGINE ELECTRONIC COMPONENT LOCATIONS — 2.0L SOHC ENGINE SHOWN

1. Fuel pressure regulator
2. Fuel rail
3. Fuel injector
4. EGR valve
5. Ignition coil
6. Throttle Position (TP) sensor
7. Mass Air Flow (MAF) sensor
8. Intake Air Temperature (IAT) sensor
9. Idle Air Control (IAC) valve

90984P01

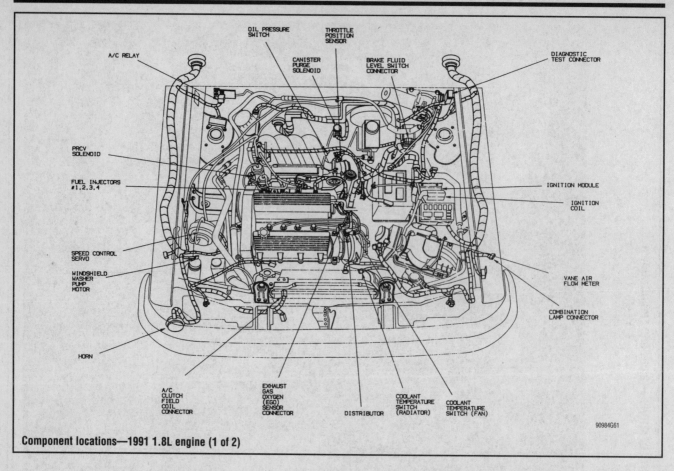

Component locations—1991 1.8L engine (1 of 2)

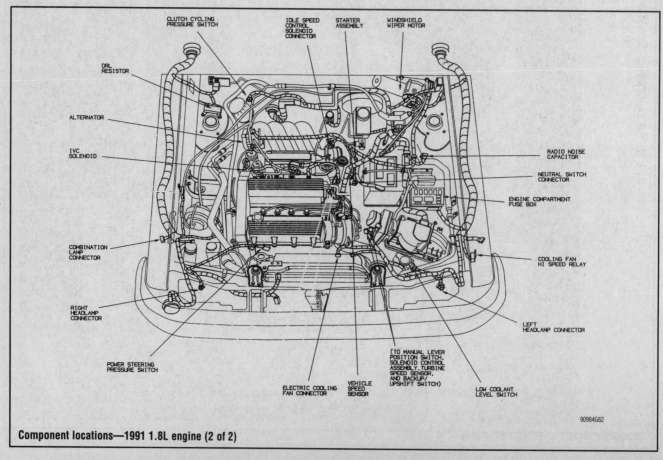

Component locations—1991 1.8L engine (2 of 2)

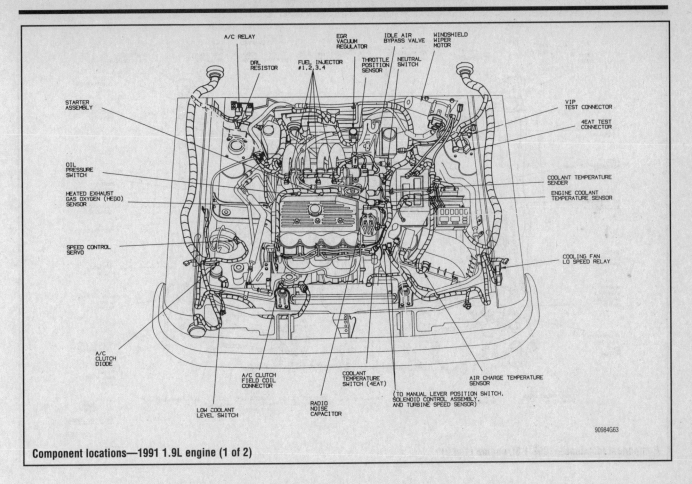

Component locations—1991 1.9L engine (1 of 2)

90984G63

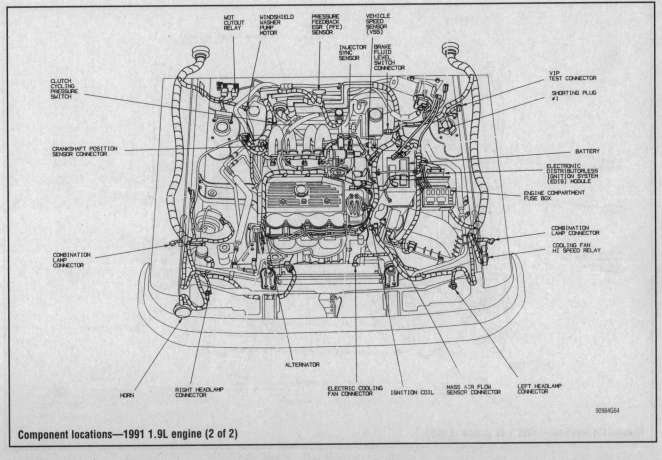

Component locations—1991 1.9L engine (2 of 2)

90984G64

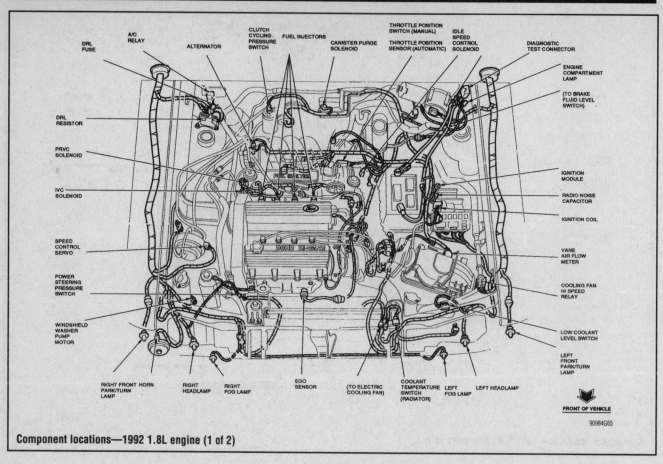

Component locations—1992 1.8L engine (1 of 2)

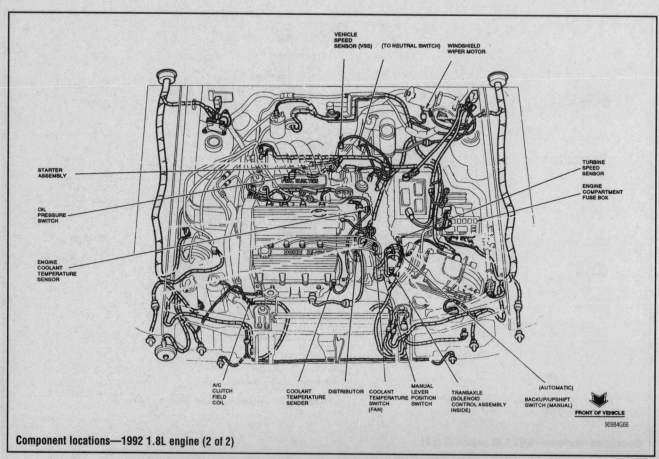

Component locations—1992 1.8L engine (2 of 2)

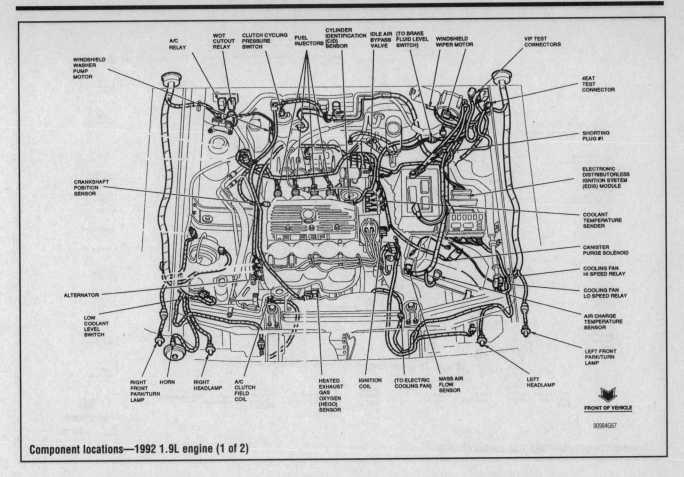

Component locations—1992 1.9L engine (1 of 2)

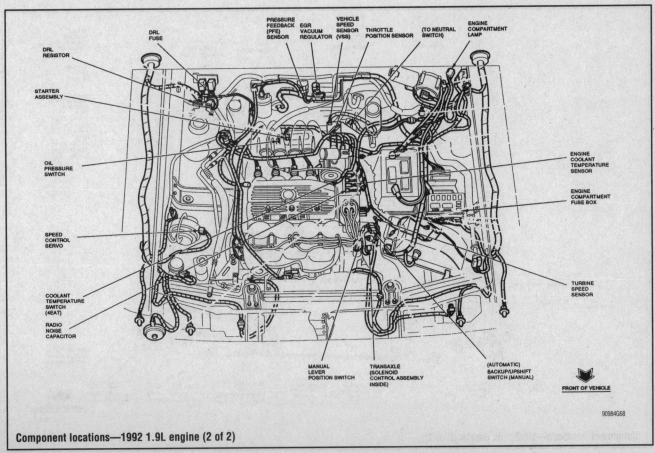

Component locations—1992 1.9L engine (2 of 2)

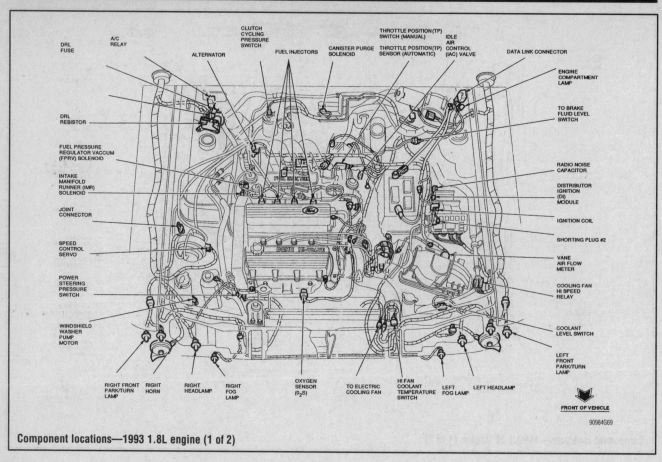

Component locations—1993 1.8L engine (1 of 2)

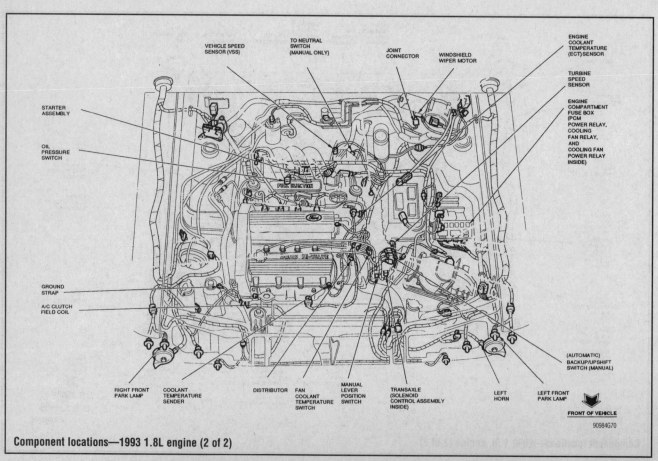

Component locations—1993 1.8L engine (2 of 2)

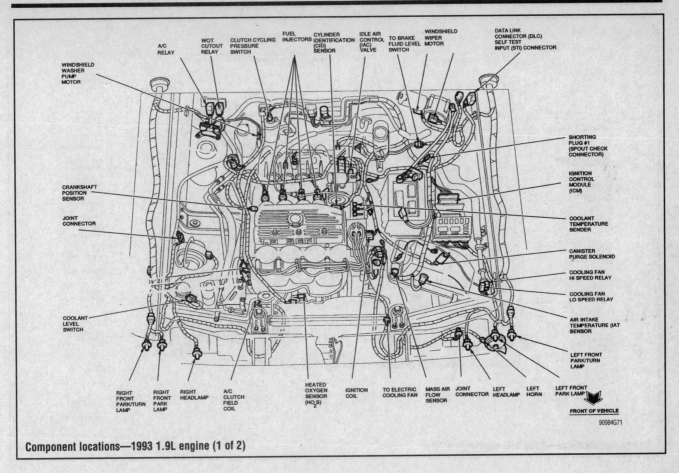

Component locations—1993 1.9L engine (1 of 2)

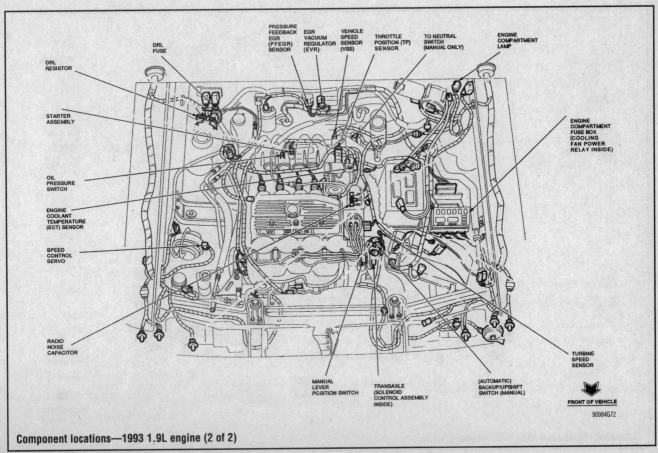

Component locations—1993 1.9L engine (2 of 2)

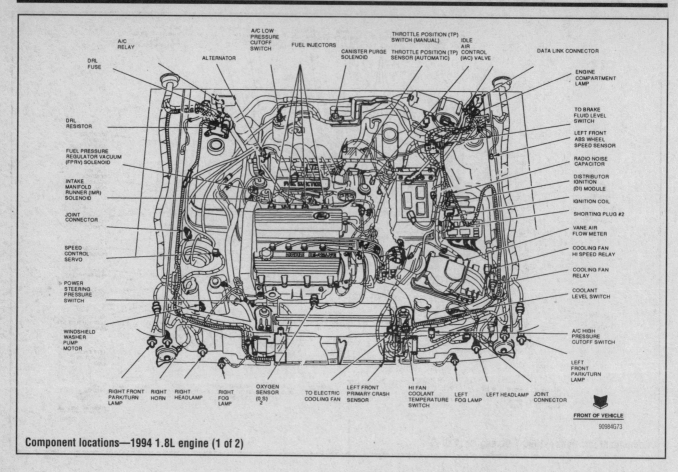

Component locations—1994 1.8L engine (1 of 2)

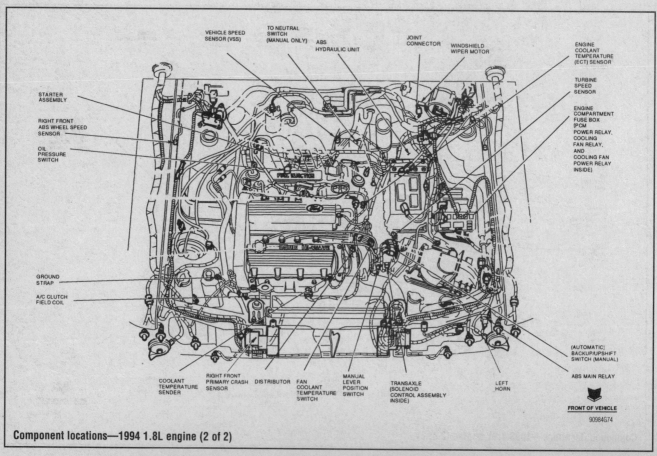

Component locations—1994 1.8L engine (2 of 2)

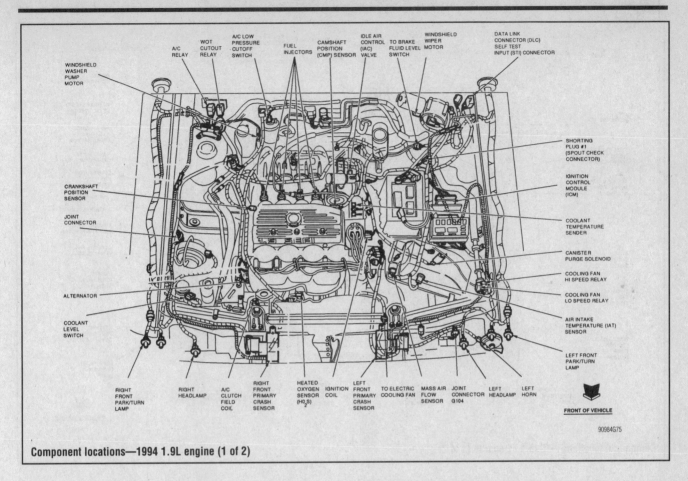

Component locations—1994 1.9L engine (1 of 2)

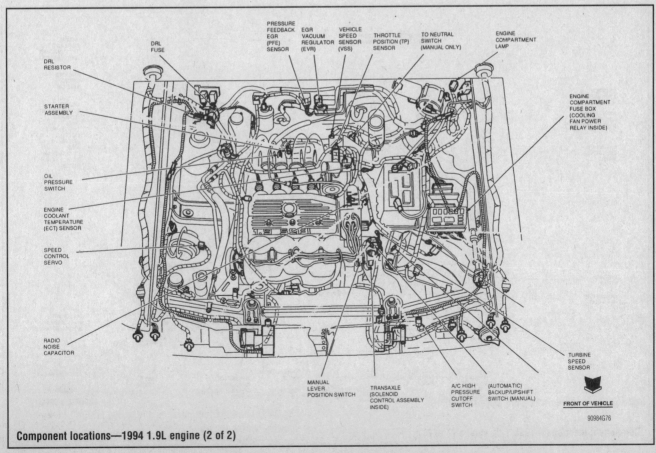

Component locations—1994 1.9L engine (2 of 2)

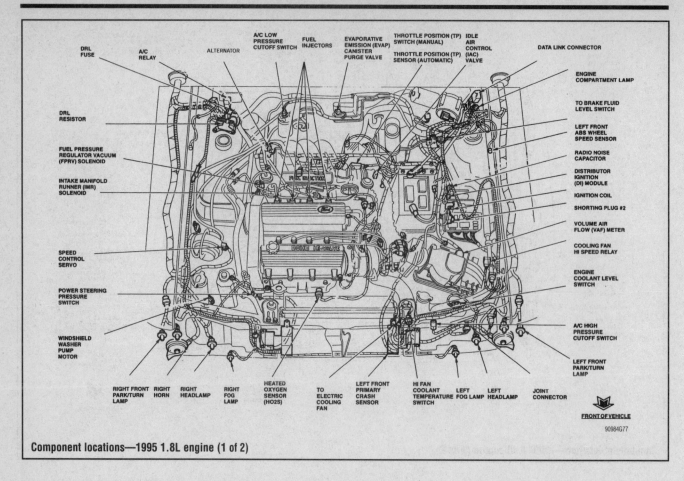

Component locations—1995 1.8L engine (1 of 2)

90984G77

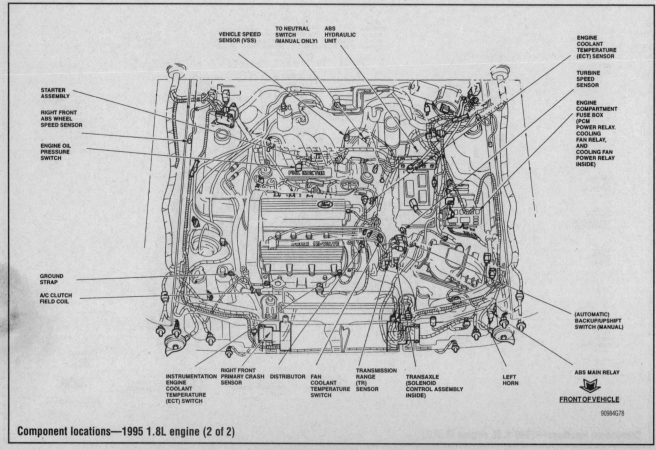

Component locations—1995 1.8L engine (2 of 2)

90984G78

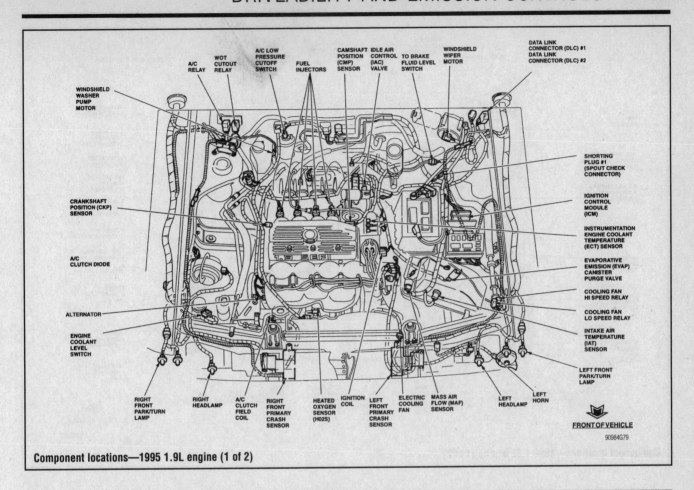

Component locations—1995 1.9L engine (1 of 2)

90984G79

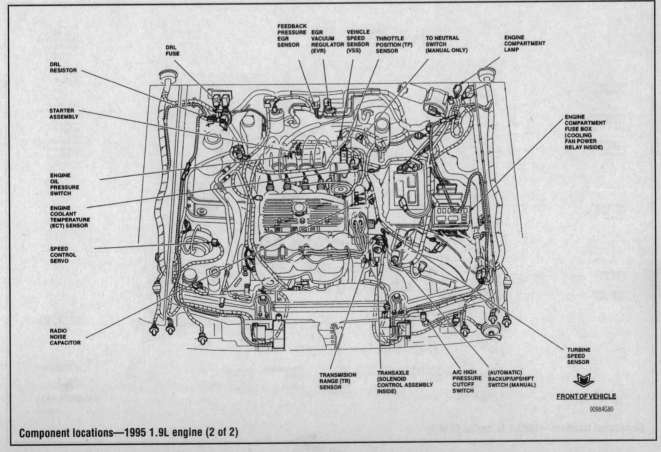

Component locations—1995 1.9L engine (2 of 2)

90984G80

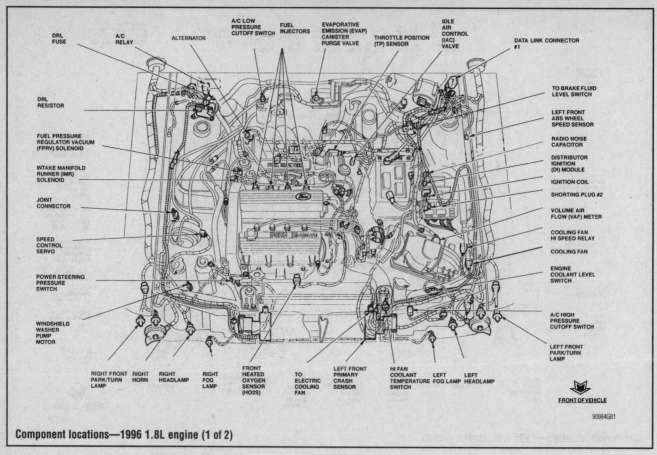

Component locations—1996 1.8L engine (1 of 2)

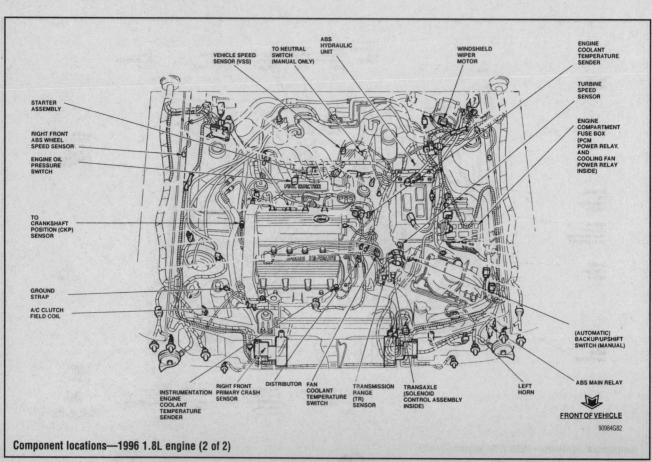

Component locations—1996 1.8L engine (2 of 2)

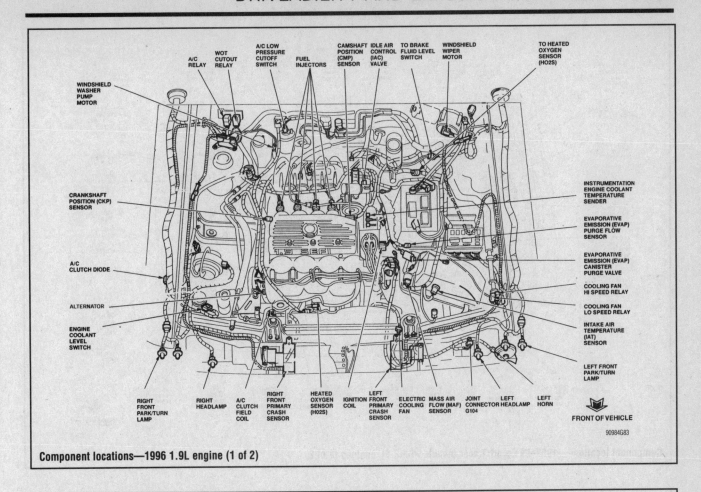

Component locations—1996 1.9L engine (1 of 2)

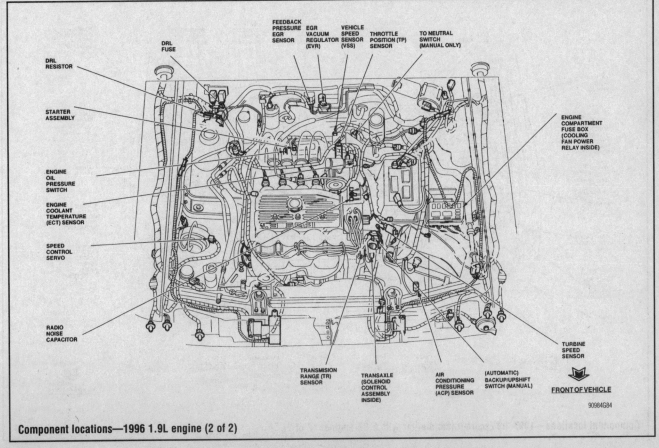

Component locations—1996 1.9L engine (2 of 2)

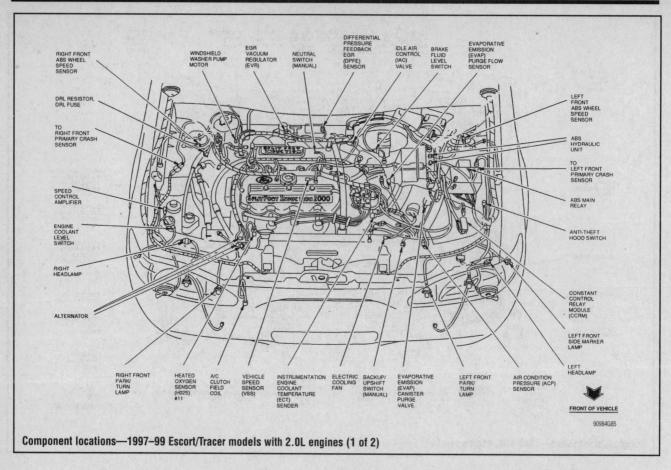

Component locations—1997–99 Escort/Tracer models with 2.0L engines (1 of 2)

90984G85

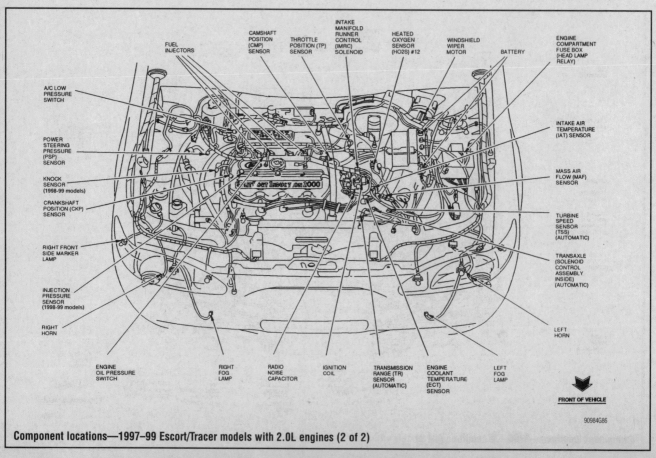

Component locations—1997–99 Escort/Tracer models with 2.0L engines (2 of 2)

90984G86

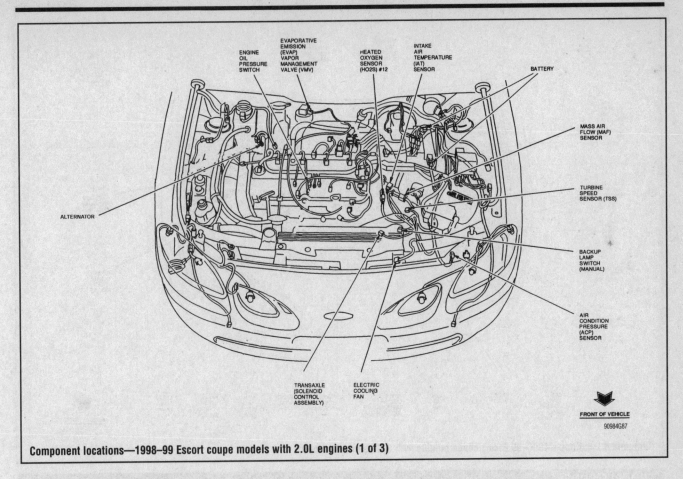

Component locations—1998–99 Escort coupe models with 2.0L engines (1 of 3)

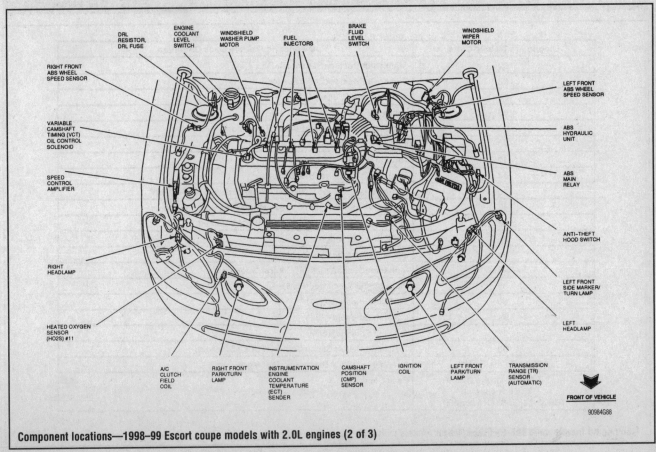

Component locations—1998–99 Escort coupe models with 2.0L engines (2 of 3)

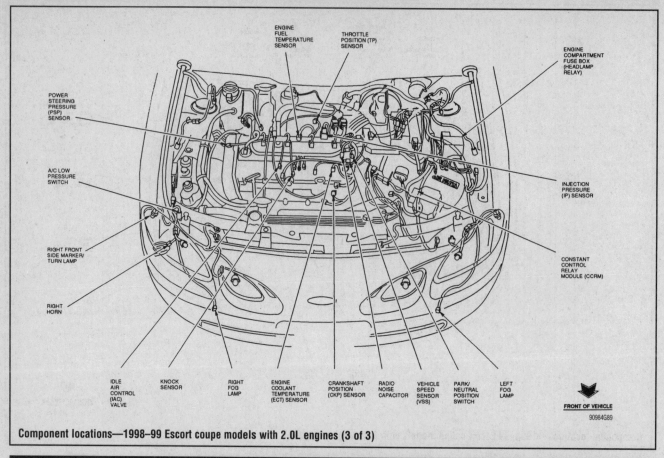

Component locations—1998–99 Escort coupe models with 2.0L engines (3 of 3)

TROUBLE CODES

Diagnostic Trouble Code	Diagnostic Trouble Code Definition
02	Crankshaft Position Sensor (CKP)
03	Camshaft Position (CMP) Sensor
06	Vehicle Speed Sensor (VSS)
08	Volume Air Flow (VAF) Sensor
09	Engine Coolant Temperature (ECT) Sensor
10	Intake Air Temperature (IAT) Sensor
12	Throttle Position (TP) Sensor
14	Barometric Pressure (BARO) Sensor
15	Heated Oxygen Sensor (HO2S) - voltage always below 0.55V
17	Heated Oxygen Sensor (HO2S) - voltage does not change
25	Fuel Pressure Regulator Control (FPRC) Solenoid
26	EVAP Canister Purge Solenoid
34	Idle Air Control (IAC) Solenoid
41	High Speed Inlet Air (HSIA) Control Solenoid
55	Pulse Signal Generator (PSG)
60	1-2 Shift Solenoid (SS1)
61	2-3 Shift Solenoid (SS2)
62	3-4 Shift Solenoid (SS3)
63	Torque Converter Clutch Control (TCCC) Solenoid
"STO LO" always ON	Not Able to Initiate Diagnostic Test Mode
"STI LO" always ON and no codes (Blank Super STAR II screen)	Pass Code

1.8L engine trouble code chart—OBD-I system

90984C06

1.9L engine trouble code chart—OBD-I system

DIAGNOSTIC TROUBLE CODES	DEFINITIONS
111	System Pass
112	Intake Air Temp (IAT) sensor circuit below minimum voltage / 254°F indicated
113	Intake Air Temp (IAT) sensor circuit above maximum voltage / -40°F indicated
114	Intake Air Temp (IAT) sensor circuit voltage higher or lower than expected
116	Engine Coolant Temp (ECT) sensor circuit voltage higher or lower than expected
117	Engine Coolant Temp (ECT) sensor circuit below minimum voltage / 254°F indicated
118	Engine Coolant Temp (ECT) sensor circuit above maximum voltage / -40°F indicated
121	Closed throttle voltage higher or lower than expected
121	Throttle position voltage inconsistent with the MAF sensor
122	Throttle Position (TP) sensor circuit below minimum voltage
123	Throttle Position (TP) sensor circuit above maximum voltage
124	Throttle Position (TP) sensor voltage higher than expected
125	Throttle Position (TP) sensor voltage lower than expected
126	MAP / BARO sensor circuit voltage higher or lower than expected
128	MAP sensor vacuum hose damaged / disconnected
129	Insufficient MAP / Mass Air Flow (MAF) change during dynamic response test KOER
136	Lack of Heated Oxygen Sensor (HO2S-2) switch during KOER, indicates lean (Bank #2)
137	Lack of Heated Oxygen Sensor (HO2S-2) switch during KOER, indicates rich (Bank #2)
139	No Heated Oxygen Sensor (HO2S-2) switches detected (Bank #2)
141	Fuel system indicates lean
144	No Heated Oxygen Sensor (HO2S-1) switches detected (Bank #1)
157	Mass Air Flow (MAF) sensor circuit below minimum voltage
158	Mass Air Flow (MAF) sensor circuit above maximum voltage
159	Mass Air Flow (MAF) sensor circuit voltage higher or lower than expected
167	Insufficient throttle position change during dynamic response test KOER
171	Fuel system at adaptive limits, Heated Oxygen Sensor (HO2S-1) unable to switch (Bank #1)
172	Lack of Heated Oxygen Sensor (HO2S-1) switches, indicates lean (Bank #1)
173	Lack of Heated Oxygen Sensor (HO2S-1) switches, indicates rich (Bank #1)
175	Fuel system at adaptive limits, Heated Oxygen Sensor (HO2S-2) unable to switch (Bank #2)
176	Lack of Heated Oxygen Sensor (HO2S-2) switches, indicates lean (Bank #2)
177	Lack of Heated Oxygen Sensor (HO2S-2) switches, indicates rich (Bank #2)
179	Fuel system at lean adaptive limit at part throttle, system rich (Bank #1)
181	Fuel system at rich adaptive limit at part throttle, system lean (Bank #1)
184	Mass Air Flow (MAF) sensor voltage higher than expected
185	Mass Air Flow (MAF) sensor voltage lower than expected
186	Injector pulsewidth higher than expected (with BARO sensor)
186	Injector pulsewidth higher or mass air flow lower than expected (without BARO sensor)
187	Injector pulsewidth lower than expected (with BARO sensor)
187	Injector pulsewidth lower or mass air flow higher than expected (without BARO sensor)
188	Fuel system at lean adaptive limit at part throttle, system rich (Bank #2)
189	Fuel system at rich adaptive limit at part throttle, system lean (Bank #2)
193	Flexible Fuel (FF) sensor circuit failure

1.9L engine trouble code chart—OBD-I system (continued)

DIAGNOSTIC TROUBLE CODES	DEFINITIONS
211	Profile Ignition Pickup (PIP) circuit failure
212	Loss of Ignition Diagnostic Monitor (IDM) input to PCM / SPOUT circuit grounded
213	SPOUT circuit open
214	Cylinder Identification (CID) circuit failure
215	PCM detected coil 1 primary circuit failure (EI)
216	PCM detected coil 2 primary circuit failure (EI)
217	PCM detected coil 3 primary circuit failure (EI)
218	Loss of Ignition Diagnostic Monitor (IDM) signal-left side (dual plug EI)
219	Spark timing defaulted to 10 degrees-SPOUT circuit open (EI)
221	Spark timing error (EI)
222	Loss of Ignition Diagnostic Monitor (IDM) signal-right side (dual plug EI)
223	Loss of Dual Plug Inhibit (DPI) control (dual plug EI)
224	PCM detected coil 1, 2, 3 or 4 primary circuit failure (dual plug EI)
225	Knock not sensed during dynamic response test KOER
226	Ignition Diagnostic Module (IDM) signal not received (EI)
232	PCM detected coil 1, 2, 3 or 4 primary circuit failure (EI)
238	PCM detected coil 4 primary circuit failure (EI)
241	ICM to PCM IDM pulsewidth transmission error (EI)
244	CID circuit fault present when cylinder balance test requested
311	AIR system inoperative during KOER (Bank #1 w/ dual HO2S)
312	AIR misdirected during KOER
313	AIR not bypassed during KOER
314	AIR system inoperative during KOER (Bank #2 w/ dual HO2S)
326	EGR (PFE / DPFE) circuit voltage lower than expected
327	EGR (EGRP / EVP / PFE / DPFE) circuit below minimum voltage
328	EGR (EVP) closed valve voltage lower than expected
332	Insufficient EGR flow detected (EGRP / EVP / DPFE)
334	EGR (EVP) closed valve voltage higher than expected
335	EGR (PFE / DPFE) sensor voltage higher or lower than expected during KOEO
336	Exhaust pressure high / EGR (PFE / DPFE) circuit voltage higher than expected
337	EGR (EGRP / EVP / PFE / DPFE) circuit above maximum voltage
338	Engine Coolant Temperature (ECT) lower than expected (thermostat test)
339	Engine Coolant Temperature (ECT) higher than expected (thermostat test)
341	Octane adjust service pin open
381	Frequent A/C clutch cycling
411	Cannot control RPM during KOER low RPM check
412	Cannot control RPM during KOER high RPM check
415	Idle Air Control (IAC) system at maximum adaptive lower limit
416	Idle Air Control (IAC) system at upper adaptive learning limit
452	Insufficient input from Vehicle Speed Sensor (VSS) to PCM
453	Servo leaking down (KOER IVSC test)
454	Servo leaking up (KOER IVSC test)
455	Insufficient RPM increase (KOER IVSC test)
456	Insufficient RPM decrease (KOER IVSC test)

DIAGNOSTIC TROUBLE CODES	DEFINITIONS
457	Speed control command switch(s) circuit not functioning (KOEO IVSC test)
458	Speed control command switch(s) stuck / circuit grounded (KOEO IVSC test)
459	Speed control ground circuit open (KOEO IVSC test)
511	PCM Read Only Memory (ROM) test failure KOEO
512	PCM Keep Alive Memory (KAM) test failure
513	PCM internal voltage failure (KOEO)
519	Power Steering Pressure (PSP) switch circuit open KOEO
519	Power Steering Pressure (PSP) sensor circuit open
521	Power Steering Pressure (PSP) switch circuit did not change states KOER
521	Power Steering Pressure (PSP) sensor circuit did not change states KOER
522	Vehicle not in PARK or NEUTRAL during KOEO / PNP switch circuit open
524	Low speed fuel pump circuit open—battery to PCM
525	Indicates vehicle in gear / A/C on
527	Park / Neutral Position (PNP) switch circuit open—A/C on KOEO
528	Clutch Pedal Position (CPP) switch circuit failure
529	Data Communication Link (DCL) or PCM circuit failure
532	Cluster Control Assembly (CCA) circuit failure
533	Data Communication Link (DCL) or Electronic Instrument Cluster (EIC) circuit failure
536	Brake On / Off (BOO) circuit failure / not actuated during KOER
538	Insufficient RPM change during KOER dynamic response test
538	Invalid cylinder balance test due to throttle movement during test (SFI only)
538	Invalid cylinder balance test due to CID circuit failure
539	A/C on / Defrost on during Self-Test
542	Fuel pump secondary circuit failure
543	Fuel pump secondary circuit failure
551	Idle Air Control (IAC) circuit failure KOEO
552	Secondary Air Injection Bypass (AIRB) circuit failure KOEO
553	Secondary Air Injection Diverter (AIRD) circuit failure KOEO
554	Fuel Pressure Regulator Control (FPRC) circuit failure
556	Fuel pump relay primary circuit failure
557	Low speed fuel pump primary circuit failure
558	EGR Vacuum Regulator (EVR) circuit failure KOEO
559	Air Conditioning On (ACON) relay circuit failure KOEO
563	High Fan Control (HFC) circuit failure KOEO
564	Fan Control (FC) circuit failure KOEO
565	Canister Purge (CANP) circuit failure KOEO
566	3-4 shift solenoid circuit failure KOEO (A4LD)
567	Speed Control Vent (SCVNT) circuit failure (KOEO IVSC test)
568	Speed Control Vacuum (SCVAC) circuit failure (KOEO IVSC test)
569	Auxiliary Canister Purge (CANP2) circuit failure KOEO
571	EGRA solenoid circuit failure KOEO
572	EGRV solenoid circuit failure KOEO
578	A/C pressure sensor circuit shorted
579	Insufficient A/C pressure change

1.9L engine trouble code chart—OBD-I system (continued)

DIAGNOSTIC TROUBLE CODES	DEFINITIONS
581	Power to Fan circuit over current
582	Fan circuit open
583	Power to Fuel pump over current
584	VCRM Power ground circuit open (VCRM Pin 1)
585	Power to A/C clutch over current
586	A/C clutch circuit open
587	Variable Control Relay Module (VCRM) communication failure
593	Heated Oxygen Sensor Heater (HO2S HTR) circuit failure
617	1-2 shift error
618	2-3 shift error
619	3-4 shift error
621	Shift Solenoid 1 (SS1) circuit failure KOEO
622	Shift Solenoid 2 (SS2) circuit failure KOEO
623	Transmission Control Indicator Lamp (TCIL) circuit failure
624	Electronic Pressure Control (EPC) circuit failure
625	Electronic Pressure Control (EPC) driver open in PCM
626	Coast Clutch Solenoid (CCS) circuit failure KOEO
627	Torque Converter Clutch (TCC) solenoid circuit failure
628	Excessive converter clutch slippage
629	Torque Converter Clutch (TCC) solenoid circuit failure
631	Transmission Control Indicator Lamp (TCIL) circuit failure KOEO
632	Transmission Control Switch (TCS) circuit did not change states during KOER
633	4x4L switch closed during KOEO
634	Transmission Range (TR) voltage higher or lower than expected
636	Transmission Fluid Temperature (TFT) higher or lower than expected
637	Transmission Fluid Temperature (TFT) sensor circuit above maximum voltage / -40°F (-40°C) indicated / circuit open
638	Transmission Fluid Temperature (TFT) sensor circuit below minimum voltage / 290°F (143°C) indicated / circuit shorted
639	Insufficient input from Turbine Shaft Speed Sensor (TSS)
641	Shift Solenoid 3 (SS3) circuit failure
643	Torque Converter Clutch (TCC) circuit failure
645	Incorrect gear ratio obtained for first gear
646	Incorrect gear ratio obtained for second gear
647	Incorrect gear ratio obtained for third gear
648	Incorrect gear ratio obtained for fourth gear
649	Electronic Pressure Control (EPC) higher or lower than expected
651	Electronic Pressure Control (EPC) circuit failure
652	Torque Converter Clutch (TCC) solenoid circuit failure
653	Transmission Control Switch (TCS) did not change states during KOER
654	Transmission Range (TR) sensor not indicating PARK during KOEO
656	Torque Converter Clutch continuous slip error
657	Transmission overtemperature condition occurred
659	High vehicle speed in park indicated
667	Transmission Range sensor circuit voltage below minimum voltage
668	Transmission Range sensor circuit voltage above maximum voltage
675	Transmission Range sensor circuit voltage out of range
998	Hard fault present—FMEM MODE

1.9L engine trouble code chart—OBD-I system (continued)

90984C14

DTC	Definition
P0732	Incorrect second gear ratio
P0733	Incorrect third gear ratio
P0734	Incorrect fourth gear ratio
P0740	Torque converter clutch system malfunction
P0745	Line pressure control solenoid malfunction
P0750	Shift solenoid 1 malfunction
P0755	Shift solenoid 2 malfunction
P0760	Shift solenoid 3 malfunction
P1000	OBD II monitoring testing not completed
P1170	Heated oxygen sensor bank 1 sensor 1 inversion
P1173	Heated oxygen sensor bank 2 sensor 1 inversion
P1195	EGR boost sensor open or short
P1196	Ignition switch (start) open or short
P1250	FPRC solenoid valve open or short
P1345	No camshaft position sensor signal
P1402	EGR valve position sensor open or short
P1485	EGR control solenoid open or short
P1486	EGR vent solenoid open or short
P1487	EGR boost check solenoid open or short
P1521	VRIS solenoid valve # 1 open or short
P1522	VRIS solenoid valve # 2 open or short
P1523	HSIA solenoid valve open or short
P1601	Serial communication error
P1608	PCM malfunction
P1794	Battery voltage or circuit fail
P1797	Neutral switch circuit failure

1.8L engine trouble code chart—OBD-II system (continued)

90984C13

DTC	Definition
P0100	Mass or volume air flow circuit malfunction
P0110	Intake air temperature circuit malfunction
P0115	Engine coolant temperature circuit malfunction
P0120	Throttle position sensor circuit malfunction
P0125	Excessive time to enter closed loop fuel control
P0130	Heated oxygen sensor bank 1 sensor 1 circuit malfunction
P0134	Heated oxygen sensor bank 1 sensor 1 circuit no activity detected
P0135	Heated oxygen sensor heater bank 1 sensor 1 circuit malfunction
P0140	Heated oxygen sensor bank 1 sensor 2 circuit no activity detected
P0150	Heated oxygen sensor bank 2 sensor 1 circuit malfunction
P0154	Heated oxygen sensor bank 2 sensor 1 circuit no activity detected
P0155	Heated oxygen sensor heater bank 2 sensor 1 circuit malfunction
P0160	Heated oxygen sensor bank 2 sensor 2 circuit no activity detected
P0170	Fuel trim bank 1 malfunction
P0173	Fuel trim bank 2 malfunction
P0300	Random misfire detected
P0301	Cylinder # 1 misfire detected
P0302	Cylinder # 2 misfire detected
P0303	Cylinder # 3 misfire detected
P0304	Cylinder # 4 misfire detected
P0305	Cylinder # 5 misfire detected
P0306	Cylinder # 6 misfire detected
P0325	Knock sensor circuit malfunction
P0335	Crankshaft position sensor circuit malfunction
P0340	Camshaft position sensor input malfunction
P0400	Exhaust gas recirculation flow malfunction
P0420	Catalyst system efficiency below threshold (bank 1)
P0430	Catalyst system efficiency below threshold (bank 2)
P0440	Evaporative emission control system malfunction
P0443	Evaporative emission control system purge control solenoid circuit malfunction
P0500	Vehicle speed sensor malfunction
P0505	Idle air control system malfunction
P0510	Idle switch malfunction
P0703	Brake on / off switch input malfunction
P0705	Transmission range sensor circuit malfunction
P0710	Transmission fluid temperature sensor circuit malfunction
P0715	Turbine speed sensor circuit malfunction
P0725	Engine speed input circuit malfunction
P0730	Incorrect gear ratio
P0731	Incorrect first gear ratio

1.8L engine trouble code chart—OBD-II system

DTC	Definitions
P0102	Mass Air Flow (MAF) sensor circuit low input
P0103	Mass Air Flow (MAF) sensor circuit high input
P0106	Barometric Pressure (BP) sensor circuit performance
P0107	Barometric Pressure (BP) sensor circuit low input
P0108	Barometric Pressure (BP) sensor circuit high input
P0112	Intake Air Temperature (IAT) sensor circuit low input
P0113	Intake Air Temperature (IAT) sensor circuit high input
P0117	Engine Coolant Temperature (ECT) sensor circuit low input
P0118	Engine Coolant Temperature (ECT) sensor circuit high input
P0121	In-range operating Throttle Position (TP) sensor circuit failure
P0122	Throttle Position (TP) sensor circuit low input
P0123	Throttle Position (TP) sensor circuit high input
P0125	Insufficient coolant temperature to enter closed loop fuel control
P0131	Upstream Heated Oxygen Sensor (HO2S 11) circuit out of range low voltage (Bank # 1)
P0133	Upstream Heated Oxygen Sensor (HO2S 11) circuit slow response (Bank # 1)
P0135	Upstream Heated Oxygen Sensor Heater (HTR 11) circuit malfunction (Bank # 1)
P0136	Downstream Heated Oxygen Sensor (HO2S 12) circuit malfunction (Bank # 1)
P0141	Downstream Heated Oxygen Sensor Heater (HTR 12) circuit malfunction (Bank # 1)
P0151	Upstream Heated Oxygen Sensor (HO2S 21) circuit out of range low voltage (Bank # 2)
P0153	Upstream Heated Oxygen Sensor (HO2S 21) circuit slow response (Bank # 2)
P0155	Upstream Heated Oxygen Sensor Heater (HTR 21) circuit malfunction (Bank # 2)
P0156	Downstream Heated Oxygen Sensor (HO2S 22) circuit malfunction (Bank # 2)
P0161	Downstream Heated Oxygen Sensor Heater (HTR 22) circuit malfunction (Bank # 2)
P0171	System (adaptive fuel) too lean (Bank # 1)
P0172	System (adaptive fuel) too rich (Bank # 1)
P0174	System (adaptive fuel) too lean (Bank # 2)
P0175	System (adaptive fuel) too rich (Bank # 2)
P0176	Fuel Composition sensor (FCS) circuit malfunction
P0182	Fuel Temperature sensor A circuit low input
P0183	Fuel Temperature sensor A circuit high input
P0187	Fuel Temperature sensor B circuit low input
P0188	Fuel Temperature sensor B circuit high input
P0191	Injector Pressure sensor circuit performance
P0192	Injector Pressure sensor circuit low input
P0193	Injector Pressure sensor circuit high input
P0222	Throttle Position Sensor B (TP-B) circuit low input
P0223	Throttle Position Sensor B (TP-B) circuit high input
P0230	Fuel Pump primary circuit malfunction
P0231	Fuel Pump secondary circuit low
P0232	Fuel Pump secondary circuit high
P0300	Random Misfire detected
P0301	Cylinder #1 Misfire detected
P0302	Cylinder #2 Misfire detected
P0303	Cylinder #3 Misfire detected

90084C07

1.9L engine trouble code chart—OBD-II system

DTC	Definitions
P0304	Cylinder # 4 Misfire detected
P0305	Cylinder #5 Misfire detected
P0306	Cylinder #6 Misfire detected
P0307	Cylinder #7 Misfire detected
P0308	Cylinder #8 Misfire detected
P0320	Ignition Engine Speed (Profile Ignition Pickup (PIP)) input circuit malfunction
P0325	Knock Sensor (KS) 1 circuit malfunction
P0326	Knock Sensor (KS) 1 circuit performance
P0331	Knock Sensor (KS) 2 circuit malfunction
P0331	Knock Sensor (KS) 2 circuit performance
P0340	Camshaft Position (CMP) sensor circuit malfunction (CID)
P0350	Ignition Coil primary circuit malfunction
P0351	Ignition Coil A primary circuit malfunction
P0352	Ignition Coil B primary circuit malfunction
P0353	Ignition Coil C primary circuit malfunction
P0354	Ignition Coil D primary circuit malfunction
P0385	Crankshaft Position (CKP) sensor malfunction
P0400	Exhaust Gas Recirculation (EGR) flow malfunction
P0401	Exhaust Gas Recirculation (EGR) flow insufficient detected
P0402	Exhaust Gas Recirculation (EGR) flow excess detected
P0411	Secondary Air Injection system incorrect upstream flow detected
P0412	Secondary Air Injection system switching valve A malfunction
P0413	Secondary Air Injection system switching valve A circuit open
P0414	Secondary Air Injection system switching valve A circuit shorted
P0416	Secondary Air Injection system switching valve B circuit open
P0417	Secondary Air Injection system switching valve B circuit shorted
P0420	Catalyst system efficiency below threshold (Bank # 1)
P0430	Catalyst system efficiency below threshold (Bank # 2)
P0440	Evaporative emission control system malfunction (Probe)
P0442	Evaporative emission control system small leak detected
P0443	Evaporative emission control system purge control solenoid or vapor management valve circuit malfunction
P0446	Evaporative emission control system Canister Vent (CV) solenoid control malfunction
P0452	Evaporative emission control system Fuel Tank Pressure (FTP) sensor low input
P0453	Evaporative emission control system Fuel Tank Pressure (FTP) sensor high input
P0455	Evaporative emission control system control leak detected (gross leak)
P0500	Vehicle Speed Sensor (VSS) malfunction
P0503	Vehicle Speed Sensor (VSS) circuit intermittent
P0505	Idle Air Control (IAC) system malfunction
P0552	Power Steering Pressure (PSP) sensor circuit low input
P0553	Power Steering Pressure (PSP) sensor circuit high input
P0603	Powertrain Control Module (PCM) - Keep Alive Memory (KAM) test error
P0605	Powertrain Control Module (PCM) - Read Only Memory (ROM) test error
P0703	Brake On / Off (BOO) switch input malfunction

90084C08

1.9L engine trouble code chart—OBD-II system (continued)

DTC	Definitions
P0704	Clutch Pedal Position (CPP) switch input circuit malfunction
P0707	Transmission Range (TR) sensor circuit low input
P0708	Transmission Range (TR) sensor circuit high input
P0712	Transmission Fluid Temperature (TFT) sensor circuit low input
P0713	Transmission Fluid Temperature (TFT) sensor circuit high input
P0715	Turbine Shaft Speed (TSS) sensor circuit malfunction
P0720	Output Shaft Speed (OSS) sensor circuit malfunction
P0721	Output Shaft Speed (OSS) sensor performance (noise)
P0731	Incorrect ratio for first gear
P0732	Incorrect ratio for second gear
P0733	Incorrect ratio for third gear
P0734	Incorrect ratio for fourth gear
P0736	Reverse incorrect gear ratio
P0741	Torque Converter Clutch (TCC) mechanical system performance
P0743	Torque Converter Clutch (TCC) electrical system malfunction
P0746	Electronic Pressure Control (EPC) solenoid performance
P0750	Shift Solenoid # 1 (SS1) circuit malfunction
P0751	Shift Solenoid # 1 (SS1) performance
P0755	Shift Solenoid # 2 (SS2) circuit malfunction
P0756	Shift Solenoid # 2 (SS2) performance
P0760	Shift Solenoid # 3 (SS3) circuit malfunction
P0761	Shift Solenoid # 3 (SS3) performance
P0781	1 to 2 shift error
P0782	2 to 3 shift error
P0783	3 to 4 shift error
P0784	4 to 5 shift error
P1000	OBD II Monitor Testing not complete
P1001	Key On Engine Running (KOER) Self-Test not able to complete, KOER aborted
P1100	Mass Air Flow (MAF) sensor intermittent
P1101	Mass Air Flow (MAF) sensor out of Self-Test range
P1112	Intake Air Temperature (IAT) sensor intermittent
P1116	Engine Coolant Temperature (ECT) sensor out of Self-Test range
P1117	Engine Coolant Temperature (ECT) sensor intermittent
P1120	Throttle Position (TP) sensor out of range low
P1121	Throttle Position (TP) sensor inconsistent with MAF Sensor
P1124	Throttle Position (TP) sensor out of Self-Test range
P1125	Throttle Position (TP) sensor circuit intermittent
P1127	Exhaust not warm enough, downstream Heated Oxygen Sensors (HO2Ss) not tested
P1128	Upstream Heated Oxygen Sensors (HO2Ss) swapped from bank to bank
P1129	Downstream Heated Oxygen Sensors (HO2Ss) swapped from bank to bank
P1130	Lack of upstream Heated Oxygen Sensor (HO2S 11) switch, adaptive fuel at limit (Bank # 1)
P1131	Lack of upstream Heated Oxygen Sensor (HO2S 11) switch, sensor indicates lean (Bank # 1)
P1132	Lack of upstream Heated Oxygen Sensor (HO2S 11) switch, sensor indicates rich (Bank # 1)

1.9L engine trouble code chart—OBD-II system (continued)

DTC	Definitions
P1137	Lack of downstream Heated Oxygen Sensor (HO2S 12) switch, sensor indicates lean (Bank # 1)
P1138	Lack of downstream Heated Oxygen Sensor (HO2S 12) switch, sensor indicates rich (Bank # 1)
P1150	Lack of upstream Heated Oxygen Sensor (HO2S 21) switch, adaptive fuel at limit (Bank # 2)
P1151	Lack of upstream Heated Oxygen Sensor (HO2S 21) switch, sensor indicates lean (Bank # 2)
P1152	Lack of upstream Heated Oxygen Sensor (HO2S 21) switch, sensor indicates rich (Bank # 2)
P1157	Lack of downstream Heated Oxygen Sensor (HO2S 22) switch, sensor indicates lean (Bank # 2)
P1158	Lack of downstream Heated Oxygen Sensor (HO2S 22) switch, sensor indicates rich (Bank # 2)
P1220	Series Throttle Control system malfunction
P1224	Throttle Position Sensor B (TP-B) out of Self-Test range
P1230	Fuel Pump low speed malfunction
P1231	Fuel Pump secondary circuit low with high speed pump on
P1232	Low speed Fuel Pump primary circuit malfunction
P1233	Fuel Pump Driver Module disabled or offline
P1234	Fuel Pump Driver Module disabled or offline
P1235	Fuel Pump control out of Self-Test range
P1236	Fuel Pump control out of Self-Test range
P1237	Fuel Pump secondary circuit malfunction
P1238	Fuel Pump secondary circuit malfunction
P1260	THEFT detected - engine disabled
P1270	Engine RPM or vehicle speed limiter reached
P1285	Cylinder Head over temperature sensed
P1288	Cylinder Head Temperature (CHT) sensor out of Self-Test range
P1289	Cylinder Head Temperature (CHT) sensor circuit low input
P1290	Cylinder Head Temperature (CHT) sensor circuit high input
P1299	Engine over temperature condition
P1351	Ignition Diagnostic Monitor (IDM) circuit input malfunction
P1356	PIPs occurred while IDM pulsewidth indicates engine not turning
P1357	Ignition Diagnostic Monitor (IDM) pulsewidth not defined
P1358	Ignition Diagnostic Monitor (IDM) signal out of Self-Test range
P1359	Spark output circuit malfunction
P1390	Octane Adjust (OCT ADJ) out of Self-Test range
P1400	Differential Pressure Feedback EGR (DPFE) sensor circuit low voltage detected
P1401	Differential Pressure Feedback EGR (DPFE) sensor circuit high voltage detected
P1405	Differential Pressure Feedback EGR (DPFE) sensor upstream hose off or plugged
P1406	Differential Pressure Feedback EGR (DPFE) sensor downstream hose off or plugged
P1408	Exhaust Gas Recirculation (EGR) flow out of Self-Test range
P1409	Electronic Vacuum Regulator (EVR) control circuit malfunction
P1411	Secondary Air Injection system incorrect downstream flow detected
P1413	Secondary Air Injection system monitor circuit low voltage
P1414	Secondary Air Injection system monitor circuit high voltage

1.9L engine trouble code chart—OBD-II system (continued)

DTC	Definitions
P1442	Evaporative emission control system small leak detected
P1443	Evaporative emission control system - vacuum system, purge control solenoid or vapor management valve malfunction
P1444	Purge Flow (PF) Sensor circuit low input
P1445	Purge Flow (PF) Sensor circuit high input
P1449	Evaporative emission control system unable to hold vacuum (Probe)
P1450	Unable to bleed up fuel tank vacuum
P1452	Unable to bleed up fuel tank vacuum
P1455	Evaporative emission control system control leak detected (gross leak)
P1460	Wide Open Throttle Air Conditioning Cut-off (WAC) circuit malfunction
P1461	Air Conditioning Pressure (ACP) sensor circuit low input
P1462	Air Conditioning Pressure (ACP) sensor circuit high input
P1463	Air Conditioning Pressure (ACP) sensor insufficient pressure change
P1464	Air condition (A / C) demand out of Self-Test range
P1469	Low air conditioning cycling period
P1473	Fan secondary high with fan(s) off
P1474	Low Fan Control primary circuit malfunction
P1479	High Fan Control primary circuit malfunction
P1480	Fan secondary low with low fan on
P1481	Fan secondary low with high fan on
P1483	Power to fan circuit overcurrent
P1484	Open power ground to Variable Load Control Module (VLCM)
P1500	Vehicle Speed Sensor (VSS) circuit intermittent
P1501	Vehicle Speed Sensor (VSS) out of Self-Test range
P1504	Idle Air Control (IAC) circuit malfunction
P1505	Idle Air Control (IAC) system at adaptive clip
P1506	Idle Air Control (IAC) overspeed error
P1507	Idle Air Control (IAC) underspeed error
P1512	Intake Manifold Runner Control (IMRC) malfunction (Bank # 1 stuck closed)
P1513	Intake Manifold Runner Control (IMRC) malfunction (Bank # 2 stuck closed)
P1516	Intake Manifold Runner Control (IMRC) Input error (Bank # 1)
P1517	Intake Manifold Runner Control (IMRC) Input error (Bank # 2)
P1518	Intake Manifold Runner Control (IMRC) malfunction (stuck open)
P1519	Intake Manifold Runner Control (IMRC) malfunction (stuck closed)
P1520	Intake Manifold Runner Control (IMRC) circuit malfunction
P1530	Air Condition (A / C) clutch circuit malfunction
P1537	Intake Manifold Runner Control (IMRC) malfunction (Bank # 1 stuck open)
P1538	Intake Manifold Runner Control (IMRC) malfunction (Bank # 2 stuck open)
P1539	Power to Air Condition (A / C) clutch circuit overcurrent
P1550	Power Steering Pressure (PSP) sensor out of Self-Test range
P1605	Powertrain Control Module (PCM) - Keep Alive Memory (KAM) test error
P1625	B(+) supply to Variable Load Control Module (VLCM) fan circuit malfunction
P1626	B(+) supply to Variable Load Control Module (VLCM) Air Condition (A / C) circuit malfunction
P1650	Power Steering Pressure (PSP) switch out of Self-Test range

90984C11

1.9L engine trouble code chart—OBD-II system (continued)

DTC	Definitions
P1651	Power Steering Pressure (PSP) switch input malfunction
P1701	Reverse engagement error
P1703	Brake On / Off (BOO) switch out of Self-Test range
P1705	Transmission Range (TR) Sensor out of Self-Test range
P1709	Park or Neutral Position (PNP) switch is not indicating neutral during KOEO Self-Test
P1711	Transmission Fluid Temperature (TFT) sensor out of Self-Test range
P1728	Transmission slip fault
P1729	4x4 Low switch error
P1741	Torque Converter Clutch (TCC) control error
P1742	Torque Converter Clutch (TCC) solenoid failed on (turns on MIL)
P1743	Torque Converter Clutch (TCC) solenoid failed on (turns on TCIL)
P1744	Torque Converter Clutch (TCC) system mechanically stuck in off position
P1746	Electronic Pressure Control (EPC) solenoid open circuit (low input)
P1747	Electronic Pressure Control (EPC) solenoid short circuit (high input)
P1749	Electronic Pressure Control (EPC) solenoid failed low
P1751	Shift Solenoid # 1 (SS1) performance
P1754	Coast Clutch Solenoid (CCS) circuit malfunction
P1756	Shift Solenoid #2 (SS2) performance
P1761	Shift Solenoid #3 (SS3) performance
P1780	Transmission Control switch (TCS) circuit out of Self-Test range
P1781	4x4 Low switch out of Self-Test range
P1783	Transmission overtemperature condition
P1788	3-2 Timing / Coast Clutch Solenoid (3-2 / CCS) circuit open
P1789	3-2 Timing / Coast Clutch Solenoid (3-2 / CCS) circuit shorted
U1021	SCP indicating the lack of Air Condition (A / C) clutch status response
U1039	SCP indicating the vehicle speed signal missing or incorrect
U1051	SCP indicating the brake switch signal missing or incorrect
U1073	SCP indicating the lack of engine coolant fan status response
U1131	SCP indicating the lack of Fuel Pump status response
U1135	SCP indicating the ignition switch signal missing or incorrect
U1256	SCP indicating a communications error
U1451	Lack of response from Passive Anti-Theft system (PATS) module - engine disabled

90984C12

1.9L engine trouble code chart—OBD-II system (continued)

4 Digit	Description
—	System Pass (No DTCs Available) — California and all Econoline
P0107	BARO Circuit Low Input
P0108	BARO Circuit High Input
P0112	IAT Sensor Circuit Low Input
P0113	IAT Sensor Circuit High Input
P0122*	Accelerator Pedal Sensor Circuit Low Input
P0123*	Accelerator Pedal Sensor Circuit High Input
P0196	EOT Sensor Circuit Performance
P0197*	EOT Sensor Circuit Low Input
P0198*	EOT Sensor Circuit High Input
P0220*	Throttle Switch B Circuit Malfunction
P0221*	Throttle Switch B Circuit Malfunction
P0236*	Turbo Boost Sensor A Circuit Performance
P0237*	Turbo Boost Sensor A Circuit Low Input
P0238*	Turbo Boost Sensor A Circuit High Input
P0261*	Injector Circuit Low — Cylinder 1
P0262	Injector Circuit High — Cylinder 1
P0263	Cylinder 1 Contribution / Balance Fault
P0264*	Injector Circuit Low — Cylinder 2
P0265	Injector Circuit High — Cylinder 2
P0266	Cylinder 2 Contribution / Balance Fault
P0267*	Injector Circuit Low — Cylinder 3
P0268	Injector Circuit High — Cylinder 3
P0269	Cylinder 3 Contribution / Balance Fault
P0270*	Injector Circuit Low — Cylinder 4
P0271	Injector Circuit High — Cylinder 4
P0272	Cylinder 4 Contribution / Balance Fault
P0273*	Injector Circuit Low — Cylinder 5
P0274	Injector Circuit High — Cylinder 5
P0275	Cylinder 5 Contribution / Balance Fault
P0276*	Injector Circuit Low — Cylinder 6
P0277	Injector Circuit High — Cylinder 6
P0278	Cylinder 6 Contribution / Balance Fault
P0279*	Injector Circuit Low — Cylinder 7
P0280	Injector Circuit High — Cylinder 7
P0281	Cylinder 7 Contribution / Balance Fault
P0282*	Injector Circuit Low — Cylinder 8
P0283	Injector Circuit High — Cylinder 8

2.0L engine trouble code chart—1997–99 OBD-II system

90994C15

4 Digit	Description
P0284	Cylinder 8 Contribution / Balance Fault
P0340	CMP Sensor Circuit Malfunction
P0341*	CMP Sensor Circuit Performance
P0344*	CMP Sensor Circuit Intermittent
P0380	Glow Plug Circuit Malfunction
P0381	Glow Plug Indicator Circuit Malfunction
P0470	Exhaust Back Pressure Sensor Circuit Malfunction
P0471	Exhaust Back Pressure Sensor Circuit Performance
P0472	Exhaust Back Pressure Sensor Circuit Low Input
P0473	Exhaust Back Pressure Sensor Circuit High Input
P0475	Exhaust Pressure Control Valve Malfunction
P0476	Exhaust Pressure Control Valve Performance
P0478	Exhaust Pressure Control Valve High Input
P0500	Vehicle Speed Sensor Malfunction — KOER Tests
P0560	System Voltage Malfunction
P0562	System Voltage Low
P0563	System Voltage High
P0565	Cruise "On" Signal Malfunction
P0566	Cruise "Off" Signal Malfunction
P0567	Cruise "Resume" Signal Malfunction
P0568	Cruise "Set" Signal Malfunction
P0569	Cruise "Coast" Signal Malfunction
P0571	Brake Switch A Circuit Malfunction
P0603	Internal Control Module KAM Error
P0605	Internal Control Module ROM Error
P0606	PCM Processor Fault
P0703	Brake Switch B Circuit Malfunction
P0704	Clutch Pedal Position Switch Input Circuit Malfunction
P0705**	TR Sensor Circuit Malfunction
P0707**	TR Sensor Circuit Low Input
P0708**	TR Sensor Circuit High Input
P0712	Transmission Fluid Temp. Sensor CKT Low Input
P0713	Transmission Fluid Temp. Sensor CKT High Input
P0741	TCC Circuit Performance
P0743	Torque Converter Clutch System Electrical Failure
P0750	Shift Solenoid 1 Malfunction

2.0L engine trouble code chart—1997–99 OBD-II system (continued)

90994C16

4 Digit	Description
P1283*	IPR Circuit Failure
P1284	ICP Failure — Aborts KOER or CCT Test
P1291	High Side No. 1 (Right) Short to GND or B+
P1292	High Side No. 2 (Left) Short to GND or B+
P1293	High Side Open Bank No. 1 (Right)
P1294	High Side Open Bank No. 2 (Left)
P1295*	Multiple Faults on Bank No. 1 (Right)
P1296*	Multiple Faults on Bank No. 2 (Left)
P1297	High Sides Shorted Together
P1298	IDM Failure
P1316	Injector Circuit/IDM Codes Detected
P1391	Glow Plug Circuit Low Input Bank No. 1 (Right)
P1392	Glow Plug Circuit High Input Bank No. 1 (Right)
P1393	Glow Plug Circuit Low Input Bank No. 2 (Left)
P1394	Glow Plug Circuit High Input Bank No. 2 (Left)
P1395	Glow Plug Monitor Fault Bank No. 1
P1396	Glow Plug Monitor Fault Bank No. 2
P1397	System Voltage out of Self Test Range
P1464	A/C On During KOER or CCT Test
P1501	Vehicle Moved During Testing
P1502	Invalid Self Test — APCM Functioning
P1531	Invalid Test — Accelerator Pedal Movement
P1536	Parking Brake Applied Failure
P1660	Output Circuit Check Signal High
P1661	Output Circuit Check Signal Low
P1662	IDM_EN Circuit Failure
P1663	FDCS Circuit Failure
P1667	CID Circuit Failure
P1668	PCM — IDM Diagnostic Communication Error
P1670	EF Feedback Signal Not Detected
P1704	Digital TRS Failed to Transition State
P1705	TR Sensor out of Self Test Range
P1706**	High Vehicle Speed in Park
P1711	TFT Sensor Out of Self Test Range
P1714	Shift Solenoid A Inductive Signature Malfunction
P1715	Shift Solenoid B Inductive Signature Malfunction
P1727	Coast Clutch Solenoid Inductive Signature Malfunction
P1728**	Transmission Slip Error — Converter Clutch Failed

2.0L engine trouble code chart—1997–99 OBD-II system (continued)

90984C18

4 Digit	Description
P0751	Shift Solenoid A Performance
P0755	Shift Solenoid 2 Malfunction
P0756	Shift Solenoid B Performance
P0760	Shift Solenoid C Malfunction
P0781	1-2 Shift Malfunction
P0781**	1-2 Shift Malfunction
P0782**	2-3 Shift Malfunction
P0783**	3-4 Shift Malfunction
P1000	OBDII Monitor Checks Not Complete, More Driving Required
P1111	System Pass — 49-State except Econoline
P1184	Engine Oil Temp Sensor Circuit Performance
P1209	Injection Control System Pressure Peak Fault
P1210	Injection Control Pressure Above Expected Level
P1211*	ICP Not Controllable — Pressure Above/Below Desired
P1212*	ICP Voltage Not at Expected Level
P1218	CID Stuck High
P1248	Turbo Boost Pressure Not Detected
P1261	High to Low Side Short — Cylinder 1
P1262	High to Low Side Short — Cylinder 2
P1263	High to Low Side Short — Cylinder 3
P1264	High to Low Side Short — Cylinder 4
P1265	High to Low Side Short — Cylinder 5
P1266	High to Low Side Short — Cylinder 6
P1267	High to Low Side Short — Cylinder 7
P1268	High to Low Side Short — Cylinder 8
P1271	High to Low Side Open — Cylinder 1
P1272	High to Low Side Open — Cylinder 2
P1273	High to Low Side Open — Cylinder 3
P1274	High to Low Side Open — Cylinder 4
P1275	High to Low Side Open — Cylinder 5
P1276	High to Low Side Open — Cylinder 6
P1277	High to Low Side Open — Cylinder 7
P1278	High to Low Side Open — Cylinder 8
P1280*	ICP Circuit Out of Range Low
P1281*	ICP Circuit Out of Range High
P1282	Excessive ICP

2.0L engine trouble code chart—1997–99 OBD-II system (continued)

90984C17

4 Digit	Description
P 1740	Torque Converter Clutch Inductive Signature Malfunction
P 1742	Torque Converter Clutch Failed On
P 1744	Torque Converter Clutch System Performance
P 1746	EPC Solenoid Open Circuit
P 1747	EPC Solenoid Short Circuit
P 1748**	EPC Malfunction
P 1751	Shift Solenoid A Performance
P 1754	CCS (Solenoid) Circuit Malfunction
P 1756	Shift Solenoid B Performance
P 1779	TCIL Circuit Malfunction
P 1780	TCS Circuit out of Self Test Range
P 1783**	Transmission Overtemperature Condition
No Code	No Communication
No Code	Auxiliary Powertrain Control System
No Code	Tachometer

* Check Engine light illuminates when fault is present. On California and all Econoline, CHECK ENGINE light will turn off if no fault is detected for four consecutive drive cycles.

** Transmission Control Indicator Light (TCIL) flashes when fault is present.

*** Refer to the Powertrain/Transmission Group in the Service Manual for diagnostic procedures.

NOTE: Speed control DTCs will be set during KOER Switch Test if the vehicle is not equipped with speed control. This is a normal condition. On these vehicles ignore the following DTCs P0565-P0566-P0567-P0568-P0569.

90984C19

2.0L engine trouble code chart—1997–99 OBD-II system (continued)

EEC-IV System

GENERAL INFORMATION

One part of the Powertrain Control Module (PCM) is devoted to monitoring both input and output functions within the system. This ability forms the core of the self-diagnostic system. If a problem is detected within a circuit, the controller will recognize the fault, assign it an identification code, and store the code in a memory section. Depending on the year and model, the fault code(s) may be represented by two or three-digit numbers. The stored code(s) may be retrieved during diagnosis.

While the EEC-IV system is capable of recognizing many internal faults, certain faults will not be recognized. Because the computer system sees only electrical signals, it cannot sense or react to mechanical or vacuum faults affecting engine operation. Some of these faults may affect another component which will set a code. For example, the PCM monitors the output signal to the fuel injectors, but cannot detect a partially clogged injector. As long as the output driver responds correctly, the computer will read the system as functioning correctly. However, the improper flow of fuel may result in a lean mixture. This would, in turn, be detected by the oxygen sensor and noticed as a constantly lean signal by the PCM. Once the signal falls outside the pre-programmed limits, the engine control assembly would notice the fault and set an identification code.

Failure Mode Effects Management (FMEM)

The PCM contains back-up programs which allow the engine to operate if a sensor signal is lost. If a sensor input is seen to be out of range—either high or low—the FMEM program is used. The processor substitutes a fixed value for the missing sensor signal. The engine will continue to operate, although performance and driveability may be noticeably reduced. This function of the controller is sometimes referred to as the limp-in or fail-safe mode. If the missing sensor signal is restored, the FMEM system immediately returns the system to normal operation. The dashboard warning lamp will be lit when FMEM is in effect.

Diagnostic Link Connector

➡ **Some of the vehicles covered by this manual utilize two Diagnostic Link Connectors (DLCs), both of which are in the same vicinity.**

The Diagnostic Link Connector(s) (DLC) may be found in the following locations:
- 1.8L engines: at the rear corner of the engine compartment
- 1.9L engines: at the rear corner of the engine compartment

The DLC is rectangular in design and capable of allowing access to 16 terminals. The connector has keying features that allow easy connection. The test equipment and the DLC have a latching feature to ensure a good mated connection.

Hardware Limited Operation Strategy (HLOS)

This mode is only used if the fault is too extreme for the FMEM circuit to handle. In this mode, the processor has ceased all computation and control; the entire system is run on fixed values. The vehicle may be operated but performance and driveability will be greatly reduced. The fixed or default settings provide minimal calibration, allowing the vehicle to be carefully driven in for service. The dashboard warning lamp will be lit when HLOS is engaged. Codes cannot be read while the system is operating in this mode.

HAND-HELD SCAN TOOLS

▶ **See Figure 75**

Although stored codes may be read through the flashing of the CHECK ENGINE or SERVICE ENGINE SOON lamp, the use of hand-held scan tools such as Ford's Self-Test Automatic Readout (STAR) tester or the second generation SUPER STAR II tester or their equivalent is highly recommended. There are many manufacturers of these tools; the purchaser must be certain that the tool is proper for the intended use.

The scan tool allows any stored faults to be read from the engine controller memory. Use of the scan tool provides additional data during troubleshooting, but does not eliminate the use of the charts. The scan tool makes collecting information easier, but the data must be correctly interpreted by an operator familiar with the system.

TCCS4P11

Fig. 75 Inexpensive scan tools, such as this Auto Xray®, are available to interface with your Ford vehicle

ELECTRICAL TOOLS

The most commonly required electrical diagnostic tool is the digital multimeter, also known as a Digital Volt Ohmmeter (DVOM), which permits voltage, resistance (ohmmage) and amperage to be read by one instrument. Many of the diagnostic charts require the use of a volt or ohmmeter during diagnosis.

The multimeter must be a high impedance unit, with 10 megohms of impedance in the voltmeter. This type of meter will not place an additional load on the circuit it is testing; this is extremely important in low voltage circuits. The multimeter must be of high quality in all respects. It should be handled carefully and protected from impact or damage. Replace the batteries frequently in the unit.

Additionally, an analog (needle type) voltmeter may be used to read stored fault codes if the STAR tester is not available. The codes are transmitted as visible needle sweeps on the face of the instrument.

Almost all diagnostic procedures will require the use of a Breakout Box, a device which connects into the EEC-IV harness and provides testing ports for the 60 wires in the harness. Direct testing of the harness connectors at the terminals or by backprobing is not recommended; damage to the wiring and terminals is almost certain to occur.

Other necessary tools include a quality tachometer with inductive (clip-on) pickup, a fuel pressure gauge with system adapters and a vacuum gauge with an auxiliary source of vacuum.

Reading Codes

Diagnosis of a driveability problem requires attention to detail and following the diagnostic procedures in the correct order. Resist the temptation to begin extensive testing before completing the preliminary diagnostic steps. The preliminary or visual inspection must be completed in detail before diagnosis begins. In many cases this will shorten diagnostic time and often cure the problem without electronic testing.

VISUAL INSPECTION

This is possibly the most critical step of diagnosis. A detailed examination of all connectors, wiring and vacuum hoses can often lead to a repair without further diagnosis. Performance of this step relies on the skill of the technician performing it; a careful inspector will check the undersides of hoses as well as the integrity of hard-to-reach hoses blocked by the air cleaner or other components. Wiring should be checked carefully for any sign of strain, burning, crimping or terminal pull-out from a connector.

Checking connectors at components or in harnesses is required; usually, pushing them together will reveal a loose fit. Pay particular attention to ground circuits, making sure they are not loose or corroded. Remember to inspect connectors and hose fittings at components not mounted on the engine, such as the evaporative canister or relays mounted on the fender aprons. Any component or wiring in the vicinity of a fluid leak or spillage should be given extra attention during inspection.

Additionally, inspect maintenance items such as belt condition and tension, battery charge and condition and the radiator cap carefully. Any of these very simple items may affect the system enough to set a fault.

ELECTRONIC TESTING

If a code was set before a problem self-corrected (such as a momentarily loose connector), the code will be erased if the problem does not reoccur within 80 warm-up cycles. Codes will be output and displayed as numbers on the hand-held scan tool, such as 23. If the codes are being read on an analog voltmeter, the needle sweeps indicate the code digits. code 23 will appear as two needle pulses (sweeps) then, after a 1.6 second pause, the needle will pulse (sweep) three times.

Key On Engine Off (KOEO) Test

▶ **See Figures 76, 77 and 78**

1. Connect the scan tool to the self-test connectors. Make certain the test button is unlatched or up.
2. Start the engine and run it until normal operating temperature is reached.
3. Turn the engine **OFF** for 10 seconds.
4. Activate the test button on the STAR tester.
5. Turn the ignition switch **ON** but do not start the engine.

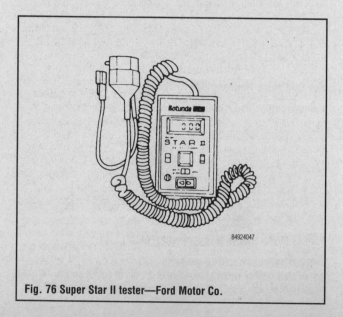

84924047

Fig. 76 Super Star II tester—Ford Motor Co.

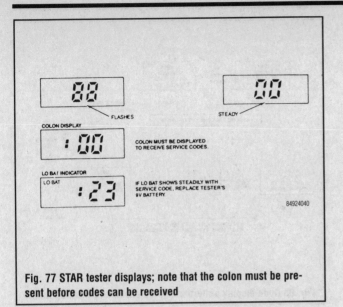

Fig. 77 STAR tester displays; note that the colon must be present before codes can be received

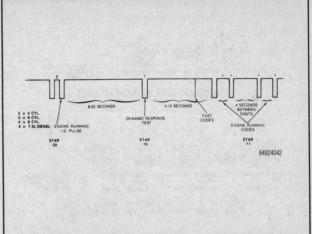

Fig. 79 Code transmission during KOER testing begins with the engine identification pulse and may include a dynamic response prompt

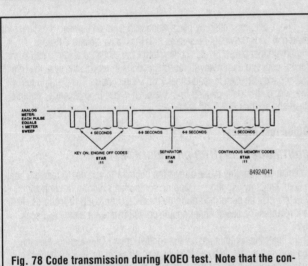

Fig. 78 Code transmission during KOEO test. Note that the continuous memory codes are transmitted after a pause and a separator pulse

6. The KOEO codes will be transmitted. Six to nine seconds after the last KOEO code, a single separator pulse will be transmitted. Six to nine seconds after this pulse, the codes from the Continuous Memory will be transmitted.

7. Record all service codes displayed. Do not depress the throttle on gasoline engines during the test.

Key On Engine Running (KOER) Test

♦ See Figures 76, 77 and 79

1. Make certain the self-test button is released or de-activated on the STAR tester.

2. Start the engine and run it at 2000 rpm for two minutes. This action warms up the oxygen sensor.

3. Turn the ignition switch **OFF** for 10 seconds.

4. Activate or latch the self-test button on the scan tool.

5. Start the engine. The engine identification code will be transmitted. This is a single digit number representing ½ the number of cylinders in a gasoline engine. On the STAR tester, this number may appear with a zero, such as 20 = 2. The code is used to confirm that the correct processor is installed and that the self-test has begun.

6. If the vehicle is equipped with a Brake On/Off (BOO) switch, the brake pedal must be depressed and released after the ID code is transmitted.

7. If the vehicle is equipped with a Power Steering Pressure Switch (PSPS), the steering wheel must be turned at least ½ turn and released within 2 seconds after the engine ID code is transmitted.

8. Certain Ford vehicles will display a Dynamic Response code 6–20 seconds after the engine ID code. This will appear as one pulse on a meter or as a 10 on the STAR tester. When this code appears, briefly take the engine to wide open throttle. This allows the system to test the throttle position, MAF and MAP sensors.

9. All relevant codes will be displayed and should be recorded. Remember that the codes refer only to faults present during this test cycle. Codes stored in Continuous Memory are not displayed in this test mode.

10. Do not depress the throttle during testing unless a dynamic response code is displayed.

Reading Codes With Analog Voltmeter

♦ See Figures 80 and 81

In the absence of a scan tool, an analog voltmeter may be used to retrieve stored fault codes. Set the meter range to read DC 0–15 volts. Connect the + lead of the meter to the battery positive terminal and connect the - lead of the meter to the self-test output pin of the diagnostic connector.

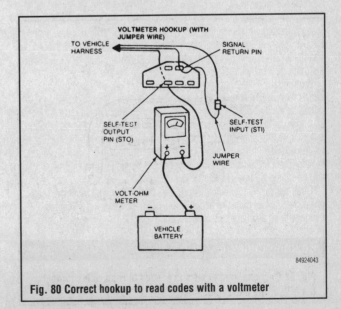

Fig. 80 Correct hookup to read codes with a voltmeter

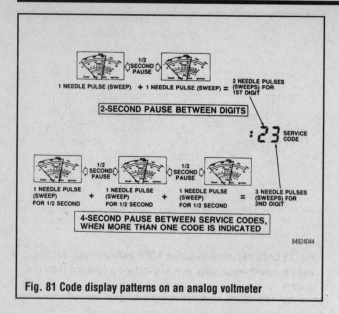

Fig. 81 Code display patterns on an analog voltmeter

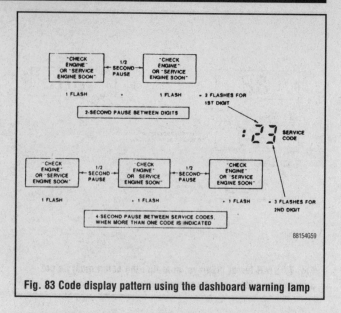

Fig. 83 Code display pattern using the dashboard warning lamp

Follow the directions given previously for performing the KOEO and KOER tests. To activate the tests, use a jumper wire to connect the signal return pin on the diagnostic connector to the self-test input connector. The self-test input line is the separate wire and connector with or near the diagnostic connector.

The codes will be transmitted as groups of needle sweeps. This method may be used to read either 2 or 3-digit codes. The Continuous Memory codes are separated from the KOEO codes by 6 seconds, a single sweep and another 6 second delay.

Malfunction Indicator Lamp Method

▶ **See Figures 82 and 83**

The Malfunction Indicator Lamp (MIL) on the dashboard may also be used to retrieve the stored codes. This method displays only the stored codes and does not allow any system investigation. It should only be used in field conditions where a quick check of stored codes is needed.

Follow the directions given previously for performing the scan tool procedure. To activate the tests, use a jumper wire to connect the signal return pin on the diagnostic connector to the Self-Test Input (STI) connector. The self-test input line is the separate wire and connector with or near the diagnostic connector.

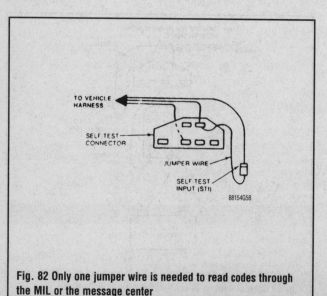

Fig. 82 Only one jumper wire is needed to read codes through the MIL or the message center

Codes are transmitted by place value with a pause between the digits; for example, code 32 would be sent as 3 flashes, a pause and 2 flashes. A slightly longer pause divides codes from each other. Be ready to count and record codes; the only way to repeat a code is to recycle the system. This method may be used to read either 2 or 3-digit codes. The Continuous Memory codes are separated from the other codes by 6 seconds, a single flash and another 6 second delay.

Other Test Modes

CONTINUOUS MONITOR OR WIGGLE TEST

Once entered, this mode allows the operator to attempt to recreate intermittent faults by wiggling or tapping components, wiring or connectors. The test may be performed during either KOEO or KOER procedures. The test requires the use of either an analog voltmeter or a hand-held scan tool.

To enter the continuous monitor mode during KOEO testing, turn the ignition switch **ON**. Activate the test, wait 10 seconds, then deactivate and reactivate the test; the system will enter the continuous monitor mode. Tap, move or wiggle the harness, component or connector suspected of causing the problem; if a fault is detected, the code will store in the memory. When the fault occurs, the dash warning lamp will illuminate, the STAR tester will light a red indicator (and possibly beep) and the analog meter needle will sweep once.

To enter this mode in the KOER test:

1. Start the engine and run it at 2000 rpm for two minutes. This action warms up the oxygen sensor.

2. Turn the ignition switch **OFF** for 10 seconds.

3. Start the engine.

4. Activate the test, wait 10 seconds, then deactivate and reactivate the test; the system will enter the continuous monitor mode.

5. Tap, move or wiggle the harness, component or connector suspected of causing the problem; if a fault is detected, the code will store in the memory.

6. When the fault occurs, the dash warning lamp will illuminate, the STAR tester will light a red indicator (and possibly beep) and the analog meter needle will sweep once.

OUTPUT STATE CHECK

This testing mode allows the operator to energize and de-energize most of the outputs controlled by the EEC-IV system. Many of the outputs may be checked at the component by listening for a click or feeling the item move or engage by a hand placed on the case. To enter this check:

1. Enter the KOEO test mode.

2. When all codes have been transmitted, depress the accelerator all the way to the floor and release it.

3. The output actuators are now all ON. Depressing the throttle pedal to the floor again switches the all the actuator outputs OFF.

4. This test may be performed as often as necessary, switching between ON and OFF by depressing the throttle.

5. Exit the test by turning the ignition switch **OFF**, disconnecting the jumper at the diagnostic connector or releasing the test button on the scan tool.

Clearing Codes

CONTINUOUS MEMORY CODES

These codes are retained in memory for 40 warm-up cycles. To clear the codes for purposes of testing or confirming repair, perform the code reading procedure. When the fault codes begin to be displayed, de-activate the test either by disconnecting the jumper wire (if using a meter, MIL or message center) or by releasing the test button on the hand scanner. Stopping the test during code transmission will erase the Continuous Memory. Do not disconnect the negative battery cable to clear these codes; the Keep Alive memory will be cleared and a new code, 19, will be stored for loss of PCM power.

KEEP ALIVE MEMORY

The Keep Alive Memory (KAM) contains the adaptive factors used by the processor to compensate for component tolerances and wear. It should not be routinely cleared during diagnosis. If an emissions related part is replaced during repair, the KAM must be cleared. Failure to clear the KAM may cause severe driveability problems since the correction factor for the old component will be applied to the new component.

To clear the Keep Alive Memory, disconnect the negative battery cable for at least 5 minutes. After the memory is cleared and the battery reconnected, the vehicle must be driven at least 10 miles (16 km) so that the processor may relearn the needed correction factors. The distance to be driven depends on the engine and vehicle, but all drives should include steady-throttle cruise on open roads. Certain driveability problems may be noted during the drive because the adaptive factors are not yet functioning.

EEC-V System

GENERAL INFORMATION

The Powertrain Control Module (PCM) is given responsibility for the operation of the emission control devices, cooling fans, ignition and advance and in some cases, automatic transmission functions. Because the EEC-V oversees both the ignition timing and the fuel injector operation, a precise air/fuel ratio will be maintained under all operating conditions. The PCM is a microprocessor or small computer which receives electrical inputs from several sensors, switches and relays on and around the engine.

Based on combinations of these inputs, the PCM controls outputs to various devices concerned with engine operation and emissions. The control module relies on the signals to form a correct picture of current vehicle operation. If any of the input signals is incorrect, the PCM reacts to whatever picture is painted for it. For example, if the coolant temperature sensor is inaccurate and reads too low, the PCM may see a picture of the engine never warming up. Consequently, the engine settings will be maintained as if the engine were cold. Because so many inputs can affect one output, correct diagnostic procedures are essential on these systems.

One part of the PCM is devoted to monitoring both input and output functions within the system. This ability forms the core of the self-diagnostic system. If a problem is detected within a circuit, the control module will recognize the fault, assign it an Diagnostic Trouble Code (DTC), and store the code in memory. The stored code(s) may be retrieved during diagnosis.

While the EEC-V system is capable of recognizing many internal faults, certain faults will not be recognized. Because the control module sees only electrical signals, it cannot sense or react to mechanical or vacuum faults affecting engine operation. Some of these faults may affect another component which will set a code. For example, the PCM monitors the output signal to the fuel injectors, but cannot detect a partially clogged injector. As long as the output driver responds correctly, the computer will read the system as functioning correctly. However, the improper flow of fuel may result in a lean mixture. This would, in turn, be detected by the oxygen sensor and noticed as a constantly lean signal by the PCM. Once the signal falls outside the pre-programmed limits, the control module would notice the fault and set an trouble code.

Additionally, the EEC-V system employs adaptive fuel logic. This process is used to compensate for normal wear and variability within the fuel system. Once the engine enters steady-state operation, the control module watches the oxygen sensor signal for a bias or tendency to run slightly rich or lean. If such a bias is detected, the adaptive logic corrects the fuel delivery to bring the air/fuel mixture towards a centered or 14.7:1 ratio. This compensating shift is stored in a non-volatile memory which is retained by battery power even with the ignition switched **OFF**. The correction factor is then available the next time the vehicle is operated.

MALFUNCTION INDICATOR LAMP

The Malfunction Indicator Lamp (MIL) is located on the instrument panel. The lamp is connected to the control unit and will alert the driver to certain malfunctions within the EEC-V system. When the lamp is illuminated, the PCM has detected a fault and stored an DTC in memory.

The light will stay illuminated as long as the fault is present. Should the fault self-correct, the MIL will extinguish but the stored code will remain in memory.

Under normal operating conditions, the MIL should illuminate briefly when the ignition key is turned **ON**. This is commonly known as a bulb check. As soon as the PCM receives a signal that the engine is cranking, the lamp should extinguish. The lamp should remain extinguished during the normal operating cycle.

Data Link Connector

The Data Link Connector (DLC) may be found in the following locations:
* 1.9L engines: under the instrument panel on the driver's side
* 2.0L engines: at the rear left-hand side of the engine compartment on the firewall

The DLC is rectangular in design and capable of allowing access to 16 terminals. The connector has keying features that allow easy connection. The test equipment and the DLC have a latching feature to ensure a good mated connection.

ELECTRICAL TOOLS

The most commonly required electrical diagnostic tool is the Digital Multimeter, allowing voltage, ohmmage (resistance) and amperage to be read by one instrument. Many of the diagnostic charts require the use of a volt or ohmmeter during diagnosis.

The multimeter must be a high impedance unit, with 10 megohms of impedance in the voltmeter. This type of meter will not place an additional load on the circuit it is testing; this is extremely important in low voltage circuits. The multimeter must be of high quality in all respects. It should be handled carefully and protected from impact or damage. Replace the batteries frequently in the unit.

Reading Codes

▶ See Figure 84

The EEC-V equipped engines utilize On Board Diagnostic II (OBD-II) DTC's, which are alpha-numeric (they use letters and numbers). The let-

Fig. 84 When using a scan tool, make sure to follow all of the manufacturer's instructions carefully to ensure proper diagnosis

ters in the OBD-II DTC's make it highly difficult to convey the codes through the use of anything but a scan tool. Therefore, to read the codes on these vehicles it is necessary to utilize an OBD-II compatible scan tool.

Since each manufacturers scan tool is different, please follow the manufacturer's instructions for connecting the tool and obtaining code information.

Clearing Codes

CONTINUOUS MEMORY CODES

These codes are retained in memory for 40 warm-up cycles. To clear the codes for the purposes of testing or confirming repair, perform the code reading procedure. When the fault codes begin to be displayed, de-activate the test by either disconnecting the jumper wire (meter, MIL or message center) or releasing the test button on the hand scanner. Stopping the test during code transmission will erase the Continuous Memory. Do not disconnect the negative battery cable to clear these codes; the Keep Alive memory will be cleared and a new code, 19, will be stored for loss of PCM power.

KEEP ALIVE MEMORY

The Keep Alive Memory (KAM) contains the adaptive factors used by the processor to compensate for component tolerances and wear. It should not be routinely cleared during diagnosis. If an emissions related part is replaced during repair, the KAM must be cleared. Failure to clear the KAM may cause severe driveability problems since the correction factor for the old component will be applied to the new component.

To clear the Keep Alive Memory, disconnect the negative battery cable for at least 5 minutes. After the memory is cleared and the battery reconnected, the vehicle must be driven at least 10 miles so that the processor may relearn the needed correction factors. The distance to be driven depends on the engine and vehicle, but all drives should include steady-throttle cruise on open roads. Certain driveability problems may be noted during the drive because the adaptive factors are not yet functioning.

VACUUM DIAGRAMS

Following are vacuum diagrams for most of the engine and emissions package combinations covered by this manual. Because vacuum circuits will vary based on various engine and vehicle options, always refer first to the vehicle emission control information label, if present. Should the label be missing, or should the vehicle be equipped with a different engine from the vehicle's original equipment, refer to the diagrams below for the same or similar configuration.

If you wish to obtain a replacement emissions label, most manufacturers make the labels available for purchase. The labels can usually be ordered from a local dealer.

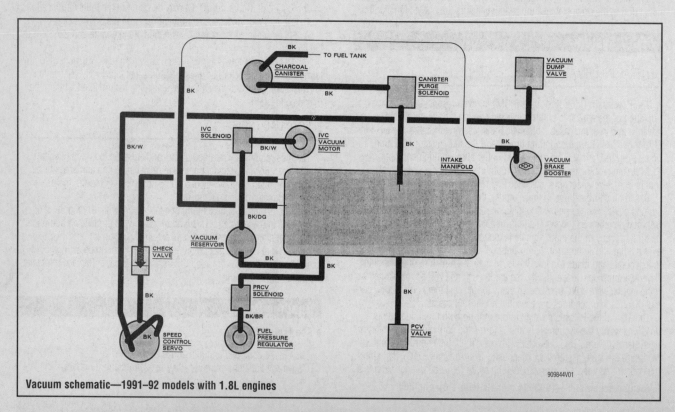

Vacuum schematic—1991–92 models with 1.8L engines

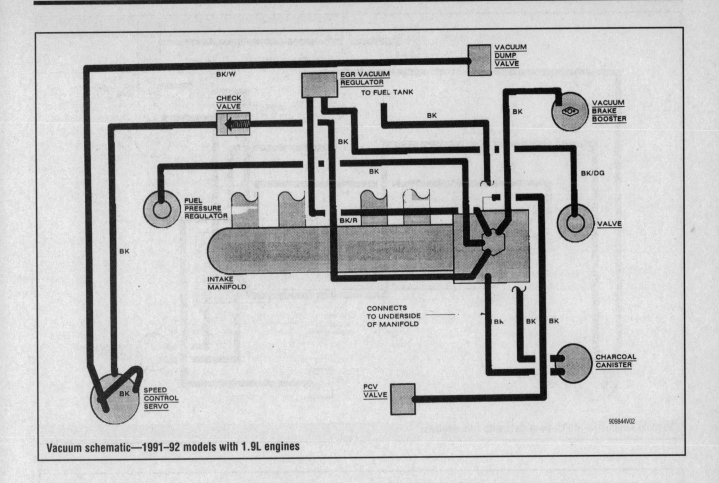

Vacuum schematic—1991–92 models with 1.9L engines

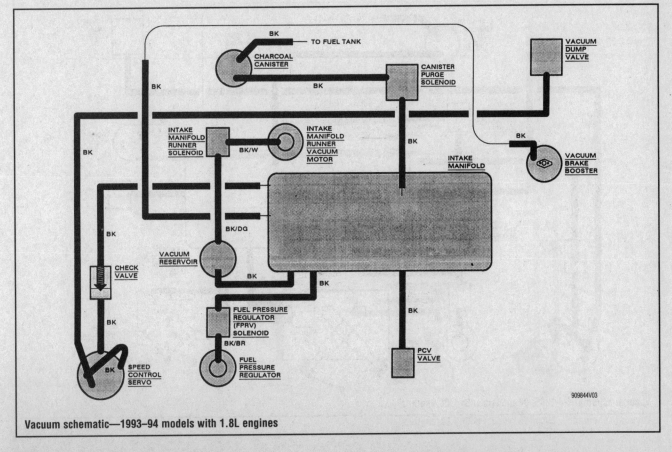

Vacuum schematic—1993–94 models with 1.8L engines

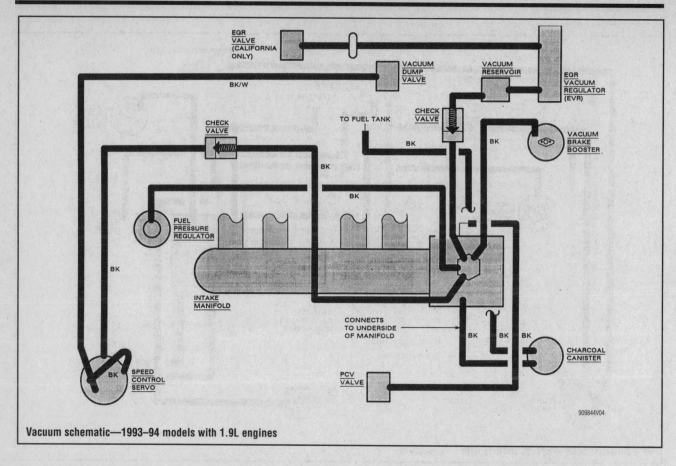

Vacuum schematic—1993–94 models with 1.9L engines

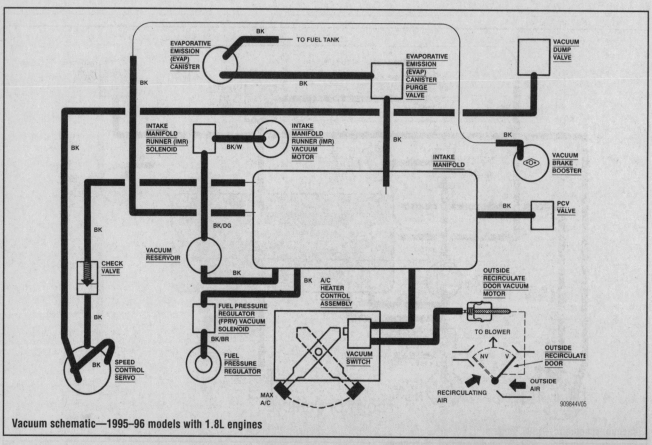

Vacuum schematic—1995–96 models with 1.8L engines

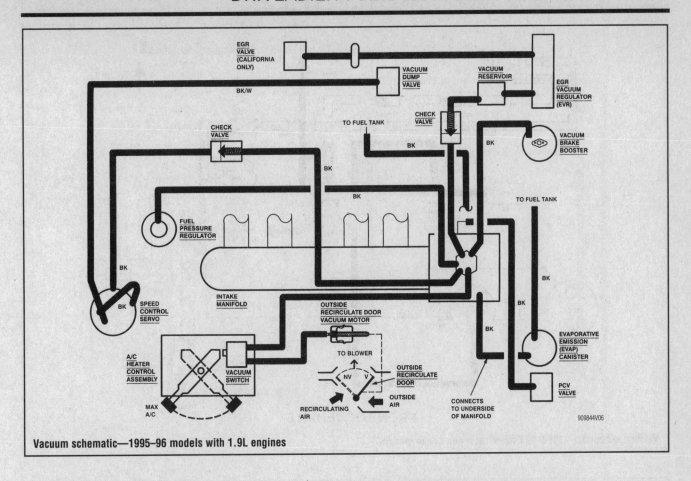

Vacuum schematic—1995–96 models with 1.9L engines

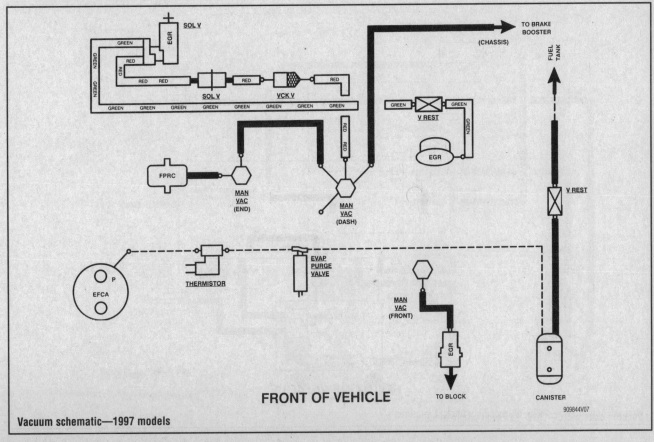

Vacuum schematic—1997 models

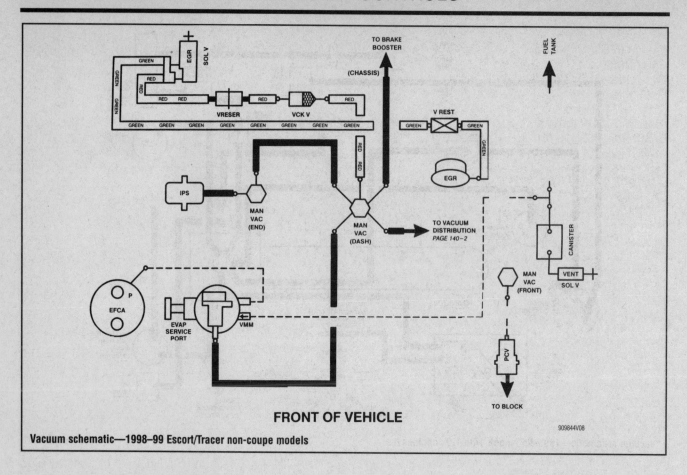

FRONT OF VEHICLE

909844V08

Vacuum schematic—1998–99 Escort/Tracer non-coupe models

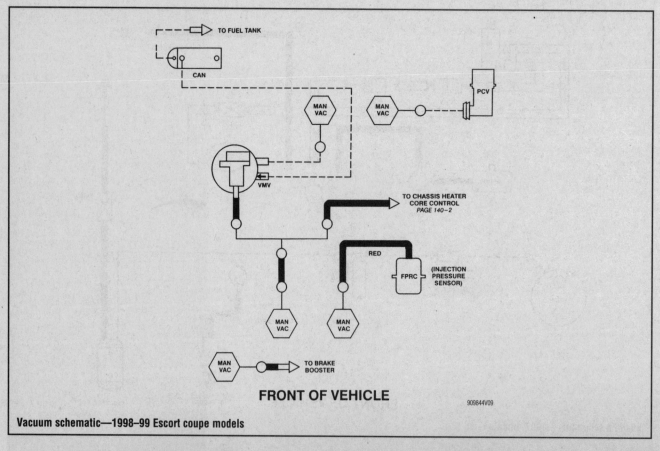

FRONT OF VEHICLE

909844V09

Vacuum schematic—1998–99 Escort coupe models

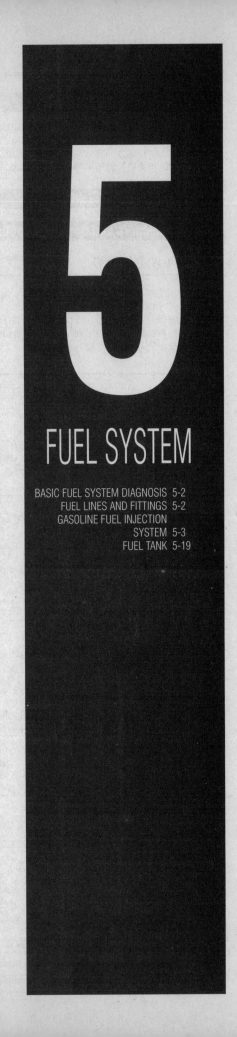

5

FUEL SYSTEM

BASIC FUEL SYSTEM DIAGNOSIS

When there is a problem starting or driving a vehicle, two of the most important checks involve the ignition and the fuel systems. The questions most mechanics attempt to answer first, "is there spark?" and "is there fuel?" will often lead to solving most basic problems. For ignition system diagnosis and testing, please refer to the information on engine electrical components and ignition systems found earlier in this manual. If the ignition system checks out (there is spark), then you must determine if the fuel system is operating properly (is there fuel?).

FUEL LINES AND FITTINGS

Push Connectors and Spring Lock Couplings

REMOVAL & INSTALLATION

The fuel system, depending on model year of the vehicle, may be equipped with push type connectors, spring lock couplings or both. When removing the fuel lines on these vehicles with spring lock couplings, it will be necessary to use Fuel Line Coupling Disconnect Tool D87L-9280-A for ⅜ inch lines or D87L-9280-B for ½ inch lines.

Spring Lock Coupling

▶ **See Figure 1**

1. Properly relieve the fuel system pressure.
Remove the retaining clip from the spring lock coupling by hand only. Do not use any sharp tool or screwdriver as it may damage the spring lock coupling.
2. Twist the fitting to free it from any adhesion at the O-ring seals.
3. Fit Spring Lock Coupling Tool D87L-9280-A/B or equivalent to the coupling.

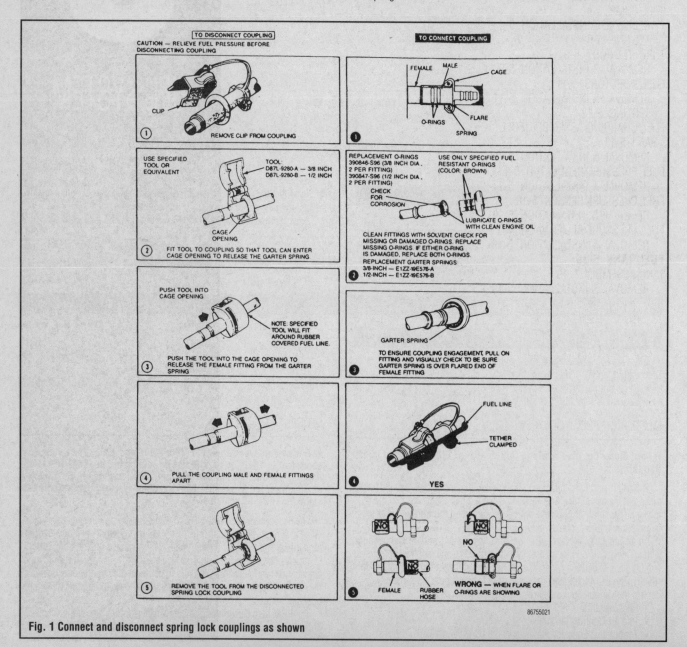

Fig. 1 Connect and disconnect spring lock couplings as shown

4. Close the tool and push it into the open side of the cage to expand garter spring and release the female fitting.

5. After the garter spring is expanded, pull the fittings apart.

6. Remove the tool from the disconnected coupling.

To install:

7. Clean all dirt from both pieces of the coupling.

8. Replace the O-rings and garter springs as necessary.

✳✳ CAUTION

Use only the specified O-rings. The use of the wrong O-rings may cause the connection to leak intermittently during engine operation.

9. Lubricate the male fitting, the O-rings and the inside of the female fitting with clean engine oil.

10. Fit the female fitting to the male fitting and push until the garter spring snaps over the flared end of the female fitting.

11. Pull on the fitting to make sure it is properly connected and visually inspect the garter spring to make sure it is over the flared end of the female fitting

➡**Some models require the large black clip to be installed on the supply side fuel line and the small gray clip to be installed on the return side.**

12. Place the retaining clip over the spring lock coupling. Firmly push the clip onto the coupling making sure the horseshoe portion of the clip is over the coupling. Do not install the clip over the rubber fuel lines.

Push Connect Fittings

▶ **See Figure 2**

1. Properly relieve the fuel system pressure.

2. Clean all dirt from the internal potion of the fitting.

✳✳ CAUTION

Do not use tools.

3. Bend the shipping tab down so that it will clear the body by bending the clips legs ⅛ inch (3.2mm) apart to disengage the body and pushing the legs into the fitting.

GASOLINE FUEL INJECTION SYSTEM

Description and Operation

There are two types of gasoline fuel injection systems used on the Ford Escort and Mercury Tracer:
- Multi-port Fuel Injection (MFI)
- Sequential Fuel Injection (SFI)

MULTI-PORT FUEL INJECTION (MFI)

➡**Ford Motor Co. also refers to this system as Electronic Fuel Injection (EFI).**

The Multi-port Fuel Injection (MFI) system is classified as a multi-point, pulse time, mass airflow fuel injection system. Fuel is metered into the intake air stream in accordance with engine demand through four injectors mounted on a tuned intake manifold.

An air induction system and a fuel injection system work in conjunction with an electronic engine control system. The electronic engine control system consists of various sensors, switches and a Powertrain Control Module (PCM). The PCM then uses the input from the switches and sensors to control the various output devices. The output devices are:
- Fuel injectors
- Idle Air Control (IAC) valve
- Evaporative Emission Canister Purge (CANP) valve

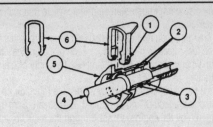

Item	Description
1	Shipping Tab
2	O-Rings
3	Spacers
4	Steel Tube
5	Body
6	Clip

90985G03

Fig. 2 Exploded view of a push connect fitting assembly

4. Lightly pull the clip from the triangular end and work it free of the tube and fitting.

5. Grasp the fitting and hose, then with a slight twisting motion, separate it from the component.

To install:

6. Inspect the clip for damage and replace as necessary.

7. Install a new clip as follows:

a. Insert the clip into any two adjacent openings with the triangular portion facing away from the fitting opening.

b. Install the clip fully to engage the body (legs of the clip locked on the outside of the body).

8. Wipe the tube end of the fitting with a clean rag , inspect the inside of the fitting for dirt or damage and lubricate it with engine oil.

9. Install the fitting into place, align the fitting and tube axial, then push the fitting onto the tube end.

10. When the fitting fully engages an audible click will be heard. Pull on the fitting to make sure it is properly fastened.

- High Speed Inlet Air (HILA) shutter valve actuator
- Fuel pressure regulator
- A/C relay
- Ignition Control Module (ICM)

By controlling these outputs, the PCM can meet the different operation and driveability needs of the engine.

SEQUENTIAL FUEL INJECTION (SFI)

➡**This system was called "SEFI" in 1991 and 1992. The name was shortened to "SFI" by Ford Motor Co. beginning in 1993. The later name is used in this manual to simplify understanding. By either designation, the Sequential Fuel Injection system is essentially the same for 1991–99 vehicles.**

The Sequential Fuel Injection (SFI) system, used on SFI engines, is classified as a multi-point, pulse time fuel injection system. Fuel is metered into each intake port by a fuel injector in sequence with the engine firing order. An on-board Powertrain Control Module (PCM) accepts electronic input signals from various engine sensors to compute the required fuel flow rate necessary to maintain a pre-determined air/fuel ratio throughout all engine operating ranges.

The PCM also determines and compensates for the age of the vehicle. This system will automatically sense and compensate for changes in altitude, and will also permit push-starting of the vehicle (manual transaxle only), if necessary.

The fuel charging manifold assembly (fuel rail) incorporates four electrically actuated fuel injectors directly above each of the engine's intake ports. Each injector, when energized, sprays a metered quantity of fuel into the intake air stream.

The system pressure is controlled by a pressure regulator connected in series with the fuel injectors and positioned downstream from them. Excess fuel, not required by the engine, passes through the regulator and returns to the fuel tank through a fuel return line.

The SFI system can be broken down into four categories:

- Fuel delivery
- Air induction
- Sensors
- PCM

The fuel system is equipped with an in-tank mounted fuel pump.

Relieving Fuel System Pressure

✳✳ CAUTION

Observe all applicable safety precautions when working around fuel. Whenever servicing the fuel system, always work in a well ventilated area. Do not allow fuel spray or vapors to come in contact with a spark or open flame. Keep a dry chemical fire extinguisher near the work area. Always keep fuel in a container specifically designed for fuel storage; also, always properly seal fuel containers to avoid the possibility of fire or explosion.

1991–96 MODELS

1. Start the engine.
2. Remove the rear seat cushion.
3. Disconnect the fuel pump electrical connectors.
4. Wait for the engine to stall, then turn the ignition switch **OFF**.
5. Connect the fuel pump electrical connectors.
6. Install the rear seat cushion.
7. Disconnect the negative battery cable.

1997–99 MODELS

▶ **See Figure 3**

1. Remove the Schrader valve cap at the end of the fuel rail and a attach a fuel pressure gauge.
2. Open the manual relief valve on the fuel pressure gauge slowly to relieve the fuel pressure.

Fuel Pump

REMOVAL & INSTALLATION

1991–96 Engines

▶ **See Figures 4 thru 13**

The fuel pump is located inside the fuel tank.

➡**This procedure will require a new fuel pump gasket for pump installation, so be sure to have one before starting.**

1. Relieve the fuel system pressure.
2. Disconnect the negative battery cable.
3. Remove the rear seat cushion and unplug the electrical connector from the fuel pump.
4. Unfasten and remove the four pump cover screws and the ground strap.

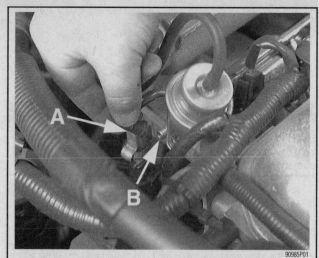
Fig. 3 Unscrew the cap (A) to access the Schrader valve (B) at the end of the fuel rail—2.0L engines

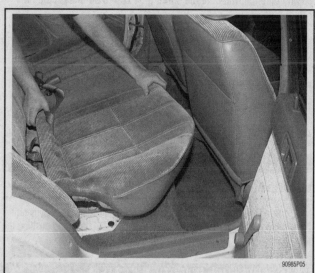
Fig. 4 Remove the rear seat cushion

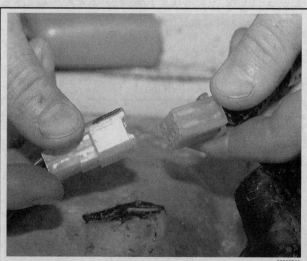
Fig. 5 Unplug the fuel pump electrical connection

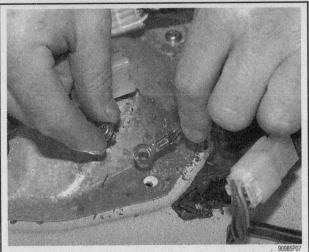

Fig. 6 Unfasten the screw attaching the ground strap to the fuel pump cover and remove the strap

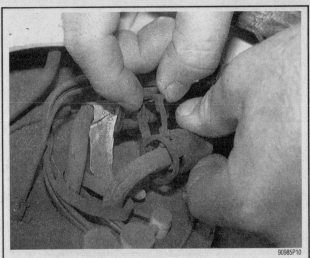

Fig. 9 Unfasten the fuel tube retaining clips and disconnect the tube from the fuel pump

Fig. 7 Unfasten the remaining fuel pump cover screws and remove the cover

Fig. 10 Place a shop rag or towel under the fuel lines to soak up or absorb any spilled fuel

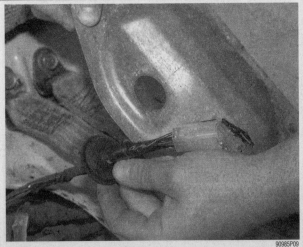

Fig. 8 To ease access, push the grommet through the hole in the cover, then pull the wire through and set the cover aside

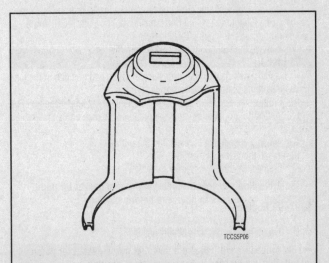

Fig. 11 A special tool is usually available to remove or install the fuel pump locking cam (retaining ring)

Fig. 12 Remove the pump retaining ring . . .

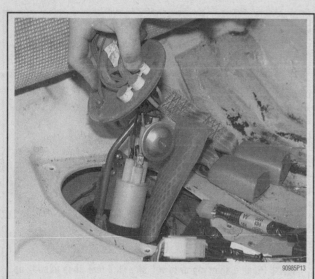

Fig. 13 . . . and remove the fuel pump assembly from the tank

5. Unfasten the fuel tube clips and disconnect the tubes from the pump.
6. Use a fuel pump locking ring removal tool or a brass drift and a hammer to unfasten the pump locking retaining ring.
7. Remove the fuel pump and gasket from the tank.
To install:
8. Install a new gasket and place the fuel pump into position in the tank.
9. Install the pump's locking retaining ring.
10. Connect the fuel tubes to the pump and install the tube retaining clips.
11. Install the ground strap and fuel pump cover, then tighten the retainers.
12. Attach the electrical connector to the pump.
13. Install the rear seat cushion.
14. Connect the negative battery cable.
15. Start the car and check for proper operation.

1997–99 Engines

The fuel pump is located inside the fuel tank.

➥This procedure will require a new fuel pump gasket for pump installation, so be sure to have one before starting.

1. Relieve the fuel system sressure.
2. Disconnect the negative battery cable.

3. Remove the rear seat cushion and unplug the electrical connectors from the fuel pump.
4. Unfasten the four pump access cover screws and remove the cover.
5. If equipped, unplug the pump electrical connector located under the cover.
6. Unfasten the fuel line clip(s) and disconnect the line(s) from the pump.
7. Use a fuel pump locking ring removal tool or a brass drift and a hammer to unfasten the pump locking retaining ring.
8. Remove the fuel pump and the gasket from the tank.
To install:
9. Install a new gasket and place the pump into position in the tank.
10. Install the pump locking retaining ring.
11. Connect the fuel line(s) to the pump and install the line retaining clip(s).
12. If equipped, attach the fuel pump electrical connection(s).
13. Install the access cover, then tighten the retainers.
14. Attach the pump electrical connector(s).
15. Install the rear seat cushion.
16. Connect the negative battery cable.
17. Start the car and check for proper operation.

TESTING

1.8L Engines

▶ See Figure 14

❊❊ CAUTION

Observe all applicable safety precautions when working around fuel. Whenever servicing the fuel system, always work in a well ventilated area. Do not allow fuel spray or vapors to come in contact with a spark or open flame. Keep a dry chemical fire extinguisher near the work area. Always keep fuel in a container specifically designed for fuel storage; also, always properly seal fuel containers to avoid the possibility of fire or explosion.

1. Check all hoses and lines for kinks and leaking. Repair as necessary.
2. Check all electrical connections for looseness and corrosion. Repair as necessary.
3. Turn the ignition key from the **OFF** position to the **RUN** position several times (do not start the engine and verify that the pump runs briefly each time, (you will here a low humming sound from the fuel tank).

➥Check that the inertia switch is reset before diagnosing power supply problems to the fuel pump.

Fig. 14 Ground the fuel pump test terminal on the DLC as shown—1.8L engines

4. Turn the ignition key **OFF** and unplug the fuel pump electrical connection at the pump.

5. Jump the fuel pump test terminal to ground. Refer to the accompanying illustration.

6. Turn the ignition key **ON**.

7. Using a high impedance Digital Volt Ohmmeter (DVOM), measure the voltage between the black wire with the pink stripe at the pump vehicle harness connector and ground. The voltage should be 10–14 volts. If not check the wire(s) for damage.

8. Relieve the fuel system pressure.

9. Connect Rotunda fuel pressure testing kit 134-R0087 or its equivalent with a Multi-port Fuel Injection (MFI) test adapter D87C-9974-A in the fuel line between the fuel rails, with its main valve open and its drain valve closed.

10. Jump the fuel pump test terminal to ground. Refer to the accompanying illustration.

11. Turn the key **ON**. The fuel pressure should be 38–46 psi (265–320 kPa).

12. If the pump pressure and supply voltage is correct the pump is fully operational, if not, replace the pump.

1.9L Engines

1991–95 MODELS

▶ See Figures 15, 16, 17, 18 and 19

※ CAUTION

Observe all applicable safety precautions when working around fuel. Whenever servicing the fuel system, always work in a well ventilated area. Do not allow fuel spray or vapors to come in contact with a spark or open flame. Keep a dry chemical fire extinguisher near the work area. Always keep fuel in a container specifically designed for fuel storage; also, always properly seal fuel containers to avoid the possibility of fire or explosion.

1. Check all hoses and lines for kinks and leaking. Repair as necessary.

2. Check all electrical connections for looseness and corrosion. Repair as necessary.

3. Check all fuses and relays.

4. Turn the ignition key from the **OFF** position to the **RUN** position several times (do not start the engine and verify that the pump runs briefly each time, (you will here a low humming sound from the fuel tank).

➡Check that the inertia switch is reset before diagnosing power supply problems to the fuel pump.

Fig. 16 Check the fuses located in the fuel pump wiring harness

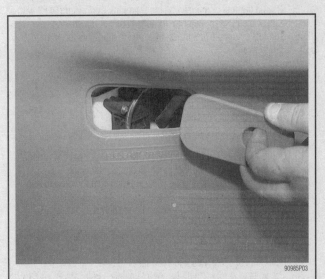

Fig. 17 Remove the inertia switch access cover in the trunk . . .

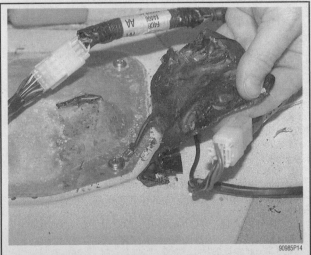

Fig. 15 Check that the fuel pump ground is corrosion free and firmly attached to the fuel pump cover

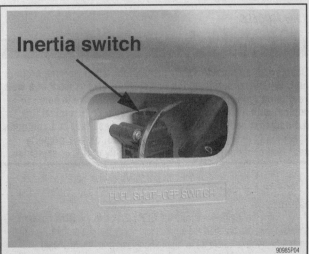

Fig. 18 . . . and check that the inertia switch is reset before diagnosing power supply problems to the fuel pump

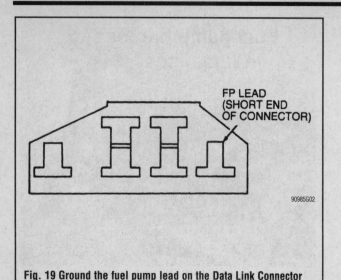

Fig. 19 Ground the fuel pump lead on the Data Link Connector (DLC) with a jumper wire at the FP lead—1991–95 1.9L engines

5. Ground the fuel pump lead on the Data Link Connector (DLC) with a jumper wire at the FP lead. Refer to the accompanying illustration.

6. Connect a suitable fuel pressure gauge to the Schrader valve teat port on the fuel rail.

7. Turn the ignition key **ON**, but do not start the engine.

8. The fuel pressure should be 30–45 psi (210–310 kPa).

9. If the pump pressure is correct the pump is fully operational.

10. Check the pump ground connection and service as necessary

11. Turn the ignition key **ON**.

12. Ground the fuel pump lead on the Data Link Connector (DLC) with a jumper wire at the FP lead.

13. Using a Digital Volt Ohmmeter (DVOM), check for battery voltage (approximately 12 volts) at the fuel pump electrical connector.

14. If the pump is getting a good voltage supply and the ground connection is good replace the pump.

15. Check the pump ground connection and service as necessary.

16. Turn the ignition key **OFF**.

17. Connect the DVOM between the inertia fuel shutoff and ground.

18. Start the engine.

19. Read the voltage at idle and 3500 rpm.

20. The voltage at idle should be approximately 9 volts at idle and 13 volts at 3500 rpm.

21. If the ground connection is good and the voltage is not within specification, replace the pump.

1996 MODELS

> ✳✳ **CAUTION**
>
> **Observe all applicable safety precautions when working around fuel. Whenever servicing the fuel system, always work in a well ventilated area. Do not allow fuel spray or vapors to come in contact with a spark or open flame. Keep a dry chemical fire extinguisher near the work area. Always keep fuel in a container specifically designed for fuel storage; also, always properly seal fuel containers to avoid the possibility of fire or explosion.**

1. Check all hoses and lines for kinks and leaking. Repair as necessary.

2. Check all electrical connections for looseness and corrosion. Repair as necessary.

3. Turn the ignition key from the **OFF** position to the **RUN** position several times (do not start the engine) and verify that the pump runs briefly each time, (you will here a low humming sound from the fuel tank).

➡ **Check that the inertia switch is reset before diagnosing power supply problems to the fuel pump.**

The use of a scan tool is required to perform these tests.

4. Turn the ignition key **OFF**.

5. Connect a suitable fuel pressure gauge to the fuel test port (Schrader valve) on the fuel rail.

6. Connect the scan tool and turn the ignition key **ON** but do not start the engine.

7. Following the scan tool manufacturer's instructions, enter the output test mode and run the fuel pump to obtain the maximum fuel pressure.

8. The fuel pressure should be between 30–40 psi (240–280 kPa).

9. If the fuel pressure is within specification the pump is working properly. If not, continue with the test.

10. Check the pump ground connection and service as necessary.

11. Turn the ignition key **ON**.

12. Using the scan tool, enter output test mode and turn on the fuel pump circuit.

13. Using a Digital Volt Ohmmeter (DVOM), check for voltage (approximately 10.5 volts) at the fuel pump electrical connector.

14. If the pump is getting a good voltage supply, the ground connection is good and the fuel pressure is not within specification, then replace the pump.

2.0L Engines

> ✳✳ **CAUTION**
>
> **Observe all applicable safety precautions when working around fuel. Whenever servicing the fuel system, always work in a well ventilated area. Do not allow fuel spray or vapors to come in contact with a spark or open flame. Keep a dry chemical fire extinguisher near the work area. Always keep fuel in a container specifically designed for fuel storage; also, always properly seal fuel containers to avoid the possibility of fire or explosion.**

1. Check all hoses and lines for kinks and leaking. Repair as necessary.

2. Check all electrical connections for looseness and corrosion. Repair as necessary.

3. Turn the ignition key from the **OFF** position to the **RUN** position several times (do not start the engine) and verify that the pump runs briefly each time, (you will here a low humming sound from the fuel tank).

➡ **Check that the inertia switch is reset before diagnosing power supply problems to the fuel pump.**

The use of a scan tool is required to perform these tests.

4. Turn the ignition key **OFF**.

5. Connect a suitable fuel pressure gauge to the fuel test port (Schrader valve) on the fuel rail.

6. Connect the scan tool and turn the ignition key **ON** but do not start the engine.

7. Following the scan tool manufacturer's instructions, enter the output test mode and run the fuel pump to obtain the maximum fuel pressure.

8. The fuel pressure should be between 30–40 psi (310–415 kPa) on 1997 models and 55–85 psi (517–862 kPa) on 1998–99 models.

9. If the fuel pressure is within specification the pump is working properly. If not, continue with the test.

10. Check the pump ground connection and service as necessary.

11. Turn the ignition key **ON**.

12. Using the scan tool, enter output test mode and turn on the fuel pump circuit.

13. Using a Digital Volt Ohmmeter (DVOM), check for voltage (approximately 10.5 volts) at the fuel pump electrical connector.

14. If the pump is getting a good voltage supply, the ground connection is good and the fuel pressure is not within specification, then replace the pump.

Throttle Body

REMOVAL & INSTALLATION

1.8L Engines

▶ See Figure 20

1. Disconnect the negative battery cable.
2. Remove the inlet air duct that connect the throttle body to the intake air resonator.
3. Unplug the throttle body electrical connection.
4. Tag and disengage the bypass air hoses from the Idle Air Control (IAC) valve.
5. Partially drain the cooling system and disconnect the coolant hoses from the IAC valve.
6. Disconnect the accelerator cable from the throttle cam.
7. If equipped with an automatic transaxle, disconnect the kickdown cable (throttle valve control actuating cable 4EAT) from the throttle cam.
8. Unfasten the throttle body retaining bolts and remove the throttle body.
9. Remove the old gasket and clean any gasket residue from both mating surfaces.

To install:

10. Install a new gasket and the throttle body.
11. Install the throttle body retaining bolts and tighten them to 14–19 ft. lbs. (19–25 Nm).
12. If equipped with an automatic transaxle, connect the kickdown cable (throttle valve control actuating cable 4EAT) to the throttle cam.
13. Connect the accelerator cable to the throttle cam.
14. Connect the coolant hoses and bypass air hoses to the IAC valve.
15. Attach the throttle body electrical connection.
16. Install the inlet air duct that connect the throttle body to the intake air resonator.
17. Fill the cooling system.
18. Connect the negative battery cable.

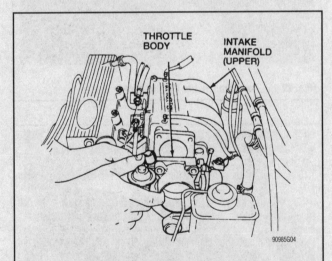

Fig. 20 Remove the throttle body from the upper intake manifold—1.8L engines

1.9L and 2.0L SOHC Engines

▶ See Figures 21 thru 28

1. Disconnect the negative battery cable.
2. Loosen the air cleaner outlet tube clamp at the throttle body and disconnect the tube from the throttle body.

Fig. 21 Unplug the Idle Air Control (IAC) valve electrical connection

Fig. 22 Unplug the Throttle Position (TP) sensor electrical connection

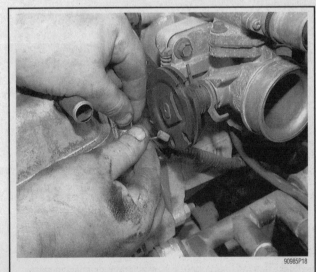

Fig. 23 Disconnect the accelerator cable from the throttle lever

3. Unplug the Throttle Position (TP) sensor and Idle Air Control (IAC) valve electrical connections.

4. Disconnect the vacuum hose from the bottom of the throttle body.

5. Disconnect the accelerator cable from the throttle lever.

6. If equipped with speed control, disconnect the speed control actuator.

7. If equipped with an automatic transaxle, disconnect the kickdown cable (throttle valve control actuating cable) from the throttle lever.

8. Unfasten the throttle body retaining bolts and remove the throttle body.

➡**If scraping is necessary to remove any gasket material, be careful not to damage the gasket mating surfaces or allow any foreign material to enter the intake manifold.**

9. Remove the old gasket and clean any gasket residue from both mating surfaces.

To install:

10. Install a new gasket and the throttle body.

11. Install the throttle body retaining bolts and tighten them to 15–22 ft. lbs. (20–30 Nm).

12. If equipped with an automatic transaxle, connect the kickdown cable (throttle valve control actuating cable) to the throttle lever.

Fig. 26 Unfasten the throttle body retaining bolts . . .

Fig. 24 If equipped with an automatic transaxle, also disconnect the kickdown cable (throttle valve control actuating cable)

Fig. 27 . . . and remove the throttle body

Fig. 25 Locations of the four throttle body retaining bolts

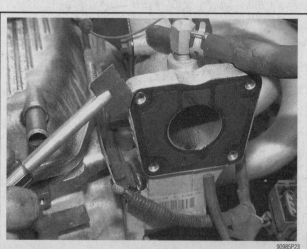

Fig. 28 Remove the old gasket, and clean any gasket residue from both mating surfaces, being careful not to damage these surfaces

13. Connect the accelerator cable to the throttle lever.
14. If equipped with speed control, connect the speed control actuator.
15. Connect the vacuum hose to the bottom of the throttle body.
16. Attach the Throttle Position (TP) sensor and Idle Air Control (IAC) valve electrical connections.
17. Connect the tube to the throttle body and tighten the clamp.
18. Connect the negative battery cable.

2.0L DOHC Engines

1. Disconnect the negative battery cable.
2. Remove the air cleaner outlet tube.
3. Unplug the Throttle Position (TP) sensor electrical connection.
4. Disconnect the accelerator cable from the throttle lever.
5. If equipped with speed control, disconnect the speed control actuator.
6. Unfasten the throttle body retaining bolts and remove the throttle body.

➡**If scraping is necessary to remove any gasket material, be careful not to damage the gasket mating surfaces or allow any foreign material to enter the intake manifold.**

7. Remove the old gasket and clean any gasket residue from both mating surfaces.

To install:

8. Install a new gasket and the throttle body.
9. Install the throttle body retaining bolts and tighten them to 71–106 inch lbs. (8–12 Nm).
10. Connect the accelerator cable to the throttle lever.
11. If equipped with speed control, connect the speed control actuator.
12. Attach the Throttle Position (TP) sensor electrical connection.
13. Connect the air cleaner outlet tube.
14. Connect the negative battery cable.

Fuel Injectors

REMOVAL & INSTALLATION

1.8L Engines

▶ **See Figure 29**

❊❊ CAUTION

Fuel injection systems remain under pressure, even after the engine has been turned OFF. The fuel system pressure must be relieved before disconnecting any fuel lines. Failure to do so may result in fire and/or personal injury.

1. Relieve the fuel system pressure.
2. Disconnect the negative battery cable.
3. Disconnect fuel supply and return lines using the proper tool for spring lock coupling removal.
4. Disconnect the crankcase ventilation hose from the valve cover and the upper intake manifold.
5. Disconnect the vacuum line from the fuel pressure regulator.
6. Unplug the fuel injector wiring harness connectors from each fuel injector.
7. Remove the three fuel injection supply manifold (fuel rail) retaining bolts and remove the fuel injection supply manifold with the fuel injectors attached.
8. Carefully remove the fuel injectors, grommets and insulators from the fuel injection supply manifold as required.
9. Once the fuel injector is removed from the fuel injection supply manifold, remove and discard the fuel injector O-rings.

To install:

10. Inspect the injector end caps (covering the injector pintle) for signs of deterioration. Replace as required. If a cap is missing, look for it in intake manifold.

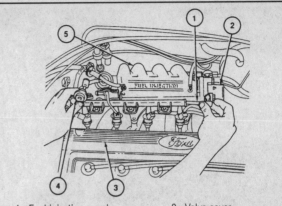

1. Fuel injection supply manifold
2. Throttle body
3. Valve cover
4. Fuel pressure regulator
5. Intake manifold, upper

90985G06

Fig. 29 Remove the fuel rail with the injectors still attached—1.8L engines

11. Install two new O-rings onto each injector and apply a small amount of clean engine oil to the O-rings.
12. Install the fuel injectors with grommets and insulators to the fuel injection supply manifold using a light twisting motion while pushing the injector into position.
13. Carefully seat the fuel injection supply manifold and injector assembly onto the intake manifold making sure the fuel injectors are fully seated. Install the three retaining bolts. Tighten the bolts to 14–19 ft. lbs. (19–25 Nm).
14. Attach the fuel injector wiring harness connectors to each fuel injector.
15. Connect the vacuum line to the fuel pressure regulator.
16. Connect the crankcase ventilation hose.
17. Connect the fuel supply and fuel return lines. Make sure the spring lock couplings are properly attached and that the fuel tube clips are properly installed.
18. Connect the negative battery cable.
19. Run the engine and check for fuel leaks.
20. Check the entire assembly for proper alignment and seating.

1.9L Engine

▶ **See Figures 30 and 31**

❊❊ CAUTION

Fuel injection systems remain under pressure, even after the engine has been turned OFF. The fuel system pressure must be relieved before disconnecting any fuel lines. Failure to do so may result in fire and/or personal injury.

1. Relieve the fuel system pressure.
2. Disconnect the negative battery cable.
3. Disconnect fuel supply and return lines using the proper tool for spring lock coupling removal.
4. Unplug the fuel injector electrical connectors.
5. Remove the two fuel injection supply manifold (fuel rail) retaining bolts.
6. Carefully disengage the fuel injection supply manifold from the fuel injectors.
7. Disconnect the vacuum line from the fuel pressure regulator and set the fuel injection supply manifold aside.
8. Grasp the fuel injectors body and pull up while gently rocking the fuel injector from side to side.
9. Once removed, inspect the fuel injector end caps and washers for signs of deterioration. Replace as required.

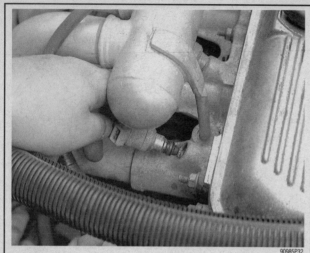

Fig. 30 Grasp the fuel injector's body and pull it out, while gently rocking the injector from side to side

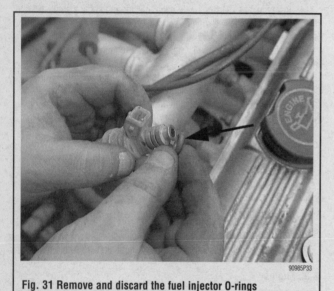

Fig. 31 Remove and discard the fuel injector O-rings

10. Remove the O-rings and discard. If an O-ring or end cap is missing, look in the intake manifold for the missing part.

To install:

11. Install two new O-rings onto each injector and apply a small amount of clean engine oil to the O-rings.

12. Install the fuel injectors using a light twisting, pushing motion into the intake manifold.

13. Carefully position the fuel injection supply manifold on top of the fuel injectors. Push the fuel injection supply manifold down onto the injectors to fully seat the O-rings.

14. Install the 2 fuel injection supply manifold retaining bolts and tighten to 15–22 ft. lbs. (20–30 Nm).

15. Connect the fuel supply and return lines making sure the spring lock couplings are fully engaged and that the fuel tube clips are properly installed.

16. Connect the vacuum line to the fuel pressure regulator.

17. Attach the fuel injector electrical harness connectors.

18. Connect the negative battery cable and turn the ignition to the **ON** position to allow the fuel pump to pressurize the system.

19. Check for any fuel leaks. If any are found, immediately turn the ignition switch to the **OFF** position and disconnect the negative battery cable. Correct any leaks found.

20. Connect the fuel injector wiring harness.

21. Connect the negative battery cable.

22. Run the engine at idle for 2 minutes, then turn the engine **OFF** and check for fuel leaks and proper operation.

2.0L Engine

▶ See Figure 32

✳✳ CAUTION

Fuel injection systems remain under pressure, even after the engine has been turned OFF. The fuel system pressure must be relieved before disconnecting any fuel lines. Failure to do so may result in fire and/or personal injury.

1. Relieve the fuel system pressure.

2. Disconnect the negative battery cable.

3. Remove the fuel injection supply manifold (fuel rail).

4. On DOHC engines, remove the injector retaining clips.

5. Grasp the fuel injectors body and pull up while gently rocking the fuel injector from side to side.

6. Once removed, inspect the fuel injector cap and body for signs of deterioration. Replace as required.

7. Remove the O-rings and discard. If an O-ring or end cap is missing, look in the intake manifold for the missing part.

To install:

8. Install new O-rings onto each injector and apply a small amount of clean engine oil to the O-rings.

9. Install the injectors using a slight twisting downward motion.

10. On DOHC engines, install the injector retaining clips.

11. Install the fuel injection supply manifold (fuel rail).

12. Connect the negative battery cable.

13. Run the engine at idle for 2 minutes, then turn the engine **OFF** and check for fuel leaks and proper operation.

Fig. 32 Grasp the fuel injector's body and pull upward, while gently rocking the fuel injector from side to side—2.0L engine

TESTING

▶ See Figures 33, 34 and 35

1. Start the car and let the engine idle.

2. Connect a tachometer to the engine.

3. Disconnect each injector one at a time and note the rpm drop. All the readings should be similar.

4. If the rpm does not drop after unplugging an injector there could be a problem with that injector.
5. Connect and operate a fuel injection tester according to the manufacturers instructions.
6. Check that the leakage and flow is within specifications according to the tool manufacturer.
7. If the leakage and flow is not within specifications, replace the injector(s).

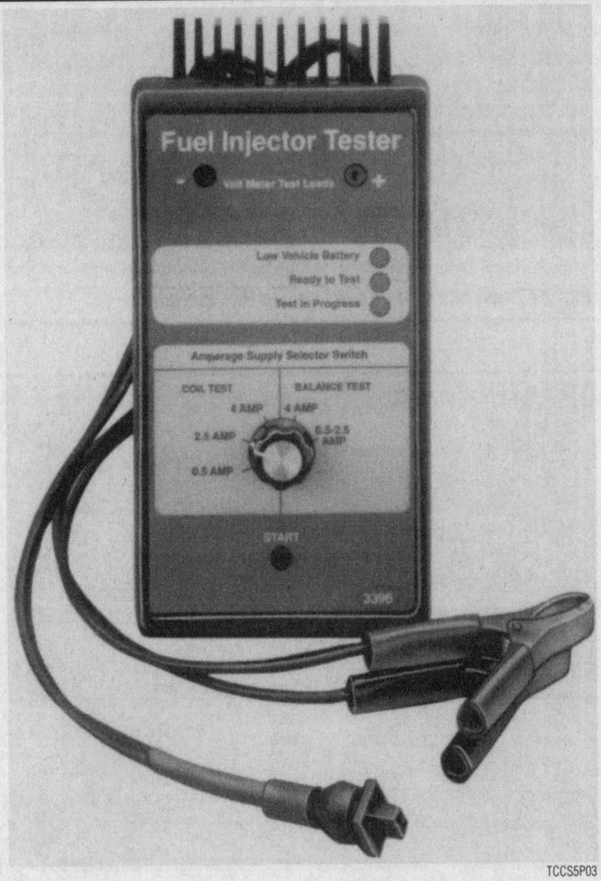

TCCS5P03

Fig. 33 Fuel injector testers can be purchased or sometimes rented

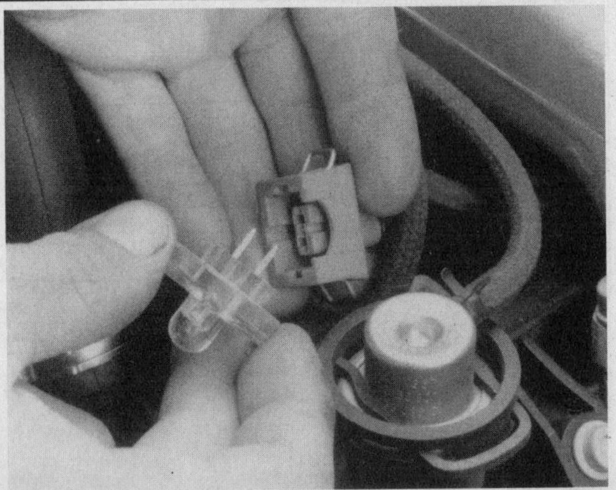

TCCS5P01

Fig. 34 A noid light can be attached to the fuel injector harness in order to test for injector pulse

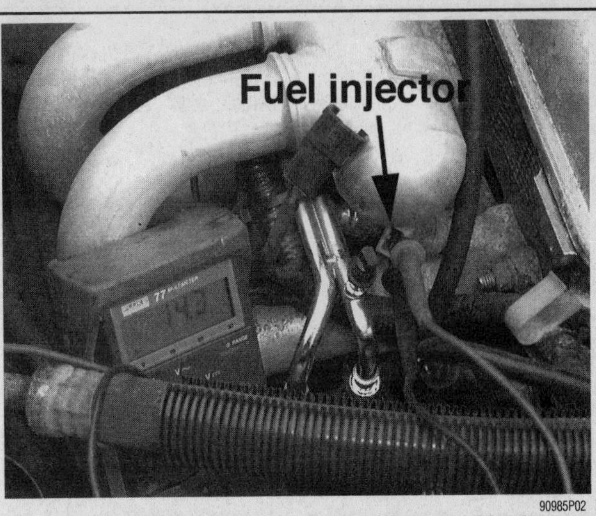

90985P02

Fig. 35 Measure the fuel injector's resistance by probing its two terminals with the positive and negative leads of a multimeter

➡Do not connect a test light to the injector harness, as this may cause damage to the Powertrain Control Module (PCM).

8. Disconnect the engine wiring harness from the injector.

➡This may require removing the upper intake manifold or other engine components.

9. Measure the resistance of the injector by probing one terminal with the positive lead, and the other injector terminal with the negative lead of a multimeter (or ohmmeter).
10. The measured resistance should be 12–16 ohms at 68°F (20°C).
11. If the resistance is not within specification, the fuel injector may be faulty.
12. If resistance is within specification, install a noid light and check for injector pulse from the PCM while cranking the engine.
13. If injector pulse is present check for proper fuel pressure.

Fuel Charging Assembly (Fuel Rail)

REMOVAL & INSTALLATION

1.8L Engine

See Figure 29

CAUTION

Fuel injection systems remain under pressure, even after the engine has been turned OFF. The fuel system pressure must be relieved before disconnecting any fuel lines. Failure to do so may result in fire and/or personal injury.

1. Relieve the fuel system pressure.
2. Disconnect the negative battery cable.
3. Disconnect fuel supply and return lines using the proper tool for spring lock coupling removal.
4. Disconnect the crankcase ventilation hose from the valve cover and the upper intake manifold.
5. Disconnect the vacuum line from the fuel pressure regulator.
6. Unplug the fuel injector wiring harness connectors from each fuel injector.
7. Remove the three fuel injection supply manifold (fuel rail) retaining bolts and remove the fuel injection supply manifold with the fuel injectors attached.

To install:

8. Carefully seat the fuel injection supply manifold and injector assembly onto the intake manifold making sure the fuel injectors are fully seated. Install the three retaining bolts. Tighten the bolts to 14–19 ft. lbs. (19–25 Nm).

9. Attach the fuel injector wiring harness connectors to each fuel injector.

10. Connect the vacuum line to the fuel pressure regulator.

11. Connect the crankcase ventilation hose.

12. Connect the fuel supply and fuel return lines. Make sure the spring lock couplings are properly attached and that the fuel tube clips are properly installed.

13. Connect the negative battery cable.

14. Run the engine and check for fuel leaks.

15. Check the entire assembly for proper alignment and seating.

1.9L Engine

▶ See Figures 36 thru 43

✳✳ CAUTION

Fuel injection systems remain under pressure, even after the engine has been turned OFF. The fuel system pressure must be relieved before disconnecting any fuel lines. Failure to do so may result in fire and/or personal injury.

1. Disconnect the negative battery cable.

2. Relieve the fuel system pressure.

3. Disconnect fuel supply and return lines, using the proper tool for spring lock coupling removal.

4. Unplug the fuel injector electrical connectors.

5. Remove the two fuel injection supply manifold (fuel rail) retaining bolts.

6. Carefully disengage the fuel injection supply manifold from the fuel injectors.

7. Disconnect the vacuum line from the fuel pressure regulator and set the fuel injection supply manifold aside.

To install:

8. Carefully position the fuel injection supply manifold on top of the fuel injectors. Push the fuel injection supply manifold down onto the injectors to fully seat the O-rings.

9. Install the 2 fuel injection supply manifold retaining bolts and torque to 15–22 ft. lbs. (20–30 Nm).

10. Connect the fuel supply and return lines making sure the spring lock couplings are fully engaged and that the fuel tube clips are properly installed.

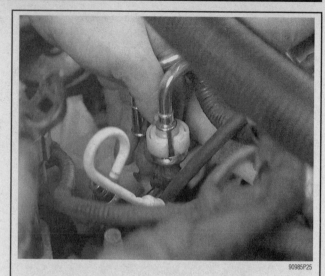

Fig. 37 Press the tool into the spring lock coupling . . .

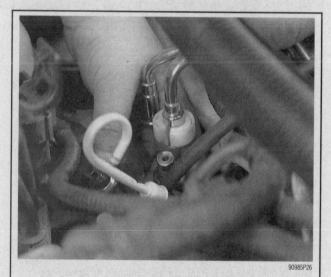

Fig. 38 . . . and separate the fuel line fitting from the hose

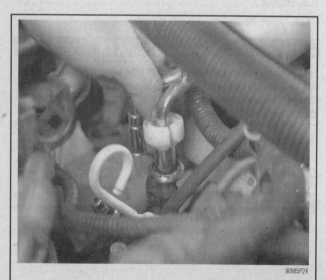

Fig. 36 Install the fuel line disconnect tool onto the fuel line

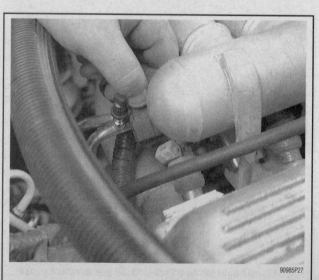

Fig. 39 Unplug the fuel injector electrical connectors

Fig. 40 Remove the two fuel injection supply manifold (fuel rail) retaining bolts

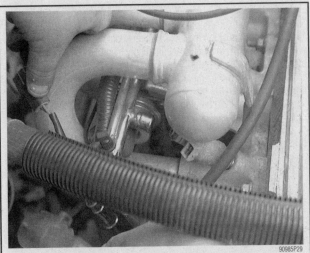

Fig. 41 Carefully disengage the fuel injection supply manifold from the fuel injectors

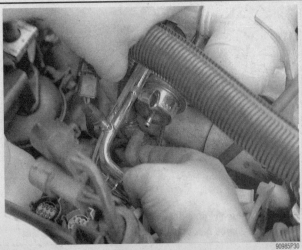

Fig. 42 Unplug the vacuum hose from the fuel pressure regulator

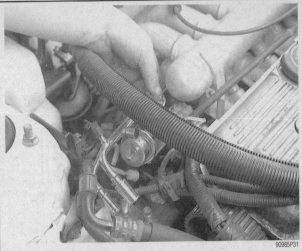

Fig. 43 Remove the fuel injection supply manifold (fuel rail) from the engine compartment

11. Connect the vacuum line to the fuel pressure regulator.

12. Attach the fuel injector electrical harness connectors.

13. Connect the negative battery cable and turn the ignition to the **ON** position to allow the fuel pump to pressurize the system.

14. Check for any fuel leaks. If any are found, immediately turn the ignition switch to the **OFF** position and disconnect the negative battery cable. Correct any leaks found.

15. Connect the fuel injector wiring harness.

16. Connect the negative battery cable.

17. Run the engine at idle for 2 minutes, then turn the engine **OFF** and check for fuel leaks and proper operation.

2.0L Engines

SOHC ENGINES

▶ See Figures 44 and 45

✳✳ CAUTION

Fuel injection systems remain under pressure, even after the engine has been turned OFF. The fuel system pressure must be relieved before disconnecting any fuel lines. Failure to do so may result in fire and/or personal injury.

1. Disconnect the negative battery cable.

2. Relieve the fuel system pressure.

3. Unplug the crankshaft position sensor electrical connection.

4. Unplug the two main engine harness connectors above the right-hand front wheel well.

5. Unplug the fuel injector electrical connectors.

6. Unplug the fuel pressure sensor and the camshaft position sensor electrical connections.

7. Grasp the plastic wiring harness routing rail, then gently pull upwards separating it from the fuel rail and set the harness aside.

8. Disconnect fuel inlet and supply lines from the manifold using the proper tool for spring lock coupling removal.

9. Unfasten the injection supply manifold retainers.

✳✳ WARNING

Use care when handling the injection supply manifold and the injectors to prevent damage to the sealing areas and sensitive fuel metering orifices.

10. Gently separate the manifold from the injectors and remove the manifold.

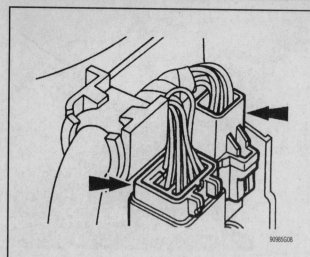

Fig. 44 Unplug the two main engine harness connectors (arrows) above the right-hand front wheel well—2.0L SOHC engines

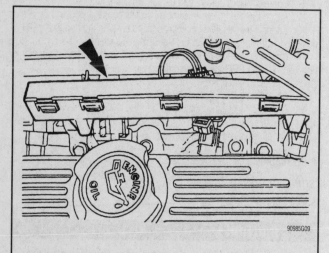

Fig. 45 Grasp the plastic wiring harness routing rail (arrow) and pull upwards to separate it from the fuel rail

To install:

11. Apply a small amount of clean engine oil to the O-rings.
12. Carefully position the fuel injection supply manifold on top of the fuel injectors. Push the fuel injection supply manifold down onto the injectors to fully seat the O-rings.
13. Install the two fuel injection supply manifold retaining bolts and tighten them to 15–22 ft. lbs. (20–30 Nm).
14. Connect the fuel return, inlet and supply lines.
15. Grasp the plastic wiring harness and slide it back into place on the manifold.
16. Attach the camshaft position sensor and the fuel pressure sensor electrical connections.
17. Attach the fuel injector and the two main harness electrical connectors.
18. Attach the crankshaft position sensor electrical connection.
19. Connect the negative battery cable.
20. Run the engine at idle for 2 minutes, then turn the engine **OFF** and check for fuel leaks and proper operation.

DOHC ENGINES

▶ See Figure 46

✳✳ CAUTION

Fuel injection systems remain under pressure, even after the engine has been turned OFF. The fuel system pressure must be relieved before disconnecting any fuel lines. Failure to do so may result in fire and/or personal injury.

1. Disconnect the negative battery cable.
2. Relieve the fuel system pressure.
3. Disconnect the spring lock coupling(s) using the appropriate tool.
4. Remove the air cleaner outlet tube.
5. Remove the throttle body.
6. Unplug the fuel injector electrical connections.
7. Unplug the electrical connection and vacuum line from the fuel pressure sensor.
8. Unplug the fuel temperature sensor electrical connection.
9. Unfasten the fuel charging wiring screws and position the wiring assembly aside.
10. Unfasten the fuel injection supply manifold (fuel rail) retainers and remove the rail.

To install:

11. Apply a small amount of clean engine oil to the O-rings.
12. Carefully position the fuel injection supply manifold on top of the fuel injectors. Push the fuel injection supply manifold down onto the injectors to fully seat the O-rings.
13. Install the two fuel injection supply manifold retaining bolts and tighten them to 71–106 inch lbs. (8–12 Nm).
14. Install the fuel charging wiring and tighten its retainers.
15. Attach the fuel temperature sensor electrical connection.
16. Attach vacuum line and electrical connection to the fuel pressure sensor.
17. Attach the fuel injector electrical connections.
18. Install the throttle body.
19. Install the air cleaner outlet tube.
20. Connect the spring lock coupling(s) using the appropriate tool.
21. Connect the negative battery cable.
22. Run the engine at idle for 2 minutes, then turn the engine **OFF** and check for fuel leaks and proper operation.

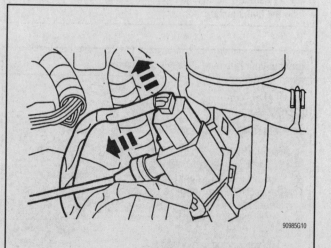

Fig. 46 Unplug the electrical connection and vacuum line (arrows) from the fuel pressure sensor—2.0L DOHC engines

Fuel Pressure Regulator

REMOVAL & INSTALLATION

1.8L Engines

▶ See Figure 47

1. Properly relieve the fuel system pressure.
2. Disconnect the negative battery cable.
3. Disconnect the vacuum line from the fuel pressure regulator.
4. Disconnect the fuel and vapor return tube from the fuel pressure regulator.
5. Unfasten the two fuel pressure regulator retaining bolts.
6. Remove the fuel pressure regulator and the O-ring. Discard the O-ring.

To install:

7. Position a new O-ring onto the fuel pressure regulator.
8. Place the fuel pressure regulator into position and install the retaining bolts. Tighten the bolts to 69–95 inch lbs. (8–11 Nm).
9. Connect the fuel and vapor return tube to the fuel pressure regulator.
10. Connect the vacuum line to the fuel pressure regulator.
11. Connect the negative battery cable.
12. Run the engine at idle for 2 minutes, then turn the engine **OFF** and check for fuel leaks and proper operation.

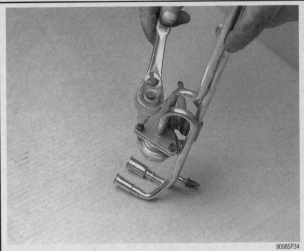

Fig. 48 Remove the Allen or Torx® head retainers that attach the fuel pressure regulator to the fuel rail

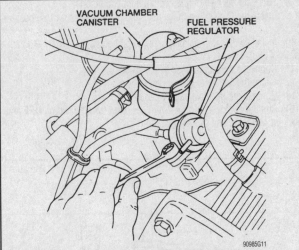

Fig. 47 A box end wrench can be used to loosen the fuel pressure regulator retaining bolts—1.8L engines

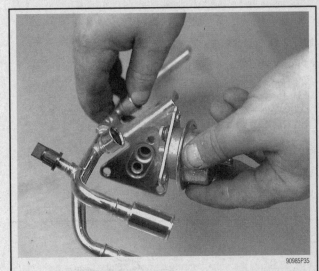

Fig. 49 Separate the fuel pressure regulator from the fuel rail

1.9L Engines

▶ See Figures 48, 49, 50 and 51

1. Properly relieve the fuel system pressure.
2. Disconnect the negative battery cable.
3. Remove the fuel injection supply manifold (fuel rail).
4. Remove the Allen or Torx® head retainers that attach the fuel pressure regulator to the fuel rail.
5. Remove the fuel pressure regulator, gasket and the O-ring. Discard the gasket and O-ring.
6. Clean any dirt and gasket residue from the fuel pressure regulator retaining screws.

To install:

7. Lubricate the new O-ring with a light engine oil.
8. Install a new gasket and O-ring on the fuel pressure regulator.
9. Place the fuel pressure regulator into position and install the retainers. Tighten the retainers to 27–40 inch lbs. (3–4 Nm).

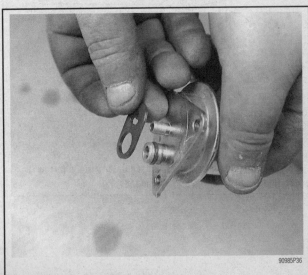

Fig. 50 Remove and discard the gasket . . .

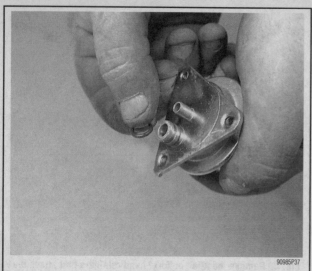

Fig. 51 . . . and the O-ring from the fuel pressure regulator

10. Install the fuel injection supply manifold (fuel rail).
11. Connect the negative battery cable.

1997 2.0L Engines

▸ See Figure 52

1. Properly relieve the fuel system pressure.
2. Disconnect the negative battery cable.
3. Disconnect the vacuum hose from the fuel pressure regulator.
4. Unfasten the two fuel pressure regulator retaining bolts.
5. Remove the fuel pressure regulator and the O-rings. Discard the O-rings.

To install:
6. Lubricate the new O-rings with a light engine oil.
7. Position a new O-rings onto the fuel pressure regulator.

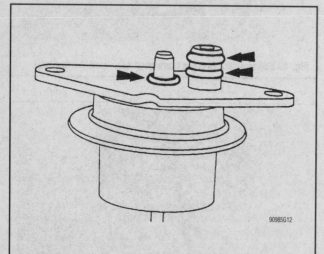

Fig. 52 Lubricate the fuel pressure regulator O-rings (arrows) with light engine oil—1997 2.0L engines

8. Place the fuel pressure regulator into position and install the retainers. Tighten the retainers to 27–40 inch lbs. (3–4 Nm).
9. Connect the vacuum line to the fuel pressure regulator.
10. Connect the negative battery cable.
11. Run the engine at idle for 2 minutes, then turn the engine **OFF** and check for fuel leaks and proper operation.

Fuel Pressure Sensor

REMOVAL & INSTALLATION

1998–99 2.0L Engines

▸ See Figure 53

➡1998–99 models do not utilize a conventional fuel pressure regulator. Instead, they contain a fuel pressure sensor, which maintains fuel pressure based on intake manifold vacuum.

1. Properly relieve the fuel system pressure.
2. Disconnect the negative battery cable.
3. Remove air cleaner outlet tube.
4. Unplug the sensor electrical connection.
5. Disconnect the vacuum hose from the sensor.
6. Unfasten the sensor retaining screws and remove the sensor.
7. Inspect the sensor O-rings and replace them as necessary.

To install:
8. Lubricate the new O-rings with a light engine oil
9. Install the O-rings on the sensor and place the sensor into position.
10. Install the sensor retaining screws and tighten them to 27–40 inch lbs. (3–4 Nm).
11. Connect the vacuum hose to the sensor.
12. Attach the sensor electrical connection.
13. Connect the negative battery cable.
14. Run the engine at idle for 2 minutes, then turn the engine **OFF** and check for fuel leaks and proper operation.

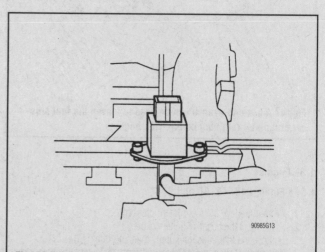

Fig. 53 The fuel pressure sensor is located on the right-hand side of the fuel supply manifold (fuel rail)—1998–99 2.0L engines

Fuel Pressure Relief Valve

REMOVAL & INSTALLATION

2.0L Engines

▶ See Figure 54

1. Properly relieve the fuel system pressure.
2. Disconnect the negative battery cable.
3. Unscrew the fuel pressure relief valve.

To install:

4. Install the valve and tighten it to 70 inch lbs. (8 Nm).
5. Connect the negative battery cable.
6. Run the engine at idle for 2 minutes, then turn the engine **OFF** and check for fuel leaks and proper operation.

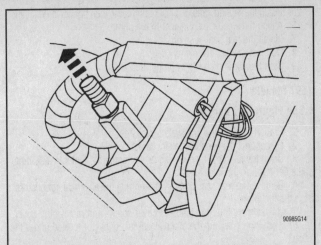

Fig. 54 Unscrew the fuel pressure relief valve from the fuel injection supply manifold

FUEL TANK

Tank Assembly

REMOVAL & INSTALLATION

1991–96 Models

▶ See Figures 55 and 56

1. Properly relieve the fuel system pressure.
2. Disconnect the negative battery cable.
3. Drain the fuel tank by pumping or siphoning the fuel into a suitable container through the filler hose.
4. Remove the rear seat and unplug the fuel pump electrical connection(s).
5. Unfasten and remove the four pump cover screws and the ground strap.
6. Unfasten the fuel tube clips and disconnect the tubes from the pump.
7. Raise the rear of the car and support it with safety stands.
8. Loosen the filler neck clamp and disconnect the hose from the filler neck.

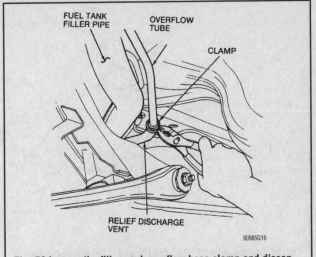

Fig. 56 Loosen the filler neck overflow hose clamp and disconnect the hose from the overflow tube—1991–96 models

9. Loosen the filler neck overflow hose clamp and disconnect the overflow hose from the overflow tube.
10. Tag and disconnect the vapor hoses from the tubes.
11. Remove the exhaust middle pipe heat shield.
12. Support the tank with a suitable jack.
13. Unfasten the fuel tank strap retaining bolts, then unclip the straps and remove them from the car.
14. Unfasten the tank heat shield attaching bolts from the tank.
15. Lower the jack slowly and remove the tank from the car.

To install:

16. Place the tank onto the jack and raise it into position.
17. Place the tank onto the fuel tank heat shield and install the heat shield attaching bolts.
18. Clip the tank straps into their mountings, then install and tighten the strap bolts to 27–38 ft. lbs. (37–52 Nm).
19. Remove the jack and install the exhaust middle pipe heat shield.
20. Connect the vapor hoses to the tubes.
21. Connect the filler neck hose to the filler neck and tighten the clamp.
22. Connect the overflow hose to the overflow tube and tighten the clamp.
23. Lower the car.
24. Connect the fuel tubes to the pump and install the tube retaining clips.

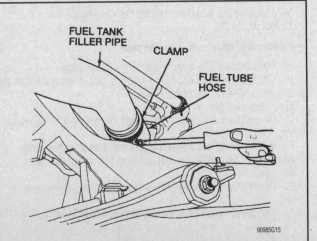

Fig. 55 Loosen the filler neck clamp and disconnect the hose from the filler neck—1991–96 models

25. Install the ground strap and fuel pump cover, then tighten the retainers.
26. Attach the electrical connector to the pump.
27. Install the rear seat cushion.
28. Connect the negative battery cable.
29. Start the car and check for proper operation.

1997 Models

▶ See Figures 57 and 58

1. Properly relieve the fuel system pressure.
2. Disconnect the negative battery cable.
3. Drain the fuel tank by pumping or siphoning the fuel into a suitable container through the filler hose.
4. Remove the rear seat cushion and unplug the electrical connectors from the fuel pump.
5. Unfasten the four pump access cover screws and remove the cover.
6. If equipped, unplug the pump electrical connector located under the cover.
7. Unfasten the fuel line clip(s) and disconnect the line(s) from the pump.
8. Raise the rear of the car and support it with safety stands.
9. Loosen the fuel line hose and relief discharge vent hose clamps, then disconnect the hoses.
10. Disconnect the tank vent line.

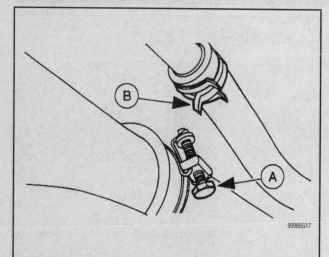

Fig. 57 Loosen the fuel line hose (A) and relief discharge vent hose (B) clamps—1997 models

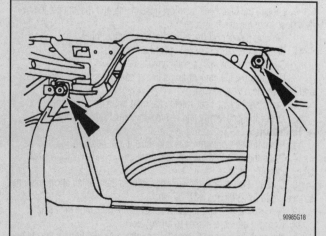

Fig. 58 Location of the fuel tank support strap retaining bolts (arrows)—1997–99 models

11. Remove the exhaust middle pipe heat shield.
12. Support the tank with a suitable jack.
13. Unfasten the fuel tank strap retaining bolts, then unclip the straps and remove them from the car.
14. Unfasten the tank heat shield attaching bolts from the tank.
15. Lower the jack slowly and remove the tank from the car.
To install:

➡ If necessary, install new fuel line clips.

16. Place the tank onto the jack and raise it into position.
17. Clip the tank straps into their mountings, then install and tighten the strap bolts to 27–38 ft. lbs. (37–52 Nm).
18. Remove the jack and install the exhaust middle pipe heat shield.
19. Connect the tank vent line.
20. Connect the fuel line hose and relief discharge vent hoses, then tighten the clamps.
21. Lower the car.
22. Connect the fuel line(s) to the pump and install the line retaining clip(s).
23. If equipped, attach the fuel pump electrical connection(s).
24. Install access cover, then tighten the retainers.
25. Attach the pump electrical connector(s).
26. Install the rear seat cushion.
27. Connect the negative battery cable.

1998–99 Models

▶ See Figure 58

1. Properly relieve the fuel system pressure.
2. Disconnect the negative battery cable.
3. Drain the fuel tank by pumping or siphoning the fuel into a suitable container through the filler hose.
4. Remove the rear seat cushion and unplug the electrical connectors from the fuel pump.
5. Unfasten the four pump access cover screws and remove the cover.
6. If equipped, unplug the pump electrical connector located under the cover.
7. Unfasten the fuel line clip(s) and disconnect the line(s) from the pump.
8. Raise the rear of the car and support it with safety stands.
9. Loosen the evaporative emission hose clamp, then disconnect the hose.
10. Loosen the fuel filler pipe and vent hose clamps and disconnect the hoses.
11. On sedan and wagon models, disconnect the fuel vapor control valve hoses.
12. Support the tank with a suitable jack.
13. Unfasten the fuel tank strap retaining bolts, then unclip the straps and remove them from the car.
14. Lower the jack slowly and remove the tank from the car.
To install:

➡ If necessary, install new fuel line clips.

15. Place the tank onto the jack and raise it into position.
16. Clip the tank straps into their mountings, then install and tighten the strap bolts to 32–44 ft. lbs. (44–60 Nm).
17. Remove the jack.
18. On sedan and wagon models, connect the fuel vapor control valve hoses.
19. Install the fuel filler pipe and vent hoses, the tighten the clamps.
20. Connect the evaporative emission hose and tighten the clamp.
21. Lower the car.
22. Connect the fuel line(s) to the pump and install the line retaining clip(s).
23. If equipped, attach the fuel pump electrical connection(s).
24. Install access cover, then tighten the retainers.
25. Attach the pump electrical connector(s).
26. Install the rear seat cushion.
27. Connect the negative battery cable.
28. Start the car and check for proper operation.

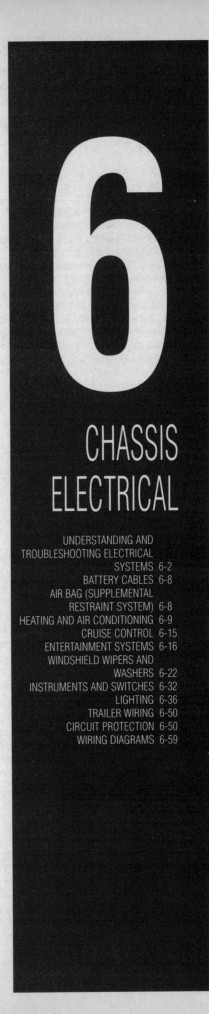

6

CHASSIS ELECTRICAL

UNDERSTANDING AND TROUBLESHOOTING ELECTRICAL SYSTEMS

Basic Electrical Theory

▶ See Figure 1

For any 12 volt, negative ground, electrical system to operate, the electricity must travel in a complete circuit. This simply means that current (power) from the positive terminal (+) of the battery must eventually return to the negative terminal (-) of the battery. Along the way, this current will travel through wires, fuses, switches and components. If, for any reason, the flow of current through the circuit is interrupted, the component fed by that circuit will cease to function properly.

Perhaps the easiest way to visualize a circuit is to think of connecting a light bulb (with two wires attached to it) to the battery—one wire attached to the negative (-) terminal of the battery and the other wire to the positive (+) terminal. With the two wires touching the battery terminals, the circuit would be complete and the light bulb would illuminate. Electricity would follow a path from the battery to the bulb and back to the battery. It's easy to see that with longer wires on our light bulb, it could be mounted anywhere. Further, one wire could be fitted with a switch so that the light could be turned on and off.

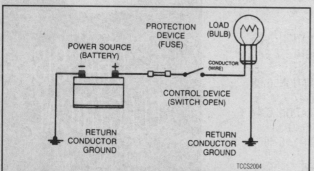

TCCS2004

Fig. 1 This example illustrates a simple circuit. When the switch is closed, power from the positive (+) battery terminal flows through the fuse and the switch, and then to the light bulb. The light illuminates and the circuit is completed through the ground wire back to the negative (-) battery terminal. In reality, the two ground points shown in the illustration are attached to the metal frame of the vehicle, which completes the circuit back to the battery

The normal automotive circuit differs from this simple example in two ways. First, instead of having a return wire from the bulb to the battery, the current travels through the frame of the vehicle. Since the negative (-) battery cable is attached to the frame (made of electrically conductive metal), the frame of the vehicle can serve as a ground wire to complete the circuit. Secondly, most automotive circuits contain multiple components which receive power from a single circuit. This lessens the amount of wire needed to power components on the vehicle.

HOW DOES ELECTRICITY WORK: THE WATER ANALOGY

Electricity is the flow of electrons—the subatomic particles that constitute the outer shell of an atom. Electrons spin in an orbit around the center core of an atom. The center core is comprised of protons (positive charge) and neutrons (neutral charge). Electrons have a negative charge and balance out the positive charge of the protons. When an outside force causes the number of electrons to unbalance the charge of the protons, the electrons will split off the atom and look for another atom to balance out. If this imbalance is kept up, electrons will continue to move and an electrical flow will exist.

Many people have been taught electrical theory using an analogy with water. In a comparison with water flowing through a pipe, the electrons would be the water and the wire is the pipe.

The flow of electricity can be measured much like the flow of water through a pipe. The unit of measurement used is amperes, frequently abbreviated as amps (a). You can compare amperage to the volume of water flowing through a pipe. When connected to a circuit, an ammeter will measure the actual amount of current flowing through the circuit. When relatively few electrons flow through a circuit, the amperage is low. When many electrons flow, the amperage is high.

Water pressure is measured in units such as pounds per square inch (psi); The electrical pressure is measured in units called volts (v). When a voltmeter is connected to a circuit, it is measuring the electrical pressure.

The actual flow of electricity depends not only on voltage and amperage, but also on the resistance of the circuit. The higher the resistance, the higher the force necessary to push the current through the circuit. The standard unit for measuring resistance is an ohm (omega). Resistance in a circuit varies depending on the amount and type of components used in the circuit. The main factors which determine resistance are:

• Material—some materials have more resistance than others. Those with high resistance are said to be insulators. Rubber materials (or rubber-like plastics) are some of the most common insulators used in vehicles as they have a very high resistance to electricity. Very low resistance materials are said to be conductors. Copper wire is among the best conductors. Silver is actually a superior conductor to copper and is used in some relay contacts, but its high cost prohibits its use as common wiring. Most automotive wiring is made of copper.

• Size—the larger the wire size being used, the less resistance the wire will have. This is why components which use large amounts of electricity usually have large wires supplying current to them.

• Length—for a given thickness of wire, the longer the wire, the greater the resistance. The shorter the wire, the less the resistance. When determining the proper wire for a circuit, both size and length must be considered to design a circuit that can handle the current needs of the component.

• Temperature—with many materials, the higher the temperature, the greater the resistance (positive temperature coefficient). Some materials exhibit the opposite trait of lower resistance with higher temperatures (negative temperature coefficient). These principles are used in many of the sensors on the engine.

OHM'S LAW

There is a direct relationship between current, voltage and resistance. The relationship between current, voltage and resistance can be summed up by a statement known as Ohm's law.

Voltage (E) is equal to amperage (I) times resistance (R): $E = I \times R$
Other forms of the formula are $R = E/I$ and $I = E/R$

In each of these formulas, E is the voltage in volts, I is the current in amps and R is the resistance in ohms. The basic point to remember is that as the resistance of a circuit goes up, the amount of current that flows in the circuit will go down, if voltage remains the same.

The amount of work that the electricity can perform is expressed as power. The unit of power is the watt (W). The relationship between power, voltage and current is expressed as:

Power (W) is equal to amperage (I) times voltage (E): $W = I \times E$

This is only true for direct current (DC) circuits; The alternating current formula is a tad different, but since the electrical circuits in most vehicles are DC type, we need not get into AC circuit theory.

Electrical Components

POWER SOURCE

Power is supplied to the vehicle by two devices: The battery and the alternator. The battery supplies electrical power during starting or during periods when the current demand of the vehicle's electrical system exceeds the output capacity of the alternator. The alternator supplies electrical current when the engine is running. Just not does the alternator supply the current needs of the vehicle, but it recharges the battery.

The Battery

In most modern vehicles, the battery is a lead/acid electrochemical device consisting of six 2 volt subsections (cells) connected in series, so that the unit is capable of producing approximately 12 volts of electrical pressure. Each subsection consists of a series of positive and negative plates held a short distance apart in a solution of sulfuric acid and water.

The two types of plates are of dissimilar metals. This sets up a chemical reaction, and it is this reaction which produces current flow from the battery when its positive and negative terminals are connected to an electrical load. The power removed from the battery is replaced by the alternator, restoring the battery to its original chemical state.

The Alternator

On some vehicles there isn't an alternator, but a generator. The difference is that an alternator supplies alternating current which is then changed to direct current for use on the vehicle, while a generator produces direct current. Alternators tend to be more efficient and that is why they are used.

Alternators and generators are devices that consist of coils of wires wound together making big electromagnets. One group of coils spins within another set and the interaction of the magnetic fields causes a current to flow. This current is then drawn off the coils and fed into the vehicles electrical system.

GROUND

Two types of grounds are used in automotive electric circuits. Direct ground components are grounded to the frame through their mounting points. All other components use some sort of ground wire which is attached to the frame or chassis of the vehicle. The electrical current runs through the chassis of the vehicle and returns to the battery through the ground (-) cable; if you look, you'll see that the battery ground cable connects between the battery and the frame or chassis of the vehicle.

➡It should be noted that a good percentage of electrical problems can be traced to bad grounds.

PROTECTIVE DEVICES

It is possible for large surges of current to pass through the electrical system of your vehicle. If this surge of current were to reach the load in the circuit, the surge could burn it out or severely damage it. It can also overload the wiring, causing the harness to get hot and melt the insulation. To prevent this, fuses, circuit breakers and/or fusible links are connected into the supply wires of the electrical system. These items are nothing more than a built-in weak spot in the system. When an abnormal amount of current flows through the system, these protective devices work as follows to protect the circuit:

• Fuse—when an excessive electrical current passes through a fuse, the fuse "blows" (the conductor melts) and opens the circuit, preventing the passage of current.

• Circuit Breaker—a circuit breaker is basically a self-repairing fuse. It will open the circuit in the same fashion as a fuse, but when the surge subsides, the circuit breaker can be reset and does not need replacement.

• Fusible Link—a fusible link (fuse link or main link) is a short length of special, high temperature insulated wire that acts as a fuse. When an excessive electrical current passes through a fusible link, the thin gauge wire inside the link melts, creating an intentional open to protect the circuit. To repair the circuit, the link must be replaced. Some newer type fusible links are housed in plug-in modules, which are simply replaced like a fuse, while older type fusible links must be cut and spliced if they melt. Since this link is very early in the electrical path, it's the first place to look if nothing on the vehicle works, yet the battery seems to be charged and is properly connected.

Always replace fuses, circuit breakers and fusible links with identically rated components. Under no circumstances should a component of higher or lower amperage rating be substituted.

SWITCHES & RELAYS

▶ See Figures 2 and 3

Switches are used in electrical circuits to control the passage of current. The most common use is to open and close circuits between the battery and the various electric devices in the system. Switches are rated according to the amount of amperage they can handle. If a sufficient amperage rated switch is not used in a circuit, the switch could overload and cause damage.

Some electrical components which require a large amount of current to operate use a special switch called a relay. Since these circuits carry a large amount of current, the thickness of the wire in the circuit is also greater. If this large wire were connected from the load to the control switch, the switch would have to carry the high amperage load and the fairing or dash

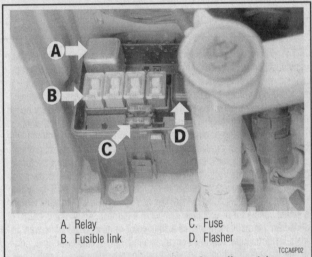

A. Relay   C. Fuse
B. Fusible link   D. Flasher

TCCA6P02

Fig. 2 The underhood fuse and relay panel usually contains fuses, relays, flashers and fusible links

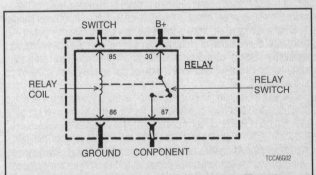

TCCA6G02

Fig. 3 Relays are composed of a coil and a switch. These two components are linked together so that when one operates, the other operates at the same time. The large wires in the circuit are connected from the battery to one side of the relay switch (B+) and from the opposite side of the relay switch to the load (component). Smaller wires are connected from the relay coil to the control switch for the circuit and from the opposite side of the relay coil to ground

would be twice as large to accommodate the increased size of the wiring harness. To prevent these problems, a relay is used.

Relays are composed of a coil and a set of contacts. When the coil has a current passed though it, a magnetic field is formed and this field causes the contacts to move together, completing the circuit. Most relays are normally open, preventing current from passing through the circuit, but they can take any electrical form depending on the job they are intended to do. Relays can be considered "remote control switches." They allow a smaller current to operate devices that require higher amperages. When a small current operates the coil, a larger current is allowed to pass by the contacts. Some common circuits which may use relays are the horn, headlights, starter, electric fuel pump and other high draw circuits.

LOAD

Every electrical circuit must include a "load" (something to use the electricity coming from the source). Without this load, the battery would attempt to deliver its entire power supply from one pole to another. This is called a "short circuit". All this electricity would take a short cut to ground and cause a great amount of damage to other components in the circuit by developing a tremendous amount of heat. This condition could develop sufficient heat to melt the insulation on all the surrounding wires and reduce a multiple wire cable to a lump of plastic and copper.

WIRING & HARNESSES

The average vehicle contains meters and meters of wiring, with hundreds of individual connections. To protect the many wires from damage and to keep them from becoming a confusing tangle, they are organized into bundles, enclosed in plastic or taped together and called wiring harnesses. Different harnesses serve different parts of the vehicle. Individual wires are color coded to help trace them through a harness where sections are hidden from view.

Automotive wiring or circuit conductors can be either single strand wire, multi-strand wire or printed circuitry. Single strand wire has a solid metal core and is usually used inside such components as alternators, motors, relays and other devices. Multi-strand wire has a core made of many small strands of wire twisted together into a single conductor. Most of the wiring in an automotive electrical system is made up of multi-strand wire, either as a single conductor or grouped together in a harness. All wiring is color coded on the insulator, either as a solid color or as a colored wire with an identification stripe. A printed circuit is a thin film of copper or other conductor that is printed on an insulator backing. Occasionally, a printed circuit is sandwiched between two sheets of plastic for more protection and flexibility. A complete printed circuit, consisting of conductors, insulating material and connectors for lamps or other components is called a printed circuit board. Printed circuitry is used in place of individual wires or harnesses in places where space is limited, such as behind instrument panels.

Since automotive electrical systems are very sensitive to changes in resistance, the selection of properly sized wires is critical when systems are repaired. A loose or corroded connection or a replacement wire that is too small for the circuit will add extra resistance and an additional voltage drop to the circuit.

The wire gauge number is an expression of the cross-section area of the conductor. Vehicles from countries that use the metric system will typically describe the wire size as its cross-sectional area in square millimeters. In this method, the larger the wire, the greater the number. Another common system for expressing wire size is the American Wire Gauge (AWG) system. As gauge number increases, area decreases and the wire becomes smaller. An 18 gauge wire is smaller than a 4 gauge wire. A wire with a higher gauge number will carry less current than a wire with a lower gauge number. Gauge wire size refers to the size of the strands of the conductor, not the size of the complete wire with insulator. It is possible, therefore, to have two wires of the same gauge with different diameters because one may have thicker insulation than the other.

It is essential to understand how a circuit works before trying to figure out why it doesn't. An electrical schematic shows the electrical current paths when a circuit is operating properly. Schematics break the entire electrical system down into individual circuits. In a schematic, usually no attempt is made to represent wiring and components as they physically appear on the vehicle; switches and other components are shown as simply as possible. Face views of harness connectors show the cavity or terminal locations in all multi-pin connectors to help locate test points.

CONNECTORS

♦ See Figures 4 and 5

Three types of connectors are commonly used in automotive applications—weatherproof, molded and hard shell.

• Weatherproof—these connectors are most commonly used where the connector is exposed to the elements. Terminals are protected against moisture and dirt by sealing rings which provide a weathertight seal. All repairs require the use of a special terminal and the tool required to service it. Unlike standard blade type terminals, these weatherproof terminals cannot be straightened once they are bent. Make certain that the connectors are properly seated and all of the sealing rings are in place when connecting leads.

• Molded—these connectors require complete replacement of the connector if found to be defective. This means splicing a new connector assembly into the harness. All splices should be soldered to insure proper

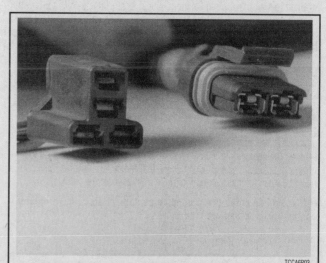

TCCA6P03

Fig. 4 Hard shell (left) and weatherproof (right) connectors have replaceable terminals

TCCA6P04

Fig. 5 Weatherproof connectors are most commonly used in the engine compartment or where the connector is exposed to the elements

contact. Use care when probing the connections or replacing terminals in them, as it is possible to create a short circuit between opposite terminals. If this happens to the wrong terminal pair, it is possible to damage certain components. Always use jumper wires between connectors for circuit checking and NEVER probe through weatherproof seals.

• Hard Shell—unlike molded connectors, the terminal contacts in hard-shell connectors can be replaced. Replacement usually involves the use of a special terminal removal tool that depresses the locking tangs (barbs) on the connector terminal and allows the connector to be removed from the rear of the shell. The connector shell should be replaced if it shows any evidence of burning, melting, cracks, or breaks. Replace individual terminals that are burnt, corroded, distorted or loose.

Test Equipment

Pinpointing the exact cause of trouble in an electrical circuit is most times accomplished by the use of special test equipment. The following describes different types of commonly used test equipment and briefly explains how to use them in diagnosis. In addition to the information covered below, the tool manufacturer's instructions booklet (provided with the tester) should be read and clearly understood before attempting any test procedures.

JUMPER WIRES

✳✳ CAUTION

Never use jumper wires made from a thinner gauge wire than the circuit being tested. If the jumper wire is of too small a gauge, it may overheat and possibly melt. Never use jumpers to bypass high resistance loads in a circuit. Bypassing resistance's, in effect, creates a short circuit. This may, in turn, cause damage and fire. Jumper wires should only be used to bypass lengths of wire or to simulate switches.

Jumper wires are simple, yet extremely valuable, pieces of test equipment. They are basically test wires which are used to bypass sections of a circuit. Although jumper wires can be purchased, they are usually fabricated from lengths of standard automotive wire and whatever type of connector (alligator clip, spade connector or pin connector) that is required for the particular application being tested. In cramped, hard-to-reach areas, it is advisable to have insulated boots over the jumper wire terminals in order to prevent accidental grounding. It is also advisable to include a standard automotive fuse in any jumper wire. This is commonly referred to as a "fused jumper". By inserting an in-line fuse holder between a set of test leads, a fused jumper wire can be used for bypassing open circuits. Use a 5 amp fuse to provide protection against voltage spikes.

Jumper wires are used primarily to locate open electrical circuits, on either the ground (-) side of the circuit or on the power (+) side. If an electrical component fails to operate, connect the jumper wire between the component and a good ground. If the component operates only with the jumper installed, the ground circuit is open. If the ground circuit is good, but the component does not operate, the circuit between the power feed and component may be open. By moving the jumper wire successively back from the component toward the power source, you can isolate the area of the circuit where the open is located. When the component stops functioning, or the power is cut off, the open is in the segment of wire between the jumper and the point previously tested.

You can sometimes connect the jumper wire directly from the battery to the "hot" terminal of the component, but first make sure the component uses 12 volts in operation. Some electrical components, such as fuel injectors or sensors, are designed to operate on about 4 to 5 volts, and running 12 volts directly to these components will cause damage.

TEST LIGHTS

▶ See Figure 6

The test light is used to check circuits and components while electrical current is flowing through them. It is used for voltage and ground tests. To

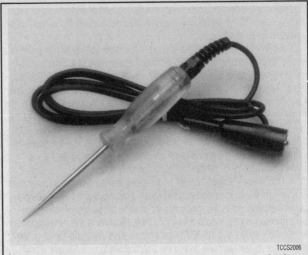

Fig. 6 A 12 volt test light is used to detect the presence of voltage in a circuit

TCCS2006

use a 12 volt test light, connect the ground clip to a good ground and probe wherever necessary with the pick. The test light will illuminate when voltage is detected. This does not necessarily mean that 12 volts (or any particular amount of voltage) is present; it only means that some voltage is present. It is advisable before using the test light to touch its ground clip and probe across the battery posts or terminals to make sure the light is operating properly.

✳✳ WARNING

Do not use a test light to probe electronic ignition, spark plug or coil wires. Never use a pick-type test light to probe wiring on computer controlled systems unless specifically instructed to do so. Any wire insulation that is pierced by the test light probe should be taped and sealed with silicone after testing.

Like the jumper wire, the 12 volt test light is used to isolate opens in circuits. But, whereas the jumper wire is used to bypass the open to operate the load, the 12 volt test light is used to locate the presence of voltage in a circuit. If the test light illuminates, there is power up to that point in the circuit; if the test light does not illuminate, there is an open circuit (no power). Move the test light in successive steps back toward the power source until the light in the handle illuminates. The open is between the probe and a point which was previously probed.

The self-powered test light is similar in design to the 12 volt test light, but contains a 1.5 volt penlight battery in the handle. It is most often used in place of a multimeter to check for open or short circuits when power is isolated from the circuit (continuity test).

The battery in a self-powered test light does not provide much current. A weak battery may not provide enough power to illuminate the test light even when a complete circuit is made (especially if there is high resistance in the circuit). Always make sure that the test battery is strong. To check the battery, briefly touch the ground clip to the probe; if the light glows brightly, the battery is strong enough for testing.

➡**A self-powered test light should not be used on any computer controlled system or component. The small amount of electricity transmitted by the test light is enough to damage many electronic automotive components.**

MULTIMETERS

Multimeters are an extremely useful tool for troubleshooting electrical problems. They can be purchased in either analog or digital form and have a price range to suit any budget. A multimeter is a voltmeter, ammeter and ohmmeter (along with other features) combined into one instrument. It is often used when testing solid state circuits because of its high input impedance (usually 10 megaohms or more). A brief description of the multimeter main test functions follows:

- Voltmeter—the voltmeter is used to measure voltage at any point in a circuit, or to measure the voltage drop across any part of a circuit. Voltmeters usually have various scales and a selector switch to allow the reading of different voltage ranges. The voltmeter has a positive and a negative lead. To avoid damage to the meter, always connect the negative lead to the negative (-) side of the circuit (to ground or nearest the ground side of the circuit) and connect the positive lead to the positive (+) side of the circuit (to the power source or the nearest power source). Note that the negative voltmeter lead will always be black and that the positive voltmeter will always be some color other than black (usually red).

- Ohmmeter—the ohmmeter is designed to read resistance (measured in ohms) in a circuit or component. Most ohmmeters will have a selector switch which permits the measurement of different ranges of resistance (usually the selector switch allows the multiplication of the meter reading by 10, 100, 1,000 and 10,000). Some ohmmeters are "auto-ranging" which means the meter itself will determine which scale to use. Since the meters are powered by an internal battery, the ohmmeter can be used like a self-powered test light. When the ohmmeter is connected, current from the ohmmeter flows through the circuit or component being tested. Since the ohmmeter's internal resistance and voltage are known values, the amount of current flow through the meter depends on the resistance of the circuit or component being tested. The ohmmeter can also be used to perform a continuity test for suspected open circuits. In using the meter for making continuity checks, do not be concerned with the actual resistance readings. Zero resistance, or any ohm reading, indicates continuity in the circuit. Infinite resistance indicates an opening in the circuit. A high resistance reading where there should be none indicates a problem in the circuit. Checks for short circuits are made in the same manner as checks for open circuits, except that the circuit must be isolated from both power and normal ground. Infinite resistance indicates no continuity, while zero resistance indicates a dead short.

✳✳ WARNING

Never use an ohmmeter to check the resistance of a component or wire while there is voltage applied to the circuit.

- Ammeter—an ammeter measures the amount of current flowing through a circuit in units called amperes or amps. At normal operating voltage, most circuits have a characteristic amount of amperes, called "current draw" which can be measured using an ammeter. By referring to a specified current draw rating, then measuring the amperes and comparing the two values, one can determine what is happening within the circuit to aid in diagnosis. An open circuit, for example, will not allow any current to flow, so the ammeter reading will be zero. A damaged component or circuit will have an increased current draw, so the reading will be high. The ammeter is always connected in series with the circuit being tested. All of the current that normally flows through the circuit must also flow through the ammeter; if there is any other path for the current to follow, the ammeter reading will not be accurate. The ammeter itself has very little resistance to current flow and, therefore, will not affect the circuit, but it will measure current draw only when the circuit is closed and electricity is flowing. Excessive current draw can blow fuses and drain the battery, while a reduced current draw can cause motors to run slowly, lights to dim and other components to not operate properly.

Troubleshooting Electrical Systems

When diagnosing a specific problem, organized troubleshooting is a must. The complexity of a modern automotive vehicle demands that you approach any problem in a logical, organized manner. There are certain troubleshooting techniques, however, which are standard:

- Establish when the problem occurs. Does the problem appear only under certain conditions? Were there any noises, odors or other unusual symptoms? Isolate the problem area. To do this, make some simple tests

and observations, then eliminate the systems that are working properly. Check for obvious problems, such as broken wires and loose or dirty connections. Always check the obvious before assuming something complicated is the cause.

- Test for problems systematically to determine the cause once the problem area is isolated. Are all the components functioning properly? Is there power going to electrical switches and motors. Performing careful, systematic checks will often turn up most causes on the first inspection, without wasting time checking components that have little or no relationship to the problem.

- Test all repairs after the work is done to make sure that the problem is fixed. Some causes can be traced to more than one component, so a careful verification of repair work is important in order to pick up additional malfunctions that may cause a problem to reappear or a different problem to arise. A blown fuse, for example, is a simple problem that may require more than another fuse to repair. If you don't look for a problem that caused a fuse to blow, a shorted wire (for example) may go undetected.

Experience has shown that most problems tend to be the result of a fairly simple and obvious cause, such as loose or corroded connectors, bad grounds or damaged wire insulation which causes a short. This makes careful visual inspection of components during testing essential to quick and accurate troubleshooting.

Testing

OPEN CIRCUITS

▸ **See Figure 7**

This test already assumes the existence of an open in the circuit and it is used to help locate the open portion.

1. Isolate the circuit from power and ground.
2. Connect the self-powered test light or ohmmeter ground clip to the ground side of the circuit and probe sections of the circuit sequentially.
3. If the light is out or there is infinite resistance, the open is between the probe and the circuit ground.
4. If the light is on or the meter shows continuity, the open is between the probe and the end of the circuit toward the power source.

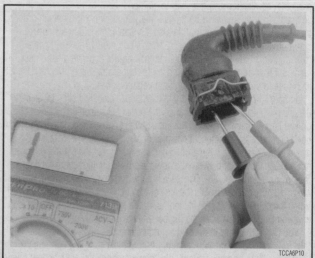

TCCA6P10

Fig. 7 The infinite reading on this multimeter (1 .) indicates that the circuit is open

SHORT CIRCUITS

➡**Never use a self-powered test light to perform checks for opens or shorts when power is applied to the circuit under test. The test light can be damaged by outside power.**

1. Isolate the circuit from power and ground.
2. Connect the self-powered test light or ohmmeter ground clip to a good ground and probe any easy-to-reach point in the circuit.
3. If the light comes on or there is continuity, there is a short somewhere in the circuit.
4. To isolate the short, probe a test point at either end of the isolated circuit (the light should be on or the meter should indicate continuity).
5. Leave the test light probe engaged and sequentially open connectors or switches, remove parts, etc. until the light goes out or continuity is broken.
6. When the light goes out, the short is between the last two circuit components which were opened.

VOLTAGE

This test determines voltage available from the battery and should be the first step in any electrical troubleshooting procedure after visual inspection. Many electrical problems, especially on computer controlled systems, can be caused by a low state of charge in the battery. Excessive corrosion at the battery cable terminals can cause poor contact that will prevent proper charging and full battery current flow.
1. Set the voltmeter selector switch to the 20V position.
2. Connect the multimeter negative lead to the battery's negative (-) post or terminal and the positive lead to the battery's positive (+) post or terminal.
3. Turn the ignition switch **ON** to provide a load.
4. A well charged battery should register over 12 volts. If the meter reads below 11.5 volts, the battery power may be insufficient to operate the electrical system properly.

VOLTAGE DROP

▶ See Figure 8

When current flows through a load, the voltage beyond the load drops. This voltage drop is due to the resistance created by the load and also by small resistance's created by corrosion at the connectors and damaged insulation on the wires. The maximum allowable voltage drop under load is critical, especially if there is more than one load in the circuit, since all voltage drops are cumulative.
1. Set the voltmeter selector switch to the 20 volt position.
2. Connect the multimeter negative lead to a good ground.
3. Operate the circuit and check the voltage prior to the first component (load).
4. There should be little or no voltage drop in the circuit prior to the first component. If a voltage drop exists, the wire or connectors in the circuit are suspect.

5. While operating the first component in the circuit, probe the ground side of the component with the positive meter lead and observe the voltage readings. A small voltage drop should be noticed. This voltage drop is caused by the resistance of the component.
6. Repeat the test for each component (load) down the circuit.
7. If a large voltage drop is noticed, the preceding component, wire or connector is suspect.

RESISTANCE

▶ See Figures 9 and 10

❋❋ WARNING

Never use an ohmmeter with power applied to the circuit. The ohmmeter is designed to operate on its own power supply. The normal 12 volt electrical system voltage could damage the meter!

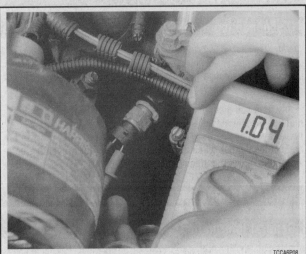

Fig. 9 Checking the resistance of a coolant temperature sensor with an ohmmeter. Reading is 1.04 kilohms

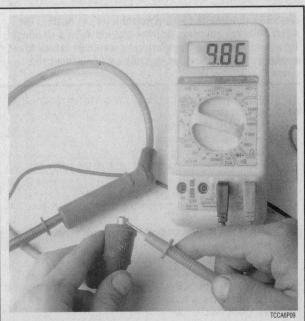

Fig. 10 Spark plug wires can be checked for excessive resistance using an ohmmeter

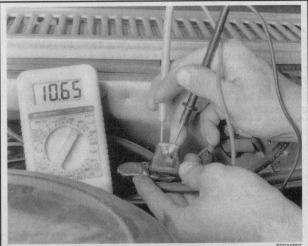

Fig. 8 This voltage drop test revealed high resistance (low voltage) in the circuit

1. Isolate the circuit from the vehicle's power source.
2. Ensure that the ignition key is **OFF** when disconnecting any components or the battery.
3. Where necessary, also isolate at least one side of the circuit to be checked, in order to avoid reading parallel resistance's. Parallel circuit resistance's will always give a lower reading than the actual resistance of either of the branches.
4. Connect the meter leads to both sides of the circuit (wire or component) and read the actual measured ohms on the meter scale. Make sure the selector switch is set to the proper ohm scale for the circuit being tested, to avoid misreading the ohmmeter test value.

Wire and Connector Repair

Almost anyone can replace damaged wires, as long as the proper tools and parts are available. Wire and terminals are available to fit almost any need. Even the specialized weatherproof, molded and hard shell connectors are now available from aftermarket suppliers.

Be sure the ends of all the wires are fitted with the proper terminal hardware and connectors. Wrapping a wire around a stud is never a permanent solution and will only cause trouble later. Replace wires one at a time to avoid confusion. Always route wires exactly the same as the factory.

➡**If connector repair is necessary, only attempt it if you have the proper tools. Weatherproof and hard shell connectors require special tools to release the pins inside the connector. Attempting to repair these connectors with conventional hand tools will damage them.**

BATTERY CABLES

Disconnecting the Cables

When working on any electrical component on the vehicle, it is always a good idea to disconnect the negative (-) battery cable. This will prevent potential damage to many sensitive electrical components such as the Engine Control Module (ECM), radio, alternator, etc.

➡**Any time you disengage the battery cables, it is recommended that you disconnect the negative (-) battery cable first. This will prevent your accidentally grounding the positive (+) terminal to the body of the vehicle when disconnecting it, thereby preventing damage to the above mentioned components.**

Before you disconnect the cable(s), first turn the ignition to the **OFF** position. This will prevent a draw on the battery which could cause arcing (electricity trying to ground itself to the body of a vehicle, just like a spark plug jumping the gap) and, of course, damaging some components such as the alternator diodes.

When the battery cable(s) are reconnected (negative cable last), be sure to check that your lights, windshield wipers and other electrically operated safety components are all working correctly. If your vehicle contains an Electronically Tuned Radio (ETR), don't forget to also reset your radio stations. Ditto for the clock.

AIR BAG (SUPPLEMENTAL RESTRAINT SYSTEM)

General Information

The Supplemental Restraint System (SRS) is designed to work in conjunction with the standard three-point safety belts to reduce injury in a head-on collision.

✳✳ WARNING

The SRS can actually cause physical injury or death if the safety belts are not used, or if the manufacturer's warnings are not followed. The manufacturer's warnings can be found in your owner's manual, or, in some cases, on your sun visors.

Depending on your vehicle, the SRS may be comprised of some or all of the following components:
- Driver's side air bag module
- Passenger's side air bag module
- Air bag diagnostic monitor computer
- Left and right-hand radiator primary crash air bag sensor and bracket
- Center cowl safing rear air bag sensor and bracket
- Left-hand kick panel safing rear air bag sensor and brackets
- Air bag warning indicator
- Tone generator (internal to the air bag diagnostic monitor)
- Electrical wiring
- Air bag Electronic Crash Sensor (ECS)

The sensors in the car are designed to detect a severe frontal impact. When at least one of the primary crash sensors and the center cowl safing rear air bag sensor close at the same time, electric current flows to the inflator and ignites the chemicals.

The chemicals burn rapidly in the metal container. This burning produces nitrogen gas and small amounts of dust, both the gas and dust are cooled and filtered during the air bag(s) inflation.

The air bag(s) split the trim covers open while inflating. The air bag(s) then rapidly unfold and inflate in front of the driver or passenger.

After the air bag(s) have inflated, the gas escapes through holes in the bag(s) and the they will deflate.

SERVICE PRECAUTIONS

✳✳ CAUTION

Some vehicles are equipped with an air bag system, also known as the Supplemental Inflatable Restraint (SIR) or Supplemental Restraint System (SRS). The system must be disabled before performing service on or around system components, steering column, instrument panel components, wiring and sensors. Failure to follow safety and disabling procedures could result in accidental air bag deployment, possible personal injury and unnecessary system repairs.

Several precautions must be observed when handling the inflator module to avoid accidental deployment and possible personal injury:
- Never carry the inflator module by the wires or connector on the underside of the module
- When carrying a live inflator module, hold securely with both hands, and ensure that the bag and trim cover are pointed away
- Place the inflator module on a bench or other surface with the bag and trim cover facing up
- With the inflator module on the bench, never place anything on or close to the module which may be thrown in the event of an accidental deployment

DISARMING THE SYSTEM

1994–99 Models

> ※※ **CAUTION**
>
> **The Supplemental Restraint System (SRS) must be disarmed before performing service around SRS components or SRS wiring. Failure to do so may cause accidental deployment of the air bag, resulting in unnecessary SRS repairs and/or personal injury.**

1. Disconnect both battery cables, negative cable first.
2. Wait at least 1 minute. This allows time for the backup power supply to deplete its stored energy.
3. Remove the driver's side air bag module and then the passenger side if required.
4. Use caution when carrying live air bags. Always place the air bag with the cover up.

> ※※ **CAUTION**
>
> **When carrying a live air bag, make sure the bag and trim cover are pointed away from the body. In the unlikely event of an acci-**

dental deployment, the bag will then deploy with minimal chance of injury. When placing a live air bag on a bench or other surface, always face the bag and trim cover up, away from the surface. This will reduce the motion of the module if it is accidentally deployed.

5. If the battery needs to be reconnected while one or both of the air bags are removed from the system, install Air Bag Simulator 105-00010 or equivalent, to the driver's side and/or passenger side air bag harness connectors as required. Before removing either air bag simulator, disconnect both battery cables and wait at least 1 minute before continuing.

ARMING THE SYSTEM

1. Once service is completed and the air bag modules are back in place, connect the negative battery cable and prove out the air bag system by turning the ignition key to the **RUN** position and visually monitoring the air bag indicator lamp in the instrument cluster. The indicator lamp should illuminate for approximately 6 seconds and then turn OFF. if the indicator lamp does not illuminate, stays ON, or flashes at any time, a fault has been detected by the air bag diagnostic monitor requiring immediate attention.

HEATING AND AIR CONDITIONING

Blower Motor

REMOVAL & INSTALLATION

1.8L and 1.9L Engines

▶ See Figures 11, 12, 13, 14 and 15

1. Disconnect the negative battery cable.
2. Remove the trim panel cover below the glove compartment.
3. Remove the wiring bracket and retaining bolt.
4. Unplug the blower motor electrical connector.
5. Unfasten the three blower motor retaining bolts and remove the blower motor assembly from the evaporator housing.
6. If necessary, disengage the blower wheel retaining clip and remove the blower wheel from the blower motor.

To install:

7. If removed, assemble the blower wheel to the motor shaft and install the retaining clip.
8. Install the blower motor and wheel assembly to the evaporator housing and secure with the three retaining bolts.
9. Attach the blower motor electrical connector.
10. Install the wiring bracket and retaining bolt.
11. Install the trim panel below the glove compartment.
12. Connect the negative battery cable.
13. Check for proper blower motor operation.

2.0L Engines

▶ See Figure 16

1. Disconnect the negative battery cable.
2. Unfasten the blower motor retaining screws.

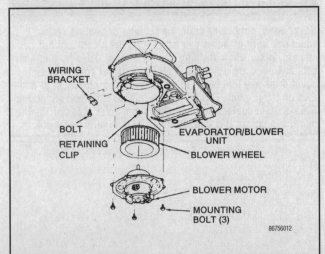

Fig. 11 Exploded view of the blower motor and wheel assembly—1.8L and 1.9L engines

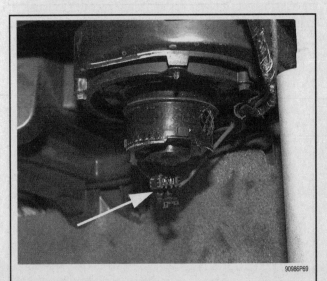

Fig. 12 Unplug the blower motor electrical connector (arrow)

Fig. 13 Location of the blower motor retaining bolts

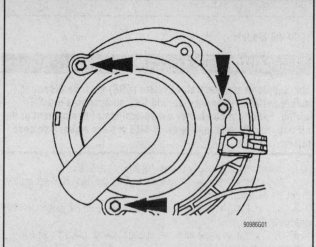

Fig. 16 Location of the blower motor retaining screws—2.0L engines

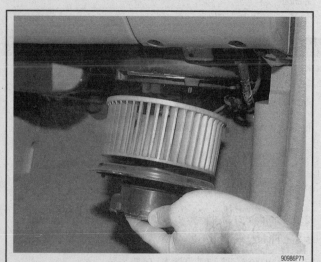

Fig. 14 Unfasten the blower motor retaining bolts and remove the blower motor

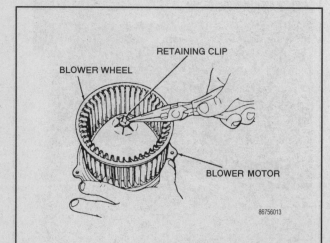

Fig. 15 If necessary, you can remove the blower wheel retaining clip with pliers

3. Unplug the blower motor electrical connector.
4. Remove the blower motor assembly from the vehicle.
5. If necessary, unfasten the blower wheel retainer and remove the blower wheel from the blower motor.

To install:

6. If removed, assemble the blower wheel to the motor shaft and install the retainer.
7. Install the blower motor and wheel assembly in its housing and secure with the three retaining screws.
8. Attach the blower motor electrical connector.
9. Connect the negative battery cable.
10. Check for proper blower motor operation.

Heater Core

REMOVAL & INSTALLATION

1.8L and 1.9L Engines

▶ See Figure 17

☀ CAUTION

Never open, service or drain the radiator or cooling system when hot; serious burns can occur from the steam and hot coolant. Also, when draining engine coolant, keep in mind that cats and dogs are attracted to ethylene glycol antifreeze and could drink any that is left in an uncovered container or in puddles on the ground. This will prove fatal in sufficient quantities. Always drain coolant into a sealable container. Coolant should be reused unless it is contaminated or is several years old.

1. Disconnect the negative battery cable. If equipped, disable the SRS system.
2. Drain the cooling system.
3. Disconnect the heater hoses at the firewall.
4. Remove the instrument panel.
5. Disconnect the mode selector and temperature control cables from the cams and retaining clips.
6. Remove the necessary defroster duct screws and loosen the capscrew that secures the heater-to-blower clamp.
7. Remove the three heater unit mounting nuts and disconnect the antenna lead from the retaining clip.
8. Remove the heater unit.

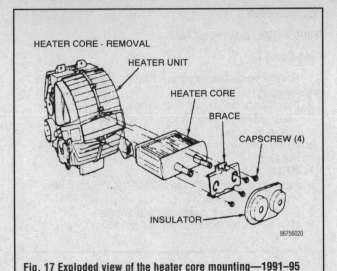

Fig. 17 Exploded view of the heater core mounting—1991–95 models

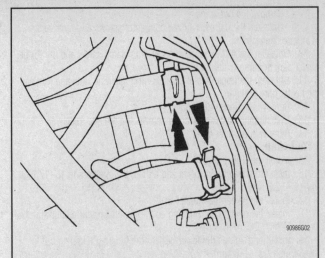

Fig. 18 Unfasten the clamps and disconnect the hoses from the heater core at the firewall—2.0L engines

9. Remove the insulator and the four brace capscrews.
10. Remove the brace.
11. Remove the heater core from the heater unit.

To install:

12. Install the heater core into the heater unit.
13. Install the brace.
14. Install the brace capscrews and the insulator.
15. Place the heater unit into position, then attach the defroster and floor ducting.
16. Install the heater unit mounting nuts.
17. Tighten the heater-to-blower clamp capscrew and install the defroster duct screws.
18. Connect the antenna lead to the retaining clip.
19. Install the instrument panel.
20. Connect and adjust the mode selector and temperature control cables.
21. Connect the heater hoses at the firewall.
22. Fill the cooling system and connect the negative battery cable.
23. Start the engine and check for leaks.
24. Check the coolant level and fill as necessary.

2.0L Engines

▶ See Figures 18, 19 and 20

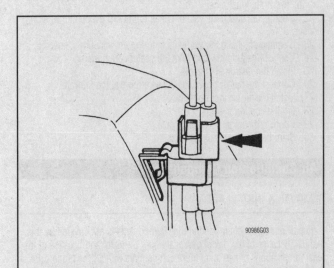

Fig. 19 If equipped, unplug the vacuum control motor's vacuum connector—2.0L engines

❄ CAUTION

Never open, service or drain the radiator or cooling system when hot; serious burns can occur from the steam and hot coolant. Also, when draining engine coolant, keep in mind that cats and dogs are attracted to ethylene glycol antifreeze and could drink any that is left in an uncovered container or in puddles on the ground. This will prove fatal in sufficient quantities. Always drain coolant into a sealable container. Coolant should be reused unless it is contaminated or is several years old.

1. Disconnect the negative battery cable.
2. Drain the cooling system.
3. Remove the air cleaner outlet tube.
4. Disconnect the heater hoses from the heater core at the firewall.
5. Remove the instrument panel.
6. Disconnect the antenna lead from the heater core housing.
7. If equipped, unplug the vacuum control motor vacuum connector.
8. If equipped, unplug the vacuum lines from the A/C evaporator housing retainer.
9. Remove the windshield defroster nozzle connectors as follows:

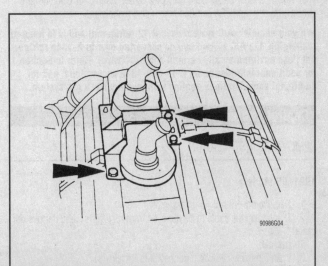

Fig. 20 Location of the heater core cover retaining screws—2.0L engines

a. Remove the pushpins.

b. Unfasten the defroster nozzle connector screws and remove the nozzle connectors.

10. Unfasten the A/C evaporator outlet duct clamp screw and the lower heater core housing retaining nut.

11. Unfasten the upper heater core housing retaining nuts and remove the heater core housing.

12. Remove the heater dash panel seal.

13. Unfasten the heater core cover screws and remove the cover.

14. Remove the heater core.

To install:

15. Install the heater core.

16. Install the heater core cover and tighten the retainers to 15–17 inch lbs. (1.7–2.0 Nm).

17. Install the heater dash panel seal.

18. Install the heater core housing and tighten the upper retaining nuts to 38–54 inch lbs. (4–6 Nm).

19. Install and tighten the lower heater core housing retaining nut to 38–54 inch lbs. (4–6 Nm).

20. Install and tighten the A/C evaporator outlet duct clamp screw.

21. Install the windshield defroster nozzle connectors as follows:

a. Install the nozzle connectors and tighten the screws.

b. Install the pushpins.

22. If equipped, attach the vacuum lines to the A/C evaporator housing retainer.

23. If equipped, attach the vacuum control motor vacuum connector.

24. Connect the antenna lead from the heater core housing.

25. Install the instrument panel.

26. Connect the heater hoses to the heater core at the firewall.

27. Install the air cleaner outlet tube.

28. Fill the cooling system.

29. Connect the negative battery cable.

30. Start the car and check for leaks.

Air Conditioning Components

REMOVAL & INSTALLATION

Repair or service of air conditioning components is not covered by this manual, because of the risk of personal injury or death, and because of the legal ramifications of servicing these components without the proper EPA certification and experience. Cost, personal injury or death, environmental damage, and legal considerations (such as the fact that it is a federal crime to vent refrigerant into the atmosphere), dictate that the A/C components on your vehicle should be serviced only by a Motor Vehicle Air Conditioning (MVAC) trained, and EPA certified automotive technician.

➡**If your vehicle's A/C system uses R-12 refrigerant and is in need of recharging, the A/C system can be converted over to R-134a refrigerant (less environmentally harmful and expensive). Refer to Section 1 for additional information on R-12 to R-134a conversions, and for additional considerations dealing with your vehicle's A/C system.**

Control Cables

REMOVAL & INSTALLATION

1991–96 Models

1. Remove the control panel assembly.

2. Disconnect the cable to be removed from its lever(s), and remove the cable.

To install:

3. Install the new cable and connect it to its lever(s).

4. Adjust the cable.

5. Install the control panel assembly.

1997–99 Models

TEMPERATURE CONTROL CABLE

▶ **See Figure 21**

1. Move the temperature control switch to the COLD position on the control assembly.

2. Unlock the cable by pulling down on the tab.

3. Disconnect the cable while holding the tab down.

4. Remove the control panel.

5. Disconnect the cable from the lever and remove it from behind the instrument panel.

To install:

6. Place the cable into position and connect it to the control lever.

7. Install the control panel.

8. Connect the cable and make sure the tab engages.

9. Make sure the temperature control switch functions properly.

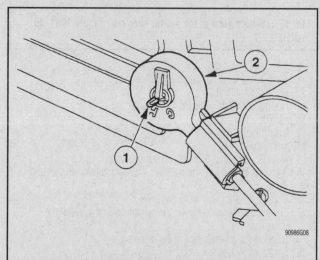

Fig. 21 Unlock the cable by pulling down on the tab (1) and disconnect the temperature cable (2)—1997–99 models

ADJUSTMENT

1991–96 Models

TEMPERATURE CONTROL

▶ **See Figure 22**

1. Move the temperature control lever to the COLD position on the control assembly.

2. To secure the cam in the proper position, insert cable locating key PNE7GH-18C408-A, or equivalent, through the cam key slot and into the heater case key boss opening.

3. Disconnect the cable from the retaining clip next to the temperature control cam.

➡**The temperature control cam is located on the left side of the heater unit.**

4. Connect the cable to the retaining clip and remove the cable locating key.

5. Make sure the temperature control lever moves its full stroke.

MODE SELECTOR

▶ **See Figure 23**

1. Move the mode selector lever to the DEFROST position on the control assembly.

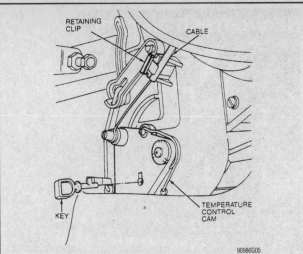

Fig. 22 Insert a cable locating key through the temperature control cam slot to hold the cam in position—1991–96 models

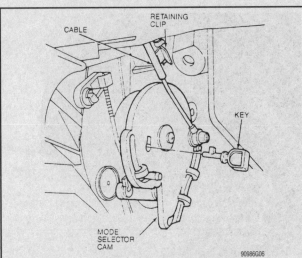

Fig. 23 Insert a cable locating key through the mode selector cam slot to secure the cam in position—1991–96 models

2. Insert cable locating key PNE7GH-18C408-A or equivalent, through the mode cam key slot and heater case key boss opening, to secure the cam in the proper position.

3. Remove the trim panel below the glove compartment, if equipped.

4. Disconnect the cable from the retaining clip next to the mode selector cam.

➡The mode selector cam is located on the right side of the heater unit.

5. Make sure the mode selector lever is in the DEFROST position.

6. Connect the cable straight to the retaining clip.

➡Do not exert any force on the cam during cable installation.

7. Remove the cable locating key.
8. Install the trim panel, if equipped.
9. Make sure the mode selector lever moves its full stroke.

➡If after performing this adjustment, air bleeds through the panel vents when in the FLOOR, MIX or DEFROST position, lengthen the adjustment rod 1–2 turns.

RECIRC/FRESH AIR SELECTOR

▸ **See Figure 24**

1. Move the control assembly's recirc/fresh air lever to the RECIRC/FRESH position on 1991–93 models, and to the DEFROST position on 1994–96 models.

2. Remove the glove compartment.

3. Insert cable locating key PNE7GH-18C408-A, or equivalent, through the fresh air door cam key slot and recirc door key boss opening to secure the cam in the proper position.

4. Disconnect the cable from the retaining clip next to the recirc/fresh air cam.

5. Connect the cable to the retaining clip and remove the cable locating key.

6. Install the glove compartment.

7. Make sure the recirc/fresh air lever moves its full stroke.

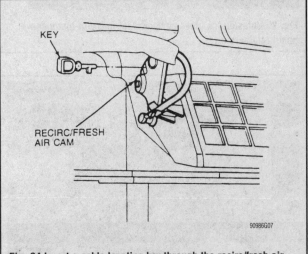

Fig. 24 Insert a cable locating key through the recirc/fresh air cam slot to secure the cam in position—1991–96 models

Control Panel

REMOVAL & INSTALLATION

1991–96 Models

▸ **See Figures 25 thru 32**

1. Unfasten the glove compartment hinge-to-instrument panel retainers and remove the glove compartment.

2. If equipped, unplug the vacuum hose from the vacuum control motor.

3. Disconnect the cable from the mode selector cam, and the retaining clip.

4. Disconnect the cable from the recirc/fresh air cam, and the cable clip.

5. Disconnect the cable from the temperature control cam and the cable clip.

6. Remove the instrument finish panel insert.

7. Unfasten the four control panel retaining screws.

8. Slide the control panel forward until you can gain access to the rear of the panel.

9. Unplug the blower motor switch and illumination lamp electrical connections.

10. Remove the control panel assembly.

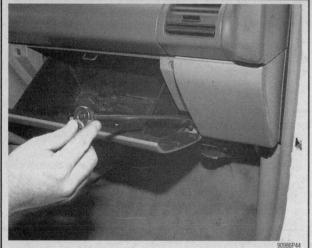

Fig. 25 Unfasten the glove compartment hinge-to-instrument panel retainers . . .

Fig. 26 . . . and remove the glove compartment

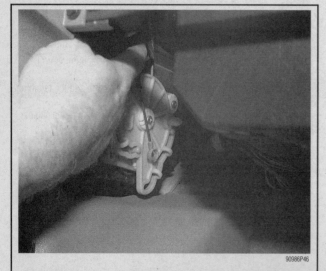

Fig. 27 Disconnect the cable from the mode selector cam

Fig. 28 Disconnect the cable from the recirc/fresh air cam

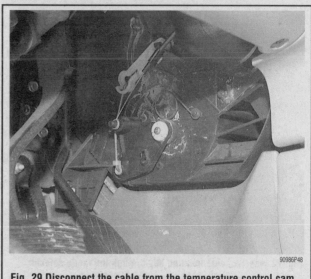

Fig. 29 Disconnect the cable from the temperature control cam

Fig. 30 Remove the instrument finish panel insert to gain access to the control panel retaining screws

Fig. 31 Unfasten the control panel retainers . . .

Fig. 32 Slide the control panel out and unplug all electrical connections from the rear of the panel

To install:
11. Route each control cable to its appropriate cam.
12. Connect the vacuum hose to the vacuum control motor.
13. Attach the blower motor switch and illumination lamp electrical connections.

14. Place the control panel into position and tighten its retaining screws.
15. Install the instrument finish panel insert.
16. Adjust the control cables.
17. Install the glove box and tighten its hinge-to-instrument panel retainers.

1997–99 Models

▶ **See Figure 33**

You will need radio removing tool T87P-19061-A or its equivalent to perform this procedure.
1. Disconnect the negative battery cable.
2. Place the temperature control switch to the COLD position.
3. Unlock the temperature cable by pulling down on the tab.
4. Disconnect the cable while holding the tab down.
5. Using the radio removal tool, pull the control panel from the instrument panel.
6. Unplug the vacuum harness, antenna lead and the electrical connections from the rear of the control panel.
7. Remove the control panel.
To install:
8. Attach the vacuum harness, antenna lead and the electrical connections to the rear of the control panel.
9. Install the control panel into the instrument panel.
10. Connect the temperature control cable.
11. Connect the negative battery cable.

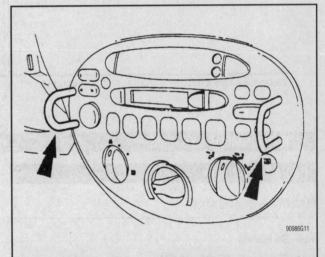

Fig. 33 Use radio removal tool T87P-19061-A or its equivalent to pull the control panel from the instrument panel

CRUISE CONTROL

The cruise control system maintains the vehicle road speed selected by the driver. When the system is turned on and the road speed is above 30 mph (48 km/h), the speed control amplifier energizes the vacuum and vent valves in the speed control servo. The vacuum valve passes vacuum to the speed control servo, where it is used to move the throttle linkage. The vent valve controls the amount of vacuum applied to the servo.

The control amplifier is operated by the control switches located on the steering wheel.

The release switches are located on the brake, clutch and accelerator pedal brackets. When the brake and clutch pedals are depressed, or the OFF switch is pressed, the system will be disengaged. As long as the OFF button has not been depressed, the vehicle can be returned to its original speed by pressing the resume button.

CRUISE CONTROL TROUBLESHOOTING

Problem	Possible Cause
Will not hold proper speed	Incorrect cable adjustment
	Binding throttle linkage
	Leaking vacuum servo diaphragm
	Leaking vacuum tank
	Faulty vacuum or vent valve
	Faulty stepper motor
	Faulty transducer
	Faulty speed sensor
	Faulty cruise control module
Cruise intermittently cuts out	Clutch or brake switch adjustment too tight
	Short or open in the cruise control circuit
	Faulty transducer
	Faulty cruise control module
Vehicle surges	Kinked speedometer cable or casing
	Binding throttle linkage
	Faulty speed sensor
	Faulty cruise control module
Cruise control inoperative	Blown fuse
	Short or open in the cruise control circuit
	Faulty brake or clutch switch
	Leaking vacuum circuit
	Faulty cruise control switch
	Faulty stepper motor
	Faulty transducer
	Faulty speed sensor
	Faulty cruise control module

Note: Use this chart as a guide. Not all systems will use the components listed.

TCCA6C01

ENTERTAINMENT SYSTEMS

Radio/Tape Player

REMOVAL & INSTALLATION

1991–96 Models

▶ **See Figures 34, 35, 36 and 37**

You will need radio removing tool T87P-19061-A or its equivalent to perform this procedure.

1. Disconnect the negative battery cable.
2. Using the radio removal tool, pull the radio out from its mounting position, so that the antenna and electrical connectors are accessible.
3. Unplug the antenna lead and the radio electrical connectors from the radio.
4. Remove the radio.

To install:

5. Attach the antenna lead and the electrical connectors to the radio.
6. Install the radio in its mounting position.
7. Connect the negative battery cable.

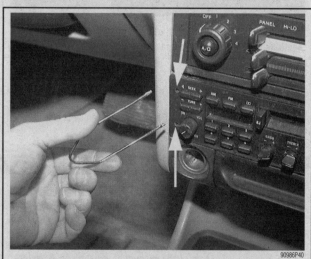

Fig. 34 A special tool must be inserted into the holes (arrows) of the radio

90986P40

Fig. 35 Insert the removal tool into the holes to disengage the retaining clips and slide the radio from the mounting bracket

Fig. 36 Slide the radio out until you can access the electrical connections at the rear . . .

Fig. 37 . . . then unplug the electrical connections and remove the radio

1997–99 Models

▶ See Figure 33

You will need radio removing tool T87P-19061-A or its equivalent to perform this procedure.
1. Disconnect the negative battery cable.
2. Place the temperature control switch to the COLD position.
3. Unlock the temperature cable by pulling down on the tab.
4. Disconnect the cable while holding the tab down.
5. Using the radio removal tool, pull the integrated control panel from the instrument panel.
6. Unplug the vacuum harness, antenna lead and the electrical connections from the rear of the control panel.
7. Remove the control panel.

To install:
8. Attach the vacuum harness, antenna lead and the electrical connections to the rear of the control panel.
9. Install the control panel into the instrument panel.
10. Connect the temperature control cable.
11. Connect the negative battery cable.

Radio Amplifier

REMOVAL & INSTALLATION

1991–96 Models

▶ See Figures 38 and 39

1. Disconnect the negative battery cable.
2. Remove the shift console.
3. Unfasten the four amplifier bracket screws.
4. If equipped with an air bag, unplug the two air bag diagnostic monitor connectors and position the diagnostic monitor aside.
5. Unplug the amplifier electrical connections and remove the amplifier assembly.

To install:
6. Place the amplifier into position and attach its electrical connections.
7. If equipped with an air bag, place the air bag diagnostic monitor into position and attach the electrical connections.
8. Tighten the four amplifier bracket screws.
9. Install the shift console.
10. Connect the negative battery cable.

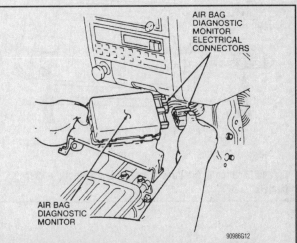

Fig. 38 If equipped with an air bag, unplug the two electrical connectors and position the air bag diagnostic monitor aside to access the amplifier—1991–96 models

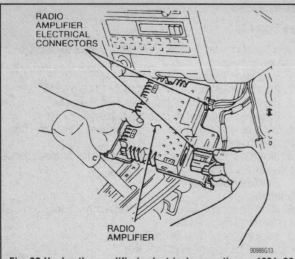

Fig. 39 Unplug the amplifier's electrical connections—1991–96 models

1997–99 Models

▶ **See Figure 40**

1. Disconnect the negative battery cable.
2. Remove the driver's seat.
3. Unfasten the three amplifier bracket bolts and unplug the amplifier electrical connections.
4. Unfasten the amplifier retaining screws and remove the amplifier.

To install:

5. Install the amplifier and its retaining screws. Tighten the screws to 17–20.5 inch lbs. (2–2.5 Nm).
6. Attach the amplifier electrical connections and install the bracket bolts. Tighten the bolts to 71 inch lbs. (8 Nm).
7. Install the driver's seat.
8. Connect the negative battery cable.

CD Changer

REMOVAL & INSTALLATION

▶ **See Figures 41 and 42**

On pre-1997 models equipped with a CD player, use the radio removal procedure to remove the CD player. The following procedure applies to 1997–99 models only.

1. Disconnect the negative battery cable.
2. Unplug the CD player electrical connection.
3. Unfasten the six CD player retaining screws and remove the CD player.

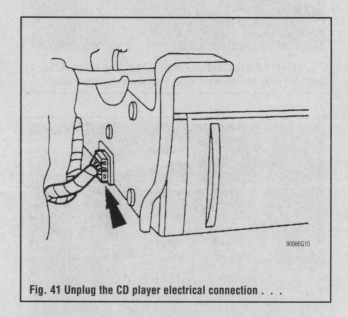

Fig. 41 Unplug the CD player electrical connection . . .

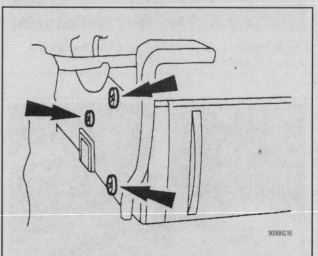

Fig. 42 . . . then unfasten the six CD player retaining screws (three on each side)—1997–99 models

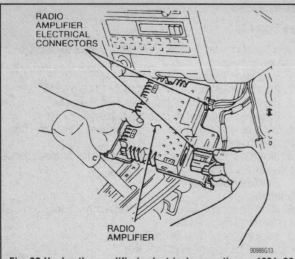

Fig. 40 Location of the three amplifier bracket bolts—1997–99 models

To install:

4. Install the CD player and tighten the six retaining screws to 45 inch lbs. (5 Nm).

5. Attach the CD player electrical connection.

6. Connect the negative battery cable.

Speakers

REMOVAL & INSTALLATION

1991–96 Models

FRONT DOOR

▶ See Figures 43, 44 and 45

1. Disconnect the negative battery cable.
2. Remove the front door trim panel.
3. Unfasten the three speaker retaining screws.
4. Pull the speaker from the door until you can access the rear of the speaker.
5. Unplug the speaker electrical connection.

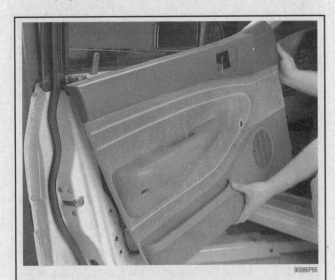

Fig. 43 Remove the front door trim panel

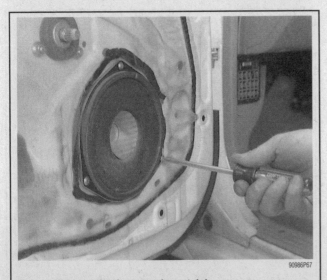

Fig. 44 Unfasten the three speaker retaining screws

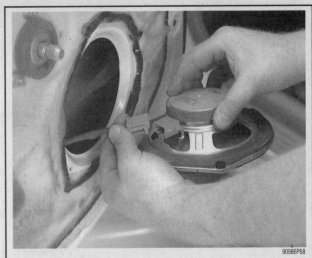

Fig. 45 Pull the speaker from the door, unplug the electrical connection and remove the speaker

6. Remove the speaker.

To install:

7. Attach the speaker electrical connection and place the speaker into position on the door.

8. Install and tighten the speaker retaining screws.

9. Install the door trim panel.

10. Connect the negative battery cable.

REAR SPEAKER—SEDAN

▶ See Figures 46, 47 and 48

1. Disconnect the negative battery cable.
2. Remove the two clips from the sides of the rear hi-mount brake light cover and unfasten its retaining screws.
3. Remove the brake light cover and set it aside.
4. Lift up the package tray panel and set it aside.
5. Unfasten the speaker retaining screws.
6. Lift the speaker up and unplug its electrical connection.
7. Remove the speaker.

To install:

8. Attach the speaker electrical connection and place the speaker into position.

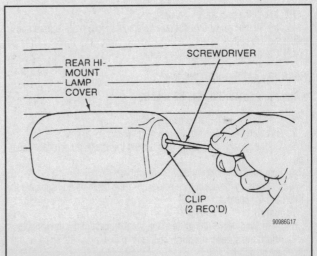

Fig. 46 To remove the rear speaker on a sedan model, remove the brake light cover . . .

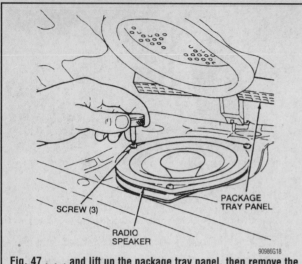

Fig. 47 . . . and lift up the package tray panel, then remove the speaker retaining screws . . .

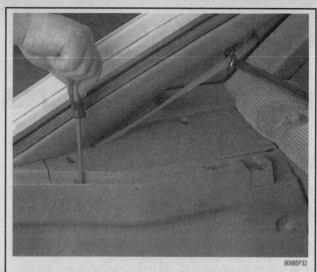

Fig. 49 Unfasten the speaker grille retaining screws . . .

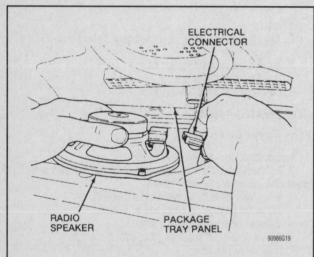

Fig. 48 . . . and lift the speaker up to unplug its electrical connection—1991–96 models

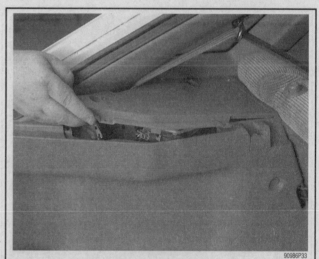

Fig. 50 . . . and lift the speaker grille to access the speaker electrical connection

9. Install and tighten the speaker retaining screws.
10. Install the package tray panel.
11. Install the rear hi-mount brake light cover, tighten the screws and install the two clips.
12. Connect the negative battery cable.

REAR SPEAKER—HATCHBACK

▶ See Figures 49, 50, 51, 52 and 53

1. Disconnect the negative battery cable.
2. Unfasten the speaker grille retaining screws.
3. Lift the speaker and grille, then unplug the speaker electrical connection.
4. Remove the speaker and grille assembly.
5. If necessary, unfasten the speaker-to-grille retainers and separate the grille from the speaker.

To install:

6. If removed, attach the grille to the speaker and tighten the fasteners.
7. Attach the speaker electrical connection, then place the speaker and grille into position.
8. Install and tighten the grille retaining screws.
9. Connect the negative battery cable.

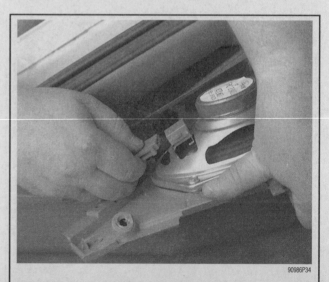

Fig. 51 Unplug the speaker electrical connection

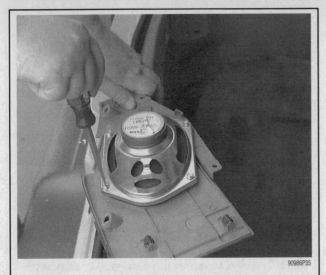

Fig. 52 Unfasten the speaker-to-grille retaining screws . . .

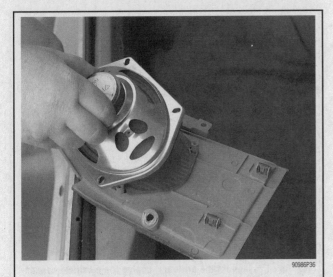

Fig. 53 . . . and separate the speaker from the grille

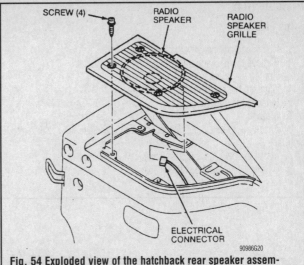

Fig. 54 Exploded view of the hatchback rear speaker assembly—1991–96 models

1997–99 Models

DOOR

▶ See Figure 55

1. Disconnect the negative battery cable.
2. Remove the door trim panel.
3. Unfasten the speaker retaining screws.
4. Pull the speaker from the door until you can access the rear of the speaker.
5. Unplug the speaker electrical connection.
6. Remove the speaker.
To install:
7. Attach the speaker electrical connection and place the speaker into position on the door.
8. Install and tighten the speaker retaining screws.
9. Install the door trim panel.
10. Connect the negative battery cable.

REAR SPEAKER—WAGON

▶ See Figure 54

1. Disconnect the negative battery cable.
2. Unfasten the four speaker grille retaining screws.
3. Lift the speaker and grille, then unplug the speaker electrical connection.
4. Remove the speaker and grille.
5. If necessary, unfasten the speaker-to-grille nuts and separate the grille from the speaker.
To install:
6. If removed, attach the grille to the speaker and tighten the nuts.
7. Attach the speaker electrical connection, then place the speaker and grille into position.
8. Install and tighten the grille retaining screws.
9. Connect the negative battery cable.

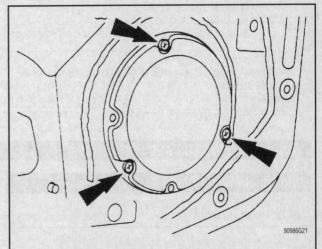

Fig. 55 Remove the door trim panel to access the three speaker retaining screws (arrows)—1997–99 models

PACKAGE TRAY

▶ **See Figure 56**

1. Disconnect the negative battery cable.
2. Remove the package tray trim panel.
3. Unplug the speaker electrical connection.
4. Unfasten the speaker retaining screws.
5. Remove the speaker.

To install:

6. Attach the speaker electrical connection and place the speaker into position.
7. Install the package tray trim panel.
8. Connect the negative battery cable.

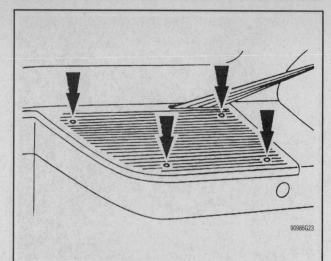

Fig. 57 To remove the quarter trim panel speaker, unfasten the four grille retaining screws . . .

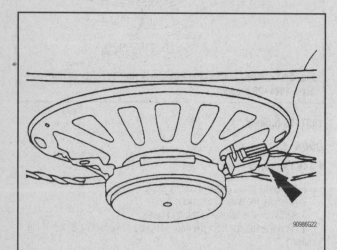

Fig. 56 Unplug the package tray speaker electrical connection (arrow)—1997–99 models

QUARTER TRIM PANEL

▶ **See Figures 57 and 58**

1. Disconnect the negative battery cable.
2. Unfasten the speaker grille retaining screws.
3. Lift the speaker and grille, then unplug the speaker electrical connection.
4. Remove the speaker and grille.
5. If necessary, unfasten the speaker-to-grille screws and separate the grille from the speaker.

To install:

6. If removed, attach the grille to the speaker and tighten the screws.

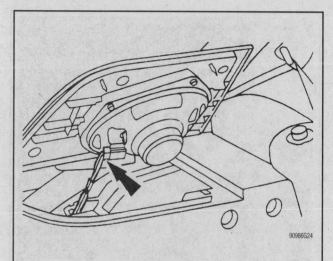

Fig. 58 . . . then lift the grille up, unplug the electrical connection and remove the speaker assembly—1997–99 models

7. Attach the speaker electrical connection, then place the speaker and grille into position.
8. Install and tighten the grille retaining screws.
9. Connect the negative battery cable.

WINDSHIELD WIPERS AND WASHERS

Windshield Wiper Blade

REMOVAL & INSTALLATION

Front

1991–95 MODELS

▶ **See Figure 59**

1. Use a prytool to push down on the wiper blade spring coil.
2. Move the wiper blade back and forth to remove it from the wiper arm.

To install:

3. Move the wiper blade back and forth to install it on the wiper arm.

1996–99 MODELS

▶ **See Figures 60 and 61**

➡The left-hand windshield wiper blade is 20 inches (51cm) long and the right-hand wiper blade is 17 inches (43cm) long. Make sure that you replace the blades one at time to avoid any confusion, and to make sure that each blade is placed on its correct side.

1. Pull the wiper arm away from the windshield.
2. Push the wiper blade clip down and remove the blade from the arm.
3. Installation is the reverse of removal.

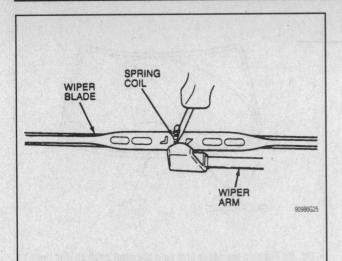

Fig. 59 Use a prytool to push down on the wiper blade spring coil—1991–95 models

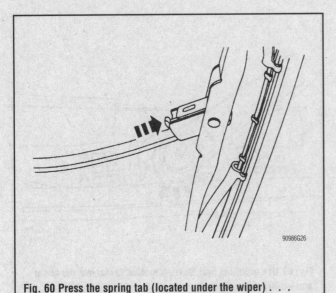

Fig. 60 Press the spring tab (located under the wiper) . . .

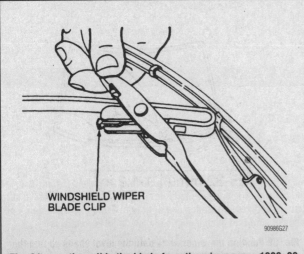

Fig. 61 . . . then slide the blade from the wiper arm—1996–99 models

Rear

1991–96 MODELS

♦ See Figures 60 and 61

1. Press the spring tab (located under the wiper) and slide the blade towards the wiper motor until it is loose.
2. Remove the blade from the wiper arm.
To install:
3. Insert the hooked end of the wiper arm into the opening in the blade.
4. Slide the blade into the hook (away from the motor) until the locking tab snaps into the arm.
5. Make sure the blade is firmly attached.

1997–99 MODELS

1. Pull the wiper arm away from the windshield.
2. Push the wiper blade clip down and remove the blade from the arm.
3. Installation is the reverse of removal.

Wiper Arm

REMOVAL & INSTALLATION

Front

1991–96 MODELS

♦ See Figures 62, 63, 64, 65 and 66

1. Remove the wiper arm attaching nut cover.
2. Unfasten the attaching nut and pull the wiper arm from the pivot shaft.
To install:
3. Turn the wiper switch **ON** and allow the wiper pivot shafts to move through three or four cycles, then turn the switch **OFF**.
4. Position the wiper arm onto the pivot shaft so that the tip of the blade is 1.10–1.28 inches (28–32mm) from the cowl grille.
5. Install the wiper arm nut and tighten it to 142–177 inch lbs. (16–20 Nm).
6. Install the wiper arm attaching nut cover.

1997–99 MODELS

♦ See Figures 67 and 68

1. Remove the wiper arm attaching nut cover.
2. Unfasten the attaching nut, then pull upwards and twist the wiper arm to remove it from the pivot shaft.

Fig. 62 Remove the wiper arm attaching nut cover

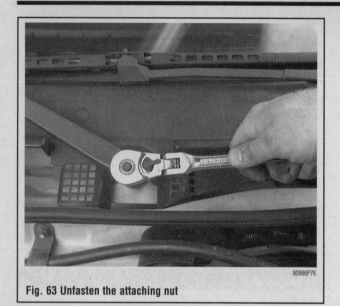

Fig. 63 Unfasten the attaching nut

Fig. 64 If reinstalling the old wiper arm, it may help to match-mark the wiper arm and pivot shaft before removal

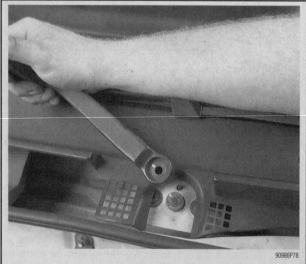

Fig. 65 Grasp the arm and pull it from the pivot shaft

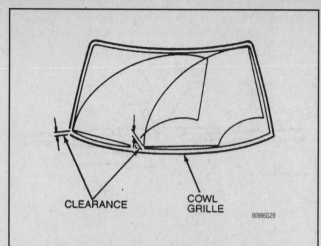

Fig. 66 Position the wiper arm onto the pivot shaft so that the tip of the blade is 1.10–1.28 inches (28–32mm) from the cowl grille—1991–96 models

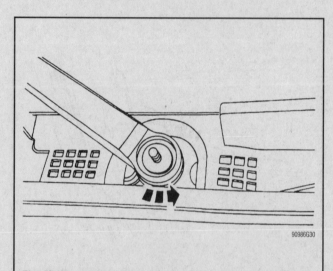

Fig. 67 Use a pulling and twisting motion to remove the wiper arm—1997–99 models

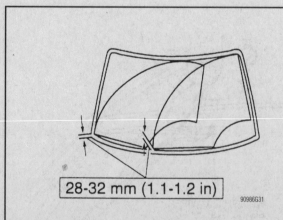

Fig. 68 Position the wiper arms onto the pivot shafts so that the tips of the blades are 1.1–1.2 inches (28–32mm) from the cowl grille—1997 models

To install:

3. Turn the wiper switch **ON** and allow the wiper pivot shafts to move through three or four cycles, then turn the switch **OFF**.

4. Position the wiper arms onto the pivot shafts so that the tips of the blades are 1.1–1.2 inches (28–32mm) from the cowl grille on 1997 models, or 0.8–1.2 inches (20–30mm) on 1998–99 models.

5. Install the wiper arm nut and tighten it to 12–14 ft. lbs. (16–19 Nm).

6. Install the wiper arm attaching nut cover.

Rear

1991–96 MODELS

▶ **See Figures 69 and 70**

1. Remove the wiper arm attaching nut cover.

2. Unfasten the attaching nut and pull the wiper arm from the pivot shaft.

To install:

3. Turn the wiper switch **ON** and allow the wiper pivot shafts to move through three or four cycles, then turn the switch **OFF**.

4. Position the wiper arm onto the pivot shaft so that the tip of the blade is 0.79–0.98 inches (20–25mm) from the rear window molding.

5. Install the wiper arm nut and tighten it to 61–87 inch lbs. (7–10 Nm).

6. Install the wiper arm attaching nut cover.

1997–99 MODELS

▶ **See Figures 71 and 72**

1. Remove the wiper arm attaching nut cover.

2. Unfasten the attaching nut, then pull upwards and twist to remove the wiper arm from the pivot shaft.

To install:

3. Turn the wiper switch **ON** and allow the wiper pivot shafts to move through three or four cycles, then turn the switch **OFF**.

4. Position the wiper arm onto the pivot shaft so that the tip of the blade is 0.8–1.1 inches (20–30mm) from the rear window molding.

5. Install the wiper arm nut and tighten it to 52–86 inch lbs. (6–10 Nm).

6. Install the wiper arm attaching nut cover.

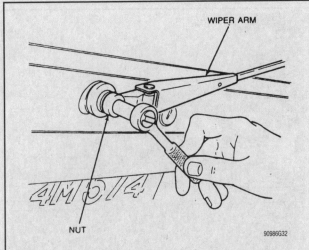

Fig. 69 Loosening the rear wiper arm retaining nut—1991–96 models

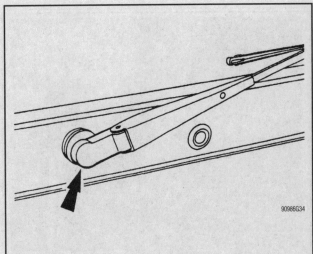

Fig. 71 Remove the wiper arm attaching nut cover—1997–99 models

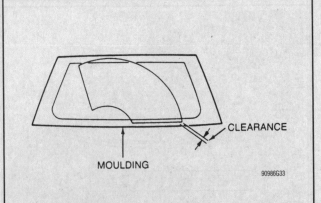

Fig. 70 Position the wiper arm onto the pivot shaft so that the tip of the blade is 0.79–0.98 inches (20–25mm) from the rear window molding—1991–96 models

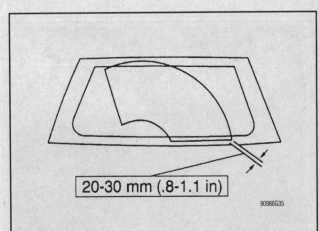

Fig. 72 Position the wiper arm onto the pivot shaft so that the tip of the blade is 0.8–1.1 inches (20–30mm) from the rear window molding—1997–99 models

Windshield Wiper Motor

REMOVAL & INSTALLATION

1991–96 Models

FRONT WIPER MOTOR

▶ **See Figures 73 thru 82**

1. Make sure the wiper motor switch is in the **OFF** position.
2. Disconnect the negative battery cable.
3. Remove the windshield wiper arms.
4. With the hood closed, remove the cowl grille screw covers.
5. Unfasten the cowl grille retaining screws and remove the cowl grille.
6. Pry up the baffle retaining clips and remove the baffle trim piece.

➡**Make sure the wiper motor is in the park position before disconnecting the linkage.**

7. Remove the wiper linkage retaining clip and disconnect the wiper linkage from the motor.

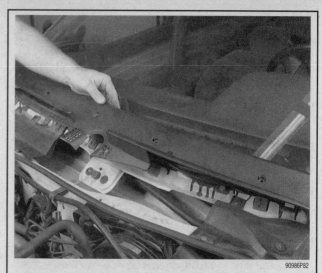
Fig. 75 Unfasten the retainers and remove the cowl grille

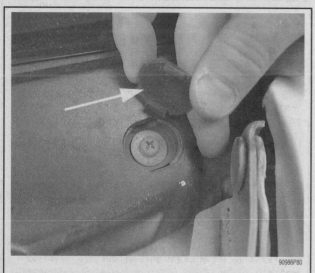
Fig. 73 Remove the cowl grille screw covers

Fig. 76 Remove the baffle trim piece retaining clips . . .

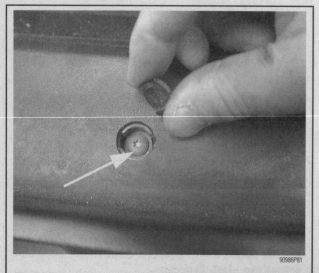
Fig. 74 The cowl cover may be retained by Torx® head screws

Fig. 77 . . . and remove the baffle trim piece

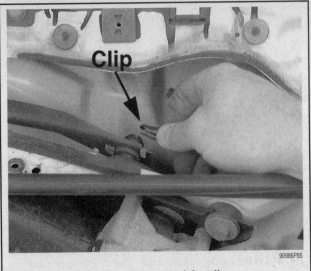

Fig. 78 Remove the wiper linkage retaining clip . . .

90986P85

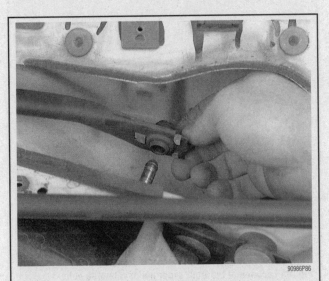

Fig. 79 . . . then separate the wiper linkage from the motor

90986P86

Fig. 80 Unplug the two wiper motor electrical connectors

90986P87

Fig. 81 Unfasten the wiper motor retaining bolts

90986P88

Fig. 82 Remove the wiper motor from the engine compartment

90986P89

8. Unplug the two wiper motor electrical connectors.

9. Unfasten the wiper motor retaining bolts until they are loose from the sheet metal mounting surface.

10. Remove the wiper motor from the vehicle.

To install:

11. Place the wiper motor into position and install the retaining bolts. Tighten the bolts to 61–79 inch lbs. (7–9 Nm).

12. Attach the wiring connectors to the wiper motor.

13. Temporarily install the negative battery cable.

14. Turn the wiper switch to the **ON** and then **OFF** positions and allow the wiper motor to stop in the **PARK** position.

15. Remove the negative battery cable.

16. Connect the wiper linkage and the retaining clip.

17. Install the baffle trim piece and retaining clips.

18. Install the cowl grille and the retaining screws. Install the screw covers.

19. Install the wiper arms.

20. Connect the negative battery cable.

21. Run the wipers at all speeds and make sure the wiper arms park in their correct positions when the wiper switch is turned **OFF**. Adjust the wiper arms if necessary.

REAR WIPER MOTOR

▶ **See Figure 83**

1. Disconnect the negative battery cable.
2. Remove the wiper arm.
3. Remove the shaft seal from the outer bushing retaining nut.
4. Unfasten the outer bushing attaching nut and remove the outer bushing.
5. Remove the liftgate trim panel.
6. Unplug the wiper motor electrical connector.
7. Remove the wiper motor retaining bolts and washers.
8. Remove the wiper motor.

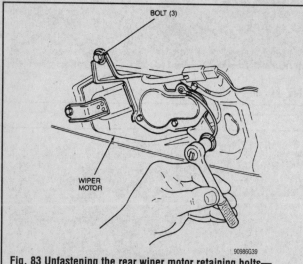

Fig. 83 Unfastening the rear wiper motor retaining bolts—1991–96 models

To install:

9. Place the rear wiper motor into position and install the retaining bolts. Tighten the wiper motor bolts to 61–79 inch lbs. (7–9 Nm).
10. Install the outer bushing and tighten the nut to 35–52 inch lbs. (4–6 Nm).
11. Install the shaft seal.
12. Attach the rear wiper motor wiring connector.
13. Install the negative battery cable.
14. Turn the wiper switch to the **ON** and then **OFF** positions and allow the wiper motor to stop in the **PARK** position.
15. Install the wiper arm. Tighten the wiper arm nut to 61–87 inch lbs. (7–9 Nm).
16. Run the rear wiper motor at all speeds and make sure the wiper arm parks in its correct position when the wiper switch is turned **OFF**. Adjust the wiper arm if necessary.
17. Install the liftgate trim panel.

1997–99 Models

FRONT WIPER MOTOR

▶ **See Figures 84 and 85**

➡ **Park the wiper blades at their highest position on the windshield, then turn the wiper switch to the OFF position.**

1. Disconnect the negative battery cable.
2. Remove the wiper arms.
3. Open and support the hood.
4. Unfasten the five center cowl vent grille retainers and screws and the two outer cowl top vent grille retainers, screws and washers.

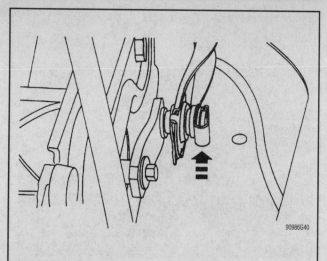

Fig. 84 Lift the clip up and off of the wiper mounting arm and pivot shaft—1997–99 models

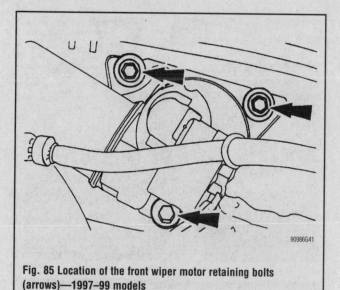

Fig. 85 Location of the front wiper motor retaining bolts (arrows)—1997–99 models

5. Remove the cowl vent grille.
6. Lift the clip up and off the wiper mounting arm and pivot shaft.
7. Slide the wiper mounting arm and pivot shaft off the wiper motor.
8. Unplug the wiper motor electrical connection.
9. Unfasten the wiper bolts and remove it from the vehicle.

To install:

➡ **Make sure the wiper motor is in the PARK position before installing it.**

10. Install the wiper motor and its retaining bolts. Tighten the bolts to 62–79 inch lbs. (7–9 Nm).
11. Attach the wiper motor electrical connection.
12. Slide the wiper mounting arm and pivot shaft onto the wiper motor.
13. Attach the clip to the wiper mounting arm and pivot shaft.
14. Install the cowl vent grille and tighten its retainers.
15. Install and adjust the wiper arms.
16. Connect the negative battery cable.
17. Check the wiper motor for proper operation and the arms for proper adjustment.

REAR WIPER MOTOR

♦ See Figure 86

1. Disconnect the negative battery cable.
2. Remove the wiper arm and blade assembly.
3. Remove the liftgate trim panel and peel back the watershield.
4. Unplug the wiper motor electrical connection.
5. Unfasten the retaining bolts and remove the wiper motor from the vehicle.

To install:

6. Install the wiper motor and its retaining bolts. Tighten the bolts to 62–79 inch lbs. (7–9 Nm).
7. Attach the wiper motor electrical connection.
8. Attach the liftgate watershield and install the trim panel.
9. Position and install the wiper arm/blade assembly.
10. Connect the negative battery cable.
11. Check the wiper motor for proper operation and the arm for proper alignment.

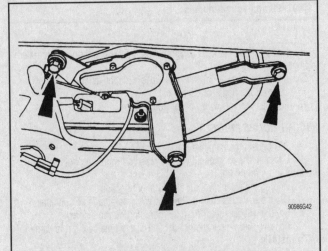

Fig. 86 Location of the rear wiper motor retaining bolts—1997–99 models

Windshield Washer Motor

REMOVAL & INSTALLATION

Front Washer Motor

1.8L ENGINE MODELS

1. Unfasten the two power steering fluid reservoir mounting bolts and position the reservoir aside.
2. If equipped, unfasten the two cruise control servo bracket mounting bolts and position the bracket aside.
3. Unfasten the windshield washer reservoir mounting bolts and unplug the washer motor electrical connection.
4. Pull the hose from the washer motor and remove the reservoir from the engine compartment.
5. Using a suitable prytool, pry the motor from the reservoir.

To install:

6. Install the motor onto the reservoir.
7. Attach the hose to the washer motor and place the reservoir into position.
8. Attach the washer motor electrical connection and install the reservoir retaining bolts. Tighten the bolts to 61–79 inch lbs. (7–9 Nm).

9. If equipped, place the cruise control servo bracket into place and tighten the mounting bolts.
10. Place the power steering reservoir into position, then install and tighten the retaining bolts.

1.9L ENGINE MODELS

♦ See Figures 87 and 88

1. Unfasten the windshield washer reservoir mounting bolts and nut.
2. Unplug the washer motor electrical connection.
3. Pull the hose from the washer motor and remove the reservoir from the engine compartment.
4. Using a suitable prytool, pry the motor from the reservoir.

To install:

5. Install the motor onto the reservoir.
6. Attach the hose to the washer motor and place the reservoir into position.
7. Attach the washer motor electrical connection.
8. Install the reservoir mounting bolts and nut. Tighten the retainers to 61–79 inch lbs. (7–9 Nm).

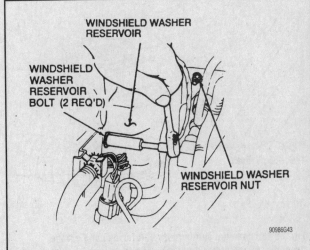

Fig. 87 Remove the front windshield washer reservoir bolts and nut—models with 1.9L engines

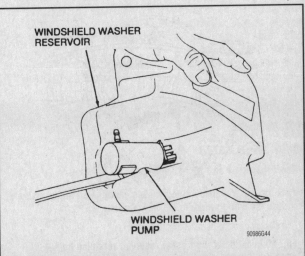

Fig. 88 Using a suitable prytool, pry the washer motor from the reservoir—models with 1.9L engines

2.0L ENGINE MODELS—EXCEPT ESCORT COUPE

▶ See Figures 89, 90 and 91

1. Disconnect the negative battery cable.
2. Unplug the engine sub-harness electrical connection.
3. Unfasten the sub-harness bolt and set the assembly to one side.
4. Unfasten the windshield washer reservoir mounting bolts and pull the reservoir straight up.
5. Unplug the washer motor electrical connection and hose.
6. Drain the washer fluid in the reservoir into a suitable container.
7. Pry the washer motor from its mounting on the reservoir.
8. Remove the washer motor seal and discard the seal if it is damaged.

To install:

9. If necessary, install a new seal.
10. Install the washer motor onto the reservoir.
11. Attach the washer motor electrical connection and hose.
12. Place the reservoir into position and tighten its retaining bolts to 61–86 inch lbs. (7–10 Nm).

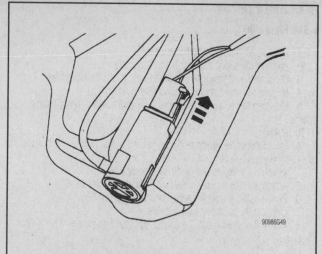

Fig. 91 Unplug the washer motor's electrical connector—1997–99 non-coupe models

13. Place the sub-harness assembly into position and tighten its retaining bolt.
14. Attach the engine sub-harness electrical connection.
15. Connect the negative battery cable.
16. Fill the reservoir with washer fluid.

ESCORT COUPE MODELS

1. Disconnect the negative battery cable.
2. Unfasten the windshield washer reservoir mounting nuts and pull the reservoir straight up.
3. Unplug the washer motor electrical connection.
4. Drain the washer fluid in the reservoir into a suitable container.
5. Pry the washer motor from its mounting on the reservoir.
6. Remove the washer motor seal and discard the seal if it is damaged.

To install:

7. If necessary, install a new seal.
8. Install the washer motor onto the reservoir.
9. Attach the reservoir electrical connection.
10. Place the reservoir into position and tighten its retaining bolts to 61–86 inch lbs. (7–10 Nm).
11. Connect the negative battery cable.
12. Fill the reservoir with washer fluid.

Rear Washer Motor

1991–96 MODELS

▶ See Figures 92 and 93

1. Remove the lower right rear quarter trim panel.
2. Unfasten the three reservoir mounting bolts.
3. Unplug the washer motor electrical connection.
4. Pull the hose from the washer motor and remove the rear window washer reservoir.
5. Gently pry the washer motor from the grommet in the reservoir.

To install:

6. Install the washer motor into the grommet on the fluid reservoir.
7. Connect the hose to the washer motor and place the reservoir into position.
8. Attach the washer motor electrical connection.
9. Install the reservoir mounting bolts. Tighten the retainers to 61–79 inch lbs. (7–9 Nm).

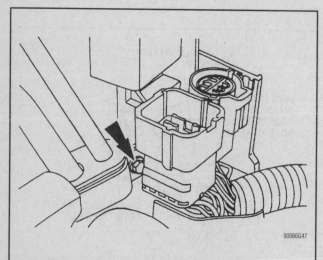

Fig. 89 Unfasten the sub-harness bolt (arrow) and set the assembly to one side—1997–99 non-coupe models

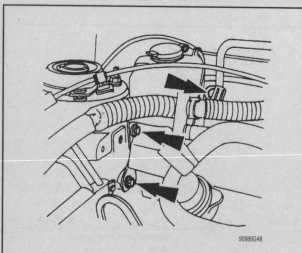

Fig. 90 Location of the washer reservoir retaining bolts—1997–99 non-coupe models

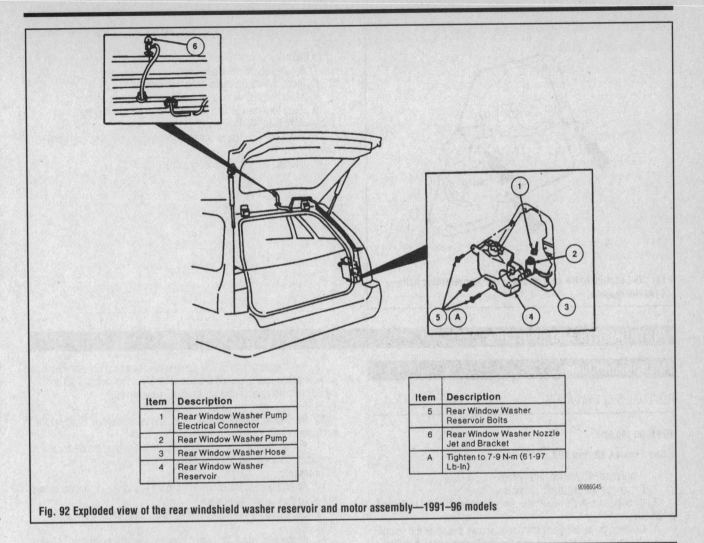

Item	Description
1	Rear Window Washer Pump Electrical Connector
2	Rear Window Washer Pump
3	Rear Window Washer Hose
4	Rear Window Washer Reservoir

Item	Description
5	Rear Window Washer Reservoir Bolts
6	Rear Window Washer Nozzle Jet and Bracket
A	Tighten to 7-9 N·m (61-97 Lb-In)

90986G45

Fig. 92 Exploded view of the rear windshield washer reservoir and motor assembly—1991–96 models

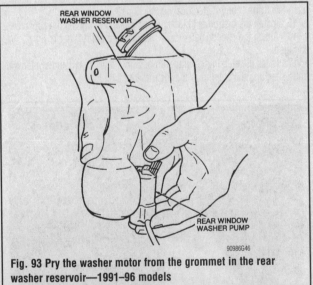

90986G46

Fig. 93 Pry the washer motor from the grommet in the rear washer reservoir—1991–96 models

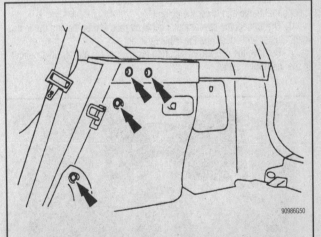

90986G50

Fig. 94 Remove the right-hand quarter trim panel pushpins and panel to gain access to the rear washer reservoir—1997–99 models

1997–99 MODELS

▶ See Figures 94 and 95

1. Disconnect the negative battery cable.
2. Unfasten the pushpins from the right-hand quarter trim panel.

3. Unfasten the rear washer reservoir bolts and pull the reservoir straight up.
4. Unplug the washer motor electrical connection and pull the hose from the washer motor.
5. Drain the washer fluid in the reservoir into a suitable container.

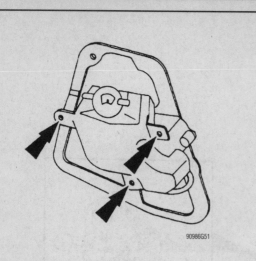

Fig. 95 Location of the rear washer reservoir retaining bolts—1997–99 models

6. Remove the washer motor seal and discard the seal if it is damaged.

To install:

7. If necessary, install a new seal.

8. Install the washer motor onto the reservoir.

9. Attach the washer motor hose and electrical connection.

10. Place the reservoir into position, install its retaining bolts and tighten them to 62–72 inch lbs. (7–9 Nm).

11. Install the right-hand quarter trim panel and its retaining push-pins.

12. Connect the negative battery cable.

INSTRUMENTS AND SWITCHES

Instrument Cluster

REMOVAL & INSTALLATION

1991–96 Models

▶ **See Figures 96 thru 107**

1. If equipped, disable the SRS system.
2. Disconnect the negative battery cable.
3. If equipped with a tilt columns, lower the steering wheel to the lowest position.
4. Unfasten the steering column shroud screws and lower the shroud.
5. Unfasten the four bolts securing the steering column to the instrument panel frame and lower the column.
6. Disconnect the speedometer cable by reaching up behind the instrument cluster and squeezing the cable retainer.
7. Remove the capscrews securing the instrument cluster finish panel to the instrument panel.

8. Pull the instrument cluster finish panel away from the instrument panel and if equipped, unplug the heated back window switch, light and outside rear view mirror control electrical connections.

9. Remove the finish panel.

10. Remove the screws and bolts securing the instrument cluster to the instrument panel.

11. Pull the instrument cluster out slightly and unplug the electrical connectors from the rear of the instrument cluster.

To install:

12. Attach the electrical connections to the rear of the instrument cluster and place the cluster into position.

13. Install and tighten the cluster-to-instrument panel screws and bolts.

14. If equipped, attach the heated back window switch, light and outside rear view mirror control electrical connections.

15. Install the instrument cluster finish panel and tighten the capscrews.

16. Attach the speedometer cable making sure the retainer is fully engaged.

17. Raise the steering column into position, then install and tighten the bolts attaching the column to the instrument panel frame.

Fig. 96 Unfasten the four bolts securing the steering column to the instrument panel frame . . .

Fig. 97 . . . and lower the column

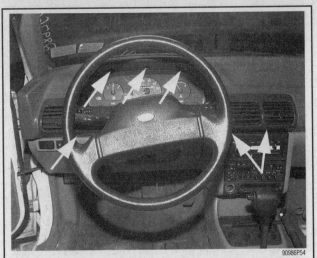

Fig. 98 Location of the capscrews which secure the instrument cluster finish panel to the instrument panel

90986P54

Fig. 101 . . . and unplug the electrical connections from the rear of the panel

90986P57

Fig. 99 Remove the capscrews . . .

90986P55

Fig. 102 Unfasten the lower instrument cluster screws . . .

90986P58

Fig. 100 . . . then pull the instrument cluster finish panel away from the instrument panel . . .

90986P56

Fig. 103 . . . and the upper instrument cluster screws

90986P59

Fig. 104 Slide the cluster forward to access the electrical connections at the rear of the cluster

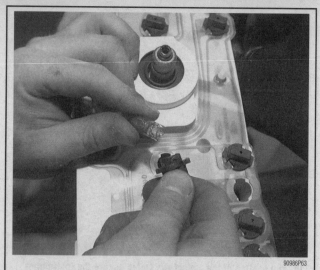

Fig. 107 . . . and pull the bulb from the socket

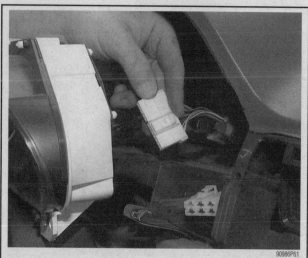

Fig. 105 Unplug the electrical connections from the rear of the cluster, then remove the cluster

18. Place the steering column in position and tighten its retaining screws.

19. If equipped with a tilt column, place the steering wheel in its normal position.

20. Connect the negative battery cable.

1997–99 Models

EXCEPT ESCORT COUPE

▶ See Figures 108 and 109

1. Disconnect the negative battery cable.

2. Unfasten the nut on the back of the hood latch pull handle and remove the handle.

3. Unfasten the instrument panel steering column cover screw and remove the cover.

4. Unfasten the five instrument panel upper finish panel screws and remove the panel.

5. Unfasten the four instrument cluster screws and slide the cluster forward until you can access the rear of the cluster.

6. Unplug the electrical connections from the rear of the cluster and remove the cluster from the instrument panel.

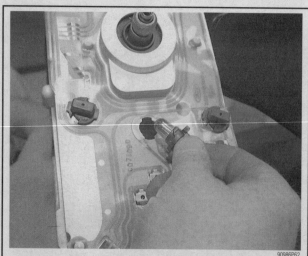

Fig. 106 To replace an instrument cluster gauge bulb, simply remove the socket assembly from the rear of the cluster . . .

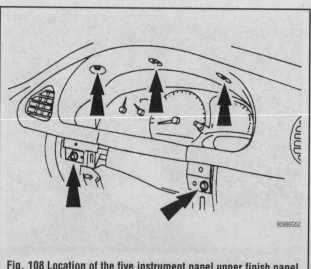

Fig. 108 Location of the five instrument panel upper finish panel screws—1997–99 models except Escort coupe

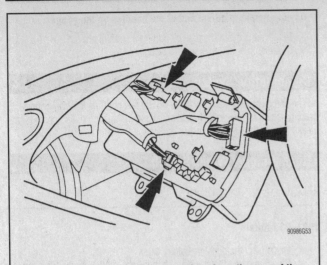

Fig. 109 Unplug the electrical connections from the rear of the cluster—1997–99 models except Escort coupe

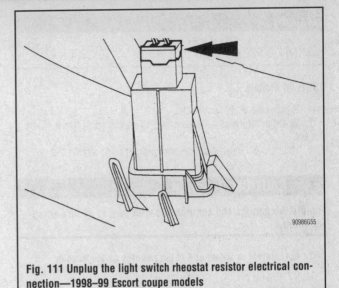

Fig. 111 Unplug the light switch rheostat resistor electrical connection—1998–99 Escort coupe models

To install:

7. Attach the electrical connections to the rear of the cluster and place the cluster into position.

8. Install and tighten the cluster retaining screws.

9. Install the instrument panel upper finish panel and tighten its retaining screws.

10. Install the instrument panel steering column cover and tighten the screw.

11. Install the hood latch pull handle and tighten its retaining nut.

12. Connect the negative battery cable.

ESCORT COUPE MODELS

▶ **See Figures 110, 111 and 112**

1. Disconnect the negative battery cable.

2. Remove the instrument panel upper finish panel insert.

3. Unfasten the nut on the back of the hood latch pull handle and set the handle aside.

4. Unfasten the instrument panel steering column cover screw and remove the cover.

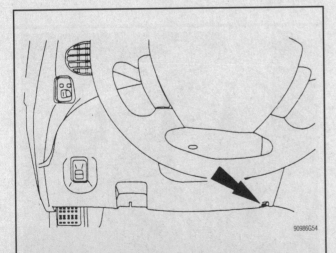

Fig. 110 Location of the instrument panel steering column cover screw—1998–99 Escort coupe models

Fig. 112 Location of the instrument panel upper finish panel screws—1998–99 Escort coupe models

5. Unplug the light switch rheostat resistor electrical connection.

6. Unfasten the instrument panel upper finish panel screws and remove the panel.

7. Unplug the power mirror switch electrical connection.

8. Unfasten the four instrument cluster screws and slide the cluster forward until you can access the rear of the cluster.

9. Unplug the electrical connections from the rear of the cluster and remove the cluster from the instrument panel.

To install:

10. Attach the electrical connections to the rear of the cluster and place the cluster into position.

11. Install and tighten the cluster retaining screws.

12. Attach the power mirror switch electrical connection.

13. Install the instrument panel upper finish panel and tighten its retaining screws.

14. Attach the light switch rheostat resistor electrical connection.

15. Install the instrument panel steering column cover and tighten the screw.

16. Install the hood latch pull handle and tighten its retaining nut.

17. Connect the negative battery cable.

Gauges

REMOVAL & INSTALLATION

1991–96 Models

1. Remove the instrument cluster.
2. Unfasten the instrument cluster lens-to-mask screws, then remove the lens.
3. Unfasten the cluster mask retaining screws and remove the mask.

✳✳ CAUTION

Handle the gauges and components with care to avoid damaging them.

➡**Do not attempt to adjust and of the needles on the gauges.**

4. Remove the desired gauge by pulling it straight out.
5. Installation is the reverse of removal.

1997–99 Models

1. Remove the instrument cluster.
2. Unfasten the instrument cluster mask screws, then remove the mask and lens.

✳✳ CAUTION

Handle the gauges and components with care to avoid damaging them.

LIGHTING

Headlights

REMOVAL & INSTALLATION

1991–96 Models

▶ **See Figures 113, 114 and 115**

1. Turn the headlight switch **OFF**.
2. Unplug the headlight bulb electrical connection.
3. Unscrew the headlight bulb retaining ring counterclockwise about ¼ turn, then pull the bulb assembly from the headlight.

✳✳ WARNING

Do not touch the glass bulb with your fingers. Oil from your fingers can severely shorten the life of the bulb. If necessary, wipe off any dirt or oil from the bulb with rubbing alcohol before completing installation.

4. Pinch the sides off the connector to separate the electrical connector from the bulb.
   To install:
5. Install the bulb in the headlight socket.
6. Align the slots in the bulb flange with the tabs on the headlight and push the bulb firmly into position.
7. Place the headlight bulb retaining ring in position and tighten it by turning it clockwise. A stop will be felt when the retaining ring is fully engaged.
8. Attach the headlight electrical connection.
9. Turn the headlight switch **ON** and check for proper operation.

➡**Do not attempt to adjust and of the needles on the gauges.**

3. Remove the desired gauge by pulling it straight out.
4. Installation is the reverse of removal.

Combination Switch

The combination switch on 1991–96 models controls the front wipers, headlights and turn signals. For removal and installation of this component, please refer to the Steering portion in Section 8 of this manual.

Rear Window Wiper Switch

REMOVAL & INSTALLATION

1991–93 Models

1. Disconnect the negative battery cable.
2. Detach the hood latch control handle and cable from the left-hand lower instrument panel steering column cover.
3. Unfasten the left-hand lower instrument panel steering column cover screws and remove the cover.
4. Unplug the wiper/washer switch electrical connection.
5. Squeeze the two switch lock tabs and remove the switch.
   To install:
6. Install the switch making sure the lock tabs are engaged.
7. Attach the wiper/washer switch electrical connection.
8. Install the left-hand lower instrument panel steering column cover and tighten the screws.
9. Attach hood latch control handle and cable to the left-hand lower instrument panel steering column cover.
10. Connect the negative battery cable.

1997–99 Models

▶ **See Figures 116, 117, 118, 119 and 120**

1. If necessary for access, disconnect the turn signal lamp socket from the lens.
2. If necessary for access, disconnect the cornering lamp socket from the lens.
3. Remove the headlight electrical connection from the access cover and unplug it.

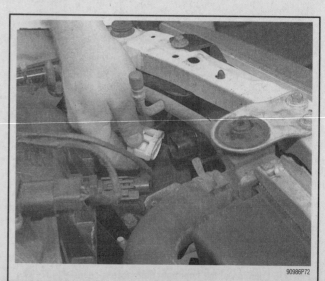

90986P72

Fig. 113 Unplug the headlight bulb electrical connection

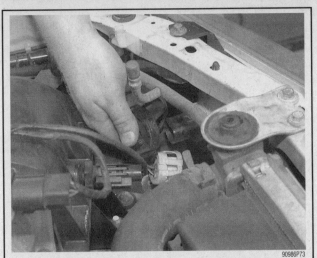

Fig. 114 Unscrew the headlight bulb retaining ring counterclockwise about ¼ turn . . .

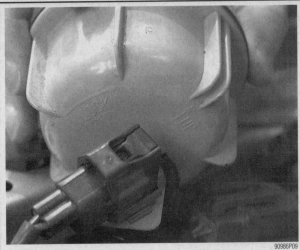

Fig. 117 Remove the bulb access cover by rotating it counterclockwise

Fig. 115 . . . and pull the bulb assembly from the headlight

Fig. 118 Unplug the electrical connector from the bulb by pulling it rearward

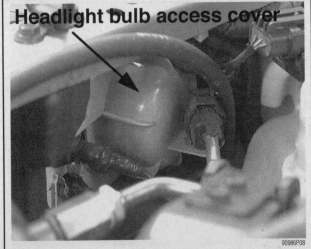

Fig. 116 Location of the headlight bulb access cover—1997–99 models

Fig. 119 Rotate the bulb retaining ring ¼ turn counterclockwise and remove it

Fig. 120 Remove the bulb from the assembly by pulling it rearward

4. Remove the bulb access cover by rotating it counterclockwise.
5. Unplug the connector from the bulb by pulling it rearward.
6. Rotate the bulb retaining ring ¼ turn counterclockwise and remove the bulb from the headlamp by pulling it rearward.

To install:

7. Install the new bulb by pushing it straight in with the bulb's plastic base facing up. You may need to turn the bulb slightly to align the grooves in the base with the tabs in the socket.
8. Slip the retaining ring over the plastic base and rotate the ring clockwise until it locks into position.
9. Attach the bulb access cover by turning it clockwise.
10. Attach the bulb electrical connection and install it on the access cover.
11. If removed, attach the cornering lamp socket to the lens.
12. If removed, attach the turn signal lamp to the lens.
13. Turn the headlight switch **ON** and check for proper operation.

AIMING THE HEADLIGHTS

▶ See Figures 121, 122, 123, 124 and 125

The headlights must be properly aimed to provide the best, safest road illumination. The lights should be checked for proper aim and adjusted as necessary. Certain state and local authorities have requirements for headlight aiming; these should be checked before adjustment is made.

❈❈ CAUTION

About once a year, when the headlights are replaced or any time front end work is performed on your vehicle, the headlight should be accurately aimed by a reputable repair shop using the proper equipment. Headlights not properly aimed can make it virtually impossible to see and may blind other drivers on the road, possibly causing an accident. Note that the following procedure is a temporary fix, until you can take your vehicle to a repair shop for a proper adjustment.

Headlight adjustment may be temporarily made using a wall, as described below, or on the rear of another vehicle. When adjusted, the lights should not glare in oncoming car or truck windshields, nor should they illuminate the passenger compartment of vehicles driving in front of you. These adjustments are rough and should always be fine-tuned by a repair shop which is equipped with headlight aiming tools. Improper adjustments may be both dangerous and illegal.

For most of the vehicles covered by this manual, horizontal and vertical aiming of each sealed beam unit is provided by two adjusting screws which

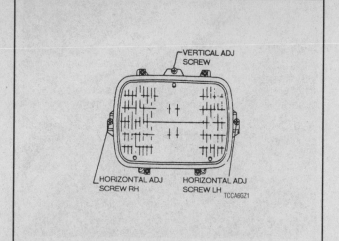

Fig. 121 Location of the aiming screws on most vehicles with sealed beam headlights

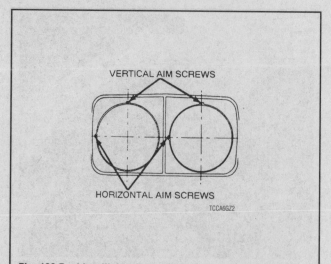

Fig. 122 Dual headlight adjustment screw locations—one side shown here (other side should be a mirror image)

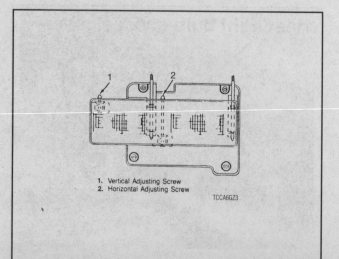

Fig. 123 Example of headlight adjustment screw location for composite headlamps

move the retaining ring and adjusting plate against the tension of a coil spring. There is no adjustment for focus; this is done during headlight manufacturing.

→**Because the composite headlight assembly is bolted into position, no adjustment should be necessary or possible. Some applications, however, may be bolted to an adjuster plate or may be retained by adjusting screws. If so, follow this procedure when adjusting the lights, BUT always have the adjustment checked by a reputable shop.**

Before removing the headlight bulb or disturbing the headlamp in any way, note the current settings in order to ease headlight adjustment upon reassembly. If the high or low beam setting of the old lamp still works, this can be done using the wall of a garage or a building:

1. Park the vehicle on a level surface, with the fuel tank about ½ full and with the vehicle empty of all extra cargo (unless normally carried). The vehicle should be facing a wall which is no less than 6 feet (1.8m) high and 12 feet (3.7m) wide. The front of the vehicle should be about 25 feet (7.6m) from the wall.

2. If aiming is to be performed outdoors, it is advisable to wait until dusk in order to properly see the headlight beams on the wall. If done in a garage, darken the area around the wall as much as possible by closing shades or hanging cloth over the windows.

3. Turn the headlights **ON** and mark the wall at the center of each light's low beam, then switch on the brights and mark the center of each light's high beam. A short length of masking tape which is visible from the front of the vehicle may be used. Although marking all four positions is advisable, marking one position from each light should be sufficient.

4. If neither beam on one side is working, and if another like-sized vehicle is available, park the second one in the exact spot where the vehicle was and mark the beams using the same-side light. Then switch the vehicles so the one to be aimed is back in the original spot. It must be parked no closer to or farther away from the wall than the second vehicle.

5. Perform any necessary repairs, but make sure the vehicle is not moved, or is returned to the exact spot from which the lights were marked. Turn the headlights **ON** and adjust the beams to match the marks on the wall.

6. Have the headlight adjustment checked as soon as possible by a reputable repair shop.

Signal and Marker Lights

REMOVAL & INSTALLATION

Front Turn Signal and Parking Lights

1991–96 MODELS

▶ See Figures 126, 127, 128 and 129

1. Remove the lens upper retaining screw and the fender side retaining screw.

2. Slide the lens assembly forward until access to the rear is possible.

3. If necessary, unplug the bulb electrical connection.

4. Turn the bulb socket assembly counterclockwise and remove it from the lens.

5. Depress and twist the bulb approximately ⅛ turn counterclockwise, then remove it from the socket.

To install:

6. Align the bulb's locating pins, then install the bulb in the socket.

7. Attach the socket to the lens and turn it clockwise to engage it.

8. If removed, attach the bulb electrical connection.

9. Place the lens into position, then tighten the fender side and upper retaining screws.

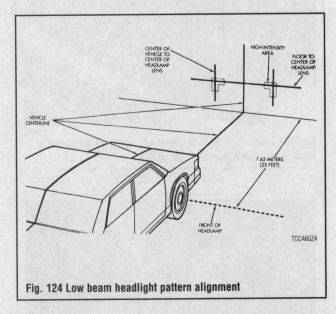

Fig. 124 Low beam headlight pattern alignment

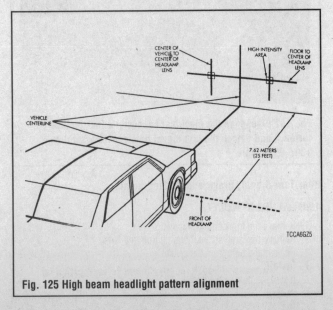

Fig. 125 High beam headlight pattern alignment

Fig. 126 Remove the lens upper retaining screw and the fender side retaining screw

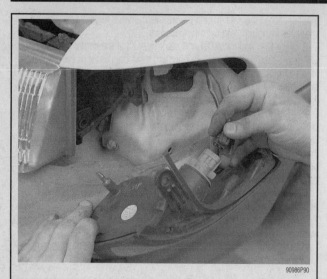

Fig. 127 If necessary, unplug the bulb's electrical connection

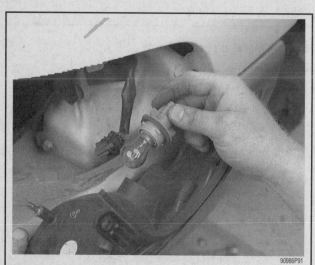

Fig. 128 Turn the bulb socket assembly counterclockwise and remove it from the lens

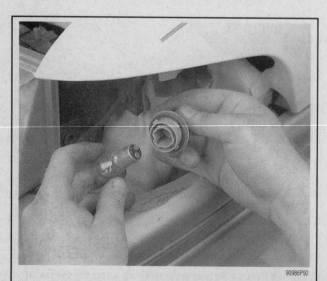

Fig. 129 Remove the bulb from the socket

1997–99 MODELS

▶ See Figures 130 and 131

1. Unplug the bulb socket's electrical connection.
2. Turn the socket assembly counterclockwise to remove it from the lens.
3. Remove the bulb from the socket.

To install:

4. Install the bulb in the socket.
5. Install the socket assembly in the lens and turn it clockwise to engage it.
6. Attach the socket electrical connection.

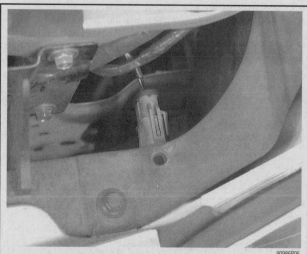

Fig. 130 Location of the turn signal and parking light socket's electrical connection—1997–99 models

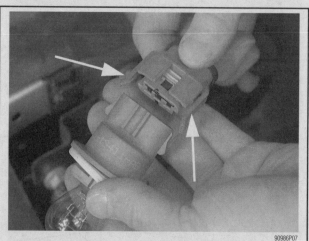

Fig. 131 Disengage the electrical connector's locking tabs (arrows) and detach the turn signal bulb/socket assembly—1997–99 models

Rear Turn Signal, Brake and Parking Lights

1991–96 SEDAN MODELS

1. Remove the trunk end trim panel.
2. Remove the lamp socket/housing from the lens.
3. Remove the bulb from the socket.

To install:

4. Install the bulb in the socket.

5. Install the socket in the lens.
6. Install the trim panel.

1991–96 HATCHBACK MODELS

▶ See Figures 132, 133 and 134

1. Remove the access cover.
2. Turn the socket assembly counterclockwise and remove it from the lens.
3. Depress and twist the bulb approximately ⅛ turn counterclockwise, then remove it from the socket.

To install:
4. Align the locating pins and install the bulb in the socket.
5. Install the socket in the lens.
6. Install the access cover.

1991–96 WAGON MODELS

1. Unfasten the lens assembly retaining screws.
2. Remove the socket(s) from the lens.
3. Remove the bulb(s) from the socket(s).

To install:
4. Install the bulb(s) in the socket(s).

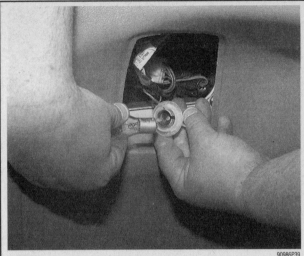

Fig. 134 Remove the bulb from the socket

5. Install the socket(s).
6. Install the lens and tighten the screws.

1997–99 SEDAN MODELS

▶ See Figures 135 thru 140

1. Unfasten the lens retaining screws and remove the lens.
2. Remove the socket from the lens.
3. Remove the bulb from the socket.

To install:
4. Install the bulb in the socket.
5. Attach the socket to the lens.
6. Install the lens and tighten the retaining screws.

1997–99 WAGON MODELS

1. Unfasten the lens retaining screws and remove the lens.
2. Remove the socket(s) from the lens.
3. Remove the bulb(s) from the socket.

To install:
4. Install the bulb(s) in the socket(s).
5. Attach the socket(s) to the lens.
6. Install the lens and tighten the retaining screws.

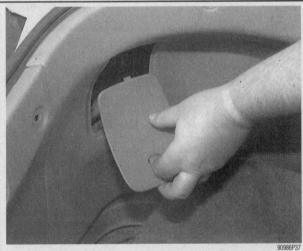

Fig. 132 Remove the cover to access the bulb assemblies—1991–96 hatchback models

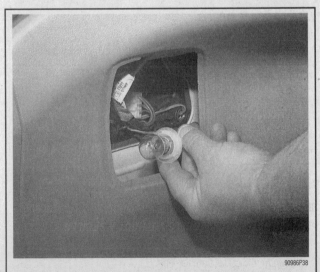

Fig. 133 Disengage the socket and bulb assembly from the lens

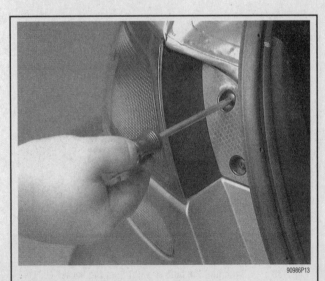

Fig. 135 Unfasten the rear lens retaining screws . . .

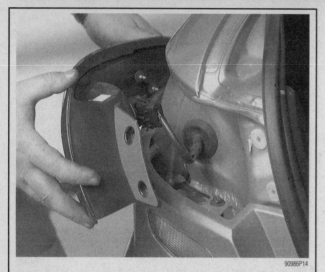

Fig. 136 . . . and separate the lens from the body

Fig. 137 Twist and remove the socket from the lens assembly . . .

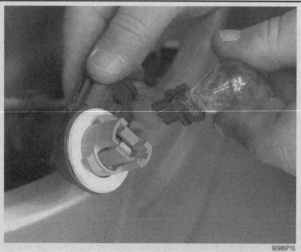

Fig. 138 . . . then pull the bulb straight from the socket—1997–99 sedan models

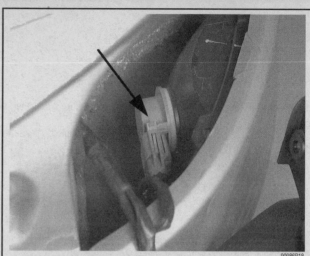

Fig. 139 The back-up light socket assembly (arrow) can also be accessed when the rear lens is removed

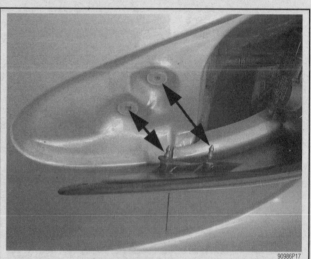

Fig. 140 When installing the lens, make sure to align the pins with the holes in the plastic retainers

1998–99 COUPE MODELS

1. Unfasten the lens retaining screws.
2. Push the lamp housing outward to separate it from the mounting clips and to gain access to the rear of the lens.
3. Remove the socket from the lens.
4. Remove the bulb from the socket.

To install:

5. Install the bulb in the socket.
6. Install the socket in the lens.
7. Position the lens assembly on the clips and gently push inward to attach the lens to the clips until an audible click is heard.
8. Install the top lens screw and then the bottom lens screw.
9. Tighten the screws to 9 inch lbs. (1 Nm).

Side Marker Lights

1991–96 WAGON MODELS

1. Remove the quarter trim panel.
2. Remove the socket from the lens.
3. Remove the bulb from the socket.

To install:
4. Install the bulb in the socket.
5. Install the socket in the lens.
6. Install the trim cover.

Cornering Lights

1997–99 WAGON MODELS

▶ See Figures 141, 142, 143 and 144

1. Remove the access cover.
2. Remove the socket from the lens.
3. Remove the bulb from the socket.
To install:
4. Install the bulb in the socket.
5. Install the socket in the lens.
6. Install the access cover.

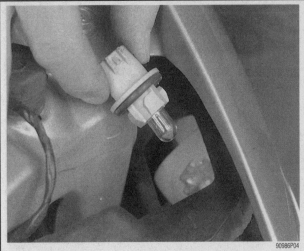

Fig. 143 Remove the socket assembly from the lens by turning it counterclockwise

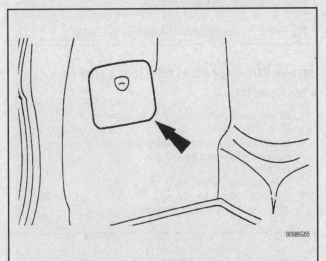

Fig. 141 Location of the cornering bulb access cover—1997–99 wagon models

Fig. 144 Pull the bulb straight from the socket

High-Mount Brake Light

1991–96 SEDAN MODELS

▶ See Figures 145, 146, 147 and 148

1. Remove the push-in retainers from the light cover.
2. Remove the cover.
3. Twist the socket/bulb assembly approximately ¼ turn counterclockwise and remove it from the lens.
4. Pull the bulb straight from the socket.
To install:
5. Install the bulb in the socket.
6. Install the socket in the lens.
7. Install the cover and its retaining pins.

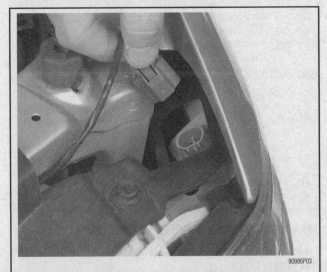

Fig. 142 Unplug the front cornering light electrical connection

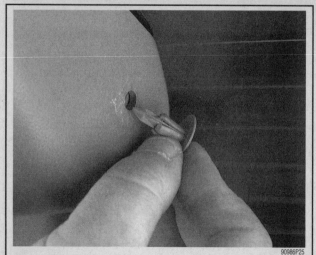

Fig. 145 Remove the push-in retainers from the high-mount brake light cover

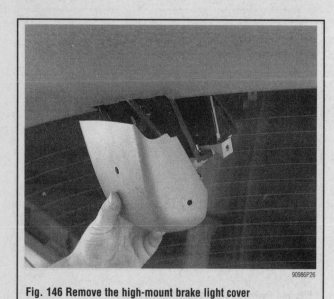

Fig. 146 Remove the high-mount brake light cover

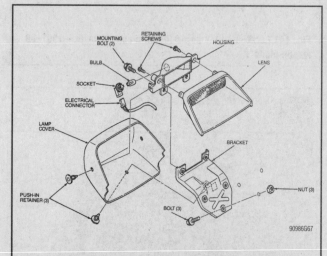

Fig. 147 Detach the socket and bulb assembly from the lens . . .

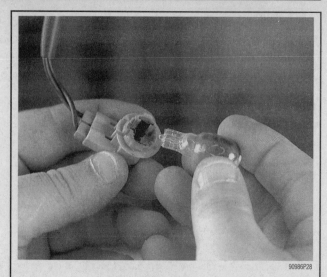

Fig. 148 . . . then remove the bulb from the socket

1991–96 HATCHBACK MODELS WITHOUT A SPOILER

▶ **See Figure 149**

1. Remove the push-in retainers from the light cover.
2. Remove the cover.
3. Detach the socket assembly from the lens.
4. Remove the bulb from the socket.

To install:

5. Install the bulb in the socket.
6. Install the socket in the lens.
7. Install the cover and its retaining pins.

Fig. 149 Exploded view of the high-mount brake light assembly—1991–96 hatchback models without a spoiler

1991–96 HATCHBACK MODELS WITH A SPOILER

▶ **See Figure 150**

The bulb is located in the center of the rear spoiler.

1. Unfasten the lens retaining screws, then remove the lens.
2. Detach the socket from the lens.
3. Remove the bulb from the socket.

To install:

4. Install the bulb in the socket.

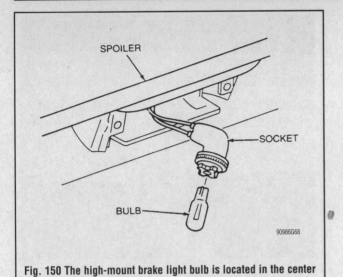

Fig. 150 The high-mount brake light bulb is located in the center of the rear spoiler—1991–96 hatchback models with a spoiler

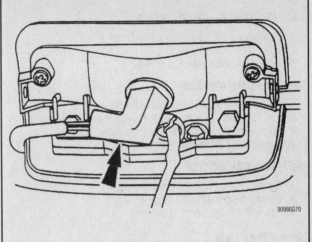

Fig. 152 Remove the bulb socket from the high-mount brake light assembly

5. Install the socket in the lens.
6. Install the lens and its retaining screws.

1997–99 MODELS

▶ See Figures 151 and 152

1. Remove the retainers located on the side of the light cover.
2. Remove the cover and detach the bulb socket from the assembly.
3. Remove the bulb from the socket.
To install:
4. Install the bulb in the socket.
5. Install the socket in the lens.
6. Install the cover and tighten the retainers.

Dome Light

▶ See Figures 153 and 154

1. Carefully pry the dome light lens from the housing.
2. Pull the bulb from the housing.
3. Installation is the reverse of removal.

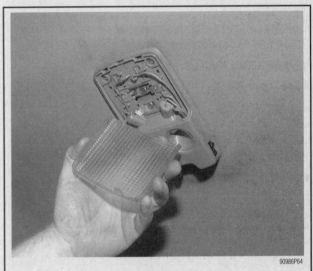

Fig. 153 Gently pry the dome light lens from its housing

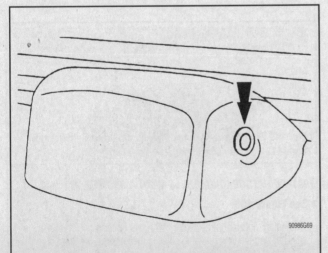

Fig. 151 Location of the high-mount brake light cover retainers—1997–99 sedan and coupe model shown, others similar

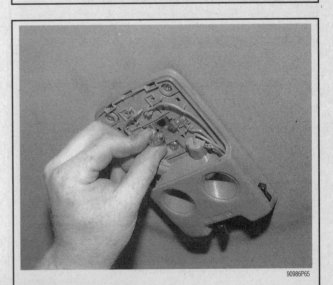

Fig. 154 Pull the bulb from the housing

Cargo Light

1991–96 MODELS—EXCEPT SEDAN

1. Carefully pry the light lens from the housing.
2. Pull the bulb from the housing.
3. Installation is the reverse of removal.

1991–96 SEDAN MODELS

1. Pull the light lens off the mounting bracket.
2. Pull the socket out of the back of the rear shelf extension panel.
3. Remove the bulb by pulling it from the socket.
4. Installation is the reverse of removal.

1997–99 SEDAN MODELS

1. Carefully pry the light lens from the housing.
2. Remove the bulb from the housing.
3. Installation is the reverse of removal.

License Plate Light

1991–96 HATCHBACK AND WAGON MODELS

▶ See Figures 155, 156, 157 and 158

1. Unfasten the lens retaining screws and remove the lens.
2. Remove the bulb straight from the socket.
3. Installation the reverse of removal.

1991–96 SEDAN MODELS

▶ See Figure 159

1. Open the trunk.
2. Locate the bulb and remove it from the socket.
3. Installation is the reverse of removal.

1997–99 MODELS

▶ See Figures 160, 161 and 162

1. Unfasten the lens retaining screws and remove the lens.
2. Twist the socket/bulb assembly approximately ¼ turn counterclockwise, then remove it from the lens.
3. Withdraw the bulb from the socket.
4. Installation is the reverse of removal.

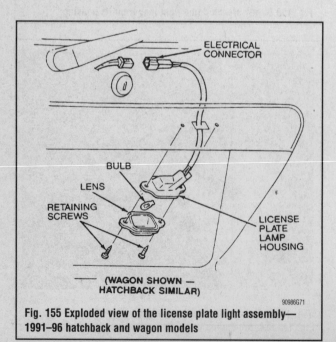

Fig. 155 Exploded view of the license plate light assembly—1991–96 hatchback and wagon models

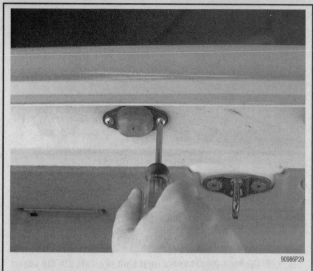

Fig. 156 Loosen the license plate lens retaining screws . . .

Fig. 157 . . . then remove the lens assembly to access the bulb

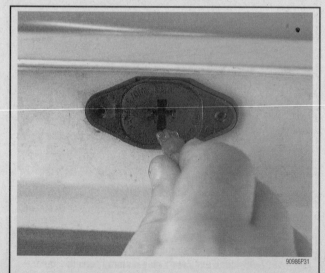

Fig. 158 Remove the license plate light bulb from the socket

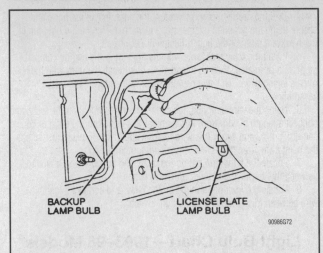

Fig. 159 Locate and remove the license plate bulb from the socket in the trunk-mounted lens—1991–96 sedan models

Fig. 160 Unfasten the license plate light lens retaining screws—1997–99 models

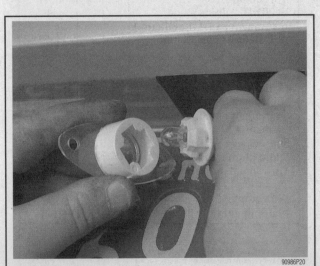

Fig. 161 Detach the socket and bulb assembly from the lens . . .

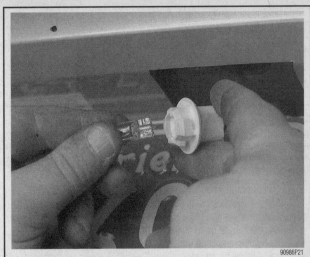

Fig. 162 . . . then pull the license plate light bulb straight from the socket

Fog/Driving Lights

REMOVAL & INSTALLATION

1991–96 Models

▶ See Figure 163

1. Unfasten the fog light lens retaining screws.
2. Remove the lens from the bumper.
3. Turn the socket assembly counterclockwise and remove it from the lens.
4. Remove the bulb from the socket.
To install:
5. Install the bulb in the socket.
6. Attach the socket to the lens and turn the socket assembly clockwise to engage it.
7. Place the lens into position and tighten the retaining screws.

1997–99 Models

1. Raise the car and support it with safety stands.
2. Unplug the fog light electrical connection from the back of the lens assembly.

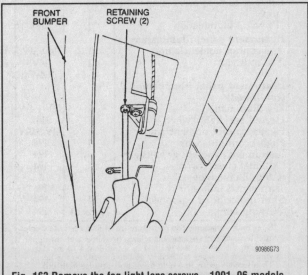

Fig. 163 Remove the fog light lens screws—1991–96 models

3. Twist, then pull the bulb from the assembly.

To install:

4. Install a new bulb and attach the electrical connection to the back of the light assembly.

5. Lower the car.

INSTALLING AND WIRING AFTERMARKET LIGHTS

➡️**Before installing any aftermarket light, make sure it is legal for road use. Most acceptable lights will have a DOT approval number. Also check your local and regional inspection regulations. In certain areas, aftermarket lights must be installed in a particular manner or they may not be legal for inspection.**

1. Disconnect the negative battery cable.

2. Unpack the contents of the light kit purchased. Place the contents in an open space where you can easily retrieve a piece if needed.

3. Choose a location for the lights. If you are installing fog lights, below the bumper and apart from each other is desirable. Most fog lights are mounted below or very close to the headlights. If you are installing driving lights, above the bumper and close together is desirable. Most driving lights are mounted between the headlights.

4. Drill the needed hole(s) to mount the light. Install the light, and secure using the supplied retainer nut and washer. Tighten the light mounting hardware, but not the light adjustment nut or bolt.

5. Install the relay that came with the light kit in the engine compartment, in a rigid area, such as a fender. Always install the relay with the terminals facing down. This will prevent water from entering the relay assembly.

6. Using the wire supplied, locate the ground terminal on the relay, and connect a length of wire from this terminal to a good ground source. You can drill a hole and screw this wire to an inside piece of metal; just scrape the paint away from the hole to ensure a good connection.

7. Locate the light terminal on the relay; and attach a length of wire between this terminal and the fog/driving lamps.

8. Locate the ignition terminal on the relay, and connect a length of wire between this terminal and the light switch.

Light Bulb Chart—1991–92 Models

Function	Number Of Bulbs	Trade Number
Exterior illumination		
Front park/turn lamps	2	1157
Fog lamps-GT	2	881
Headlamps—aero high & low beam	2	9004**
Rear license plate lamp 2-Door, 4-door	1	168
High-mount brakelamp 2-Door & 4-door	1	921
Rear, brakelamp & backup turn lamp	1/2	1157/1156
Liftgate station wagon		
Rear license plate lamp	2	168
Rear side marker lamp	2	194
Interior illumination		
Cargo lamp—liftgate station wagon	1	12V/5W
Dome lamp	1	12V/10W
Dome/map lamp	1/2	12V/6W
Engine compartment lamp	1	D8BB 13465CA (12.8W)
Luggage compartment lamp—(opt.)	1	5W
"PRNDL" illumination	1	1445
Instrument panel illumination		
A/C control nomenclature	1	14V/3W
A/C indicator	1	14V 1.4W
Instrument panel illumination (continued)		
Key illumination	1	12V/1.4W
Heated backlight switch	1	2102
Heater control nomenclature	1	14V/3.0W
High beam indicator	1	194
Instrument panel gauge (cluster)	4	194
Optional cluster w/tach.	5	194
Radio illumination		*
Turn signal indicator	2	194
Shift indicator (if equipped)	1	194
Warning lamps—all	(1 each)	194

*Refer bulb replacement to Ford Authorized Radio Service Center.

***After removal of three attaching screws, two lower and one upper inboard, the lamp is still retained by a stud into a spring clip which may be easily released by pulling forward on the lamp. Then remove socket and bulb from lamp. Replace bulb and reattach by reversing the above sequence.

Light Bulb Chart—1993–96 Models

Function	Number Of Bulbs	Trade Number
Exterior illumination		
Front park/turn lamps	2	3157K
Fog lamps—(if equipped)	2	881
Headlamps—aero high & low beam	2	9004**
Rear license plate lamp 2-Door, 4-Door	2	168
High-mount brakelamp	1	921
Hatchback brakelamp/ backup lamp/turn lamps	2/4	3157K/ 3156K
Notchback—Backup lamp	2	3156K
Notchback—Brakelamp	2	3156K
Notchback—Rear/turn/ sidemarker	2	3357
Liftgate station wagon		
Rear license plate lamp	2	168
Rear side marker lamp	2	168
Interior illumination		
Cargo lamp—liftgate station wagon	1	12V/5W
Dome lamp	1	12V/10W
Dome/map lamp	1/2	12V/6W
Engine compartment lamp	1	D8BB 13465CA (12.8W)
Luggage compartment lamp— (if equipped)	1	5W
"PRNDL" illumination	1	1445
Instrument panel illumination		
A/C control nomenclature	1	14V/3W
A/C indicator	1	14V/ 1.4W
Rear defroster switch	1	2102
Heater control nomenclature	1	14V/3.0W
High beam indicator	1	194
Instrument panel gauge (cluster)	4	194
Sport cluster w/tach.	5	194
Radio illumination		*
Turn signal indicator	2	194
Upshift indicator (if equipped)	1	194
Warning lights—all	(1 each)	194

*Refer bulb replacement to Ford Authorized Radio Service Center.

**After removal of three attaching screws, two lower and one upper inboard, the lamp is still retained by a stud into a spring clip which may be easily released by pulling forward on the lamp. Then remove socket and bulb from lamp. Replace bulb and reattach by reversing the above sequence.

9. Find a suitable mounting location for the light switch and install. Some examples of mounting areas are a location close to the main light switch, auxiliary light position in the dash panel, if equipped, or in the center of the dash panel.

10. Depending on local and regional regulations, the other end of the switch can be connected to a constant power source like the battery, an ignition opening in the fuse panel, or a parking or headlight wire.

11. Locate the power terminal on the relay, and connect a wire with an in-line fuse of at least 10 amperes between the terminal and the battery.

12. With all the wires connected and tied up neatly, connect the negative battery cable.

13. Turn the lights ON and adjust the light pattern if necessary.

AIMING

1. Park the vehicle on level ground, so it is perpendicular to and, facing a flat wall about 25 ft. (7.6m) away.

2. Remove any stone shields, if equipped, and switch ON the lights.

3. Loosen the mounting hardware of the lights so you can aim them as follows:

   a. The horizontal distance between the light beams on the wall should be the same as between the lights themselves.

   b. The vertical height of the light beams above the ground should be 4 in. (10cm) less than the distance between the ground and the center of the lamp lenses for fog lights. For driving lights, the vertical height should be even with the distance between the ground and the center of the lamp.

4. Tighten the mounting hardware.

5. Test to make sure the lights work correctly, and the light pattern is even.

Light Bulb Chart—1997–99 Models

Function	Number of bulbs	Trade number
Exterior illumination		
Front park/turn lamps	2	3457
Foglamps (if equipped)	2	881
Headlamps — aero high and low beam	2	9007
Rear license plate lamp	2	168
High-mount brakelamp	1	921
Notchback — Backup lamp	2	3156
Notchback — Brakelamp	2	3157
Notchback — Rear/turn/side marker	2	3157
Liftgate wagon rear side marker lamp	2 (1 each side)	168
Interior illumination		
Cargo lamp liftgate (wagon)	1	12V/5W
Interior overhead lamp	2	12V/10W
Luggage compartment lamp (if equipped)	1	5W
PRNDL illumination	1	197
Heater control nomenclature	1	14V/3.0
High beam indicator	1	W
Instrument panel gauge (cluster)	4	194
Sport cluster w/ tachometer	2	194
Turn signal indicator	1	194
Upshift indicator (if equipped)	(1 each)	194
Warning lights — all		194
Anti-theft LED	1 LED	See your dealer to order replacement assembly, service part #F57Z13B765-A

90986C03

TRAILER WIRING

Wiring the vehicle for towing is fairly easy. There are a number of good wiring kits available and these should be used, rather than trying to design your own.

All trailers will need brake lights and turn signals as well as tail lights and side marker lights. Most areas require extra marker lights for overwide trailers. Also, most areas have recently required back-up lights for trailers, and most trailer manufacturers have been building trailers with back-up lights for several years.

Additionally, some Class I, most Class II and just about all Class III and IV trailers will have electric brakes. Add to this number an accessories wire, to operate trailer internal equipment or to charge the trailer's battery, and you can have as many as seven wires in the harness.

Determine the equipment on your trailer and buy the wiring kit necessary. The kit will contain all the wires needed, plus a plug adapter set which includes the female plug, mounted on the bumper or hitch, and the male plug, wired into, or plugged into the trailer harness.

When installing the kit, follow the manufacturer's instructions. The color coding of the wires is usually standard throughout the industry. One point to note: some domestic vehicles, and most imported vehicles, have separate turn signals. On most domestic vehicles, the brake lights and rear turn signals operate with the same bulb. For those vehicles without separate turn signals, you can purchase an isolation unit so that the brake lights won't blink whenever the turn signals are operated.

One, final point, the best kits are those with a spring loaded cover on the vehicle mounted socket. This cover prevents dirt and moisture from corroding the terminals. Never let the vehicle socket hang loosely; always mount it securely to the bumper or hitch.

CIRCUIT PROTECTION

Fuses

▶ See Figures 164 thru 182

REPLACEMENT

Fuses are a one-time circuit protection. If a circuit is overloaded or shorts, the thin metal fuse acts like a weak (and expendable) link in a chain by burning. This cuts off electrical flow before the circuit is damaged. Fuses inserted to replace blown fuses will continue to blow unless the circuit is first repaired.

The interior fuse panel can be found below the instrument panel and the exterior fuse panel beneath the hood, near the battery.

1. Remove the fuse panel cover.
2. Locate the fuse to be removed.
3. If equipped with a small fuse removal tool (usually attached to the inside of the fuse panel cover), use the tool to grasp the fuse. Otherwise, you can use your fingers to pull the fuse from the panel. Remove the fuse and inspect it to see if the filament is blown.
4. If the fuse is blown, replace it with a fuse of the same amperage rating.
5. Replace the fuse removal tool, if applicable, then install the fuse panel cover.
6. If the fuse continues to blow, check the circuit or component that the fuse is protecting, and repair it as necessary.

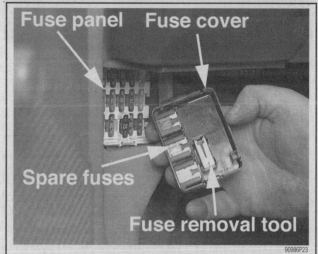

Fig. 165 Remove the fuse panel cover to gain access to the fuse panel and, if equipped, the spare fuses or fuse removal tool

Fig. 164 The interior fuse panel is located below the driver's side of the instrument panel

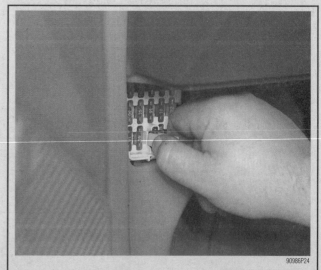

Fig. 166 Grasp the fuse and pull it straight from the fuse panel

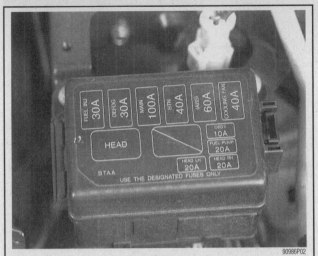

Fig. 167 The underhood mounted (exterior) fuse panel may have the fuse locations marked on its cover

Fig. 168 Remove the cover from the exterior fuse panel to access the fuses

Fuse Panel* Cavity Number	Fuse Rating	Color	Protected Component
REAR WIPER	10 amp	Red	Rear wiper and washer motor, WAC and A/C relay DRL relay (Canada), A/C switch INO lamp
HAZARD	15 amp circuit breaker	Blue	Front and rear turn lamp, turn indicator lamp, flasher.
ROOM	10 amp	Red	Dome & map lamp, TWS unit, IG key illumination, luggage lamp, vanity mirror lamp, radio (memory), door lock relay, shift-lock system, EAT module, EEC module (1.9L engine), EGI module (1.8L engine)
ENGINE	15 amp	Blue	Fan #1 relay, IG relay, EEC relay
RADIO	15 amp	Blue	Radio, premium sound amplifier. Remote control mirror, panel light resistor
DOOR LOCK	30 amp	Light green	Door lock motor
BELT	30 amp	Light green	Passive belt control module, passive belt motor
POWER WIND	30 amp	Light green	Power window motor
METER	15 amp	Blue	Cluster, backup lamp, turn lamp, auto cruise, shift-lock system, TWS unit, flasher unit EAT module, passive belt control module, flasher unit
WIPER	20 amp	Yellow	Front wiper and washer motor, I.W.W. relay unit
STOP	20 amp	Yellow	Brakelamp, horn, high-mount brakelamp, shift interlock system, auto cruise, EAT module, EGI module
TAIL	15 amp	Blue	Exterior lamps, interior illumination, engine room lamp, TNS relay, TWS unit, EGI module (1.8L engine)
SUN ROOF	15 amp	Blue	Moon roof motor
—	—	—	—
DEFOG	20 amp	Yellow	Rear window defrost, EGI module (1.8L engine)
HEATER	30 amp circuit breaker	—	Blower motor, EGI module (1.8L engine)
HEGO	10 amp	Red	HEGO sensor (1.9L engine)

Fig. 169 Interior fuse location, rating, color and which circuit it protects—1991–92 models

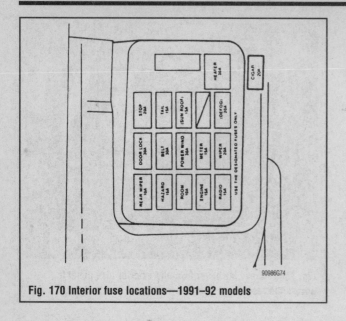

Fig. 170 Interior fuse locations—1991–92 models

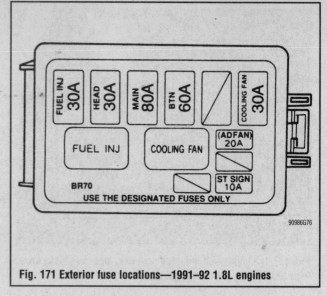

Fig. 171 Exterior fuse locations—1991–92 1.8L engines

Position	Description	Color	Protected Component
Fuel INJ	30 amp	Pink	Fuel injection system
HEAD	30 amp F.L.	Pink	Headlamps, high beam indicator, fog lamp Daytime Running Lights (Canada)
Main	100 amp F.L. (1.9L engine)	Blue	Alternator, wiper and washer motors, audio system,
	80 amp F.L. (1.8L engine)	Black	Turn signal lamp, backup lamps, cigar lighter, power window cluster, shift-lock system, moon roof motor.
BTN	60 amp F.L. (1.8L engine)	Yellow	Belt, hazard, room, door lock, stop and tail; charging system
	40 amp F.L. (1.9L engine)	Green	
Cooling Fan	40 amp (1.9L engine)	Green	Cooling fan motor
	30 amp (1.8L engine)	Pink	
Electrical Fan	30 amp (1.8L engine, M/T)	Pink	
Air cond. (1.9L engine)	10 amp (1.9 liter engine)	Red	A/C magnet clutch, EEC module (1.9L engine)
ST SIGN (1.8L engine)	10 amp	Red	Circuit relay EGI module

Fig. 172 Exterior fuse location, rating, color and which circuit it protects—1991–92 models

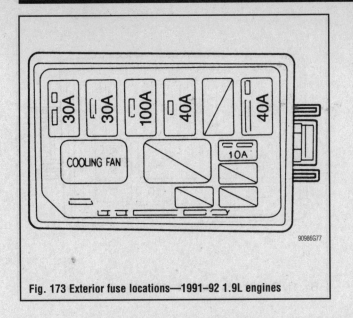

Fig. 173 Exterior fuse locations—1991–92 1.9L engines

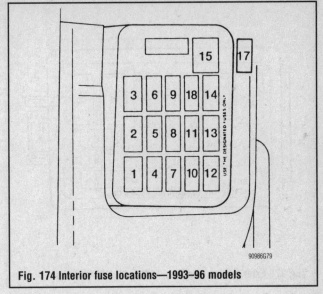

Fig. 174 Interior fuse locations—1993–96 models

Fuse/C.B. Relay Location	Fuse Amp Rating	Description
1	10 amp	A/C On Indicator, Air Conditioner Relay, Air Conditioner Switch, Daytime Running Lamp Module, Daytime Running Lamp Relay, Rear Wiper and Washer Motor, Wide-Open Throttle Cutout Relay
2	30 amp	Door Lock Motor
3	20 amp	Brakelamp, Electronic Automatic Transaxle Module, Powertrain Control Module, High-Mount Brakelamp, Horn, Shift Interlock System, Speed Control
4	15 amp	Hazard Flashers, Front and Rear Turn Lamp, Turn Indicator Lamp
5	30 amp	Passive Belt Control Module, Passive Belt Motor
6	15 amp	Powertrain Control Module (1.8L engine), Exterior Lamps, Interior Illumination, Parking Lamp Relay, Warning Chime Module
7	15 amp 1.8L engine / 15 amp 1.9L engine	Dome and Map Lamp, Door Lock Switch, Engine Room, Ignition Key Illumination, Luggage Lamp, Premium Sound Amplifier, Radio (memory), Powertrain Control Module, Shift Interlock System, Visor Mirror Lamp, Warning Chime Module
8	30 amp	Power Window Motor
9	15 amp	Moon Roof Motor
10	15 amp	Cooling Fan System, Powertrain Control Module Power Relay
11	15 amp	Air Bag Diagnostic Module, Backup Lamps, Cluster, Flasher Unit, Passive Belt Control Module, Powertrain Control Module (Canada Only), Shift-Lock System, Speed Control, Turn Signal Flashers, Warning Chime
12	15 amp	Instrument Panel Dimmer Module, Radio, Remote Control Mirror
13	20 amp	Front Wiper and Washer Motor, Interval Governor, Interval Wiper and Washer Switch
14	20 amp	Powertrain Control Module (1.8L engine), Rear Window Defrost
15	30 amp circuit breaker	Blower Motor, Powertrain Control Module (1.8L engine)
16	10 amp (1.9L engine) / 20 amp (1.8L engine)	Heated Exhaust Gas Oxygen Sensor (1.9L engine) (on joint box side, not shown) / Horn (on joint box side, not shown)
17	20 amp	Cigar Lighter (on joint box side)
18	10 amp	Anti-lock Brake System (1.8L engine)

Fig. 175 Interior fuse location, rating, and which circuit it protects—1993–96 models

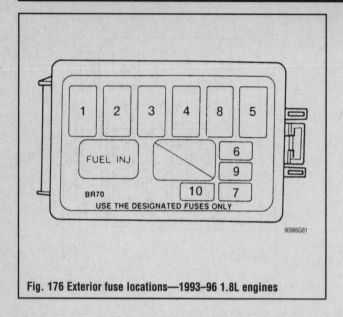

Fig. 176 Exterior fuse locations—1993–96 1.8L engines

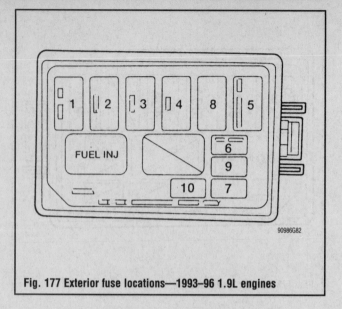

Fig. 177 Exterior fuse locations—1993–96 1.9L engines

Fuse/C.B. Relay Location	Fuse Amp Rating	Description
1	30 amp	Charging System (1.8L Engine), Fuel Injection System
2	30 amp FL	Daytime Running Lamps (Canada), Fog Lamps, Headlamps, High Beam Indicator
3	80 amp FL (1.8L engine) / 100 amp FL (1.9L engine)	Charging System, Engine Compartment Fuse Panel (ABS, A/C, BTN, Fan, Horn [1.8L Engine]), Engine Controls, Instrument Cluster (Manual Transaxle Only), Instrument Panel Fuse Panel (Cigar, Defrost, Engine ABS, Heater, HEGO [1.9L Engine], Meter, Power Window, Radio, Rear Wiper, Sun Roof), Starting System
4	60 amp FL (1.8L engine) / 40 amp FL (1.9L engine)	Charging System (1.9L Engine), Instrument Panel Fuse Panel (Belt, Door Lock, Hazard, Room, Stop, Tail)
5	30 amp (1.8L MTX engine) / 40 amp (1.9L engine) (1.8L ATX engine)	Cooling Fan System
6	10 amp (1.9L engine) / 20 amp (1.8L engine)	Air Conditioner Magnet Clutch, Powertrain Control Module (1.9L engine)
7	10 amp FL (1.8L engine)	Fuel Pump Relay, Powertrain Control Module
	20 amp (1.9L engine)	Fuel Pump
8	60 amp (1.8L engine)	Anti-lock Brake System
9	10 amp	Air Bag Diagnostic Module
10	20 amp (1.8L engine)	Fuel pump
	10 amp (1.9L engine)	OBD-II (Data link connector)

Fig. 178 Exterior fuse location, rating, and which circuit it protects—1993–96 models

Fuse/Relay Location	Fuse Amp Rating	Description
DRL	10A	Daytime running lamps
HAZARD	15A	Hazard flasher
ROOM	10A	Engine controls, RAP system, radio, shift lock, courtesy lamps, starting system, warning chime, instrument cluster
ENGINE	15A	Electronic automatic transaxle, ignition system, constant control relay module (PCM relay)
RADIO	5A	Power mirrors, radio, RAP system
DOOR LOCK	30A	Power door locks
HORN	15A	Horn, shift lock
AIR COND	15A	A/C-Heater, ABS
METER	10A	Backup lamps, engine coolant level switch, instrument cluster, rear window defrost, shift lock, warning chime, turn signal switch
WIPER	20A	Wiper/washer, blower motor relay
STOP	20A	Stop lamps, brake pressure switch
TAIL	15A	Exterior lamps, instrument illumination
SUN ROOF	15A	Power moonroof
ASC	10A	Speed control
P. WINDOW (C.B.)	30A	Power windows
CIGAR	20A	Cigar lighter
AIR BAG	10A	Air bags
FOG	10A	Fog lamps, daytime running lamps (DRL)
AUDIO	15A	Premium sound amplifier, CD changer
FUEL INJ.	10A	H02S, evaporative emission purge flow sensor
BLOWER (C.B.)	30A	Blower motor relay

90986G85

Fig. 179 Interior fuse location, rating, and which circuit it protects—1997–99 models

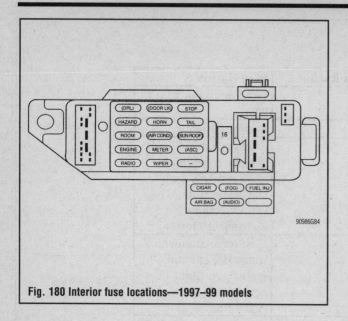

Fig. 180 Interior fuse locations—1997–99 models

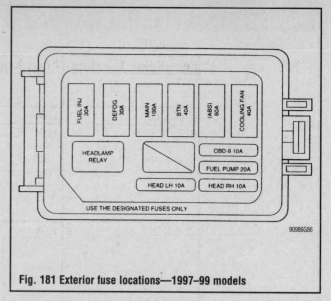

Fig. 181 Exterior fuse locations—1997–99 models

Fuse/Relay Location	Fuse Amp Rating	Description
FUEL INJ.	30A	Air bags, constant control relay module (PCM relay), generator
DEFOG	30A	Rear window defrost
MAIN	100A	Overall circuit protection
BTN	40A	Hazard, stop, door lock, tail, room and horn fuses of the I/P fuse panel
ABS	60A	ABS main relay
COOLING FAN	40A	Constant control relay module (Cooling fan)
OBD-II	10A	Data link connector (DLC), instrument cluster
FUEL PUMP	20A	Constant control relay module (fuel pump)
HEAD RH	10A	Headlamps
HEAD LH	10A	Headlamps

Fig. 182 Exterior fuse location, rating, and which circuit it protects—1997–99 models

Fusible Link

▶ **See Figure 183**

The fuse link is a short length of wire, integral with the engine compartment wiring harness and should not be confused with standard wire. The fusible link wire gauge is smaller than the circuit which it protects. Under no circumstances should a fuse link replacement repair be made using a length of standard wire cut from bulk stock or from another wiring harness.

Fusible link wire is covered with a special thick, non-flammable insulation. An overload condition causes the insulation to blister. If the overall condition continues, the wire will melt. To check a fusible link, look for blistering insulation. If the insulation is okay, pull gently on the wire. If the fusible link stretches, the wire has melted.

Fusible links are often identified by the color coding of the insulation. Refer to the accompanying illustration for wire link size and color.

FUSIBLE LINK COLOR CODING	
WIRE LINK SIZE	**INSULATION COLOR**
20 GA	Blue
18 GA	Brown or Red
16 GA	Black or Orange
14 GA	Green
12 GA	Gray

90986G89

Fig. 183 Common fusible link color coding

Circuit Breakers

▶ **See Figure 184**

RESETTING

Circuit breakers are used to protect the various components of the electrical system, such as headlights and windshield wipers.

Circuit Protected	Size	Location
Blower motor, PCM Module (1.8L engine)	30 amp	Power distribution box above fuse panel

90986G88

Fig. 184 Circuit breaker location, rating, and which circuit it protects—1991–96 models

Circuit breakers operate when an electrical circuit overloads, or exceeds its rated amperage. Once activated, they may be reset.

There are two kinds of circuit breakers. One type will automatically reset itself after a given length of time, the second will not reset itself until the problem in the circuit has been repaired.

Flashers

The flasher is located on the interior fuse panel. Refer to the fuse panel illustrations in this section for the location of the flasher.

REPLACEMENT

1. Locate the flasher unit on the fuse panel.
2. Grasp the unit and pull it from the panel.
3. Install the new unit in its location on the fuse panel and press it into place until firmly seated.
4. Check for proper operation.

Troubleshooting Basic Turn Signal and Flasher Problems

Most problems in the turn signals or flasher system can be reduced to defective flashers or bulbs, which are easily replaced. Occasionally, problems in the turn signals are traced to the switch in the steering column, which will require professional service.
F = Front   R = Rear   • = Lights off   o = Lights on

Problem		Solution
Turn signals light, but do not flash		• Replace the flasher
No turn signals light on either side		• Check the fuse. Replace if defective. • Check the flasher by substitution • Check for open circuit, short circuit or poor ground
Both turn signals on one side don't work		• Check for bad bulbs • Check for bad ground in both housings
One turn signal light on one side doesn't work		• Check and/or replace bulb • Check for corrosion in socket. Clean contacts. • Check for poor ground at socket
Turn signal flashes too fast or too slow		• Check any bulb on the side flashing too fast. A heavy-duty bulb is probably installed in place of a regular bulb. • Check the bulb flashing too slow. A standard bulb was probably installed in place of a heavy-duty bulb. • Check for loose connections or corrosion at the bulb socket
Indicator lights don't work in either direction		• Check if the turn signals are working • Check the dash indicator lights • Check the flasher by substitution
One indicator light doesn't light		• On systems with 1 dash indicator: See if the lights work on the same side. Often the filaments have been reversed in systems combining stoplights with taillights and turn signals. Check the flasher by substitution • On systems with 2 indicators: Check the bulbs on the same side Check the indicator light bulb Check the flasher by substitution

TCCA6C02

INDEX OF WIRING DIAGRAMS

90986W01

SAMPLE DIAGRAM: HOW TO READ & INTERPRET WIRING DIAGRAMS

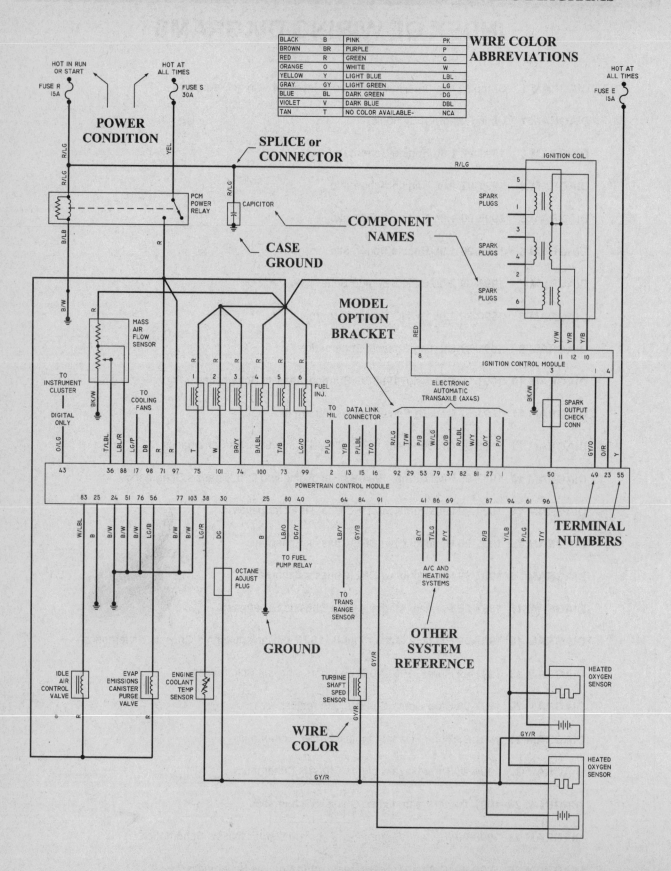

DIAGRAM 1

TCCA6W01

WIRING DIAGRAM SYMBOLS

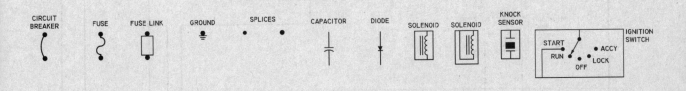

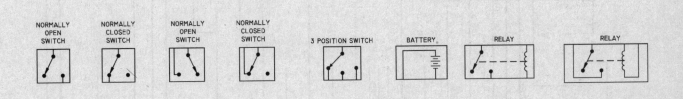

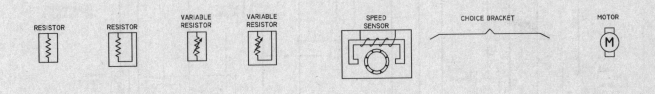

DIAGRAM 2

TCCA6W02

1991-92 1.8L ENGINE SCHEMATIC

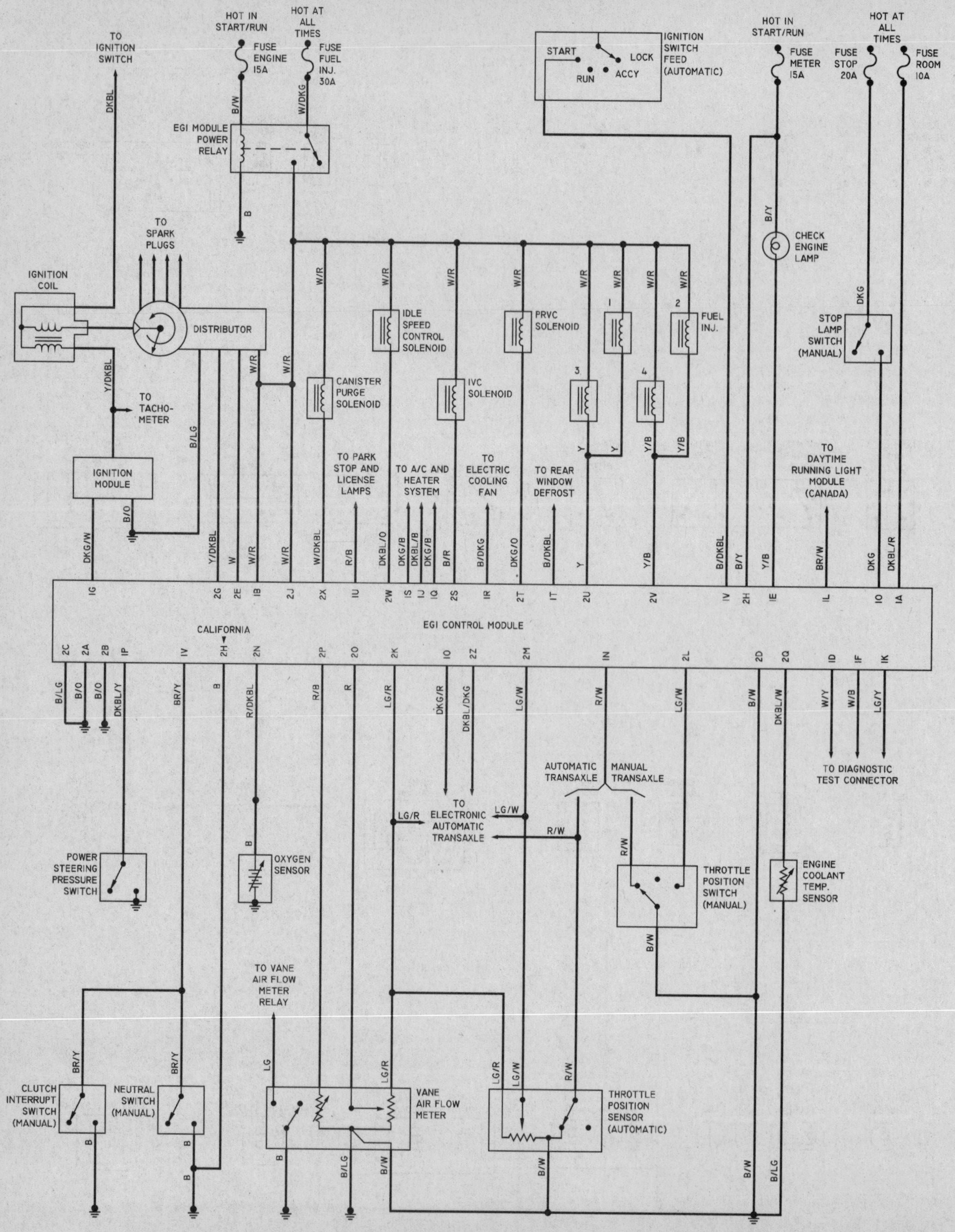

DIAGRAM 3

90986E01

1991-92 1.9L ENGINE SCHEMATIC

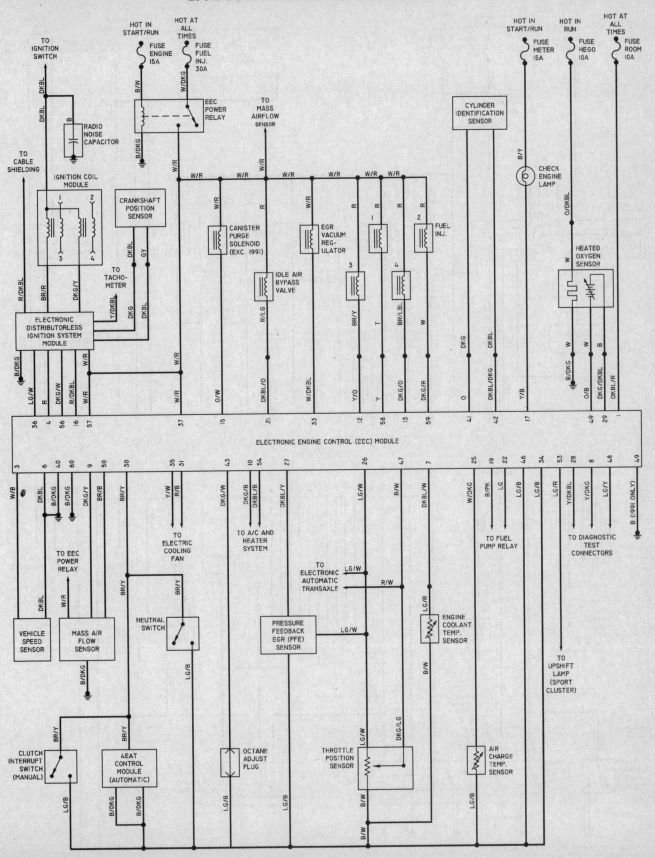

DIAGRAM 4

90986E02

1993-96 1.8L ENGINE SCHEMATIC

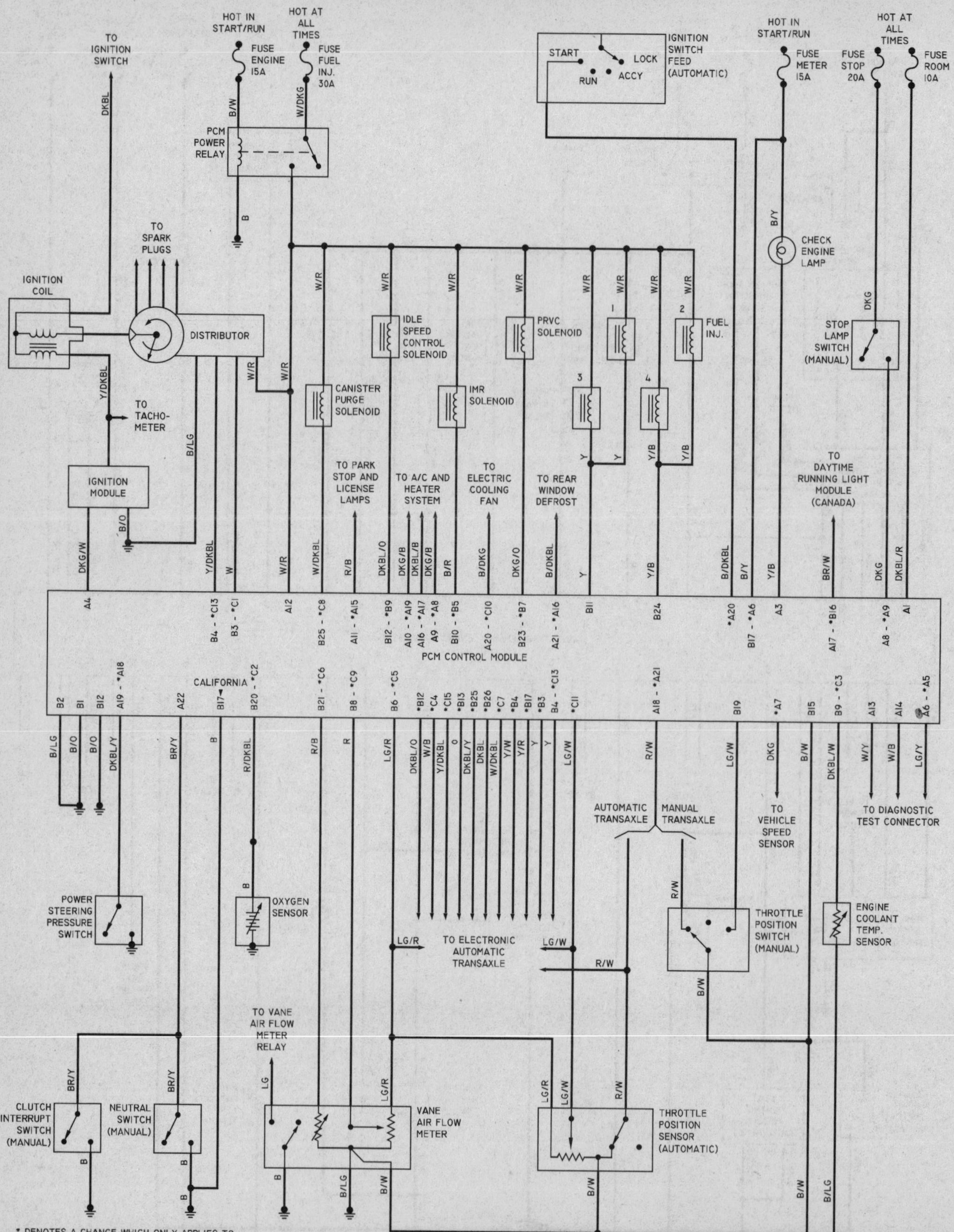

* DENOTES A CHANGE WHICH ONLY APPLIES TO AUTOMATIC TRANSMISSIONS

DIAGRAM 5

90986E03

1993-96 1.9L ENGINE SCHEMATIC

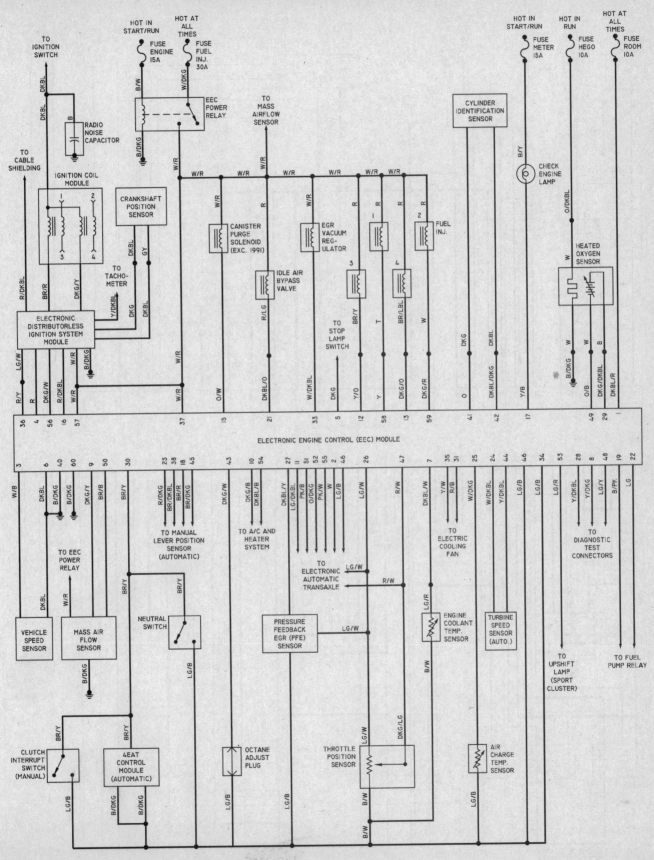

DIAGRAM 6

90986E04

1997-99 2.0L SOHC ENGINE SCHEMATIC

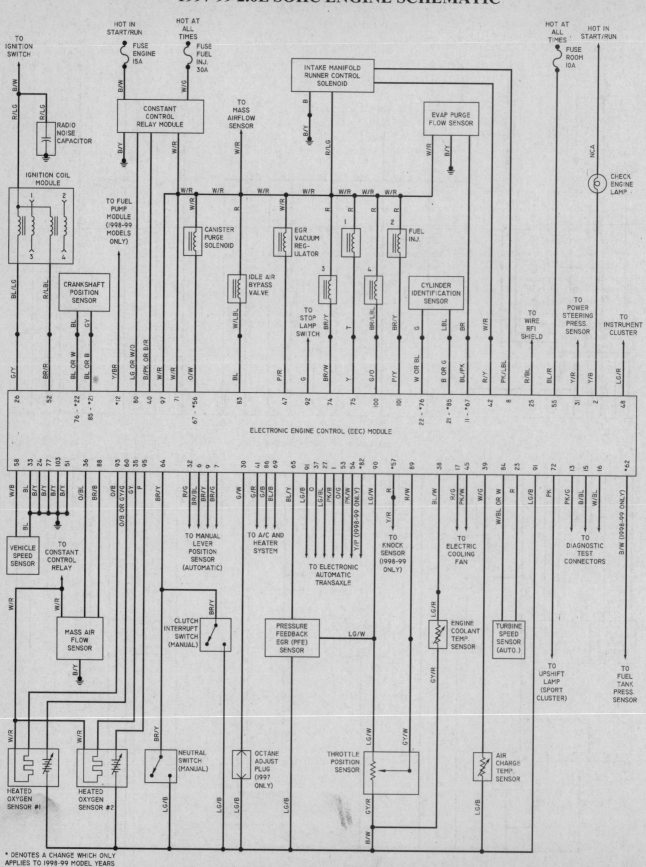

* DENOTES A CHANGE WHICH ONLY
APPLIES TO 1998-99 MODEL YEARS

DIAGRAM 7

90986E05

1998-99 2.0L DOHC ENGINE SCHEMATIC

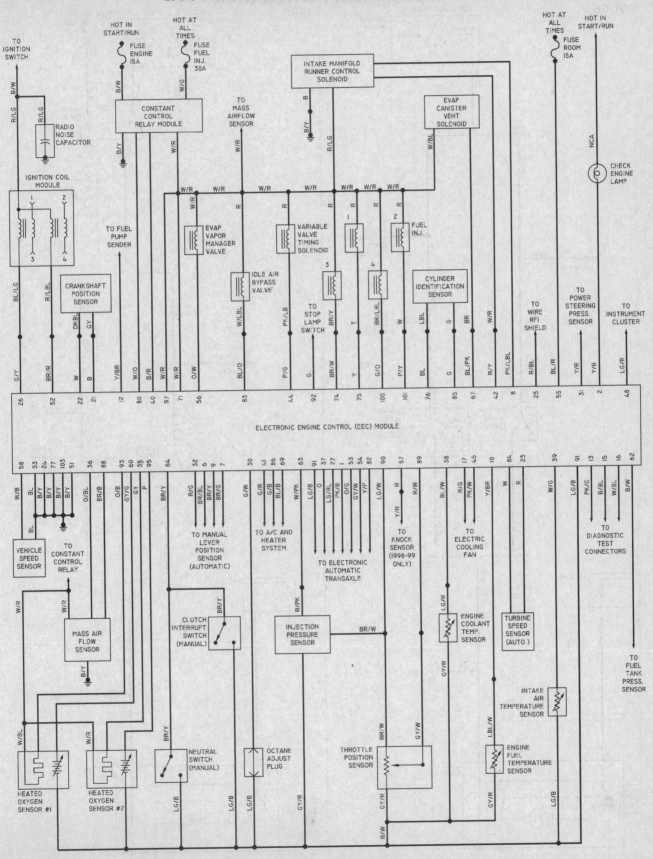

DIAGRAM 8

90986E06

1991-97 ESCORT/TRACER

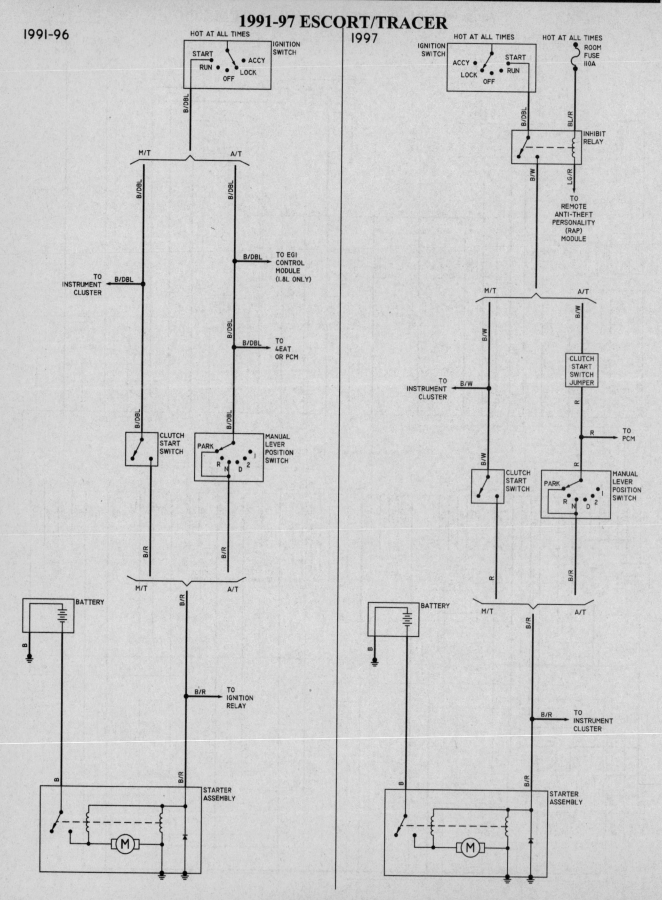

DIAGRAM 9

90986B01

1991-99 ESCORT/TRACER

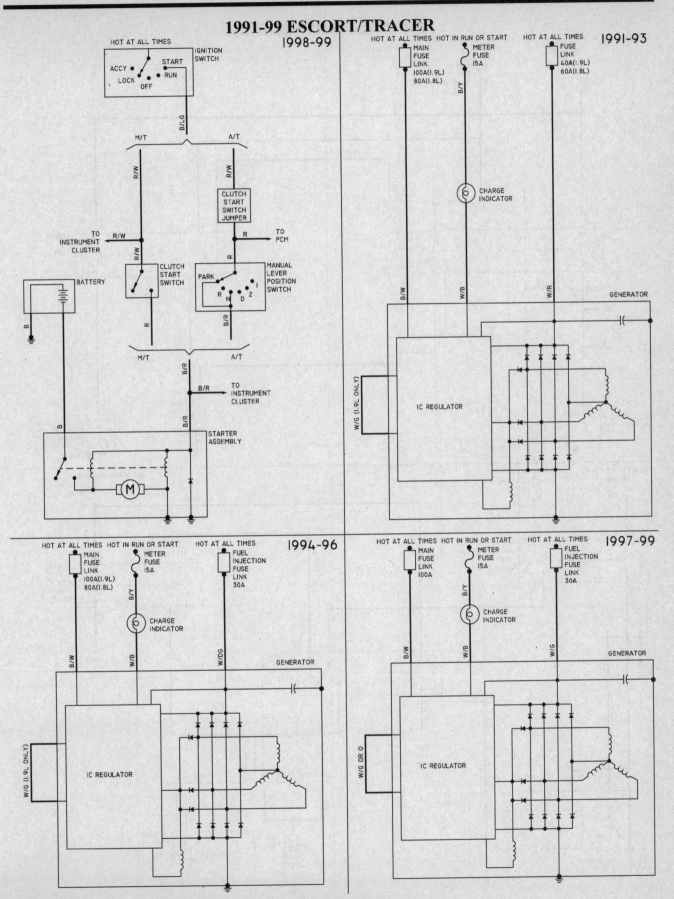

DIAGRAM 10

90986B02

1991-97 ESCORT/TRACER

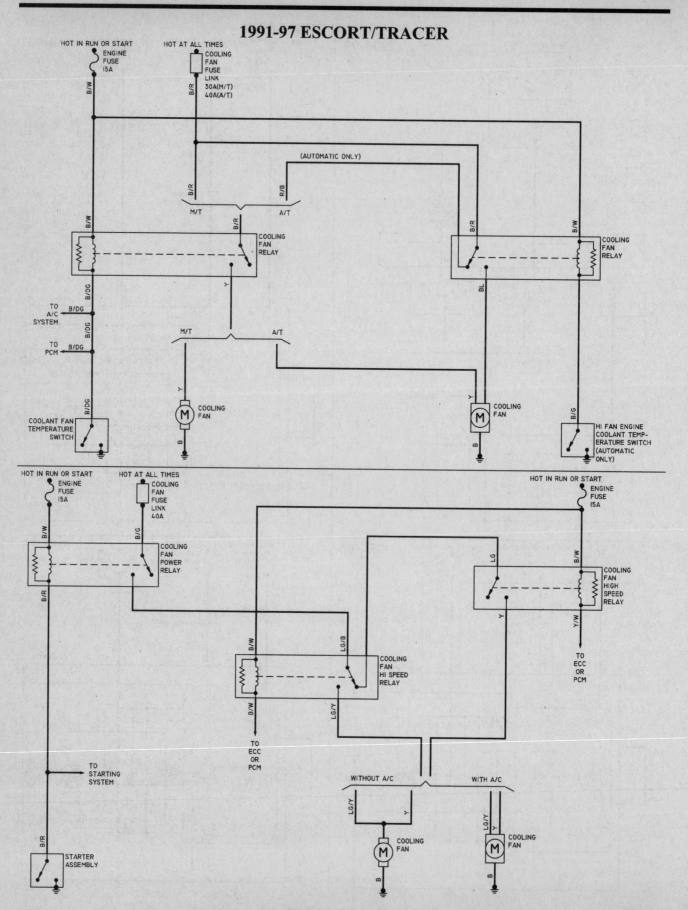

DIAGRAM 11

90986B03

1991-99 ESCORT/TRACER

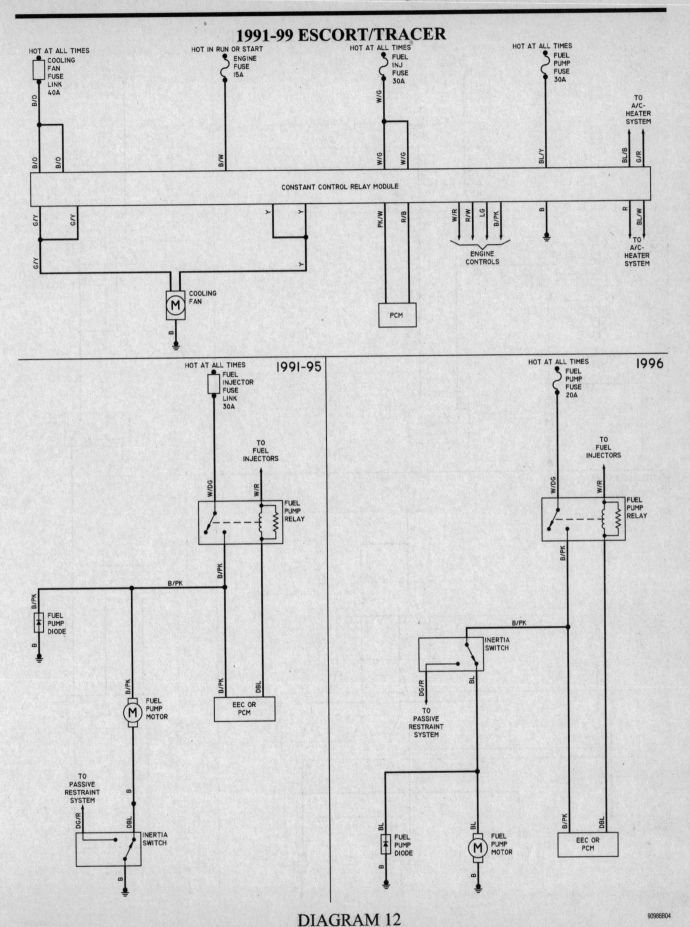

DIAGRAM 12

1991-99 ESCORT/TRACER

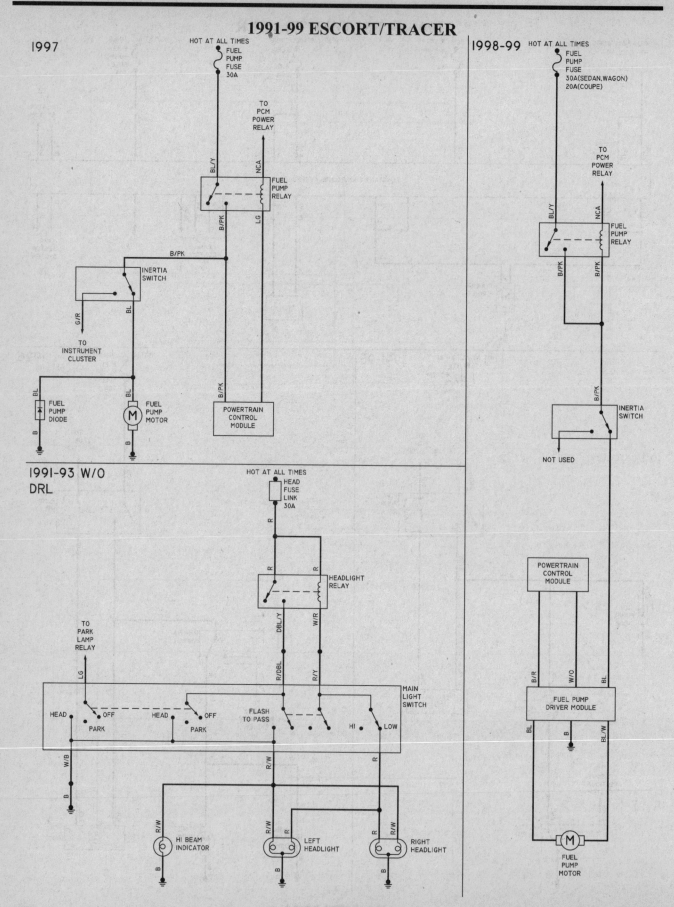

DIAGRAM 13

90986B05

1994-99 ESCORT/TRACER

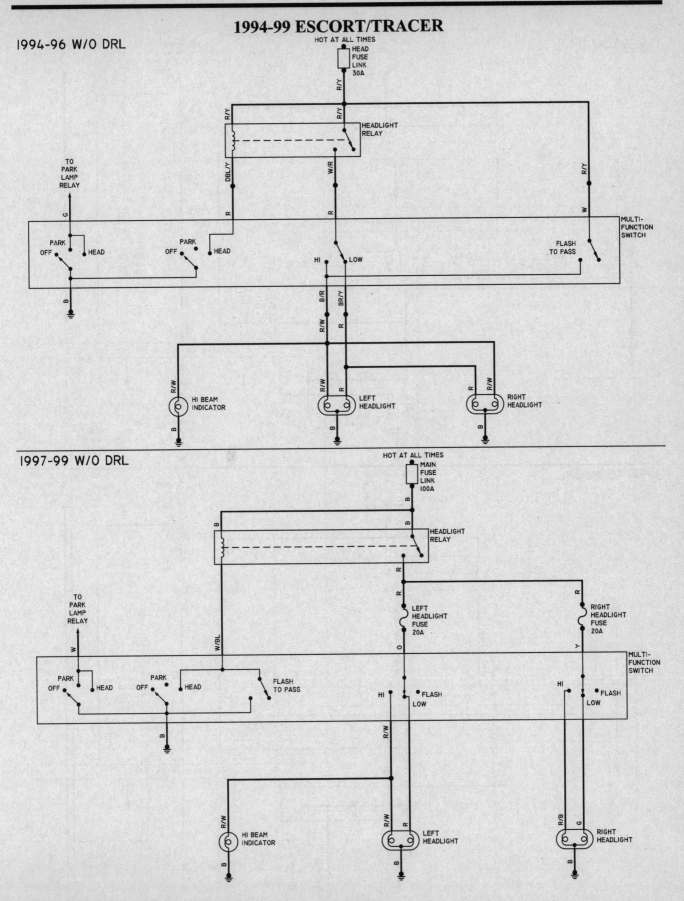

DIAGRAM 14

90986B06

1991-96 ESCORT/TRACER

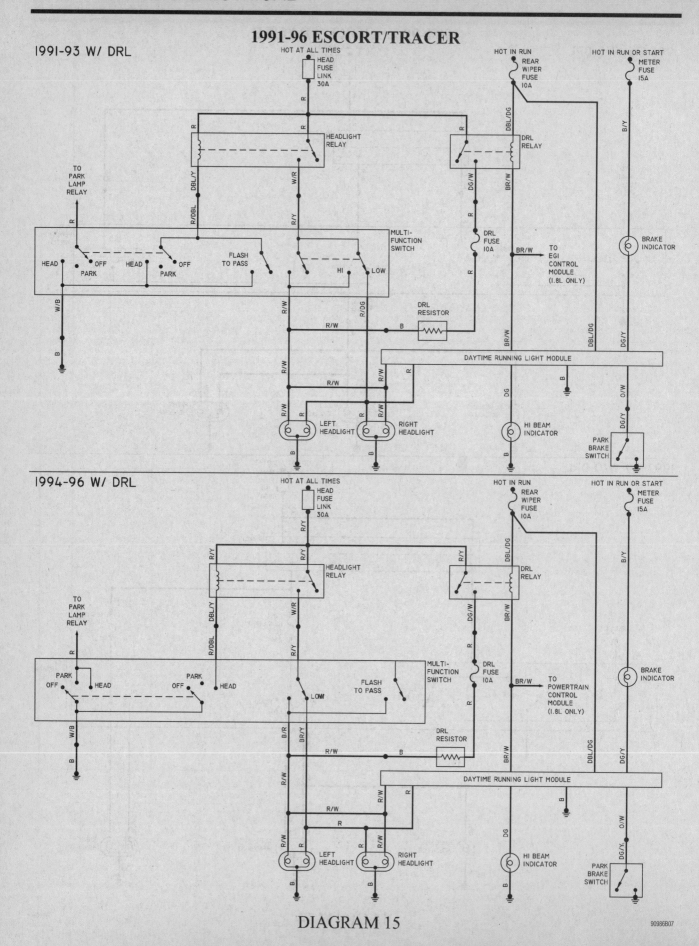

DIAGRAM 15

90986B07

1997-99 ESCORT/TRACER

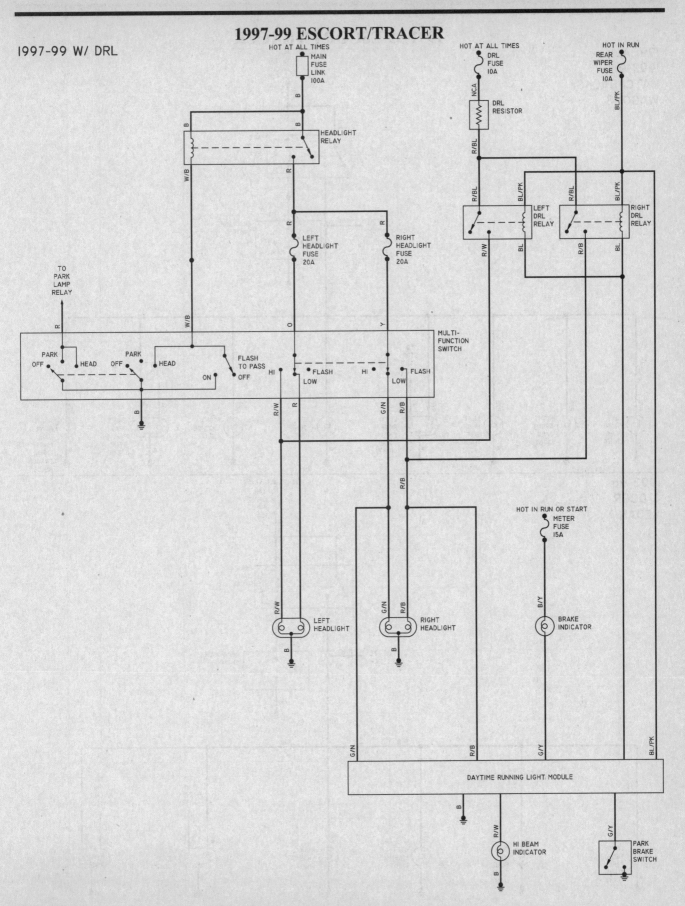

DIAGRAM 16

90986B09

1991-99 ESCORT/TRACER

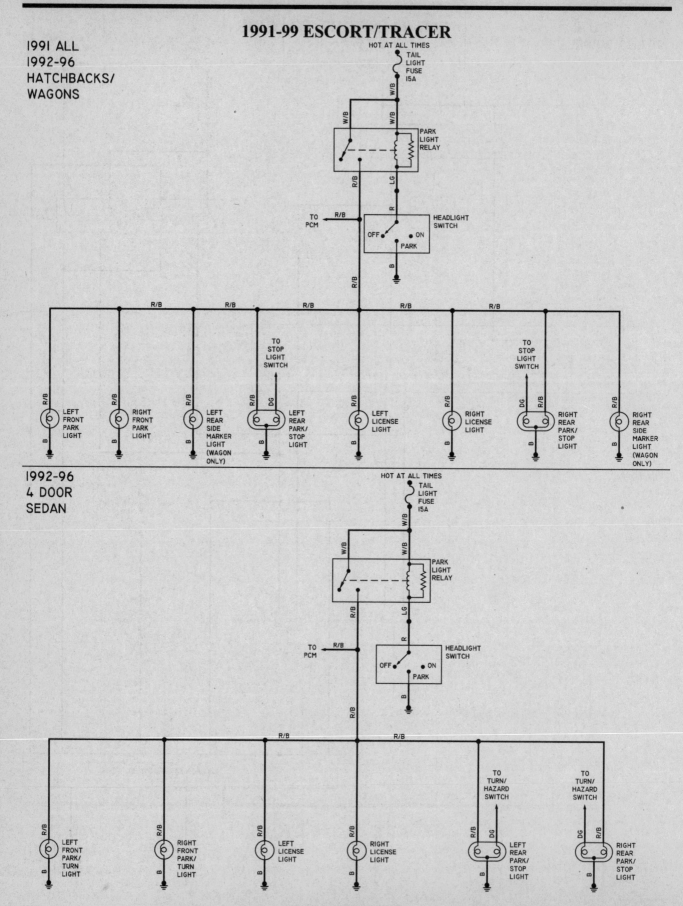

DIAGRAM 17

90986B08

1991-99 ESCORT/TRACER

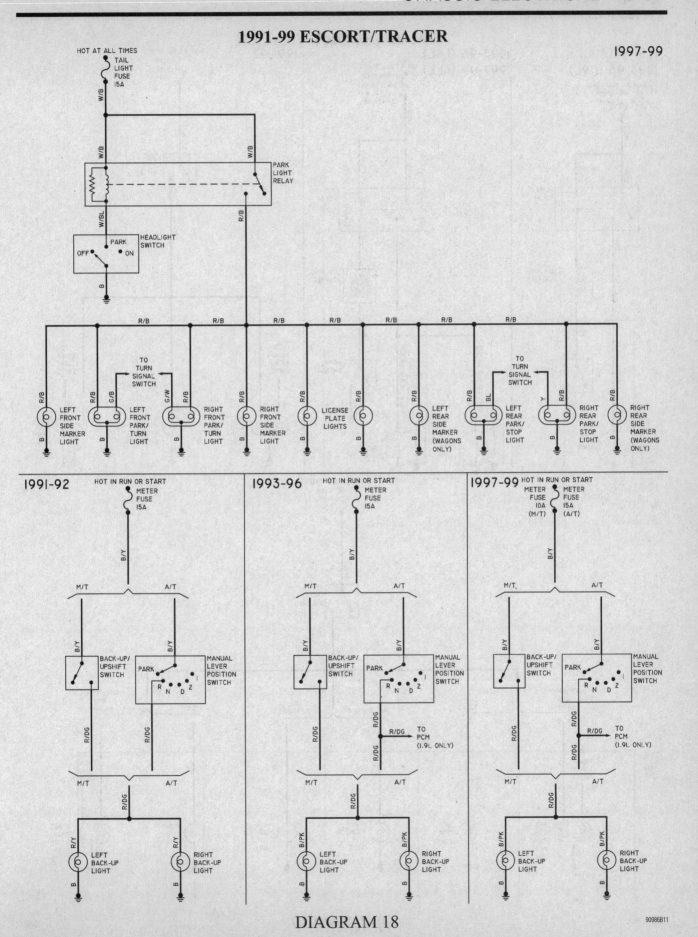

DIAGRAM 18

1991-99 ESCORT/TRACER

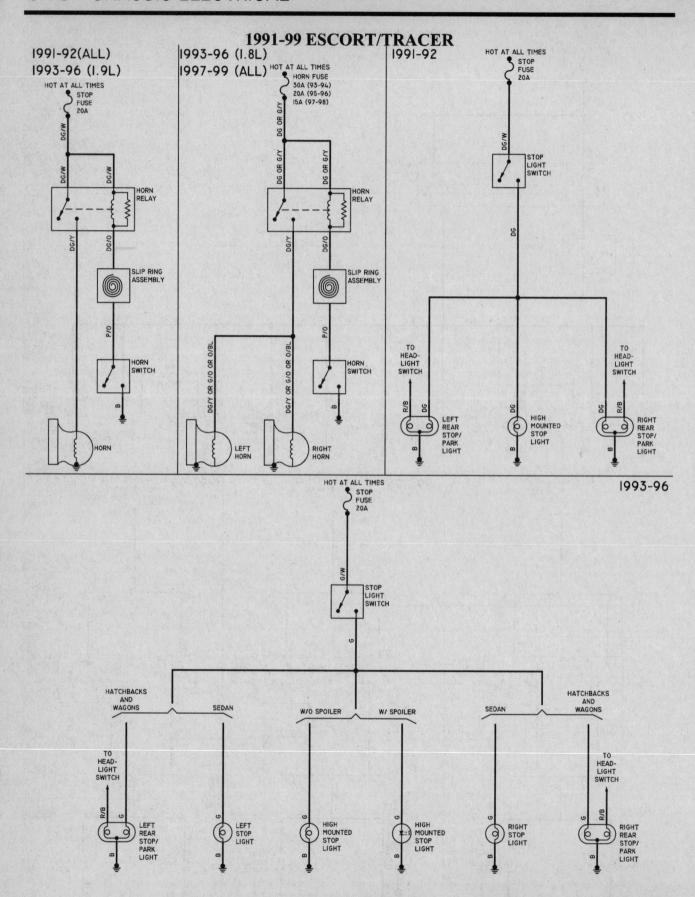

DIAGRAM 19

90986B12

1997-99 ESCORT/TRACER

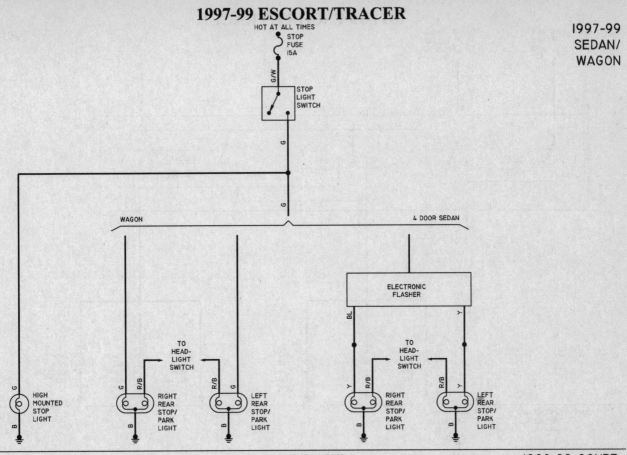

1998-99 COUPE

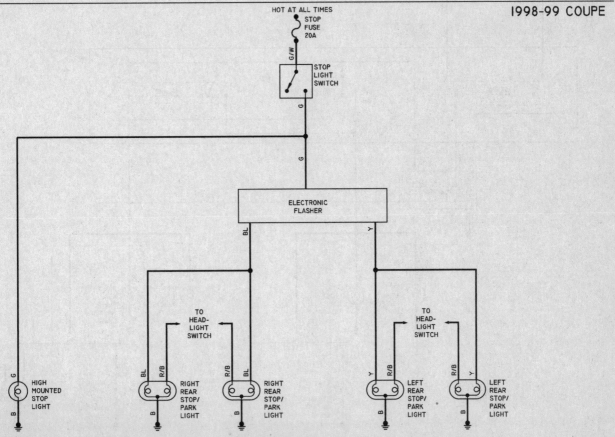

DIAGRAM 20

90986B15

1991-93 ESCORT/TRACER

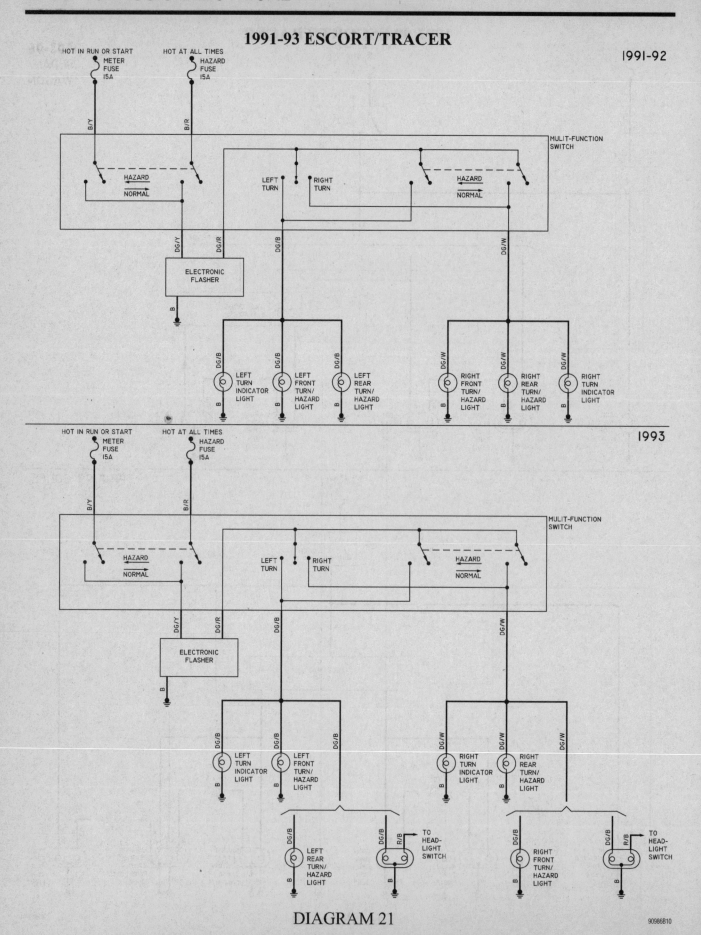

1991-92

1993

DIAGRAM 21

90986B10

1994-96 ESCORT/TRACER

1994-96

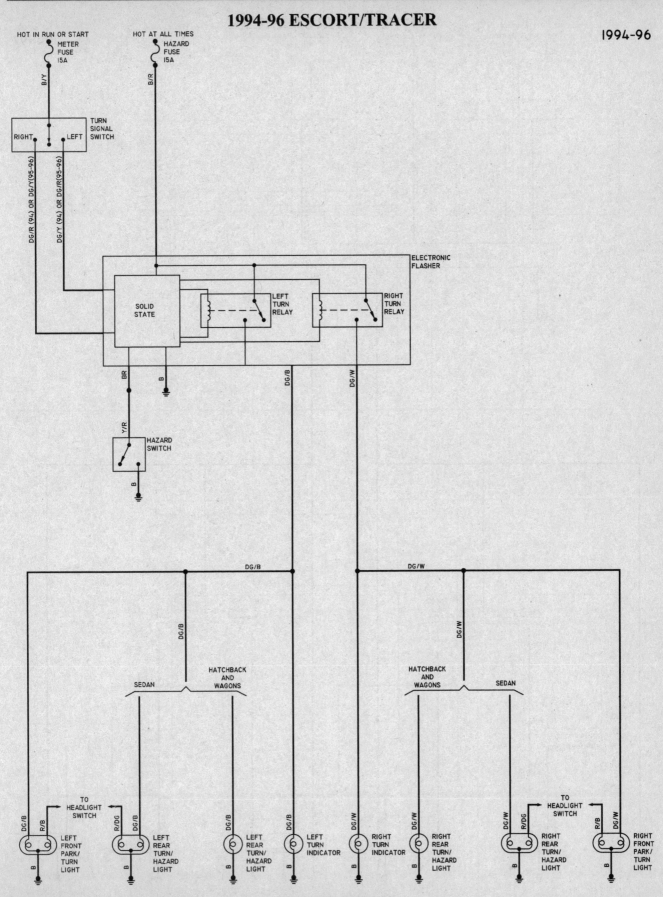

DIAGRAM 22

90986B14

1997 ESCORT/TRACER

1997

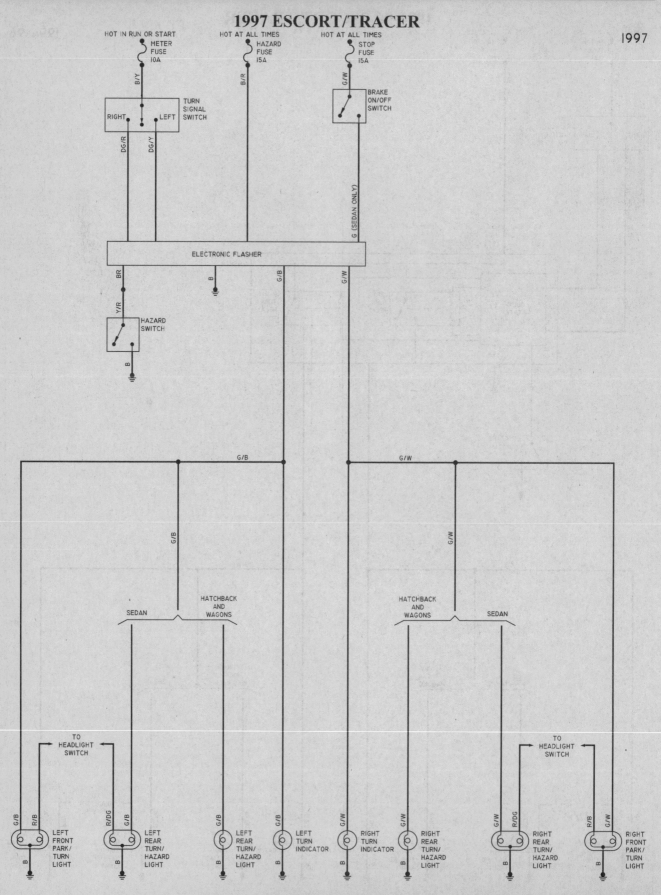

DIAGRAM 23

90986B16

1998-99 ESCORT/TRACER

1998-99 SEDAN/WAGON

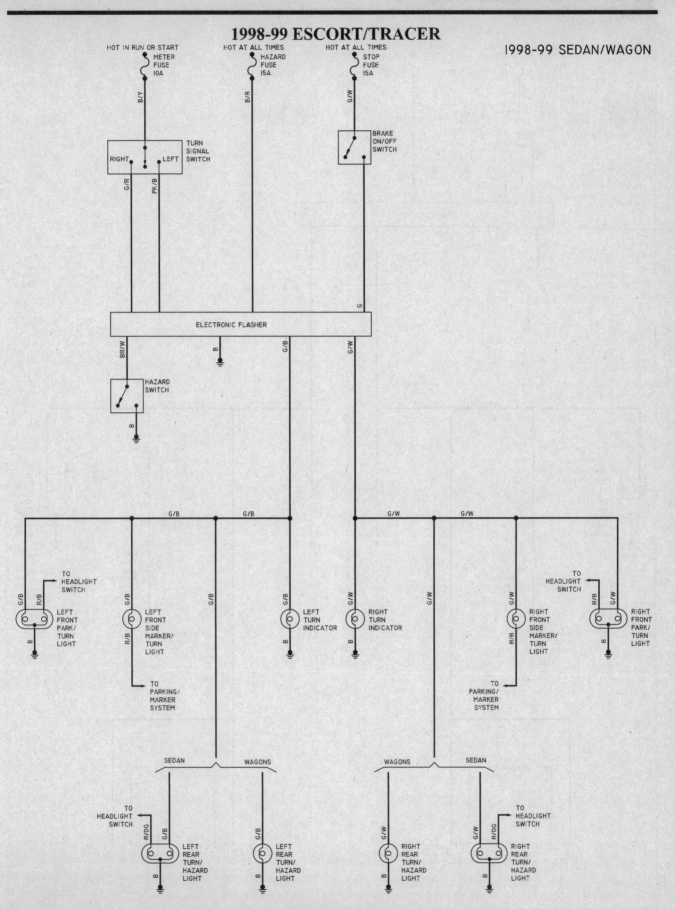

DIAGRAM 24

90986B17

1998-99 ESCORT COUPE

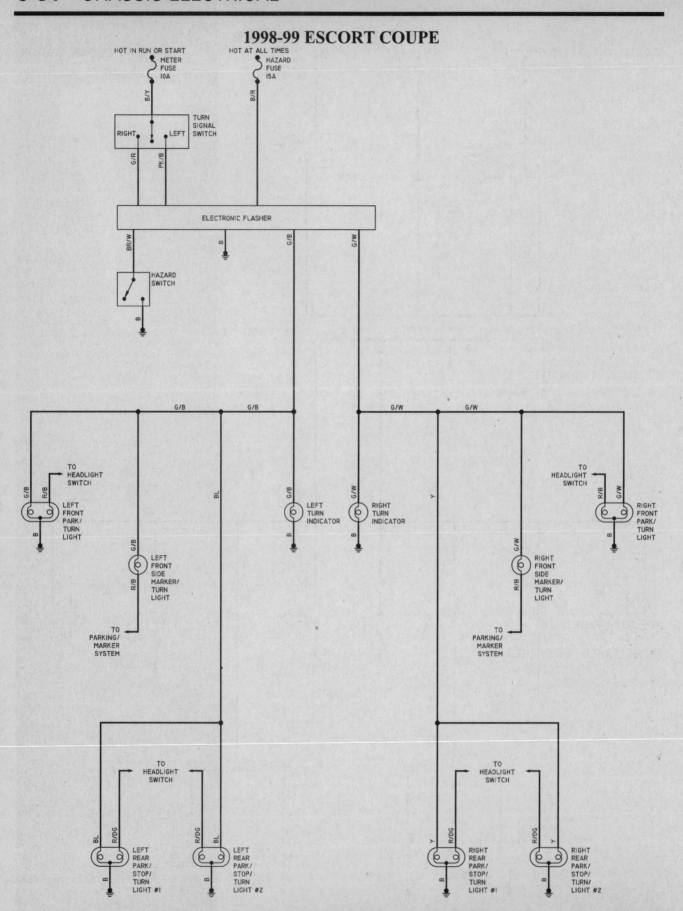

DIAGRAM 25

90986B18

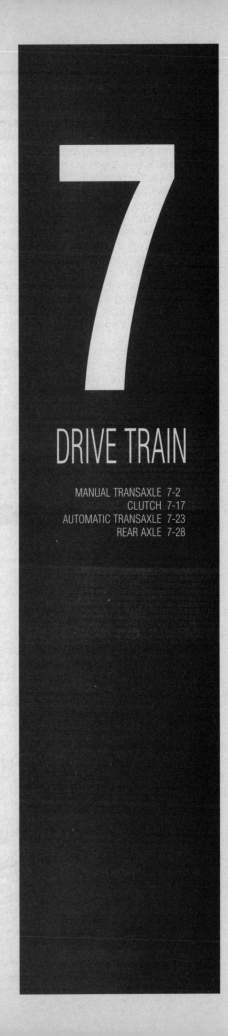

7

DRIVE TRAIN

MANUAL TRANSAXLE

Understanding the Manual Transaxle

Because of the way an internal combustion engine breathes, it can produce torque, or twisting force, only within a narrow speed range. Most modern, overhead valve pushrod engines must turn at about 2500 rpm to produce their peak torque. By 4500 rpm they are producing so little torque that continued increases in engine speed produce no power increases. The torque peak on overhead camshaft engines is generally much higher, but much narrower.

The manual transaxle and clutch are employed to vary the relationship between engine speed and the speed of the wheels so that adequate engine power can be produced under all circumstances. The clutch allows engine torque to be applied to the transaxle input shaft gradually, due to mechanical slippage. Consequently, the vehicle may be started smoothly from a full stop. The transaxle changes the ratio between the rotating speeds of the engine and the wheels by the use of gears. The gear ratios allow full engine power to be applied to the wheels during acceleration at low speeds and at highway/passing speeds.

In a front wheel drive transaxle, power is usually transmitted from the input shaft to a mainshaft or output shaft located slightly beneath and to the side of the input shaft. The gears of the mainshaft mesh with gears on the input shaft, allowing power to be carried from one to the other. All forward gears are in constant mesh and are free from rotating with the shaft unless the synchronizer and clutch is engaged. Shifting from one gear to the next causes one of the gears to be freed from rotating with the shaft and locks another to it. Gears are locked and unlocked by internal dog clutches which slide between the center of the gear and the shaft. The forward gears employ synchronizers; friction members which smoothly bring gear and shaft to the same speed before the toothed dog clutches are engaged.

Back-Up Light Switch

REMOVAL & INSTALLATION

1991–96 Models

▶ See Figure 1

1. Disconnect the negative battery cable.
2. Raise and support the car with safety stands.
3. Drain the transaxle fluid into a suitable container.
4. Unplug the backup switch electrical connection.
5. Remove the back-up switch and discard the washer.

To install:
6. Install a new washer and the switch. Tighten the switch to 14–22 ft. lbs. (20–29 Nm).
7. Attach the switch electrical connector.
8. Lower the car and refill the transaxle with the proper type and amount of fluid.
9. Connect the negative battery cable.

1997–99 Models

1. Disconnect the negative battery cable.
2. Drain the transaxle fluid into a suitable container.
3. Unplug the back-up light switch electrical connection.
4. Unscrew the switch with an open end wrench.
To install:
5. Install a new switch and tighten it to 15–21 ft. lbs. (20–25 Nm).
6. Attach the back-up light switch electrical connection.
7. Fill the transaxle with the proper type and amount of fluid.
8. Connect the negative battery cable.

Manual Transaxle Assembly

REMOVAL & INSTALLATION

1.8L and 1.9L Engines

▶ See Figures 2, 3 and 4

1. Disconnect both battery cables, negative cable first.
2. Remove the battery and battery tray.
3. Remove the engine air cleaner tube and the air intake resonator.
4. Disconnect the speedometer cable at the transaxle.
5. Remove the slave cylinder line-to- slave cylinder hose retaining clip, then disconnect the slave cylinder line from the slave cylinder hose and plug the hose.
6. Disconnect the ground strap from the transaxle.
7. Remove the tie wrap and unplug the three electrical connectors located above the transaxle.
8. Remove the electrical connector support bracket.
9. Install Engine Support Bar 014–00750 or equivalent, and attach it to the engine lifting eyes with suitable chains or cables.
10. If equipped, remove the three nuts from the left-hand engine support bracket.

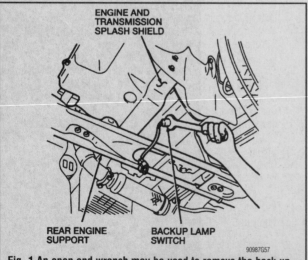

Fig. 1 An open end wrench may be used to remove the back-up light switch—1991–96 models with a manual transaxle

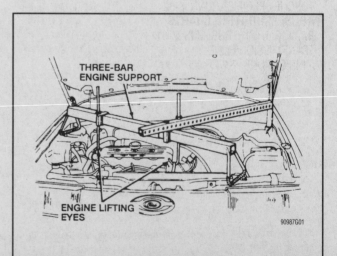

Fig. 2 Install a suitable engine support bar and attach it to the engine lifting eyes—1.8L and 1.9L engines

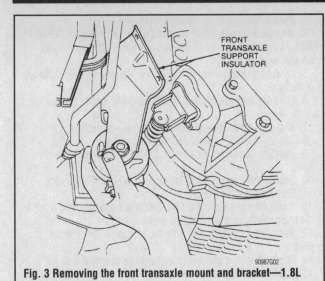

Fig. 3 Removing the front transaxle mount and bracket—1.8L and 1.9L engines

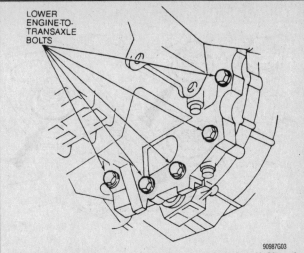

Fig. 4 Location of the lower engine-to-transaxle bolts—1.8L and 1.9L engines

11. Loosen the mount pivot nut and rotate the mount out of the way.

12. Remove the three bolts and the left-hand engine support mount.

13. Remove the two upper transaxle-to-engine bolts.

14. Raise and safely support the vehicle.

15. Remove the front wheel and tire assemblies.

16. Remove the inner fender splash shields.

17. Drain the transaxle fluid and install the drain plug.

18. Remove the halfshafts.

19. Install Transaxle Plugs T88C-7025-AH or equivalent, between the differential side gears.

✳✳ WARNING

Failure to install the transaxle plugs may cause the differential side gears to become improperly positioned. If the gears become misaligned, the differential will have to be removed from the transaxle to align them.

20. If equipped with the 1.8L engine, remove the intake manifold support bolts and the support.

21. Remove the starter motor.

22. Unfasten the gearshift stabilizer bar nut and washers. Remove the stabilizer bar and bracket from the transaxle.

23. Unfasten the shift control rod-to-transaxle bolt and nut and remove the shift control rod from the transaxle.

24. Remove both lower splash shields.

25. Unfasten the transaxle mount-to-crossmember bolts and nuts and remove the lower crossmember (rear engine support).

26. Position and secure a suitable transaxle jack under the transaxle.

27. Remove the front transaxle mount and bracket.

28. Remove the lower engine-to-transaxle bolts and slowly lower the transaxle out of the vehicle.

To install:

29. Apply a thin coating of suitable grease to the spline of the input shaft.

30. Place the transaxle onto a suitable transaxle jack. Make sure the transaxle is secure.

31. Raise the transaxle into position.

32. Install the lower engine-to-transaxle bolts and tighten to 27–38 ft. lbs. (37–52 Nm).

33. Install the front transaxle mount and bracket. Tighten the bolts to 12–17 ft. lbs. (16–23 Nm).

34. Remove the transaxle jack.

35. Install the lower crossmember. Tighten the support bolts to 47–66 ft. lbs. (64–89 Nm) and the transaxle support insulator-to-rear engine support nuts to 27–38 ft. lbs. (37–52 Nm).

36. Install both lower splash shields.

37. Install the shift control rod bolt and nut and tighten to 12–17 ft. lbs. (16–23 Nm).

38. Install the stabilizer bracket and stabilizer bar with the nut and washers and tighten to 23–34 ft. lbs. (31–46 Nm).

39. Install the starter motor.

40. If equipped with the 1.8L engine, install the intake manifold support and tighten the retaining bolts to 27–38 ft. lbs. (37–52 Nm).

41. Remove the transaxle plugs and install the halfshafts.

42. Install the inner fender splash shields.

43. Install the wheel and tire assemblies.

44. Lower the vehicle.

45. Install the upper engine-to-transaxle bolts and tighten to 47–66 ft. lbs. (64–89 Nm).

46. Install the left-hand engine support mount and tighten 3 bolts to 32–45 ft. lbs. (43–61 Nm) for 1.8L engine or 41–59 ft. lbs. (55–80 Nm) for 1.9L engine.

47. Rotate the left-hand engine support bracket into position and tighten the pivot nut.

48. Install and tighten the left-hand engine support bracket nuts and tighten to 47–66 ft. lbs. (64–89 Nm).

49. Remove the engine support bar.

50. Install the electrical connector support bracket. Attach the electrical connectors and secure with a new tie wrap.

51. Connect the ground strap to the transaxle.

52. Connect the slave cylinder line to the slave cylinder hose and install the retaining clip.

53. Add the proper type and amount of fluid to the transaxle.

54. Connect the speedometer cable.

55. Install the engine air cleaner tube and the air intake resonator.

56. Install the battery tray and the battery.

57. Connect the battery cables, negative cable last.

58. Check for fluid leaks and proper clutch operation.

59. Road test the vehicle and check for proper transaxle operation.

2.0L Engines

▶ **See Figures 5, 6, 7 and 8**

1. Disconnect both battery cables, negative cable first.

2. Remove the battery and battery tray.

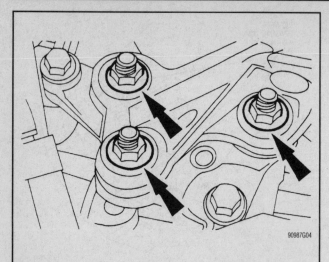

Fig. 5 Location of the left-hand engine support bracket nuts—2.0L engines

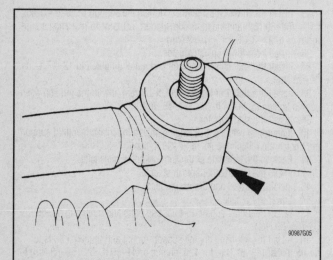

Fig. 6 Remove the gearshift stabilizer bar and support from the transaxle—2.0L engines

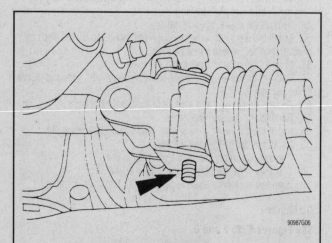

Fig. 7 Loosen the transaxle gearshift bolt, then remove the gearshift rod and clevis pin from the input shift shaft—2.0L engines

3. Remove the engine air cleaner outlet tube.

4. If necessary, unplug the Constant Control Relay Module (CCRM) electrical connection, loosen its retainers and remove the module and bracket as an assembly.

5. Disconnect the slave cylinder line from the slave cylinder hose and plug the hose.

6. Unfasten the slave cylinder line retaining clip and remove the line from the bracket.

7. Unplug the heated oxygen sensor electrical connection.

8. Unplug the back-up light electrical connection.

9. Unfasten the electrical connector bracket bolt and remove the bracket.

10. Unplug the Vehicle Speed Sensor (VSS) electrical connection.

11. Remove the halfshafts.

12. Install Engine Support Bar D88–6000A or equivalent, and attach it to the engine lifting eyes with suitable chains or cables.

13. Remove the insulator nuts from the left-hand engine support bracket.

14. Remove the front and rear upper transaxle-to-engine bolts.

15. Raise and safely support the vehicle.

16. Drain the transaxle fluid and install the drain plug.

17. Disconnect the A/C line from the retainer located on the engine support crossmember.

18. Unfasten the engine support crossmember bolts and nuts, then remove the crossmember.

19. Unfasten the gearshift stabilizer bar-to-transaxle nut, then remove the stabilizer bar and support from the transaxle.

20. Unfasten the transaxle gearshift rod nut.

21. Unfasten the transaxle gearshift bolt and remove the gearshift rod and clevis pin from the input shift shaft.

22. Remove the starter motor.

23. Disconnect the lower slave cylinder tube and remove the slave cylinder.

24. Unfasten the lower transaxle-to-engine bolts.

25. Position and secure a suitable transaxle jack under the transaxle.

26. Remove the catalytic converter.

27. Unfasten the middle transaxle-to-engine bolts and remove the transaxle from the car.

To install:

28. Apply a thin coating of suitable grease to the spline of the input shaft.

29. Place the transaxle onto a suitable transaxle jack. Make sure the transaxle is secure.

30. Raise the transaxle into position.

31. Install the middle transaxle-to-engine bolts and tighten them to 23–38 ft. lbs. (38–51 Nm).

32. Install the lower engine-to-transaxle bolts and tighten them to 23–38 ft. lbs. (38–51 Nm).

33. Install the clutch slave cylinder and tighten the nuts to 12–17 ft. lbs. (16–23 Nm).

34. Connect the lower slave cylinder tube and tighten the fitting to 10–16 ft. lbs. (13–21 Nm).

35. Install the starter motor.

36. Place the gearshift rod and clevis into position on the input shift shaft, then install gearshift bolt and gearshift rod nut and tighten to 12–17 ft. lbs. (16–23 Nm).

37. Install the gearshift stabilizer bar and tighten the nut to 23–34 ft. lbs. (31–46 Nm).

38. Install the halfshafts and the catalytic converter.

39. Install the engine support crossmember. Tighten the crossmember bolts and nuts to 47–65 ft. lbs. (64–89 Nm) and the insulator nuts to 28–37 ft. lbs. (38–51 Nm).

40. Install the front and rear upper transaxle-to-engine bolt and tighten it to 28–38 ft. lbs. (38–51 Nm).

41. Install the left-hand engine support insulator nuts and tighten them to 50–68 ft. lbs. (67–93 Nm).

42. Remove the engine support bar.

43. Install the electrical connector support bracket.

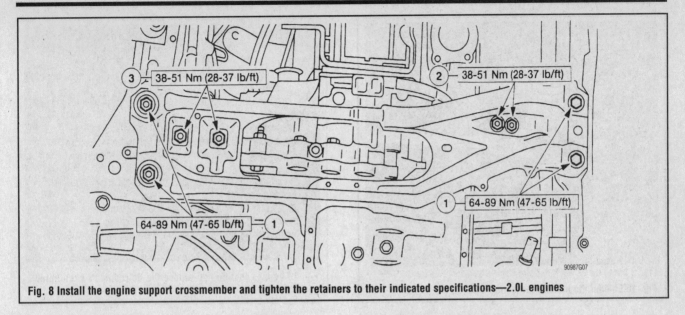

Fig. 8 Install the engine support crossmember and tighten the retainers to their indicated specifications—2.0L engines

44. Attach all the electrical connectors.

45. Connect the slave cylinder line to the slave cylinder hose and install the retaining clip. Tighten the fitting to 10–16 ft. lbs. (13–21 Nm).

46. Bleed the clutch hydraulic system.

47. Add the proper type and amount of fluid to the transaxle.

48. If removed, install the CCRM and bracket assembly. Tighten the retainers and attach the electrical connection.

49. Install the engine air cleaner tube.

50. Install the battery tray and the battery.

51. Connect the battery cables, negative cable last.

52. Check for fluid leaks and proper clutch operation.

53. Road test the vehicle and check for proper transaxle operation.

Halfshafts

REMOVAL & INSTALLATION

1991–96 Models

1.9L ENGINE AND LEFT SIDE OF 1.8L ENGINE

♦ See Figures 9 thru 27

➡Before continuing with any halfshaft procedure, make sure to have available, new halfshaft retaining nuts and circlips. Once removed, these parts loose their torque holding ability or retention capability and must not be reused.

1. Disconnect the negative battery cable.

2. With the vehicle sitting on the ground, carefully raise the staked portion of the halfshaft retaining nut using a suitable small chisel. Loosen the nut.

3. Raise and safely support the vehicle.

4. Remove the wheel and tire assembly.

5. Remove the splash shield.

6. Remove and discard the halfshaft retaining nut.

7. Remove the cotter pin and castellated nut from the tie rod end, and separate the tie rod end from the steering knuckle using a suitable removal tool. Discard the cotter pin.

8. In some cases, it may be necessary to remove the sway bar nut before prying down on the control arm.

9. Remove the lower ball joint pinch bolt. Carefully pry down on the lower control arm to separate the ball joint stud from the steering knuckle.

10. Pull outward on the steering knuckle/brake assembly. Carefully pull the halfshaft from the hub and position it aside.

11. Removal of the left side halfshaft requires removal of the crossmember to allow access with a prybar as follows:

   a. Support the transaxle with a suitable transaxle jack.

   b. Remove the four transaxle mount-to-crossmember retaining nuts.

   c. Remove the two crossmember retaining nuts at the rear of the crossmember.

   d. While supporting the rear of the crossmember, unfasten the two front mounting bolts and remove the crossmember.

12. Position a drain pan under the transaxle.

13. Insert a prybar between the halfshaft and the transaxle case. Gently pry outward to release the halfshaft from the differential side gear. Be careful not to damage the transaxle case, oil seal, CV-joint or CV-joint boot.

14. Remove the halfshaft.

➡Install suitable plug(s) after removing the halfshaft(s) to prevent the differential side gears from moving out of place. Should the gears become misaligned, the differential will have to be removed from the transaxle to align the gears.

To install:

15. Position a new circlip on the inner CV-joint spline so the circlip gap is at the top. Lubricate the splines lightly with a suitable grease.

16. Remove the plugs that were installed in the differential side gears.

Fig. 9 With the vehicle on the ground, carefully raise the staked portion of the halfshaft retaining nut with a small chisel

Fig. 10 Loosen the halfshaft retaining nut

Fig. 11 Remove and discard the halfshaft retaining nut

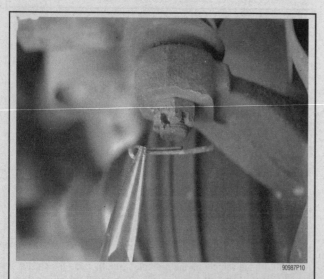

Fig. 12 Remove the cotter pin from the tie rod end

Fig. 13 Loosen, but do not remove the tie rod end's castellated nut

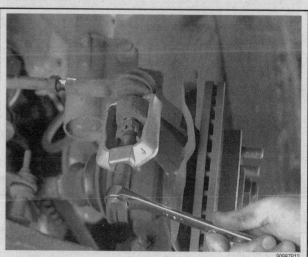

Fig. 14 Separate the tie rod end from the steering knuckle using a suitable removal tool

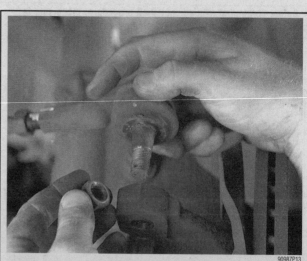

Fig. 15 Remove the castellated nut and disengage the tie rod end from the steering knuckle

Fig. 16 In some cases, it may be necessary to loosen the sway bar nut . . .

Fig. 19 . . . then remove the pinch bolt and nut

Fig. 17 . . . then remove the nut, washer and bushing. This will make it easier to separate the ball joint stud

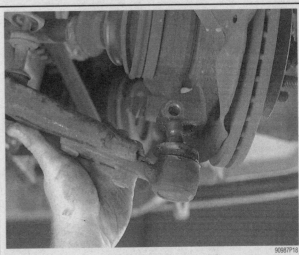

Fig. 20 Carefully pry down on the lower control arm to separate the ball joint stud from the steering knuckle

Fig. 18 Unfasten the lower ball joint pinch bolt . . .

Fig. 21 Pull outward on the steering knuckle/brake assembly. Separate the hub from the halfshaft and position it aside

Fig. 22 Insert a prybar between the halfshaft and transaxle case. Gently pry outward to release the halfshaft from the differential side gear

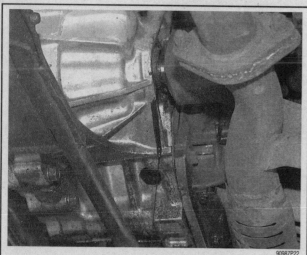

Fig. 23 Place a drain pan beneath the transaxle to catch any fluid that could drain from the transaxle during halfshaft removal

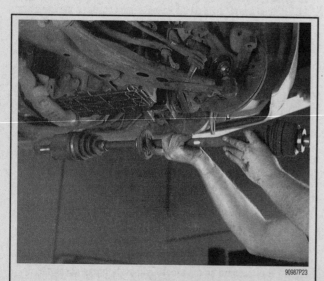

Fig. 24 Remove the halfshaft from the vehicle . . .

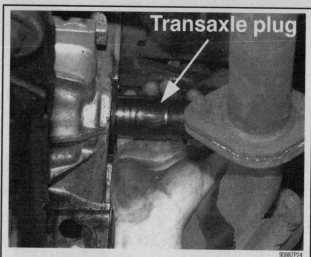

Fig. 25 . . . and install a suitable plug to prevent the differential side gears from moving out of place

17. Position the halfshaft so the CV-joint splines are aligned with the differential side gear splines. Push the halfshaft into the differential. When seated properly, the circlip can be felt snapping into the differential side gear groove.

18. Pull outward on the steering knuckle/brake assembly and insert the halfshaft into the hub.

19. Pry downward on the lower control arm and position the lower ball joint stud in the steering knuckle.

20. Install the crossmember and the crossmember-to-frame nuts and bolts. Tighten the nuts to 27–38 ft. lbs. (37–52 Nm) and the bolts to 47–66 ft. lbs. (64–89 Nm).

21. Install the four transaxle mount-to-crossmember nuts and tighten to 27–38 ft. lbs. (37–52 Nm).

22. Remove the transaxle jack.

23. Install the lower ball joint pinch bolt and tighten to 32–43 ft. lbs. (43–59 Nm).

24. Attach the tie rod end to the steering knuckle. Install the castellated nut and tighten to 31–42 ft. lbs. (42–57 Nm). Install a new cotter pin.

25. If removed, attach the sway bar nut and tighten to specification.

26. Install the splash shield.

27. Install the wheel and tire assembly.

28. Install a new halfshaft retaining nut and tighten to 174–235 ft. lbs. (235–319 Nm). Stake the halfshaft retaining nut using a suitable chisel with a rounded cutting edge.

Fig. 26 Remove the old circlip from the inner CV-joint spline, then install a new circlip with the gap at the top

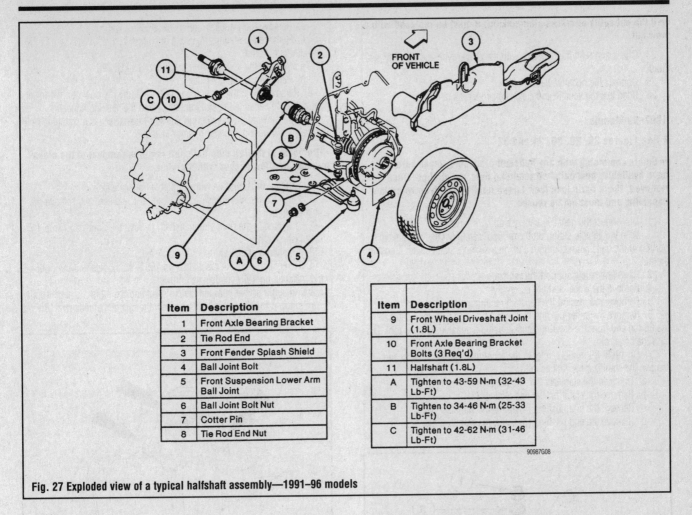

Item	Description
1	Front Axle Bearing Bracket
2	Tie Rod End
3	Front Fender Splash Shield
4	Ball Joint Bolt
5	Front Suspension Lower Arm Ball Joint
6	Ball Joint Bolt Nut
7	Cotter Pin
8	Tie Rod End Nut

Item	Description
9	Front Wheel Driveshaft Joint (1.8L)
10	Front Axle Bearing Bracket Bolts (3 Req'd)
11	Halfshaft (1.8L)
A	Tighten to 43-59 N·m (32-43 Lb-Ft)
B	Tighten to 34-46 N·m (25-33 Lb-Ft)
C	Tighten to 42-62 N·m (31-46 Lb-Ft)

90987G08

Fig. 27 Exploded view of a typical halfshaft assembly—1991–96 models

➡**If the nut splits or cracks after staking, replace it with a new nut.**

29. Check and refill the transaxle with the proper type and quantity of fluid.

30. Connect the negative battery cable.

31. Road test the vehicle and check for proper operation.

RIGHT SIDE OF 1.8L ENGINE

➡**The right side halfshaft assembly is a two piece shaft with a bearing support bracket positioned between the two halves. The bearing support bracket is mounted on the cylinder block and must be unbolted if the entire halfshaft assembly is to be removed. If only the CV-joints/boots are to be serviced, the outboard shaft assembly may be removed, leaving the bearing support bracket mounted on the engine cylinder block.**

1. Disconnect the negative battery cable.

2. With the vehicle sitting on the ground, carefully raise the staked portion of the halfshaft retaining nut using a suitable small chisel. Loosen the nut.

3. Raise and safely support the vehicle.

4. Remove the right front wheel and tire assembly.

5. Remove the splash shield.

6. Remove and discard the halfshaft retaining nut.

7. Remove the cotter pin and castellated nut from the tie rod end and separate the tie rod end from the steering knuckle using a suitable removal tool. Discard the cotter pin.

8. Remove the lower ball joint pinch bolt. Carefully pry down on the lower control arm to separate the ball joint stud from the steering knuckle.

9. Pull outward on the steering knuckle/brake assembly. Carefully pull the halfshaft from the hub and position it aside.

10. Position a drain pan under the transaxle.

11. Remove the three bearing support bracket mounting bolts.

12. Insert a prybar between the bearing support bracket and the starter bracket. Gently pry outward on the damper until the halfshaft disengages from the differential side gear.

13. Remove the halfshaft assembly. Install an appropriate differential plug in the differential side gear.

To install:

14. Position a new circlip on the inner CV-joint spline so the circlip gap is at the top. Lubricate the splines lightly with a suitable grease.

15. Remove the differential plug from the side gear. Position the halfshaft assembly so the shaft splines are aligned with the differential side gear splines. Push the halfshaft into the differential. When seated properly, the circlip can be felt snapping into the differential side gear groove.

16. Pull outward on the steering knuckle/brake assembly and insert the halfshaft into the hub.

17. Pry downward on the lower control arm and position the lower ball joint stud into the steering knuckle. Install the lower ball joint pinch bolt and tighten to 32–43 ft. lbs. (43–59 Nm).

18. Install the tie rod end to the steering knuckle. Install the castellated nut and tighten to 31–42 ft. lbs. (42–57 Nm). Install a new cotter pin.

19. Position the bearing support bracket and install the three retaining bolts. Tighten the outer bolt first, then the top inner, then the bottom inner. Tighten the bolts to 31–46 ft. lbs. (42–62 Nm).

20. Install the splash shield.

21. Install the wheel and tire assembly.

22. Lower the vehicle.

23. Install a new halfshaft retaining nut and tighten to 174–235 ft. lbs. (235–319 Nm). Stake the retaining nut using a suitable chisel with the cutting edge rounded off.

➡️If the nut splits or cracks after staking, it must be replaced with a new nut.

24. Check and refill the transaxle with the proper type and quantity of fluid.

25. Connect the negative battery cable.

26. Road test the vehicle and check for proper operation.

1997–99 Models

▶ **See Figures 28, 29, 30, 31 and 32**

➡️Before continuing with any halfshaft procedure, make sure to have available, new halfshaft retaining nuts and circlips. Once removed, these parts lose their torque holding ability or retention capability and must not be reused.

1. Disconnect the negative battery cable.

2. With the vehicle sitting on the ground, carefully raise the staked portion of the halfshaft retaining nut using a suitable small chisel. Loosen the nut.

3. Raise and safely support the vehicle.

4. Remove the wheel and tire assembly.

5. Remove and discard the halfshaft retaining nut.

6. Remove the cotter pin and nut from the tie rod end, then separate the tie rod end from the steering knuckle using a suitable removal tool. Discard the cotter pin.

7. On 1998–99 models, refer to the accompanying illustration and remove the stabilizer bar link as follows:

    a. Unfasten the stabilizer bar end nut (1) and bolt (2).

    b. Remove the stabilizer bar end retainer (3).

    c. Remove the end bushing (4) above the stabilizer bar.

    d. Remove the end bushing (5) below the stabilizer bar.

    e. Remove the stabilizer bar spacer (6).

    f. Remove the stabilizer bar end bushings from above (7) and below (8) the sub-frame

    g. Remove the lower stabilizer bar end retainer (9).

    h. Remove the stabilizer bar.

8. Remove the ball joint bolt and nut. Carefully pry down on the lower control arm to separate the ball joint stud from the steering knuckle.

9. Pull outward on the steering knuckle/brake assembly. Carefully pull the halfshaft from the hub and position it aside.

➡️Removal of the left side halfshaft requires removal of the cross-member to allow access with a prybar.

10. Support the transaxle with a suitable transaxle jack.

11. Unfasten the four transaxle crossmember retainers and remove the crossmember.

12. If removing the right side halfshaft, remove the right-hand shield and splash shield.

13. Position a drain pan under the transaxle.

14. Remove the left-hand halfshaft on 1997–99 models and the right-hand halfshaft on 1997 models as follows:

    a. Insert a prybar between the halfshaft and the transaxle case. Gently pry outward to release the halfshaft from the differential side gear. Be

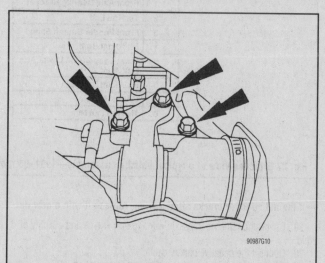

Fig. 29 On 1998–99 models with a manual transaxle, unfasten the center support bearing bolts

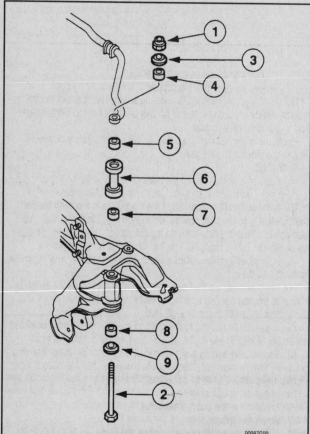

Fig. 28 Exploded view of the stabilizer bar link assembly—1998–99 models. (Refer to the text for component identification)

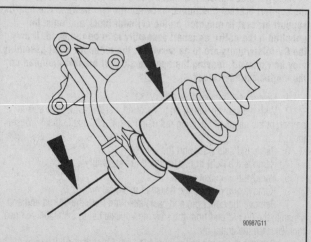

Fig. 30 Separate the halfshaft from the center support bearing, and remove the halfshaft from the vehicle—1998–99 models with a manual transaxle

careful not to damage the transaxle case, oil seal, CV-joint or CV-joint boot.

    b. Remove the halfshaft.

15. On 1998–99 models, remove the right-hand halfshaft as follows:

    a. On models with a manual transaxle, unfasten the center support bearing bolts.

    b. Lower the halfshaft and remove it from the transaxle.

    c. Seperate the halfshaft from the center support bearing and remove the halfshaft from the vehicle.

    d. Inspect the center support bearing for damage and replace as necessary.

➡**Install suitable plugs after removing the halfshafts to prevent the differential side gears from moving out of place. Should the gears become misaligned, the differential will have to be removed from the transaxle to align the gears.**

To install:

16. Position a new circlip on the inner CV-joint spline so the circlip gap is at the top. Lubricate the splines lightly with a suitable grease.

17. Remove the plugs that were installed in the differential side gears.

18. On all models except 1998–99 models wit a manual transaxle, position the halfshaft so the CV-joint splines are aligned with the differential side gear splines. Push the halfshaft into the differential.

➡**When seated properly, the circlip can be felt snapping into the differential side gear groove.**

19. Install the right-hand halfshaft on 1998–99 models with a manual transaxle as follows:

    a. Position the halfshaft and joint so that the splines line up with the splines in the halfshaft, and push the halfshaft, joint and halfshaft together with the center support bearing.

    b. Install the halfshaft in the transaxle.

20. Place the center support bearing into position and tighten it retaining bolts to 32–46 ft. lbs. (46–62 Nm).

    a. Install the right-hand shield and splash shield.

21. Pull outward on the steering knuckle/brake assembly and insert the halfshaft into the hub.

22. Pry downward on the lower control arm and position the lower ball joint stud in the steering knuckle.

23. Install the crossmember and the crossmember-to-frame bolts. Tighten the bolts to 69–93 ft. lbs. (94–126 Nm).

24. Remove the transaxle jack.

25. Install the steering knuckle and ball joint nut and bolt. Tighten the nut and bolt to 32–43 ft. lbs. (43–59 Nm).

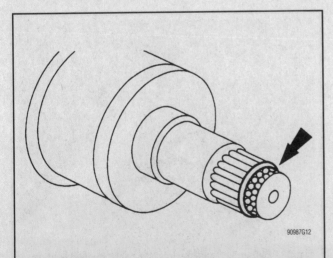

Fig. 31 Install a new circlip on the inner CV-joint spline, so that the circlip gap is at the top

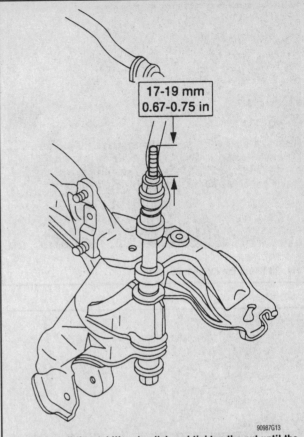

Fig. 32 Install the stabilizer bar link and tighten the nut until the protruding end bolt length is within specification

26. On 1998–99 models, install the stabilizer bar link in reverse order of removal and tighten the bar end nut until the protruding bar end bolt length is 0.67–75 inch (17–19mm).

27. Install the tie rod end to the steering knuckle. Install the nut and tighten to 25–33 ft. lbs. (34–46 Nm) on 1997 models and 32–41 ft. lbs. (43–56 Nm) on 1998–99 models. Install a new cotter pin.

28. Install the wheel and tire assembly.

29. Install a new halfshaft retaining nut and tighten to 174–235 ft. lbs. (235–319 Nm). Stake the halfshaft retaining nut using a suitable chisel with a rounded cutting edge.

➡**If the nut splits or cracks after staking, replace it with a new nut.**

30. Check and refill the transaxle with the proper type and quantity of fluid.

31. Connect the negative battery cable.

32. Road test the vehicle and check for proper operation.

CV-JOINTS OVERHAUL

1991–96 Models

▶ **See Figures 33 thru 46**

➡**The outboard CV-joint is permanently fitted onto the halfshaft and cannot be removed. To replace the outboard CV-joint boot, the inner CV-joint must be removed. If a boot has failed due to age or wear, all boots should be replaced at the same time.**

1. Raise and safely support the vehicle.

2. Remove the halfshaft from the vehicle. Support the assembly in a vise with soft jaws.

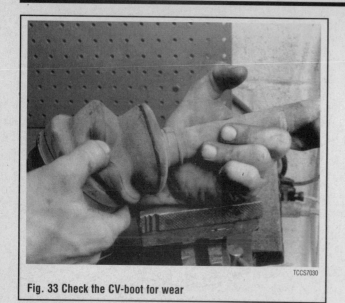

Fig. 33 Check the CV-boot for wear

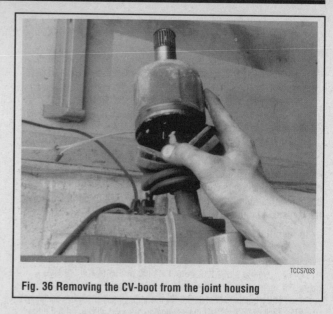

Fig. 36 Removing the CV-boot from the joint housing

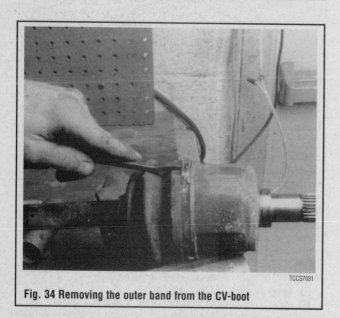

Fig. 34 Removing the outer band from the CV-boot

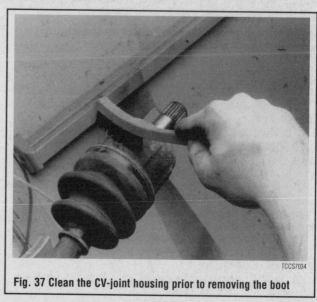

Fig. 37 Clean the CV-joint housing prior to removing the boot

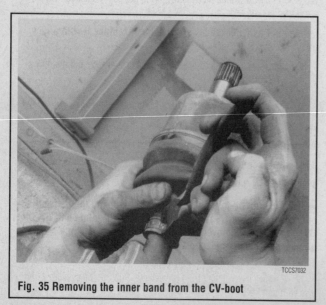

Fig. 35 Removing the inner band from the CV-boot

Fig. 38 Removing the CV-joint housing assembly

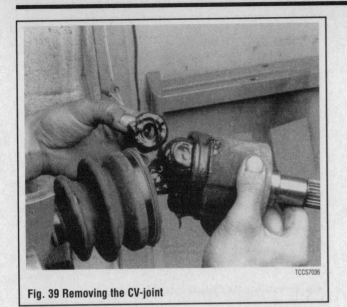

Fig. 39 Removing the CV-joint

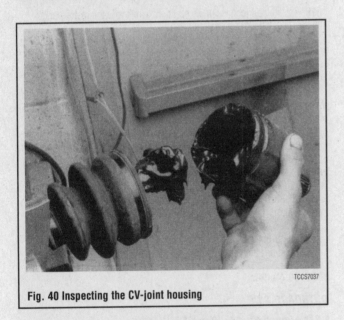

Fig. 40 Inspecting the CV-joint housing

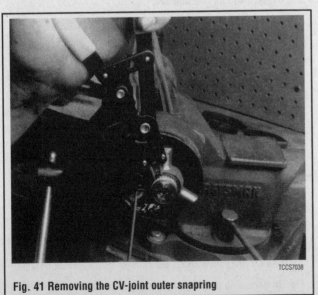

Fig. 41 Removing the CV-joint outer snapring

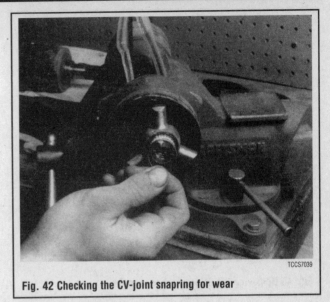

Fig. 42 Checking the CV-joint snapring for wear

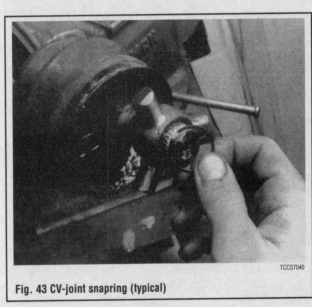

Fig. 43 CV-joint snapring (typical)

Fig. 44 Removing the CV-joint assembly

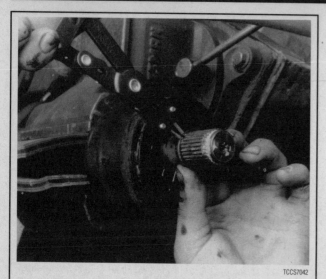

Fig. 45 Removing the CV-joint inner snapring

Fig. 46 Installing the CV-joint assembly (typical)

3. Remove the large boot clamp from the inboard CV-joint and roll the boot back over the shaft.

4. Matchmark the outer race, axle shaft and tripot bearing for reassembly. Remove the wire ring bearing retainer from inside the outer race/housing and remove the outer race.

5. Matchmark the tripot bearing and the shaft. Remove the tripot bearing snapring.

6. Remove the tripot bearing from the shaft. It may be necessary to drive the tripot off the shaft with a brass drift.

7. Remove the small clamp and the CV-joint boot from the halfshaft.

8. To remove the outboard CV-joint boot, remove the clamps and slide the boot off the shaft from the inboard side. If equipped with the 1.9L engine, remove the dynamic damper and mark its location on the halfshaft for installation.

To install:

9. The inner and outer CV-joint boots are different. To make sure the boot is being installed in the correct location, measure the outer diameter of the large end of the boot:

- **1.8L engine**
- Outer boot—3.35 inches (85.2mm)
- Inner boot—3.54 inches (89.9mm)
- **1.9L engine**
- Outer boot—3.50 inches (89.0mm)
- Right side inner boot—3.31 inches (84.0mm)
- Left side inner boot—3.54 inches (90.0mm)

10. Wrap smooth electrical tape around the halfshaft spline to ease installation of the boot. Slide the clamps and the outboard boot onto the shaft.

11. Before positioning the boot over the CV-joint, pack the CV-joint and boot with grease. Be sure to use all of the grease in the pouch supplied with the boot kit.

12. Fit the boot into place on the CV-joint, making sure it is fully seated in the grooves in the shaft and outer race. Insert a suitable tool between the boot and the outer bearing race to allow trapped air to escape from the boot.

13. Install the boot clamps, wrapping them around the boots in the opposite direction of halfshaft rotation. Pull the clamps tight with a suitable tool and bend the locking tabs to secure in position.

14. On models equipped with the 1.9L engine, after installing the outboard CV-joint boot, install the dynamic damper onto the halfshaft at its original location. Make sure the band is tightened properly and the locking clip is secured.

15. Fit the inboard CV-joint boot and clamps onto the halfshaft and remove the electrical tape.

16. Install the tripot assembly on the halfshaft with the matchmarks aligned. Install the tripot retaining ring.

17. Fill the CV-joint outer race with CV-joint grease. Make sure the boot is also greased to prevent wear from internal contact of the ribs.

18. Install the outer race over the tripot joint with the matchmarks aligned and install the wire ring bearing retainer.

19. Fit the boot into place on the CV-joint, making sure it is fully seated in the grooves in the shaft and outer race. Insert a suitable tool between the boot and the outer bearing race to allow trapped air to escape from the boot.

20. Install the boot clamps, wrapping them around the boots in the opposite direction of halfshaft rotation. Pull the clamps tight with a suitable tool and bend the locking tabs to secure in position.

21. Work the CV-joint through its full range of travel at various angles. The joint should flex, extend, and compress smoothly. Wipe away any excess grease.

22. Install the halfshaft in the vehicle using new circlips.

23. Lower the vehicle.

24. Road test the vehicle and check for proper operation.

1997–99 Models

OUTBOARD SIDE

▶ See Figures 47, 48, 49 and 50

1. Remove the halfshaft from the vehicle. Support the assembly in a vise with soft jaws.

2. If equipped with an Anti-lock Brake System (ABS), use a punch to drive the front brake anti-lock sensor indicator off the halfshaft.

3. Remove and discard the two halfshaft boot clamps.

4. Slide the boot back out of the way to access the outboard joint.

5. Matchmark the joint-to-halfshaft for reassembly.

6. Use a soft faced mallet to separate the outboard joint by gently tapping it off the halfshaft.

7. Remove and discard the halfshaft bearing retaining circlip.

8. Remove the snapring from the outboard side of the halfshaft.

➡Do not remove the tape until after installation of the boot.

9. Wrap the outboard halfshaft splines with tape and then slide the boot from the shaft.

10. Clean and inspect the outboard bearings for damage, grit in the grease, pitting or cracks and replace as necessary.

To install:

11. Lubricate the joint bearings with constant velocity grease E43Z-19590-A or equivalent.

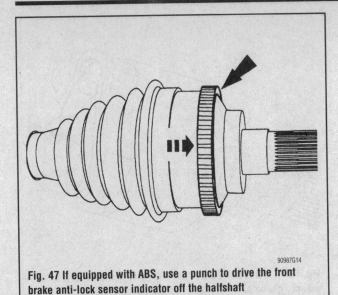

90987G14

Fig. 47 If equipped with ABS, use a punch to drive the front brake anti-lock sensor indicator off the halfshaft

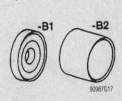

90987G17

Fig. 50 Use sensing ring replacer tool T94P-20202-B or equivalent to install the front brake anti-lock sensor indicator onto the halfshaft

12. Install the boot and remove the tape.

13. Install the snapring on the outboard side of the halfshaft.

14. Install a new bearing retaining circlip.

15. Use a soft faced mallet to install the outboard joint by gently tapping it onto the halfshaft.

16. Remove any excess grease from the mating surfaces and slide the boot forward onto the joint.

17. Insert a suitable cloth covered tool between the boot and the outer bearing race to allow trapped air to escape from the boot.

18. Use boot clamp pliers to install two new boot clamps.

19. If equipped with anti-lock brakes, use sensing ring replacer tool T94P-20202-B or equivalent, to install the front brake anti-lock sensor indicator onto the halfshaft.

20. Install the halfshaft.

INBOARD SIDE

▶ See Figures 51, 52, 53, 54 and 55

1. Remove the halfshaft from the vehicle. Support the assembly in a vise with soft jaws.

➡The right-hand side halfshaft on models equipped with a manual transaxle do not have an inboard circlip.

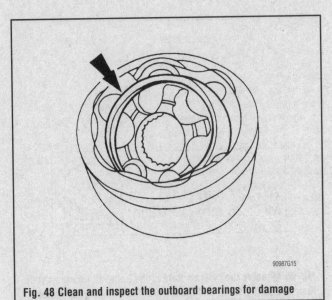

90987G15

Fig. 48 Clean and inspect the outboard bearings for damage

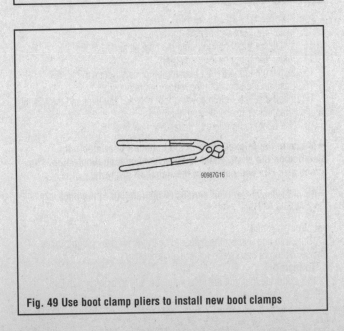

90987G16

Fig. 49 Use boot clamp pliers to install new boot clamps

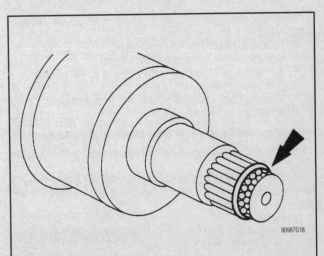

90987G18

Fig. 51 Remove and discard the bearing retaining circlip from the inboard joint housing

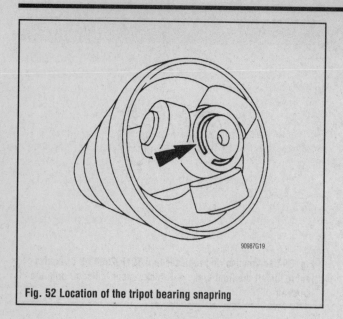

Fig. 52 Location of the tripot bearing snapring

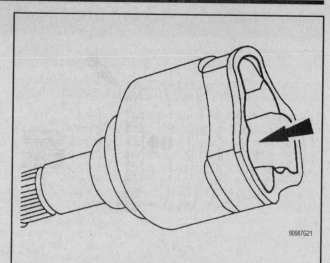

Fig. 54 . . . and outboard joint housing for damage, grit in the grease, pitting or cracks, and replace as necessary

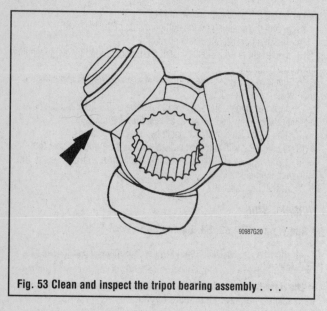

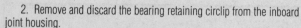

Fig. 53 Clean and inspect the tripot bearing assembly . . .

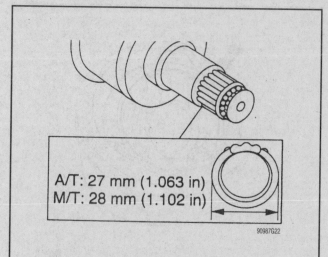

A/T: 27 mm (1.063 in)
M/T: 28 mm (1.102 in)

Fig. 55 Measure the relaxed state of the halfshaft bearing circlip installed on the shaft, and make sure it is within specification

2. Remove and discard the bearing retaining circlip from the inboard joint housing.
3. Remove and discard the joint boot clamps.
4. Sepearte the joint boot from the joint housing.
5. Remove the joint housing from the tripot bearing and halfshaft.
6. Remove the tripot bearing snapring.
7. Matchmark the tripot bearing-to-halfshaft for reassembly.
8. Remove the tripot bearing from the halfshaft.

➡ Do not remove the tape until after installation of the boot.

9. Wrap the halfshaft splines with tape and then slide the boot from the shaft.
10. Clean and inspect the tripot bearing assembly and outboard joint housing for damage, grit in the grease, pitting or cracks and replace as necessary.

To install:

11. Lubricate the tripot bearing and inboard joint housing with constant velocity grease E43Z-19590-A or equivalent.

12. Install the boot and remove the tape.
13. Install the tripot bearing onto the halfshaft.
14. Install the tripot bearing snapring.
15. Install the inboard joint housing onto the tripot bearing.
16. Position the boot onto the inboard joint housing.
17. Insert a suitable cloth covered tool between the boot and the bearing to allow trapped air to escape from the boot.
18. Use boot clamp pliers to install two new boot clamps.

➡ Measure the relaxed state of the halfshaft bearing circlip installed on the shaft. Refer to the accompanying illustration. The wrong size clip will not retain the halfshaft properly.

19. Install a new halfshaft bearing retainer circlip of the correct size onto the outboard halfshaft joint.

CLUTCH

Understanding the Clutch

✶✶ CAUTION

The clutch driven disc may contain asbestos, which has been determined to be a cancer causing agent. Never clean clutch surfaces with compressed air! Avoid inhaling any dust from any clutch surface! When cleaning clutch surfaces, use a commercially available brake cleaning fluid.

The purpose of the clutch is to disconnect and connect engine power at the transaxle. A vehicle at rest requires a lot of engine torque to get all that weight moving. An internal combustion engine does not develop a high starting torque (unlike steam engines) so it must be allowed to operate without any load until it builds up enough torque to move the vehicle. Torque increases with engine rpm. The clutch allows the engine to build up torque by physically disconnecting the engine from the transaxle, relieving the engine of any load or resistance.

The transfer of engine power to the transaxle (the load) must be smooth and gradual; if it weren't, drive line components would wear out or break quickly. This gradual power transfer is made possible by gradually releasing the clutch pedal. The clutch disc and pressure plate are the connecting link between the engine and transaxle. When the clutch pedal is released, the disc and plate contact each other (the clutch is engaged) physically joining the engine and transaxle. When the pedal is pushed inward, the disc and plate separate (the clutch is disengaged) disconnecting the engine from the transaxle.

Most clutches utilize a single plate, dry friction disc with a diaphragm-style spring pressure plate. The clutch disc has a splined hub which attaches the disc to the input shaft. The disc has friction material where it contacts the flywheel and pressure plate. Torsion springs on the disc help absorb engine torque pulses. The pressure plate applies pressure to the clutch disc, holding it tight against the surface of the flywheel. The clutch operating mechanism consists of a release bearing, fork and cylinder assembly.

The release fork and actuating linkage transfer pedal motion to the release bearing. In the engaged position (pedal released) the diaphragm spring holds the pressure plate against the clutch disc, so engine torque is transmitted to the input shaft. When the clutch pedal is depressed, the release bearing pushes the diaphragm spring center toward the flywheel. The diaphragm spring pivots the fulcrum, relieving the load on the pressure plate. Steel spring straps riveted to the clutch cover lift the pressure plate from the clutch disc, disengaging the engine drive from the transaxle and enabling the gears to be changed.

The clutch is operating properly if:
1. It will stall the engine when released with the vehicle held stationary.
2. The shift lever can be moved freely between 1st and reverse gears when the vehicle is stationary and the clutch disengaged.

Driven Disc and Pressure Plate

REMOVAL & INSTALLATION

1991–96 Models

▶ See Figures 56, 57 and 58

1. Disconnect the negative battery cable.
2. Raise and safely support the vehicle.
3. Remove the transaxle assembly.
4. If the clutch assembly is to be reused, matchmark the pressure plate and the flywheel so they can be assembled in the same position.
5. Install flywheel holding tool T84P-6375-A or equivalent, in a transaxle mounting hole on the engine and engage the tooth of the holding tool into the flywheel ring gear.

6. Loosen the pressure plate-to-flywheel retaining bolts one turn at a time, in a crisscross pattern, until the spring tension is relieved, to prevent pressure plate cover distortion.
7. Support the pressure plate and unfasten the retaining bolts. Remove the pressure plate and clutch disc from the flywheel.

➡ If the flywheel shows any signs of overheating (blue discoloration) or if it is badly grooved or scored, it should be refaced or replaced.

8. Inspect the flywheel, clutch disc, pressure plate, release bearing, pilot bearing and the clutch fork for wear. Replace parts as needed.
   To install:
9. If removed, install a new pilot bearing using a suitable installation tool.
10. If removed, install the flywheel. Make sure the flywheel and crankshaft flange mating surfaces are clean. Tighten the flywheel retaining bolts to 71–76 ft. lbs. (96–103 Nm) on the 1.8L engine or 54–67 ft. lbs. (73–91 Nm) on the 1.9L engine.
11. Clean the pressure plate and flywheel surfaces thoroughly. Position the clutch disc and pressure plate into the installed position and support

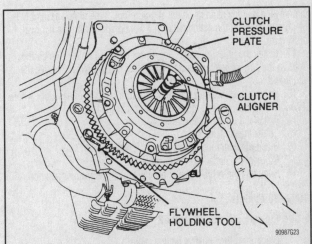

Fig. 56 Install a flywheel holding tool in a transaxle mounting hole on the engine, and engage the tooth of the tool into the flywheel ring gear

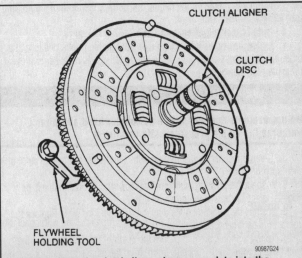

Fig. 57 Position the clutch disc and pressure plate into the installed position and support them with a clutch aligning tool

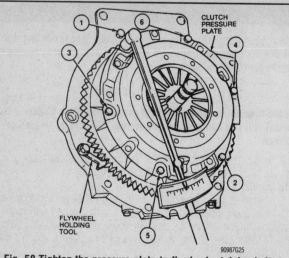

Fig. 58 Tighten the pressure plate-to-flywheel retaining bolts to specification in the sequence illustrated

them with a dummy shaft or clutch aligning tool. If the clutch assembly is being reused, align the matchmarks that were made during the removal procedure.

12. Install the pressure plate-to-flywheel retaining bolts. Tighten the bolts in the correct sequence to 13–20 ft. lbs. (18–26 Nm). Remove the alignment tool.

13. If the release bearing was removed, lubricate the release fork where it contacts the bearing and install the bearing in the fork.

14. Install the transaxle assembly.

15. Lower the vehicle.

16. Bleed the hydraulic clutch system, if needed.

17. Connect the negative battery cable.

18. Road test the vehicle and check the clutch for proper operation.

1997–99 Models

▶ **See Figures 59, 60, 61 and 62**

1. Disconnect the negative battery cable.
2. Raise and safely support the vehicle.
3. Remove the transaxle assembly.
4. If the clutch assembly is to be reused, matchmark the pressure plate and the flywheel so they can be assembled in the same position.
5. Install flywheel holding tool T74P-7337-K or equivalent, in a transaxle mounting hole on the engine and engage the tooth of the holding tool into the flywheel ring gear.
6. Install clutch alignment tool T74P-7137-K or equivalent.
7. Loosen the pressure plate-to-flywheel retaining bolts one turn at a time, in a crisscross pattern, until the spring tension is relieved, to prevent pressure plate damage.

✳✳ WARNING

Do not use any cleaners with a petroleum base and do not immerse the clutch pressure plate in solvent.

8. Clean the clutch pressure plate with a suitable commercial alcohol base solvent.
9. Inspect the pressure plate surface for burns, scores, flatness or ridges. Reface or replace the pressure plate.
10. Inspect the pressure plate diaphragm fingers for wear. Replace the pressure plate if necessary.
11. Using a slide caliper, measure the depth of the rivet heads. If the rivet head is within 0.012 inch (0.3mm) from the clutch surface, replace the clutch.

✳✳ WARNING

If the clutch disc is saturated with oil, inspect the rear engine crankshaft seal for leakage. If the seal is leaking, it must be replaced before installing the clutch.

➡**Use emery cloth to remove minor imperfections from the clutch disc lining surface.**

12. Inspect the clutch disc for the following:
- Oil or grease saturation
- Worn or loose facings
- Warpage or loose rivets at the hub
- Loose or broken torsion dampening springs
- Wear or rust on the splines

13. If the clutch disc shows any of these conditions, it should be replaced.

14. Use a dial indicator mounted on a metal base to measure the clutch disc run-out. If the run-out exceeds 0.0276 inch (0.700mm), replace the disc.

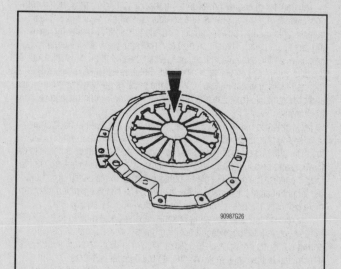

Fig. 59 Inspect the pressure plate diaphragm fingers for wear

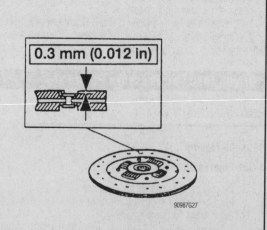

Fig. 60 Use a slide caliper to measure the depth of the rivet heads. Replace the disc if not within specification

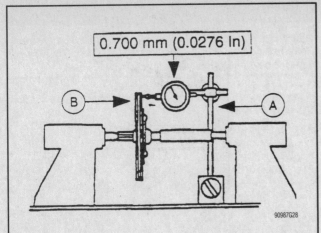

Fig. 61 Use a dial indicator mounted on a metal base to measure the clutch disc run-out. If the run-out exceeds specification, replace the disc

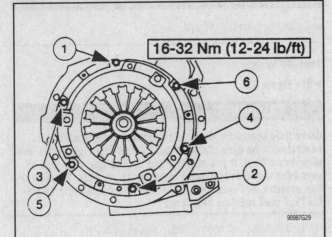

Fig. 62 Tighten the pressure plate-to-flywheel retaining bolts to specification in the sequence illustrated

15. Inspect the clutch release for distortion, cracks, excessive release bearing surface wear or damaged tines and replace as necessary.

To install:

16. Clean the pressure plate and flywheel surfaces thoroughly. Position the clutch disc and pressure plate into the installed position and support them with clutch aligning tool T74P-7137-K or equivalent. If the clutch assembly is being reused, align the matchmarks that were made during the removal procedure.

17. Install the pressure plate-to-flywheel retaining bolts. Tighten the bolts in the correct sequence to 12–24 ft. lbs. (16–32 Nm). Remove the alignment tool.

18. Install the transaxle assembly.
19. Lower the vehicle.
20. Bleed the hydraulic clutch system.
21. Adjust the clutch pedal free-play.
22. Connect the negative battery cable.
23. Road test the vehicle and check the clutch for proper operation.

ADJUSTMENTS

Pedal Free-Play

1991–96 MODELS

To determine if the clutch pedal free-play needs adjusting, depress the clutch pedal by hand until resistance is felt. Using a ruler, measure the distance between the upper clutch pedal height and where the resistance is felt.

Free-play should be 0.20–0.51 inch (5–13mm). If not, proceed as follows:

1. Loosen the clutch pedal to clutch master cylinder rod locknut.
2. Turn the clutch pedal to clutch master cylinder rod until the free-play is within specification.
3. Check that the disengagement height is within specification. Minimum disengagement height is 1.6 inches (41mm).
4. Tighten the clutch pedal-to-clutch master cylinder rod locknut to 9–12 ft. lbs. (12–17 Nm).
5. Check clutch pedal free-play to verify proper adjustment.

1997–99 MODELS

▶ See Figures 63 and 64

1. Depress the clutch pedal until resistance can be felt, and measure the distance between the upper clutch height and where the resistance is felt. The free-play should be 0.0–0.40 inch (5.0–13.9mm).
2. If an adjustment is necessary, turn the locknut and equalizer bar-to-clutch release lever rod.
3. After adjustment, measure the disengagement height from the upper surface of the clutch pedal pad to the carpet. The distance should be 2.3 inches (59mm).

Pedal Height

1991–96 MODELS

▶ See Figure 65

To determine if the pedal height requires adjustment, measure the distance from the bulkhead to the upper center of the pedal pad. The distance should be 7.72–8.03 in. (196–204mm). If adjustment is necessary, proceed as follows:

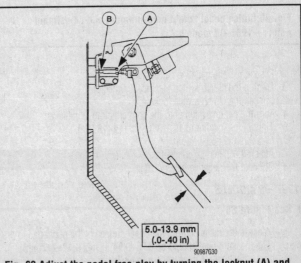

Fig. 63 Adjust the pedal free-play by turning the locknut (A) and equalizer bar-to-clutch release lever rod (B)

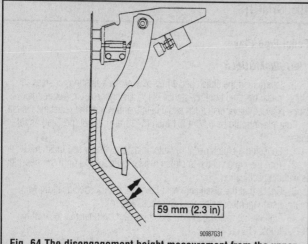

Fig. 64 The disengagement height measurement from the upper surface of the clutch pedal pad to the carpet should be 2.3 inches (59mm) for 1997–99 models

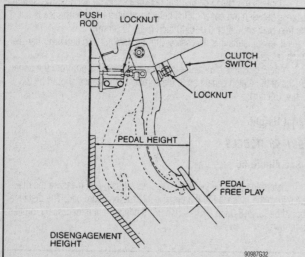

Fig. 65 Clutch pedal height measurement and adjustment points—1991–96 models

1. Disconnect the negative battery cable.
2. Unplug the clutch switch electrical connector.
3. Loosen the clutch switch locknut.
4. Turn the clutch switch until the correct height is achieved.
5. Tighten the locknut to 10–13 ft. lbs. (14–18 Nm).
6. Measure the pedal free-play.
7. Attach the electrical connector.
8. Connect the negative battery cable.

1997–99 MODELS

▶ See Figure 66

1. Measure the distance from the upper surface of the pedal pad to the carpet. The measurement should be 8.35–8.54 inches (212–217mm).
2. If an adjustment is necessary, turn the locknut and the Clutch Pedal Position (CPP) switch until the pedal height is correct.

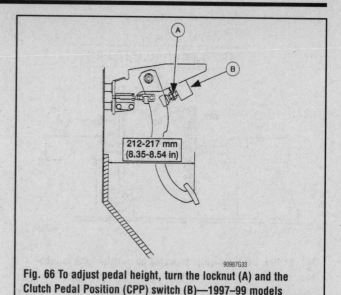

Fig. 66 To adjust pedal height, turn the locknut (A) and the Clutch Pedal Position (CPP) switch (B)—1997–99 models

Master Cylinder

REMOVAL & INSTALLATION

1991–96 Models

▶ See Figure 67

✳✳ CAUTION

Brake fluid contains polyglycol ethers and polyglycols. Avoid contact with the eyes and wash your hands thoroughly after handling brake fluid. If you do get brake fluid in your eyes, flush your eyes with clean, running water for 15 minutes. If eye irritation persists, or if you have taken brake fluid internally, IMMEDIATELY seek medical assistance.

1. Disconnect both battery cables, negative cable first.
2. Remove the battery and battery tray.
3. Disconnect the clutch tube from the clutch master cylinder using a suitable line wrench.
4. Disengage the clamp and remove the master cylinder reservoir hose from the clutch master cylinder. Prevent excess fluid loss by plugging the hose.
5. Remove the external retaining nut.
6. Remove the internal retaining nut from inside the passenger compartment.
7. Remove the clutch master cylinder.
To install:
8. Align the clutch pedal push rod and install the clutch master cylinder.
9. Install the external and internal retaining nuts and tighten to 14–19 ft. lbs. (19–25 Nm).
10. Connect the clutch tube and tighten the tube nut to 10–16 ft. lbs. (13–22 Nm).
11. Install the master cylinder reservoir hose and the clamp to the clutch master cylinder.
12. Install the battery and battery tray.
13. Bleed the air from the hydraulic clutch system.

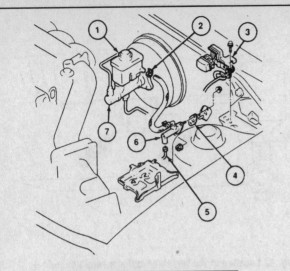

Item	Description
1	Brake Master Cylinder Reservoir
2	Clamp
3	Data Link Connector (DLC)
4	Gasket
5	Lower Clutch Slave Cylinder Tube
6	Clutch Master Cylinder
7	Brake Master Cylinder

90987G34

Fig. 67 Exploded view of the clutch master cylinder assembly for 1991–96 models

14. Test the clutch system and make sure there is no leakage.
15. Connect both battery cables, negative cable last.
16. Road test the vehicle and check for proper operation.

1997–99 Models

▶ See Figures 68, 69 and 70

✳✳ CAUTION

Brake fluid contains polyglycol ethers and polyglycols. Avoid contact with the eyes and wash your hands thoroughly after handling brake fluid. If you do get brake fluid in your eyes, flush your eyes with clean, running water for 15 minutes. If eye irritation persists, or if you have taken brake fluid internally, IMMEDIATELY seek medical assistance.

1. Disconnect the clutch master cylinder hose from the clutch master cylinder. Prevent excess fluid loss by plugging the hose.
2. Disconnect the lower clutch slave cylinder tube from the clutch master cylinder.
3. Unfasten the clutch master cylinder retaining nut located inside the passenger compartment.
4. Unfasten the clutch master cylinder retaining nut located inside the engine compartment and remove the master cylinder.

To install:
5. Align the clutch pedal-to-clutch release lever rod with the master cylinder and install the master cylinder.
6. Install the external and internal retaining nuts and tighten to 14–18 ft. lbs. (19–25 Nm).
7. Connect the lower clutch slave cylinder tube and tighten the tube nut to 10–16 ft. lbs. (13–22 Nm).

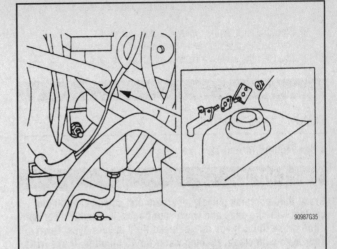

90987G35

Fig. 68 Unfasten the clutch master cylinder retaining nut inside the passenger compartment . . .

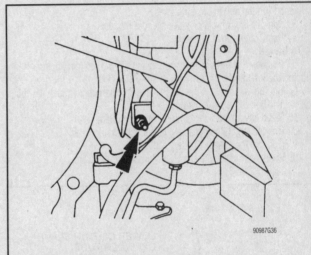

90987G36

Fig. 69 . . . and the clutch master cylinder retaining nut inside the engine compartment

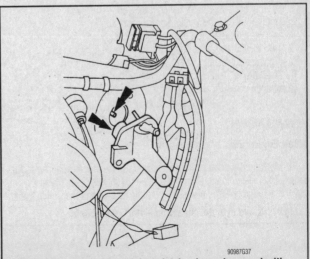

90987G37

Fig. 70 Align the clutch pedal-to-clutch release lever rod with the master cylinder

8. Connect the clutch master cylinder hose to the clutch master cylinder.

9. Bleed the air from the hydraulic clutch system.

10. Test the clutch system and make sure there is no leakage.

11. Road test the vehicle and check for proper operation.

Slave Cylinder

REMOVAL & INSTALLATION

♦ See Figures 71 and 72

✷✷ CAUTION

Brake fluid contains polyglycol ethers and polyglycols. Avoid contact with the eyes and wash your hands thoroughly after handling brake fluid. If you do get brake fluid in your eyes, flush your eyes with clean, running water for 15 minutes. If eye irritation persists, or if you have taken brake fluid internally, IMMEDIATELY seek medical assistance.

1. Disconnect the negative battery cable.

2. Disconnect the clutch slave cylinder tube from the clutch slave cylinder. Plug the line to prevent leakage.

3. Remove the two clutch slave cylinder retainers.

4. Remove the slave cylinder.

To install:

5. Position the slave cylinder and install the two retaining bolts. Tighten the retaining bolts to 12–17 ft. lbs. (16–23 Nm).

6. Unplug and connect the clutch slave cylinder tube. Tighten the tube nut to 10–16 ft. lbs. (13–22 Nm).

7. Bleed any air from the hydraulic clutch system.

8. Operate the clutch pedal and check for leaks.

9. Connect the negative battery cable.

10. Road test the vehicle and check for proper operation.

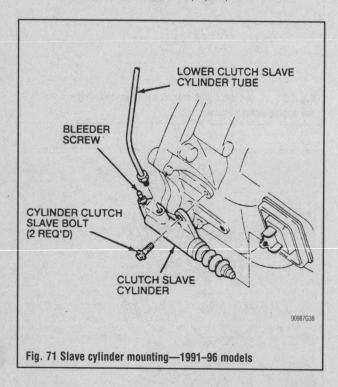

Fig. 71 Slave cylinder mounting—1991–96 models

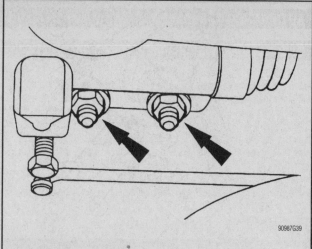

Fig. 72 Location of the two slave cylinder retaining nuts—1997–99 models

HYDRAULIC SYSTEM BLEEDING

♦ See Figure 73

1. Check that the brake master cylinder is at least ¾ full during the entire bleeding process.

2. Remove the bleeder screw cap from the clutch slave cylinder and attach a hose to the bleeder screw. Place the other end of the hose into a container to catch the fluid.

3. Have an assistant slowly pump the clutch pedal several times and then hold the clutch pedal down.

4. Loosen the bleeder screw to release the fluid and air. Tighten the bleeder screw.

5. Repeat the bleeding procedure until no more air bubbles are seen in the fluid.

6. Tighten the bleeder screw to 52–78 inch lbs. (6–9 Nm).

7. Top off the brake master cylinder to the full line.

8. Check for proper clutch system operation.

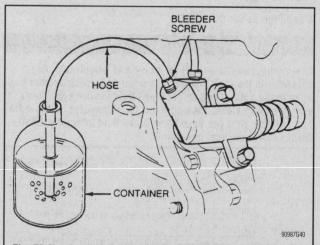

Fig. 73 Attach a hose to the bleeder screw and place the other end of the hose into a container to catch the fluid—1991–96 model shown

AUTOMATIC TRANSAXLE

Understanding the Automatic Transaxle

The automatic transaxle allows engine torque and power to be transmitted to the front wheels within a narrow range of engine operating speeds. It will allow the engine to turn fast enough to produce plenty of power and torque at very low speeds, while keeping it at a sensible rpm at high vehicle speeds (and it does this job without driver assistance). The transaxle uses a light fluid as the medium for the transmission of power. This fluid also works in the operation of various hydraulic control circuits and as a lubricant. Because the transaxle fluid performs all of these functions, trouble within the unit can easily travel from one part to another. For this reason, and because of the complexity and unusual operating principles of the transaxle, a very sound understanding of the basic principles of operation will simplify troubleshooting.

Neutral Safety Switch

The neutral safety switch is also referred to as the Transmission Range Switch (TRS) or the Manual Lever Position Switch (MLPS). Though different names are used, the switch still performs the same functions. This switch also functions as the back-up light switch, which is an integral part of the neutral safety switch on models equipped with an automatic transaxle.

REMOVAL & INSTALLATION

1991–96 Models

▶ See Figure 74

1. Disconnect the negative battery cable.
2. Remove the air cleaner outlet tube.

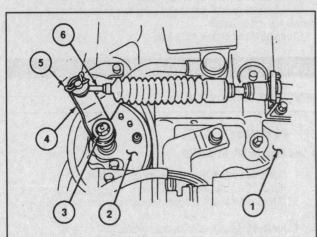

Item	Description
1	Transaxle Case
2	Transmission Range (TR) Switch
3	Manual Control Lever Nut
4	Manual Control Shift Outer Lever
5	Clip
6	Shift Cable and Bracket

90987G58

Fig. 74 Assembled view of the transmission range switch and its related components—1991–96 models

3. Unfasten the nut attaching the manual control shift outer lever to the manual control lever.
4. Seperate the manual control shift outer lever from the manual control lever.
5. Unplug the solenoid electrical connections located on the top and front side of the transaxle.
6. Unfasten the transmission range switch bolts.
7. Unfasten the bolts attaching the solenoid electrical connector bracket to the transaxle case.
8. Remove the transmission range switch from the manual control lever.
To install:
9. Place the switch into position on the manual control lever.
10. Install the bolts attaching the solenoid electrical connector bracket to the transaxle case.
11. Install, but do not tighten, the transmission range switch bolts.
12. Attach the solenoid electrical connections located on the top and front side of the transaxle.
13. Adjust the switch, as outlined later in this section.
14. Attach the manual control shift outer lever the manual control lever and tighten the nut to 33–47 ft. lbs. (44–64 Nm).
15. Install the air cleaner outlet tube.
16. Connect the negative battery cable.

1997–99 Models

▶ See Figures 75, 76, 77 and 78

1. Disconnect the negative battery cable.
2. Remove the air cleaner outlet tube.
3. Unfasten the shift cable and bracket retaining nut and the control cable front clamp.
4. Unfasten the manual lever control nut and remove the manual control shift outer lever.
5. Unplug the transmission range switch electrical connection.
6. Unfasten the switch bolts and remove the switch.
To install:
7. Shift the transaxle into NEUTRAL, then align the marks on the transmission range switch and the manual control lever.
8. Install and finger-tighten the switch retaining bolts.
9. Attach an ohmmeter between terminals **A** and **B** on the switch as shown in the accompanying illustration.
10. Adjust the switch by rotating the switch housing on the manual control lever until there is no continuity between the terminals.

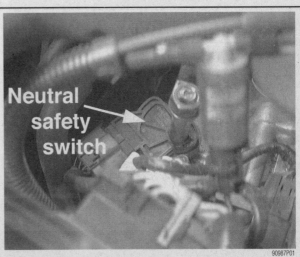

90987P01

Fig. 75 Location of the neutral safety switch (transmission range switch) on 1997–99 models with an automatic transaxle

Fig. 76 Align the marks on the transmission range switch and the manual control lever

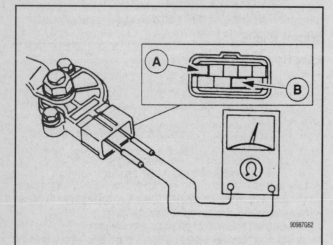

Fig. 77 Attach an ohmmeter to terminals A and B on the transmission range switch

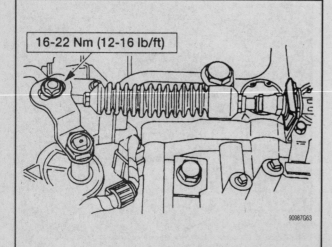

Fig. 78 Adjust the shift cable, then tighten the transmission range switch cable nut to specification

11. Hold the switch in place, then tighten its retaining bolts to 70–95 inch lbs. (8–11 Nm).

12. Remove the ohmmeter and attach the switch electrical connection.

13. Place the manual control shift outer lever in position and tighten its retaining nut to 33–47 ft. lbs. (44–64 Nm).

14. Install the shift cable and bracket, and tighten the retaining nut to 12–16 inch lbs. (16–22 Nm).

15. Move the gearshift lever to the PARK position.

16. Loosen the transmission range switch cable nut.

17. Manually move the shift cable rearward as far as possible.

18. Check the cable for any tension or restriction of movement and tighten the transmission range switch cable nut to 12–16 ft. lbs. (16–22 Nm).

19. Install the air cleaner tube and connect the negative battery cable.

ADJUSTMENT

1991–96 Models

▶ See Figure 79

1. Remove the air cleaner outlet tube.

2. Remove the clip that attaches the shift cable and bracket to the manual control shift outer lever.

3. Remove the manual control shift outer lever from the shift cable and bracket.

4. Turn the manual control shift lever to the Neutral position.

5. Remove the screw from the access hole on the transmission range switch.

6. Using a 5/64 inch (2.0mm) pin or drill bit shank, insert the pin inside the access hole and align the indentation inside the switch with the access hole.

7. Tighten the switch retaining bolts to 69–95 inch lbs. (8–11 Nm) and remove the pin.

8. Install the screw in the access hole on the switch.

9. Attach the manual control shift outer lever to the shift cable and bracket and install the clip.

10. Install the air cleaner outlet tube.

Automatic Transaxle Assembly

REMOVAL & INSTALLATION

1991–96 Models

▶ See Figures 80, 81 and 82

1. Disconnect both battery cables, negative cable first.

2. Remove the battery and battery tray.

3. Disconnect the wiring harness retaining clip from the battery tray.

4. Remove the engine air cleaner assembly.

5. Disconnect the shift control cable from the manual shift lever on the transaxle.

6. Disengage the retaining clip, then unsnap the speedometer cable from the Vehicle Speed Sensor (VSS) at the transaxle.

7. Unplug the transaxle electronic control electrical connectors and separate the harness from the transaxle clips.

8. Remove the Manual Lever Position (MLP) switch wiring brackets and disconnect the ground cables from the top of the transaxle.

9. Remove the starter motor.

10. Unplug the MLP switch wiring connectors.

11. Install Engine Support D88L-6000-A or equivalent, to the engine. The engine must be properly supported for transaxle removal.

12. Disconnect the kickdown cable (also known as the throttle valve cable) at the throttle cam on the throttle body.

13. Place a suitable drain pan under the transaxle and disconnect the transaxle cooler lines at the transaxle.

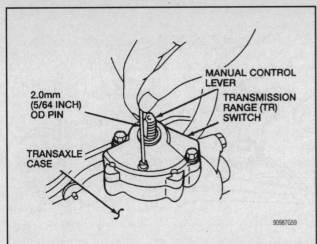

Fig. 79 Use a ⁵⁄₆₄ inch (2.0mm) pin or drill bit shank to align the indentation inside the switch with the access hole—1991–96 models

Fig. 80 Disengage the clip, then unsnap the speedometer cable from the vehicle speed sensor at the transaxle

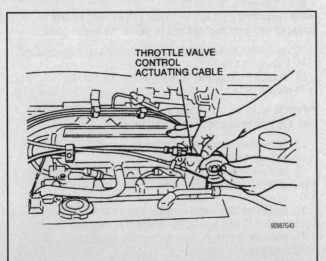

Fig. 81 Disconnect the throttle valve cable (kickdown cable) at the cam on the throttle body

→In some later models, the upper transaxle cooler line has a spring and a check ball under the fitting.

14. Remove the left-hand engine mount bolts and the mount.
15. Remove the upper transaxle housing bolts.
16. Unplug the Oxygen Sensor (O2S) and/or Heated Oxygen Sensor (HO2S) electrical connector, the transaxle vent hose and the electrical connector at the VSS.
17. Raise and safely support the vehicle.
18. Separate the halfshafts from both steering knuckles.
19. Remove the three engine/transaxle lower splash shield bolts and the torque converter inspection plate.
20. Remove the four nuts securing the torque converter to the flexplate.
21. Remove the bolts securing the lower transaxle to the engine oil pan.
22. Unfasten the rear engine support-to-vehicle chassis bolt and remove the transaxle support crossmember from the vehicle chassis.
23. Unfasten the rear engine support-to-transaxle mount nuts and remove the transaxle support crossmember from the transaxle mounts.
24. Remove both halfshafts from the transaxle. Install two transaxle plugs T88C-7025-AH or equivalent, into the differential side gears.

✳✳ WARNING

Failure to install the transaxle plugs may cause the differential side gears to become improperly positioned. If the gears become misaligned, the differential will have to be removed from the transaxle to align them.

25. Position a drain pan and remove the drain plug from the transaxle. Drain the fluid from the differential cavity. Remove the transaxle pan and drain the remaining transaxle fluid, then install the pan and drain plug.
26. Position a suitable transaxle jack under the transaxle. Secure the transaxle to the jack.
27. Remove the lower transaxle-to-engine bolts.
28. Slowly lower the transaxle out of the vehicle.
29. Inspect all components including mounts and brackets.
To install:

→A pin is used for securing the throttle control lever in a fixed position on new and rebuilt transaxles. This pin must be removed to allow proper transaxle operation. If the pin is not removed, the throttle lever will remain in a fixed position. After removing the pin, apply sealant to the bolt from the previous transaxle. Install the bolt and tighten to 69–95 inch lbs. (8–11 Nm).

30. If rebuilding or replacing the transaxle, make sure to completely flush the transaxle cooler and cooler lines before installing the transaxle.

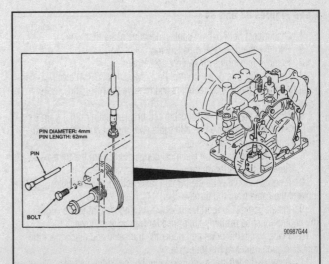

Fig. 82 Be sure to remove the pin used for securing the throttle control lever in a fixed position on new and rebuilt transaxles

31. Remove the pin securing the throttle control lever, if installed.

32. Secure the transaxle on the transaxle jack.

33. Carefully raise the transaxle into position and install the lower transaxle-to-engine bolts. Tighten the bolts to 41–59 ft. lbs. (55–80 Nm).

34. Position the torque converter to the flexplate and install the retaining nuts. Tighten the nuts to 25–36 ft. lbs. (34–49 Nm). Install the torque converter inspection plate.

35. Remove the transaxle plugs and install the halfshafts.

36. Connect the crossmember to the transaxle mounts and the chassis. Tighten the crossmember-to-transaxle mount nuts to 27–38 ft. lbs. (37–52 Nm). Tighten the crossmember-to-chassis nuts and bolts to 47–66 ft. lbs. (64–89 Nm).

37. Install the lower transaxle-to-engine oil pan bolts and tighten to 27–38 ft. lbs. (37–52 Nm). Install the engine/transaxle splash shields.

38. Install the starter motor.

39. Lower the vehicle.

40. Install the upper transaxle-to-engine bolts and tighten to 41–59 ft. lbs. (55–80 Nm).

41. Install the left-hand engine mount and tighten the nuts to 49–69 ft. lbs. (67–93 Nm).

42. Attach the transaxle vent hose, the electrical connector at the VSS, the speedometer cable and the Oxygen Sensor (O2S) and/or Heated Oxygen Sensor (HO2S) connector.

43. Install the check ball and spring under the cooler line fitting if equipped, then connect the transaxle cooler lines.

44. Connect the kickdown cable at the throttle body.

45. Remove the engine support.

46. Engage the ground wires to the transaxle and attach the MLP sensor bracket and wiring connectors.

47. Connect the shift control cable to the manual shift lever on the transaxle. Tighten the selector lever attaching locknut to 33–47 ft. lbs. (44–64 Nm).

➡ Do not use any type of power wrench to tighten the locknut. Damage to the transaxle may result.

48. Install the battery tray and battery. Connect the wiring harness retaining clip to the battery tray.

49. Install the engine air cleaner assembly.

50. Connect both battery cables, negative cable last.

51. Add the proper type and quantity of transaxle fluid.

52. Check the transaxle for leaks and for proper operation.

53. Check the manual lever position sensor for proper adjustment.

54. Road test the vehicle and check for proper operation.

1997–99 Models

♦ See Figures 83 and 84

1. Disconnect both battery cables, negative cable first.

2. Remove the battery and battery tray.

3. Remove the engine air cleaner assembly.

4. Unplug the Computer Control Relay Module (CCRM) electrical connections, unfasten the relay retainers and remove the relay and bracket from the engine.

5. Unfasten the shift control cable and bracket retaining nut from the manual shift lever , remove the shift cable and bracket clip, then set the bracket and cable assembly aside.

6. Tag and disconnect all electrical connections from the transaxle.

7. Remove the starter motor.

8. If equipped, unfasten the throttle valve actuating cable bolts and disconnect the cable from the throttle cam.

9. Install Engine Support D88L-6000-A or equivalent to the engine. The engine must be properly supported for transaxle removal.

10. Place a suitable drain pan under the transaxle and disconnect the transaxle cooler lines at the transaxle.

11. Remove the left-hand engine mount bolts and the mount.

12. Remove the upper transaxle housing bolts.

Fig. 83 Unfasten the shift control cable and bracket retaining nut (1), then remove the shift cable and bracket clip (2)

13. Raise and safely support the vehicle.

14. If equipped, remove the left-hand splash shields.

15. Remove the transaxle plug and drain the fluid.

16. Remove the halfshafts. Install two transaxle plugs T88C-7025-AH or equivalent, into the differential side gears.

✳✳ WARNING

Failure to install the transaxle plugs may cause the differential side gears to become improperly positioned. If the gears become misaligned, the differential will have to be removed from the transaxle to align them.

17. Remove the engine support crossmember and the catalytic converter.

18. Disconnect the A/C line from the retainer located on the engine support crossmember.

19. Unfasten the transaxle support crossmember bolts and nuts, the left-hand engine isolator nuts, and then remove the crossmember.

20. Unfasten the transaxle housing cover bolts and remove the cover.

21. Remove the four flywheel-to-torque converter nuts.

22. Position a suitable transaxle jack under the transaxle. Secure the transaxle to the jack.

23. Remove the remaining transaxle-to-engine bolts.

➡ The upper front transaxle-to-engine bolt on 1997 models is equipped with a retainer and will remain in the engine block.

24. On 1997 models, unfasten the upper front transaxle-to-engine bolt.

25. Slowly lower the transaxle out of the vehicle.

26. Inspect all components including mounts and brackets.

To install:

➡ Prior to installing the transaxle, lubricate the torque converter pilot hub with multi-purpose grease.

27. Align the torque converter studs to the flywheel.

28. Secure the transaxle on the transaxle jack.

29. Carefully raise the transaxle into position and install the middle and lower transaxle-to-engine bolts. Tighten the bolts to 40–58 ft. lbs. (55–80 Nm).

30. On 1997 models, install the upper front transaxle-to-engine bolt. Tighten the bolt to 40–58 ft. lbs. (55–80 Nm).

31. Install the flywheel-to-converter nuts and tighten them to 26–36 ft. lbs. (35–49 Nm).

32. Install the transaxle housing cover and tighten the bolts to 40–58 ft. lbs. (55–80 Nm).

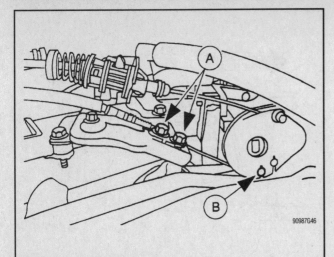

Fig. 84 Connect the throttle valve cable at the throttle cam (B) and tighten the cable retaining bolts (A)

33. Install the engine support crossmember. Tighten the crossmember bolts and nuts to 47–65 ft. lbs. (64–89 Nm) and the insulator nuts to 28–37 ft. lbs. (38–51 Nm).

34. Install the front and rear upper transaxle-to-engine bolt and tighten it to 28–38 ft. lbs. (38–51 Nm).

35. Remove the transaxle plugs and install the halfshafts.

36. Connect the crossmember to the transaxle mounts and the chassis. Tighten the crossmember-to-transaxle mount nuts to 27–38 ft. lbs. (37–52 Nm). Tighten the crossmember-to-chassis nuts and bolts to 47–66 ft. lbs. (64–89 Nm).

37. Install the lower transaxle-to-engine oil pan bolts and tighten to 27–38 ft. lbs. (37–52 Nm).

38. Install the engine/transaxle splash shields.

39. Install the starter motor.

40. Attach all the electrical connections.

41. Lower the vehicle.

42. Install the upper transaxle-to-engine bolts and tighten to 40–58 ft. lbs. (55–80 Nm).

43. Install the left-hand engine mount and tighten the nuts to 50–68 ft. lbs. (67–93 Nm).

44. If equipped, connect the throttle valve cable at the throttle cam. Adjust the cable as outlined in this section.

45. Remove the engine support.

46. Attach the shift cable and bracket to the manual shift lever, install the shift cable and bracket clip. Tighten the nut to 12–16 ft. lbs. (16–22 Nm).

47. Install the engine air cleaner assembly. Adjust the cable as outlined in this section.

48. Install the battery tray and battery.

49. Connect both battery cables, negative cable last.

50. Add the proper type and quantity of transaxle fluid.

51. Check the transaxle for leaks and for proper operation.

52. Check the manual lever position sensor for proper adjustment.

53. Road test the vehicle and check for proper operation.

ADJUSTMENTS

Throttle Linkage

▶ **See Figures 85, 86 and 87**

➡ The Throttle Valve (TV) linkage adjustment is set at the factory and is critical in establishing automatic transaxle upshift and down-shift timing and feel. Any time the engine, transaxle or throttle link-

age components are removed, it is recommended that the TV linkage adjustment be reset after the component installation or replacement.

➡ The TV cable adjustment for the 4-speed Electronically Activated Transmission (4EAT) requires a transmission test adapter, part No. D87C-77000-A, or equivalent and a line pressure gauge, part No. T57L-77820-A, or equivalent.

1. If necessary, install the ends of the TV control actuating cable to the transaxle and the throttle control lever.

2. If necessary, install the throttle cable bracket to the intake manifold bracket.

3. Remove the left front engine/transmission shields.

4. Remove the square head plug (marked **L**) and install the transmission test adapter, or equivalent, and a suitable line pressure gauge.

5. Start the car and let it reach normal operating temperature.

6. Apply the parking brake and make sure the idle speed is within the 670–730 rpm range.

➡ **You must loosen bolt 1 before loosening bolt 2.**

7. Loosen bolt **1** and then bolt **2**.

8. Make sure the throttle plate is fully closed.

9. Tighten the bolt **1** at the bracket (closest to the throttle control lever) to 61–87 inch lbs. (7–10 Nm). Refer to the accompanying illustration.

10. Pull the throttle cable conduit in the direction of the arrows (refer to the illustration), to increase or decrease line pressure.

11. Adjust the throttle valve control actuating cable until the line pressure reaches 57–60 psi (393–413 kPa) for 1.8L engines and 71–74 psi (490–510 kPa) for 1.9L and 2.0L engines.

12. After the line pressure is within specifications, tighten bolt **2** to 61–87 inch lbs. (7–10 Nm).

13. Apply slight downward pressure to the cable with a finger to make sure all slack is removed.

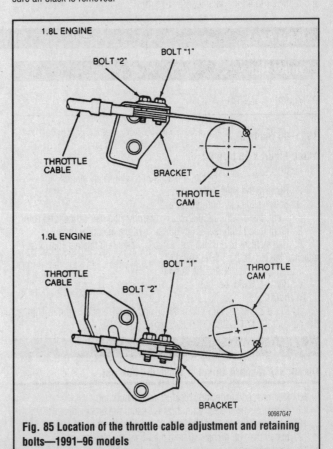

Fig. 85 Location of the throttle cable adjustment and retaining bolts—1991–96 models

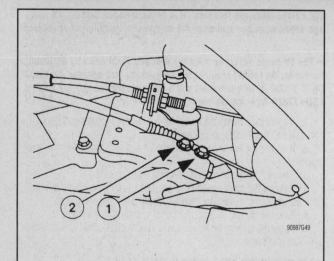

Fig. 86 Location of the throttle cable adjustment and retaining bolts—1997–99 models

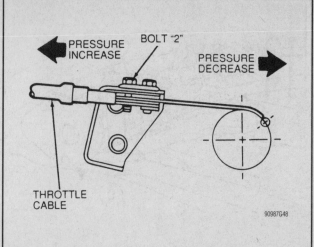

Fig. 87 Loosely tighten bolt "2" and adjust the cable—1991–96 models

14. Turn the engine **OFF** and verify that the throttle valve control actuating cable operates smoothly.

15. Restart the engine and press the accelerator slightly, then run the engine at idle.

16. Verify that the line pressure is within 51–64 psi (352–441 kPa) on 1.8L engines and 65–78 psi (448–537 kPa) on 1.9L engines.

17. If the line pressure is not within specifications, repeat the procedure beginning with step 7.

18. Turn the engine **OFF**.

19. Remove the gauge and install a new square head oil passage plug and tighten it to 43–87 inch lbs. (5–10 Nm).

Halfshafts

REMOVAL & INSTALLATION

The Halfshaft removal and installation procedure for automatic transaxle equipped models is covered in the manual transaxle portion of this section.

REAR AXLE

Wheel Hub

REMOVAL & INSTALLATION

1991–96 Models

▶ **See Figures 88 thru 93**

1. Raise the rear of the car and support it with safety stands.
2. Remove the wheel assembly.
3. Remove the rear hub grease cap.
4. If equipped with rear disc brakes, remove the rear caliper and rotor.
5. If equipped with rear drum brakes, remove the brake drum.
6. Use a chisel to unstake the rear axle wheel hub retainer (nut) that attaches the hub to the wheel spindle.
7. Remove and discard the hub nut.
8. Remove the wheel hub.

To install:

9. Place the wheel hub into position and install a new hub nut. Tighten the nut to 130–174 ft. lbs. (177–235 Nm).

✳✳ WARNING

Do not use a sharp chisel to stake the hub nut.

10. Using a cape or round chisel, stake the hub nut.
11. If equipped with rear drum brakes, install the brake drum.
12. If equipped with rear disc brakes, install the rotor and caliper.
13. Install the hub grease cap and the wheel assembly.
14. Lower the car.

1997–99 Models

1. Raise the rear of the car and support it with safety stands.
2. Remove the wheel assembly.
3. If equipped with rear disc brakes, remove the rear caliper and rotor.
4. If equipped with rear drum brakes, remove the brake drum.

Fig. 88 Remove the rear hub grease cap

Fig. 89 Use a cape or round chisel to unstake the hub nut retainer

Fig. 92 . . . then slide the rear wheel hub from the spindle

Fig. 90 Use a wrench to loosen . . .

Fig. 93 Use a torque wrench to tighten the new hub nut retainer to specification

5. Use a chisel to unstake the rear axle wheel hub retainer (nut) that attaches the hub to the wheel spindle.

6. Remove and discard the hub nut.

7. Remove the wheel hub.

To install:

8. If necessary, use a press and a steel plate to install a new anti-lock brake sensor indicator on the hub.

9. Place the wheel hub into position and install a new hub nut. Tighten the nut to 130–174 ft. lbs. (177–235 Nm).

✳✳ WARNING

Do not use a sharp chisel to stake the hub nut.

10. Using a cape or round chisel, stake the hub nut.

11. If equipped with rear drum brakes, install the brake drum.

12. If equipped with rear disc brakes, install the rotor and caliper.

13. Install the wheel assembly.

14. Lower the car.

Fig. 91 . . . and remove the rear hub nut . . .

Wheel Spindle

REMOVAL & INSTALLATION

1991–96 Models

▶ See Figures 94 and 95

1. Remove the wheel hub.
2. If equipped with disc brakes, unfasten the four disc brake shield retaining bolts and remove the shield.
3. If equipped with drum brakes, remove the brake backing plate.
4. Remove the retainers attaching the rear shock absorber and strut mounting to the wheel spindle.
5. Remove the rear suspension trailing link bolt that attaches the trailing link to the suspension.
6. Remove the stabilizer bar links.
7. Remove the rear suspension arm and bushing rear nut from the spindle.
8. Remove the spindle.
   To install:
9. Place the spindle into position.

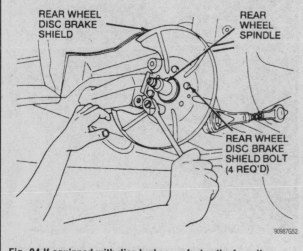

Fig. 94 If equipped with disc brakes, unfasten the four disc brake shield retaining bolts and remove the shield

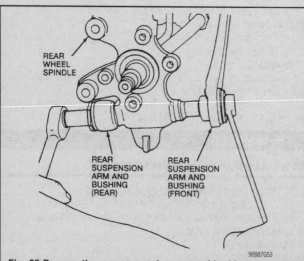

Fig. 95 Remove the rear suspension arm and bushing rear nut from the spindle

10. Attach the rear shock absorber and strut mounting to the spindle. Tighten the shock absorber-to-spindle retainers to 69–93 ft. lbs. (93–127 Nm).
11. Attach the trailing link to the spindle. Install the trailing link rear bolt and tighten the bolt to 69–93 ft. lbs. (93–127 Nm).
12. Position the rear suspension arm and bushing on the spindle and secure each of them with a nut and bolt. Tighten the retainers to 63–86 ft. lbs. (85–117 Nm).
13. Install the stabilizer bar links.
14. If equipped with drum brakes, install the brake backing plate.
15. If equipped with disc brakes, install the brake shield and tighten the retaining bolts.
16. Install the wheel hub.

1997–99 Models

▶ See Figure 96

1. Remove the wheel hub.
2. If equipped with disc brakes, unfasten the four disc brake shield retaining bolts.
3. If equipped with drum brakes, remove the brake backing plate.
4. If equipped with an Anti-lock Brake System (ABS), unfasten the ABS sensor bracket bolt.
5. Remove the two lower shock absorber nuts and bolts.
6. If equipped with ABS, unfasten the ABS sensor bolt and remove the sensor.
7. Unfasten the trailing link bolt.
8. Unfasten the rear suspension arm and bushing nut and bolt, then remove the spindle.
   To install:
9. Place the spindle into position.
10. Install the rear suspension arm bushing nut and bolt. Tighten the nut and bolt to 64–86 ft. lbs. (87–116 Nm).
11. Install the trailing link bolt and tighten to 69–94 ft. lbs. (94–126 Nm).
12. If equipped with ABS, install the ABS sensor and tighten the bolt to 14–18 ft. lbs. (19–25 Nm).
13. If equipped with ABS, tighten the ABS sensor bracket bolt to 14–18 ft. lbs. (19–25 Nm).
14. Install the two lower shock absorber nuts and bolt. Tighten the bolt and nut to 76–100 ft. lbs. (103–136 Nm).
15. If equipped with drum brakes, install the brake backing plate.
16. If equipped with disc brakes, install the brake shield and tighten the retaining bolts.
17. Install the wheel hub.

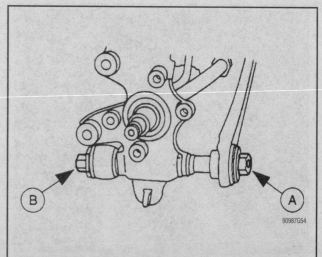

Fig. 96 Remove the rear suspension arm and bushing nut (A) and bolt (B) before removing the spindle—1997–99 models

Troubleshooting Basic Clutch Problems

Problem	Cause
Excessive clutch noise	Throwout bearing noises are more audible at the lower end of pedal travel. The usual causes are: • Riding the clutch • Too little pedal free-play • Lack of bearing lubrication A bad clutch shaft pilot bearing will make a high pitched squeal, when the clutch is disengaged and the transmission is in gear or within the first 2″ of pedal travel. The bearing must be replaced. Noise from the clutch linkage is a clicking or snapping that can be heard or felt as the pedal is moved completely up or down. This usually requires lubrication. Transmitted engine noises are amplified by the clutch housing and heard in the passenger compartment. They are usually the result of insufficient pedal free-play and can be changed by manipulating the clutch pedal.
Clutch slips (the car does not move as it should when the clutch is engaged)	This is usually most noticeable when pulling away from a standing start. A severe test is to start the engine, apply the brakes, shift into high gear and SLOWLY release the clutch pedal. A healthy clutch will stall the engine. If it slips it may be due to: • A worn pressure plate or clutch plate • Oil soaked clutch plate • Insufficient pedal free-play
Clutch drags or fails to release	The clutch disc and some transmission gears spin briefly after clutch disengagement. Under normal conditions in average temperatures, 3 seconds is maximum spin-time. Failure to release properly can be caused by: • Too light transmission lubricant or low lubricant level • Improperly adjusted clutch linkage
Low clutch life	Low clutch life is usually a result of poor driving habits or heavy duty use. Riding the clutch, pulling heavy loads, holding the car on a grade with the clutch instead of the brakes and rapid clutch engagement all contribute to low clutch life.

TCCA7C01

Transmission Fluid Indications

The appearance and odor of the transmission fluid can give valuable clues to the overall condition of the transmission. Always note the appearance of the fluid when you check the fluid level or change the fluid. Rub a small amount of fluid between your fingers to feel for grit and smell the fluid on the dipstick.

If the fluid appears:	It indicates:
Clear and red colored	• Normal operation
Discolored (extremely dark red or brownish) or smells burned	• Band or clutch pack failure, usually caused by an overheated transmission. Hauling very heavy loads with insufficient power or failure to change the fluid, often result in overheating. Do not confuse this appearance with newer fluids that have a darker red color and a strong odor (though not a burned odor).
Foamy or aerated (light in color and full of bubbles)	• The level is too high (gear train is churning oil) • An internal air leak (air is mixing with the fluid). Have the transmission checked professionally.
Solid residue in the fluid	• Defective bands, clutch pack or bearings. Bits of band material or metal abrasives are clinging to the dipstick. Have the transmission checked professionally.
Varnish coating on the dipstick	• The transmission fluid is overheating

TCCA7C02

TORQUE SPECIFICATIONS

Components	Ft. Lbs.	Nm
Manual Transaxle		
Back-Up Light Switch		
1991–96 Models	14-22	20-29
1997–99 Models	15-21	20-25
Manual Transaxle Assembly		
1.8L and 1.9L Engines		
Lower engine-to-transaxle bolts	27-38	37-52
Front transaxle mount and bracket bolts	12-17	16-23
Lower crossmember support bolts	47-66	64-89
Transaxle support insulator-to-rear engine support nuts	27-38	37-52
Shift control rod bolt and nut	12-17	16-23
Stabilizer bracket and stabilizer bar nut	23-34	31-46
Intake manifold support bolts	27-38	37-52
1.8L engine		
Upper engine-to-transaxle bolts	47-66	64-89
Left-hand engine support mount bolts		
1.8L engine	32-45	43-61
1.9L engine	41-59	55-80
Left-hand engine support bracket nuts	47-66	64-89
2.0L Engines		
Transaxle-to-engine bolts	23-38	38-51
Clutch slave cylinder nuts	12-17	16-23
Lower slave cylinder tube fitting	10-16	13-21
Gearshift bolt and gearshift rod nut	12-17	16-23
Gearshift stabilizer bar nut	23-34	31-46
Engine support crossmember bolts and nuts	47-65	64-89
Left-hand engine support insulator nuts	50-68	67-93
Slave cylinder line fitting	10-16	13-21
Halfshafts		
1991–96 Models		
1.9L engine and left side of 1.8L engine		
Crossmember-to-frame		
Nuts	27-38	37-52
Bolts	47-66	64-89
Transaxle mount-to-crossmember nuts	27-38	37-52
Lower ball joint pinch bolt	32-43	43-59
Tie rod end nut	31-42	42-57
Halfshaft retaining nut	174-235	235-319
Right side of 1.8L engine		
Lower ball joint pinch bolt	32-43	43-59
Tie rod end nut	31-42	42-57
Bearing support bracket bolts	31-46	42-62
Halfshaft retaining nut	174-235	235-319
1997–99 Models		
Center support bearing bolts	32-46	46-62
Crossmember-to-frame bolts	69-93	94-126
Ball joint nut and bolt	32-43	43-59
Tie rod end nut		
1997 models	25-33	34-46
1998–99 models	32-41	43-56
Halfshaft retaining nut	174-235	235-319

90987C01

TORQUE SPECIFICATIONS

Components	Ft. Lbs.	Nm
Clutch		
Driven Disc and Pressure Plate		
1991–96 Models		
Flywheel bolts		
1.8L engine	71-76	96-103
1.9L engine	54-67	73-91
Pressure plate-to-flywheel bolts	13-20	18-26
1997–99 Models		
Pressure plate-to-flywheel bolts	12-24	16-32
Clutch Master Cylinder		
Clutch master cylinder nuts	14-19	19-25
Clutch tube nut	10-16	13-22
Clutch Slave Cylinder		
Slave cylinder bolts	12-17	16-23
Clutch slave cylinder tube nut	10-16	13-22
Automatic Transaxle		
Neutral Safety Switch		
1991–96 Models		
Manual control shift outer lever-to-manual control lever nut	33-47	44-64
1997–99 Models		
Switch bolts	70-95 inch lbs.	8-11
Manual control shift outer lever nut	33-47	44-64
Shift cable bracket nut	12-16 inch lbs.	16-22
Automatic Transaxle Assembly		
1991–96 Models		
Throttle control lever bolt	69-95 inch lbs.	8-11
Transaxle-to-engine bolts	41-59	55-80
Torque converter-to-flexplate nuts	25-36	34-49
Crossmember-to-transaxle mount nuts	27-38	37-52
Crossmember-to-chassis nuts and bolts	47-66	64-89
Lower transaxle-to-engine oil pan bolts	27-38	37-52
Left–hand engine mount nuts	49-69	67-93
1997–99 Models		
Middle and lower transaxle-to-engine bolts	40-58	55-80
Upper front transaxle-to-engine bolt		
1997 models	40-58	55-80
Flywheel-to-converter nuts	26-36	35-49
Transaxle housing cover bolts	40-58	55-80
Engine support crossmember bolts and nuts	47-65	64-89
Engine support insulator nuts	28-37	38-51
Front and rear upper transaxle-to-engine bolt	28-37	38-51
Crossmember-to-transaxle mount nuts	28-37	38-51
Crossmember-to-chassis nuts and bolts	47-66	64-89
Lower transaxle-to-engine oil pan bolts	27-38	37-51
Upper transaxle-to-engine bolts	40-58	55-80
Left-hand engine mount nuts	50-68	67-93
Halfshafts		
1991–96 Models		
1.9L engine and left side of 1.8L engine		
Crossmember-to-frame nuts	27-38	37-52
Crossmember-to-frame bolts	47-66	64-89

90987C02

TORQUE SPECIFICATIONS

Components	Ft. Lbs.	Nm
Halfshafts (cont.)		
1991-96 Models		
1.9L engine and left side of 1.8L engine		
Transaxle mount-to-crossmember nuts	27-38	37-52
Lower ball joint pinch bolt	32-43	43-59
Tie rod end nut	31-42	42-57
Halfshaft retaining nut	174-235	235-319
Right side of 1.8L engine		
Lower ball joint pinch bolt	32-43	43-59
Tie rod end nut	31-42	42-57
Bearing support bracket bolts	31-46	42-62
Halfshaft retaining nut	174-235	235-319
1997–99 Models		
Center support bearing bolts	32-46	46-62
Crossmember-to-frame bolts	69-93	94-126
Ball joint nut and bolt	32-43	43-59
Tie rod end nut		
1997 models	25-33	34-46
1998–99 models	32-41	43-56
Halfshaft retaining nut	174-235	235-319
Rear Axle		
Wheel Hub		
Wheel hub retainer	130-174	177-235
Wheel Spindle		
1991–96 Models		
Shock absorber-to-spindle retainers	69-93	93-127
Trailing link rear bolt	69-93	93-127
Rear suspension arm bushing nut and bolt	63-86	85-117
1997–99 Models		
Rear suspension arm bushing nut and bolt	64-86	87-116
Trailing link bolt	69-94	94-126
ABS sensor bolt	14-18	19-25
ABS sensor bracket bolt	14-18	19-25
Lower shock absorber nuts and bolt	76-100	103-136

90987C03

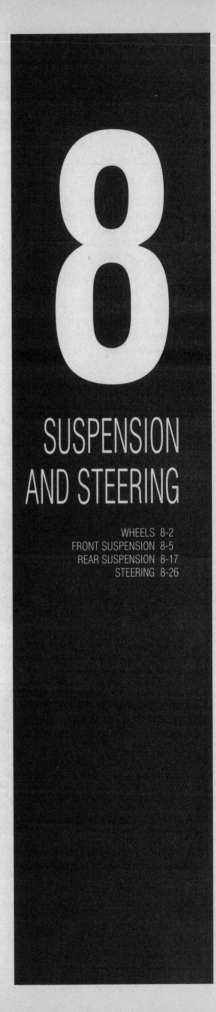

8

SUSPENSION AND STEERING

WHEELS

Wheels

REMOVAL & INSTALLATION

▶ **See Figures 1 thru 7**

1. Park the vehicle on a level surface.
2. Remove the jack, tire iron and, if necessary, the spare tire from their storage compartments.
3. Check the owner's manual or refer to Section 1 of this manual for the jacking points on your vehicle. Then, place the jack in the proper position.
4. If equipped with lug nut trim caps, remove them by either unscrewing or pulling them off the lug nuts, as appropriate. Consult the owner's manual, if necessary.
5. If equipped with a wheel cover or hub cap, insert the tapered end of the tire iron in the groove and pry off the cover.
6. Apply the parking brake and block the diagonally opposite wheel with a wheel chock or two.

➡Wheel chocks may be purchased at your local auto parts store, or a block of wood cut into wedges may be used. If possible, keep one or two of the chocks in your tire storage compartment, in case any of the tires has to be removed on the side of the road.

7. If equipped with an automatic transaxle, place the selector lever in **P** or Park; with a manual transmission/transaxle, place the shifter in Reverse.
8. With the tires still on the ground, use the tire iron/wrench to break the lug nuts loose.

➡**If a nut is stuck, never use heat to loosen it or damage to the wheel and bearings may occur. If the nuts are seized, one or two heavy hammer blows directly on the end of the bolt usually loosens the rust. Be careful, as continued pounding will likely damage the brake drum or rotor.**

9. Using the jack, raise the vehicle until the tire is clear of the ground. Support the vehicle safely using jackstands.
10. Remove the lug nuts, then remove the tire and wheel assembly.

TCCA8P00

Fig. 1 Place the jack at the proper lifting point on your vehicle

TCCA8P02

Fig. 3 With the vehicle still on the ground, break the lug nuts loose using the wrench end of the tire iron

TCCA8P01

Fig. 2 Before jacking the vehicle, block the diagonally opposite wheel with one or, preferably, two chocks

TCCA8P03

Fig. 4 After the lug nuts have been loosened, raise the vehicle using the jack until the tire is clear of the ground

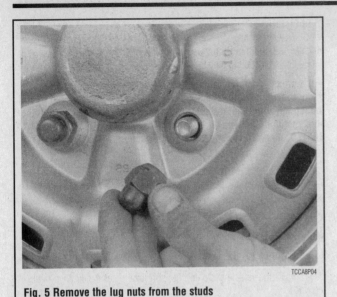

Fig. 5 Remove the lug nuts from the studs

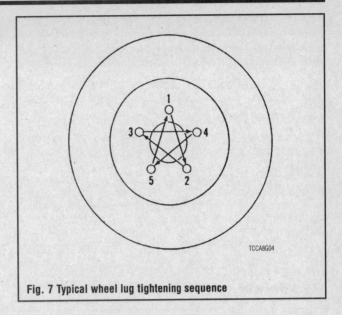

Fig. 7 Typical wheel lug tightening sequence

Fig. 6 Remove the wheel and tire assembly from the vehicle

16. If so equipped, install the wheel cover or hub cap. Make sure the valve stem protrudes through the proper opening before tapping the wheel cover into position.

17. If equipped, install the lug nut trim caps by pushing them or screwing them on, as applicable.

18. Remove the jack from under the vehicle, and place the jack and tire iron/wrench in their storage compartments. Remove the wheel chock(s).

19. If you have removed a flat or damaged tire, place it in the storage compartment of the vehicle and take it to your local repair station to have it fixed or replaced as soon as possible.

INSPECTION

Inspect the tires for lacerations, puncture marks, nails and other sharp objects. Repair or replace as necessary. Also check the tires for treadwear and air pressure as outlined in Section 1 of this manual.

Check the wheel assemblies for dents, cracks, rust and metal fatigue. Repair or replace as necessary.

Wheel Lug Studs

REMOVAL & INSTALLATION

With Disc Brakes

▶ See Figures 8, 9 and 10

1. Raise and support the appropriate end of the vehicle safely using jackstands, then remove the wheel.

2. Remove the brake pads and caliper. Support the caliper aside using wire or a coat hanger. For details, please refer to Section 9 of this manual.

3. Remove the outer wheel bearing and lift off the rotor. For details on wheel bearing removal, installation and adjustment, please refer to Section 1 of this manual.

4. Properly support the rotor using press bars, then drive the stud out using an arbor press.

➡If a press is not available, CAREFULLY drive the old stud out using a blunt drift. MAKE SURE the rotor is properly and evenly supported or it may be damaged.

To install:

11. Make sure the wheel and hub mating surfaces, as well as the wheel lug studs, are clean and free of all foreign material. Always remove rust from the wheel mounting surface and the brake rotor or drum. Failure to do so may cause the lug nuts to loosen in service.

12. Install the tire and wheel assembly and hand-tighten the lug nuts.

13. Using the tire wrench, tighten all the lug nuts, in a crisscross pattern, until they are snug.

14. Raise the vehicle and withdraw the jackstand, then lower the vehicle.

15. Using a torque wrench, tighten the lug nuts in a crisscross pattern to 65–87 ft. lbs. (88–118 Nm) on 1991–97 models and 73–99 ft. lbs. (100–135 Nm) on 1998–99 models. Check your owner's manual or refer to Section 1 of this manual for the proper tightening sequence.

✷✷ WARNING

Do not overtighten the lug nuts, as this may cause the wheel studs to stretch or the brake disc (rotor) to warp.

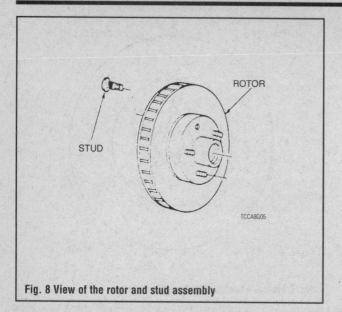

Fig. 8 View of the rotor and stud assembly

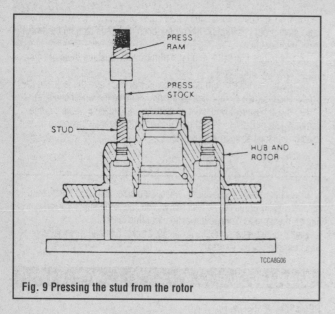

Fig. 9 Pressing the stud from the rotor

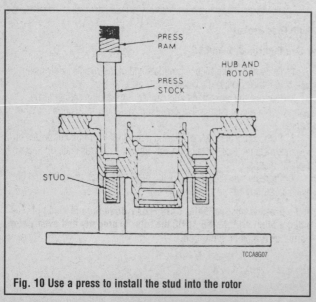

Fig. 10 Use a press to install the stud into the rotor

To install:

5. Clean the stud hole with a wire brush and start the new stud with a hammer and drift pin. Do not use any lubricant or thread sealer.

6. Finish installing the stud with the press.

➡️If a press is not available, start the lug stud through the bore in the hub, then position about 4 flat washers over the stud and thread the lug nut. Hold the hub/rotor while tightening the lug nut, and the stud should be drawn into position. **MAKE SURE THE STUD IS FULLY SEATED, then remove the lug nut and washers.**

7. Install the rotor and adjust the wheel bearings.

8. Install the brake caliper and pads.

9. Install the wheel, then remove the jackstands and carefully lower the vehicle.

10. Tighten the lug nuts to the proper torque.

With Drum Brakes

▶ **See Figures 11, 12 and 13**

1. Raise the vehicle and safely support it with jackstands, then remove the wheel.

2. Remove the brake drum.

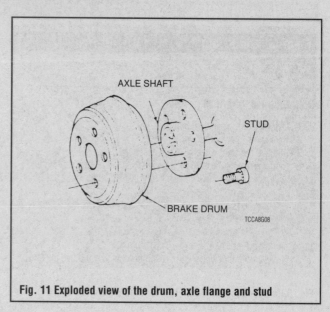

Fig. 11 Exploded view of the drum, axle flange and stud

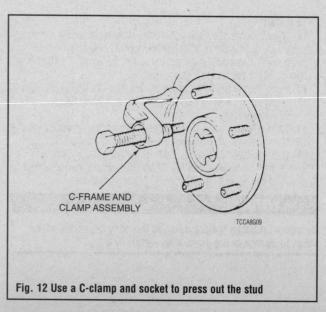

Fig. 12 Use a C-clamp and socket to press out the stud

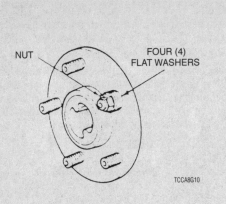

Fig. 13 Force the stud onto the axle flange using washers and a lug nut

3. If necessary to provide clearance, remove the brake shoes, as outlined in Section 9 of this manual.

4. Using a large C-clamp and socket, press the stud from the axle flange.

5. Coat the serrated part of the stud with liquid soap and place it into the hole.

To install:

6. Position about 4 flat washers over the stud and thread the lug nut. Hold the flange while tightening the lug nut, and the stud should be drawn into position. MAKE SURE THE STUD IS FULLY SEATED, then remove the lug nut and washers.

7. If applicable, install the brake shoes.

8. Install the brake drum.

9. Install the wheel, then remove the jackstands and carefully lower the vehicle.

10. Tighten the lug nuts to the proper torque.

FRONT SUSPENSION

MacPherson Struts

REMOVAL & INSTALLATION

▶ See Figures 14 thru 21

1. Disconnect the negative battery cable.
2. Raise and safely support the vehicle.
3. Remove the front wheel and tire assembly.
4. Remove the clip securing the brake hose to the strut (spring and shock) assembly. If equipped with anti-lock brakes, remove the anti-lock brake harness cable and clip.
5. Unfasten the two nuts and two bolts securing the strut assembly to the steering knuckle.
6. If equipped, unfasten the A/C line-to-strut stud retaining nut and set the hose and bracket aside.
7. Unfasten the four upper strut retaining nuts and remove the strut assembly from the vehicle.

✳✳ CAUTION

Never remove the strut piston rod nut unless the coil spring is compressed. Always wear safety glasses when using a spring compressor.

8. Inspect all components and replace as needed.

To install:

9. Position the strut assembly into the wheel housing. Make sure the direction indicator on the upper mounting bracket faces inboard.

10. Secure the upper mounting bracket to the strut tower with the retaining nuts. Tighten the nuts to 22–30 ft. lbs. (29–40 Nm).

11. Attach the strut assembly to the steering knuckle and install the retaining bolts and nuts. Tighten to 69–93 ft. lbs. (93–127 Nm).

12. Position the brake hose on the strut assembly and secure it with the brake hose clip. If equipped with anti-lock brakes, install the anti-lock harness cable and clip.

13. Install the front wheel and tire assembly.

14. Lower the vehicle.

FRONT SUSPENSION AND STEERING COMPONENT LOCATIONS—EARLY MODELS

1. Strut assembly
2. Stabilizer bar
3. Tie rod end (behind CV-boot)
4. Lower control arm
5. Ball joint

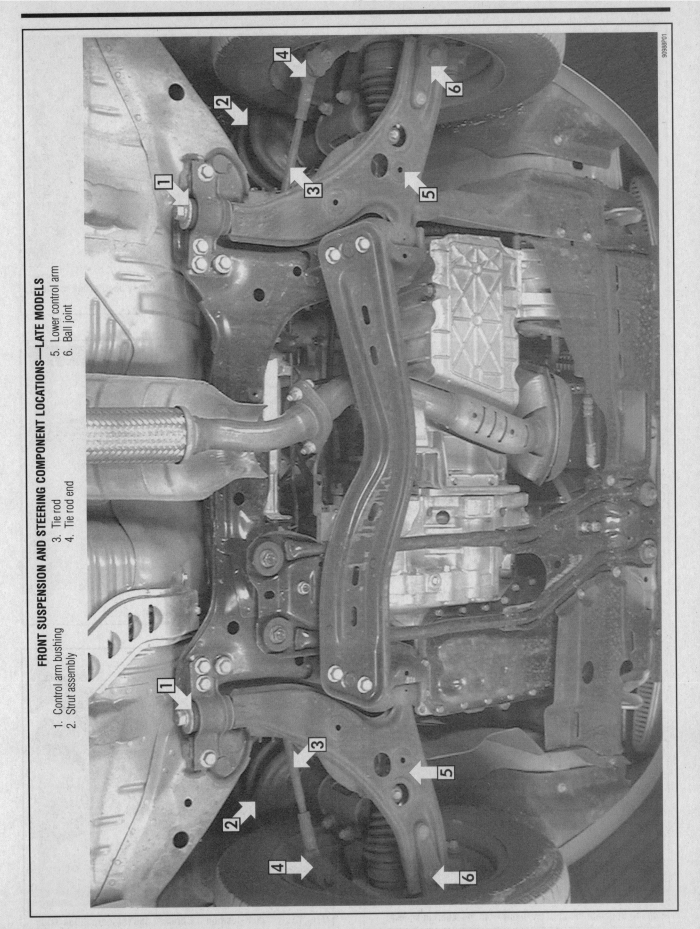

FRONT SUSPENSION AND STEERING COMPONENT LOCATIONS—LATE MODELS

1. Control arm bushing
2. Strut assembly
3. Tie rod
4. Tie rod end
5. Lower control arm
6. Ball joint

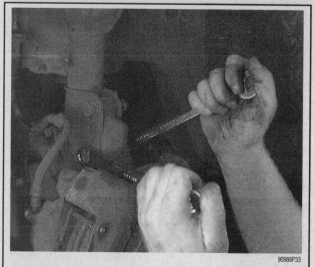

Fig. 14 Use a pair of wrenches to loosen . . .

Fig. 15 . . . and remove the two nuts and bolts which secure the strut assembly to the steering knuckle

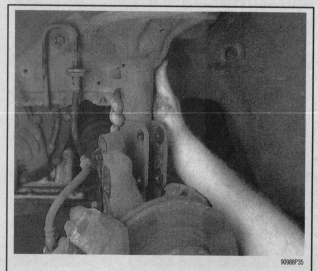

Fig. 16 Separate the strut assembly from the steering knuckle

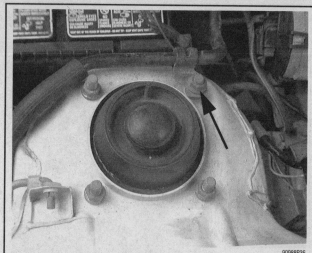

Fig. 17 An A/C refrigerant line bracket may be attached to one of the strut's upper mounting studs

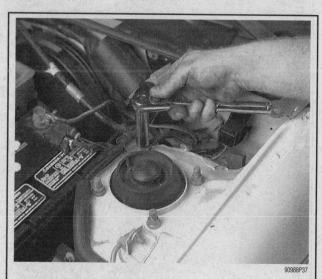

Fig. 18 Loosen the bracket retaining nut . . .

Fig. 19 . . . then position the bracket and refrigerant line aside

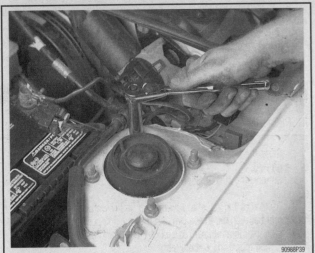

Fig. 20 Unfasten the front strut assembly's upper mount retaining nuts . . .

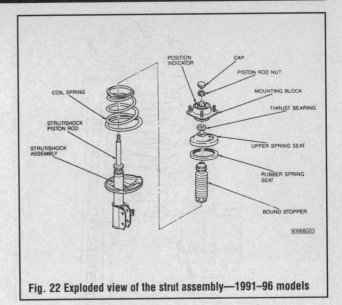

Fig. 22 Exploded view of the strut assembly—1991–96 models

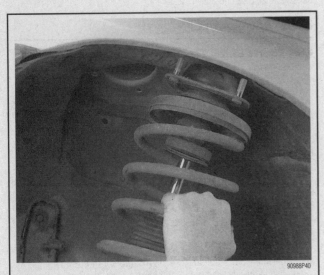

Fig. 21 . . . and remove the strut assembly from the vehicle

15. Connect the negative battery cable.
16. Check the front wheel alignment.
17. Road test the vehicle and check for proper operation.

OVERHAUL

1991–96 Models

▶ See Figure 22

1. Remove the strut assembly.
2. Remove the cap from the top of the strut.
3. Place the strut assembly in a vise, hold the piston rod in position and loosen the piston rod nut.

✳✳ CAUTION

Always wear goggles when using a spring compressor.

4. Install a suitable spring compressor tool onto the coil spring.

5. Compress the spring using the tool.
6. Remove the strut piston rod nut, front mounting block, thrust bearing, upper spring seat, rubber spring seat, coil spring and bound stopper.

To assemble:
7. Place the bound stopper onto the strut.
8. With coil spring compressed, position the spring onto the strut assembly.
9. Install the rubber spring seat, upper spring seat, thrust bearing, mounting block and piston rod nut. Tighten the piston rod nut to 58–81 ft. lbs. (79–110 Nm).
10. After the piston rod nut has been tightened to specification, carefully remove the compressor tool from the spring while making sure the spring is properly seated in the upper and lower spring seats.
11. Install the cap on top of the strut.

➡**The position indicator on the mounting block faces inboard during installation.**

12. Install the strut assembly in the vehicle.
13. Have the vehicle alignment checked and if necessary, adjusted.

1997–99 Models

▶ See Figures 23 and 24

1. Remove the strut assembly.
2. Place the strut assembly in a vise.

✳✳ CAUTION

Always wear goggles when using a spring compressor.

3. Install a suitable spring compressor tool onto the coil spring and compress the spring.
4. Unfasten the piston rod nut and remove the upper mounting bracket.
5. Remove the bound stopper, dust boot, rubber spring seat, spring, upper spring seat and thrust bearing.

To assemble:
6. Install the thrust bearing, upper spring seat, spring, rubber spring seat, dust boot and the bound stopper.
7. Install the piston rod nut and tighten it to 58–81 ft. lbs. (79–110 Nm).

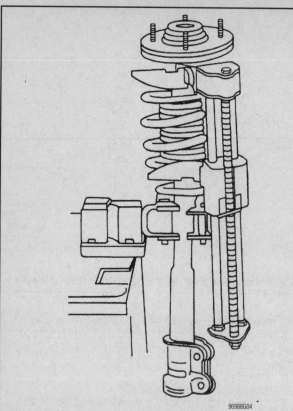

Fig. 23 Use a suitable spring compressor tool to safely compress the spring

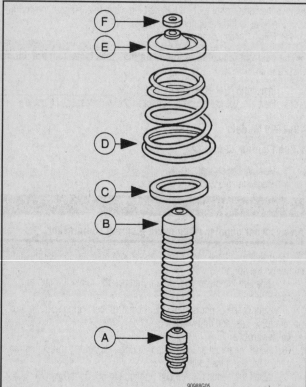

Fig. 24 Remove the bound stopper (A), dust boot (B), rubber spring seat (C), spring (D), upper spring seat (E) and thrust bearing (F)—1996–97 models

8. After the piston rod nut has been tightened to specification, carefully remove the compressor tool from the spring while making sure the spring is properly seated in the upper and lower spring seats.

9. Install the strut assembly in the vehicle.

10. Have the vehicle alignment checked and if necessary, adjusted.

Lower Ball Joint

INSPECTION

1. Raise the front of the car until the wheel and tire assembly are clear of the ground.

2. Support the suspension lower arm until there is no load on the shock absorber.

3. Try to rock the wheel top-to-bottom; if any wobble is felt, look for movement between the lower arm and the wheel knuckle.

4. If the ball joint appears to be tight, check and adjust the front wheel bearing, then repeat the wobble test.

5. If any movement is present, this would probably indicate ball joint wear and the ball joint should be replaced.

6. If wear is present, check the tie rod end. The lower arm and stabilizer bar should also be checked.

REMOVAL & INSTALLATION

♦ **See Figures 25, 26, 27, 28 and 29**

1. Raise the front of the car and support it with safety stands.

2. Remove the wheel assembly.

3. Unfasten the pinch bolt attaching the lower ball joint to the steering knuckle.

4. Separate the ball joint from the steering knuckle.

5. Unfasten the lower control arm ball joint nuts and bolt. Remove the ball joint.

To install:

6. Place the ball joint into position on the lower control arm. Install the ball joint-to-lower control arm retainers. Tighten the nuts and bolt to 69–86 ft. lbs. (93–117 Nm).

7. Apply Loctite 290® threadlocking compound or equivalent to the ball joint nut and threads.

8. Attach the ball joint to the steering knuckle and install the pinch bolt. Tighten the pinch bolt to 32–43 ft. lbs. (43–59 Nm).

9. Install the wheel assembly and lower the car.

10. Have the vehicle alignment checked and if necessary, adjusted.

Fig. 25 Loosen the pinch bolt attaching the lower ball joint to the steering knuckle . . .

Fig. 26 . . . then remove the pinch bolt and nut

Fig. 27 Separate the ball joint from the steering knuckle

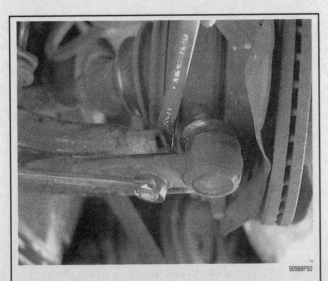

Fig. 28 Unfasten the lower arm ball joint nuts and bolt . . .

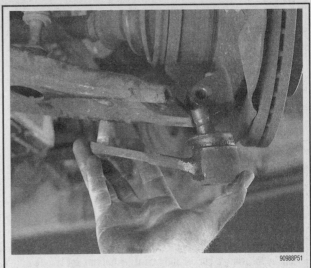

Fig. 29 . . . and remove the ball joint from the vehicle

Lower Ball Joint Dust Seal

REMOVAL & INSTALLATION

1991–96 Models

1. Remove the ball joint and place it in a vise.
2. Position a chisel between the ball joint and the dust seal. Lightly tap on the chisel to separate the dust seal from the ball joint.
   To install:
3. Place the new dust seal into position and use an appropriate tool to seat the dust boot onto the ball joint.
4. Install the ball joint.

Stabilizer Bar

REMOVAL & INSTALLATION

1991–96 Models

▶ See Figures 30 and 31

1. Disconnect the negative battery cable.
2. Support the engine and transaxle assembly with Engine Support D88L-6000-A, or equivalent.
3. Raise and safely support the vehicle.
4. Remove the front wheel and tire assemblies.
5. Unfasten the four retaining nuts securing the rack and pinion (steering gear) mounting brackets and position the rack and pinion slightly forward.
6. Unfasten the stabilizer bar nuts, washers, bushings, sleeves and bolts from the lower control arm.
7. Unfasten the rear crossmember retaining nuts from the rear transaxle mount and the vehicle frame.
8. Loosen the front crossmember retaining bolts and nuts from the front transaxle mount and the vehicle frame. Lower the rear end of the crossmember.
9. Remove the nuts and bolts securing the sub-frame to the vehicles frame. Lower the sub-frame enough for removal of the sway bar.

➡The engine and transaxle mounts will support the sub-frame from falling when it is unbolted from the vehicle frame.

10. Unbolt the sway bar from the sub-frame and remove.

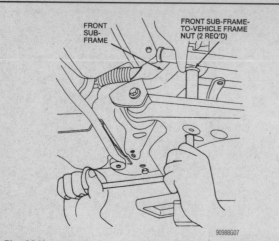

Fig. 30 You can access some of the sub-frame-to-vehicle frame nuts by inserting a socket and extension bar through a hole in the control arm—1991–96 models

To install:

11. Position the sway bar to the sub-frame.

12. Secure the sway bar to the sub-frame with the retaining bolts. Tighten the bolts to 32–43 ft. lbs. (43–59 Nm).

13. Install the sub-frame to the vehicle frame with the bolts and nuts. Tighten the bolts and nuts to 69–93 ft. lbs. (93–127 Nm).

14. Position the crossmember to the vehicle frame and the transaxle mounts. Tighten the retaining nuts and/or bolts to insulator mounts to 27–38 ft. lbs. (37–52 Nm) and the crossmember to frame retaining nuts and/or bolts to 47–66 ft. lbs. (64–89 Nm).

15. Install the sway bar bolts, sleeves, bushings, washers and nuts. Tighten the sway bar bolts so 0.67–0.75 inches (17–19mm) of thread is exposed at the end of the bolt.

16. Position the rack and pinion (steering gear) and secure it with the brackets and nuts. Tighten the nuts to 28–38 ft. lbs. (37–52 Nm).

17. Install the front wheel and tire assemblies. Tighten the lug nuts to 65–87 ft. lbs. (88–118 Nm).

18. Lower the vehicle.

19. Remove the engine support.

20. Connect the negative battery cable.

➡Whenever the vehicles sub-frame is removed or lowered, the wheel alignment should be checked.

21. Check the wheel alignment.

22. Road test the vehicle and check for proper operation.

1997–99 Models

▶ See Figures 32 and 33

1. Disconnect the negative battery cable.

2. Support the engine and transaxle assembly with Engine Support D88L-6000-A, or equivalent.

3. Raise and safely support the vehicle.

4. Remove the front wheel and tire assemblies.

5. Unfasten the crossmember bolts and remove the crossmember.

6. Unfasten the retaining nuts securing the steering gear mounting brackets and position the steering gear slightly forward.

7. Unfasten the stabilizer bar nuts, washers, bushings, sleeves and bolts from the lower control arm.

8. Unfasten the rear crossmember retaining nuts from the rear transaxle mount and the vehicle frame.

9. Loosen the transaxle crossmember retaining bolts and nuts from the front transaxle mount and the vehicle frame. Lower the rear end of the crossmember.

10. Place a transmission jack under the sub-frame to support it.

Fig. 32 Use a transmission jack to support the sub-frame— 1997–99 models

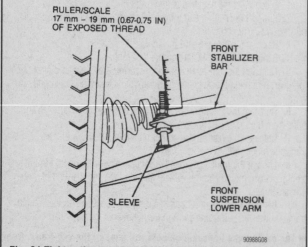

Fig. 31 Tighten the sway bar bolts until 0.67–0.75 inches (17–19mm) of thread is exposed at the end of the bolt

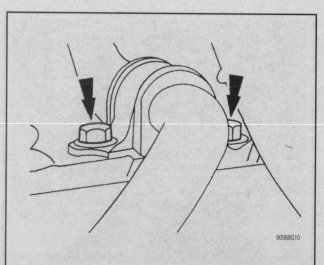

Fig. 33 Location of the stabilizer bar retaining bolts (arrows)— 1997–99 models

11. Remove the nuts and bolts securing the sub-frame to the vehicles frame. Lower the sub-frame enough for removal of the sway bar.

12. Unbolt the sway bar from the sub-frame and remove.

To install:

13. Position the sway bar to the sub-frame.

14. Secure the sway bar to the sub-frame with the retaining bolts. Tighten the bolts to 32–43 ft. lbs. (43–59 Nm).

15. Install the sub-frame to the vehicle frame with the bolts and nuts. Tighten the bolts and nuts to 69–93 ft. lbs. (93–127 Nm).

16. Remove the transmission jack.

17. Position the crossmember to the vehicle frame and the transaxle mounts. Tighten the retaining nuts and/or bolts to insulator mounts to 27–38 ft. lbs. (37–52 Nm) and the crossmember to frame retaining nuts and/or bolts to 47–66 ft. lbs. (64–89 Nm).

18. Install the sway bar bolts, sleeves, bushings, washers and nuts. Tighten the sway bar bolts so 0.67–0.75 inches (17–19mm) of thread is exposed at the end of the bolt.

19. Position the steering gear and secure it with the brackets and nuts. Tighten the nuts to 28–38 ft. lbs. (37–52 Nm).

20. Install the crossmember and tighten the bolts to 47–66 ft. lbs. (64–89 Nm).

21. Install the front wheel and tire assemblies.

22. Lower the vehicle.

23. Remove the engine support.

24. Connect the negative battery cable.

➥**Whenever the vehicles sub-frame is removed or lowered, the wheel alignment should be checked.**

25. Check the wheel alignment.

26. Road test the vehicle and check for proper operation.

Lower Control Arm

REMOVAL & INSTALLATION

1991–96 Models

▶ **See Figure 34**

1. Raise and safely support the vehicle.

2. Remove the front wheel and tire assembly.

3. Remove the stabilizer bar link nuts, retainers, bushings, bolts and sleeves.

4. Unfasten the pinch bolt and nut securing the ball joint to the steering knuckle.

5. Separate the lower ball joint from the steering knuckle by prying the lower control arm down with a prybar.

6. Unfasten the bolt and washer securing the front bushing of the lower control arm.

7. Remove the bolts securing the lower control arm rear bushing retaining strap.

8. Remove the lower control arm.

9. Inspect the lower control arm, lower control arm bushings and the lower ball joint. The ball joint and bushings can be replaced individually.

To install:

10. If required, install new bushings to the lower control arm.

11. If replacing the lower ball joint, position the ball joint to the steering knuckle. Install the ball joint retaining nuts and bolt and tighten to 32–43 ft. lbs. (43–59 Nm). Apply a suitable threadlock sealer to the nut and bolt threads prior to installation.

12. Install the lower control arm rear bushing retaining strap to the lower frame. Install the bolts and tighten to 69–86 ft. lbs. (93–117 Nm).

13. Install the lower control arm front pivot bolt and washer. Tighten the nut to 69–93 ft. lbs. (93–127 Nm).

14. Install the stabilizer bolts, washers, bushings, sleeves and nuts. Tighten the stabilizer nuts so 0.67–0.75 inches (17–19mm) of thread is exposed at the end of the bolt.

15. Install the wheel and tire assembly.

16. Lower the vehicle.

17. Check the front wheel alignment.

18. Road test the vehicle and check for proper operation.

1997–99 Models

▶ **See Figures 35, 36 and 37**

1. Raise and safely support the vehicle.

2. Remove the front wheel and tire assembly.

3. Remove the stabilizer bar link nuts, retainers, bushings, bolts and sleeves.

4. Unfasten the pinch bolt and nut securing the ball joint to the steering knuckle.

5. Separate the lower ball joint from the steering knuckle by prying the lower control arm down with a prybar.

6. Unfasten the front lower control arm pivot bolt.

7. Unfasten the three lower control arm retaining bolts and remove the lower control arm.

8. Inspect the lower control arm, lower control arm bushings and the lower ball joint. The ball joint and bushings can be replaced individually.

To install:

9. Place the lower control arm into position at the bushings.

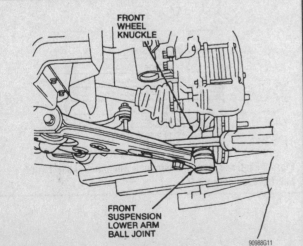

Fig. 34 Use a prybar to separate the lower ball joint from the steering knuckle

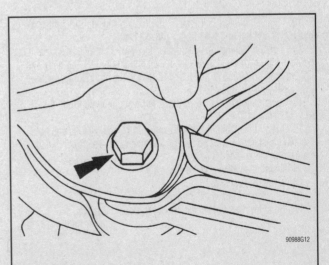

Fig. 35 Unfasten of the lower control arm pivot bolt (arrow)— 1997–99 models

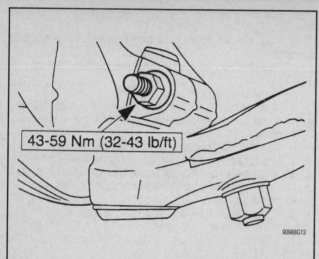

Fig. 36 Engage the lower ball joint to the steering knuckle and tighten the pinch bolt and nut to specification—1997–99 models

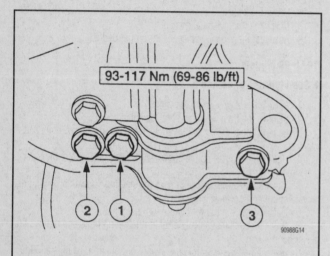

Fig. 37 Tighten the lower control arm retaining bolts in the sequence shown to the proper specification—1997–99 models

10. Attach the lower ball joint to the steering knuckle and tighten the pinch bolt and nut to 32–43 ft. lbs. (43–59 Nm).

11. Use a transmission jack to raise the lower control arm so that it is parallel with the ground, then install the control arm retaining bolts and tighten them to 69–86 ft. lbs. (93–117 Nm) in the order shown in the accompanying illustration.

12. Install and tighten the control arm pivot bolt to 69–86 ft. lbs. (93–117 Nm).

13. Install the stabilizer bolts, washers, bushings, sleeves and nuts. Tighten the stabilizer nuts so 0.67–0.75 inches (17–19mm) of thread is exposed at the end of the bolt.

14. Install the wheel and tire assembly.

15. Lower the vehicle.

16. Check the front wheel alignment.

17. Road test the vehicle and check for proper operation.

Wheel Hub, Knuckle and Bearing

REMOVAL & INSTALLATION

▶ **See Figure 38**

1. With the vehicle sitting on the ground, carefully raise the staked portion of the halfshaft retaining nut using a suitable small chisel. Loosen the nut.

2. Raise the front of the car and support it with safety stands.

3. Remove the wheel and tire assembly.

➡ **Do not disconnect the brake hose from the caliper.**

4. Remove the brake caliper and secure it out of the way with a piece of mechanic's wire. Do not let the caliper hang on the hose.

5. Remove the brake rotor.

6. Remove the halfshaft retaining nut and discard it.

7. Remove the cotter pin and castellated nut from the tie rod end and separate the tie rod end from the steering knuckle using a suitable removal tool. Discard the cotter pin.

8. Use the appropriate tool to separate the tie rod end from the wheel knuckle.

9. If equipped with an Anti-lock Brake System (ABS), unfasten the ABS sensor bolt and remove the sensor.

10. Remove the strut mounting nuts and the studs which attach the strut assembly to the steering knuckle.

11. Seperate the strut from the steering knuckle.

12. Remove the lower ball joint pinch bolt. Carefully pry down on the lower control arm to separate the ball joint stud from the steering knuckle.

13. Remove the wheel hub, knuckle and bearing assembly from the vehicle.

To install:

14. Apply Loctite 290® threadlocking compound or equivalent to the ball joint nut and threads.

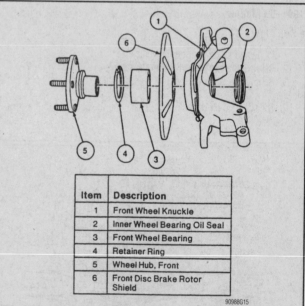

Item	Description
1	Front Wheel Knuckle
2	Inner Wheel Bearing Oil Seal
3	Front Wheel Bearing
4	Retainer Ring
5	Wheel Hub, Front
6	Front Disc Brake Rotor Shield

Fig. 38 Exploded view of a common wheel hub, knuckle and bearing assembly

15. Install the wheel hub, knuckle and bearing assembly onto the ball joint and tighten the pinch bolt and nut to 32–43 ft. lbs. (43–59 Nm).

16. Install the tie rod end and tighten the nut to 25–33 ft. lbs. (34–46 Nm). Install a new cotter pin.

17. If equipped with an Anti-lock Brake System (ABS), install the ABS sensor and tighten the bolt.

18. Attach the knuckle to the strut assembly and tighten the strut mounting nuts to 69–93 ft. lbs. (93–127 Nm).

19. Install a new halfshaft retaining nut and tighten to 174–235 ft. lbs. (235–319 Nm). Stake the retaining nut using a suitable chisel with the cutting edge rounded off.

➡️If the nut splits or cracks after staking, it must be replaced with a new nut.

20. Install the brake rotor and caliper.
21. Install the wheel and tire assembly.
22. Lower the vehicle.
23. Check the front wheel alignment.
24. Road test the vehicle and check for proper operation.

DISASSEMBLY

▶ See Figures 39, 40, 41 and 42

1. Remove the wheel hub, knuckle and bearing assembly from the vehicle.
2. Remove and discard the inner wheel bearing oil seal.
3. Place the wheel hub, knuckle and bearing assembly on a press.
4. Using an appropriate tool, press the wheel hub out of the knuckle. If the bearing inner race remains on the hub, use a grinder to grind a section of the inner race until only 0.020 inch (0.5mm) remains, then remove inner race with a chisel.
5. Remove the retainer ring from the steering knuckle.
6. Place the knuckle assembly on a press.
7. Use an appropriate bearing remover to press the bearing from the knuckle.
8. Scribe a matchmark on the brake rotor shield and knuckle.

➡️If the brake rotor shield is removed, a new rotor shield must be installed.

9. Use a chisel to remove the rotor shield.

➡️Do not remove the wheel lug bolts if they are not damaged.

10. Use the press and an appropriate tool to remove the lug bolts.
To assemble:
11. If removed, use the press and an appropriate tool to install new lug bolts.

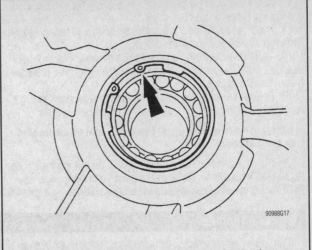

Fig. 40 Remove the retainer ring (arrow) from the steering knuckle

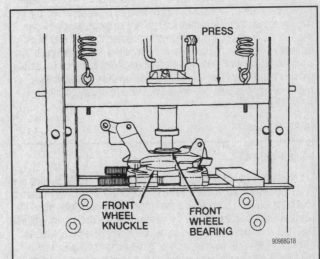

Fig. 41 Use a press and an appropriate tool to remove the wheel bearing

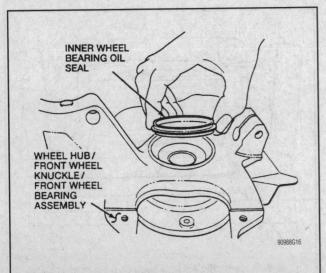

Fig. 39 Remove and discard the inner wheel bearing oil seal

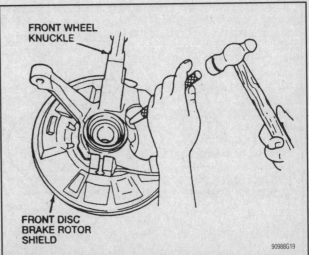

Fig. 42 A chisel can be used to remove the brake rotor shield. If the shield is removed, always replace it with a new one

12. Scribe a mark on the new brake rotor shield in the same location that was marked on the previous shield.

13. Align the rotor shield and knuckle matchmarks, the using the press and an appropriate tool, install the shield.

14. Apply Threadlock 262® or equivalent to the wheel bearing outer race, then using the press and an appropriate bearing installer, press the bearing into the knuckle.

15. Position the wheel hub onto the knuckle, then the press and an appropriate tool press the hub into the wheel bearing and knuckle.

➡**Always use a new inner wheel bearing oil seal on the inboard side of the knuckle.**

16. Use an appropriate seal installer to install the new inner wheel bearing oil seal. Make sure the seal is mounted flush with the knuckle.

17. Install the wheel hub, knuckle and bearing assembly on the vehicle.

Wheel Alignment

If the tires are worn unevenly, if the vehicle is not stable on the highway or if the handling seems uneven in spirited driving, the wheel alignment should be checked. If an alignment problem is suspected, first check for improper tire inflation and other possible causes. These can be worn suspension or steering components, accident damage or even unmatched tires. If any worn or damaged components are found, they must be replaced before the wheels can be properly aligned. Wheel alignment requires very expensive equipment and involves minute adjustments which must be accurate; it should only be performed by a trained technician. Take your vehicle to a properly equipped shop.

Following is a description of the alignment angles which are adjustable on most vehicles and how they affect vehicle handling. Although these angles can apply to both the front and rear wheels, usually only the front suspension is adjustable.

CASTER

▶ **See Figure 43**

Looking at a vehicle from the side, caster angle describes the steering axis rather than a wheel angle. The steering knuckle is attached to a control arm or strut at the top and a control arm at the bottom. The wheel pivots around the line between these points to steer the vehicle. When the upper point is tilted back, this is described as positive caster. Having a positive caster tends to make the wheels self-centering, increasing directional stability. Excessive positive caster makes the wheels hard to steer, while an uneven caster will cause a pull to one side. Overloading the vehicle or sagging rear springs will affect caster, as will raising the rear of the vehicle. If the rear of the vehicle is lower than normal, the caster becomes more positive.

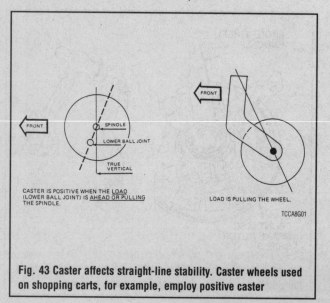

Fig. 43 Caster affects straight-line stability. Caster wheels used on shopping carts, for example, employ positive caster

CAMBER

▶ **See Figure 44**

Looking from the front of the vehicle, camber is the inward or outward tilt of the top of wheels. When the tops of the wheels are tilted in, this is negative camber; if they are tilted out, it is positive. In a turn, a slight amount of negative camber helps maximize contact of the tire with the road. However, too much negative camber compromises straight-line stability, increases bump steer and torque steer.

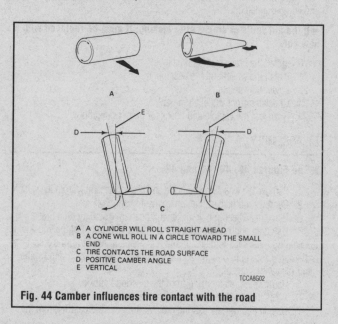

A A CYLINDER WILL ROLL STRAIGHT AHEAD
B A CONE WILL ROLL IN A CIRCLE TOWARD THE SMALL END
C TIRE CONTACTS THE ROAD SURFACE
D POSITIVE CAMBER ANGLE
E VERTICAL

TCCA8G02

Fig. 44 Camber influences tire contact with the road

TOE

▶ **See Figure 45**

Looking down at the wheels from above the vehicle, toe angle is the distance between the front of the wheels, relative to the distance between the back of the wheels. If the wheels are closer at the front, they are said to be toed-in or to have negative toe. A small amount of negative toe enhances directional stability and provides a smoother ride on the highway.

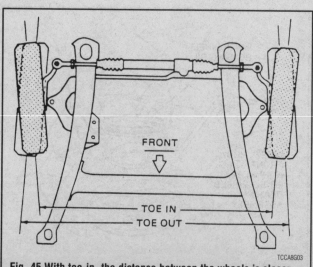

TCCA8G03

Fig. 45 With toe-in, the distance between the wheels is closer at the front than at the rear

REAR SUSPENSION

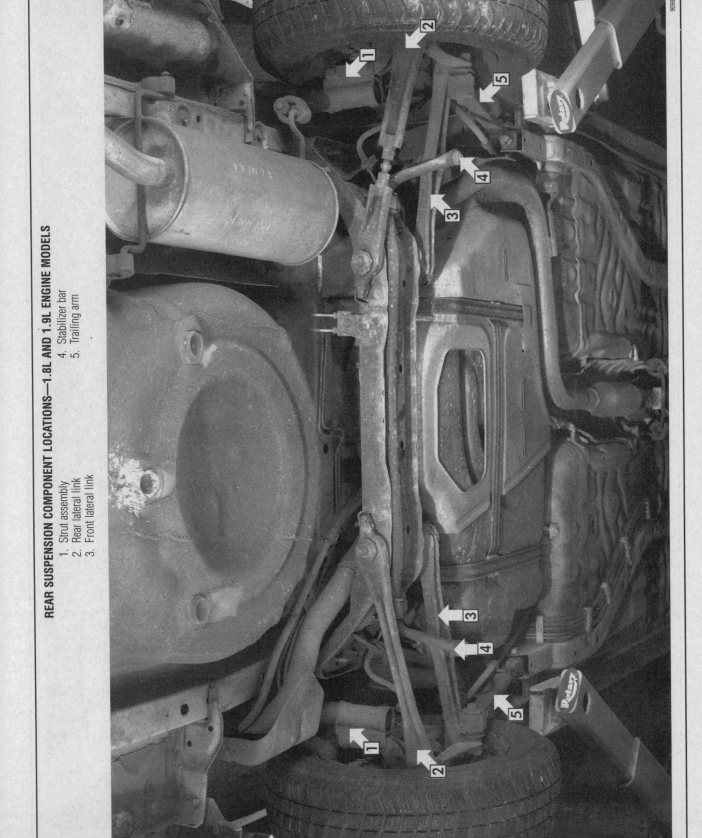

REAR SUSPENSION COMPONENT LOCATIONS—1.8L AND 1.9L ENGINE MODELS

1. Strut assembly
2. Rear lateral link
3. Front lateral link
4. Stabilizer bar
5. Trailing arm

REAR SUSPENSION COMPONENT LOCATIONS—2.0L ENGINE MODELS

1. Strut assembly
2. Rear lateral link
3. Stabilizer bar
4. Front lateral link
5. Trailing link

MacPherson Struts

REMOVAL & INSTALLATION

1991–96 Models

▶ **See Figures 46 thru 56**

1. Disconnect the negative battery cable.
2. Raise and safely support the vehicle.
3. Remove the wheel and tire assembly.
4. Remove the clip securing the brake hose to the rear strut assembly.
5. If equipped with anti-lock brakes, remove the ABS harness from the clip on the strut assembly.
6. Remove the nuts and bolts securing the rear strut assembly to the wheel spindle.
7. Partially lower the vehicle.
8. On hatchback and wagon models, remove the quarter trim panel.
9. Unfasten the two upper strut insulator retaining nuts and, if equipped, bend back the retaining clip.
10. Remove the rear strut assembly from the vehicle.

Fig. 48 . . . then remove the strut-to-spindle nuts and bolts

Fig. 46 Remove the clip securing the brake hose to the rear strut assembly

Fig. 49 On hatchback and wagon models, to remove the rear quarter trim panel . . .

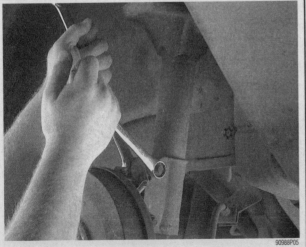

Fig. 47 Unfasten the nuts and bolts securing the rear strut assembly to the wheel spindle . . .

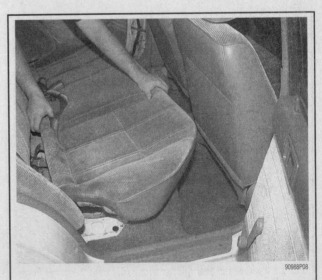

Fig. 50 . . . first remove the rear seat

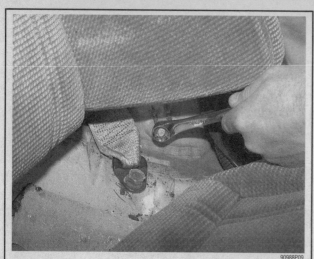

Fig. 51 It may be necessary to remove the rear seat extension retaining bolt . . .

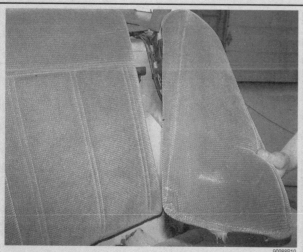

Fig. 52 . . . then lift the seat extension up to disengage the rear clip and remove the seat extension

Fig. 53 Remove the rear quarter trim panel from the cargo compartment

Fig. 54 Unfasten the two upper strut insulator retaining nuts

Retaining clip

Fig. 55 If equipped, bend back the retaining clip on top of the strut . . .

Fig. 56 . . . and remove the strut assembly from the vehicle

To install:

11. Position the strut assembly into the vehicle wheel housing.

12. Install the two upper strut insulator retaining nuts and tighten to 22–27 ft. lbs. (29–40 Nm).

13. On hatchback and wagon models, install the quarter trim panel.

14. Install the nuts and bolts securing the strut assembly to the rear wheel spindle assembly. Tighten the lower strut bolts and nuts to 69–93 ft. lbs. (93–127 Nm).

15. Install the clip securing the flexible brake hose to the rear strut assembly.

16. If equipped with anti-lock brakes, install the ABS harness to the clip.

17. Install the wheel and tire assembly.

18. Lower the vehicle.

19. Connect the negative battery cable.

20. Check the rear wheel alignment.

21. Road test the vehicle and check for proper operation.

1997–99 Models

▶ **See Figure 57**

1. Disconnect the negative battery cable.

2. On sedan and coupe models, remove the package tray trim panel.

3. On wagon models, remove the quarter trim panel.

4. Unfasten the two upper strut retaining nuts.

5. Raise and safely support the vehicle.

6. Remove the wheel and tire assembly.

7. Remove the clip securing the brake hose to the rear strut assembly.

8. If equipped with anti-lock brakes, unfasten the ABS sensor bolt.

9. Remove the nuts and bolts securing the rear strut assembly to the wheel spindle.

10. Remove the strut assembly from the vehicle.

To install:

11. Position the strut assembly into the vehicle wheel housing.

12. Install the nuts and bolts securing the strut assembly to the rear wheel spindle assembly. Tighten the lower strut bolts and nuts to 76–100 ft. lbs. (103–136 Nm).

13. If equipped with anti-lock brakes, tighten the ABS sensor bolt.

14. Install the clip securing the flexible brake hose to the rear strut assembly.

15. Install the wheel and tire assembly.

16. Lower the vehicle.

17. Install the two upper strut retaining nuts and tighten to 34–46 ft. lbs. (47–62 Nm).

18. Install the trim panel.

19. Connect the negative battery cable.

20. Check the rear wheel alignment.

21. Road test the vehicle and check for proper operation.

OVERHAUL

1991–96 Models

▶ **See Figures 58 thru 67**

1. Position the strut assembly in a vise and secure the assembly at the upper insulator bracket.

2. Remove the cap and loosen the piston rod nut 1 turn. Do not remove the piston rod nut at this time.

> ✳✳ **CAUTION**
>
> **Attempting to remove the spring from the strut without first compressing the spring with a tool designed for that purpose could cause bodily injury.**

3. Install an appropriate coil spring compressor and compress the coil spring.

Fig. 58 Remove the cap from the strut assembly

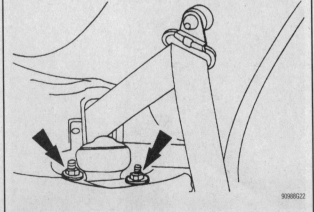

Fig. 57 Location of the two upper strut retaining nuts (arrows)—1997–99 models

Fig. 59 Loosen the piston rod nut one turn, but do not remove the piston rod nut at this time

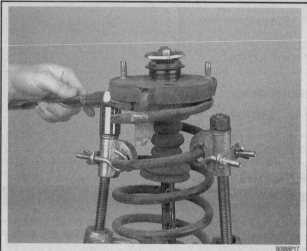

Fig. 60 Install an appropriate coil spring compressor and compress the coil spring

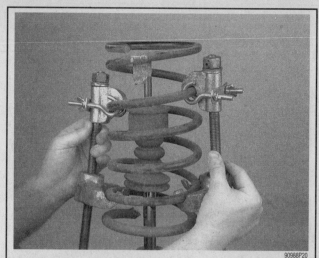

Fig. 63 Remove the coil spring with the compressor tool attached

Fig. 61 Remove the piston rod nut and washer

Fig. 64 Remove the stopper seat . . .

Fig. 62 Remove the retainer and anti-rattle plate

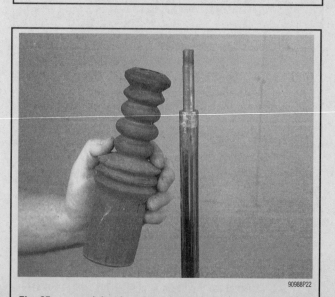

Fig. 65 . . . and dust boot from the strut piston

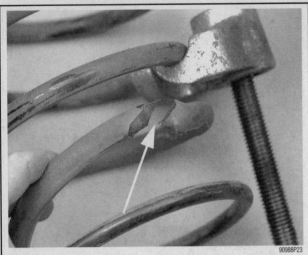

Fig. 66 Check the coil spring for cracks and breaks. As you can see, this spring is broken and must be replaced

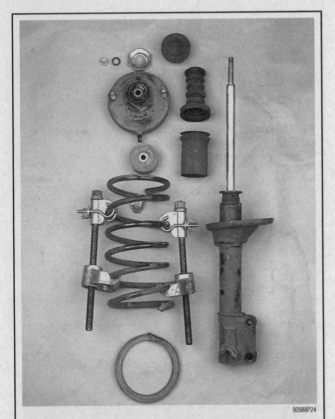

Fig. 67 Typical rear MacPherson strut components

4. Remove the piston rod nut, washer, retainer, anti-rattle plate and insulator.

5. Remove the coil spring.

6. Remove the stopper seat and dust boot from the strut piston.

To assemble:

7. Position the strut assembly in a vise and secure.

8. Install the dust boot and the stopper seat onto the strut piston rod.

9. Compress the coil spring and install on the strut assembly.

10. Install the upper strut insulator, then align the upper strut insulator mounting studs and the lower bracket of the strut assembly.

11. Install the retainer, washer and piston rod nut. Tighten the nut to 41–50 ft. lbs. (55–68 Nm).

12. Make sure the spring is properly aligned and carefully release the spring into the seats of the strut.

13. Remove the spring compressor from the coil spring and install the cap.

1997–99 Models

▶ **See Figures 68 and 69**

1. Remove the strut assembly.
2. Place the strut assembly in a vise.

✳✳ CAUTION

Always wear goggles when using a spring compressor.

3. Install a suitable spring compressor tool onto the coil spring and compress the spring.

4. Remove the rear strut assembly top mounting cover.

5. Unfasten the piston rod nut and remove the retainer.

6. Remove the strut insulator.

7. Carefully remove the spring compressor.

8. Remove the rear strut dust boot and stopper seat.

9. Remove the spring and the rear strut insulator.

To assemble:

10. Place the strut assembly in a vise.

11. Install the strut insulator and spring.

12. Install the stopper seat and dust boot.

13. Use the spring compressor tool to compress the strut spring.

14. Remove the strut insulator and the retainer.

15. Install the piston rod nut and tighten it to 41–49 ft. lbs. (55–67 Nm).

16. Install the top mounting cover.

17. Make sure the spring is properly aligned and carefully release the spring into the seats of the strut.

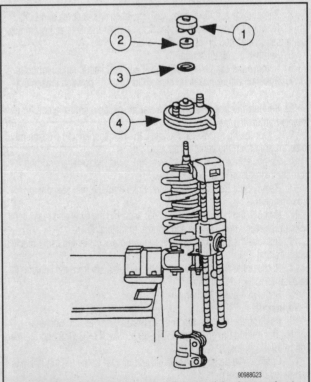

Fig. 68 Remove the strut top mounting cover (1), piston rod nut (2), retainer (3) and insulator (4)—1997–99 models

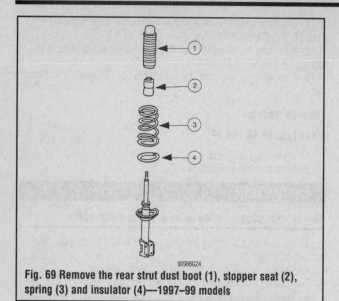

Fig. 69 Remove the rear strut dust boot (1), stopper seat (2), spring (3) and insulator (4)—1997–99 models

18. Remove the spring compressor from the coil spring.
19. Install the strut assembly.

Lateral Links and Trailing Link

REMOVAL & INSTALLATION

1991–96 Models

▶ See Figures 70 and 71

1. Raise the car and support it with safety stands.
2. Remove the wheel and tire assembly.
3. Remove the stabilizer nuts, washers, bushings, sleeves and bolts.
4. Remove the bolts securing the stabilizer bar brackets and grommets to the rear suspension crossmember.
5. Remove the stabilizer bar.
6. Remove the cap covering the front and rear lateral link pivot bolts.
7. Position a floor jackstand beneath the rear suspension crossmember.
8. Remove the bolts securing the rear suspension crossmember to the vehicle frame.
9. Lower the floor jackstand to allow the rear suspension crossmember to be lowered from the vehicle frame.
10. Remove the front and rear lateral link pivot nut, washer and bolt from the rear suspension crossmember.
11. Remove the front and rear lateral links from the rear suspension crossmember.
12. Remove the bolt, washers and nut securing the front and rear lateral links to the rear wheel spindle and remove the lateral links.
13. Remove the nuts securing the parking brake cable and cable bracket to the trailing link.
14. Remove the rear trailing link bolts and washers from the vehicle frame and rear wheel spindle.
15. Remove the rear trailing link.

To install:
16. Position the rear trailing link and install the bolts and washers. Tighten the trailing link front bolt to 46–69 ft. lbs. (63–93 Nm) and the rear bolt to 69–93 ft. lbs. (93–127 Nm).
17. Position the parking brake cable and bracket to the trailing link and secure it with the nuts.
18. Position the front and rear lateral links to the rear wheel spindle and install the washers, bolt and nut. Tighten the front and rear lateral link nut at the rear wheel spindle to 63–86 ft. lbs. (85–117 Nm).

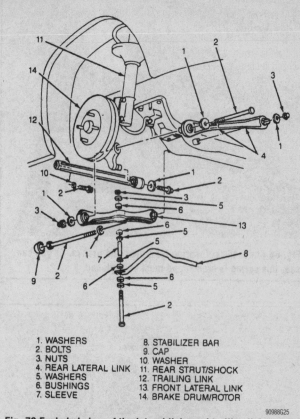

1. WASHERS	8. STABILIZER BAR
2. BOLTS	9. CAP
3. NUTS	10. WASHER
4. REAR LATERAL LINK	11. REAR STRUT/SHOCK
5. WASHERS	12. TRAILING LINK
6. BUSHINGS	13. FRONT LATERAL LINK
7. SLEEVE	14. BRAKE DRUM/ROTOR

Fig. 70 Exploded view of the lateral links and trailing link components—1991–96 models

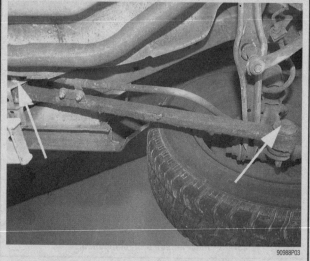

Fig. 71 Location of the rear trailing link retaining bolts (arrows)

19. Position the front and rear lateral links to the rear suspension crossmember. Tighten the front and rear lateral link nut at the rear suspension crossmember to 50–70 ft. lbs. (68–95 Nm).
20. Install the cap.
21. Raise the floor jackstand to position the rear suspension crossmember to the vehicle frame. Install and tighten the bolts. Remove the floor jackstand from under the vehicle.
22. Position the grommets onto the stabilizer bar and align the grommets to the positions painted on the bar.

23. Position the stabilizer bar to the rear suspension crossmember and secure it in place with the straps and bolts. Tighten the bolts to 32–43 ft. lbs. (43–59 Nm).

24. Install the stabilizer bolts, washers, grommets, sleeves and nuts. Tighten the stabilizer nuts so 0.64–0.71 in. (16.2–18.2mm) of thread is exposed at the end of the bolt.

25. Install the wheel and tire assembly.

26. Check the wheel alignment and lower the vehicle.

Control Arm

REMOVAL & INSTALLATION

1997–99 Models

▶ **See Figures 72 and 73**

1. Raise the car and support it with safety stands.
2. Position a floor jackstand beneath the rear suspension crossmember.
3. Remove the wheel and tire assembly.
4. Remove the stabilizer nuts, washers, bushings, sleeves and bolts.

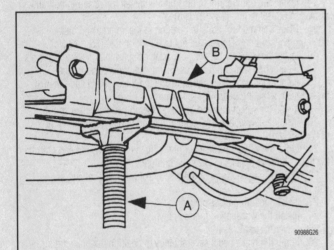

Fig. 72 Support the rear suspension crossmember (B) with a floor jackstand (A)—1997–99 models

Fig. 73 Unfasten the rear suspension crossmember bolts, then lower the floor jackstand and crossmember

5. Remove the bolts securing the stabilizer bar brackets and grommets to the rear suspension crossmember.

6. Remove the stabilizer bar.

7. Remove the bolts securing the rear suspension crossmember to the vehicle frame.

8. Lower the floor jackstand to allow the rear suspension crossmember to be lowered from the vehicle frame.

9. Remove the control arm and bushing nut.

10. Unfasten the control arm and bushing bolt, then remove the control arm.

To install:

11. Place the control arm into position, install the retaining bolt and tighten it to 50–70 ft. lbs. (68–95 Nm).

12. Install the control arm and bushing retaining nut, then tighten the nut to 64–86 ft. lbs. (87–116 Nm).

13. Raise the floor jack and place the crossmember into position. Install the crossmember bolts and tighten them to 34–46 ft. lbs. (47–62 Nm).

14. Position the grommets onto the stabilizer bar and align the grommets to the positions painted on the bar.

15. Position the stabilizer bar to the rear suspension crossmember and secure it in place with the straps and bolts. Tighten the bolts to 32–43 ft. lbs. (43–59 Nm).

16. Install the stabilizer bolts, washers, grommets, sleeves and nuts. Tighten the stabilizer nuts so 0.64–0.71 in. (16.2–18.2mm) of thread is exposed at the end of the bolt.

17. Install the wheel and tire assembly.

18. Check the wheel alignment and lower the vehicle.

Sway Bar

REMOVAL & INSTALLATION

▶ **See Figures 74 and 75**

1. Raise and safely support the vehicle.
2. Remove the sway (stabilizer) bar link nuts, retainers, washers, bushings, sleeves and bolts.

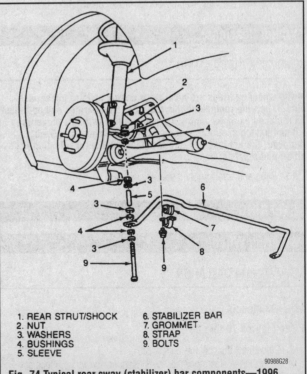

1. REAR STRUT/SHOCK
2. NUT
3. WASHERS
4. BUSHINGS
5. SLEEVE
6. STABILIZER BAR
7. GROMMET
8. STRAP
9. BOLTS

Fig. 74 Typical rear sway (stabilizer) bar components—1996 models shown, others similar

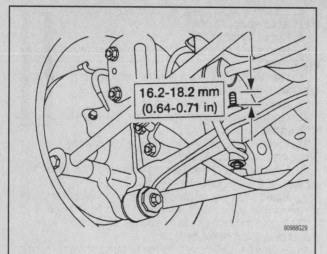

Fig. 75 Tighten the sway bar link nuts until 0.64–0.71 inch (16.2–18.2mm) of thread is exposed at the end of the bolt

3. Remove the sway bar bracket retaining bolts and brackets.
4. Remove the sway bar from the vehicle.
5. Inspect the sway bar bracket insulators and link bushings. Replace as needed.

To install:

6. If removed, install the insulators on the sway bar and align the insulators to the positions painted on the sway bar.
7. Place the sway bar to the floor crossmember and secure it in place with the sway bar brackets and bolts. Tighten the bolts to 32–43 ft. lbs. (43–59 Nm).
8. Install the sway bar link bolts, retainers, bushings, sleeves and nuts. Tighten the sway bar link nuts so 0.64–0.71 inch (16.2–18.2mm) of thread is exposed at the end of the bolt.
9. Install the wheel and tire assembly.
10. Lower the vehicle.
11. Road test the vehicle and check for proper operation.

Wheel Bearings

REMOVAL & INSTALLATION

➡The wheel bearings are a cartridge design and are not serviceable. If bearing replacement is required, the bearings and hub must be replaced as an assembly. Do not continue with this procedure without having available a new wheel hub retainer nut. Once removed, the nut loses its torque holding ability (or retention capability) and must not be reused.

1. Raise and safely support the vehicle.

STEERING

Steering Wheel

REMOVAL & INSTALLATION

1991–93 Models

♦ See Figures 76 thru 83

1. Disconnect the negative battery cable.
2. Unfasten the steering wheel cover retaining screws from the back side of the steering wheel and remove the cover.

2. Remove the wheel and tire assembly.
3. Remove the hub grease cap.
4. Remove the brake drum or disc brake caliper and rotor, as necessary.
5. Unstake and remove the wheel hub retainer nut securing the hub to the spindle and remove the hub and bearing assembly. Discard the hub retainer nut.
6. If equipped with disc brakes, remove the disc brake shield retaining bolts and the shield.
7. If equipped with drum brakes, remove the backing plate.
8. Remove the strut-to-spindle retaining bolts and nuts.
9. Remove the trailing arm bolt securing the trailing arm to the spindle.
10. Remove the stabilizer bar link nuts, retainers, bushings, sleeves and bolts.
11. Remove the control arm nut and bolt securing both control arms to the wheel spindle and remove the spindle from the vehicle.
12. Inspect all components. If the wheel spindle is damaged, replace it. Wheel bearings are sealed and must be replaced if damaged with the wheel hub.

To install:

13. Place the wheel spindle in position to the strut and install the retaining bolts and nuts. Tighten to 69–93 ft. lbs. (93–127 Nm).
14. Install the trailing arm to the spindle. Install the retaining bolt and tighten to 69–93 ft. lbs. (93–127 Nm).
15. Place both control arms in position to the spindle and install the retaining bolt and nut. Tighten the nut to 63–86 ft. lbs. (85–117 Nm).
16. Install the stabilizer bar link nuts, retainers, bushings, sleeves and bolts.
17. If equipped with drum brakes, install the brake backing plate.
18. If equipped with disc brakes, install the brake shield and the disc brake shield retaining bolts. Tighten securely.
19. Install the wheel hub and bearing assembly to the wheel spindle.
20. Install a new wheel hub retainer nut and tighten to 130–174 ft. lbs. (177–235 Nm).
21. Stake the wheel hub retainer nut using a cape or round end chisel. Do not use a sharp chisel to stake the hub nut.
22. Install the brake drum or the disc brake rotor and caliper, as equipped.
23. Install the hub grease cap.
24. Install the wheel and tire assembly.
25. Lower the vehicle.
26. Pump the brake pedal several times to position the brake lining before attempting to move the vehicle.
27. Road test the vehicle and check for proper operation.

ADJUSTMENT

The bearings on the front and rear wheels are a lone piece cartridge design and cannot be adjusted. Wheel bearing play can be checked with a dial indicator. If wheel bearing play exceeds 0.002 inch (0.05mm) check the wheel hub retainer nut for proper torque. If the torque is correct, replacement of the wheel bearing is required.

➡On the two-spoke steering wheels there are two retaining screws, and on four-spoke steering wheels there are four retaining screws.

3. Disengage the horn and if equipped, speed control electrical connectors.
4. Remove the steering wheel mounting nut, then scribe matchmarks on the steering wheel and shaft to assure installation in the proper alignment.
5. Remove the steering wheel with a suitable puller. DO NOT USE a knock-off type puller. It will cause damage to the collapsible steering column.

Fig. 76 Unfasten the steering wheel cover retaining screws from the back side of the steering wheel

Fig. 79 Matchmark the steering shaft, wheel and retaining nut prior to removal. This will aid in alignment during installation

Fig. 77 Separate the steering wheel cover from the steering wheel . . .

Fig. 80 Unfasten the steering wheel retaining nut . . .

Fig. 78 . . . then unplug the horn electrical connection and remove the cover

Fig. 81 . . . and remove the nut from the shaft

Fig. 82 Use a suitable steering wheel puller to remove the steering wheel

Fig. 83 Upon installation, use a torque wrench to tighten the steering wheel mounting nut to specification

To install:

6. Position the steering wheel, aligning the matchmarks made earlier, then install the mounting nut. Tighten the nut to 34–46 ft. lbs. (46–63 Nm).

7. Attach the horn and if equipped, the speed control electrical connectors.

8. Position the steering wheel cover and install the retaining screws.

9. Connect the negative battery cable.

1994–99 Models

▸ See Figure 84

✳✳ CAUTION

Some models covered by this manual are equipped with a Supplemental Restraint System (SRS), which uses an air bag. Whenever working near any of the SRS components, such as the impact sensors, the air bag module, steering column and instrument panel, disable the SRS, as described in Section 6.

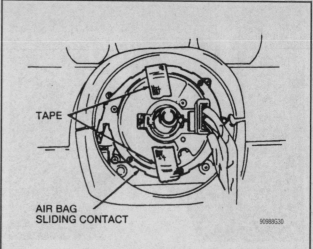
Fig. 84 Tape the air bag sliding contact to prevent disturbing its alignment

➡ Before continuing with this procedure, make sure to have available a new steering wheel retaining bolt. Once removed, the bolt loses its torque holding ability (or retention capability) and must not be reused.

1. Make sure the front wheels are in the straight-ahead position.

2. Disarm the air bag system.

3. Remove the two air bag module retaining bolts from the rear of the steering wheel. Pull the air bag module up and away from the steering wheel and unplug the module electrical connector from the air bag sliding contact.

✳✳ CAUTION

When carrying a live air bag, make sure the bag and trim cover are pointed away from the body. In the unlikely event of an accidental deployment, the bag will then deploy with minimal chance of injury. When placing a live air bag on a bench or other surface, always face the bag and trim cover up, away from the surface. This will reduce the motion of the module, if accidentally deployed.

4. Remove the air bag module from the steering wheel.

5. Remove the steering wheel retaining bolt and the steering wheel, using a suitable puller. Discard the steering wheel retaining bolt.

6. Tape the air bag sliding contact to prevent disturbing the air bag sliding contact alignment.

To install:

7. Remove the tape from the air bag sliding contact.

8. Install the steering wheel with a new retaining bolt. Tighten to 34–46 ft. lbs. (46–63 Nm).

9. Attach the air bag module electrical connector and install the module to the steering wheel. Install 2 module retaining bolts and tighten to 35–53 inch lbs. (4–6 Nm) on 1994–96 models and 70–103 inch lbs. (8–12 Nm) on 1997–99 models.

10. Connect the negative battery cable.

11. Confirm operational status of the air bag system by turning the ignition key to the **RUN** position and visually monitoring the air bag indicator lamp in the instrument cluster. The indicator lamp should illuminate for approximately 6 seconds and then turn OFF. If the indicator lamp does not illuminate, stays ON, or flashes at any time, a fault has been detected by the air bag diagnostic monitor.

12. Check the steering wheel, horn and if equipped cruise control for proper operation.

Combination Switch

REMOVAL & INSTALLATION

1991–93 Models

▶ See Figure 85

✳✳ CAUTION

Some models covered by this manual are equipped with a Supplemental Restraint System (SRS), which uses an air bag. Whenever working near any of the SRS components, such as the impact sensors, the air bag module, steering column and instrument panel, disable the SRS, as described in Section 6.

➡ Before continuing with this procedure, make sure to have available a new steering wheel retaining bolt. Once removed, the bolt loses its torque holding ability (or retention capability) and must not be reused.

1. Disarm the air bag system.
2. Disconnect the negative battery cable.
3. Remove the steering wheel according to the appropriate procedure.
4. Unfasten the four screws that retain the lower steering column cover and remove the cover.
5. Remove the upper steering column cover.
6. Unplug the three multi-function switch electrical connectors.
7. Remove the multi-function switch retaining screw.
8. Pull the multi-function switch electrical connectors from the brackets and remove the combination switch.

To install:

9. Press the combination switch electrical connectors into the retaining brackets and place the switch into position.
10. Install and tighten the switch retaining screw.
11. Attach the switch electrical connectors.
12. Install the upper and lower steering column covers and the lower column cover retaining screws.
13. Install the steering wheel.
14. Connect the negative battery cable and check for proper switch operation.

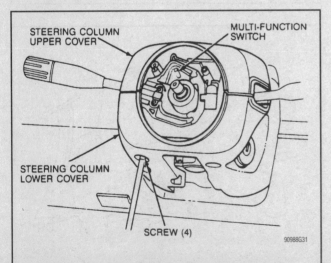

Fig. 85 The combination switch is accessed by removing the steering wheel and column covers—1991–93 models

STEERING COLUMN UPPER COVER

MULTI-FUNCTION SWITCH

STEERING COLUMN LOWER COVER

SCREW (4)

90988G31

1994–96 Models

✳✳ CAUTION

Some models covered by this manual are equipped with a Supplemental Restraint System (SRS), which uses an air bag. Whenever working near any of the SRS components, such as the impact sensors, the air bag module, steering column and instrument panel, disable the SRS, as described in Section 6.

➡ Before continuing with this procedure, make sure to have available a new steering wheel retaining bolt. Once removed, the bolt loses its torque holding ability (or retention capability) and must not be reused.

1. Remove the steering wheel according to the appropriate procedure.
2. Place tape on the air bag sliding contact to prevent it from moving.
3. Remove the four retaining screws from the steering column lower cover.
4. Unplug the ignition switch lock cylinder illumination lamp socket, if equipped.
5. Remove the steering column lower and upper covers.
6. Unplug the combination switch electrical connectors.
7. Remove the combination switch retaining screws.
8. Remove the electrical connectors from the retaining brackets and remove the switch.

To install:

9. Place the combination switch in position to the steering column.
10. Install the switch retaining screws and tighten securely.
11. Position the electrical connector harnesses to the retaining brackets and attach the connectors to the switch.
12. Install the steering column upper cover.
13. Install the ignition switch lock cylinder illumination lamp socket to the lower cover, if equipped.
14. Install the steering column lower cover and the retaining screws.
15. Remove the tape from the air bag sliding contact.
16. Install the steering wheel and a new retaining bolt.
17. Connect the negative battery cable.
18. Confirm operational status of the air bag system by turning the ignition key to the **RUN** position and visually monitoring the air bag indicator lamp in the instrument cluster. The indicator lamp should illuminate for approximately 6 seconds and then turn OFF. If the indicator lamp does not illuminate, stays ON, or flashes at any time, a fault has been detected by the air bag diagnostic monitor.
19. Check all combination switch functions for proper operation.

1997–99 Models

EXCEPT 1998–99 ESCORT/TRACER (NON-COUPE MODELS)

✳✳ CAUTION

Some models covered by this manual are equipped with a Supplemental Restraint System (SRS), which uses an air bag. Whenever working near any of the SRS components, such as the impact sensors, the air bag module, steering column and instrument panel, disable the SRS, as described in Section 6.

1. On 1998–99 coupe models, remove the steering wheel according to the appropriate procedure.
2. Place tape on the air bag sliding contact to prevent it from moving.
3. Unfasten the lower steering column cover retaining screws and remove the upper and lower column covers.
4. Remove the combination switch retaining screws.
5. Unplug the combination switch electrical connectors.
6. Remove the switch.

To install:

7. Place the combination switch in position.

8. Attach the switch electrical connectors.
9. Install the switch retaining screws and tighten securely.
10. Install the steering column covers and tighten the screws securely.
11. Remove the tape from the air bag sliding contact.
12. If removed, install the steering wheel and a new retaining bolt.
13. Connect the negative battery cable.
14. Confirm operational status of the air bag system by turning the ignition key to the **RUN** position and visually monitoring the air bag indicator lamp in the instrument cluster. The indicator lamp should illuminate for approximately 6 seconds and then turn OFF. If the indicator lamp does not illuminate, stays ON, or flashes at any time, a fault has been detected by the air bag diagnostic monitor.
15. Check all combination switch functions for proper operation.

1998–99 ESCORT/TRACER (NON-COUPE MODELS)

♦ **See Figures 86 thru 93**

On 1998–99 Escort/Tracer models, different components such as the combination housing or turn signal switch may be removed separately. If you are removing for example, the turn signal switch, you may not need to use all the steps in the following procedure. Read the procedure first to determine which steps you need to perform to gain access to and remove the switch or component you wish to replace.

The removal of the combination switch housing requires the removal of the steering wheel, but if you are just removing the turn signal, hazard/flasher or the wiper/washer switch, then you may not have to remove the steering wheel, only the steering column covers.

❋❋ CAUTION

Some models covered by this manual are equipped with a Supplemental Restraint System (SRS), which uses an air bag. Whenever working near any of the SRS components, such as the impact sensors, the air bag module, steering column and instrument panel, disable the SRS, as described in Section 6.

1. To remove the combination switch housing and switch(s) proceed as follows:
   a. Disarm the air bag system.
   b. Disconnect the negative battery cable.
   c. Make sure the wheels are in the straight ahead position.
   d. Remove the air bag module and the steering wheel.
   e. Unfasten the steering column cover retaining screws, then remove the upper and lower covers.
   f. Place tape on the air bag sliding contact to prevent it from moving.
   g. Unplug the air bag sliding contact electrical connectors.

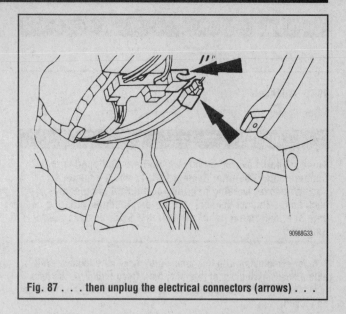

Fig. 87 . . . then unplug the electrical connectors (arrows) . . .

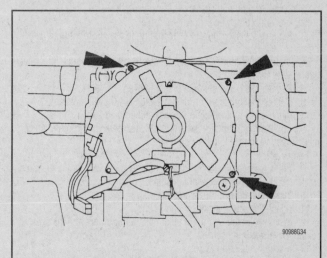

Fig. 88 . . . and unfasten the air bag sliding contact retaining screws—1998–99 Escort/Tracer models

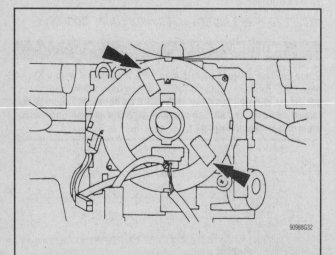

Fig. 86 Place tape on the air bag sliding contact to prevent it from moving . . .

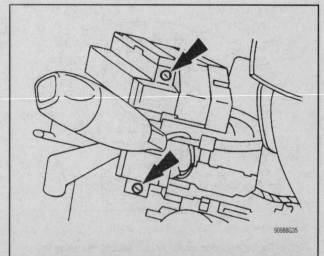

Fig. 89 Location of the windshield wiper/washer switch retaining screws—1998–99 Escort/Tracer models

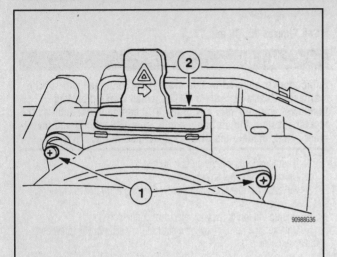

Fig. 90 Unfasten the hazard/flasher switch (2) retaining screws (1)—1998–99 Escort/Tracer models

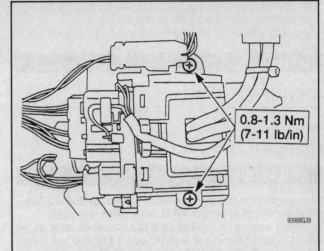

Fig. 92 Tighten the turn signal switch retaining screws—1998–99 Escort/Tracer models

h. Unfasten the sliding contact retaining screws and remove the contact.

i. Unplug the electrical connector from the turn signal switch.

j. Unfasten the turn signal switch retaining screws and unplug the electrical connectors.

k. Remove the turn signal switch.

l. Unfasten the windshield wiper/washer switch retaining screws.

m. Unplug the windshield wiper/washer switch electrical connectors.

n. Remove the windshield wiper/washer switch.

o. Unfasten the hazard/flasher switch retaining screws and separate the switch from the combination switch housing.

p. Unplug the hazard/flasher switch electrical connector and remove the switch.

q. Unfasten the combination switch housing retaining screws and remove the housing.

To install:

2. Install the housing or switch(s).

a. Install the combination switch housing and tighten the retaining screws to 9 inch lbs. (1 Nm).

b. Attach the hazard/flasher switch electrical connector, install the switch and tighten its retaining screws to 4.5–5 inch lbs. (0.5–0.6 Nm).

c. Install the windshield wiper/washer switch.

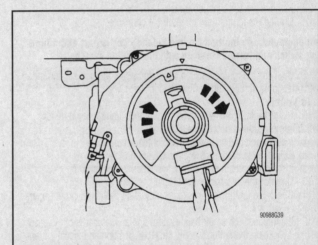

Fig. 93 If the air bag sliding contact becomes misaligned, turn it clockwise to lock, then back it off 3½ turns to center, and align the arrows before installing—1998–99 Escort/Tracer models

d. Attach the windshield wiper/washer switch electrical connectors.

e. Install and tighten the windshield wiper/washer switch retaining screws to 7–11 inch lbs. (0.8–1.3 Nm).

f. Install the turn signal switch.

g. Attach the turn signal switch electrical connectors.

h. Install and tighten the turn signal switch retaining screws 7–11 inch lbs. (0.8–1.3 Nm).

➡ If the air bag sliding contact becomes misaligned, turn the sliding contact clockwise to lock, then back off 3.5 turns to center and align the arrows before installing.

i. Install the air bag sliding contact switch and tighten its retaining screws.

j. Attach the air bag sliding contact electrical connectors.

k. Remove the tape from the air bag sliding contact.

l. Install the steering column covers and tighten the screws securely.

m. If removed, install the steering wheel and air bag module.

n. Connect the negative battery cable.

o. Confirm operational status of the air bag system by turning the ignition key to the **RUN** position and visually monitoring the air bag indicator lamp in the instrument cluster. The indicator lamp should illuminate for approximately 6 seconds and then turn OFF. If the indicator

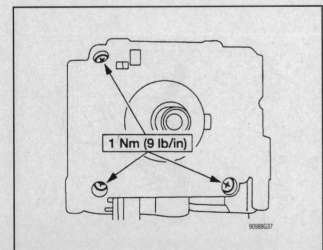

Fig. 91 Tighten the combination switch housing retaining screws—1998–99 Escort/Tracer models

lamp does not illuminate, stays ON, or flashes at any time, a fault has been detected by the air bag diagnostic monitor.

   p. Check the switch(s) for proper operation.

Ignition Switch

REMOVAL & INSTALLATION

1991–96 Models

▶ See Figure 94

❋❋ CAUTION

Some models covered by this manual are equipped with a Supplemental Restraint System (SRS), which uses an air bag. Whenever working near any of the SRS components, such as the impact sensors, the air bag module, steering column and instrument panel, disable the SRS, as described in Section 6.

1. If equipped, disarm the air bag system.
2. Disconnect the negative battery cable.
3. Remove the combination switch.
4. Unplug the ignition switch electrical connector.

➡**If equipped, the ignition key reminder switch is part of the ignition switch and is only serviced with the ignition switch.**

   5. Unfasten the ignition switch and if equipped, ignition key reminder switch retaining screws and remove the ignition switch.

To install:

   6. Place the ignition switch and if equipped, ignition key reminder switch into position on the steering column.

   7. Install the retaining screws and tighten securely.

   8. Attach the ignition switch electrical connector.

   9. Install the combination switch and steering column trim.

   10. Connect the negative battery cable.

   11. Check the ignition switch and combination switch for proper operation.

   12. If equipped with an air bag, confirm operational status of the air bag system by turning the ignition key to the **RUN** position and visually monitoring the air bag indicator lamp in the instrument cluster. The indicator lamp should illuminate for approximately 6 seconds and then turn OFF. If the indicator lamp does not illuminate, stays ON, or flashes at any time, a fault has been detected by the air bag diagnostic monitor.

1997–99 Models

▶ See Figures 95, 96 and 97

❋❋ CAUTION

Some models covered by this manual are equipped with a Supplemental Restraint System (SRS), which uses an air bag. Whenever working near any of the SRS components, such as the impact sensors, the air bag module, steering column and instrument panel, disable the SRS, as described in Section 6.

1. If equipped, disarm the air bag system.
2. Disconnect the negative battery cable.
3. Unfasten the steering column cover screws and remove the upper and lower covers.
4. Unplug the ignition switch electrical connector(s).
5. Unfasten the ignition switch electrical connector cover screw and remove the cover.

➡**The ignition key reminder switch is part of the ignition switch and is only serviced with the ignition switch.**

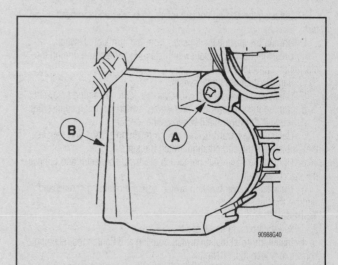

Fig. 95 Unfasten the ignition switch electrical connector cover screw (A) and remove the cover (B)—1997–99 models

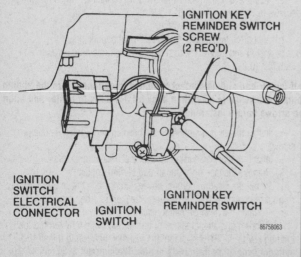

Fig. 94 Typical ignition switch components—1991–96 models

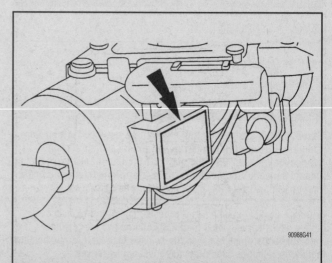

Fig. 96 If equipped, remove the ignition key reminder switch cover (arrow) . . .

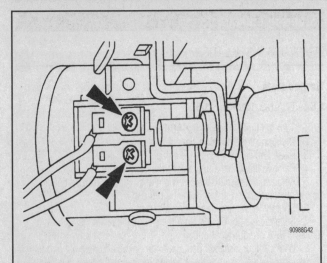

Fig. 97 . . . and unfasten the two ignition key reminder switch screws (arrows)

6. If equipped, remove the ignition key reminder switch cover.

7. Unfasten the two ignition key reminder switch screws.

8. Remove the ignition switch.

To install:

9. Install the ignition switch.

10. Tighten the two ignition key reminder switch screws.

11. If equipped, install the ignition key reminder switch cover.

12. Install the ignition switch electrical connector and tighten the retaining screw to 12–14 inch lbs. (1.4–1.6 Nm).

13. Attach the ignition switch electrical connector.

14. Install the steering column covers and screws, tighten the screws securely.

15. Connect the negative battery cable.

16. Check the ignition switch and combination switch for proper operation.

17. Confirm operational status of the air bag system by turning the ignition key to the **RUN** position and visually monitoring the air bag indicator lamp in the instrument cluster. The indicator lamp should illuminate for approximately 6 seconds and then turn OFF. If the indicator lamp does not illuminate, stays ON, or flashes at any time, a fault has been detected by the air bag diagnostic monitor.

Ignition Lock Cylinder

REMOVAL & INSTALLATION

1991–96 Models

▶ See Figures 98 and 99

✳✳ CAUTION

Some models covered by this manual are equipped with a Supplemental Restraint System (SRS), which uses an air bag. Whenever working near any of the SRS components, such as the impact sensors, the air bag module, steering column and instrument panel, disable the SRS, as described in Section 6.

➡Before continuing with this procedure, make sure to have available a new steering wheel retaining bolt and two lock cylinder retaining bolts. Once removed, these parts lose their torque holding ability (or retention capability) and must not be reused.

1. If equipped, disarm the air bag system and disconnect the negative battery cable.

2. Remove the steering wheel.

3. Remove the combination switch.

4. Unplug the wiring connector to the ignition switch.

5. Remove the ignition and shifter interlock cable mounting bracket bolt and position the assembly to one side.

6. Remove the four steering column bracket bolts and lower the steering column.

7. Cut a groove in the ignition cylinder bracket bolts with a chisel and hammer or use a similar method.

8. Using a screwdriver, remove and discard the bracket bolts.

9. Remove the ignition switch lock cylinder and bracket.

To install:

10. Install the new ignition switch and the bracket into position on the steering column tube.

11. Install the new lock cylinder bolts and tighten the bolts enough to hold the switch in position.

12. Check for proper switch operation by rotating the key to each position. If necessary, reposition the lock cylinder until it operates properly.

13. If positioned properly, tighten the retaining bolts until the bolt head shears off.

14. Raise and position the steering column. Tighten the bracket bolts to 80–124 inch lbs. (9–14 Nm).

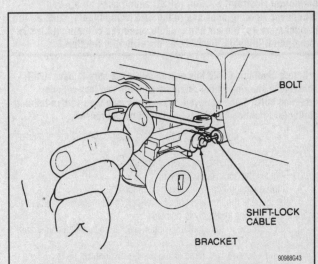

Fig. 98 Unfasten the ignition and shifter interlock cable mounting bracket bolt, and position the assembly to one side

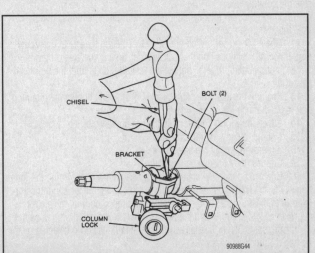

Fig. 99 Use a chisel and hammer to cut a groove in the ignition cylinder bracket bolts—1991–96 models shown; 1997–99 models similar

15. If equipped with tilt column, remove the upper mounting bracket retaining pin.

16. Position the interlock cable bracket. Install and tighten the retaining bolt to 35–53 inch lbs. (4–6 Nm).

17. Attach the wiring connector to the ignition switch.

18. Install the combination switch.

19. Connect the negative battery cable.

20. Confirm operational status of the air bag system by turning the ignition key to the **RUN** position and visually monitoring the air bag indicator lamp in the instrument cluster. The indicator lamp should illuminate for approximately 6 seconds and then turn OFF. If the indicator lamp does not illuminate, stays ON, or flashes at any time, a fault has been detected by the air bag diagnostic monitor.

21. Check the steering wheel, horn and combination switch functions for proper operation.

1997–99 Models

▶ See Figures 98 and 99

☀ CAUTION

Some models covered by this manual are equipped with a Supplemental Restraint System (SRS), which uses an air bag. Whenever working near any of the SRS components, such as the impact sensors, the air bag module, steering column and instrument panel, disable the SRS, as described in Section 6.

➡ Before continuing with this procedure, make sure to have available a new steering wheel retaining bolt and two lock cylinder retaining bolts. Once removed, these parts lose their torque holding ability (or retention capability) and must not be reused.

1. If equipped, disarm the air bag system and disconnect the negative battery cable.

2. If necessary, remove the steering wheel.

3. Remove the combination switch.

4. Unplug the ignition switch wiring connectors.

5. Remove the ignition and shifter interlock cable mounting bracket bolt and position the assembly to one side.

6. Cut a groove in the ignition cylinder bracket bolts with a chisel and hammer or use a similar method.

7. Using a screwdriver, remove and discard the bracket bolts.

8. Remove the ignition switch lock cylinder and bracket.

To install:

9. Install the new ignition switch and the bracket into position on the steering column tube.

10. Install the new lock cylinder bolts and tighten the bolts enough to hold the switch in position.

11. Check for proper switch operation by rotating the key to each position. If necessary, reposition the lock cylinder until it operates properly.

12. If positioned properly, tighten the retaining bolts until the bolt head shears off.

13. Position the interlock cable bracket. Install and tighten the retaining bolt to 35–53 inch lbs. (4–6 Nm).

14. Attach the wiring connector to the ignition switch.

15. Install the combination switch.

16. If removed, install the steering wheel.

17. Connect the negative battery cable.

18. Confirm operational status of the air bag system by turning the ignition key to the **RUN** position and visually monitoring the air bag indicator lamp in the instrument cluster. The indicator lamp should illuminate for approximately 6 seconds and then turn OFF. If the indicator lamp does not illuminate, stays ON, or flashes at any time, a fault has been detected by the air bag diagnostic monitor.

19. Check the steering wheel, horn and combination switch functions for proper operation.

Steering Linkage

REMOVAL & INSTALLATION

Tie Rod Ends

▶ See Figures 100 thru 106

1. Turn the ignition key to the **ACC** position.

2. Disconnect the negative battery cable.

3. Raise and safely support the vehicle.

4. Remove the wheel and tire assembly.

5. Remove and discard the cotter pin and unfasten (but do not yet remove) the castellated nut from the tie rod end.

6. Slightly loosen the tie rod end jam nut.

7. Separate the tie rod end from the steering knuckle, using tool T85M-3395-A or equivalent puller.

8. With paint or a marker pen, mark the tie rod end, jam nut and tie rod to make installation easier, without having to change the toe-in setting.

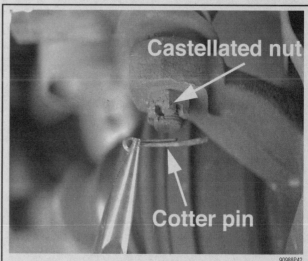

90988P42

Fig. 100 Remove and discard the cotter pin

90988P43

Fig. 101 Loosen, but do not remove, the castellated nut from the tie rod end

Fig. 102 Loosen the tie rod end jam nut

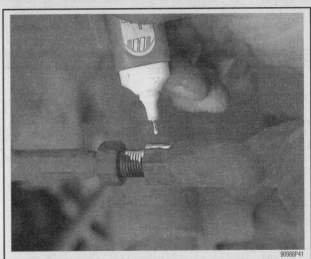
Fig. 105 With paint or a marker pen, mark the tie rod end, jam nut and tie rod to make installation easier

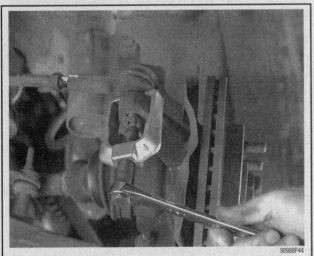
Fig. 103 Using a suitable puller, separate the tie rod end from the steering knuckle

Fig. 106 Unscrew the tie rod end from the inner tie rod

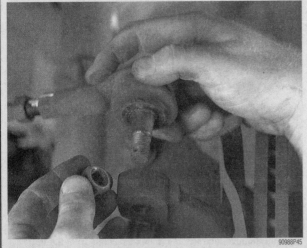
Fig. 104 Remove the castellated nut and disengage the tie rod end from the steering knuckle

9. Further loosen the jam nut and unscrew the tie rod end from the inner tie rod.

10. Remove the steering ball dust boot.

To install:

11. Install a new steering ball dust boot.

12. Clean the inner tie rod threads. Apply a light coating of suitable grease to the threads.

13. If removed, install the jam nut.

14. Thread the new tie rod end onto the inner tie rod and align the marks made before removal. Tighten the jam nut to 25–37 ft. lbs. (34–50 Nm).

15. Connect the tie rod end stud to the steering knuckle.

16. Install the castellated nut onto the tie rod end stud. Tighten the nut to the following specifications:

• 1991–99 models—except 1998–99 Escort/Tracer (non-coupe): 25–33 ft. lbs. (34–46 Nm)

• 1998–99 Escort/Tracer (non-coupe) models: 32–41 ft. lbs. (43–56 Nm)

17. Align the next slot with the cotter pin hole in the tie rod end stud. Install a new cotter pin.

18. Install the wheel and tire assembly.

19. Lower the vehicle.

20. Check the front wheel alignment and adjust as necessary.
21. Road test the vehicle and check for proper steering system operation.

Manual Rack and Pinion

REMOVAL & INSTALLATION

1991–96 Models

▶ **See Figure 107**

1. Disconnect the negative battery cable.
2. Working from inside the vehicle, unfasten the five nuts securing the steering column tube boot and remove the boot.
3. Remove the intermediate shaft-to-pinion shaft coupling bolt from inside the vehicle.
4. Raise and safely support the vehicle.
5. Remove the front wheel and tire assemblies.
6. Remove the cotter pins and castellated nuts securing the tie rod ends to the steering knuckles. Separate the tie rod ends from the steering knuckles. Discard the cotter pins.
7. If equipped with a manual transaxle, unfasten the gearshift lever stabilizer bar nut and disconnect the bar and support from the transaxle.
8. Unfasten the nuts securing the rack and pinion (steering gear) mounting brackets to the firewall. Remove the mounting brackets.
9. Remove the rack and pinion assembly from the vehicle.
To install:
10. Position the rack and pinion assembly to its mounting position and install the mounting brackets and retaining nuts. Tighten the nuts to 27–38 ft. lbs. (37–52 Nm).
11. If equipped with a manual transaxle, connect the gearshift lever stabilizer bar. Tighten the nut to 23–34 ft. lbs. (31–46 Nm).
12. Install the tie rod ends to the steering knuckles. Install the castellated nuts and tighten to specifications. Install new cotter pins.
13. Install the front wheel and tire assemblies.
14. Lower the vehicle.
15. Install the intermediate shaft-to-pinion shaft bolt and tighten to 13–20 ft. lbs. (18–27 Nm) for 1991–94 vehicles or 33 ft. lbs. (45 Nm) for 1995–96 vehicles.
16. Install the steering column tube boot and 5 retaining nuts. Tighten to 35 inch lbs. (4 Nm).
17. Connect the negative battery cable.
18. Check the alignment and adjust the toe as required.
19. Road test the vehicle and check the steering system for proper operation.

Power Rack and Pinion

REMOVAL & INSTALLATION

1991–96 Models

▶ **See Figure 108**

1. Disconnect the negative battery cable.
2. From inside the passenger compartment, remove the steering column tube boot nuts at the base of the column and remove the tube boots.
3. Remove the intermediate shaft-to-pinion shaft bolt.
4. Raise and safely support the vehicle.
5. Remove the front wheel and tire assemblies.
6. Remove the left-hand splash shield.
7. Remove the cotter pins and castellated nuts from the tie rod ends. Using a suitable tool, separate the tie rod ends from the steering knuckles. Discard the cotter pins.
8. Remove the strap that holds the power steering lines to the rack and pinion (steering gear) housing and discard the strap.
9. Disconnect the pressure and return lines from the rack and pinion assembly and plug the lines.
10. If equipped with a manual transaxle, disconnect the gearshift stabilizer bar and shift control rod from the transaxle.
11. Remove the retaining nuts from the rack and pinion mounting brackets.
12. Remove the rack and pinion assembly from the left-hand side of the vehicle.
To install:
13. Place the rack and pinion assembly in its mounting location.
14. Install the rack and pinion mounting brackets. Install the retaining nuts and tighten to 28–38 ft. lbs. (37–57 Nm).
15. If equipped with a manual transaxle, connect the gearshift stabilizer bar and shift control rod. Tighten the gearshift stabilizer bar nut to 23–34 ft. lbs. (31–46 Nm) and the shift control rod nut to 12–17 ft. lbs. (16–23 Nm).
16. Remove the plugs and connect the pressure and return lines to the rack and pinion assembly. Tighten the flare nuts to 22–28 ft. lbs. (29–39 Nm).
17. Install a new strap to hold the power steering lines to the rack and pinion housing.
18. Install the tie rod ends to the steering knuckles and install the castellated nuts. Tighten to specification. Install new cotter pins.
19. Install the left-hand splash shield.
20. Install the wheel and tire assemblies.
21. Lower the vehicle.

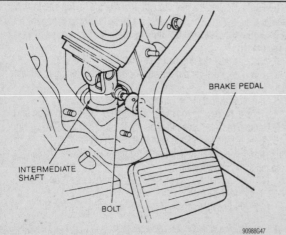

Fig. 107 Unfasten the intermediate shaft-to-pinion shaft coupling bolt from inside the vehicle—1991–96 models with manual rack and pinion

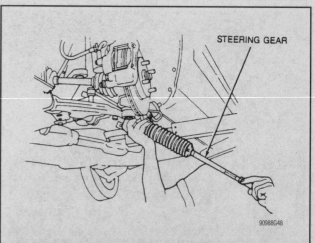

Fig. 108 Remove the rack and pinion assembly from the left-hand side of the vehicle—1991–96 models with power rack and pinion

22. From inside the vehicle, install the intermediate shaft-to-pinion shaft bolt. Tighten the bolt to 13–20 ft. lbs. (18–27 Nm) for 1991–94 vehicles or 30–36 ft. lbs. (40–50 Nm) for 1995–96 vehicles.

23. Install the steering column tube boot and the five retaining nuts. Tighten the retaining nuts to 35 inch lbs. (4 Nm).

24. Connect the negative battery cable.

25. Fill and bleed the power steering system.

26. Check the alignment and adjust as required.

27. Start the engine and check for leaks.

28. Road test the vehicle and check for proper steering system operation.

1997–99 Models

▶ See Figures 109, 110 and 111

1. Turn the key to the **ACC** position.

2. From inside the passenger compartment, remove the steering column tube boot nuts at the base of the column and remove the tube boots.

3. Remove the steering column input shaft coupling-to-steering gear input shaft pinch bolt.

4. Raise and safely support the vehicle.

5. Remove the front wheel and tire assemblies.

6. Using a suitable tool, separate the tie rod ends from the steering knuckles. Discard the cotter pins.

7. Remove the right-hand lower splash shield.

8. Unfasten the bolts and remove the crossmember.

9. Disconnect the pressure and return lines from the rack and pinion assembly and plug the lines.

10. Remove and discard the strap holding the hoses to the steering gear.

11. If equipped with a manual transaxle, disconnect the gearshift rod and clevis from the transaxle.

12. If equipped with a manual transaxle, unfasten the extension bar nut and disconnect the gearshift lever stabilizer bar and support from the transaxle.

13. Unfasten the retaining nuts from the rack and pinion mounting brackets and remove the brackets.

14. Remove the pushpin and position the right-hand boot shield aside.

15. Remove the rack and pinion assembly from the right-hand side of the vehicle.

To install:

16. Place the rack and pinion assembly in its mounting location.

17. Align the steering column input shaft coupling and the steering gear input shaft.

18. Install the rack and pinion mounting brackets. Install the retaining nuts and tighten to 28–38 ft. lbs. (37–57 Nm).

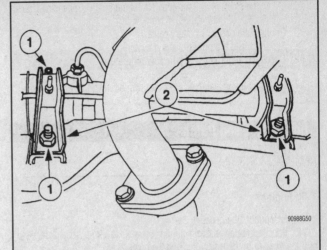

Fig. 110 Unfasten the retaining nuts (1) from the rack and pinion mounting brackets, then remove the brackets (2)

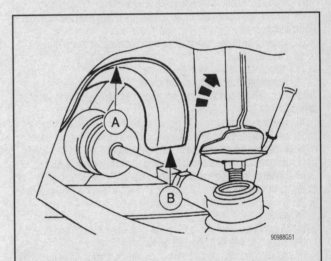

Fig. 111 Remove the pushpin (A) and position the right-hand boot shield (B) aside

19. If equipped with a manual transaxle, connect the gearshift stabilizer bar, support and the gearshift rod and clevis.

➡ Install new Teflon® seals on the power steering pressure hose fitting and make sure the threads are clean before connecting the hose.

20. Remove the plugs and connect the pressure and return lines to the rack and pinion assembly. Tighten the pressure hose to 21–25 ft. lbs. (28–33 Nm) and the return line fitting to 20–25 ft. lbs. (27–34 Nm).

21. Install a new strap to hold the power steering lines to the rack and pinion housing.

22. Install the crossmember and tighten the bolts to 69–97 ft. lbs. (94–131 Nm).

23. Place the right-hand boot shield into position and install the push pin.

24. Install the right-hand splash shield.

25. Install the tie rod ends to the steering knuckles and install the castellated nuts. Tighten to specification. Install new cotter pins.

26. Install the wheel and tire assemblies.

27. Lower the vehicle.

28. Install the steering column input shaft coupling-to-steering gear input shaft pinch bolt and tighten the bolt to 30–36 ft. lbs. (40–50 Nm).

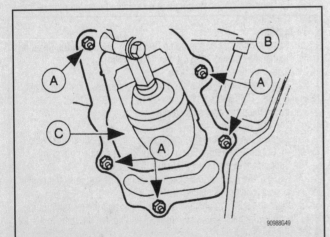

Fig. 109 Unfasten the nuts (A) at the base of the steering column, then remove the steering column tube boot (B) and inner steering column tube boot (C)—1997–99 models

29. Install the steering column tube boots and the five retainers. Tighten the retainers to 18–52 inch lbs. (2–6 Nm).

30. Connect the negative battery cable.

31. Fill and bleed the power steering system.

32. Check the alignment and adjust as required.

33. Start the engine and check for leaks.

34. Road test the vehicle and check for proper steering system operation.

Power Steering Pump

REMOVAL & INSTALLATION

1.8L Engines

1. Disconnect the negative battery cable.

2. Loosen the power steering fluid reservoir-to-pump hose clamp and pull the hose from the reservoir. Plug the hose.

3. Remove the reservoir retaining bolts and lift the reservoir from its mounting position.

4. Loosen the return hose clamp and pull the return hose from the reservoir. Plug the hose and remove the reservoir.

5. Unplug the electrical connector from the Power Steering Pressure (PSP) switch.

6. Loosen the pressure line fitting and disconnect the line from the pump. Plug the line.

7. Raise and safely support the vehicle.

8. Remove the right-hand splash shield.

9. Unfasten the belt tensioner adjustment bolt and remove the accessory drive belt from the pulley.

10. Lower the vehicle.

11. Unfasten the three power steering pump mounting bracket retaining bolts and remove the steering pump and the bracket.

12. Remove the bolt attaching the pump to the mounting bracket.

13. Unfasten the nut and bolt attaching the tensioner to the pump mounting bracket and remove the nut and bolt attaching the tensioner to the pump.

To install:

14. Position the tensioner to the pump and install the bolt and nut. Tighten the nut to 14–19 ft. lbs. (19–25 Nm).

15. Position the tensioner to the pump mounting bracket and install the bolt and nut. Tighten the nut to 23–34 ft. lbs. (31–46 Nm).

16. Install the bolt that attaches the pump to the mounting bracket and tighten to 27–40 ft. lbs. (36–54 Nm).

17. Position the pump and bracket, then install the 3 pump mounting bracket retaining bolts. Tighten the bolts to 27–38 ft. lbs. (37–54 Nm).

18. Raise and safely support the vehicle.

19. Position the accessory drive belt on the pulley and install the belt tensioner adjustment bolt.

20. Position the right front splash shield and install the 5 retaining bolts.

21. Lower the vehicle.

22. Unplug and connect the pressure line to the power steering pump. Tighten the line fitting to 12–17 ft. lbs. (16–24 Nm).

23. Attach the PSP switch electrical connector.

24. Unplug and connect the return hose to the reservoir. Tighten the clamp.

25. Position the reservoir and install the retaining bolts.

26. Unplug and connect the pump hose to the reservoir. Tighten the clamp.

27. Adjust the accessory drive belt tension.

28. Fill the system with power steering fluid.

29. Connect the negative battery cable.

30. Bleed air from the power steering system.

31. Start the engine and check for leaks.

32. Road test the vehicle and check for proper steering system operation.

1.9L Engines

✸✸ CAUTION

Never open, service or drain the radiator or cooling system when hot; serious burns can occur from the steam and hot coolant. Also, when draining engine coolant, keep in mind that cats and dogs are attracted to ethylene glycol antifreeze and could drink any that is left in an uncovered container or in puddles on the ground. This will prove fatal in sufficient quantities. Always drain coolant into a sealable container. Coolant should be reused unless it is contaminated or is several years old.

1. Disconnect the negative battery cable.

2. Drain the engine cooling system into a suitable container.

3. Loosen the drive belt tensioner and remove the drive belt from the pulley.

4. If necessary, unfasten the belt tensioner bolt and remove the tensioner.

5. Support the engine with a suitable floor jack.

6. If equipped, remove the speed control servo and bracket and move aside.

7. If necessary, unfasten the engine vibration damper nut and bolt, then remove the damper.

8. Unfasten the right-hand engine support insulator nut and through-bolt. Remove the support insulator.

9. Remove the two front engine mount nuts. Loosen the engine mount pivot bolt and nut and position the engine mount aside.

10. Raise the engine using the floor jack, to gain access to the power steering pump pulley.

11. Hold the pulley in position with a suitable tool and unfasten the three pulley retaining bolts. Remove the pulley and lower the engine.

12. Position the engine mount and install the retaining nuts.

13. Loosen the clamp and disconnect the return line from the pump. Loosen the line fitting from the pressure line and disconnect the line from the pump. Plug both power steering lines.

14. If required, remove the A/C tube bracket bolt from the power steering pump support.

15. Raise and safely support the vehicle.

16. Remove the passenger side splash shields.

17. If equipped with A/C, remove the A/C compressor retaining bolts and position the A/C compressor aside.

18. Remove the lower radiator hose.

19. Unfasten the power steering pump retaining bolts and remove the power steering pump.

To install:

20. Place the power steering pump in position and install the retaining bolts. Tighten the bolts to 30–41 ft. lbs. (40–55 Nm).

21. Install the lower radiator hose.

22. If equipped with A/C, position the A/C compressor and install the retaining bolts. Tighten the bolts to 15–22 ft. lbs. (20–30 Nm).

23. Install the passenger side splash shields.

24. Lower the vehicle.

25. Connect the pressure line to the power steering pump and tighten the fitting. Connect the return line to the pump and position the clamp.

26. Support the engine with a suitable floor jack.

27. Remove the front engine mount retaining nuts and raise the engine to gain access to the pulley using the floor jack.

28. Place the pulley in position and loosely install the retaining bolts. Hold the pulley in place with a suitable tool and tighten the bolts to 15–22 ft. lbs. (20–30 Nm).

29. Lower the engine.

30. Position the engine mount and install 2 retaining nuts. Tighten the engine mount pivot bolt and nut.

31. Position the engine support insulator and install the bolt and nut.

32. Remove the floor jack.

33. Position the belt tensioner and loosely install the bolt. Position the accessory drive belt on the pulley and tighten the tensioner mounting bolt to 30–41 ft. lbs. (40–55 Nm).

34. Fill the engine cooling system.

35. Add the proper type and quantity of power steering fluid to the power steering fluid reservoir.

36. Connect the negative battery cable.

37. Bleed the air from the power steering system.

38. Start the engine and check for leaks.

39. Road test the vehicle and check the power steering system for proper operation.

2.0L Engines

SOHC MODELS

▶ See Figures 112, 113, 114 and 115

1. Disconnect the negative battery cable.

2. Loosen the power steering reservoir-to-pump hose clamp and disconnect the hose from the reservoir.

3. Loosen the power steering return hose-to-reservoir clamp and disconnect the hose from the reservoir.

4. Unfasten the two power steering reservoir retaining bolts and remove the reservoir.

5. Unfasten the bolts from the power steering pressure hose brackets and set the hose assembly aside.

6. Unfasten the two power steering hose support bracket bolts and move the bracket aside.

7. Remove the accessory drive belt.

8. Unfasten the alternator mounting bolts and position the alternator aside.

9. Using strap wrench D85L-6000-A or equivalent to hold the power steering pump stationary, unfasten the pulley retaining bolts.

10. Remove the power steering pump pulley from the engine compartment.

11. Raise the front of the car and support it with safety stands.

12. Remove the right-hand splash shield.

13. Disconnect the power steering pressure hose from the pump.

14. Lower the car and loosen the power steering reservoir-to-pump hose clamp, then disconnect the hose from the pump.

15. Unfasten the three power steering pump mounting bolts and remove the pump.

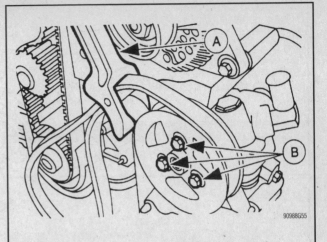

Fig. 113 Use a strap wrench (A) to hold the power steering pump stationary, then unfasten the pulley retaining bolts (B)— 2.0L SOHC engines

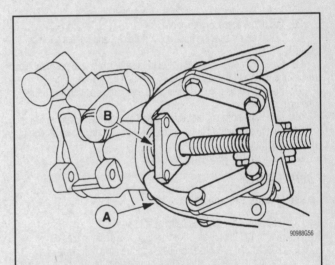

Fig. 114 If removing the power steering pump pulley hub (B), use puller T71P-19703-B or equivalent (A)

16. If it is necessary to remove the power steering pump pulley hub, use puller T71P-19703-B or equivalent to remove the hub from the pump.

To install:

17. If removed, install the power steering pump hub onto the pump using replacer tool T91P-3A733-A or equivalent.

18. Place the pump into position and install the pump mounting bolts. Tighten the bolts to 30–41 ft. lbs. (40–55 Nm).

19. Raise the front of the car and support it with safety stands.

➡After disconnecting the power steering pressure hose, install a new Teflon® seal # 388898-S or equivalent onto the pressure hose fitting before reconnecting the hose.

20. Connect the power steering pressure hose to the pump and tighten the fitting to 40–54 ft. lbs. (57–73 Nm).

21. Install the right-hand splash shield.

22. Lower the car and place the power steering pump pulley into position.

23. Install the power steering pump pulley bolts finger-tight.

24. Use strap wrench D85L-6000-A or equivalent to hold the power steering pump stationary, and tighten the pulley retaining bolts to 15–22 ft. lbs. (20–30 Nm).

Fig. 112 Unfasten the power steering pump reservoir retainers (A) and remove the reservoir (B)

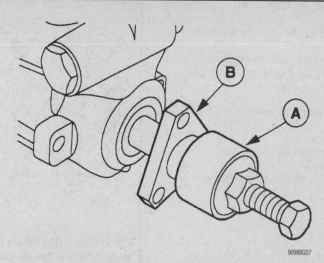

90988G57

Fig. 115 If removed, install the power steering pump hub (B) onto the pump using replacer tool T91P-3A733-A or equivalent (A)

25. Install the alternator and tighten the mounting bolts.

26. Install the accessory drive belt.

27. Install power steering hose support bracket and tighten the retaining bolts.

28. Place the power steering pressure hose brackets into position, then install the bolts and tighten them to 64–87 inch lbs. (8–11 Nm).

29. Place the power steering pump reservoir into position and tighten the bolts securely.

30. Attach the hoses to the reservoir and engage their retaining clamps.

31. Fill the reservoir to the proper level with Mercon power steering fluid or equivalent.

32. Connect the negative battery cable.

DOHC MODELS

▶ See Figures 116 and 117

1. Disconnect the negative battery cable.
2. Disconnect the radiator overflow tube and position it aside.
3. Unfasten the A/C hose clamp bolt and remove the clamp.
4. Unclip the speed control actuator cable from the A/C hose bracket.
5. Unfasten the A/C hose bracket bolt and remove the bracket.

6. Raise and support the car with safety stands.

7. Remove the right-hand lower splash shield.

8. Turn the belt tensioner bolt clockwise and remove the accessory belt.

9. Disconnect the power steering pressure hose from the pump.

10. Lower the car and disconnect the power steering pressure hoses from each other.

11. Unfasten the power steering pressure hose bracket bolts and set the brackets aside.

12. Unplug the Heated Oxygen Sensor (HO2S) electrical connection.

13. Unfasten the engine block ground bracket bolts and remove the bracket.

14. Disconnect the power steering return hose from the pump.

15. Raise the car and support it with safety stands.

16. Remove the power steering hose from the car.

17. Unfasten the power steering pump bolts and remove the pump.

18. Discard the power steering pump heat shield.

To install:

19. Install a new power steering pump heat shield.

20. Place the power steering pump into position, install the bolts and tighten them to 15–22 ft. lbs. (20–30 Nm).

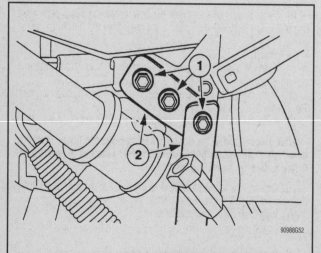

90988G52

Fig. 116 Unfasten the power steering pressure hose bracket bolts (1) and set the brackets (2) aside—2.0L DOHC engine

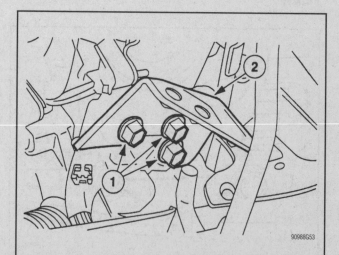

90988G53

Fig. 117 Unfasten the engine block ground bracket bolts (1) and remove the bracket (2)—2.0L DOHC engine

21. Place the power steering pressure hose in the car.

22. Lower the car and connect the power steering return hose to the pump.

23. Install the engine block ground bracket and tighten the bolts to 71–89 inch lbs. (8–10 Nm).

24. Attach the Heated Oxygen Sensor (HO2S) electrical connection.

25. Install the power steering pressure hose bracket and the retaining bolts. Tighten the bolts to 71–89 inch lbs. (8–10 Nm).

26. Connect the power steering pressure hoses together.

27. Raise the car and support it with safety stands.

28. Connect the power steering pressure hose to the pump and tighten the fitting to 40–54 ft. lbs. (57–73 Nm).

29. Install the accessory drive belt and install the right-hand splash shield.

30. Lower the car, place the A/C hose bracket in position and install the bolt. Tighten the bolt to 15–22 ft. lbs. (20–30 Nm).

31. Place the speed control actuator cable into the A/C hose bracket.

32. Place the A/C hose clamp into position and install the bolt. Tighten the bolt to 71–89 inch lbs. (8–10 Nm).

33. Connect the radiator overflow tube.

34. Add the proper type and quantity of power steering fluid to the power steering fluid reservoir.

35. Connect the negative battery cable.

36. Bleed the air from the power steering system.

37. Start the engine and check for leaks.

38. Road test the vehicle and check the power steering system for proper operation.

BLEEDING

1991–96 Models

Normally the power steering system will expel any trapped air during normal operation. If the power steering system is noisy due to trapped air, turn the steering wheel left to right several times with the front wheels off the ground and the vehicle properly secured, to release the trapped air.

1997–99 Models

1. Raise the car until the front tires are clear of the ground.

2. Check the power steering pump fluid level and add fluid if necessary.

3. Unplug the ignition coil electrical connector to prevent the engine from starting.

➡**Do not hold the steering wheel "on stops" (at the fully turned right or left position).**

4. Crank the engine for 30 seconds while cycling the steering wheel fully to the left and right.

5. Check the fluid level again and add fluid if necessary.

6. Attach the ignition coil electrical connector.

7. Check for proper and quiet pump operation, then lower the car.

TORQUE SPECIFICATIONS

Components	Ft. Lbs.	Nm
Wheels		
1991-97 models	65-87	88-118
1998-99 models	73-99	100-135
Front Suspension		
MacPherson Struts		
Upper mounting bracket-to-strut tower nuts	22-30	29-40
Strut assembly-to-steering knuckle bolts and nuts	69-93	93-127
Strut Overhaul		
Piston rod nut	58-81	79-110
Lower Ball Joint		
Ball joint-to-lower control arm nuts and bolt	69-86	93-117
Ball joint-to-steering knuckle nut and bolt	32-43	43-59
Stabilizer Bar		
1991-96 models		
Sway bar-to- sub-frame bolts	32-43	43-59
Sub-frame-to-vehicle frame bolts and nuts	69-93	93-127
Sway bar bolts	①	①
Steering gear nuts	28-38	37-52
1997-99 models		
Sway bar-to-sub-frame bolts	32-43	43-59
Sub-frame-to-vehicle frame bolts and nuts	69-93	93-127
Sway bar bolts	①	①
Steering gear nuts	28-38	37-52
Crossmember bolts	47-66	64-89
Lower Control Arm		
1991-96 models		
Lower control arm rear bushing retaining strap bolts	69-86	93-117
Lower control arm front pivot bolt and nut	69-93	93-127
1997-99 models		
Lower control arm bolts	69-86	93-117
Lower control arm pivot bolt	69-86	93-117
Wheel Hub, Knuckle and Bearing		
Wheel hub, knuckle and bearing assembly pinch bolt and nut	32-43	43-59
Tie rod end castellated nut	25-33	34-46
Halfshaft retaining nut	174-235	235-319
Rear Suspension		
MacPherson Struts		
1991-96 models		
Upper strut insulator retaining nuts	22-27	29-40
Lower strut bolts and nuts	69-93	93-127
1997-99 models		
Lower strut bolts and nuts	76-100	103-136
Upper strut retaining nuts	34-46	47-62
Strut Overhaul		
Piston rod nut	41-50	55-68
Lateral Links and Trailing Link		
1991-96 models		
Rear trailing link front bolt	46-69	63-93
Rear trailing link rear bolt	69-93	93-127

TORQUE SPECIFICATIONS

Components	Ft. Lbs.	Nm
Lateral Links and Trailing Link (cont.)		
Front and rear lateral link nut-to-rear wheel spindle	63-86	85-117
Front and rear lateral link nut-to-rear suspension crossmember	50-70	68-95
Control Arm		
1997-99 models		
Control arm bolt	50-70	68-95
Control arm and bushing nut	64-86	87-116
Crossmember bolts	34-46	47-62
Sway Bar		
Sway bar bracket bolts	32-43	43-59
Steering		
Steering Wheel		
Steering wheel nut	34-46	46-63
Air bag module bolts		
1994-96 models	35-53 inch lbs.	4-6
1997-99 models	70-103 inch lbs.	8-12
Steering Linkage		
Tie Rod Ends		
Jam nut	25-37	34-50
Castellated nut		
Except 1998-99 Escort/Tracer non-coupe models	25-33	34-46
1998-99 Escort/Tracer non-coupe models	32-41	43-56
Manual Rack and Pinion		
Rack and pinion assembly mounting brackets nuts	27-38	37-52
Intermediate shaft-to-pinion shaft bolt		
1991-94 models	13-20	18-27
1995-96 models	33	45
Steering column tube boot nuts	35 inch lbs.	4
Power Rack and Pinion		
1991-96 models		
Rack and pinion mounting bracket nuts	28-38	37-57
Pressure and return line fitting-to-rack and pinion nuts	22-28	29-39
Intermediate shaft-to-pinion shaft bolt		
1991-94 models	13-20	18-27
1995-96 models	30-36	40-50
Steering column tube boot nuts	35 inch lbs.	4
1997-99 models		
Rack and pinion mounting brackets nuts	28-38	37-57
Pressure line fitting	21-25	28-33
Return line fitting	20-25	27-34
Crossmember bolts	69-97	94-131
Steering column input shaft coupling-to-steering gear input shaft bolt	30-36	40-50
Steering column tube boot retainers	18-52 inch lbs.	2-6
Power Steering Pump		
1991-96 models		
1.8L Engine		
Tensioner-to-pump bolt and nut	14-19	19-25
Tensioner-to-pump mounting bracket bolt and nut	23-34	31-46
Pump-to-mounting bracket bolt	27-40	36-54

90988C02

TORQUE SPECIFICATIONS

Components	Ft. Lbs.	Nm
Power Steering Pump (cont.)		
1.8L Engine		
Pump mounting bracket bolts	27-38	37-53
Pressure line-to-power steering pump fitting	12-17	16-24
1.9L Engine		
Power steering pump bolts	30-41	40-55
A/C compressor bolts	15-22	20-30
Power steering pump pulley bolts	15-22	20-30
Belt tensioner mounting bolt	30-41	40-55
1997-99 models		
2.0L SOHC Engine		
Power steering pump bolts	30-41	40-55
Power steering pressure hose-to-pump fitting	40-54	57-73
Power steering pump pulley bolts	15-22	20-30
Power steering pressure hose brackets bolts	64-87 inch lbs.	8-11
2.0L DOHC (zetec) engine		
Power steering pump bolts	15-22	20-30
Engine block ground bracket bolts	71-89 inch lbs.	8-10
Power steering pressure hose bracket bolts	71-89 inch lbs.	8-10
Power steering pressure hose-to-pump fitting	40-54	57-73
A/C hose bracket bolt	15-22	20-30
A/C hose clamp bolt	71-89 inch lbs.	8-10

① Tighten the bolt until 0.67-0.75 inches (17-19mm) of thread is exposed at the end of the bolt

90988C03

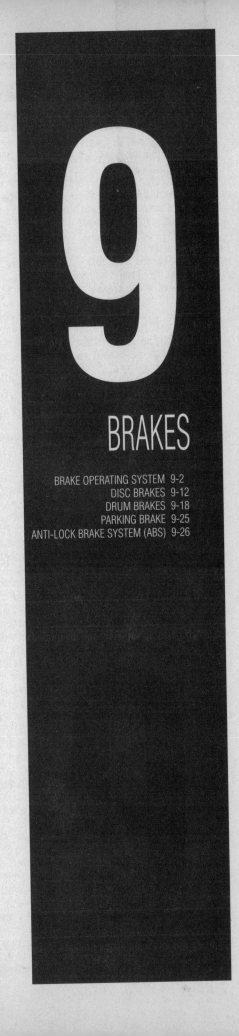

9

BRAKES

BRAKE OPERATING SYSTEM

Basic Operating Principles

Hydraulic systems are used to actuate the brakes of all modern automobiles. The system transports the power required to force the frictional surfaces of the braking system together from the pedal to the individual brake units at each wheel. A hydraulic system is used for two reasons.

First, fluid under pressure can be carried to all parts of an automobile by small pipes and flexible hoses without taking up a significant amount of room or posing routing problems.

Second, a great mechanical advantage can be given to the brake pedal end of the system, and the foot pressure required to actuate the brakes can be reduced by making the surface area of the master cylinder pistons smaller than that of any of the pistons in the wheel cylinders or calipers.

The master cylinder consists of a fluid reservoir along with a double cylinder and piston assembly. Double type master cylinders are designed to separate the front and rear braking systems hydraulically in case of a leak. The master cylinder coverts mechanical motion from the pedal into hydraulic pressure within the lines. This pressure is translated back into mechanical motion at the wheels by either the wheel cylinder (drum brakes) or the caliper (disc brakes).

Steel lines carry the brake fluid to a point on the vehicle's frame near each of the vehicle's wheels. The fluid is then carried to the calipers and wheel cylinders by flexible tubes in order to allow for suspension and steering movements.

In drum brake systems, each wheel cylinder contains two pistons, one at either end, which push outward in opposite directions and force the brake shoe into contact with the drum.

In disc brake systems, the cylinders are part of the calipers. At least one cylinder in each caliper is used to force the brake pads against the disc.

All pistons employ some type of seal, usually made of rubber, to minimize fluid leakage. A rubber dust boot seals the outer end of the cylinder against dust and dirt. The boot fits around the outer end of the piston on disc brake calipers, and around the brake actuating rod on wheel cylinders.

The hydraulic system operates as follows: When at rest, the entire system, from the piston(s) in the master cylinder to those in the wheel cylinders or calipers, is full of brake fluid. Upon application of the brake pedal, fluid trapped in front of the master cylinder piston(s) is forced through the lines to the wheel cylinders. Here, it forces the pistons outward, in the case of drum brakes, and inward toward the disc, in the case of disc brakes. The motion of the pistons is opposed by return springs mounted outside the cylinders in drum brakes, and by spring seals, in disc brakes.

Upon release of the brake pedal, a spring located inside the master cylinder immediately returns the master cylinder pistons to the normal position. The pistons contain check valves and the master cylinder has compensating ports drilled in it. These are uncovered as the pistons reach their normal position. The piston check valves allow fluid to flow toward the wheel cylinders or calipers as the pistons withdraw. Then, as the return springs force the brake pads or shoes into the released position, the excess fluid reservoir through the compensating ports. It is during the time the pedal is in the released position that any fluid that has leaked out of the system will be replaced through the compensating ports.

Dual circuit master cylinders employ two pistons, located one behind the other, in the same cylinder. The primary piston is actuated directly by mechanical linkage from the brake pedal through the power booster. The secondary piston is actuated by fluid trapped between the two pistons. If a leak develops in front of the secondary piston, it moves forward until it bottoms against the front of the master cylinder, and the fluid trapped between the pistons will operate the rear brakes. If the rear brakes develop a leak, the primary piston will move forward until direct contact with the secondary piston takes place, and it will force the secondary piston to actuate the front brakes. In either case, the brake pedal moves farther when the brakes are applied, and less braking power is available.

All dual circuit systems use a switch to warn the driver when only half of the brake system is operational. This switch is usually located in a valve body which is mounted on the firewall or the frame below the master cylinder. A hydraulic piston receives pressure from both circuits, each circuit's pressure being applied to one end of the piston. When the pressures are in balance, the piston remains stationary. When one circuit has a leak, however, the greater pressure in that circuit during application of the brakes will push the piston to one side, closing the switch and activating the brake warning light.

In disc brake systems, this valve body also contains a metering valve and, in some cases, a proportioning valve. The metering valve keeps pressure from traveling to the disc brakes on the front wheels until the brake shoes on the rear wheels have contacted the drums, ensuring that the front brakes will never be used alone. The proportioning valve controls the pressure to the rear brakes to lessen the chance of rear wheel lock-up during very hard braking.

Warning lights may be tested by depressing the brake pedal and holding it while opening one of the wheel cylinder bleeder screws. If this does not cause the light to go on, substitute a new lamp, make continuity checks, and, finally, replace the switch as necessary.

The hydraulic system may be checked for leaks by applying pressure to the pedal gradually and steadily. If the pedal sinks very slowly to the floor, the system has a leak. This is not to be confused with a springy or spongy feel due to the compression of air within the lines. If the system leaks, there will be a gradual change in the position of the pedal with a constant pressure.

Check for leaks along all lines and at wheel cylinders. If no external leaks are apparent, the problem is inside the master cylinder.

DISC BRAKES

Instead of the traditional expanding brakes that press outward against a circular drum, disc brake systems utilize a disc (rotor) with brake pads positioned on either side of it. An easily-seen analogy is the hand brake arrangement on a bicycle. The pads squeeze onto the rim of the bike wheel, slowing its motion. Automobile disc brakes use the identical principle but apply the braking effort to a separate disc instead of the wheel.

The disc (rotor) is a casting, usually equipped with cooling fins between the two braking surfaces. This enables air to circulate between the braking surfaces making them less sensitive to heat buildup and more resistant to fade. Dirt and water do not drastically affect braking action since contaminants are thrown off by the centrifugal action of the rotor or scraped off the by the pads. Also, the equal clamping action of the two brake pads tends to ensure uniform, straight line stops. Disc brakes are inherently self-adjusting. There are three general types of disc brake:

1. A fixed caliper.
2. A floating caliper.
3. A sliding caliper.

The fixed caliper design uses two pistons mounted on either side of the rotor (in each side of the caliper). The caliper is mounted rigidly and does not move.

The sliding and floating designs are quite similar. In fact, these two types are often lumped together. In both designs, the pad on the inside of the rotor is moved into contact with the rotor by hydraulic force. The caliper, which is not held in a fixed position, moves slightly, bringing the outside pad into contact with the rotor. There are various methods of attaching floating calipers. Some pivot at the bottom or top, and some slide on mounting bolts. In any event, the end result is the same.

DRUM BRAKES

Drum brakes employ two brake shoes mounted on a stationary backing plate. These shoes are positioned inside a circular drum which rotates with the wheel assembly. The shoes are held in place by springs. This allows them to slide toward the drums (when they are applied) while keeping the linings and drums in alignment. The shoes are actuated by a wheel cylinder which is mounted at the top of the backing plate. When the brakes are applied, hydraulic pressure forces the wheel cylinder's actuating links outward. Since these links bear directly against the top of the brake shoes, the tops of the shoes are then forced against the inner side of the drum. This action forces the bottoms of the two shoes to contact the brake drum by rotating the entire assembly slightly (known as servo action). When pressure within the wheel cylinder is relaxed, return springs pull the shoes back away from the drum.

Most modern drum brakes are designed to self-adjust themselves during application when the vehicle is moving in reverse. This motion causes both shoes to rotate very slightly with the drum, rocking an adjusting lever, thereby causing rotation of the adjusting screw. Some drum brake systems are designed to self-adjust during application whenever the brakes are applied. This on-board adjustment system reduces the need for maintenance adjustments and keeps both the brake function and pedal feel satisfactory.

POWER BOOSTERS

Virtually all modern vehicles use a vacuum assisted power brake system to multiply the braking force and reduce pedal effort. Since vacuum is always available when the engine is operating, the system is simple and efficient. A vacuum diaphragm is located on the front of the master cylinder and assists the driver in applying the brakes, reducing both the effort and travel he must put into moving the brake pedal.

The vacuum diaphragm housing is normally connected to the intake manifold by a vacuum hose. A check valve is placed at the point where the hose enters the diaphragm housing, so that during periods of low manifold vacuum brakes assist will not be lost.

Depressing the brake pedal closes off the vacuum source and allows atmospheric pressure to enter on one side of the diaphragm. This causes the master cylinder pistons to move and apply the brakes. When the brake pedal is released, vacuum is applied to both sides of the diaphragm and springs return the diaphragm and master cylinder pistons to the released position.

If the vacuum supply fails, the brake pedal rod will contact the end of the master cylinder actuator rod and the system will apply the brakes without any power assistance. The driver will notice that much higher pedal effort is needed to stop the car and that the pedal feels harder than usual.

Vacuum Leak Test

1. Operate the engine at idle without touching the brake pedal for at least one minute.
2. Turn off the engine and wait one minute.
3. Test for the presence of assist vacuum by depressing the brake pedal and releasing it several times. If vacuum is present in the system, light application will produce less and less pedal travel. If there is no vacuum, air is leaking into the system.

System Operation Test

1. With the engine **OFF**, pump the brake pedal until the supply vacuum is entirely gone.
2. Put light, steady pressure on the brake pedal.
3. Start the engine and let it idle. If the system is operating correctly, the brake pedal should fall toward the floor if the constant pressure is maintained.

Power brake systems may be tested for hydraulic leaks just as ordinary systems are tested.

Brake Light Switch

REMOVAL & INSTALLATION

1991–96 Models

▶ See Figure 1

1. Disconnect the negative battery cable.
2. In some cases, it may be necessary to remove the underdash panel to access the switch.
3. Unplug the switch electrical connection.
4. Unscrew the switch and remove it from the pedal.
To install:
5. Install the switch on the pedal and finger-tighten the switch locknut.

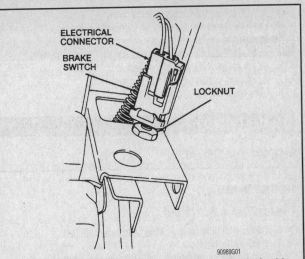

Fig. 1 Unplug the electrical connector and loosen the locknut to remove the brake light switch from the pedal

6. Measure the distance from the center of the brake pedal pad to the floor. The distance should be 7.60–7.72 inches (193–196mm).
7. If the pedal height is correct, tighten the switch locknut to specification and attach the electrical connection.
8. If the pedal height is not within specification, loosen the brake light switch locknut and turn the switch until it does not contact the pedal.
9. Loosen the locknut pushrod locknut and turn the rod until the pedal height is within specification.
10. Turn the brake light switch until it contacts the pedal, then turn it an additional half turn.
11. Tighten the switch locknut to 10–13 ft. lbs. (14–17 Nm).
12. Tighten the pushrod locknut.
13. Attach the switch electrical connection.
14. If removed, install the underdash panel.
15. Connect the negative battery cable.

1997–99 Models

▶ See Figure 2

1. Disconnect the negative battery cable.
2. In some cases, it may be necessary to remove the underdash panel to access the switch.

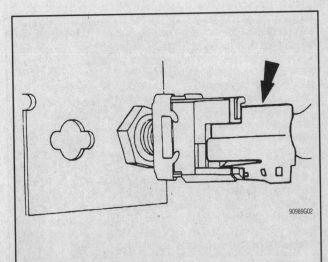

Fig. 2 The electrical connector (arrow) plugs directly into the brake light switch

3. Unplug the switch electrical connection.
4. Unscrew the switch and remove it from the pedal.

To install:

5. Install the switch on the pedal and tighten the switch locknut.
6. Attach the switch electrical connection.
7. If removed, install the underdash panel.
8. Connect the negative battery cable.

Master Cylinder

REMOVAL & INSTALLATION

1991–96 Models

▶ See Figures 3, 4, 5, 6 and 7

1. Disconnect both battery cables, negative cable first.
2. Remove the battery.
3. Remove the speed control cable from its bracket, if equipped.
4. Unplug the low fluid level sensor electrical connector.
5. Pump the brake pedal to exhaust the brake booster vacuum.

Fig. 5 . . . and disconnect the lines from the master cylinder

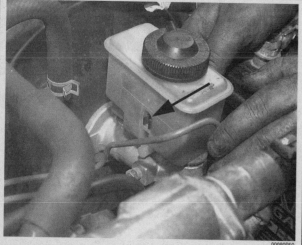

Fig. 3 Unfasten the fluid level sensor electrical connector clips and detach the connector from the master cylinder

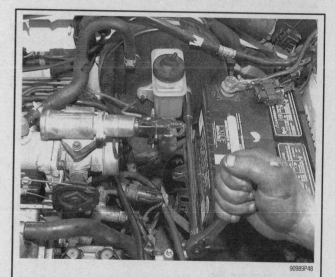

Fig. 6 Unfasten the master cylinder mounting nuts . . .

Fig. 4 Use a flare nut wrench to loosen the front brake line fittings . . .

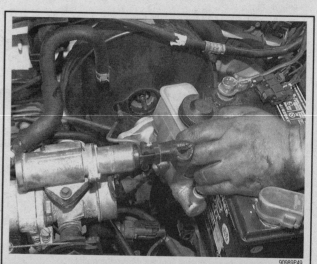

Fig. 7 . . . then remove the master cylinder from the engine compartment

6. Loosen the brake line fittings and disconnect the brake lines from the master cylinder.

7. Cap the brake lines and the master cylinder ports.

8. If equipped with a manual transaxle, remove the clamp and pull the clutch hose from the brake/clutch fluid reservoir.

9. Cap the clutch master cylinder hose and reservoir port.

10. Unfasten the mounting nuts and remove the master cylinder assembly.

To install:

11. If a new master cylinder is being installed, adjust the master cylinder piston-to-brake booster pushrod clearance as outlined in this section.

12. Position the master cylinder over the booster pushrod and booster mounting studs. Install the mounting nuts and tighten to 8–12 ft. lbs. (10–16 Nm).

13. Install the speed control cable to its bracket, if removed.

14. If equipped with manual transaxle, connect the clutch hose onto the brake/clutch fluid reservoir and install the clamp.

15. Remove the caps and connect the brake lines. Tighten the brake line fittings.

16. Make sure the master cylinder reservoir is full and bleed it.

17. Attach the low fluid level sensor electrical connector.

18. Install the battery.

19. Connect both battery cables, negative cable last.

20. Make sure the master cylinder reservoir is full. Bleed the brake system.

21. Bleed the clutch hydraulic system, if required.

22. Check for brake fluid leaks and brake pedal operation.

23. Road test the vehicle and check the brake system for proper operation.

1997–99 Models

➡A scan tool is absolutely necessary to bleed the brake hydraulic system on 1997–99 models equipped with an Anti-lock Brake System (ABS). If your vehicle is equipped with ABS, be sure to refer to the ABS bleeding procedures in this section before performing any work on your vehicle's brake hydraulic system.

1. Remove the air cleaner outlet tube.

2. Disconnect the negative battery cable.

3. Unplug the low fluid level sensor electrical connector.

4. Remove the reservoir cap and use a suction device such as a turkey baster, to remove the brake fluid from the reservoir

5. Loosen the brake line fittings and disconnect the brake lines from the master cylinder.

6. Cap the brake lines and the master cylinder ports.

7. If equipped with a manual transaxle, remove the clamp and pull the clutch hose from the brake/clutch fluid reservoir.

8. Cap the clutch master cylinder hose and reservoir port.

9. Unfasten the mounting nuts and remove the master cylinder assembly.

To install:

10. On 1998–99 models, if installing a new master cylinder, transfer the master cylinder reservoir to the new master cylinder as follows:

  a. Carefully pry up on the reservoir to separate it from the master cylinder.

  b. Lubricate two new grommets with brake fluid.

  c. Insert the grommets into the master cylinder.

  d. Place the master cylinder reservoir into position and press down on the reservoir until it snaps into place securely.

11. Position the master cylinder over the booster pushrod and booster mounting studs. Install the mounting nuts and tighten to 8–12 ft. lbs. (10–16 Nm).

12. If equipped with manual transaxle, connect the clutch hose onto the brake/clutch fluid reservoir and install the clamp.

13. Remove the caps and connect the brake lines. Tighten the brake line fittings.

14. Make sure the master cylinder reservoir is full and bleed it.

15. Attach the low fluid level sensor electrical connector.

16. Install the air cleaner outlet tube.

17. Connect the negative battery cable.

18. Make sure the master cylinder reservoir is full. Bleed the brakes system.

19. Bleed the clutch hydraulic system, if required.

20. Check for brake fluid leaks and brake pedal operation.

21. Road test the vehicle and check the brake system for proper operation.

Power Brake Booster

REMOVAL & INSTALLATION

1991–96 Models

▶ See Figure 8

➡The power brake booster is the same for all 1991–96 vehicles, including those equipped with an Anti-Lock Brake System (ABS).

1. Disconnect the negative battery cable.

2. Remove the master cylinder assembly.

3. Loosen the vacuum hose clamp and remove the hose from the power brake booster.

4. From inside the vehicle, remove the pin and discard.

5. Remove the clevis pin.

6. Unfasten the four booster mounting nuts and remove the booster. Remove and discard the gasket.

To install:

7. Install a new gasket over the studs and position the power brake booster.

8. From inside the vehicle, install the four mounting nuts and tighten to 14–19 ft. lbs. (19–25 Nm).

9. Lubricate the clevis pin with white lithium grease and install.

10. Install a new pin.

11. Position the vacuum hose to the booster and install the clamp.

12. Install the master cylinder, making sure to check the master cylinder pushrod clearance.

13. Adjust the brake pedal as follows:

  a. Press the brake pedal several times to eliminate the vacuum in the booster.

  b. Carefully press the pedal and measure the amount of free-play until resistance is felt. If the free-play is 0.16–0.28 in. (4–7mm), the pedal free-play is within specification. If the free-play is not within specification, continue with the procedure.

  c. Loosen the rod locknut and rotate the rod either in or out, as necessary, to obtain the specified free-play.

  d. While holding the rod in position, tighten the rod locknut.

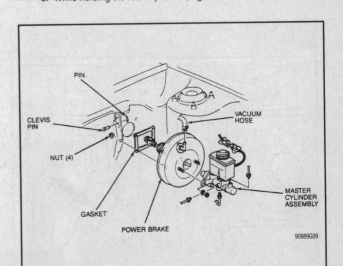

Fig. 8 Exploded view of the power brake booster mounting— 1991–96 models

e. Measure the distance from the center of the brake pedal to the floor. If the distance measures 7.60–7.72 in. (193–196mm), the pedal height is within specification. If the pedal height is not within specification, continue with the procedure.

f. Unplug the brake light switch electrical connector, loosen the switch locknut and turn the switch until it does not contact the brake pedal.

g. Loosen the rod locknut and turn the rod until the brake pedal height is within specification.

h. Turn the brake light switch until it contacts the brake pedal, then turn it an additional ½ turn. Tighten the brake light locknut and the rod locknut.

i. Attach the brake light switch electrical connector.

14. Connect the negative battery cable.

15. Bleed the brake system.

16. Check the operation of the brake lights and brake system.

1997–99 Models

▶ See Figures 9, 10 and 11

➡ A scan tool is absolutely necessary to bleed the brake hydraulic system on 1997–99 models equipped with an Anti-lock Brake System (ABS). If your vehicle is equipped with ABS, be sure to refer to

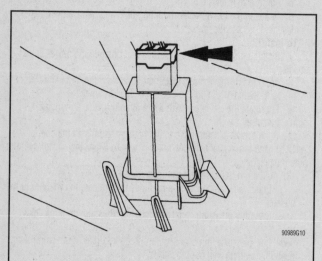

Fig. 9 Unplug the light switch rheostat resistor electrical connection—1997–99 models

Fig. 10 Remove the self-locking pin (arrow) . . .

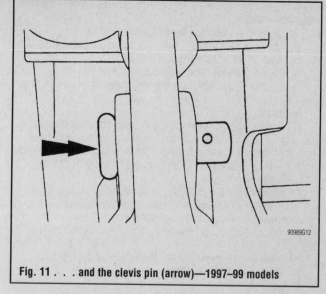

Fig. 11 . . . and the clevis pin (arrow)—1997–99 models

the ABS bleeding procedures in this section before performing any work on your vehicle's brake hydraulic system.

1. Disconnect the negative battery cable.

2. Unfasten the brake booster hose clamp and disconnect the hose.

3. If necessary, remove the battery tray.

4. Remove the master cylinder.

5. On 1998–99 models, unfasten the nut on the back side of the hood release handle and set the handle aside.

6. Unfasten the instrument panel steering column cover retainer(s) and remove the cover.

7. Unplug the light switch rheostat resistor electrical connection.

8. Remove the self-locking pin and the clevis pin.

9. Unfasten the four brake booster nuts and the booster.

To install:

10. Install the brake booster into position.

11. Install the booster nuts and tighten them to 14–19 ft. lbs. (19–25 Nm).

12. Install the clevis pin and self-locking pin.

13. Attach the light switch rheostat resistor electrical connection.

14. Install the instrument panel steering column cover and tighten the retainer(s).

15. On 1998–99 models, place hood release handle in position and tighten the retaining nut on the back side of the handle.

16. Install the master cylinder.

17. If removed, install the battery tray.

18. Attach the brake booster hose and engage the clamp.

19. Bleed the brake system.

20. Check the operation of the brake system.

Brake Booster Pushrod

ADJUSTMENT

1991–96 Models

MANUAL TRANSAXLE MODELS WITHOUT ANTI-LOCK BRAKES (ABS)

▶ See Figures 12 and 13

The use of master cylinder gauge T87C-2500-A or equivalent, is required for this procedure.

1. Remove the master cylinder.

2. Position master cylinder gauge T87C-2500-A or equivalent on the end of the master cylinder, loosen the setscrew and push the gauge plunger against the bottom of the primary piston.

1. Remove the master cylinder and mount it in a soft jawed vise.
2. Loosen the brass holding screw on the master cylinder gauge tool T92C-2500-A or equivalent and retract the gauge rod.
3. Attach the gauge to the power brake booster and tighten the gauge nuts to 8–12 ft. lbs. (10–16 Nm).
4. Start the engine and let it idle for about 15 seconds.
5. Push lightly on the end of the gauge rod until the gauge rod just contacts the brake booster pushrod.

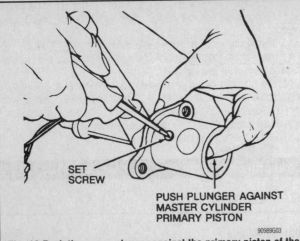

Fig. 12 Push the gauge plunger against the primary piston of the master cylinder, then tighten the setscrew—1991–96 manual transaxle models without ABS

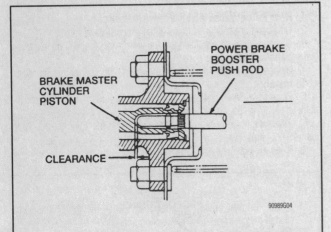

Fig. 13 Adjust the brake booster pushrod length to achieve the proper master cylinder piston-to-pushrod clearance—1991–96 manual transaxle models without ABS

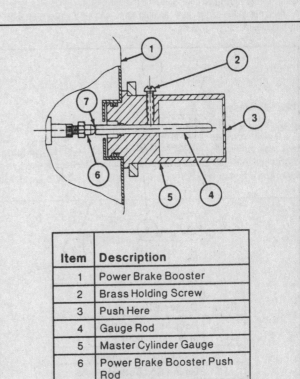

Item	Description
1	Power Brake Booster
2	Brass Holding Screw
3	Push Here
4	Gauge Rod
5	Master Cylinder Gauge
6	Power Brake Booster Push Rod
7	Touches Here

Fig. 14 Sectional view of the power brake booster with a gauge installed—1991–96 vehicles except manual transaxle models without ABS

3. While holding the gauge in position, tighten the setscrew.
4. Use a vacuum pump to apply 19.7 in. Hg (66 kPa) of vacuum to the power brake booster.
5. Invert the gauge and place it over the power brake pushrod.
6. Check that there is no space between the gauge and the pushrod.
7. If there is space between the gauge and pushrod, loosen the pushrod locknut and adjust the pushrod until there is no space. Tighten the pushrod locknut.
8. Install the master cylinder.

EXCEPT MANUAL TRANSAXLE MODELS WITHOUT ANTI-LOCK BRAKES (ABS)

▶ See Figures 14, 15, 16 and 17

➡A scan tool is absolutely necessary to bleed the brake hydraulic system on 1997–99 models equipped with an Anti-lock Brake System (ABS). If your vehicle is equipped with ABS, be sure to refer to the ABS bleeding procedures in this section before performing any work on your vehicle's brake hydraulic system.

The use of master cylinder gauge T92C-2500-A or equivalent is required for this procedure.

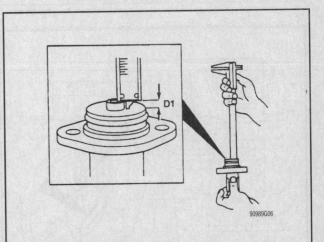

Fig. 15 Use a depth gauge to measure the height of the master cylinder gauge rod (D1)—1991–96 vehicles except manual transaxle models without ABS

6. Tighten the brass holding screw on the gauge securing the gauge rod in place.

➡️**Use care when removing the gauge from the master cylinder. If the gauge rod setting is changed during removal, a faulty measurement will be taken which could lead to a unnecessary adjustment of the brake booster pushrod.**

7. Use a depth gauge to measure the height of the master cylinder gauge rod as illustrated and record the measurement.

8. Loosen the gauge brass holding screw and set the gauge on the master cylinder as illustrated.

9. Push lightly on the end of the gauge rod, until the end of the gauge rod just bottoms in the master cylinder piston and tighten the brass holding screw.

10. Remove the gauge from the master cylinder.

11. Use a depth gauge to measure the height of the gauge rod as illustrated and record the measurement.

12. Determine the difference between measurements D1 and D2. If D2 is larger than D1, subtract D1 from D2. If D1 is larger than D2, subtract D2 from D1. Adjust the brake booster pushrod nut to lengthen or shorten the pushrod the amount equal to the difference between D1 and D2.

13. Install the master cylinder.

Proportioning Valve

REMOVAL & INSTALLATION

1991–92 Models

▶ **See Figure 18**

➡️**1991–92 models use a proportioning valve which regulates hydraulic pressure to the rear brakes. 1993–96 models use two brake pressure differential valves.**

1. Raise the car and support it with safety stands.
2. Unfasten the brake line fittings at the proportioning valve.
3. Disconnect the brake lines from the valve and cap the lines to prevent leakage and contamination.
4. Unfasten the proportioning valve mounting bolts and remove the valve.

To install:

5. Place the valve in position and install the mounting bolts. Tighten the bolts to 14–17 ft. lbs. (19–23 Nm).
6. Attach the brake lines to the valve and tighten the fittings to 10–16 ft. lbs. (13–22 Nm).
7. Bleed the brake system.

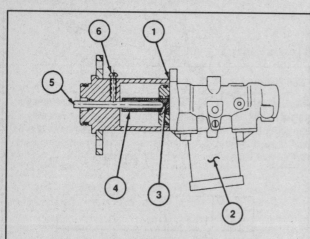

Item	Description
1	Hold Flush With Brake Master Cylinder
2	Brake Master Cylinder
3	Gauge Rod Bottoms Here
4	Brake Master Cylinder Piston
5	Push Here
6	Brass Holding Screw

90989G07

Fig. 16 Attach the gauge to the master cylinder—1991–96 vehicles except manual transaxle models without ABS

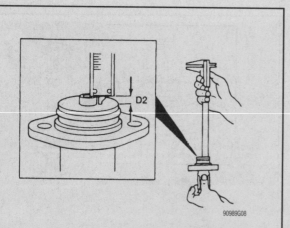

90989G08

Fig. 17 Use a depth gauge to measure the height of the gauge rod (D2)—1991–96 vehicles except manual transaxle models without ABS

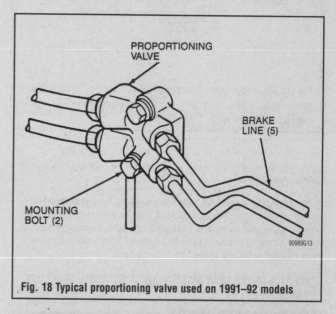

90989G13

Fig. 18 Typical proportioning valve used on 1991–92 models

Brake Pressure Differential Valve

REMOVAL & INSTALLATION

▶ **See Figures 19 and 20**

Two brake pressure differential valves are located on the brake master cylinder. When you apply the brake pedal, full rear brake circuit pressure passes through the differential valves to the rear brakes. This creates bal-

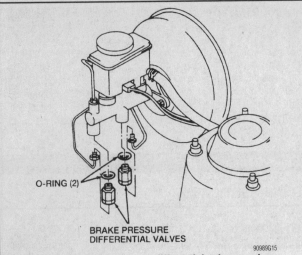

Fig. 19 Common brake pressure differential valves used on 1994–99 models without ABS

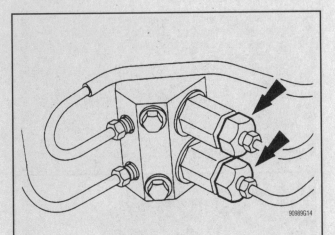

Fig. 20 Typical brake pressure differential valves (arrows) used on 1997–99 models with ABS

anced braking between the front and rear wheels and maintains a balanced hydraulic pressure at the rear wheels.

➡A scan tool is absolutely necessary to bleed the brake hydraulic system on 1997–99 models equipped with an Anti-lock Brake System (ABS). If your vehicle is equipped with ABS, be sure to refer to the ABS bleeding procedures in this section before performing any work on your vehicle's brake hydraulic system.

The brake pressure differential valve is used control hydraulic pressure to the rear brakes.
1. Unfasten the brake line-to-brake pressure differential valve fittings.
2. Disconnect the brake lines from the valves and plug the lines to avoid leakage and contamination.
3. Unscrew the valves, then remove the valves and if equipped, the O-rings. Discard the O-rings.

To install:
4. If equipped, install new O-rings and the valves Tighten the valves to 33–40 ft. lbs. (44–54 Nm).
5. Attach the brake lines to the valves and tighten the fittings to10–16 ft. lbs. (13–22 Nm).
6. Bleed the brake system.

Brake Hoses and Lines

Metal lines and rubber brake hoses should be checked frequently for leaks and external damage. Metal lines are particularly prone to crushing and kinking under the vehicle. Any such deformation can restrict the proper flow of fluid and therefore impair braking at the wheels. Rubber hoses should be checked for cracking or scraping; such damage can create a weak spot in the hose and it could fail under pressure.

Any time the lines are removed or disconnected, extreme cleanliness must be observed. Clean all joints and connections before disassembly (use a stiff bristle brush and clean brake fluid); be sure to plug the lines and ports as soon as they are opened. New lines and hoses should be flushed clean with brake fluid before installation to remove any contamination.

REMOVAL & INSTALLATION

♦ See Figures 21 thru 26

➡A scan tool is absolutely necessary to bleed the brake hydraulic system on 1997–99 models equipped with an Anti-lock Brake System (ABS). If your vehicle is equipped with ABS, be sure to refer to the ABS bleeding procedures in this section before performing any work on your vehicle's brake hydraulic system.

1. Disconnect the negative battery cable.
2. Raise and safely support the vehicle on jackstands.
3. Remove any wheel and tire assemblies necessary for access to the particular line you are removing.
4. Thoroughly clean the surrounding area at the joints to be disconnected.
5. Place a suitable catch pan under the joint to be disconnected.
6. Using two wrenches (one to hold the joint and one to turn the fitting), disconnect the hose or line to be replaced.
7. Disconnect the other end of the line or hose, moving the drain pan if necessary. Always use a back-up wrench to avoid damaging the fitting.
8. Disconnect any retaining clips or brackets holding the line and remove the line from the vehicle.

➡If the brake system is to remain open for more time than it takes to swap lines, tape or plug each remaining clip and port to keep contaminants out and fluid in.

To install:
9. Install the new line or hose, starting with the end farthest from the master cylinder. Connect the other end, then confirm that both fittings are correctly threaded and turn smoothly using finger pressure. Make sure the new line will not rub against any other part. Brake lines must be at least 1/2 in. (13mm) from the steering column and other moving parts. Any

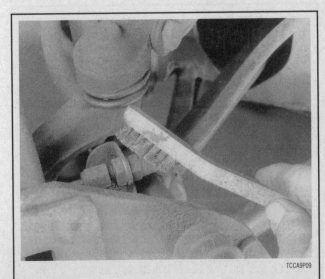

Fig. 21 Use a brush to clean the fittings of any debris

90989P39

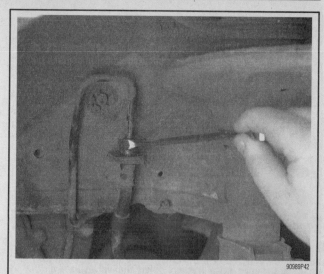

Fig. 22 Loosen the banjo bolt fitting from the rear of the caliper

90989P40

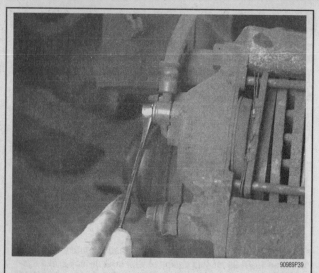

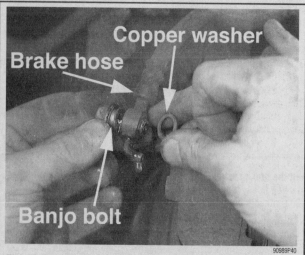

Fig. 23 Remove the hose from the caliper and discard the copper washers

90989P41

Fig. 24 A flare nut type wrench is preferable for loosening any brake line fittings

90989P42

Fig. 25 Use a flare nut wrench to loosen the brake line fitting

90989P43

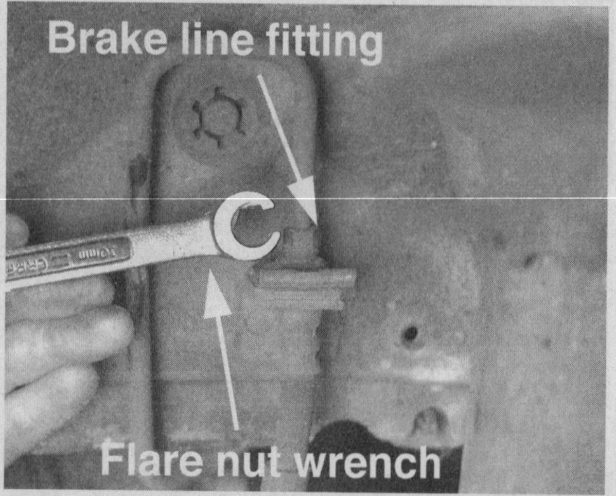

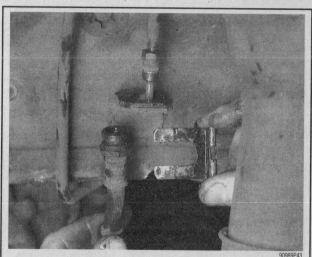

Fig. 26 Remove the hose retaining clip and separate the hose from the brake line

protective shielding or insulators must be reinstalled in the original location.

WARNING

Make sure the hose is NOT kinked or touching any part of the frame or suspension after installation. These conditions may cause the hose to fail prematurely.

10. Using two wrenches as before, tighten each fitting.
11. Install any retaining clips or brackets on the lines.
12. If removed, install the wheel and tire assemblies, then carefully lower the vehicle to the ground.
13. Refill the brake master cylinder reservoir with clean, fresh brake fluid, meeting DOT 3 specifications. Properly bleed the brake system.
14. Connect the negative battery cable.

Bleeding the Brake System

See Figures 27, 28 and 29

Bleeding the hydraulic brake system on 1991–99 models without ABS is performed using the following procedure. On 1994–96 models with ABS, you

also may also use the following procedure. However, a scan tool is absolutely necessary to bleed the brake hydraulic system on 1997–99 models equipped with an Anti-lock Brake System (ABS). If your 1997–99 vehicle is equipped with ABS, be sure to refer to the ABS bleeding procedures in this section before performing any work on your vehicle's brake hydraulic system.

1. Clean the area around the master cylinder filler cap and remove the cap.

2. Fill the reservoir with clean brake fluid and install the cap.

3. If the master cylinder is known or suspected to have air in the bore, it must be bled before any of the wheel cylinders or calipers. To bleed the master cylinder, position a shop towel under the rear master cylinder outlet fitting and loosen the fitting approximately ¾ turn. Have an assistant depress the brake pedal slowly through its full range of travel. Close the outlet fitting and let the pedal return slowly to the fully released position. Wait 5 seconds, then repeat the operation until all air bubbles disappear.

❊❊ WARNING

Be careful not to spill brake fluid on painted surfaces, as it can destroy the finish. If any brake fluid is spilled, rinse the area immediately with water.

4. Repeat the master cylinder bleeding procedure at the front master cylinder outlet fitting.

5. Position a correct size box-end wrench or flare nut wrench on the bleeder screw at the right rear wheel.

➡**Always bleed the longest line first, which is the right rear line.**

6. Attach one end of a clear ose to the brake bleeder screw and the other end into a container half full of clean brake fluid.

7. Loosen the bleeder screw while an assistant apply the brake pedal slowly through its entire travel.

8. Close the brake bleeder and then have the assistant release the brake pedal.

9. Continue bleeding the right rear wheel until the fluid is free of air bubbles.

➡**DO NOT allow the master cylinder to run out of brake fluid. Only use fresh DOT 3 or equivalent brake fluid from a closed container.**

10. Repeat the procedure on the left front wheel, then the left rear and finally the right front wheel.

11. Throughout the brake bleeding process, continually check the brake master cylinder and top off the fluid as required.

12. If the brake pedal is spongy, repeat the brake bleeding procedure.

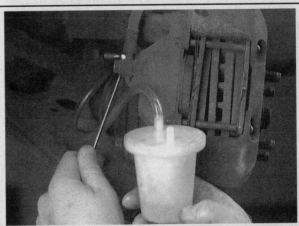

Fig. 28 Attach one end of a clear hose to the bleeder screw and place the other end in a clear container half full of clean brake fluid, then use a suitable wrench to open and close the bleeder

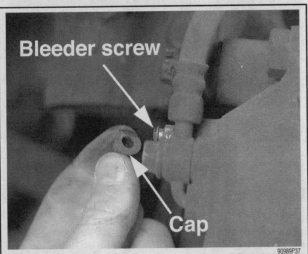

Fig. 27 If so equipped, remove the protective cap from the bleeder screw—disc brake caliper shown

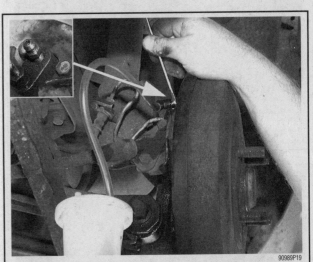

Fig. 29 On drum brakes, the bleeder screw is located behind the wheel cylinder, adjacent to the brake line fitting

DISC BRAKES

Brake Pads

REMOVAL & INSTALLATION

Front Brakes

♦ **See Figures 30 thru 37**

1. Remove the master cylinder reservoir cap and check the fluid level in the reservoir. Remove brake fluid until the reservoir is ½ full. Discard the removed fluid.
2. Raise and safely support the vehicle.
3. Remove the wheel and tire assembly.
4. Remove the M-spring.
5. Remove the W-spring.
6. Remove the two disc brake pad locating pins.
7. Remove the brake pads and shims from the brake caliper.
8. Inspect the brake rotor. Resurface or replace if needed.

To install:

9. Use a suitable tool to push the piston into the brake caliper bore.

10. Apply a suitable grease between the shims and the disc brake pad guide plates and position the brake pads and shims into the brake caliper.
11. Install the two brake pad locating pins.
12. Install the W-spring.
13. Install the M-spring.
14. Install the wheel and tire assembly.
15. Lower the vehicle.
16. Pump the brake pedal several times prior to moving the vehicle to position the brake pads.
17. Check the fluid level in the master cylinder reservoir and fill as needed.
18. Road test the vehicle and check for proper brake system operation.

Rear Brakes

1. Remove the master cylinder reservoir cap and check the fluid level in the reservoir. Remove brake fluid until the reservoir is ½ full. Discard the removed fluid.
2. Raise and safely support the vehicle.
3. Remove the wheel and tire assembly.
4. If necessary, remove the screw plug and turn the adjustment gear counterclockwise with an Allen wrench to pull the piston fully inward.

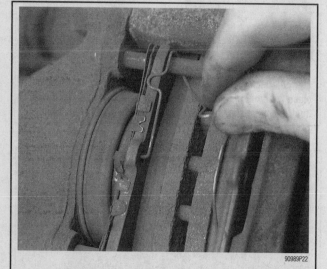

90989P22

Fig. 30 Remove the M-spring from the locating pin

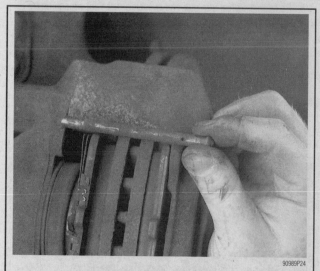

90989P24

Fig. 32 Remove the locating pins from the caliper assembly

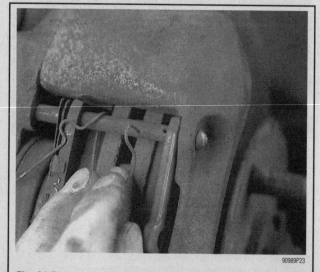

90989P23

Fig. 31 Remove the W-spring from the locating pin

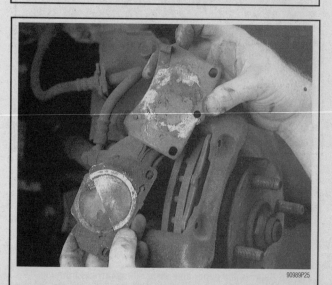

90989P25

Fig. 33 Remove the inner brake pad and shim from the caliper

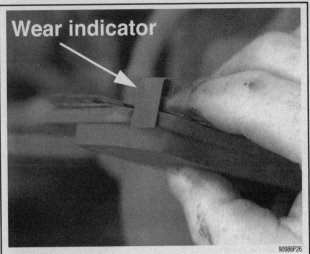

Fig. 34 A brake pad wear indicator will rub against the rotor and cause a squealing sound when the pads are worn

Fig. 35 Remove the outer brake pad from the caliper

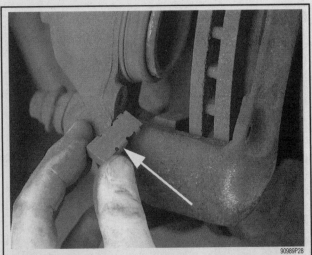

Fig. 36 Remove the upper and lower shims (arrow) from the caliper

Fig. 37 A C-clamp and socket placed on the outside of the outer pad (see inset) can be used to press the caliper piston into its bore

5. Remove the lower brake caliper bolt.

6. Using a small prybar, pivot the caliper on its mounting bracket to access the brake pads. If the upper lock bolt requires lubrication or service, remove it and suspend the caliper with mechanic's wire.

7. Remove the brake pads, M-spring and if equipped, shims and guides.

8. Inspect the brake rotor. Resurface or replace if needed.

To install:

9. Apply an appropriate brake pad grease between the shims and brake pads.

10. Pivot the caliper on its mounting bracket and position the brake pads, shims, spring and guides to the brake rotor.

11. Lubricate and install the caliper bolt(s). Tighten the bolt(s) to 33–43 ft. lbs. (45–59 Nm).

12. Turn the adjustment gear clockwise with an Allen wrench until the brake pads just touch the rotor, then loosen the gear 1/3 of a turn. Install the screw plug and tighten to 9–12 ft. lbs. (12–16 Nm).

13. Install the wheel and tire assembly.

14. Lower the vehicle.

15. Pump the brake pedal several times prior to moving the vehicle to position the brake pads.

16. Check the brake fluid level in the master cylinder reservoir and fill if needed.

17. Road test the vehicle and check for proper brake system operation.

INSPECTION

Inspect the brake pads for wear using a ruler or Vernier caliper. The maximum thickness is 0.39 inch (10mm) and the minimum thickness allowable is 0.08 inch (2.0mm). If the lining is thinner than specification or there is evidence of the lining being contaminated by brake fluid or oil, replace all brake pad assemblies (a complete axle set).

Brake Caliper

REMOVAL & INSTALLATION

Front Brakes

▶ See Figures 38 thru 43

➡A scan tool is absolutely necessary to bleed the brake hydraulic system on 1997–99 models equipped with an Anti-lock Brake System (ABS). If your vehicle is equipped with ABS, be sure to refer to the ABS bleeding procedures in this section before performing any work on your vehicle's brake hydraulic system.

1. Raise and safely support the vehicle.
2. Remove the wheel and tire assembly.
3. Remove the disc brake pads.
4. Unfasten the two brake caliper retaining bolts and remove the brake caliper.
5. Either support the caliper with a piece of mechanic's wire, or unfasten the banjo bolt securing the brake hose to the brake caliper and remove the caliper from the vehicle. Discard the two copper sealing washers.

To install:

6. Place the brake caliper in position and install the two brake caliper retaining bolts. Tighten the bolts to 29–36 ft. lbs. (39–49 Nm) on 1991–96 models and 36–43 ft. lbs. (49–59 Nm) on 1997–99 models.
7. If removed, attach the brake hose to the brake caliper and install the banjo bolt with two new copper sealing washers. Tighten the banjo bolt to 16–20 ft. lbs. (22–29 Nm).
8. Install the disc brake pads.
9. Bleed the brake system.
10. Install the wheel and tire assembly.
11. Lower the vehicle.
12. Pump the brake pedal several times to position the brake pads to the brake rotor.
13. Road test the vehicle and check the brake system for proper operation.

Fig. 40 Remove the caliper assembly from its mounting . . .

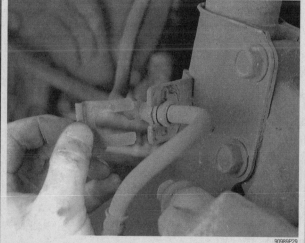

Fig. 38 If necessary, remove the clip that attaches the hose to the front strut

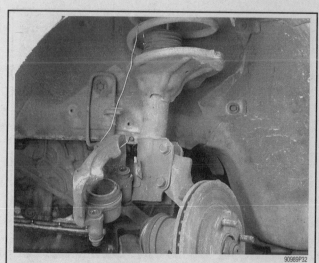

Fig. 41 . . . and support the caliper with a piece of mechanic's wire

Fig. 39 Unfasten the disc brake caliper retaining bolts (arrows)

Fig. 42 Unfasten the banjo bolt securing the brake hose to the brake caliper . . .

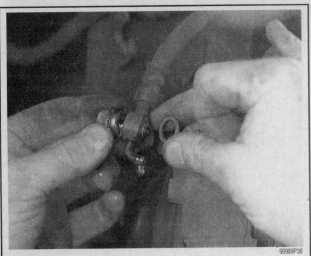

Fig. 43 . . . then detach the brake hose and discard the copper washers

Rear Brakes

➡A scan tool is absolutely necessary to bleed the brake hydraulic system on 1997–99 models equipped with an Anti-lock Brake System (ABS). If your vehicle is equipped with ABS, be sure to refer to the ABS bleeding procedures in this section before performing any work on your vehicle's brake hydraulic system.

1. Raise and safely support the vehicle.
2. Remove the wheel and tire assembly.
3. Remove the disc brake pads.
4. Remove the parking brake cable bracket bolt and position the bracket aside.
5. Remove the parking brake cable from the operating lever.
6. Unfasten the banjo bolt securing the brake hose to the brake caliper. Discard the two copper sealing washers.
7. Remove the upper brake caliper retaining bolt.
8. Slide the brake caliper off the mounting bracket and remove from the vehicle.

To install:

9. Place the brake caliper on the mounting bracket and slide into position.
10. Install the upper brake caliper retaining bolt. Tighten the bolt to 33–43 ft. lbs. (45–59 Nm).
11. Install the brake hose to the brake caliper and secure with the banjo bolt using two new copper sealing washers. Tighten the banjo bolt to 16–22 ft. lbs. (22–29 Nm).
12. Connect the parking brake cable to the operating lever. Position the bracket and install the bracket bolt.
13. Install the disc brake pads.
14. Bleed the brake system.
15. Install the wheel and tire assembly.
16. Adjust the parking brake.
17. Lower the vehicle.
18. Pump the brake pedal several times to position the brake pads to the brake rotor.
19. Road test the vehicle and check the brake system for proper operation.

OVERHAUL

♦ **See Figures 44 thru 51**

➡A scan tool is absolutely necessary to bleed the brake hydraulic system on 1997–99 models equipped with an Anti-lock Brake System (ABS). If your vehicle is equipped with ABS, be sure to refer to the ABS bleeding procedures in this section before performing any work on your vehicle's brake hydraulic system.

➡Some vehicles may be equipped with dual piston calipers. The procedure to overhaul the caliper is essentially the same with the exception of multiple pistons, O-rings and dust boots.

1. Remove the caliper from the vehicle and place on a clean workbench.

✷✷ CAUTION

NEVER place your fingers in front of the pistons in an attempt to catch or protect the pistons when applying compressed air. This could result in personal injury!

➡Depending upon the vehicle, there are two different ways to remove the piston from the caliper. Refer to the brake pad replacement procedure to make sure you have the correct procedure for your vehicle.

2. The first method is as follows:
   a. Stuff a shop towel or a block of wood into the caliper to catch the piston.
   b. Remove the caliper piston using compressed air applied into the caliper inlet hole. Inspect the piston for scoring, nicks, corrosion and/or worn or damaged chrome plating. The piston must be replaced if any of these conditions are found.
3. For the second method, you must rotate the piston to retract it from the caliper.
4. If equipped, remove the anti-rattle clip.
5. Use a prytool to remove the caliper boot, being careful not to scratch the housing bore.
6. Remove the piston seals from the groove in the caliper bore.
7. Carefully loosen the brake bleeder valve cap and valve from the caliper housing.
8. Inspect the caliper bores, pistons and mounting threads for scoring or excessive wear.
9. Use crocus cloth to polish out light corrosion from the piston and bore.
10. Clean all parts with denatured alcohol and dry with compressed air.

To assemble:

11. Lubricate and install the bleeder valve and cap.
12. Install the new seals into the caliper bore grooves, making sure they are not twisted.
13. Lubricate the piston bore.
14. Install the pistons and boots into the bores of the calipers and push to the bottom of the bores.
15. Use a suitable driving tool to seat the boots in the housing.
16. Install the caliper in the vehicle.
17. Install the wheel and tire assembly, then carefully lower the vehicle.
18. Properly bleed the brake system.

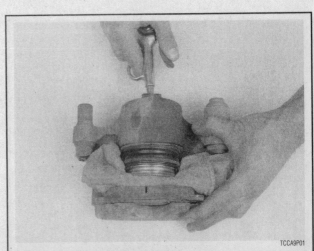

Fig. 44 For some types of calipers, use compressed air to drive the piston out of the caliper, but make sure to keep your fingers clear

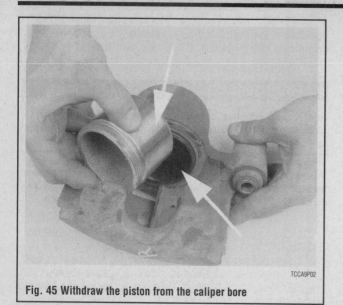

Fig. 45 Withdraw the piston from the caliper bore

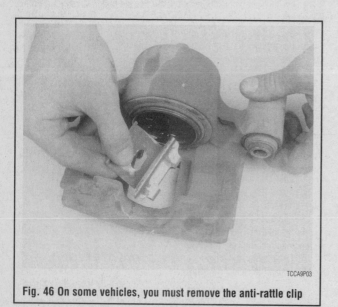

Fig. 46 On some vehicles, you must remove the anti-rattle clip

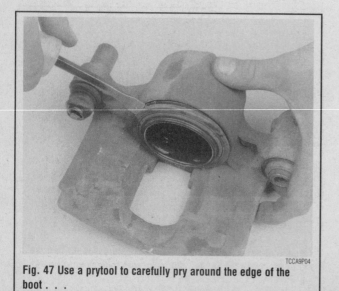

Fig. 47 Use a prytool to carefully pry around the edge of the boot . . .

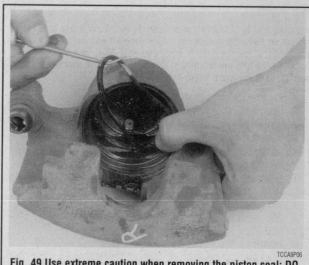

Fig. 48 . . . then remove the boot from the caliper housing, taking care not to score or damage the bore

Fig. 49 Use extreme caution when removing the piston seal; DO NOT scratch the caliper bore

Fig. 50 Use the proper size driving tool and a mallet to properly seal the boots in the caliper housing

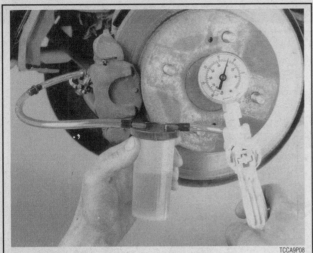

Fig. 51 There are tools, such as this Mighty-Vac, available to assist in proper brake system bleeding

Fig. 52 Remove the caliper and support it with a piece of mechanic's wire . . .

Brake Disc (Rotor)

REMOVAL & INSTALLATION

Front Brakes

▶ See Figures 52 and 53

1. Raise and safely support the vehicle.
2. Remove the wheel and tire assembly.
3. Unfasten the disc brake caliper retaining bolts.
4. Remove the disc brake caliper and secure the caliper aside with mechanic's wire. Do not disconnect the brake hose.
5. Pull the brake rotor from the hub.
6. Inspect the rotor and refinish or replace, as necessary. If refinishing, the minimum thickness rotor thickness is stamped on the brake rotor.

To install:
7. Place the brake rotor to the hub. Make sure the mating surfaces are free of rust which may prevent the brake rotor from seating properly.
8. Remove the mechanic's wire and position the brake caliper.
9. Install the brake caliper retaining bolts to specification.
10. Install the wheel and tire assembly.
11. Lower the vehicle.
12. Pump the brake pedal several times to position the brake pads before moving the vehicle.
13. Road test the vehicle and check the brake system for proper operation.

Rear Brakes

1. Raise and safely support the vehicle.
2. Remove the wheel and tire assembly.
3. On 1997–99 models, unfasten the rear disc support bracket bolts and remove the bracket.
4. Remove the two disc brake rotor retaining screws.
5. Remove the lower caliper retaining bolt.
6. Pivot the caliper and remove the disc brake pads.
7. Pivot the caliper and remove the disc brake rotor from the hub.
8. Inspect the rotor and refinish or replace, as necessary. If refinishing, the minimum thickness is stamped on the brake rotor.

To install:
9. Pivot the brake caliper and position the disc brake rotor onto the hub.
10. Install the disc brake pads and shims.
11. Install the lower brake caliper retaining bolt and tighten to specification.
12. Install the brake rotor retaining screws.
13. On 1997–99 models, install the rear disc support bracket and

Fig. 53 . . . then pull the brake rotor from the hub

tighten the bolts to 34–44 ft. lbs. (46–60 Nm).
14. Install the wheel and tire assembly.
15. Lower the vehicle.
16. Pump the brake pedal several times to position the brake pads before moving the vehicle.
17. Road test the vehicle and check the brake system for proper operation.

INSPECTION

1. Using a brake rotor micrometer or Vernier caliper, measure the rotor thickness in several places around the rotor.
2. The disc brake rotor minimum thickness is as follows:
- Front disc brake rotor—1991–99 models: 0.79 inch (20mm)
- Rear disc brake rotor—1991–96 models: 0.28 inch. (7mm)
- Rear disc brake rotor—1997–99 models: 0.04 inch (1.0mm)
3. If the rotor thickness exceeds the limit, replace the rotor.
4. Mount a magnetic base dial indicator to the strut member and zero the indicator stylus on the face of the rotor. Rotate the rotor 360 degrees by hand and record the run-out.
5. The front and rear rotor run-out should be a maximum of 0.004 inch (0.1mm) on 1991–96 models and 0.05 inch (0.002mm) on 1997–99 models. If the run-out exceeds the limit, replace the rotor.

DRUM BRAKES

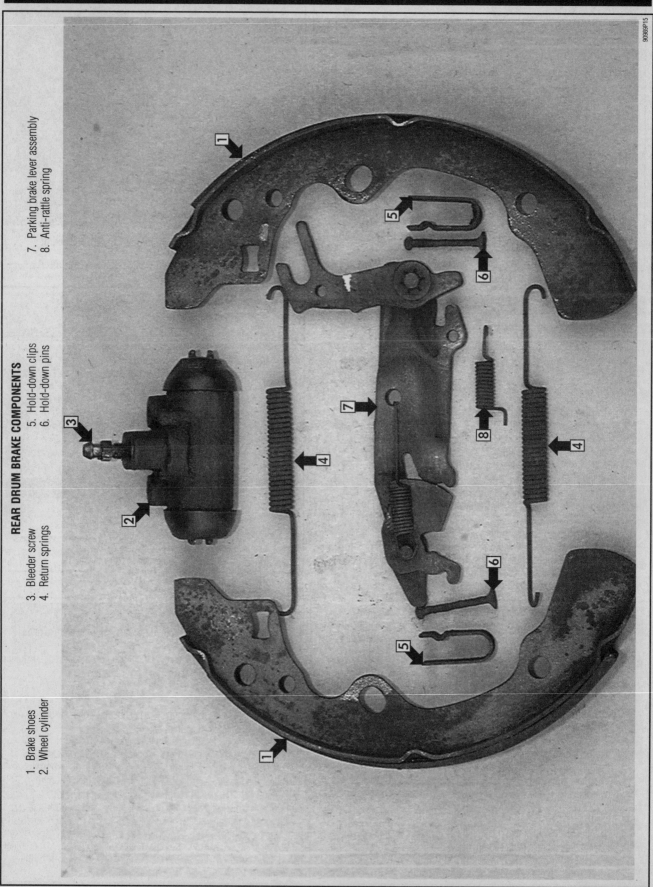

REAR DRUM BRAKE COMPONENTS

1. Brake shoes
2. Wheel cylinder
3. Bleeder screw
4. Return springs
5. Hold-down clips
6. Hold-down pins
7. Parking brake lever assembly
8. Anti-rattle spring

90989P15

Brake Drums

REMOVAL & INSTALLATION

▶ See Figures 54, 55 and 56

1. Raise and safely support the vehicle.
2. Remove the wheel and tire assembly.
3. Remove the two brake drum retaining screws.
4. Pull the brake drum from the hub.
5. If the drum will not come off, insert the screws in the other screw holes in the drum and tighten the screws. This should unseat the drum and make it easier to remove.
6. Inspect the drum and refinish or replace, as necessary. If refinishing, check the maximum inside diameter specification.

To install:

7. If necessary, adjust the brake shoes to fit the brake drum.
8. Place the brake drum on the hub.
9. Install the two brake drum retaining screws. Tighten the screws to 89–123 inch lbs. (10–14 Nm).
10. Install the wheel and tire assembly.

Fig. 56 If the drum will not come off, insert the screws in the alternate holes in the drum, then tighten the screws to unseat the drum

11. Lower the vehicle.
12. Check the brake system for proper operation.

INSPECTION

▶ See Figure 57

1. Use denatured alcohol to clean any dust, brake fluid or other contaminants from the drum.
2. Visually inspect the inside surface of the drum for scratches and uneven or abnormal wear.
3. Resurface the drum if the damage is minor and replace the drum if the damage is excessive.
4. Measure the inside diameter of the drum with a brake drum micrometer.

❊❊ WARNING

Make sure to check the drum-to-shoe contact after repairing or replacing the drum.

5. If the drum diameter exceeds 7.91 inches (201.0mm), replace the drum.

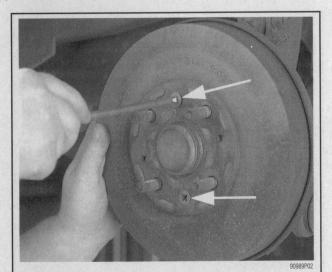

Fig. 54 Unfasten the brake drum retaining screws (arrows) . . .

Fig. 55 . . . and slide the brake drum from the hub

Fig. 57 The brake drum maximum diameter is usually stamped on the drum

Brake Shoes

INSPECTION

1. Check the brake linings for peeling, cracks or extremely uneven wear.
2. Use a Vernier caliper to measure the lining thickness.
3. If the lining thickness is less than 0.04 inch (1.0mm), replace the brake shoes.
4. If there is evidence of the lining being contaminated by brake fluid or oil, replace the shoes.
5. Always replace the brake shoe assemblies on both sides.

REMOVAL & INSTALLATION

▶ **See Figures 58 thru 68**

1. Raise and safely support the vehicle.
2. Remove the wheel and tire assembly.
3. Remove the brake drum.
4. Remove the two brake shoe return springs.
5. Remove the right-hand anti-rattle spring.

Fig. 60 Use needlenose pliers to remove the lower brake shoe return spring . . .

Fig. 58 View of the rear drum brake components in their installed positions

Fig. 61 . . . and the upper brake shoe return spring

Fig. 59 Use a spray brake parts cleaner to remove dirt, dust and grime from the rear brake components

Fig. 62 Remove the right-hand anti-rattle spring

Fig. 63 Depress the brake shoe hold-down clips and rotate them a quarter turn to release from their pins

Fig. 66 Use a wire brush to clean the dirt from the backing plate, especially the brake shoe-to-backing plate contact surfaces

Fig. 64 Remove the leading . . .

Fig. 67 If necessary, remove the parking brake actuating lever through the slot in the backing plate

6. Depress and twist the two brake shoe hold-down springs (clips) ¼ turn and remove the springs.

7. Remove the leading and trailing shoes from the brake backing plate.

8. If necessary, disconnect the parking brake cable from the parking brake actuating lever and remove the lever.

To install:

9. Use a suitable high temperature grease to lightly lubricate the brake shoe contact points on the backing plate.

➡**Make sure the wheel cylinder retaining bolts are tight.**

10. If removed, install the parking brake lever and attach the return spring and cable assembly.

11. Position the trailing brake shoe on the backing plate and install one of the brake shoe hold-down springs.

12. Position the leading brake shoe on the backing plate and install the other brake shoe hold-down spring.

13. Install the right-hand anti-rattle spring.

14. Install the two brake shoe return springs.

15. Using a brake adjusting gauge, measure the inside diameter of the brake drum.

16. Compare the brake drum measurement to the brake shoes.

Fig. 65 . . . and the trailing brake shoe from the backing plate

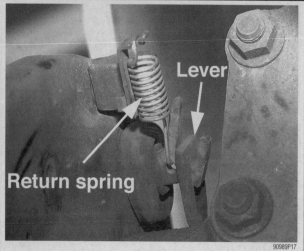

Fig. 68 Install the parking brake lever, then attach the return spring and cable assembly

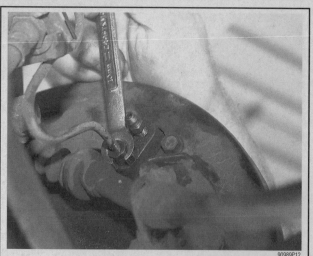

Fig. 69 Loosen the wheel cylinder-to-brake line flare nut using a suitable flare nut wrench

17. Adjust the brake shoes by inserting a brake adjustment tool into the knurled quadrant of the rear quad operating lever and adjust the shoes to the same measurement as the brake drum.

18. Install the brake drum.

19. Install the wheel and tire assembly.

20. Lower the vehicle.

21. Check the brake system operation by making several stops while driving slowly forward.

ADJUSTMENT

1. Raise and safely support the vehicle.

2. Remove the wheel and tire assembly.

3. Remove the brake drum.

4. Using a brake adjusting gauge, measure the inside diameter of the brake drum.

5. Compare the brake drum measurement to the brake shoes.

6. Adjust the brake shoes by inserting a brake adjustment tool into the knurled quadrant of the rear quad operating lever and adjust the shoes to the same measurement as the brake drum.

7. Install the brake drum.

8. Install the wheel and tire assembly.

9. Lower the vehicle.

10. Check the brake system operation by making several stops while driving slowly forward.

Wheel Cylinder

REMOVAL & INSTALLATION

▶ See Figures 69, 70 and 71

➡A scan tool is absolutely necessary to bleed the brake hydraulic system on 1997–99 models equipped with an Anti-lock Brake System (ABS). If your vehicle is equipped with ABS, be sure to refer to the ABS bleeding procedures in this section before performing any work on your vehicle's brake hydraulic system.

1. Raise and safely support the vehicle.

2. Remove the wheel and tire assembly.

3. Remove the brake drum.

4. On 1991–96 models, remove the upper brake shoe return spring.

5. On 1997–99 models, remove the brake shoes.

6. Using a suitable flare nut wrench, loosen the wheel cylinder-to-brake line flare nut.

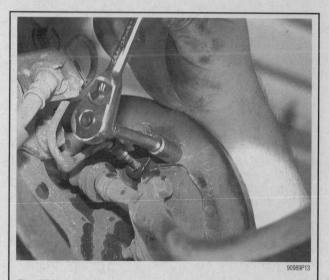

Fig. 70 Unfasten the two wheel cylinder retaining bolts . . .

Fig. 71 . . . then remove the wheel cylinder from the backing plate

7. On 1991–96 models, pull the clip from the brake line retaining bracket and remove the brake line from the retaining bracket.

8. Remove the brake line from the wheel cylinder and cap the brake line fitting.

9. Unfasten the two wheel cylinder retaining bolts and remove the wheel cylinder from the backing plate.

10. Remove and discard the wheel cylinder gasket.

To install:

11. Install a new wheel cylinder gasket onto the backing plate.

12. Position the wheel cylinder onto the backing plate and loosely install the two retaining bolts.

13. Install the brake line to the wheel cylinder and tighten the flare nut fitting to 12–16 ft. lbs. (16–22 Nm).

14. Tighten the wheel cylinder retaining bolts to 84–108 inch lbs. (10–13 Nm).

15. On 1991–96 models, attach the brake hose to the retaining bracket and install the clip.

16. On 1991–96 models, install the upper brake shoe return spring.

17. On 1997–99 models, install the brake shoes.

18. Have an assistant gently press the brake pedal to verify the operation of the automatic brake adjuster.

19. Manually adjust the brakes if required.

20. Install the brake drum.

21. Install the wheel and tire assembly.

22. Bleed the brake system.

23. Lower the vehicle.

24. Fill the brake master cylinder as required.

25. Road test the vehicle and check the brake system for proper operation.

OVERHAUL

▶ See Figures 72 thru 81

➡A scan tool is absolutely necessary to bleed the brake hydraulic system on 1997–99 models equipped with an Anti-lock Brake System (ABS). If your vehicle is equipped with ABS, be sure to refer to the ABS bleeding procedures in this section before performing any work on your vehicle's brake hydraulic system.

Wheel cylinder overhaul kits may be available, but often at little or no savings over a reconditioned wheel cylinder. It often makes sense with these components to substitute a new or reconditioned part instead of attempting an overhaul.

If no replacement is available, or you would prefer to overhaul your wheel cylinders, the following procedure may be used. When rebuilding and installing wheel cylinders, avoid getting any contaminants into the system. Always use clean, new, high quality brake fluid. If dirty or improper fluid has been used, it will be necessary to drain the entire system, flush the system with proper brake fluid, replace all rubber components, then refill and bleed the system.

1. Remove the wheel cylinder from the vehicle and place on a clean workbench.

2. First remove and discard the old rubber boots, then withdraw the pistons. Piston cylinders are equipped with seals and a spring assembly, all located behind the pistons in the cylinder bore.

3. Remove the remaining inner components, seals and spring assembly. Compressed air may be useful in removing these components. If no compressed air is available, be VERY careful not to score the wheel cylinder bore when removing parts from it. Discard all components for which replacements were supplied in the rebuild kit.

4. Wash the cylinder and metal parts in denatured alcohol or clean brake fluid.

⁕⁕ WARNING

Never use a mineral-based solvent such as gasoline, kerosene or paint thinner for cleaning purposes. These solvents will swell rubber components and quickly deteriorate them.

Fig. 72 Remove the outer boots from the wheel cylinder

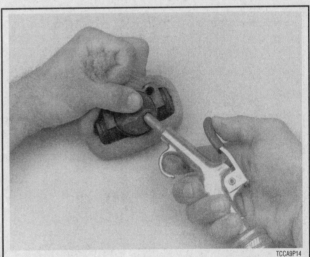
Fig. 73 Compressed air can be used to remove the pistons and seals

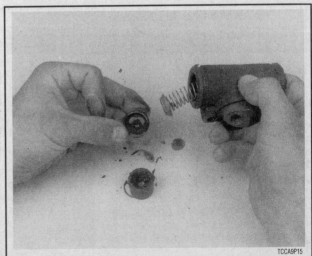
Fig. 74 Remove the pistons, cup seals and spring from the cylinder

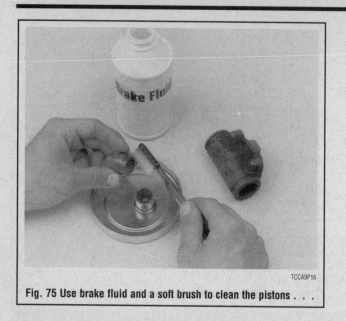

Fig. 75 Use brake fluid and a soft brush to clean the pistons . . .

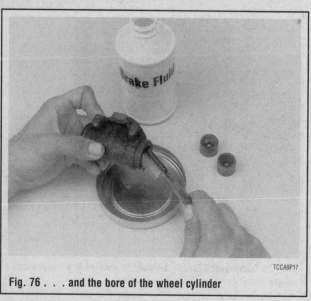

Fig. 76 . . . and the bore of the wheel cylinder

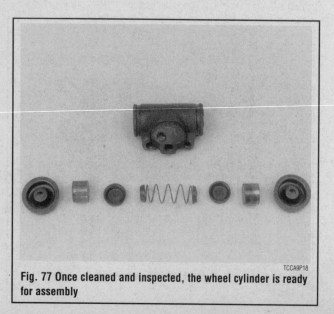

Fig. 77 Once cleaned and inspected, the wheel cylinder is ready for assembly

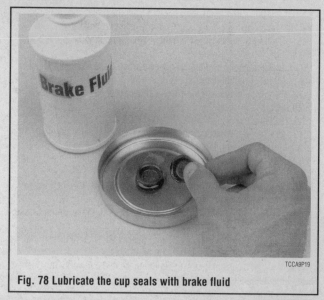

Fig. 78 Lubricate the cup seals with brake fluid

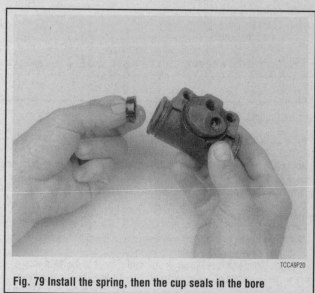

Fig. 79 Install the spring, then the cup seals in the bore

Fig. 80 Lightly lubricate the pistons, then install them

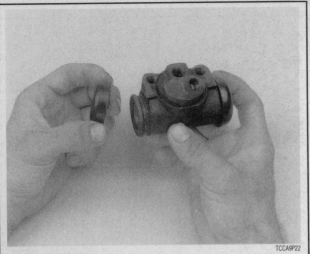

TCCA9P22

Fig. 81 The boots can now be installed over the wheel cylinder ends

5. Allow the parts to air dry or use compressed air. Do not use rags for cleaning, since lint will remain in the cylinder bore.

6. Inspect the piston and replace it if it shows scratches.

7. Lubricate the cylinder bore and seals using clean brake fluid.

8. Position the spring assembly.

9. Install the inner seals, then the pistons.

10. Install the wheel cylinder.

11. Insert the new boots into the counterbores by hand. Do not lubricate the boots.

PARKING BRAKE

Cables

REMOVAL & INSTALLATION

Front Cable

1. Disconnect the negative battery cable.

2. Remove the parking brake console.

3. Unplug the parking brake signal switch electrical connector.

4. Remove the cable adjusting nut.

5. Unfasten the two parking brake control retaining bolts and remove the parking brake control.

6. Remove the front parking brake cable and conduit from the cable guide.

7. Raise and safely support the vehicle.

8. Remove the rear exhaust pipe and resonator heat shields.

9. Remove the equalizer return spring and disconnect both rear parking brake cables from the equalizer.

10. Remove the front parking brake cable, conduit and equalizer from the vehicle.

To install:

11. Position the front parking brake cable, conduit and equalizer to the vehicle.

12. Connect the rear parking brake cables to the equalizer and install the equalizer return spring.

13. Install the exhaust heat shields.

14. Lower the vehicle.

15. Position the front parking brake cable and conduit to the cable guide.

16. Install the parking brake control and the two retaining bolts. Tighten the bolts to 14–19 ft. lbs. (19–26 Nm).

17. Fit the cable to the parking brake control and install the adjusting nut.

18. Attach the parking brake signal switch electrical connector.

19. Install the parking brake console.

20. Connect the negative battery cable.

21. Adjust the parking brake.

Rear Cable

1. Disconnect the negative battery cable.

2. Remove the parking brake console.

3. Unplug the parking brake signal switch electrical connector.

4. Remove the cable adjusting nut.

5. Raise and safely support the vehicle.

6. Remove the rear exhaust pipe and resonator heat shields.

7. Remove the equalizer return spring and disconnect both rear parking brake cables from the equalizer.

8. Unfasten the clip that attaches the cable to the retaining bracket located near the equalizer. Remove the cable from the bracket.

9. On 1991–96 models, unfasten the cable routing bracket bolt from the floorpan and remove the bracket.

10. On 1997–99 models, unfasten the bolt from the front bracket on the parking brake rear cable and remove the bracket.

11. On 1991–96 models, unfasten the two cable routing bracket nuts from the trailing link and remove the bracket.

12. On 1997–99 models, unfasten the bolt from the rear bracket on the rear cable and remove the bracket.

13. On 1991–96 models equipped with rear drum brakes, unfasten the two cable retaining bracket bolts from the backing plate and remove the bracket.

14. On 1997–99 models equipped with rear drum brakes, disconnect the cable from the parking brake actuating lever.

15. On 1991–96 models equipped with rear disc brakes, unfasten the parking brake bracket bolt and position the parking brake bracket aside.

16. On 1997–99 models equipped with rear disc brakes, remove the cable retaining clip, slide the cable from caliper bracket and disconnect the cable from the rear brake actuating lever.

17. Remove the rear cable and conduit from the parking brake actuating lever.

18. Remove the rear cable from the vehicle.

To install:

19. Position the cable onto the parking brake actuating lever.

20. On 1991–96 models equipped with rear drum brakes, position the parking brake cable bracket onto the backing plate and install the two bolts. Tighten the bolts to 14–19 ft. lbs. (19–25 Nm).

21. On 1997–99 models equipped with rear drum brakes, connect the cable to the parking brake actuating lever.

22. On 1991–96 models equipped with rear disc brakes, install the parking brake bracket and retaining bolt.

23. On 1991–96 models equipped with rear disc brakes, attach the cable to the rear brake actuating lever, slide the cable onto caliper bracket and install the cable retaining clip.

24. On 1991–96 models, position the cable routing bracket onto the trailing link and install the two nuts. Tighten the nuts to 12–17 ft. lbs. (16–23 Nm).

25. On 1997–99 models, install the rear bracket on the rear cable and tighten the bolt to 14–18 ft. lbs. (19–25 Nm).

26. On 1991–96 models, position the cable routing bracket to the floor pan and install the mounting bolt. Tighten the bolt to 14–19 ft. lbs. (19–25 Nm).

27. On 1997–99 models, install the front bracket on the parking brake rear cable and tighten the bolt to14–18 ft. lbs. (19–25 Nm).

28. Position the cable into the retaining bracket near the equalizer and install the clip.

29. Install the cables into the equalizer and install the equalizer return spring.

30. Install the rear exhaust pipe and resonator heat shields.

31. Lower the vehicle.

32. Install the adjusting nut.

33. If removed, install the parking brake console.

34. Connect the negative battery cable.

35. Adjust the parking brake.

ADJUSTMENT

♦ See Figure 82

❊❊ WARNING

Use caution when performing a parking brake adjustment which requires operating the vehicle in Reverse.

1. Start the engine and place the transaxle in **R**.
2. With the vehicle slowly moving in reverse, apply the parking brake lever several times.

Parking brake adjusting nut

90989P21

Fig. 82 Turn the parking brake adjusting nut until the parking brake control clicks 5–7 notches

3. Stop the vehicle and move the gearshift selector to the **N** or **P** position.
4. Shut the engine **OFF**.
5. Turn the parking brake adjusting nut until the parking brake control clicks 5–7 notches when pulled up with a force of 22 pounds (98 N).
6. Check the parking brake system for proper operation.

ANTI-LOCK BRAKE SYSTEM (ABS)

General Information

The Anti-lock Brake System (ABS) functions by releasing and applying fluid pressure to either the front disc brake calipers or the rear drum brake wheel cylinders during certain braking conditions. The ABS only actuates when one or more wheels approach a slip condition. The ABS automatically senses the slip and activates the fluid pressure control function.

The anti-lock actuator assembly is not used under normal braking conditions. Under normal conditions, fluid from the master cylinder enters the two inlet ports located on the actuator assembly. The fluid then flows through the normally open solenoid valves to each respective wheel location.

The anti-lock wheel speed sensors operate on the magnetic induction principle. As the teeth on the sensor indicator rotate past the stationary sensor, a signal proportional to the speed of rotation is generated and sent via a cable to the control module.

The anti-lock relay is controlled by the control module. The relay is grounded by the control module to power up the system. The control module consists of the fail safe and motor relays. The fail safe relay inhibits solenoid operation and turns the anti-lock brake warning indicator on and off. The motor relay controls pump and motor operation.

The ABS system is operated and monitored by a control module. The control receives readings from the two rear and two front wheel speed sensors and uses this information to compare wheel speeds. Once the control module senses wheel lock-up under a severe braking condition, it sends a pressure reduction signal through the anti-lock relay to the anti-lock actuator assembly. The solenoid controls the flow of hydraulic fluid into a buffer chamber located in the hydraulic anti-lock actuator assembly. This regulates the fluid entering the circuit preventing wheel lock up. When the control module senses the wheel is decelerating it sends a pressure signal through the anti-lock relay to the anti-lock actuator assembly. One signal tells the solenoid to allow hydraulic fluid pressure to increase while the other signal activates the pump motor to further increase pressure by returning fluid from the buffer chamber. This operation continues until all wheels are no longer in lockup.

Anti-lock Brake System (ABS) Components

The ABS system is comprised of the following components:
- Power brake booster
- Front and rear wheel speed sensors and indicators
- Anti-lock brake control module
- Anti-lock relay
- Hydraulic anti-lock actuator assembly
- Master cylinder
- Brake pressure control valve
- Master Cylinder
1. Front disc and rear disc or drum brakes

TESTING

The anti-lock brake warning indicator is illuminated when the engine is turned **ON**. If the light fails to go out or does not illuminate, there may be a problem with the ABS system.

Visual Check

➡It may be necessary to disengage some harness connections to perform a through inspection. Always make sure the ignition key is in the OFF position before disengaging any connections.

1. Check for a low brake fluid level, damaged sensors, leaks and a damaged hydraulic anti-lock actuator assembly.
2. Check the ABS wiring harness for proper connections, bent or broken pins, corrosion, loose wires and proper routing.
3. Check that all fuses and connected properly and are not damaged.
4. Check the control module for physical damage.

Scan Tool Test

1. Apply the parking brake and place the transaxle in **PARK** (automatic transaxle) or **NEUTRAL** (manual transaxle).

2. Block all the drive wheels.

3. Turn off all electrical loads such as the radio, lamps, heater blower, A/C system, etc.

4. With the key **OFF**, connect the scan tool to the Data Link Connector (DLC) which is located in the engine compartment.

5. Follow the tool manufacturer's instructions on the hook-up and use of the tool.

Analog Volt Ohmmeter Test

1994–96 MODELS

▶ See Figure 83

1. Turn the key **OFF**.

2. Connect a jumper wire at the Data Link Connector (DLC) between terminals GND and TBS.

3. Connect the analog volt ohmmeter between the FBS terminal and a good known engine ground.

4. Set the analog volt ohmmeter on a DC voltage range to read from zero to twenty.

The trouble code will represent itself on the analog volt ohmmeter as a needle sweep or pulse. If for example a code 51 is present, the needle will sweep or pulse across the meter five times, pause for a very short time, then it will sweep or pulse once. After all the codes have been retrieved, the meter will begin to repeat the codes.

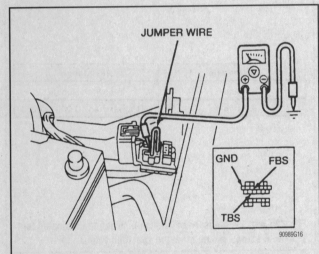

Fig. 83 Connect the analog voltmeter and jump the DLC terminals as illustrated—1991–96 models

Clearing Codes

USING AN ANALOG VOLT OHMMETER—1994–96 MODELS

1. Connect a jumper wire between terminal GND and TBS of the data Link Connector (DLC).

2. Turn the key to the **ON** position.

3. Use the analog volt ohmmeter to retrieve the trouble codes.

4. After the first code is repeated, depress the brake pedal ten times (one per second) and turn the key **OFF**.

5. Disconnect the jumper wire and analog volt ohmmeter from the DLC.

USING A SCAN TOOL—1994–96 MODELS

1. With the key **ON** and the scan tool connected to the Data Link Connector (DLC), follow the tool manufacturer's instructions and begin to retrieve the trouble codes.

2. After the first code is repeated, depress the brake pedal ten times (one per second) and turn the key **OFF**.

3. Disconnect the scan tool from the DLC.

USING A SCAN TOOL—1997–99 MODELS

1. With the key **ON** and the scan tool connected to the Data Link Connector (DLC), follow the tool manufacturer's instructions to clear the trouble codes.

2. After the codes are cleared, disconnect the scan tool from the DLC.

Wheel Speed Sensor

1994–96 MODELS

1. Check the clearance between the sensor and the trigger wheel. The measurement should be 0.030–0.050 inch (0.3–1.1mm).

2. If the measurement is not within specification, replace the sensor.

3. Disengage the sensor electrical connection.

4. Use a Digital Volt Ohmmeter (DVOM) to measure the resistance between the following pins on the connector for each sensor:

   a. Left front sensor: Black w/white stripe and orange w/white stripe wires

   b. Right front sensor: Black w/red stripe and orange wires

   c. Left rear sensor: Black w/blue stripe and red/blue stripe wires

   d. Right rear sensor: Black w/orange stripe and white wires

5. If the resistance is not 1600–2000 ohms, replace the sensor.

1997–99 MODELS

▶ See Figures 84 and 85

1. Check the clearance between the sensor and the trigger wheel. The measurement should be 0.012–0.043 inch (0.76–1.27mm).

2. If the measurement is not within specification, replace the sensor.

3. Disengage the sensor electrical connection.

4. Use a Digital Volt Ohmmeter (DVOM) to measure the resistance between the wheel speed sensor connector terminals shown in the accompanying illustration on the connector and ground. The resistance should be greater than 10,000 ohms. If not within specification, replace the sensor.

5. Use a DVOM to measure the resistance between the wheel speed sensor connector terminals shown in the accompanying illustration on the connector. The resistance should be between 2400 and 2800 ohms. If not within specification, replace the sensor.

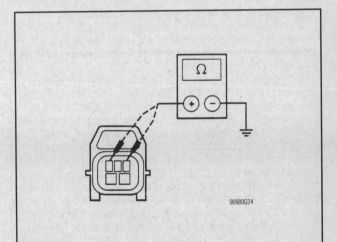

Fig. 84 Use a DVOM to measure resistance between each of the wheel speed sensor connector terminals in the illustration and ground—1997–99 models

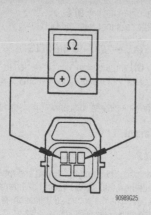

90989G25

Fig. 85 Use a DVOM to measure resistance between the two wheel speed sensor connector terminals in the illustration—1997–99 models

Anti-lock Relay

1991–96 MODELS

▶ See Figures 86, 87, 88, 89 and 90

1. Unplug the anti-lock relay.
2. Measure the resistance between the terminals in the accompanying illustration (chart 1) using a Digital Volt Ohmmeter (DVOM).
3. Apply voltage to 12 volts terminal 5 and ground terminal 4 on the relay.
4. Measure the resistance between the terminals in the accompanying illustration (chart 2) using a Digital Volt Ohmmeter (DVOM).

➡Battery voltage must remain applied to terminal 5 and ground to terminal 4 before proceeding with the next step.

5. Apply 12 volts to terminal 7 and ground terminal 8 on the relay.
6. Measure the resistance between the terminals indicated in the accompanying illustration (chart 3) using a DVOM.
7. Remove the grounds and 12 volt power sources from the relay terminals.
8. Place the DVOM on diode check.

Terminals	Resistance
5 and 4	60-100 ohms
3 and 1	Greater than 10,000 ohms
3 and 6	Less than 5 ohms
6 and 8	50-90 ohms
3 and 8	50-90 ohms
1 and 2	Greater than 10,000 ohms

90989G18

Fig. 87 Chart 1—measure resistance between the indicated terminals; readings should be within the specified ranges

Terminals	Resistance
1 and 6	Less than 5 ohms
3 and 6	Greater than 10,000 ohms

90989G19

Fig. 88 Chart 2—measure resistance between the indicated terminals; readings should meet the specified values

ANTI-LOCK RELAY

90989G22

Fig. 86 Anti-lock relay terminal identification—1991–96 models

Terminals	Resistance
1 and 2	Less than 5 ohms

90989G20

Fig. 89 Chart 3—measure resistance between terminals 1 and 2; the reading should be less than 5 ohms

Terminals	Continuity
6 (-) and 7 (+)	Yes
6 (+) and 7 (-)	No

90989G21

Fig. 90 Chart 4—check continuity between the indicated terminals, and make sure that results agree with this chart

➡ The positive (+) and negative (-) signs refer to the DVOM leads.

9. Measure the continuity between the terminals in the accompanying illustration (chart 4) using the DVOM.

10. If the relay fails any of these tests, it should be replaced.

1997–99 MODELS

▶ See Figure 91

1. Measure the resistance between relay terminal 85 and all the other terminals in the accompanying illustration using a Digital Volt Ohmmeter (DVOM). If the resistances are 5 ohms or less, replace the relay.

2. Use a jumper wire to apply battery voltage to terminals 30 and 85. Connect a jumper wire from terminal 86 to ground.

3. Use a DVOM to measure the voltage at terminal 87. If the voltage is less than 10 volts, replace the relay.

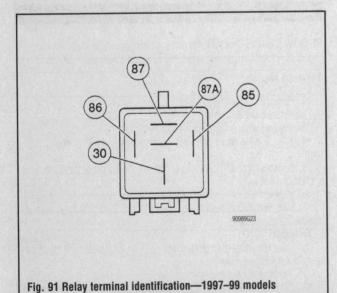

90989G23

Fig. 91 Relay terminal identification—1997–99 models

Trouble Codes

The following is a list of the ABS system trouble codes for 1994–96 models:

- Code 11: Right-hand front anti-lock sensor (wheel speed sensor) or sensor indicator
- Code 12: Left-hand front anti-lock sensor (wheel speed sensor) or sensor indicator
- Code 13: Right-hand rear anti-lock sensor (wheel speed sensor) or sensor indicator
- Code 14: Left-hand rear anti-lock sensor (wheel speed sensor) or sensor indicator
- Code 15: Front and rear anti-lock sensor (wheel speed sensor)
- Code 22: Solenoid valve
- Code 51: Fail safe relay
- Code 53: Motor relay
- Code 61: Control module

The following is a list of the ABS system trouble codes for 1997–99 models:
- Code B1318: No/low voltage to the anti-lock brake control module
- Code B1342: Anti-lock brake control module failure
- Code C1095: Pump motor shorted
- Code C1096: Pump motor open
- Code C1115: Shorted anti-lock relay
- Code C1140: Excessive dump time fault
- Code C1145: Right front anti-lock brake sensor (static)
- Code C1148/C1234: Right front anti-lock brake sensor (dynamic)
- Code C1155: Left front anti-lock brake sensor (static)
- Code C1158/C1233: Left front anti-lock brake sensor (dynamic)
- Code C1165: Right rear anti-lock brake sensor (static)
- Code C1168/C1235: Right rear anti-lock brake sensor (dynamic)
- Code C1175: Left rear anti-lock brake sensor (static)
- Code C1178/C1236: Left rear anti-lock brake sensor (dynamic)
- Code C1184: Excessive ABS isolation
- Code C1185: Open anti-lock relay
- Code C1194/C1196: Open or shorted left front dump valve solenoid
- Code C1198/C1200: Open or shorted left front isolation valve solenoid
- Code C1220: Anti-lock brake warning indicator shorted
- Code C1222: Wheel speed error
- Code C1210/C1212: Open or shorted right front dump valve solenoid
- Code C1214/C1216: Open or shorted right front isolation valve solenoid
- Code C1242/C1244: Open or shorted left rear dump valve solenoid
- Code C1246/C1248: Open or shorted right rear dump valve solenoid
- Code C1250/C1252: Open or shorted left rear isolation valve solenoid
- Code C1254/C1256: Open or shorted right rear isolation valve solenoid

ABS System Service Precautions

1. Certain components within the ABS system are not intended to be serviced or repaired individually. Only those components with removal and installation procedures should be serviced.

2. Do not use rubber hoses or other parts not specifically specified for and ABS system. When using repair kits, replace all parts included in the kit. Partial or incorrect repair may lead to functional problems and require the replacement of components.

3. Lubricate rubber parts with clean, fresh brake fluid to ease assembly. Do not use lubricated shop air to clean parts; damage to rubber components may result.

4. Use only DOT 3 brake fluid from an unopened container.

5. If any hydraulic component or line is removed or replaced, it may be necessary to bleed the entire system.

6. A clean repair area is essential. Always clean the reservoir and cap thoroughly before removing the cap. The slightest amount of dirt in the fluid may plug an orifice and impair the system function. Perform repairs have been thoroughly cleaned: use only denatures alcohol to clean components. Do not allow ABS components to come in contact with any substance containing mineral oil; this includes used shop rags.

7. The Anti-Lock control unit is a microprocessor similar to other computer units in the vehicle. Ensure that the ignition switch is **OFF** before removing or installing controller harnesses. Avoid static electricity discharge at or near the controller.

8. If any are welding is to be done on the vehicle, the ALCU connectors should be disconnected before welding operations begin.

Speed Sensors

REMOVAL & INSTALLATION

Front Wheels

1994–96 MODELS

1. Disconnect both battery cables, negative cable first.
2. Remove the battery to gain access to the left speed sensor connector.
3. Unplug the speed sensor electrical connector.
4. Pinch the grommet and push the grommet through the hole in the strut tower.
5. Raise and safely support the vehicle.
6. Remove the wheel and tire assembly.
7. Remove the retaining clips holding the wiring harness to the wheel well.
8. Remove the wiring harness bracket from the wheel well.
9. Remove the retaining clips holding the wiring harness to the top and bottom of the strut tower.
10. Unfasten the speed sensor bracket retaining bolts and remove the speed sensor.

To install:

11. Install the speed sensor bracket retaining bolts and tighten to 12–17 ft. lbs. (16–23 Nm).
12. Position the wiring and install the retaining clips holding the wiring harness to the top and bottom of the strut tower. Feed the wiring connector through the hole in the strut tower.
13. Attach the plug and position the grommet.
14. Install the wiring harness bracket to the wheel well.
15. Install the retaining clips holding the wiring harness to the wheel well.
16. Install the wheel and tire assembly.
17. Install the battery. Connect both battery cables, negative cable last.
18. Turn the ignition key to the **RUN** position. In the key ON, engine OFF position, the amber anti-lock brake indicator in the instrument cluster will illuminate continuously. Once the engine has started and for up to 60 seconds after engine start-up while the system performs a self-diagnostic check, the indicator will extinguish indicating that the anti-lock brake system is functional. If the amber indicator does not illuminate during the prove-out test, or at any time the anti-lock brake indicator illuminates after the initial prove-out or stays illuminated, a problem has been found in the anti-lock system and required immediate attention.
19. Road test the vehicle and check for proper operation.

1997–99 MODELS

1. Disconnect the negative battery cable.
2. Remove the windshield washer pump and reservoir.
3. Unplug the speed sensor electrical connector.
4. Raise and safely support the vehicle.
5. Remove the wheel and tire assembly.
6. Unfasten the upper sensor cable bracket bolt and remove the bracket.
7. Pinch the grommet and push the grommet and sensor wiring through the opening.
8. Unfasten the speed sensor cable clamp retaining bolt and remove the clamp.
9. Unfasten the sensor retaining bolts and remove the sensor.

To install:

10. Install the speed sensor retaining bolts and tighten to 12–17 ft. lbs. (16–23 Nm).
11. Install the speed sensor cable clamp and tighten the retaining bolt to 70–89 inch lbs. (8–10 Nm).
12. Route the wiring and install the grommet.
13. Install the upper sensor cable bracket and tighten the bolt.

14. Attach the sensor electrical connector.
15. Install the wheel and tire assembly.
16. Install the windshield washer pump and reservoir.
17. Connect the negative battery cable.
18. Road test the vehicle and check for proper operation.

Rear Wheels

1. Disconnect the negative battery cable.
2. On 1994–96 models, remove the quarter trim panel.
3. Unplug the speed sensor electrical connector.
4. Push the grommet through the hole in the chassis.
5. Raise and safely support the vehicle.
6. Remove the wheel and tire assembly.
7. Remove the upper and lower retaining clips holding the wiring harness to the wheel well.
8. Unfasten the speed sensor retaining bolt and remove the sensor.

To install:

9. Install the speed sensor and the retaining bolt. Tighten to 12–17 ft. lbs. (16–23 Nm) on 1994–96 models and 14–18 ft. lbs. (19–25 Nm) on 1997–99 models.
10. Position the wire and install the upper and lower retaining clips holding the wiring harness to the wheel well.
11. Attach the grommet to the hole in the chassis and attach the sensor electrical connector.
12. On 1994–96 models, install the quarter trim panel.
13. Install the wheel and tire assembly.
14. Lower the vehicle.
15. Connect the negative battery cable.
16. Turn the ignition key to the **RUN** position. In the Key On, Engine Off (KOEO) position, the amber anti-lock brake indicator in the instrument cluster will illuminate continuously. Once the engine has started and for up to 60 seconds after engine start-up while the system performs a self-diagnostic check, the indicator will extinguish indicating that the anti-lock brake system is functional. If the amber indicator does not illuminate during the prove-out test, or at any time the anti-lock brake indicator illuminates after the initial prove-out or stays illuminated, a problem has been found in the anti-lock system and required immediate attention.
17. Road test the vehicle and check for proper operation.

Anti-lock Actuator Assembly

REMOVAL & INSTALLATION

1994–96 Models

1. Remove the battery and tray.
2. Remove the acid shield.
3. Tag and unplug the electrical connections.
4. Tag the brake tubes and make corresponding marks on the ports.
5. Using an appropriate wrench, unfasten the six brake tubes from the actuator assembly.
6. Unfasten the nut on the front of the actuator assembly.
7. Unfasten the two nuts on the back of the actuator assembly and remove the assembly.

To install:

8. Place the actuator assembly into position and make sure the electrical connectors are properly routed.
9. Tighten the front and rear nuts until they are snug.
10. Connect the six brake tubes and tighten the flare nut fittings to 10–16 ft. lbs. (13–22 Nm).
11. Attach the electrical connections.
12. Install the acid shield, battery tray and battery.
13. Connect the negative battery cable.
14. Bleed the brake system.

1997–99 Models

➡**A scan tool is absolutely necessary to bleed the brake hydraulic system on 1997–99 models equipped with an Anti-lock Brake System (ABS). If your vehicle is equipped with ABS, be sure to refer to the ABS bleeding procedures in this section before performing any work on your vehicle's brake hydraulic system.**

1. Remove the battery and tray.
2. Tag and unplug the electrical connections.
3. Tag the brake tubes and make corresponding marks on the ports.
4. Using an appropriate wrench, unfasten the six brake tubes from the actuator assembly.
5. Unfasten the two actuator assembly bolts and remove the assembly.

To install:

6. Place the actuator assembly into position and make sure the electrical connectors are properly routed.
7. Tighten the actuator assembly retaining bolts to 14–18 ft. lbs. (19–25 Nm).
8. Connect the six brake tubes and tighten the flare nut fittings to 10–16 ft. lbs. (13–22 Nm).
9. Attach the electrical connections.
10. Install the battery tray and battery.
11. Connect the negative battery cable.
12. Bleed the brake system.

Sensor Indicator Ring

REMOVAL & INSTALLATION

Front

1. Remove the halfshaft from the vehicle (as described in Section 7) and insert it in a vise.
2. Use a punch to drive the front brake anti-lock sensor indicator off the halfshaft.

To install:

3. Use sensing ring replacer tool T93P-20202-A on 1994–96 models or tool T94P-20202-B on 1997–99 models, or their equivalents, to install the front brake anti-lock sensor indicator onto the halfshaft.
4. Install the halfshaft.

Rear

1. Remove the wheel hub.
2. Use a punch to remove the sensor indicator from the wheel hub.

To install:

3. Use a press and a steel plate to install the sensor indicator on the hub.
4. Install the hub.

Bleeding the ABS System

The ABS system on 1994–96 models does not require any special procedures or tools and is covered in the bleeding procedure for non-ABS systems at the start of this section.

The ABS systems on 1997–99 models requires the use of a scan tool that must be able to perform the System Bleed Function to purge the air from the Hydraulic Control Unit (HCU). An appropriate scan tool would be the New Generation Star (NGS) tester 418-F048 (007-00500) or its equivalent.

1. Start the vehicle and let the engine idle normally.
2. Following the tool manufacturer's instructions, attach a scan tool capable of performing the System Bleed Function to the Data Link Connector (DLC).
3. Depress the brake pedal to half of the full travel position.
4. Access the Function Test mode on the scan tool and activate the System Bleed Function.
5. Manually bleed the brake system as follows:
    a. Clean the area around the master cylinder filler cap and remove the cap.
    b. Fill the reservoir with clean brake fluid and install the cap.

✳✳ WARNING

Be careful not to spill brake fluid on painted surfaces, as it can destroy the finish. If any brake fluid is spilled, rinse the area immediately with water.

c. Repeat the master cylinder bleeding procedure at the front master cylinder outlet fitting.
    d. Position the correct box-end wrench on the brake bleeder on the right rear wheel.

➡**Always bleed the longest line first, which is the right rear line.**

e. Attach one end of a clear rubber hose to the brake bleeder screw and the other end into a container half full of clean brake fluid.
    f. Loosen the bleeder screw while an assistant apply the brake pedal slowly through its entire travel.
    g. Close the brake bleeder and then have the assistant release the brake pedal.
    h. Continue bleeding the right rear wheel until the fluid is free of air bubbles.

➡**DO NOT allow the master cylinder to run out of brake fluid. Only use fresh DOT 3 or equivalent brake fluid from a closed container.**

i. Repeat the procedure on the left rear wheel, then the right front, and finally the left front wheel.
    j. Throughout the brake bleeding process, continually check the brake master cylinder and top off the fluid as required.
6. Repeat the procedure, performing a total of two System Bleed Functions and two manual bleed cycles.
7. If the brake pedal is spongy, repeat the brake bleeding procedure.
8. Disconnect the scan tool and check the fluid level.
9. Test drive the vehicle and check for proper operation.

BRAKE SPECIFICATIONS
All measurements in inches unless noted

Year	Model		Brake Disc Original Thickness	Brake Disc Minimum Thickness	Maximum Run-out	Brake Drum Diameter Original Inside Diameter	Brake Drum Diameter Max. Wear Limit	Minimum Lining Thickness Front	Minimum Lining Thickness Rear
1991	Escort	F	0.870	0.790	0.004	—	—	0.080	—
		R	0.350	0.280	0.004	7.870	7.950	—	0.040
	Tracer	F	0.870	0.790	0.004	—	—	0.080	—
		R	0.350	0.280	0.004	9.000	9.040	—	0.040
1992	Escort	F	0.870	0.790	0.004	—	—	0.080	—
		R	0.350	0.280	0.004	7.870	7.950	—	0.040
	Tracer	F	0.870	0.790	0.004	—	—	0.080	—
		R	0.350	0.280	0.004	9.000	9.040	—	0.040
1993	Escort	F	0.870	0.820	0.004	—	—	0.080	—
		R	0.350	0.310	0.004	7.870	7.950	—	0.040
	Tracer	F	0.870	0.820	0.004	—	—	0.080	—
		R	0.350	0.310	0.004	7.870	7.950	—	0.040
1994	Escort	F	0.870	0.790	0.004	—	—	0.080	—
		R	0.350	0.280	0.004	7.870	7.950	—	0.040
	Tracer	F	0.870	0.790	0.004	—	—	0.080	—
		R	0.350	0.280	0.004	7.870	7.950	—	0.040
1995	Escort	F	0.870	0.790	0.004	—	—	0.080	—
		R	0.350	0.280	0.004	7.87	7.95	—	0.040
	Tracer	F	0.870	0.790	0.004	—	—	0.080	—
		R	0.350	0.280	0.004	7.87	7.95	—	0.040
1996	Escort	F	0.870	0.790	0.004	—	—	0.080	—
		R	0.350	0.280	0.004	7.87	7.95	—	0.040
	Tracer	F	0.870	0.790	0.004	—	—	0.080	—
		R	0.350	0.280	0.004	7.87	7.95	—	0.040
1997	Escort	F	0.870	0.790	0.004	—	—	0.080	—
		R	0.350	0.280	0.004	7.87	7.95	—	0.040
	Tracer	F	0.870	0.790	0.004	—	—	0.080	—
		R	0.350	0.280	0.004	7.87	7.95	—	0.040
1998	Escort	F	0.870	0.790	0.004	—	—	0.080	—
		R	0.350	0.280	0.004	7.87	7.95	—	0.040
	ZX2	F	0.870	0.790	0.004	—	—	0.080	—
		R	0.350	0.280	0.004	7.87	7.95	—	0.040
	Tracer	F	0.870	0.790	0.004	—	—	0.080	—
		R	0.350	0.280	0.004	7.87	7.95	—	0.040
1999	Escort	F	0.870	0.790	0.004	—	—	0.080	—
		R	0.350	0.280	0.004	7.87	7.95	—	0.040
	ZX2	F	0.870	0.790	0.004	—	—	0.080	—
		R	0.350	0.280	0.004	7.87	7.95	—	0.040
	Tracer	F	0.870	0.790	0.004	—	—	0.080	—
		R	0.350	0.280	0.004	7.87	7.95	—	0.040

NOTE: Follow specifications stamped on rotor or drum if figures differ from those in this chart.

F - Front

R - Rear

90989C1A

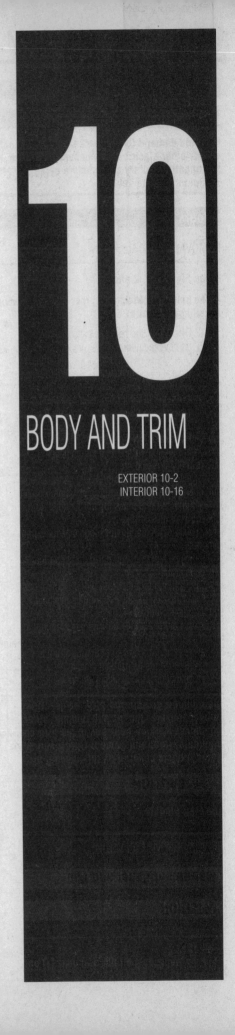

10

BODY AND TRIM

EXTERIOR

❋❋ WARNING

To avoid damage to the Electronic Engine Control (EEC) modules and/or other electrical components or wiring, always disconnect the negative battery cable before using any electric welding equipment on the vehicle.

Doors

REMOVAL & INSTALLATION

▶ See Figures 1, 2 and 3

➡The help of an assistant is recommended, when removing or installing the door(s).

1. Disconnect the negative battery cable.
2. Remove the door checker pin with a hammer and punch, or suitable tool.

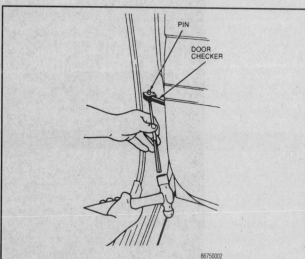

Fig. 1 Remove the door checker pin with a hammer and punch—1991–96 models

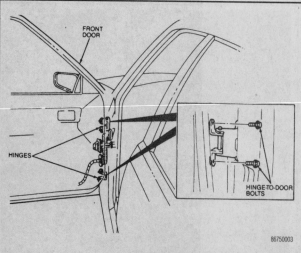

Fig. 2 Disconnect the hinges to remove the front door—1991–96 models

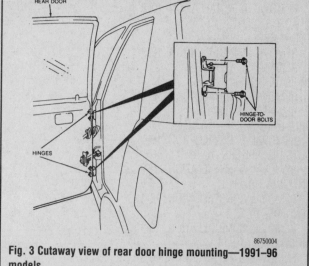

Fig. 3 Cutaway view of rear door hinge mounting—1991–96 models

3. Detach the rubber electrical conduit from the vehicle body.
4. Pry the electrical connector out of the body and unplug it.
5. Scribe marks around the hinge locations for reference during installation.
6. Unfasten the hinge bolts and remove the door.

To install:

7. Place the door into position and install the hinge bolts.
8. Align the hinges with the marks made previously.
9. Adjust the door.
10. Install the electrical conduit.
11. Install the door checker pin.
12. Connect the negative battery cable.

ADJUSTMENTS

▶ See Figures 4, 5, 6, 7 and 8

Adjusting the hinge affects the positioning of the outside surface of the door frame. Adjusting the latch striker affects the alignment of the door relative to the weatherstrip and the door closing characteristics.

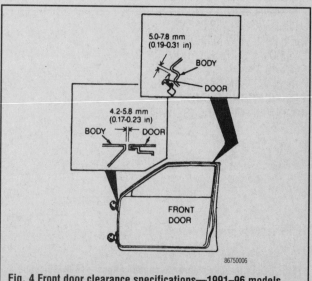

Fig. 4 Front door clearance specifications—1991–96 models

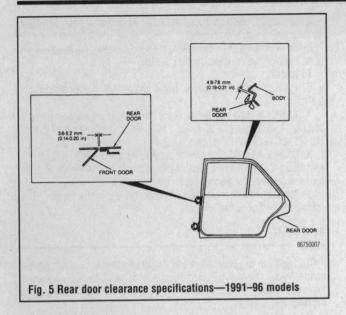

Fig. 5 Rear door clearance specifications—1991–96 models

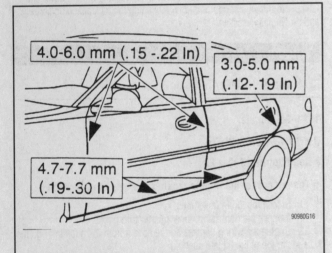

Fig. 6 Door-to-body clearance specifications—1997–99 sedan and wagon models

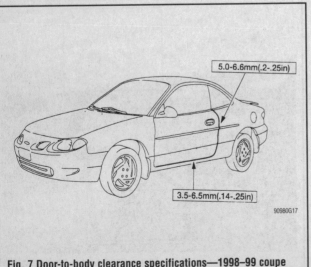

Fig. 7 Door-to-body clearance specifications—1998–99 coupe models

Fig. 8 Panel alignment specifications—1998–99 coupe models

1. Loosen the hinge bolts just enough to permit movement of the door.
2. Move the door to the desired position and tighten the hinge bolts to 13–22 ft. lbs. (18–29 Nm).
3. Check the door fit to be sure the clearances are within the specifications shown.
4. Repeat Steps 1 and 2 until the desired fit is obtained, then check the striker plate for proper door closing.

Hood

REMOVAL & INSTALLATION

▶ **See Figures 9, 10, 11 and 12**

➡ **The help of an assistant is recommended when removing or installing the hood.**

1. Open and support the hood.
2. Protect the body with covers to prevent damage to the paint.
3. Use a marker or scribe marks around the hinge locations for reference during installation.

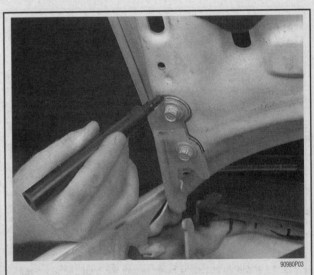

Fig. 9 Use a marker to outline the hood hinge locations

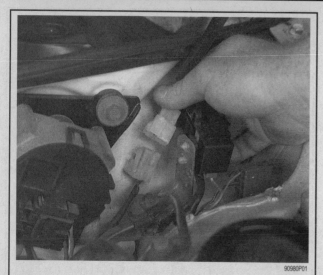

Fig. 10 Unfasten any electrical connections . . .

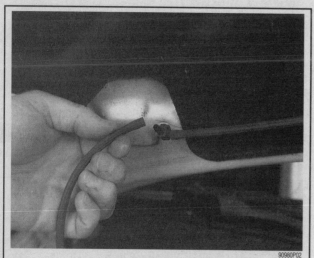

Fig. 11 . . . and windshield washer hoses which attach to the hood

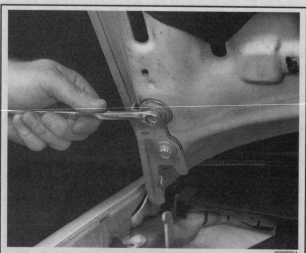

Fig. 12 While an assistant helps secure the hood, unfasten the attaching bolts

4. Unplug any electrical connections and windshield washer hoses that would interfere with hood removal.

5. While an assistant helps secure the hood, unfasten the attaching bolts, then remove the hood from the vehicle.

To install:

6. Place the hood into position. Install and partially tighten attaching bolts.

7. Adjust the hood with the reference marks and tighten the attaching bolts to 14–19 ft. lbs. (19–25 Nm) on 1991–96 models and 14–17 ft. lbs. (19–23 Nm) on 1997–99 models.

8. Check the hood for an even fit between the fenders and for flush fit with the front of the fenders. Also, check for a flush fit with the top of the cowl and fenders. If necessary, adjust the hood latch.

9. Attach any electrical connections or windshield washer hoses removed to facilitate hood removal.

ALIGNMENT

The hood can be adjusted fore and aft and side to side by loosening the hood-to-hinge attaching bolts and reposition the hood. To raise or lower the hood, loosen the hinge hood on body attaching bolts and raise or lower the hinge as necessary.

The hood lock can be moved from side-to-side and up and down and laterally to obtain a snug hood fit by loosening the lock attaching screws and moving as necessary.

Liftgate

REMOVAL & INSTALLATION

1991–96 Models

3 AND 5-DOOR MODELS

▶ See Figures 13 thru 22

➡The removal of the liftgate requires the help of an assistant.

1. Detach the lifting tray straps.
2. Remove the right-hand upper quarter trim panel.
3. Unplug the wiring harness and remove it from the body through the hole in the top of the liftgate opening.
4. On models equipped with hydraulic supports attached by a nut, unfasten the retaining nut and separate the support from the liftgate.

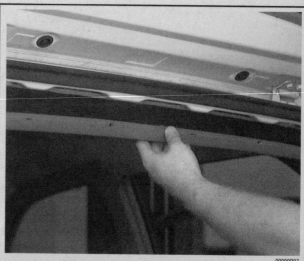

Fig. 13 If necessary, remove the upper trim panel

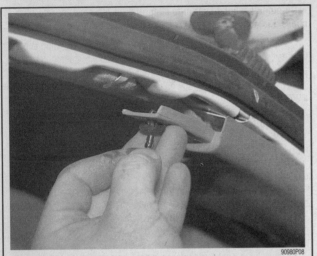

Fig. 14 Remove the upper retaining clip from the right-hand upper trim panel

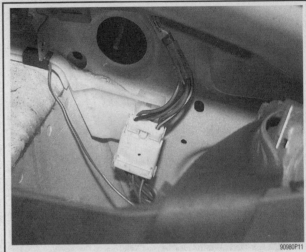

Fig. 17 Remove the trim panel to access the liftgate wiring harness connector

Fig. 15 Unclip the seat belt bolt trim cover to access the bolt

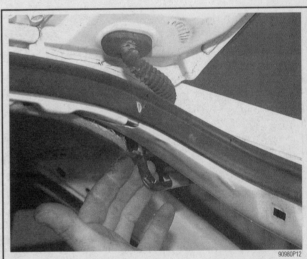

Fig. 18 Unfasten the liftgate wiring harness retaining clips and remove the wiring through the hole in the top of the body panel

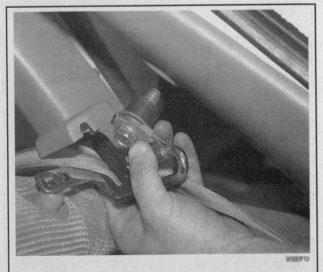

Fig. 16 Unfasten the bolt and set the seat belt assembly aside

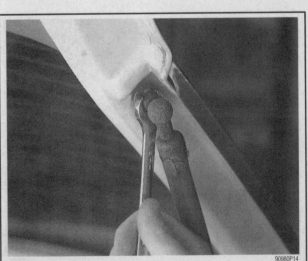

Fig. 19 On models equipped with hydraulic supports attached by a nut, unfasten the retaining nut . . .

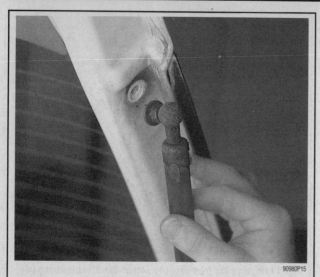
Fig. 20 . . . and separate the support from the liftgate

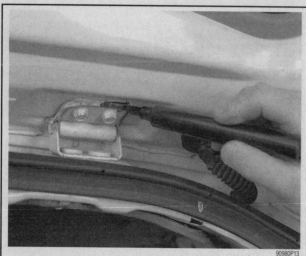
Fig. 21 Make marks around the hinge locations for reference during installation

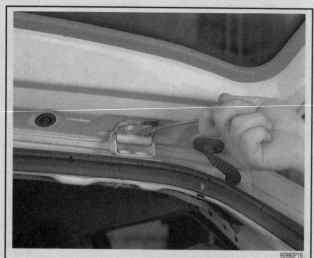
Fig. 22 A box end wrench can be used to loosen the liftgate hinge-to-body bolts

➡On models whose hydraulic supports are attached by retaining clips, it is not necessary to remove the clips from the supports.

5. On models with hydraulic supports attached by a retaining clip, have your assistant support the liftgate, and use a suitable prytool to detach the supports from the liftgate by gently prying on the clips.

6. Scribe marks around the hinge locations for reference during installation.

7. Unfasten the hinge bolts and remove the liftgate.

To install:

8. With the aid of an assistant, place the liftgate into position and loosely install the hinge bolts.

9. Attach the hydraulic supports to the liftgate and install the retainer.

10. Feed the liftgate harness through the hole and attach it to the body.

11. Adjust the liftgate until the hinges are aligned with marks made prior to removal and tighten the hinge bolts to 78–113 inch lbs. (9–13 Nm).

12. Install the right-hand upper quarter trim panel.

13. Attach the lifting tray straps.

WAGON MODELS

▶ See Figures 23 and 24

1. Open the liftgate.

2. Remove the quarter trim panel, the roof side inner molding and upper quarter trim panel.

3. Unplug the liftgate electrical connection and detach the harness from the body.

4. Remove the electrical harness through the hole in the top of the liftgate opening.

5. If equipped, lower the rear of the headliner and disconnect the washer hose.

6. On models equipped with hydraulic supports attached by a nut, unfasten the retaining nut and separate the support from the liftgate.

➡On models equipped with hydraulic supports attached by clips, it is not necessary to remove the clips from the supports.

7. On models equipped with hydraulic supports attached by a retaining clip, have your assistant support the liftgate, and use a suitable prytool to detach the supports from the liftgate by gently prying on the clips.

8. Scribe marks around the hinge locations for reference during installation.

9. Unfasten the hinge bolts and remove the liftgate.

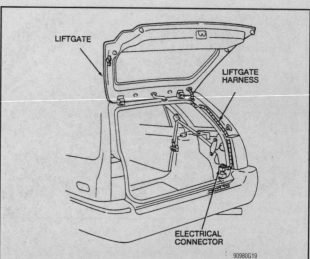
Fig. 23 Remove the trim panel to access the liftgate wiring harness and unplug the harness electrical connector

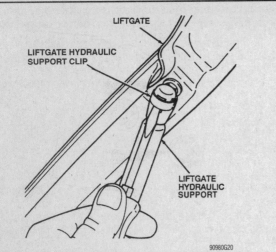

Fig. 24 Use a suitable prytool to detach the hydraulic supports from the liftgate by gently prying on the clips

To install:

10. With the aid of an assistant, place the liftgate into position and loosely install the hinge bolts.

11. Attach the gas or hydraulic supports to the liftgate and install the retainer.

12. Feed the liftgate harness through the hole and attach it to the body.

13. Attach the electrical connector.

14. Adjust the liftgate until the hinges are aligned with marks made prior to removal and tighten the hinge bolts to 78–113 inch lbs. (9–13 Nm).

15. Install the quarter trim panel, the roof side inner molding and upper quarter trim panel.

1997–99 Models

➡Removal of the liftgate requires the help of an assistant.

1. Disconnect the negative battery cable.
2. Remove the roof side inner trim molding.
3. Unplug the liftgate electrical harness.
4. If equipped, disconnect the rear washer hose.
5. Pry upwards on the luggage compartment door hydraulic support clips with a suitable prytool and detach the supports from the liftgate.
6. Have your assistant support the liftgate.
7. Scribe marks around the hinge locations for reference during installation.
8. Unfasten the hinge bolts and remove the liftgate.

To install:

9. With the aid of an assistant, place the liftgate into position and loosely install the hinge bolts.

10. Attach the hydraulic supports to the liftgate.

11. Adjust the liftgate until the hinges are aligned with marks made prior to removal and tighten the hinge bolts to 78–112 inch lbs. (9–12 Nm).

12. If equipped, connect the rear washer hose.
13. Attach the liftgate electrical harness.
14. Install the roof side inner trim molding.
15. Connect the negative battery cable.

ALIGNMENT

1. Loosen the liftgate hinge bolts.
2. Move the hood up, down or side-to-side as required.
3. When the liftgate is in the desired position, tighten the bolts to 78–113 inch lbs. (9–13 Nm).

Grille

REMOVAL & INSTALLATION

1991–96 Models

▶ See Figures 25, 26, 27 and 28

1. Remove the grille retaining screw.
2. Insert a suitable flat-bladed tool to release the five locking clips, then remove the radiator grille.

To install:

3. Install the radiator grille by positioning the grille and pressing it into place.
4. Install the retaining screws.

1997–99 Models

The radiator grille on 1997–99 models is part of the front bumper assembly, and is referred to as the front bumper cover.

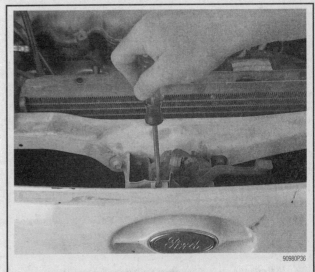

Fig. 25 Remove the grille retaining screw

Fig. 26 Release the five locking clips . . .

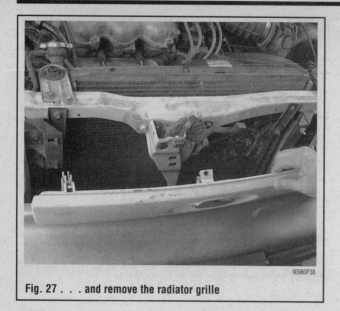

Fig. 27 . . . and remove the radiator grille

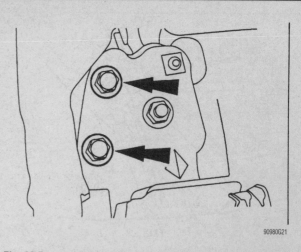

Fig. 29 From each wheel opening, unfasten the concealed bolts which attach the front fender to the front bumper cover (grille)

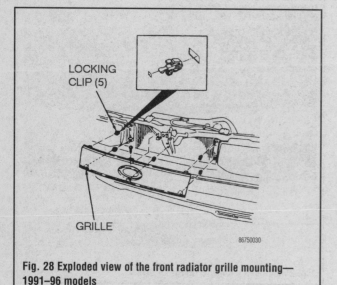

LOCKING CLIP (5)

GRILLE

Fig. 28 Exploded view of the front radiator grille mounting—1991–96 models

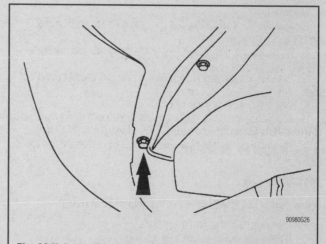

Fig. 30 Unfasten the lower front bumper cover (grille) screw from the bottom of each side of the bumper cover—1997–99 sedan and wagon models

SEDAN AND WAGON MODELS

▶ See Figures 29, 30, 31 and 32

1. Unfasten the lower front bumper cover (grille) screw from the bottom of each side of the bumper cover (grille).

2. From each wheel well, unfasten the four screws and one pushpin that attach the front fender splash shield.

3. From each wheel opening, unfasten the concealed bolts which connect the front fender to the front bumper cover (grille).

4. From each wheel opening, unfasten the screw which attaches the front bumper cover (grille) to the fender.

5. Unfasten the upper front bumper cover (grille) bolts and the plastic fastener from the top of the bumper cover (grille).

6. Remove the bumper cover (grille).

To install:

8. Place the bumper cover (grille) into position and plastic fastener to the top of the bumper cover.

9. Install the upper front bumper cover (grille) bolts and tighten them to 70–82 inch lbs. (8–9 Nm).

10. From each wheel opening, install the screw which attaches the front bumper cover (grille) to the fender. Tighten the screw to 22–31 inch lbs. (2.5–3.5 Nm).

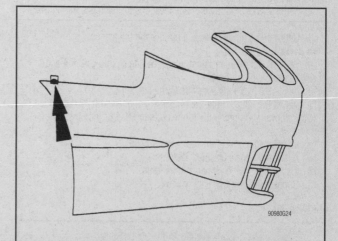

Fig. 31 From each wheel opening, unfasten the screw which attaches the front bumper cover (grille) to the fender—1997–99 sedan and wagon models

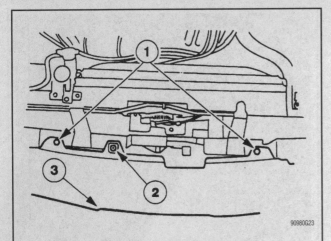

Fig. 32 Unfasten the front bumper cover (grille) bolts (1), and remove the alignment pushpin (2) before removing the bumper cover (3)

11. From each wheel opening, install the concealed bolts which connect the front fender to the front bumper cover (grille). Tighten the bolts to 61–87 inch lbs. (7–10 Nm).

12. Place the splash shield into position, install the pushpin and the screws. Tighten the screws to 23–30 inch lbs. (2.5–3.5 Nm).

13. Install the lower front bumper cover (grille) screw to the bottom of each side of the bumper cover (grille). Tighten the screws to 23–30 inch lbs. (2.5–3.5 Nm).

COUPE MODELS

▶ See Figures 29, 32 and 33

1. Disconnect the negative battery cable.
2. Unplug the combination lamp electrical connectors.
3. If equipped, unplug the fog lamp electrical connections.
4. Unfasten the splash shield screws and pushpins, then set the splash shield aside.
5. From each wheel opening, unfasten the concealed bolts which connect the front fender to the front bumper cover (grille).
6. From each wheel opening, unfasten the screw which attaches the front bumper cover (grille) to the fender.
7. Unfasten the front bumper cover (grille) bolts, then remove the alignment pushpin and remove the bumper cover (grille).

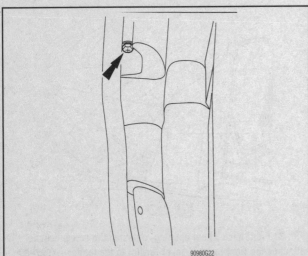

Fig. 33 From each wheel opening, unfasten the screw which attaches the front bumper cover (grille) to the fender

To install:

8. Place the bumper cover (grille) into position and install the alignment pushpin.

9. Install the bumper cover (grille) bolts and tighten them to 70–82 inch lbs. (7.8–9.2 Nm).

10. From each wheel opening, install the screw which attaches the front bumper cover (grille) to the fender. Tighten the screw to 22.3–31.2 inch lbs. (2.5–3.5 Nm).

11. From each wheel opening, install the concealed bolts which connect the front fender to the front bumper cover (grille). Tighten the bolts to 60.6–87.4 inch lbs. (6.8–9.8 Nm).

12. Place the splash shield into position, install the pushpins and the screws. Tighten the screws to 23–30 inch lbs. (2.5–3.5 Nm)

13. If equipped, attach the fog lamp electrical connections.
14. Attach the combination lamp electrical connectors.
15. Connect the negative battery cable.

Outside Mirrors

REMOVAL & INSTALLATION

1991–96 Models

REMOTE CONTROL MIRRORS

▶ See Figure 34

1. Using a small, flat-bladed tool, pry the control knob inside the locking tab slightly away from the control handle and slide the control knob off.
2. Remove the mirror trim cover from the door.
3. Remove the three retaining screws.
4. Remove the mirror.

To install:

5. Place the mirror into position and install the retaining screws.
6. Install the mirror trim cover.
7. Slide the control knob onto the control handle until it locks into position.

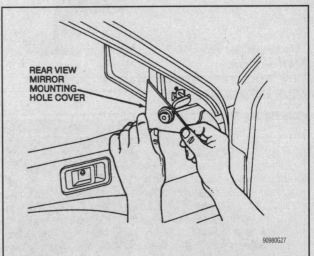

REAR VIEW MIRROR MOUNTING HOLE COVER

Fig. 34 Remove the mirror trim cover from the door to access the mirror retaining screws—1991–96 models

POWER MIRRORS

▶ See Figures 35, 36, 37 and 38

1. Remove the mirror trim cover from the door.
2. Remove the three retaining screws.
3. Unplug the mirror electrical connection.
4. Remove the mirror.

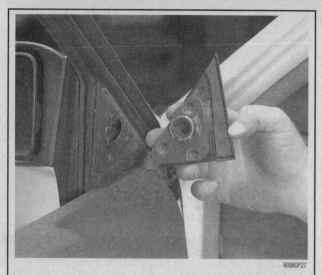

Fig. 35 Remove the outside mirror trim cover from the door

90980P27

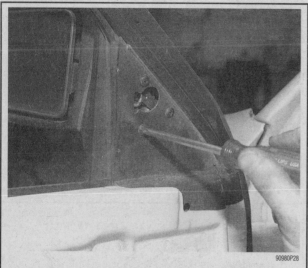

Fig. 36 Unfasten the three retaining screws

90980P28

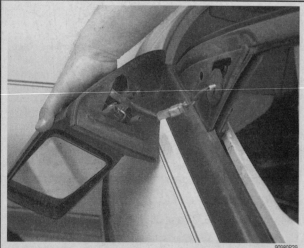

Fig. 37 Separate the mirror from its mounting until you can access the mirror electrical connection . . .

90980P29

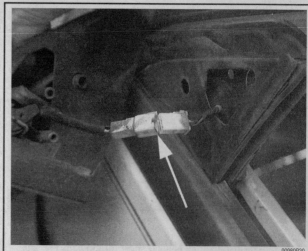

Fig. 38 . . . then unplug the electrical connection (arrow) and remove the mirror from the vehicle

90980P30

To install:

5. Place the mirror into position and install the retaining screws.
6. Attach the mirror electrical connection.
7. Install the mirror trim cover.
8. Slide the control knob onto the control handle until it locks into position.

1997–99 Models

REMOTE CONTROL MIRRORS

▶ See Figure 39

1. Unfasten the mirror interior trim panel screw and remove the panel.
2. Remove the door trim panel.
3. Remove the three retaining screws.
4. Remove the mirror.

To install:

5. Place the mirror into position and install the retaining screws.
6. Install the door trim panel.
7. Install the mirror trim panel and tighten the screw.

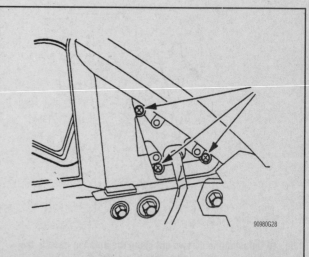

Fig. 39 Location of the mirror retaining screws—1997–99 models

90980G28

POWER MIRRORS

1. Disconnect the negative battery cable.
2. Unfasten the mirror interior trim panel screw and remove the panel.
3. Remove the door trim panel and peel back the watershield.
4. Unplug the mirror electrical connection.
5. Remove the three retaining screws.
6. Remove the mirror.

To install:

7. Place the mirror into position and install the retaining screws.
8. Attach the mirror electrical connection.
9. Install the watershield and door trim panel.
10. Install the mirror trim panel and tighten the screw.

Antenna

REMOVAL & INSTALLATION

1991–96 Models

▶ See Figures 40 and 41

1. Remove the instrument cluster.
2. Unhook the antenna cable from the clips behind the cluster.
3. Remove the radio.
4. Disconnect the antenna cable from the radio.
5. Remove the cable from the heater and retainer.
6. Unfasten the screws attaching the antenna base to the front body upper pillar.
7. Pull the antenna, base and insulating tube up until the tape is exposed.
8. Cut the old cable near the base.
9. Tape the new cable to the old cable, as this will help pull the new cable through the car.

To install:

10. While pulling on the old cable, insert the cable and insulating tube down through the body pillar.
11. Once the base is in position, tighten its retaining screws. Make sure the drain tube end fits into the drain hole.
12. Connect the cable to the wiring harness retainer on the heater and the retainer behind the cluster.
13. Remove the old cable, then install the radio and cluster.

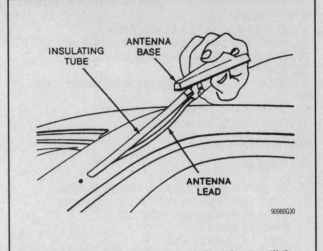

Fig. 41 Pull the antenna, base and insulating tube up until the tape is exposed—1991–96 models

1997–99 Models

CABLE—SEDAN AND WAGON

▶ See Figure 42

1. Disconnect the negative battery cable.
2. On 1997 models, remove the instrument cluster.
3. On 1998–99 models, remove the radio chassis/integrated control panel.
4. Remove the console panel and disconnect the antenna from the radio lead-in cable.
5. Attach the new cable to the end of the old antenna cable with a piece of wire or tape.
6. Disconnect the antenna cable from the wiring harness retainer.
7. Remove the antenna cable from the wiring insulators.
8. Remove the antenna base mounting screws.
9. Pull the antenna, antenna lead and insulating tube out of the body pillar. Keep pulling until the new cable is all the way through.
10. Detach the wire from the end of the antenna lead.

To install:

11. Attach the new cable to the antenna.

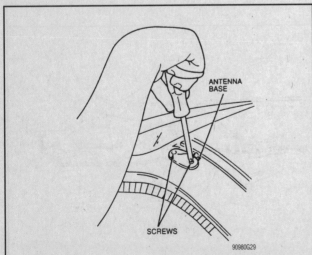

Fig. 40 Unfasten the screws attaching the antenna base to the front body upper pillar—1991–96 models

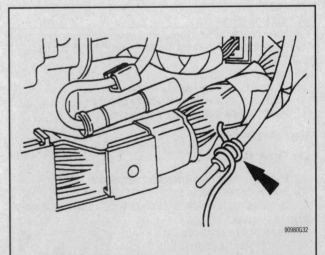

Fig. 42 Attach the new cable to the end of the old antenna cable with a piece of wire or tape—1997–99 sedan and wagon models

12. Install the mounting base and tighten the retaining screws to 9–13 inch lbs. (1–1.4 Nm).
13. Attach the antenna cable to the wiring insulators.
14. Connect the antenna cable to the wiring harness retainer.
15. Connect the antenna cable to the radio lead-in cable.
16. Install the console panel.
17. On 1998–99 models, install the radio chassis/integrated control panel.
18. On 1997 models, install the instrument cluster.
19. Connect the negative battery cable.

ANTENNA BASE—COUPE

▶ See Figure 43

1. Remove the trunk scuff plate pushpins and the scuff plate.
2. Remove the trunk side trim panel pushpins and the panel.
3. Disconnect the radio antenna lead-in cable.
4. Remove the antenna mast.
5. Unfasten the antenna base nut.
6. Remove the antenna base cover.
7. Remove the antenna base.

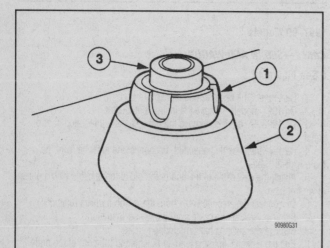

Fig. 43 Remove the antenna nut (1), cover (2) and base (3)—1998–99 coupe models

To install:
8. Install the antenna base.
9. Install the antenna base cover.
10. Install the antenna base nut. Tighten the nut to 14–26 inch lbs. (1.5–2.9 Nm).
11. Install the antenna mast.
12. Connect the radio antenna lead-in cable.
13. Install the trunk side trim panel and the pushpins.
14. Install the trunk scuff plate and the pushpins.

FRONT CABLE—COUPE

▶ See Figure 44

1. Remove the radio chassis/integrated control panel.
2. Remove the center console.
3. Disconnect the front radio antenna lead-in cable from the rear radio antenna lead-in cable.
4. Remove the cable from the clips.
5. Remove the front antenna cable.
To install:
6. Install the front antenna cable.
7. Attach the cable to the clips.

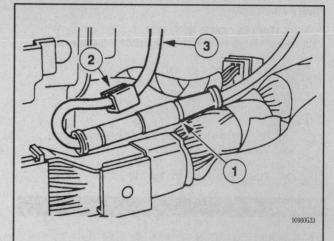

Fig. 44 Disconnect the front radio antenna lead-in cable (3) from the rear radio antenna lead-in cable (1) and detach the cable from the clips (2)—1998–99 coupe models

8. Connect the front radio antenna lead-in cable to the rear radio antenna lead-in cable.
9. Install the center console.
10. Install the radio chassis/integrated control panel.

REAR CABLE—COUPE

▶ See Figure 45

1. Disconnect the negative battery cable.
2. Remove the trunk scuff plate pushpins and the scuff plate.
3. Remove the trunk side trim panel pushpins and the panel.
4. Disconnect the radio antenna lead-in cable.
5. Remove the front seat.

➡The anti-lock control module is located under the passenger's seat.

6. Remove the anti-lock control module as follows:
   a. Unfasten module electrical connector bolt and unplug the connector.
   b. Unfasten the module retaining bolts and remove the module.
7. Remove the door scuff plate by pulling it upwards.

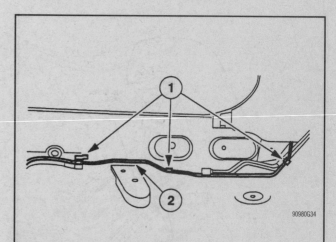

Fig. 45 Disconnect the rear radio antenna lead-in cable (2) from the clips (1)

8. Remove the quarter trim panel.

➡**Do not attempt to remove the front safety belt lower anchor bolt from the front safety belt anchor, as it is part of the assembly.**

9. Use safety belt bolt bit T77L-2100A or its equivalent to loosen the safety belt lower bolt.

10. Position the carpet aside.

11. Disconnect the rear radio antenna lead-in cable from the clips and remove the lead-in cable from the vehicle.

To install:

12. Install the lead-in cable and attach the lead-in cable to the clips.

13. Place the carpet into position.

14. Use safety belt bolt bit T77L-2100A or its equivalent to tighten the safety belt lower bolt to 25–33 ft. lbs. (34–46 Nm).

15. Install the quarter trim panel.

16. Install the door scuff plate.

17. Install the anti-lock control module as follows:

a. Install the module and tighten the retaining bolts to 61–86 inch lbs. (7–10 Nm).

b. Attach the module electrical connector, install the bolt and tighten it to 53–62 inch lbs. (6–7 Nm).

18. Install the front seat.

19. Connect the radio antenna lead-in cable.

20. Install the trunk side trim panel and the pushpins.

21. Install the trunk scuff plate and the pushpins.

22. Connect the negative battery cable.

Fenders

REMOVAL & INSTALLATION

1991–96 Models

▶ **See Figure 46**

1. Remove the radiator grille.
2. Remove the parking/turn signal lamp and headlamp.

3. Unfasten the sill molding retainers and remove the sill molding as follow:

a. Pull the bottom of the sill molding out and lift the top of the sill molding out of the retainer.

b. If necessary, remove the rivets from the retainer.

4. Remove the splash shield and mud flap attaching screws.

5. Unfasten the fender mounting bolts and nuts. Remove the fender.

To install:

6. Place the fender into position. Install the retaining bolts and nuts. Tighten to 61–87 inch lbs. (7–10 Nm).

7. Install the splash shield and mud flap attaching screws.

8. Install the sill molding retainer and the molding.

9. Install the parking/turn signal lamp and headlamp.

10. Install the radiator grille.

1997–99 Models

▶ **See Figures 47, 48, 49 and 50**

1. If equipped, unfasten the stone guard pushpins and screws, then remove the stone guard.

2. Remove the six front fender splash shield pushpins and the seven splash shield screws.

3. Remove the splash shield.

4. Remove the bumper cover (grille). Refer to the grille removal and installation procedure in this section.

5. Unfasten the three front bumper bracket nuts from each side of the bumper, then remove the bumper from the vehicle.

6. Unplug the headlamp electrical connections.

7. Unfasten the two nuts and two headlamp housing bolts.

8. Unfasten the headlamp housing nut and (if applicable) the bolt, which are accessed through the front wheel well opening.

9. Remove the headlamp housing.

10. Unfasten the eleven front fender bolts and remove the fender.

To install:

11. Install the fender and tighten the retaining bolts to the specifications shown in the accompanying illustrations.

12. Place the headlamp housing into position.

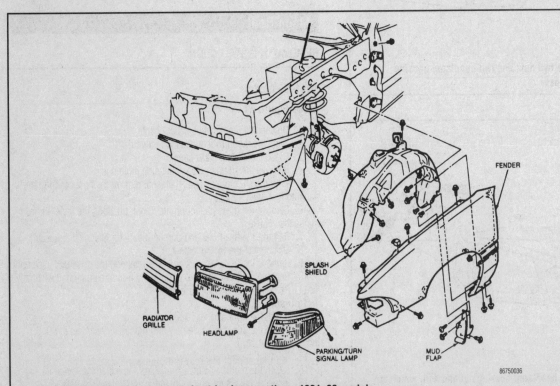

RADIATOR GRILLE

HEADLAMP

PARKING/TURN SIGNAL LAMP

SPLASH SHIELD

FENDER

MUD FLAP

86750036

Fig. 46 Exploded view of the common front fender mounting—1991–96 models

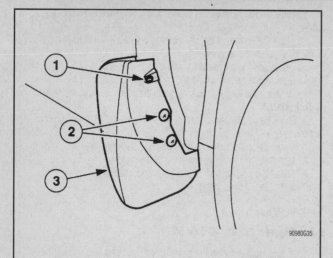

Fig. 47 If equipped, unfasten the stone guard pushpins (2) and screw (1), then remove the stone guard (3)—1997–99 models

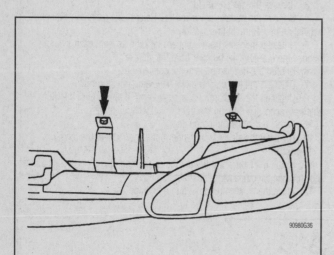

Fig. 48 Unfasten the two nuts and two headlamp housing bolts—1997–99 models

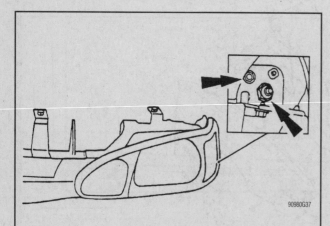

Fig. 49 Unfasten the headlamp housing nut and bolt, which are accessed through the front wheel well opening—1997–99 models

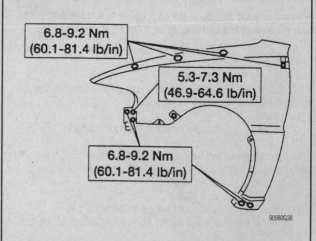

Fig. 50 Install the fender and tighten the retaining bolts to the indicated specifications—1997–99 models

13. Install the headlamp housing nut and, if applicable, the bolt through the front wheel well opening. Tighten the nut and bolt to 47–65 inch lbs. (5.5–7.5 Nm).

14. Install the two nuts and two headlamp housing bolts. Tighten the nuts and bolts to 47–65 inch lbs. (5.5–7.5 Nm).

15. Attach the headlamp electrical connections.

16. Place the bumper into position and install the three front bumper bracket nuts on each side of the bumper. Tighten the nuts to 12–16 ft. lbs. (16–22 Nm).

17. Install the bumper cover (grille). Refer to the grille removal and installation procedure, earlier in this section.

18. Install the splash shield, splash shield screws and pushpins. Tighten the splash shield screws to 23–30 inch lbs. (2.5–3.5 Nm).

19. If equipped, install the stone guard, pushpins and screws. Tighten the screws to 23–30 inch lbs. (2.5–3.5 Nm).

Moon Roof

REMOVAL & INSTALLATION

1991–96 Models

▶ See Figure 51

1. Disconnect the negative battery cable.
2. Slide the moon roof sunshade rearward.
3. Close the sliding glass panel.
4. Remove the sliding glass panel side moldings.
5. With the sliding glass panel closed, remove the nuts securing the panel to its frame.
6. Remove the glass panel from its frame, by lifting the panel up from inside the vehicle.
7. Remove the headliner and unplug the motor electrical connector.
8. Disconnect the wiring fasteners.
9. Remove the bolts, screws and nuts retaining the drive unit assembly.
10. Remove the front and rear drain tubes from the guide unit assembly.
11. Remove the drive unit assembly.

To install:

12. Install the front and rear drain tubes.
13. Install the drive unit assembly and tighten its retainers to 69–95 inch lbs. (8–11 Nm).
14. Connect the wiring fasteners.
15. Attach the motor electrical connector and install the headliner.
16. Install the glass panel into its frame and tighten the nuts.
17. Install the sliding glass panel side moldings.

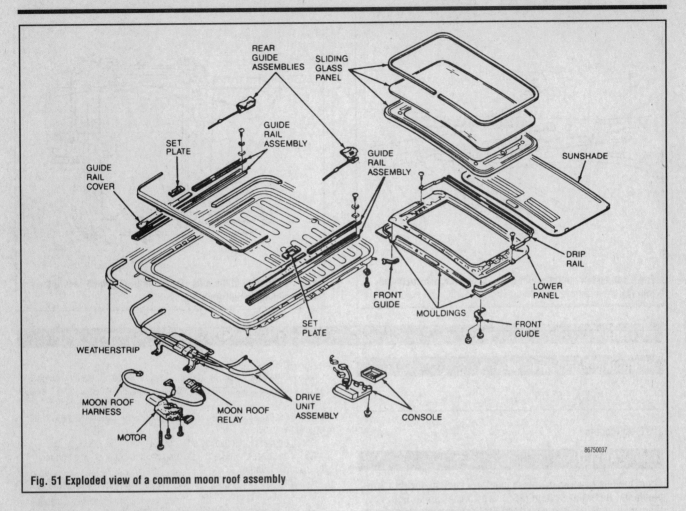

Fig. 51 Exploded view of a common moon roof assembly

18. Connect the negative battery cable and check for proper moon roof operation.
19. Make all necessary adjustments.

1997–99 Models

♦ See Figures 52, 53 and 54

1. Disconnect the negative battery cable.
2. Unfasten the visor retaining screws and remove the visors.
3. Unfasten the visor arm clip screws and remove the clips.
4. Remove the dome lamp.
5. Remove the moon roof trim panel.
6. Remove the three pushpins from the headliner.
7. Remove the headliner.
8. Open the opening shield.
9. Unfasten the glass panel retaining nuts and remove the panel.
10. Unfasten the lifter arm bolts (two on each arm).
11. Remove the lifter arms.
12. Realease the opening shield pins and remove the opening shield.
13. Remove the roof side inner front molding.
14. Disconnect the four drain hoses from the roof opening panel frame.
15. Unfasten the roof opening panel frame nuts and bolts.
16. Remove the opening panel frame.

To install:

17. Place the opening panel frame into position.
18. Install the opening panel frame nuts and bolts. Tighten the nuts and bolts to 70–95 inch lbs. (8–11 Nm).
19. Connect the four drain hoses to the roof opening panel frame.
20. Install the roof side inner front molding.
21. Install the opening shield and engage the pins.
22. Install the lifter arms.

23. Install and tighten the lifter arm bolts (two on each arm).
24. Install the glass panel and tighten the retaining nuts. Tighten the nuts bolts to 70–95 inch lbs. (8–11 Nm).
25. Install the headliner and the pushpins.
26. Install the moon roof trim panel.
27. Install the dome lamp.
28. Install the visor arm clips and tighten the screws.
29. Install the visors and tighten the screws.
30. Install the roof side inner front molding.

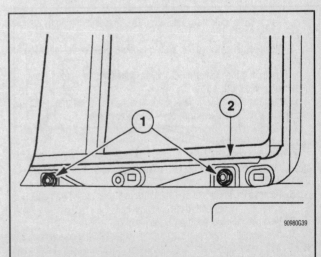

Fig. 52 Unfasten the glass panel retaining nuts (1) and remove the panel (2)—1997-99 models

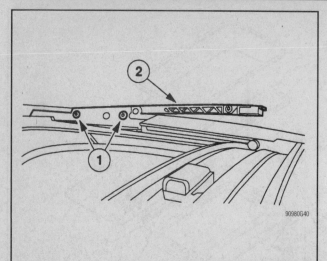

Fig. 53 Unfasten the lifter arm bolts (1) and remove each lifter arm (2)

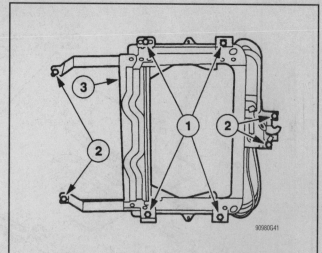

Fig. 54 Location of the nuts (1) and bolts (2) which secure the roof opening panel frame (3)

INTERIOR

Instrument Panel and Pad

REMOVAL & INSTALLATION

1991–96 Models

> ❋❋ **CAUTION**
>
> **Some models covered by this manual are equipped with a Supplemental Restraint System (SRS), which uses an air bag. Whenever working near any of the SRS components, such as the impact sensors, the air bag module, steering column and instrument panel, disable the SRS, as described in Section 6.**

1. Disconnect the negative battery cable.
2. Remove the instrument cluster.
3. Unfasten the glove compartment hinge retainers and remove the glove compartment.
4. On models equipped with a passenger side air bag module, remove the module as follows:
   a. Unfasten the air bag module retainers.
   b. Pull the module from the instrument panel and unplug its electrical connection.
5. When working with a live air bag module, observe the following precautions:
   • Never carry the inflator module by the wires or connector on the underside of the module
   • When carrying a live inflator module, hold securely with both hands, and ensure that the bag and trim cover are pointed away
   • Place the inflator module on a bench or other surface with the bag and trim cover facing up
   • With the inflator module on the bench, never place anything on or close to the module which may be thrown in the event of an accidental deployment
6. Remove the hood release cable from the lower dash trim panel.
7. Carefully pry out both dash side panels.
8. Remove the lower dash trim side panels.
9. If equipped, unfasten the instrument panel steering column cover screws, remove the cover and unplug the light switch rheostat resistor and fog lamp switch electrical connections.
10. Remove the climate control assembly.

11. Remove the ashtray.
12. Remove the center instrument panel finish panel retaining screws.
13. Unplug all radio and cigar lighter electrical connectors and the radio antenna.
14. If necessary, unfasten the right-hand instrument panel screws and remove the panel.
15. If equipped, remove the shift console.
16. If necessary, remove the steering column support bolts and lower the steering column.
17. On 1994–96 models, unfasten the left and right-hand control box side cover pins and remove the covers.
18. On 1994–96 models, perform the following steps:
    a. Slide the air bag diagnostic monitor off the mounting bracket.
    b. Unplug the diagnostic monitor electrical connections.
19. Unplug the amplifier connectors.
20. Remove the instrument panel to floor pan attaching bolts.
21. On 1994–96 models, unfasten the air bag diagnostic monitor bracket bolts and remove the bracket.
22. Remove the bolts from the lower and upper instrument panel mounts.
23. On 1991–93 models, unfasten the defroster duct bezel retaining screw and remove the bezel.
24. Unfasten the instrument panel upper finish panel retainer(s) and remove the upper finish panel.
25. Remove the mounting bolts that attach the upper instrument panel to the cowl.
26. Pull the instrument panel forward, then disconnect the heating and A/C ducts and unplug all electrical connections.
27. Carefully remove the instrument panel from the vehicle.
28. Transfer all attaching components to the replacement panel.
To install:
29. While holding the instrument panel close to installed position, route all wire harness's, connectors and the heater ducts to their proper locations.
30. Place the instrument panel into position and install the retaining bolts.
31. Install the mounting bolts that attach the upper instrument panel to the cowl. Tighten the bolts to 69–104 inch lbs. (8–12 Nm).
32. Install the instrument panel upper finish panel and tighten the retainer(s) to 69–104 inch lbs. (8–12 Nm).
33. On 1991–93 models, install the defroster duct bezel and tighten the retaining screw.
34. Install the bolts to the lower and upper instrument panel mounts. Tighten the bolts to 69–104 inch lbs. (8–12 Nm).

35. On 1994–96 models, install the air bag diagnostic monitor bracket and tighten the bolts. and remove the bracket.

36. Install the instrument panel to floor pan attaching bolts. Tighten the bolts to 69–104 inch lbs. (8–12 Nm).

37. Attach the amplifier connectors.

38. On 1994–96 models perform the following steps:
  a. Slide the air bag diagnostic monitor onto the mounting bracket.
  b. Attach the diagnostic monitor electrical connections.

39. On 1994–96 models, install the left and right-hand control box side covers and pins.

40. If removed, raise the steering column and tighten the steering column support bolts. Tighten the bolts to 80–123 inch lbs. (9–14 Nm).

41. If removed, install the right-hand instrument panel and tighten the screws.

42. If removed, install the shift console.

43. Attach all radio and cigar lighter electrical connectors and the radio antenna.

44. Install the center instrument panel finish panel retaining screws.

45. Install the ashtray.

46. Install the climate control assembly.

47. If equipped, attach the light switch rheostat resistor and fog lamp switch electrical connections then install the instrument panel steering column cover and screws,

48. Install the trim side panels.

49. Attach the hood release cable to the lower dash trim panel.

50. On models equipped with a passenger side air bag module, install the module as follows:
  a. Press the module mounting tabs down 0.08–0.11 inch (2–3mm).
  b. Attach the module electrical connection and position the module on the instrument.
  c. Install and tighten the air bag module retainers to 61–79 inch lbs. (7–9 Nm).

51. Install the glove compartment and tighten the hinge retainers to 69–104 inch lbs. (8–12 Nm).

52. Install the instrument cluster.

53. Connect the negative battery cable.

1997–99 Models

▶ See Figures 55 thru 65

✷✷ CAUTION

Some models covered by this manual are equipped with a Supplemental Restraint System (SRS), which uses an air bag. Whenever working near any of the SRS components, such as the impact sensors, the air bag module, steering column and instrument panel, disable the SRS, as described in Section 6.

1. Disconnect the negative battery cable.

2. On 1997 models, remove the parking brake and shift consoles.

3. On 1998–99 models, remove the floor console.

4. Remove the screw from the center instrument panel finish panel.

5. Pull the center instrument panel finish panel straight out from the instrument panel reinforcement and remove it.

6. On 1997 models, unplug the cigar lighter electrical connection, remove the cigar lighter knob and element. Twist the cigar lighter socket from the lighter retainer and remove the socket.

7. On 1998–99 models, unplug the cigar lighter electrical connection.

8. Remove the center instrument panel finish panel.

9. Unfasten the left-hand and right-hand control box cover pushpins and remove the covers.

10. Disconnect the radio antenna lead-in cable from the instrument panel reinforcement.

11. Unplug the lead-in cable.

12. If equipped, unplug the amplifier electrical connection.

13. Unfasten the transaxle control lever dial bezel screws and position the dial bezel sideways.

14. Unfasten the Powertrain Control Module (PCM) electrical connector bolt, unplug the connector and move it aside.

15. Unfasten the two rear side PCM bracket bolts and the front bolts, then remove the PCM.

16. On 1997 models, remove the integrated control panel (radio and heater panel.

17. On 1998–99 models, rotate the temperature control switch to the cool position and disconnect the temperature control cable.

18. Remove the steering wheel.

19. Unfasten the hood control latch nut, then position the latch and cable aside.

20. Unfasten the Powertrain Control Module (PCM) electrical connector bolt, unplug the connector and move it aside

21. On 1998–98 models, unplug the light switch rheostat connector and remove the steering column cover.

22. Unfasten the steering column bracket bolts and lower the column.

23. Unfasten the finish panel screws and remove the panel.

24. On 1997 models, remove the instrument cluster.

25. Remove both the front door scuff plates by pulling them upward.

26. Unfasten each cowl side trim panel pushpins and remove the panels.

27. On 1997 models, remove both front door seam welts.

28. On 1998–99 models, unplug the interior fuse junction panel connector.

29. On 1998–99 models, unplug the in-line electrical connector located on the left-hand side of the lower instrument panel reinforcement.

30. On 1997 models, remove both roof side inner moldings by pulling them outward.

31. On 1997 models, remove the fuse panel cover and unplug the main fuse junction panel electrical connectors.

32. Push in on the glove compartment door tabs and lower the door.

33. Unfasten the glove compartment hinge-to-instrument panel screws and remove the glove compartment.

34. When working with a live air bag module, observe the following precautions:
  • Never carry the inflator module by the wires or connector on the underside of the module.
  • When carrying a live inflator module, hold securely with both hands, and ensure that the bag and trim cover are pointed away
  • Place the inflator module on a bench or other surface with the bag and trim cover facing up
  • With the inflator module on the bench, never place anything on or close to the module which may be thrown in the event of an accidental deployment

35. Remove the passenger side air bag module as follows:
  a. Unfasten the passenger side air bag module bolts.
  b. Slide the module from the instrument panel and unplug the electrical connector.

36. Tag and unplug the vacuum line harness connector.

37. On 1997 models, pry off both instrument panel end panels with a suitable pry tool.

38. On 1998–99 models, unplug the in-line electrical connector located on the right-hand side of the lower instrument panel reinforcement

39. On 1998–99 models, unplug the blower motor resistor electrical connector.

40. Unfasten both the left-hand and right-hand center instrument panel reinforcement bolts.

41. Unfasten both the left-hand and right-hand lower instrument panel reinforcement bolts.

42. Remove the cover and unfasten the upper instrument panel reinforcement bolt.

43. Pull the instrument panel slightly away from the mounting brackets and unplug all remaining electrical connections.

44. Remove the instrument panel from the vehicle.

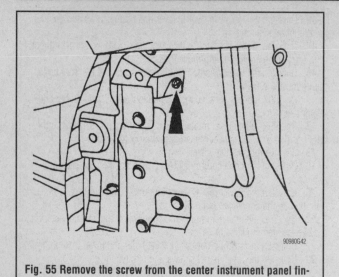

Fig. 55 Remove the screw from the center instrument panel finish panel

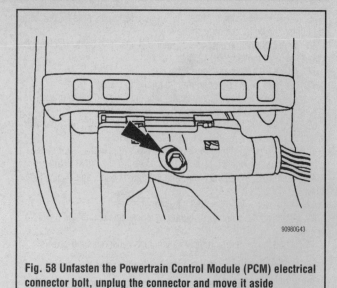

Fig. 58 Unfasten the Powertrain Control Module (PCM) electrical connector bolt, unplug the connector and move it aside

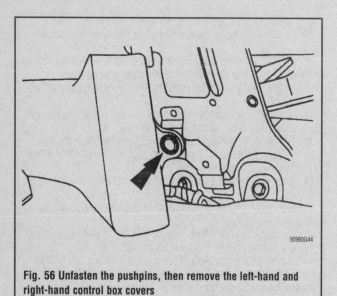

Fig. 56 Unfasten the pushpins, then remove the left-hand and right-hand control box covers

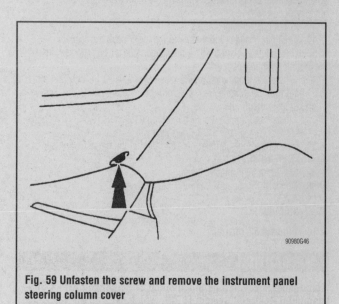

Fig. 59 Unfasten the screw and remove the instrument panel steering column cover

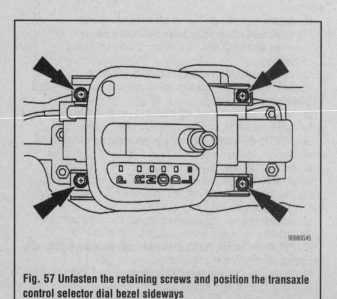

Fig. 57 Unfasten the retaining screws and position the transaxle control selector dial bezel sideways

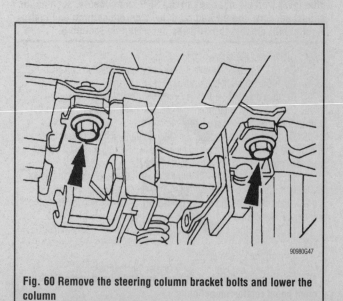

Fig. 60 Remove the steering column bracket bolts and lower the column

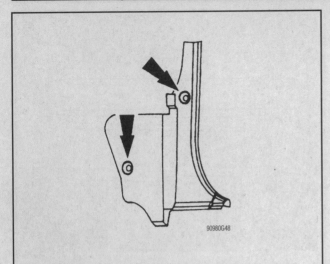

Fig. 61 Remove the pushpins from each cowl side trim panel, and remove the panels

Fig. 64 Unfasten both the left-hand and right-hand lower instrument panel reinforcement bolts

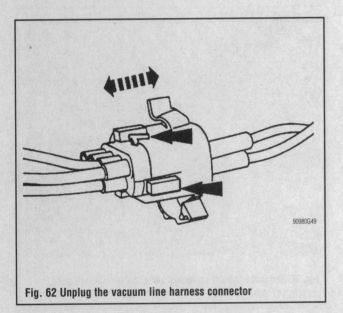

Fig. 62 Unplug the vacuum line harness connector

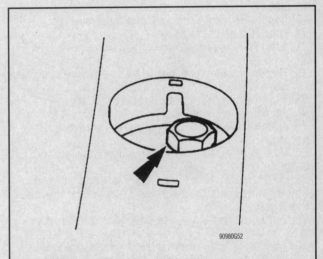

Fig. 65 Remove the cover and unfasten the upper instrument panel reinforcement bolt

Fig. 63 Unfasten both the left-hand and right-hand center instrument panel reinforcement bolts

To install:

45. Attach the electrical connections to the instrument panel and place the panel into position.

46. Install the upper instrument panel reinforcement bolt. Tighten the bolt to 70–94 inch lbs. (8–11 Nm) and install the cover.

47. Install both the left-hand and right-hand lower instrument panel reinforcement bolts. Tighten the bolts to 14–18 ft. lbs. (19–25 Nm).

48. Install both the left-hand and right-hand center instrument panel reinforcement bolts. Tighten the bolt to 70–94 inch lbs. (8–11 Nm).

49. On 1998–99 models, attach the in-line electrical connector located on the right-hand side of the lower instrument panel reinforcement.

50. On 1998–99 models, attach the blower motor resistor electrical connector.

51. Install both instrument panel end panels.

52. Attach the vacuum line harness connector.

53. Install the passenger side air bag module as follows:

    a. Attach the module electrical connector and place the module into position.

    b. Install the passenger side air bag module bolts. Tighten the bolts to 70–103 inch lbs. (8–12 Nm).

54. Install the glove compartment and tighten the hinge-to-instrument panel screws.
55. Engage the glove compartment door tabs.
56. Attach the main fuse junction panel electrical connectors and install the fuse panel cover.
57. Install both roof side inner moldings.
58. On 1997 models, install both front door seam welts.
59. On 1998–99 models, attach the interior fuse junction panel connector.
60. On 1998–99 models, attach the in-line electrical connector located on the left-hand side of the lower instrument panel reinforcement.
61. Install the cowl side trim panel and attach the pushpins.
62. Install both the front door scuff plates.
63. On 1997 models, install the instrument cluster.
64. Install the finish panel and tighten the screws.
65. Raise the steering column, install the bracket bolts and tighten the bolts to 80–124 inch lbs. (9–14 Nm).
66. On 1997 models, install the instrument panel steering column cover and tighten the screw.
67. On 1998–98 models, attach the light switch rheostat connector and install the steering column cover.
68. Install the steering wheel.
69. On 1997 models, install the integrated control panel (radio and heater panel).
70. On 1998–99 models, connect the temperature control cable.
71. Install PCM and the bracket bolts.
72. Attach the PCM electrical connector and tighten the retaining bolt.
73. Place the transaxle control lever dial bezel into position and tighten the screws.
74. If equipped, attach the amplifier electrical connection.
75. Attach the antenna lead-in cable.
76. Attach the radio antenna lead-in cable to the instrument panel reinforcement.
77. Install the left-hand and right-hand control box cover and attach pushpins.
78. On 1997 models, install the cigar lighter socket into the lighter retainer and twist it to engage it into position. Install the cigar lighter element and knob.
79. On 1998–99 models, attach the cigar lighter electrical connection.
80. Install the instrument panel finish panel and tighten the screw.
81. On 1997 models, install the shift and parking brake consoles.
82. On 1998–99 models, install the floor console.
83. Connect the negative battery cable.

Parking Brake Console

REMOVAL & INSTALLATION

1991–96 Models

▶ See Figures 66, 67 and 68

1. Place both front seats in their rearmost positions.
2. If necessary, remove the rear passenger ashtray.
3. Unfasten the two front screws from the parking brake console.
4. Recline both front seats.
5. Unfasten the two rear screws from the parking brake console.
6. Raise the parking brake lever and remove the console.

To install:

7. Feed the safety belt ends through the holes in the console.
8. Install the console and lower the lever.
9. Install the four console retaining screws.
10. Place the seats in their original positions.
11. If removed, install the rear passenger ashtray.

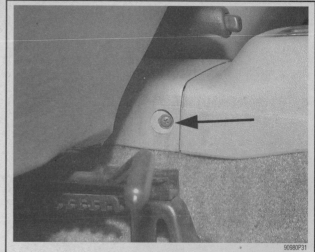
Fig. 66 Unfasten the screw(s) from the front of the parking brake console

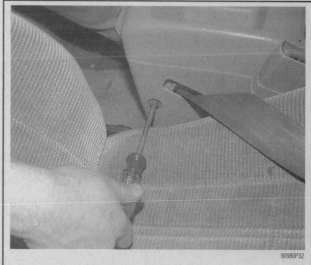
Fig. 67 Unfasten the rear console screws . . .

Fig. 68 . . . and remove the parking brake console

1997–99 Models

▶ **See Figure 69**

1. Place both front seats in their foremost positions.
2. Unfasten the two screws from the parking brake console.
3. Raise the parking brake lever and remove the console.

To install:

4. Install the console and tighten the screws.
5. Return the seats to their original positions.

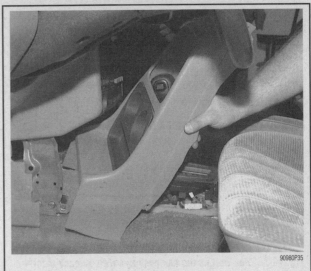

Fig. 71 . . . then remove the console

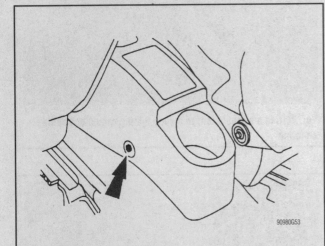

Fig. 69 Unfasten the two screws from the parking brake console—1997–99 models

3. On models equipped with a manual transaxle, unscrew the gearshift lever knob.
4. Remove the shift console.
5. Installation is the reverse of removal.

1997–99 Models

▶ **See Figures 72, 73 and 74**

1. Remove the parking brake console.
2. Unfasten the two shift console screws.
3. Remove the four pushpins (two on each side).
4. On 1997 models with an automatic transaxle, loosen the gearshift knob screws and remove the knob.
5. On 1998–99 models, place the gearshift selector in low gear.
6. On 1998–99 models, remove the beverage holder from the console.
7. On models with a manual transaxle, remove the gearshift knob.
8. Lift up and remove the console.
9. On 1998–99 models, place the gearshift selector in the PARK position.

To install:

10. On 1998–99 models, place the gearshift selector in low gear.
11. Install the console.

Shift Console

REMOVAL & INSTALLATION

1991–96 Models

▶ **See Figures 70 and 71**

1. Remove the parking brake console.
2. Unfasten the two shift console screws.

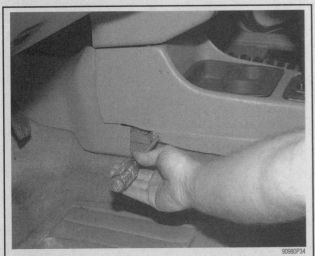

Fig. 70 Unfasten the two shift console screws (one on each side) . . .

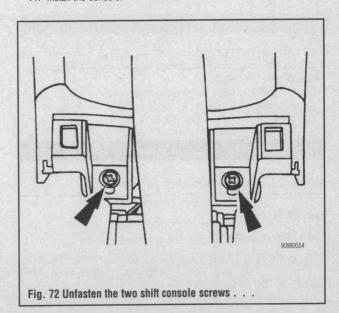

Fig. 72 Unfasten the two shift console screws . . .

Fig. 73 . . . as well as the four pushpins (two on each side)—1997–99 models

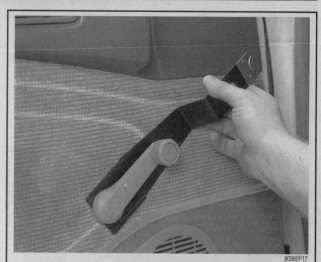

Fig. 75 Use a suitable tool to disengage the regulator handle snapring

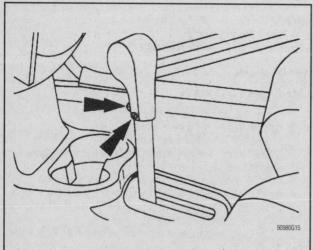

Fig. 74 On 1997 models with an automatic transaxle, loosen the gearshift knob screws and remove the knob

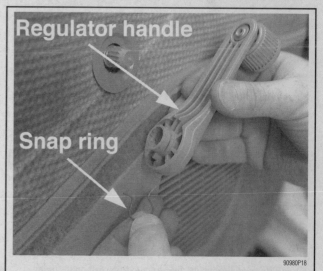

Fig. 76 Remove the regulator handle and snapring

12. On 1998–99 models, place the gearshift selector in the PARK position.

13. On models with a manual transaxle, install the gearshift knob.

14. On 1997 models with an automatic transaxle, install the gearshift knob and tighten the screws.

15. On 1998–99 models, install the beverage holder.

16. Install the four pushpins.

17. Install the parking brake console.

Door Panels

REMOVAL & INSTALLATION

1991–96 Models

▶ See Figures 75 thru 81

1. Disconnect the negative battery cable.

2. Remove the window regulator handle, using a suitable tool to disengage the regulator handle snapring.

3. Remove the power window switch, if equipped.

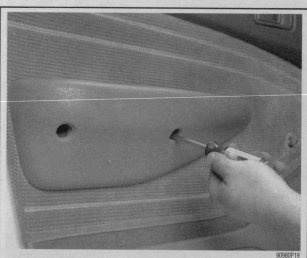

Fig. 77 Unfasten the armrest screws and, if necessary, remove the armrest

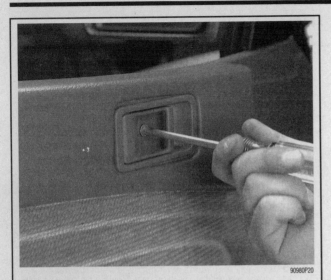

Fig. 78 Remove the inside door handle retaining screw

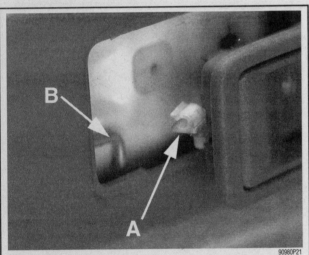

Fig. 79 Remove the inside door handle after disengaging the handle clip (A) from the lock mechanism (B)

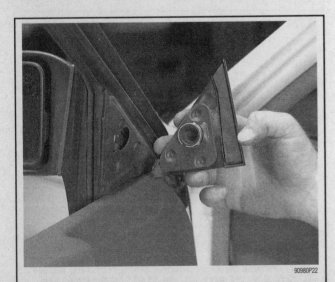

Fig. 80 Remove the outside mirror's trim cover

Fig. 81 Remove the trim panel by lifting it up and sliding it rearward to clear the sheet metal

4. Remove the outside mirror's trim cover (and remote control handle, if so equipped).

5. Unfasten the armrest screws and, if necessary, remove the armrest.

6. Slide a flat-bladed tool behind each of the retaining clips and twist to disengage the clips from the door shell.

7. Remove the trim panel by lifting it up and sliding it rearward to clear the sheet metal.

To install:

8. Replace all damaged trim panel retainers.

9. If removed, install the watershield.

10. Place the trim panel into position on the door and, if applicable, insert the outside mirror's remote control handle through the opening.

11. Attach the outside mirror's trim cover.

12. Install the power window switch, if equipped.

13. Install the armrest and tighten the screws.

14. Install the window regulator handle.

15. Connect the negative battery cable.

1997–99 Models

COUPE

♦ See Figures 82, 83 and 84

1. Disconnect the negative battery cable.

2. Remove the screw covers, screws and pushpin, then remove the door pull handle appliqué.

3. If equipped, unplug the regulator switch plate electrical connector.

4. Mark the position of the window regulator handle, then remove the handle using a suitable tool to disengage the regulator handle snapring.

5. Remove the pushpins from the trim panel.

6. Slide a flat-bladed tool behind each of the retaining clips and twist to disengage the clips from the door shell.

7. Remove the trim panel by lifting it up and sliding it rearward to clear the sheet metal.

To install:

8. Replace all damaged trim panel retainers.

9. If removed, install the watershield.

10. Place the trim panel into position on the door and insert the door handle through the opening.

11. Attach the door panel fasteners.

12. Install the pushpins on the trim panel.

13. Install the regulator handle.

14. If equipped, attach the regulator switch plate electrical connector.

15. Install the door pull handle appliqué cover, the screws, screw covers and the pushpin.

16. Connect the negative battery cable.

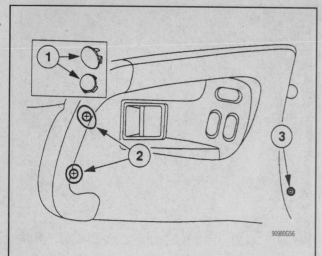

Fig. 82 Remove the door pull handle appliqué's screw covers (1), screws (2) and pushpin (3)—1998–99 coupe models

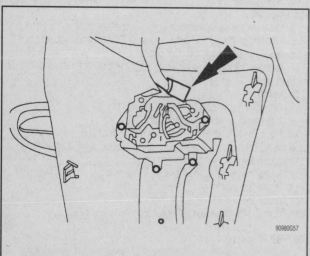

Fig. 83 If equipped, unplug the regulator switch plate electrical connector

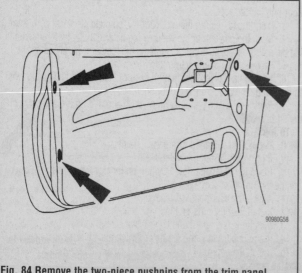

Fig. 84 Remove the two-piece pushpins from the trim panel

SEDAN AND WAGON—FRONT DOORS

▶ **See Figures 85, 86, 87 and 88**

1. Disconnect the negative battery cable.
2. Remove the front door interior pull handle screw.
3. Remove the screw cap and the screw from the inside door handle.
4. Slide the handle rearward to disengage the hook from the sheet metal.
5. Disconnect the handle from the door latch link.
6. Mark the position of the window regulator handle, then remove the handle using a suitable tool to disengage the regulator handle snapring.
7. Remove the two-piece pushpins from the trim panel.
8. Slide a flat-bladed tool behind each of the retaining clips and twist to disengage the clips from the door shell.
9. Remove the trim panel.
10. If equipped, unplug the power window electrical connector.
11. Pull out on the cup retainer tabs and remove the power window regulator control switch electrical connector from the retainer.

To install:

12. Attach the power window regulator control switch electrical connector to the retainer and secure the retainer tabs.
13. Install the trim panel and engage its fasteners.

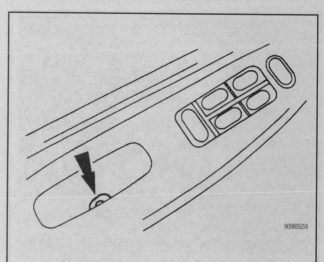

Fig. 85 Remove the front door interior pull handle screw— 1997–99 sedan and wagon models

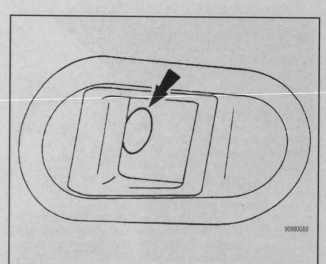

Fig. 86 Remove the screw cap and screw from the inside door handle

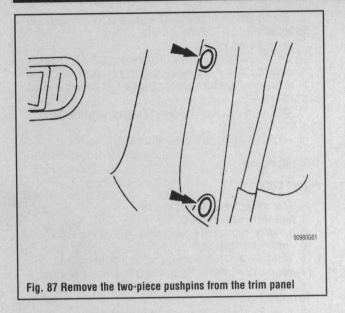

Fig. 87 Remove the two-piece pushpins from the trim panel

Fig. 89 Remove the rear door cup screw

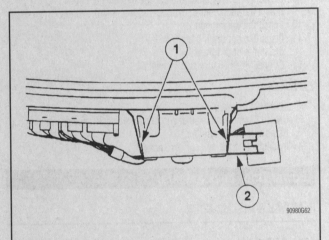

Fig. 88 Pull outward on the cup retainer tabs (1) to remove the master window regulator control switch panel, then detach the electrical connector from the retainer (2)

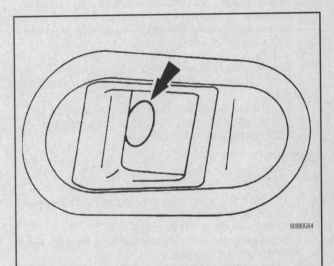

Fig. 90 Remove the screw cap and screw from the inside door handle

14. Install the two-piece pushpins which attach the trim panel.
15. Install the regulator handle.
16. Attach the door handle to the latch link.
17. Install the screw and screw cap.
18. Install the front door interior pull handle screw.
19. Connect the negative battery cable.

SEDAN AND WAGON—REAR DOORS

▶ See Figures 89, 90 and 91

1. Disconnect the negative battery cable.
2. Remove the rear door cup screw.
3. Remove the screw cap and the screw from the inside door handle.
4. Slide the handle rearward to disengage the hook from the sheet metal.
5. Disconnect the handle from the door latch link.
6. Mark the position of the window regulator handle, then remove the handle using a suitable tool to disengage the regulator handle snapring.
7. Slide a flat-bladed tool behind each of the retaining clips and twist to disengage the clips from the door shell.
8. Remove the trim panel.

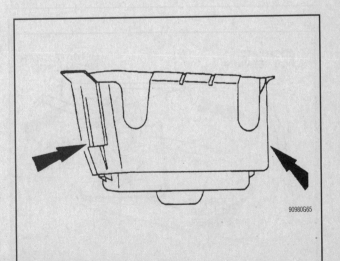

Fig. 91 Remove the door pull cup retainer by pulling outwards on the locking tabs—1997–99 sedan and wagon models

9. Remove the door pull cup retainer by pulling outwards on the locking tabs.

To install:

10. Install the door pull cup and engage the tabs.
11. Install the trim panel.
12. Install the regulator handle.
13. Attach the door handle to the latch link.
14. Install the screw and screw cap.
15. Install the rear door cup screw.
16. Connect the negative battery cable.

Door Lock Cylinder

REMOVAL & INSTALLATION

1991–96 Models

FRONT AND REAR DOORS

➡When a lock cylinder must be replaced, replace both locks in the set to avoid carrying an extra key which fits only one lock.

1. Remove the door trim panel and the watershield.
2. Remove the clip attaching the lock cylinder rod to the lock cylinder.
3. Slide the lock cylinder retainer out from the top of the lock cylinder.
4. Remove the lock cylinder from the door.

To install:

5. Work the cylinder lock assembly into the outer door panel.
6. Install the cylinder retainer into its slot and push the retainer onto the lock cylinder.
7. Install the lock cylinder rod with the clip onto the lock assembly.
8. Lock and unlock the door to check the lock cylinder operation.
9. Install the watershield and door trim panel.

LIFTGATE

▶ See Figure 92

1. On 3 and 5 door models, unfasten the luggage compartment rear cover pushpins and remove the cover.
2. On wagon models, remove the trim panel.
3. Disengage the door latch rod retainer and detach the liftgate latch release rod from the door lock cylinder.
4. Slide the lock cylinder retainer out from the side of the door lock cylinder.
5. On GT models, unfasten the four screws and remove the rear reflector.

6. Remove the lock cylinder from the outside of the rear body panel.

To install:

7. Install the lock cylinder.
8. On GT models, install the rear reflector and fasten the retaining screws.
9. Install the lock cylinder retainer through the side of the lock cylinder.
10. Attach the liftgate latch release rod to the door lock and engage the door latch retainer.
11. On 3 and 5-door models, install the luggage compartment rear cover and the pushpins.
12. On wagon models, install the trim panel.

1997–99 Models

FRONT DOOR

1. Disconnect the negative battery cable.
2. Remove the door trim panel.
3. Unfasten the door pull bracket screw.
4. Remove the watershield.
5. Detach the latch control cylinder rod from the lock cylinder.
6. Remove the retainer clip by expanding the brass spring outward.
7. Remove the lock cylinder.

To install:

8. Install the lock cylinder and engage the retainer clip.
9. Attach the latch control cylinder rod to the lock cylinder.
10. Install the watershield.
11. Install the door pull bracket screw.
12. Install the door trim panel.
13. Connect the negative battery cable.

LIFTGATE

1. Remove the trim panel.
2. Detach the lock rod retainer and remove the lock cylinder retaining clip.
3. Remove the lock cylinder.
4. Installation is the reverse of removal.

Power Door Lock Actuator

REMOVAL & INSTALLATION

1991–96 Models

▶ See Figures 93 and 94

1. Disconnect the negative battery cable.
2. Remove the door trim panel.

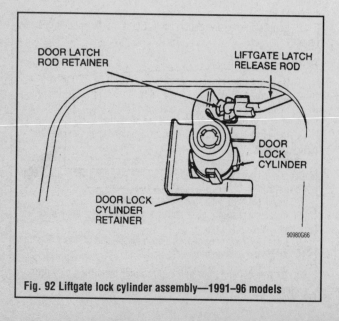

Fig. 92 Liftgate lock cylinder assembly—1991–96 models

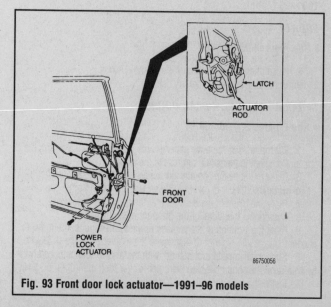

Fig. 93 Front door lock actuator—1991–96 models

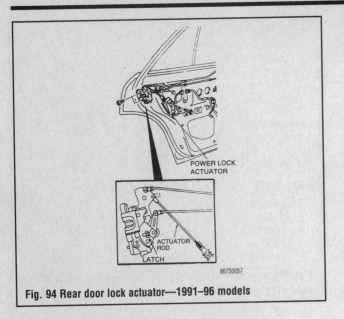

Fig. 94 Rear door lock actuator—1991–96 models

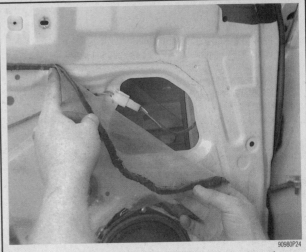

Fig. 95 Peel back the watershield to access the two door glass retaining bolts

3. Disconnect the actuator rod from the door latch.
4. Unplug the actuator electrical connection.
5. Unfasten the actuator bolts and remove the actuator.
6. Installation is the reverse of removal.
7. Tighten the actuator bolts to 61–89 inch lbs. (7–9 Nm).

1997–99 Models

1. Disconnect the negative battery cable.
2. Remove the door trim panel.
3. Unfasten the actuator nuts.
4. Disconnect the actuator from the door latch and unplug the actuator electrical connector.
5. Remove the actuator.
6. Installation is the reverse of removal.
7. Tighten the actuator nuts to 70–96 inch lbs. (7–10 Nm).

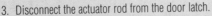

Door Glass

REMOVAL & INSTALLATION

1991–96 Models

FRONT

▶ **See Figures 95 and 96**

1. Raise the front door glass 4.3 inches (110mm) from the fully open position.
2. Disconnect the negative battery cable.
3. Remove the door trim panel and watershield.
4. Remove the two glass retaining bolts. Allow the glass to remain supported on the glass plastic clips.
5. Tilt the front of the door glass downward to disengage if from the channel and pull the glass up and out of the door.
6. Place the glass on a protected surface.
To install:
7. Place the glass in the door and tilt the front end downward.
8. Engage the rear edge of the glass into the channel.
9. Bring the front edge of the glass upward and engage it into the channel.
10. Support the glass on the slider with the plastic clips and install the two glass retainer bolts. Tighten the bolts to 2–3 inch lbs. (0.23–0.35 Nm).
11. Install the trim panel and watershield.

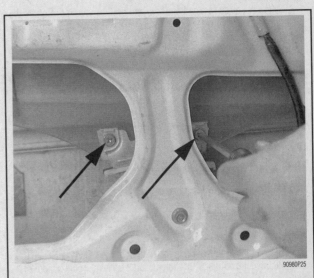

Fig. 96 Unfasten the two glass retaining bolts (arrows)

12. Connect the negative battery cable. Check that the window operates properly.

REAR

1. Open the rear door glass fully.
2. Disconnect the negative battery cable.
3. Remove the door trim panel and watershield.
4. Detach the weatherstrip from the top of the door.
5. Remove the two glass retainers, retaining the center channel and channel protector.
6. Remove the window regulator roller through the large hole in the lift bracket and remove the rear door glass. Pull the fixed glass out of the channel.
To install:
7. Install the fixed glass to the door channel.
8. Install the rear door glass and engage the regulator roller into the large hole.
9. Install the center channel, channel protector and retainers.
10. Attach the weatherstrips.
11. Install the door trim panel.
12. Connect the negative battery cable. Check that the window operates properly.

1997–99 Models

1. Lower the window glass.
2. Remove the door trim panel.
3. If equipped, remove the door armrest bracket screw.
4. Remove the watershield.
5. Unfasten the access panel screws and remove the access panel.
6. Unfasten the nut and bolt attaching the glass to the regulator and remove the glass.

To install:

7. Install the glass and tighten the nut and bolt to 2–3 inch lbs. (0.23–0.35 Nm).
8. Check the operation of the window and adjust as necessary.
9. Install the access panel and tighten the screws.
10. Install the watershield.
11. If equipped, install the door armrest bracket screw.
12. Install the trim panel.

ADJUSTMENTS

1. Remove the door trim panel and watershield.
2. Loosen the nut and washer assemblies retaining the glass run and bracket assembly.
3. Move the glass fore and aft (or in and out), as required. Tighten the nut and washer assemblies.
4. Check the operation of the window.
5. Install the trim panel and watershield.

Window Regulator

REMOVAL & INSTALLATION

1991–96 Models

MANUAL WINDOW—FRONT DOOR

▶ **See Figures 97 and 98**

1. Remove the front door glass.
2. Remove the two regulator retaining nuts and one regulator retaining screw.
3. Remove the regulator drive retaining nuts.
4. Remove the regulator through the large opening in the bottom of the door.

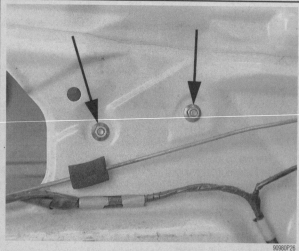

Fig. 97 Remove the two window regulator retaining nuts (arrows)

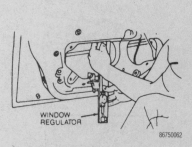

Fig. 98 Remove the window regulator through the bottom of the door—1991–96 models

To install:

5. Rotate the regulator drive unit 180⁻ to install, so that the gray cable is toward the glass and the black cable is toward the inner door panel.
6. Install the regulator through the large opening in the bottom of the door.
7. Install the regulator drive retaining nuts. Tighten to 61–87 inch lbs. (7–9 Nm).
8. Install the two regulator retaining nuts and one regulator retaining screw.
9. Install the front door glass.

MANUAL WINDOW—REAR DOOR

1. Remove the rear door glass.
2. Remove the three retaining bolts.
3. Remove the regulator through the large opening in the bottom of the door.
4. Install the regulator in the reverse order of removal. Tighten the bolts to 61–87 inch lbs. (7–9 Nm).

POWER WINDOW—FRONT DOOR

▶ **See Figure 99**

1. Disconnect the negative battery cable.
2. Remove the front door glass.
3. Twist the retainers to release the conduit from the door.
4. Unplug the electrical connector.
5. Remove the two upper regulator mounting nuts.
6. Remove the three lower regulator mounting bolts.
7. Remove the regulator through the large opening in the bottom of the door.

To install:

8. Install the regulator through the large opening in the bottom of the door.
9. Install the lower and upper regulator retaining nuts and bolts. Tighten to 61–87 inch lbs. (7–9 Nm).
10. Attach the electrical connector.
11. Twist the retainers to secure the conduit from the door.
12. Install the front door glass.
13. Connect the negative battery cable.
14. Cycle the glass up and down to check for smooth operation.

POWER WINDOW—REAR DOOR

1. Remove the rear door glass.
2. Disconnect the negative battery cable.

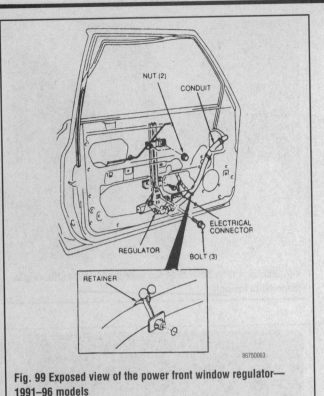

Fig. 99 Exposed view of the power front window regulator—1991-96 models

3. Unplug the electrical connector and remove the four retaining bolts.

4. Remove the regulator through the large opening in the bottom of the door.

5. Install the regulator in the reverse order of removal. Tighten the bolts to 61–87 inch lbs. (7–9 Nm).

1997–99 Models

EXCEPT COUPE MODELS

1. Remove the door glass.
2. Unfasten the five regulator nuts and one bolt.
3. Remove the regulator.
4. Installation is the reverse of removal.
5. Tighten the nuts and bolt to 62–79 inch lbs. (7–9 Nm).

COUPE MODELS

1. Remove the door glass.
2. If equipped, unplug the window regulator motor electrical connection.
3. Unfasten the motor and regulator nuts.
4. Remove the regulator.
5. Installation is the reverse of removal.
6. Tighten the motor nuts to 62–86 inch lbs. (7–10 Nm) and the regulator nuts to 14–18 ft. lbs. (18–25 Nm).

Electric Window Motor

REMOVAL & INSTALLATION

1. Remove the door trim panel and watershield.
2. If necessary, remove the glass.
3. Disconnect the negative battery cable.
4. Unplug the motor electrical connection.
5. If necessary and possible, remove the regulator assembly.
6. If the regulator is attached with rivets, drill out the rivets.
7. If the motor is retained by fasteners, remove the fasteners.
8. Remove the motor.

To install:

9. Install the motor making sure the to engage it to the regulator.
10. If removed, install the regulator.
11. Attach new rivets or fasteners.
12. Attach the motor electrical connection.
13. If removed, install the glass.
14. Connect the negative battery cable.
15. Check for proper window operation.
16. Install the trim panel and watershield.

Windshield and Fixed Glass

REMOVAL & INSTALLATION

If your windshield, or other fixed window, is cracked or chipped, you may decide to replace it with a new one yourself. However, there are two main reasons why replacement windshields and other window glass should be installed only by a professional automotive glass technician: safety and cost.

The most important reason a professional should install automotive glass is for safety. The glass in the vehicle, especially the windshield, is designed with safety in mind in case of a collision. The windshield is specially manufactured from two panes of specially-tempered glass with a thin layer of transparent plastic between them. This construction allows the glass to "give" in the event that a part of your body hits the windshield during the collision, and prevents the glass from shattering, which could cause lacerations, blinding and other harm to passengers of the vehicle. The other fixed windows are designed to be tempered so that if they break during a collision, they shatter in such a way that there are no large pointed glass pieces. The professional automotive glass technician knows how to install the glass in a vehicle so that it will function optimally during a collision. Without the proper experience, knowledge and tools, installing a piece of automotive glass yourself could lead to additional harm if an accident should ever occur.

Cost is also a factor when deciding to install automotive glass yourself. Performing this could cost you much more than a professional may charge for the same job. Since the windshield is designed to break under stress, an often life saving characteristic, windshields tend to break VERY easily when an inexperienced person attempts to install one. Do-it-yourselfers buying two, three or even four windshields from a salvage yard because they have broken them during installation are common stories. Also, since the automotive glass is designed to prevent the outside elements from entering your vehicle, improper installation can lead to water and air leaks. Annoying whining noises at highway speeds from air leaks or inside body panel rusting from water leaks can add to your stress level and subtract from your wallet. After buying two or three windshields, installing them and ending up with a leak that produces a noise while driving and water damage during rainstorms, the cost of having a professional do it correctly the first time may be much more alluring. We here at Chilton, therefore, advise that you have a professional automotive glass technician service any broken glass on your vehicle.

WINDSHIELD CHIP REPAIR

♦ See Figures 100 thru 114

➡Check with your state and local authorities on the laws for state safety inspection. Some states or municipalities may not allow chip repair as a viable option for correcting stone damage to your windshield.

Although severely cracked or damaged windshields must be replaced, there is something that you can do to prolong or even prevent the need for replacement of a chipped windshield. There are many companies which offer windshield chip repair products, such as Loctite's® Bullseye™ windshield repair kit. These kits usually consist of a syringe, pedestal and a sealing adhesive. The syringe is mounted on the pedestal and is used to create a vacuum which pulls the plastic layer against the glass. This helps make the chip transparent. The adhesive is then injected which seals the chip and helps to prevent further stress cracks from developing. Refer to the sequence of photos to get a general idea of what windshield chip repair involves.

➡Always follow the specific manufacturer's instructions.

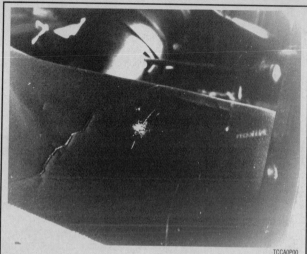

Fig. 100 Small chips on your windshield can be fixed with an aftermarket repair kit, such as the one from Loctite®

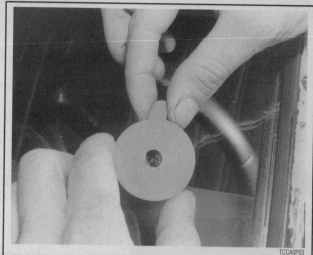

Fig. 103 . . . then press it on the windshield so that the chip is centered in the hole

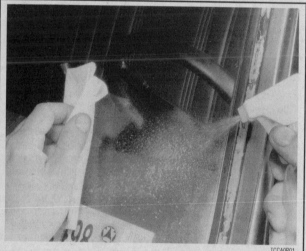

Fig. 101 To repair a chip, clean the windshield with glass cleaner and dry it completely

Fig. 104 Be sure that the tab points upward on the windshield

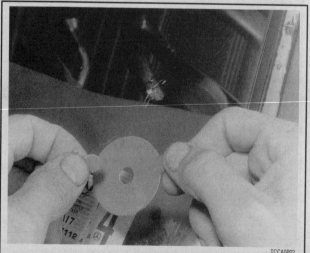

Fig. 102 Remove the center from the adhesive disc and peel off the backing from one side of the disc . . .

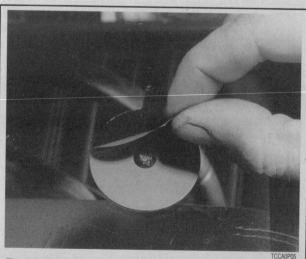

Fig. 105 Peel the backing off the exposed side of the adhesive disc . . .

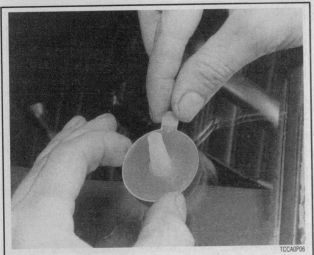

Fig. 106 . . . then position the plastic pedestal on the adhesive disc, ensuring that the tabs are aligned

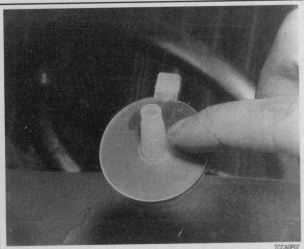

Fig. 107 Press the pedestal firmly on the adhesive disc to create an adequate seal . . .

Fig. 108 . . . then install the applicator syringe nipple in the pedestal's hole

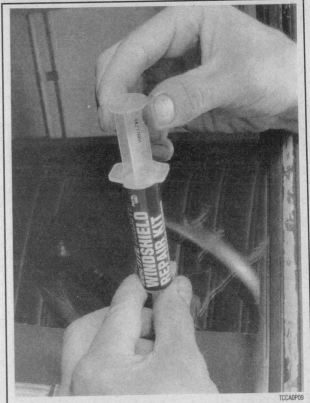

Fig. 109 Hold the syringe with one hand while pulling the plunger back with the other hand

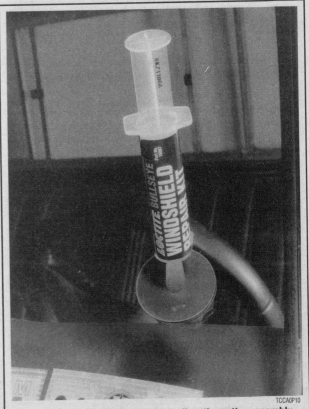

Fig. 110 After applying the solution, allow the entire assembly to sit until it has set completely

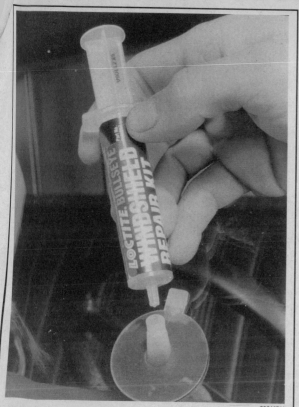

Fig. 111 After the solution has set, remove the syringe from the pedestal . . .

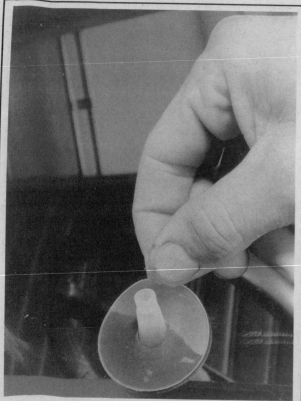

Fig. 112 . . . then peel the pedestal off of the adhesive disc . . .

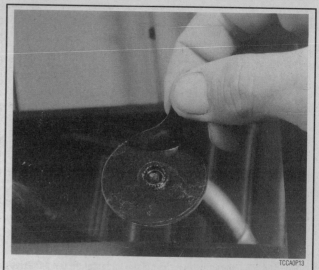

Fig. 113 . . . and peel the adhesive disc off of the windshield

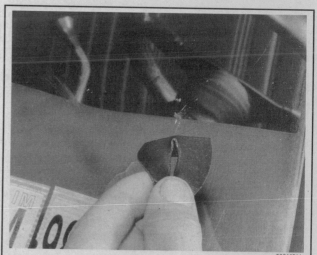

Fig. 114 The chip will still be slightly visible, but it should be filled with the hardened solution

Inside Rear View Mirror

REMOVAL & INSTALLATION

1991–93 Models

1. Grasp the rear view mirror firmly.
2. Insert rear view mirror removal tool T91T-17700-A or equivalent into the screwless mount slot until the spring clip is contacted.
3. Push on the spring clip with the tool and pull the mirror to remove it from the mounting bracket.

To install:
4. Install the mirror onto the mounting bracket until it firmly fits in place.

1994–99 Models

1. Grasp the inside rear view mirror firmly.
2. Tap gently on the mirror with a rubber mallet to remove it from the mounting bracket.

To install:
3. Install the mirror onto the mounting bracket until it firmly fits in place.

Seats

REMOVAL & INSTALLATION

Front

1. Disconnect the negative battery cable.
2. Slide the seat rearward.
3. Unfasten the two front seat track-to-floor bolts.
4. Slide the seat forward.
5. Unfasten the screws attaching the seat track covers on the track and remove the covers.
6. Unfasten the two rear seat track-to-floor mounting bolts.
7. Unplug the seat belt electrical connection.
8. Remove the front seat.

To install:

9. Install the seat and attach the seat belt electrical connection.
10. Install the two rear seat track-to-floor mounting bolts. Tighten the bolts to 28–38 ft. lbs. (38–51 Nm).
11. Install the seat track covers and their retaining screws.
12. Install the two front seat track-to-floor bolts. Tighten the bolts to 28–38 ft. lbs. (38–51 Nm).
13. Connect the negative battery cable.

Rear Seat Cushion

▶ See Figures 115, 116 and 117

1. Depress the two rear seat cushion retaining clips which attach the front of the seat cushion to the floor.

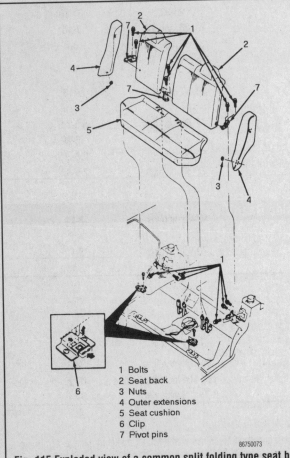

1 Bolts
2 Seat back
3 Nuts
4 Outer extensions
5 Seat cushion
6 Clip
7 Pivot pins

86750073

Fig. 115 Exploded view of a common split folding type seat back and cushion—1991–96 models

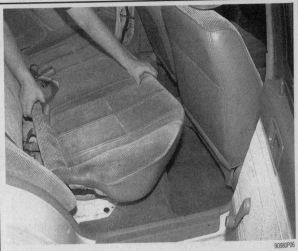

90980P06

Fig. 116 Remove the seat cushion after disengaging the retaining clips

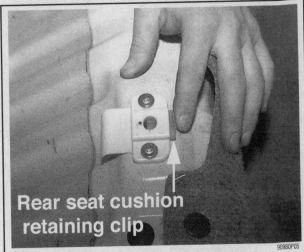

90980P05

Fig. 117 Typical rear seat cushion retaining clip used on 1991–96 models

2. Remove the seat cushion.

To install:

3. Place the seat cushion into position, making sure the safety belt buckles are over the rear seat cushion.
4. Align the cushion's retaining pins with the retaining clips and attach the cushion, making sure the pins are firmly engaged.

Split Rear Seat Back

1. Fold the rear seat back down.
2. Unfasten the rear seat back pivot bolts and remove the seat back from the pivot.
3. Installation is the reverse of removal. Tighten the outer pivot bolts to 16–22 ft. lbs. (22–30 Nm).

TORQUE SPECIFICATIONS

Components	Ft. Lbs.	Nm
Exterior		
Hood		
1991-96 models	14-19	19-25
1997-99 models	14-17	19-23
Liftgate		
Hinge bolts	78-113 inch lbs.	9-13
Grille		
1997-99 models		
Coupe models		
Bumper cover bolts	70-82 inch lbs.	8-10
Front bumper cover-to-fender screw	23-30 inch lbs.	2.5-3.5
Front fender-to-front bumper cover concealed bolts	60-87 inch lbs.	7-10
Splash shield screws	23-30 inch lbs.	2.5-3.5
Sedan and wagon models		
Upper front bumper cover bolts	70-82 inch lbs.	8-10
Front bumper cover-to-fender screw	23-30 inch lbs.	2.5-3.5
Front fender-to-front bumper cover concealed bolts	60-87 inch lbs.	7-10
Splash shield screws	23-30 inch lbs.	2.5-3.5
Lower front bumper cover screw	23-30 inch lbs.	2.5-3.5
Antenna		
1997-99 models		
Coupe models		
Antenna base nut	14-26 inch lbs.	1.5-2.9
Rear cable		
Safety belt lower bolt	25-33	34-46
Anti-lock control module bolts	61-86 inch lbs.	7-10
Anti-lock module electrical connector bolt	53-62 inch lbs.	6-7
Fenders		
1991-96 models		
Fender retaining bolts and nuts	61-87 inch lbs.	7-10
1997-99 models		
Headlamp housing nuts/bolts	47-65 inch lbs.	5.5-7.5
Front bumper bracket nuts	12-16	16-22
Splash shield screws	23-30 inch lbs.	2.5-3.5
Stone guard screws	23-30 inch lbs.	2.5-3.5
Moon Roof		
1991-96 models		
Drive unit assembly retainers	69-95 inch lbs.	8-11
1997-99 models		
Opening panel frame nuts and bolts	70-95 inch lbs.	8-11
Glass panel retaining nuts	70-95 inch lbs.	8-11
Interior		
Instrument Panel and Pad		
1991-96 models		
Upper instrument panel-to-cowl bolts	69-104 inch lbs.	8-12
Instrument panel upper finish panel retainers	69-104 inch lbs.	8-12
Lower and upper instrument panel mount bolts	69-104 inch lbs.	8-12
Instrument panel-to-floor pan attaching bolts	69-104 inch lbs.	8-12
Steering column support bolts	80-123 inch lbs.	9-14

90980C01

TORQUE SPECIFICATIONS

Components	Ft. Lbs.	Nm
Interior (con't)		
Instrument Panel and Pad		
1991-96 models		
Air bag module retainers	61-79 inch lbs.	7-9
Glove compartment hinge retainers	69-104 inch lbs.	8-12
1997-99 models		
Upper instrument panel reinforcement bolt	70-94 inch lbs.	8-11
Left and right-hand lower instrument panel reinforcement bolts	14-18	19-25
Left and right-hand center instrument panel reinforcement bolts	70-94 inch lbs.	8-11
Passenger side air bag module bolts	70-103 inch lbs.	8-12
Steering column bracket bolts	80-124 inch lbs.	9-14
Power door lock actuator		
1991-96 models		
Actuator bolts	61-89 inch lbs.	7-9
1997-99 models		
Actuator nuts	70-96 inch lbs.	7-10
Door glass		
1991-99 models		
Glass retainers	0.20-0.30 inch lbs.	0.023-0.035
Window regulator		
1991-96 models		
Regulator retainers	61-79 inch lbs.	7-9
1997-99 models		
Except coupe models		
Regulator nuts and bolt	61-79 inch lbs.	7-9
Coupe models		
Motor nuts	62-86 inch lbs.	7-10
Regulator nuts	14-18	18-25
Seats		
1991-99 models		
Front		
Seat track-to-floor mounting bolts	28-38	38-51
Split rear seat back		
Outer pivot bolts	16-22	22-30

90980C02

GLOSSARY

AIR/FUEL RATIO: The ratio of air-to-gasoline by weight in the fuel mixture drawn into the engine.

AIR INJECTION: One method of reducing harmful exhaust emissions by injecting air into each of the exhaust ports of an engine. The fresh air entering the hot exhaust manifold causes any remaining fuel to be burned before it can exit the tailpipe.

ALTERNATOR: A device used for converting mechanical energy into electrical energy.

AMMETER: An instrument, calibrated in amperes, used to measure the flow of an electrical current in a circuit. Ammeters are always connected in series with the circuit being tested.

AMPERE: The rate of flow of electrical current present when one volt of electrical pressure is applied against one ohm of electrical resistance.

ANALOG COMPUTER: Any microprocessor that uses similar (analogous) electrical signals to make its calculations.

ARMATURE: A laminated, soft iron core wrapped by a wire that converts electrical energy to mechanical energy as in a motor or relay. When rotated in a magnetic field, it changes mechanical energy into electrical energy as in a generator.

ATMOSPHERIC PRESSURE: The pressure on the Earth's surface caused by the weight of the air in the atmosphere. At sea level, this pressure is 14.7 psi at 32°F (101 kPa at 0°C).

ATOMIZATION: The breaking down of a liquid into a fine mist that can be suspended in air.

AXIAL PLAY: Movement parallel to a shaft or bearing bore.

BACKFIRE: The sudden combustion of gases in the intake or exhaust system that results in a loud explosion.

BACKLASH: The clearance or play between two parts, such as meshed gears.

BACKPRESSURE: Restrictions in the exhaust system that slow the exit of exhaust gases from the combustion chamber.

BAKELITE: A heat resistant, plastic insulator material commonly used in printed circuit boards and transistorized components.

BALL BEARING: A bearing made up of hardened inner and outer races between which hardened steel balls roll.

BALLAST RESISTOR: A resistor in the primary ignition circuit that lowers voltage after the engine is started to reduce wear on ignition components.

BEARING: A friction reducing, supportive device usually located between a stationary part and a moving part.

BIMETAL TEMPERATURE SENSOR: Any sensor or switch made of two dissimilar types of metal that bend when heated or cooled due to the different expansion rates of the alloys. These types of sensors usually function as an on/off switch.

BLOWBY: Combustion gases, composed of water vapor and unburned fuel, that leak past the piston rings into the crankcase during normal engine operation. These gases are removed by the PCV system to prevent the buildup of harmful acids in the crankcase.

BRAKE PAD: A brake shoe and lining assembly used with disc brakes.

BRAKE SHOE: The backing for the brake lining. The term is, however, usually applied to the assembly of the brake backing and lining.

BUSHING: A liner, usually removable, for a bearing; an anti-friction liner used in place of a bearing.

CALIPER: A hydraulically activated device in a disc brake system, which is mounted straddling the brake rotor (disc). The caliper contains at least one piston and two brake pads. Hydraulic pressure on the piston(s) forces the pads against the rotor.

CAMSHAFT: A shaft in the engine on which are the lobes (cams) which operate the valves. The camshaft is driven by the crankshaft, via a belt, chain or gears, at one half the crankshaft speed.

CAPACITOR: A device which stores an electrical charge.

CARBON MONOXIDE (CO): A colorless, odorless gas given off as a normal byproduct of combustion. It is poisonous and extremely dangerous in confined areas, building up slowly to toxic levels without warning if adequate ventilation is not available.

CARBURETOR: A device, usually mounted on the intake manifold of an engine, which mixes the air and fuel in the proper proportion to allow even combustion.

CATALYTIC CONVERTER: A device installed in the exhaust system, like a muffler, that converts harmful byproducts of combustion into carbon dioxide and water vapor by means of a heat-producing chemical reaction.

CENTRIFUGAL ADVANCE: A mechanical method of advancing the spark timing by using flyweights in the distributor that react to centrifugal force generated by the distributor shaft rotation.

CHECK VALVE: Any one-way valve installed to permit the flow of air, fuel or vacuum in one direction only.

CHOKE: A device, usually a moveable valve, placed in the intake path of a carburetor to restrict the flow of air.

CIRCUIT: Any unbroken path through which an electrical current can flow. Also used to describe fuel flow in some instances.

CIRCUIT BREAKER: A switch which protects an electrical circuit from overload by opening the circuit when the current flow exceeds a predetermined level. Some circuit breakers must be reset manually, while most reset automatically.

COIL (IGNITION): A transformer in the ignition circuit which steps up the voltage provided to the spark plugs.

COMBINATION MANIFOLD: An assembly which includes both the intake and exhaust manifolds in one casting.

COMBINATION VALVE: A device used in some fuel systems that routes fuel vapors to a charcoal storage canister instead of venting them into the atmosphere. The valve relieves fuel tank pressure and allows fresh air into the tank as the fuel level drops to prevent a vapor lock situation.

COMPRESSION RATIO: The comparison of the total volume of the cylinder and combustion chamber with the piston at BDC and the piston at TDC.

CONDENSER: 1. An electrical device which acts to store an electrical charge, preventing voltage surges. 2. A radiator-like device in the air conditioning system in which refrigerant gas condenses into a liquid, giving off heat.

CONDUCTOR: Any material through which an electrical current can be transmitted easily.

CONTINUITY: Continuous or complete circuit. Can be checked with an ohmmeter.

COUNTERSHAFT: An intermediate shaft which is rotated by a mainshaft and transmits, in turn, that rotation to a working part.

CRANKCASE: The lower part of an engine in which the crankshaft and related parts operate.

CRANKSHAFT: The main driving shaft of an engine which receives reciprocating motion from the pistons and converts it to rotary motion.

CYLINDER: In an engine, the round hole in the engine block in which the piston(s) ride.

CYLINDER BLOCK: The main structural member of an engine in which is found the cylinders, crankshaft and other principal parts.

CYLINDER HEAD: The detachable portion of the engine, usually fastened to the top of the cylinder block and containing all or most of the combustion chambers. On overhead valve engines, it contains the valves and their operating parts. On overhead cam engines, it contains the camshaft as well.

DEAD CENTER: The extreme top or bottom of the piston stroke.

DETONATION: An unwanted explosion of the air/fuel mixture in the combustion chamber caused by excess heat and compression, advanced timing, or an overly lean mixture. Also referred to as "ping".

DIAPHRAGM: A thin, flexible wall separating two cavities, such as in a vacuum advance unit.

DIESELING: A condition in which hot spots in the combustion chamber cause the engine to run on after the key is turned off.

DIFFERENTIAL: A geared assembly which allows the transmission of motion between drive axles, giving one axle the ability to turn faster than the other.

DIODE: An electrical device that will allow current to flow in one direction only.

DISC BRAKE: A hydraulic braking assembly consisting of a brake disc, or rotor, mounted on an axle, and a caliper assembly containing, usually two brake pads which are activated by hydraulic pressure. The pads are forced against the sides of the disc, creating friction which slows the vehicle.

DISTRIBUTOR: A mechanically driven device on an engine which is responsible for electrically firing the spark plug at a predetermined point of the piston stroke.

DOWEL PIN: A pin, inserted in mating holes in two different parts allowing those parts to maintain a fixed relationship.

DRUM BRAKE: A braking system which consists of two brake shoes and one or two wheel cylinders, mounted on a fixed backing plate, and a brake drum, mounted on an axle, which revolves around the assembly.

DWELL: The rate, measured in degrees of shaft rotation, at which an electrical circuit cycles on and off.

ELECTRONIC CONTROL UNIT (ECU): Ignition module, module, amplifier or igniter. See Module for definition.

ELECTRONIC IGNITION: A system in which the timing and firing of the spark plugs is controlled by an electronic control unit, usually called a module. These systems have no points or condenser.

END-PLAY: The measured amount of axial movement in a shaft.

ENGINE: A device that converts heat into mechanical energy.

EXHAUST MANIFOLD: A set of cast passages or pipes which conduct exhaust gases from the engine.

FEELER GAUGE: A blade, usually metal, or precisely predetermined thickness, used to measure the clearance between two parts.

FIRING ORDER: The order in which combustion occurs in the cylinders of an engine. Also the order in which spark is distributed to the plugs by the distributor.

FLOODING: The presence of too much fuel in the intake manifold and combustion chamber which prevents the air/fuel mixture from firing, thereby causing a no-start situation.

FLYWHEEL: A disc shaped part bolted to the rear end of the crankshaft. Around the outer perimeter is affixed the ring gear. The starter drive engages the ring gear, turning the flywheel, which rotates the crankshaft, imparting the initial starting motion to the engine.

FOOT POUND (ft. lbs. or sometimes, ft.lb.): The amount of energy or work needed to raise an item weighing one pound, a distance of one foot.

FUSE: A protective device in a circuit which prevents circuit overload by breaking the circuit when a specific amperage is present. The device is constructed around a strip or wire of a lower amperage rating than the circuit it is designed to protect. When an amperage higher than that stamped on the fuse is present in the circuit, the strip or wire melts, opening the circuit.

GEAR RATIO: The ratio between the number of teeth on meshing gears.

GENERATOR: A device which converts mechanical energy into electrical energy.

HEAT RANGE: The measure of a spark plug's ability to dissipate heat from its firing end. The higher the heat range, the hotter the plug fires.

HUB: The center part of a wheel or gear.

HYDROCARBON (HC): Any chemical compound made up of hydrogen and carbon. A major pollutant formed by the engine as a byproduct of combustion.

HYDROMETER: An instrument used to measure the specific gravity of a solution.

INCH POUND (inch lbs.; sometimes in.lb. or in. lbs.): One twelfth of a foot pound.

INDUCTION: A means of transferring electrical energy in the form of a magnetic field. Principle used in the ignition coil to increase voltage.

INJECTOR: A device which receives metered fuel under relatively low pressure and is activated to inject the fuel into the engine under relatively high pressure at a predetermined time.

INPUT SHAFT: The shaft to which torque is applied, usually carrying the driving gear or gears.

INTAKE MANIFOLD: A casting of passages or pipes used to conduct air or a fuel/air mixture to the cylinders.

JOURNAL: The bearing surface within which a shaft operates.

KEY: A small block usually fitted in a notch between a shaft and a hub to prevent slippage of the two parts.

MANIFOLD: A casting of passages or set of pipes which connect the cylinders to an inlet or outlet source.

MANIFOLD VACUUM: Low pressure in an engine intake manifold formed just below the throttle plates. Manifold vacuum is highest at idle and drops under acceleration.

MASTER CYLINDER: The primary fluid pressurizing device in a hydraulic system. In automotive use, it is found in brake and hydraulic clutch systems and is pedal activated, either directly or, in a power brake system, through the power booster.

MODULE: Electronic control unit, amplifier or igniter of solid state or integrated design which controls the current flow in the ignition primary circuit based on input from the pick-up coil. When the module opens the primary circuit, high secondary voltage is induced in the coil.

NEEDLE BEARING: A bearing which consists of a number (usually a large number) of long, thin rollers.

OHM: (Ω) The unit used to measure the resistance of conductor-to-electrical flow. One ohm is the amount of resistance that limits current flow to one ampere in a circuit with one volt of pressure.

OHMMETER: An instrument used for measuring the resistance, in ohms, in an electrical circuit.

OUTPUT SHAFT: The shaft which transmits torque from a device, such as a transmission.

OVERDRIVE: A gear assembly which produces more shaft revolutions than that transmitted to it.

OVERHEAD CAMSHAFT (OHC): An engine configuration in which the camshaft is mounted on top of the cylinder head and operates the valve either directly or by means of rocker arms.

OVERHEAD VALVE (OHV): An engine configuration in which all of the valves are located in the cylinder head and the camshaft is located in the cylinder block. The camshaft operates the valves via lifters and pushrods.

OXIDES OF NITROGEN (NOx): Chemical compounds of nitrogen produced as a byproduct of combustion. They combine with hydrocarbons to produce smog.

OXYGEN SENSOR: Use with the feedback system to sense the presence of oxygen in the exhaust gas and signal the computer which can reference the voltage signal to an air/fuel ratio.

PINION: The smaller of two meshing gears.

PISTON RING: An open-ended ring with fits into a groove on the outer diameter of the piston. Its chief function is to form a seal between the piston and cylinder wall. Most automotive pistons have three rings: two for compression sealing; one for oil sealing.

PRELOAD: A predetermined load placed on a bearing during assembly or by adjustment.

PRIMARY CIRCUIT: the low voltage side of the ignition system which consists of the ignition switch, ballast resistor or resistance wire, bypass, coil, electronic control unit and pick-up coil as well as the connecting wires and harnesses.

PRESS FIT: The mating of two parts under pressure, due to the inner diameter of one being smaller than the outer diameter of the other, or vice versa; an interference fit.

RACE: The surface on the inner or outer ring of a bearing on which the balls, needles or rollers move.

REGULATOR: A device which maintains the amperage and/or voltage levels of a circuit at predetermined values.

RELAY: A switch which automatically opens and/or closes a circuit.

RESISTANCE: The opposition to the flow of current through a circuit or electrical device, and is measured in ohms. Resistance is equal to the voltage divided by the amperage.

RESISTOR: A device, usually made of wire, which offers a preset amount of resistance in an electrical circuit.

RING GEAR: The name given to a ring-shaped gear attached to a differential case, or affixed to a flywheel or as part of a planetary gear set.

ROLLER BEARING: A bearing made up of hardened inner and outer races between which hardened steel rollers move.

ROTOR: 1. The disc-shaped part of a disc brake assembly, upon which the brake pads bear; also called, brake disc. 2. The device mounted atop the distributor shaft, which passes current to the distributor cap tower contacts.

SECONDARY CIRCUIT: The high voltage side of the ignition system, usually above 20,000 volts. The secondary includes the ignition coil, coil wire, distributor cap and rotor, spark plug wires and spark plugs.

SENDING UNIT: A mechanical, electrical, hydraulic or electro-magnetic device which transmits information to a gauge.

SENSOR: Any device designed to measure engine operating conditions or ambient pressures and temperatures. Usually electronic in nature and designed to send a voltage signal to an on-board computer, some sensors may operate as a simple on/off switch or they may provide a variable voltage signal (like a potentiometer) as conditions or measured parameters change.

SHIM: Spacers of precise, predetermined thickness used between parts to establish a proper working relationship.

SLAVE CYLINDER: In automotive use, a device in the hydraulic clutch system which is activated by hydraulic force, disengaging the clutch.

SOLENOID: A coil used to produce a magnetic field, the effect of which is to produce work.

SPARK PLUG: A device screwed into the combustion chamber of a spark ignition engine. The basic construction is a conductive core inside of a ceramic insulator, mounted in an outer conductive base. An electrical charge from the spark plug wire travels along the conductive core and jumps a preset air gap to a grounding point or points at the end of the conductive base. The resultant spark ignites the fuel/air mixture in the combustion chamber.

SPLINES: Ridges machined or cast onto the outer diameter of a shaft or inner diameter of a bore to enable parts to mate without rotation.

TACHOMETER: A device used to measure the rotary speed of an engine, shaft, gear, etc., usually in rotations per minute.

THERMOSTAT: A valve, located in the cooling system of an engine, which is closed when cold and opens gradually in response to engine heating, controlling the temperature of the coolant and rate of coolant flow.

TOP DEAD CENTER (TDC): The point at which the piston reaches the top of its travel on the compression stroke.

TORQUE: The twisting force applied to an object.

TORQUE CONVERTER: A turbine used to transmit power from a driving member to a driven member via hydraulic action, providing changes in drive ratio and torque. In automotive use, it links the driveplate at the rear of the engine to the automatic transmission.

TRANSDUCER: A device used to change a force into an electrical signal.

TRANSISTOR: A semi-conductor component which can be actuated by a small voltage to perform an electrical switching function.

TUNE-UP: A regular maintenance function, usually associated with the replacement and adjustment of parts and components in the electrical and fuel systems of a vehicle for the purpose of attaining optimum performance.

TURBOCHARGER: An exhaust driven pump which compresses intake air and forces it into the combustion chambers at higher than atmospheric pressures. The increased air pressure allows more fuel to be burned and results in increased horsepower being produced.

VACUUM ADVANCE: A device which advances the ignition timing in response to increased engine vacuum.

VACUUM GAUGE: An instrument used to measure the presence of vacuum in a chamber.

VALVE: A device which control the pressure, direction of flow or rate of flow of a liquid or gas.

VALVE CLEARANCE: The measured gap between the end of the valve stem and the rocker arm, cam lobe or follower that activates the valve.

VISCOSITY: The rating of a liquid's internal resistance to flow.

VOLTMETER: An instrument used for measuring electrical force in units called volts. Voltmeters are always connected parallel with the circuit being tested.

WHEEL CYLINDER: Found in the automotive drum brake assembly, it is a device, actuated by hydraulic pressure, which, through internal pistons, pushes the brake shoes outward against the drums.